23 - 39 / New York –   Europe – 55000
/ Asheville –   N.Y. Asheville – 5600
/ Europe   other places
/ etc   Marine
                Philadelphia, 1 000
                etc   _____
                                 6 1 6 0 0

30 - 34   25 000

Thus, I have traveled not
less than 125 - 150
000 miles in my 34 years
at not methat, considerable
sugare of variety –

have seen a great deal
of the life of
the states of the _____ as
well as variety of _____
Bermuda England, Norway
Italy, Switzerland, Austria
_____ Czechoslovakia, _____
_____ Belgium, ___ Denmark

THE NOTEBOOKS OF

Thomas Wolfe

THE NOTEBOOKS OF
Thomas Wolfe

Edited by
R I C H A R D   S .   K E N N E D Y
and
P A S C H A L   R E E V E S

Volume II

THE UNIVERSITY OF
NORTH CAROLINA PRESS
Chapel Hill

Abbreviations

FDTM	*From Death to Morning* (New York, 1935).
HB	*The Hills Beyond* (New York, 1941).
Letters	*The Letters of Thomas Wolfe*, ed. Elizabeth Nowell (New York, 1956).
LHA	*Look Homeward, Angel* (New York, 1929).
LTM	*The Letters of Thomas Wolfe to His Mother*, ed. C. Hugh Holman and Sue Fields Ross (Chapel Hill, 1968).
OT&R	*Of Time and the River* (New York, 1935).
PN	Pocket Notebook. There are thirty-five pocket notebooks, HCL*46AM-7(69), in the Wisdom Collection at Harvard.
SN	*The Story of a Novel* (New York, 1936).
Short Novels	*The Short Novels of Thomas Wolfe*, ed. C. Hugh Holman (New York, 1961).
W&R	*The Web and the Rock* (New York, 1939).
YCGHA	*You Can't Go Home Again* (New York, 1940).

Contents

Volume II

PART FOUR ~

THE SEARCH
FOR A SECOND NOVEL

Pocket Notebook 13

February, 1930, to May, 1930

After Wolfe resigned in mid-year from New York University, he lived on his royalties until he was awarded a Guggenheim fellowship. While he made his preparations to go to Europe, he began to assemble notes, drafts, and plans for "The October Fair," including the development of another autobiographical character, David Hawke (who years later came to light as "Monk" Webber in The Web and the Rock). *But during the three-month period before he sailed he was upset by the distractions of being a celebrity and by his renewed determination to end his relationship with Mrs. Bernstein.*

The notes and diary entries of this time show him diligently recording impressions of city life and writing episodes about Esther Jacobs and her circle. But the emotional stress he was undergoing is reflected in many of these passages: they display guilt, jealousy, grief, and anxiety of various sorts. Because Wolfe was working almost daily on his notes for "The October Fair," for which he was using a large accounting ledger, he wrote most of his diary entries in that ledger. In editing Pocket Notebook 13, we have extracted these entries, plus a sample of his October Fair notes, from the ledger and placed them where they seem to belong chronologically in the material from the notebook. The Pocket Notebook itself is largely filled with talk that Wolfe overheard in public places, and we have included only a representative portion of it.

[*From the October Fair ledger*]

Feb. 3, 1930: [1]

Mr. _____ the English novelist took me out to lunch. "I like the companionship of men better than that of women," he said. "I have never married . . . I am sorry men are not equipped to love one another . . . I suppose you will get married . . . you are so very masculine . . . I can just see now the kind of woman you will marry

---

1. Although this item and the third item are dated, they are fictional renderings of Wolfe's experience and feeling which he has expressed in the first person.

[413]

. . . she will be big and placid . . . just your opposite in temperament . . . you will have children . . . she will cook and mend for you . . . she will be a good woman to get into bed with."

I saw the picture suddenly and I thought of big women from Kansas, and it looked very good to me. I said "By *God!* By *God!* I hope so."

Snodgrass *solus* again: I have heard that a man should sleep alone and down a long hall-way, so that when he has relations with his wife he must rise and walk down a cold passage. People should sleep upon hard mattresses—I have heard that soft ones make for sloth and weaken moral fibre. I never eat meat for luncheon.

Sunday, Feb. 9 [2] . . . I thought of Esther's daughter, Alma, as exclusively the growth of this world, a plant that did not belong to any vegetable or animal life, a plant that belonged to stone and steel, to money and the inside of vast apartments. She was like one of those strange and lovely plants that one sees in the collection of Glass Flowers at Harvard: she might be broken but she would not bleed. Wherever I saw her small bloodless face I always thought with wonder of Esther's small rosy one that was so full of glowing warmth and health, and that by contrast seemed so near akin to all rich things that grow in the earth, to fruit and flowers and grain, and to all the joyful business of life.

I thought that Mona wanted to have love affairs with literary men, and if possible with literary men of T. S. Eliot's school. I do not think she could have considered going to bed with one of the constant contributors to the *Saturday Evening Post*, but she might have been more favorably disposed to one of the *New Republic* group. She kept her eye pretty carefully peeled on the fashionable trends.

"I knew this would happen when I read your book," she said. "I wept over it; and I wanted to be some part of it."

"Now listen, God-damn it" I said, "no more of this cheap New York wise-cracking. Go get your mother and get her now—at once. Do you hear?" I heard her take in her breath a little. Then there was silence: she hung the phone up suddenly while I waited. I put the

---

2. Penciled revisions of this item show Wolfe's attempt to make these thoughts be the speculations of Stephen Hook. The passage actually continues, for one more paragraph, into a paranoiac vision of his humiliation, at which the young girl stares, "cool and slightly smiling."

receiver on the hook, full of shame over what I had done, my anger half-appeased but lashing itself to a new frenzy as I sought to justify myself. I waited, cursing, for the call that I knew would come from Esther in a few moments.

Jacobs looked at me with his strained bitter smile that now somehow had such power to move me.

"Vot's the matter, Chene?" he said. "You look unhappy too. Are you sad because we are having to give up the apartment?"

A little retort rose swiftly to my lips; then died suddenly. He was wrong in what he said, and I think he knew he was wrong, and was a little ashamed of it. But he was full of grief and trouble, as we all were, and he had reason for his little complaint at life.

"No, Fritz," I said, "I do not care about you having to give up your apartment. You know I never came here much until three months ago: I am thinking of troubles of my own."

"Go on!" he said roughly, changing quickly to another mood. "Vot are you talking about? You are a young fellow who's begun to get famous—everyone's after you now, and you have your whole life in front of you. You ought to be the happiest fellow in the world."

I entered into a bitter indictment of Marie Doyle—"this damned fat woman who wants to drink my heart's blood."

But all the time, I think, our sad minds looked at each other and at Esther, and I think we felt some pity and affection for each other. My sad mind kept saying: [*breaks off*]

THE OCTOBER FAIR (Part I)

Characters who appear in the Sleep Scene: Esther, Alma, Eliza, Mona (?), Eugene, Croly (?), Fritz, Snodgrass, Kansas (?)

Plan for The October Fair

(Part I: The Fast Express)
I Introduction
    a) "October had come again," etc.
    b) "Whoever lays a rail across this dust."
    c) The Fathers ("Cynewulf"; Crockett; Thomas Pentland the First; Greeley—etc.)
    d) A Letter.
    e) The Train—Tom Cline, the Men Inside, Darkness coming in Washington, Virginia by Moonlight, Moonlight, Moonlight.

f) America By Night—"All through the night in darkness rivers run."

g) Sleep and A Dozen of the Sleepers.

Part II Antaeus.

Part III Telemachus (?)

The burlesk shows—the rapt dark-jawed faces of the men—the dull beast-faces feeding upon flesh—the conventions of burlesk.

Yes, I said, you're coming right out of there. What do you think of that, I said. You're going to take that little tin hearse of yours right out of there. O yeah? he says. Yea, I says, and how! [3]

Mr. Schwertberg (*sol.*): A bit seedy too. No one would ever call him a snappy dresser. That suit he's wearing is about shot. When they start to go at the cuffs there's not much to be done.

"Wine, women and song" for the asking. Here you take 'em out, buy them a swell meal with some good drinks, get two orchestra seats that sets you back $8.80, and what do you get? "You may kiss my little hand." You may kiss my little _____, that's what you may do. You're out 20 bucks on the evening and all you get is a lot of stale baloney. You get *ausgeboozled!* Low! Most of 'em are about six inches lower than a snake's belly—and when your dough is gone, you're out! And I don't mean maybe! [4]

Good scenes from Novels

1) Moll Flanders telling her husband in Virginia he is her brother (incest); 2) Harry Richmond at unveiling of statues in Germany, 3) Gulliver awaking and finding himself trussed up and Lilliputians swarming on his face, 4) Leopold Bloom in the Ormond Bar, 5) Family meeting of the Forsytes, 6) The fucking scene in the Pheasant House in *Lady Chatterly's Lover*, 7) The execution of Tess, 8) Quentin Durward's meeting with Louis XI, 9) My Uncle Toby and the death bed of the Frenchwoman, 10) Ishmael and Queequeg eating clam chowder.

In Search of My Father.

Upon Fifth Avenue several hundred thousand people were coming, going, swarming, seething, entering buildings, pausing in front of

3. Wolfe reworked these notes for the Voice of the City in OT&R, pp. 417.

4. This material ultimately became part of the complaint against American women uttered by the expatriated New Yorker in France, OT&R, pp. 861-62.

shops, getting on buses, hailing taxis, descending from buses, crossing at corners, being held back at corners, dodging in front, between, and behind trucks and motors, jostling, pushing, milling, tramping steadily in undulant tides along the pavement—dots, points, masses, in themselves nothing, in themselves fenced, measured by ticking time, but together part of an unceasing, unending, infinite river.

What sort of husband do you call yourself? By God, you'd make the bed for her to lie in with her lovers and bring them toast and coffee in the morning. "Good morning, sir. I hope you passed a pleasant night with my wife. I am very glad to hear it, sir—I know she always tries to give satisfaction, and though I do say it myself, as shouldn't, I think the best critics agree she generally does. How will you have your eggs, sir . . . . Four minutes . . . . Very good, sir . . . . Are you both quite warm enough . . . . Thank you, sir."

What kind of man are you? Why don't you kill me? That's right, Goddam it, kill me, shoot me through the head, spatter my brains out on the pavement, hire thugs and gunmen, have me tied up naked to a post and spit on me, vomit over me, urinate on me, and debagg me, castrate me with a rabbi's circumcision knife, and feed my genitals to ladies' lap-dogs.

Feb. 17—at Louis—8:30:
3 Martini Secs—Shall I have another or go on to eat, to eat?
When I passed it they signed it without his OK—I didn't sign it. . . . just menshoned the fact that a certain engineer . . . well, I said, . . . Lissen, I had laundry on there, I had several pers. tel. calls. . . . I checked them off . . . I didn't like it a bit, see . . . an' I said . . . It's impossible that I didn't . . . when I *knew* it. He threw it up to me in such a sarcastic way, you know . . . well, I *undoubtedly* will find out. Leave it, just leave it, leave it.

(Another party:)
We never got down to the point where they're thoroughly sold on a campaign as they're sold on this.
. . . my gosh if you don't get here pretty quick, we were goin' to tell 'em about . . . Now the first thing I'm gonna tell 'em is . . . that's fer *attention* . . . that's fer *interest* . . . attention is promise . . . then interest.

Smartest guy in the world . . . thoroughly sold on as now . . . he says I says . . . he says . . . .

Bar none . . . he's the only boy in the world who thinks . . . I don't give a damn what you think . . . Bar *none.*

He said, *How'd* you find out? . . . I said, how'd I find *out?* I know why I got fired—God damn it, I know why I got fired.

Tues. Feb 18:

Eating at Charles—How many times have I eaten at Charles? . . . I write this under the table because two people—a man and a woman—across the room are watching me—with superior smiles mixed with indecent curiosity—the man is middle-aged—on to 50—healthy-looking—like old Doc MacNider[5]—the woman is a *fuckable* middle age—and he is worried, and superior—Is it a *Comedy*, after all?

The elevated goes by outside with not unpleasant rumble—Clanging of a street car bell—it passes . . . The streets are soupy with running slush and water today—It has become mild. I talk with the black-haired dish-faced waiter of Vienna—a mild winter all over Europe he says.

O golden and abundant life—come, come.

Read Miss Latimer's book last night.[6]

Save yourself? What are you saving yourself for?

Having conviction and "having the courage of your convictions" are two very different things. I think it is better to live than to die, although I could not explain this.

Room 806—6:40–8:10—Wash. Sq. Coll.—The Amer. Novel —Friday, Feb. 21, 1930. [*A lecture Wolfe was invited to deliver.*]

Waiter *2nd Avenue:*

Nikolaus I says that's just it, you got to cater to the public and *not no few.*

I says leave it alone—People don't come in here for no artistic effect you may have in your dining room. People come in here to eat and drink and dance an' you gotta give it to 'em.

Another—a dark Jew:

Listen, I don't care for no one—all I want to know is am I right an' then I go ahead. I don't care if it's the best man in the world—

5. Dr. William de B. MacNider was a professor of medicine at The University of North Carolina when Wolfe was an undergraduate.
6. Margery Latimer, *This Is My Body* (New York, 1930).

Tues. Feb. 25 at 12 o'clock in Child's at 11th St.—Two Burlesk girls next to me—blonde—beautiful and empty faces—went to Mario's tonight (conversation of Mario's wife in table next to me) later to 14th St. Burlesk.

[*At this point, Wolfe makes a scurrilous remark about Jewish women whom he thinks follow fashion in their sexual interests. He then explains his comment:* "This was written in Mario's when I saw the beautiful J____ Jewess—She was in here with the Jap sculptor."]

As I sit here in a speakeasy I hear the shouts of children in a school playground nearby—Their screams, shrieks, shouts.

Thus in the night great ships are passing on the seas, but if they lead to glory joy and wisdom; and if men find strange shores and happy lands, who knows how?

But Rosenberg is leaning on a First Class rail.
With good American dollars he has plumbed strange seas.

Two Irish girls, two lovely ladies, two nice girls in a speakeasy:
"You're an Italian aren't you Nick?"
"Ah-h I speak every language in the Balkan states," (he said with tension).
Well then, you're a Greek— . . . I suppose you wanta hit us, doncha?
Why? . . . He's not ashamed of being a Greek, is he? . . .
When Greek meets Greek . . . etc.
Now dontcha be ashamed of bein' a Greek, Nick . . . There ain't nothin' t' be ashamed of.
Where's your wife—out front?
I'm a stonethrower, you're a stonethrower—so lets both keep our mouth shut.

[*Wolfe developed the notes above into the following vignette, which has never been published. Later he intended to include it in his "Walpurgis Night" or "Hound of Darkness" sequence.*]

"You're an Eyetalian, ain't you, Nick?" one of the ladies asked.
Nick's tar-black eyes shifted nervously in his head, his short hairy fingers took his chewed cigar from the table edge.
"Ah-h," he said gutterally, jocosely, and with an air of embarrassed and clumsy evasion, "I spik every language in the Balkan States."

"Well, then, he's a Greek," the lady said positively. "I knew the minute I first saw him he was either an Eyetalian or a Greek—yuh can't fool me."

"No, no, no!" the gentleman who had been addressed as George said, slowly and heavily. "You got it all wrong! Whatcha tryin' to give us? Nick's no Greek and I'll bet on it. What about it, Nick?" he demanded.

Nick took the cigar in his short hairy fingers again, and made the slighted motion of his heavy shoulders.

"Eet's all the same. Wot t'hell," he said. "Doesn't matter wat you are. Pipple all de same all over de world," he declared now with great earnestness, leaning forward and tapping heavily upon the table. "Grik, Italian, Armenian, Rooshian—I don't gif a damn wat dey are, pipple all de same!"

"I suppose you wanta hit us wit' somethin', doncha, Nick?" The other lady, who had up to this time taken no part in the conversation, now demanded.

"Why? He's not ashamed of being a Greek, is he?" the lady who had originally uttered the charge now said.

"When Greek meets Greek, they open a restaurant, eh Nick?" the other lady now laughingly remarked.

"They open a 49th St. Speak-Gently, you mean?" George said with a burst of infectious laughter.

"Now dontcha be ashamed of bein' a Greek, Nick," the first lady, who had been somewhat lost in a rapt contemplation of her glass, now said, severely and admonishingly. "There ain't nothin' to be ashamed of. A Greek's youman just like everybody else."

"Why, Jesus!" said George philosophically, at this juncture, "We ain't got nothin' to do with where we come from. A guy can't pick out the place he wants to get born in, can he? You know we can't *all* be Amurricans: there's got to be *some* foreigners left in the world. Do you ever go back to the Old Country, Nick?" George added.

"Sure, sure," said Nick, with a vigorous nod, "I go four times."

"You're quite a traveller, ain't you, Nick?" one of the ladies remarked. "Do you take the wife along?"

"Nah-h!" Nick said with an impatient and disdainful movement, "She say 'What t'hell! Why you don't stay here at home. You got good place here, what you go for?' Women no like to travel." He pressed the cigar to his full firm meditative lips.

"Dontcha ever do it, Nick," the lady continued as if she had never been interrupted. "Dontcha ever go back on the Old Country. It ain't where you come from that counts, it's whatcha are. Am I right?"

"Sure! Sure!" said Nick taking the cigar from his mouth, and nodding vigorously.

"Why, Jesus," George remarked again, "A Greek's ev'ry damn bit as good as an Eyetalian, if you ask me!"

"Why, certainly!" the lady declared, impatiently, as if the matter admitted of no doubt. "It's what you *are* that counts, Nick," she went on earnestly, "See."

"Sure, sure," Nick agreed, nodding seriously.

"People are *people*," George declared profoundly, "I don't give a damn where they come from. It's the same the world over. We all got something to be proud of, I don't give a damn who we are."

"Why sure," the other lady now diplomatically remarked, "I bet at that Greece is a swell country. You Greeks got quite a history, ain't you, Nick?"

"Sure! Sure!" said Nick. "Big history." He held two thick fingers up to a waiter. "Jack," he said gutterally, "fill 'em up again. This one is on the house," he said.

Jeez (woman) I wouldn't dare call up my mother tonight. They both died when they was a year old an' this is their birthday. They'd a been 26 years old if they lived.

(Tenderly)—I was only teasin' yuh (some horrible insult).

(Papa) Ah y' oughtn'd to beat her.

I did, I hit her very hard, my hand was burnin' fer a half hour. I smacked her on the behind, papa.

Ah I do it t' make 'em mind me, see. I don't want 'em to get too fresh, see.

That's my only reason fer that—that's my only reason fer hittin' her—I'm afraid she'll hurt the baby—She bends her fingers back.[7]

Childhood Reminiscences:

I said fer God's sake please don't do that, I gotta headache. I said, Mama I didn't do that—She hits an' clouts.

I said, I'll never forgive yuh fer that—an' I never (an' what a crack!) did—I tell it every time I get drunk.

That's true yuh never forget a thing like that.

7. Wolfe used a good deal of this and the following material for the "sweet accent of maternal tribulation" in OT&R, p. 418.

I came in while they was sayin prayers, see . . . an' I couldn't explain why I was late.

. . . May'll say: "Ah-h-ah- yer not goin t'hit me, are ye Mama?"

A big rawboned kid. If ye ever get it from him ye'll know it. If he turned on ye—

He wouldn't turn on yuh.

Nah, Marian's like I am—I can't stop with a slap—

Nah, if I couldn't manage Jimmy without tellin Jule what respec' he's gotta have fer me . . . .

I said, Jimmy: I want to tell y' somethin; yer goin to lose yer allowance fer a week. That does more good.

Those days people didn' have nerves . . . These days people live on their nerves.

. . . Those days, what days?

I just blow up . . . This fella's in the bathroom callin' fer his eggs, the baby's yellin fer his bottle, Marian's . . . an' I just blow up.

[From the October Fair ledger]

Item—forgotten—on way to Langner's [8] we stop in to see Aline. Mina there. Aline, who was about to kill herself today at two o'clock, dancing around—so Stott says—exhibiting new ball dress.

My dear Tom Wolfe, there's nothing more to learn about these people—four years is a full university period, and Mr. Wolfe has not wholly misused his time.

Sunday, March 3—

Up at one. Aline in at 12:30—left—Wasson [9] called later—lunch with Wasson at Algonquin—Harvard Club during afternoon—talk with Wasson—Munn and woman at H. Club—Later with Wasson to rooms, 47th and Lexington—Drink there—then to Aline's for dinner—Teddy, Edla, Clara Weiss [10]—splendid dinner—Music, Strauss, Tchai-

---

8. Lawrence Langner, an outstanding patent attorney and one of the directors of the Theatre Guild, was a good friend of Aline Bernstein's. Wolfe first met him in 1923 when Langner guaranteed him a production of *Welcome To Our City* if he would cut the play.

9. Ben Wasson, a friend of Aline Bernstein's and a literary agent.

10. Mrs. Bernstein's son, Theodore Bernstein, Jr.; her daughter Edla; and her old friend.

kovsky 1812, popular songs—then to Emily's [11]—the little Frenchman, fair haired Dutch P'boy, Emily's cousin (husband dead) & later much Bacardi—home.

Alma said with her groping hit-or-miss malice: "Let's have a Strange Interlude game."

"Very well," he said roughly, "If you're willing, I'm willing. It's a game at which I would do fully as well as anyone here"

Ethel's [*Ethel Frankau's*] long hearty laughter at young Dutchman's joke—not at the joke but at its clumsiness, looking at Emily saying "I caught that—I saw that" etc. Meaning Emily's look.

Today [*March*] 3-4 Monday–Tues—4:30 A.M.:

Back from Mrs. Ulmann's at 3:00—Young Jewish writer much-travelled there—Two entire days now devoted to parties, smell of cunt, food, quarrels, introductions—Nothing done!!!

Terrible scene with Aline to begin day—the poison in mind beginning—Last night at Emily's left over—She screamed and cried bitterly—Later we make up somewhat—I kiss her tears away—she leaves with red eyes, red face, and tear-stained face. She is growing old and she is still a child. Edla to be operated on tomorrow.

Scribner's—Lacy Meredith [12]—Harvard Club—Doris Ulmann's —Aline called me sobbing over phone—said Teddy was by her. Later I called—gravely he answered phone, said mother was asleep—that she was ill, "something has worn her out"—that they had given her sleeping powders.

Last night (Sunday—before Emily's):

The grand music (Strauss Wiener Wald) began and the women began to dance around by themselves. Esther held her small hands out, swaying to the music; she began to dance proposing her dainty legs and feet to each side comically. She nodded her head slightly and briskly

11. Emily Davies Thayer, whom Mrs. Bernstein had met during her European trip in 1928. She was an attractive, vivacious, and aggressive young woman who was divorced and remarried. Part of Wolfe's fascination with her lay in the fact that her first husband was William H. Vanderbilt. Wolfe used her complex personality as the basis for fictional characters more than once. She is treated most fully as "Amy Carleton" in "The Party at Jack's." Her life ended pathetically in suicide in May, 1935. See Pocket Notebook 14 for her association with Wolfe in Paris.

12. A friend of Wolfe's from North Carolina who had aspirations to be an actor, but who meanwhile worked as a night cashier at the Hotel McAlpin. He appears in Wolfe's later fiction as Monty Bellamy.

from side to side to the music and she looked at him comically. He looked at her sad face, her sad child's face with the droop that had come to the mouth during the past year and he saw that she was a child trying to be gay for a moment. The mighty music soared, slowly and daintily she danced by herself; he looked at that small child's face in which age and grief had settled; he thought of the great distance they had come together; and suddenly he turned his face away and wept, bitterly and silently.

Wanted—a dark name [13]—and a physical picture of my soul—a mixture of the ape and the angel—a fierce delicate demon's face which seemed to have been broken by some terrific smash of living—mixture of ape and angel.

He was about a middling height, but the stoop of his heavy shoulders and the great length of his arms which dangled grotesquely and apishly almost to his knees made him appear at first sight a good deal shorter. When he walked indeed his motion was a curious loping prowl that suggested the motion of a gorilla getting over the ground at great speed. Because of his gait and structure his schoolmates in childhood had given him the name of "Jocko."

Allusions in the October Fair

English: *King Lear*, The Rime, *Ulysses*, *Beowulf*, Egdon Heath, *Tom Jones*, The Anatomy, Diary of Daniel Boone, Donne ("The Funeral"), Prufrock, "Anna Livia Plurabelle," *Confessions of Eng. Opium Eater*.

Figures in nat'l history: Nathaniel Greene, The pioneers (autobiography of America), Dan'l Drew, Barnum, Dempsey, Ward McAllister, The Governors of North Carolina and South Carolina, Joaquin Miller, Sarnoff, Cole L. Blease, J. E. B. Stuart, Theodore Roosevelt, John D., Chester Arthur, Big Bill the Builder, Scarface Al Capone, Gyp the Blood, Boss Croker, Roger Williams, Sheriff Bob Chambers.

Jason Gudger, Hugh Weaver.

Craig, David, Joseph, Arthur, Albert, Edward, Philip, Stephen, Junius, John.

John Crockett.

His name was John [14] Crockett Hawke, and his arms were so

---

13. In the margin the names "Ernest" and "James" are crossed out. On the next page is a list of twenty-two names, all crossed out except the last, "David."
14. In a revision for typescript Wolfe changed this to "Daniel."

long they dangled upon the floor when he sat in high chairs. Physically he was lazy and he could reach many things without moving from his seat—books from high shelves, cigarettes from the pockets of a hanging overcoat, and food, food, food, rich, abundant, succulent food from all ends and corners of a table. *Crockett* had been his mother's family name: he no longer used it in his signature. Wherever he went he signed his name "John Hawke" and he had been to many places. Yet, few people had ever called him John during his childhood. He had been known as Crockett to his elders, and at first as "Crock" to other boys. But very early the name, coupled with his extraordinary physique, and the incredible length of his arms, which dangled apishly almost to his knees, had had its suggestive effect upon his companions. The "Crock" became "Jock," and in a very short time "Jocko."

When it did, he stopped climbing trees, an accomplishment in which he had exulted all through his boyhood, and in which he had possessed the agility of a cat or a monkey. He could climb anything— trees, barns, houses, the flush wall of a cliff, pulling himself up in a sinuous feline twist, secure and certain as long as his prehensile toes and fingers had an inch to grip on.

He could leap five feet above him for the limb of an oak and whatever his fingers touched they held. Yet, strangely, he had an insane horror of high places: he shrank back from them, fearful of a fall, with queasy bowels.

Dark angels hovered at his birth, and a strange dark light shone on him.

March 12–13—

At 1:10 A.M. in subway—first Aline's for drinks, then H. Club, then 49th St. Grill—A man *dead* in B.M.T. subway at Times Square. I came down steps and saw beyond turnstiles hungry crowd pressing in a semicircle. Frantically I searched for nickel and rushed through. The dead man, a shabby fellow of 45–55 sat slumped in one of the subway benches—a small puddle of urine stained the concrete at his feet. "No matter where they kick off," said a big soldier to a little dish-faced Irishman, "they always leave that black mark." His voice was quiet, hard, casual. "You said it!" said the Irishman.

[*At this point Wolfe turned to a full and detailed rendering with characterizations, dialogue, and a style characteristic of his fiction. The material runs for several pages. At the top of the entry he has placed a title, "Death in the Subway." Later the episode became part of "Death, the Proud Brother."*]

We do not need the words of the abstract philosophers. We need the words of men who have drawn their breaths in labor, and yet have known sweet sleep.

What do I want? In the agony of New York life a woman asks me this, as if there is no answer save in my mind and soul. And Horace said we could change our skies but not our souls. But I do not want to change my soul: I want to change my skies and pavements. What do I want at present? Thirty days in a town of 14000 people, a river with slow barges, a tapestried spring all gold and white, small streets with leaning houses, a tavern with deep beds and rough white linens, two good restaurants, one café, and a house with several clean and jolly whores.

Abe came at eleven o'clock—and at the station people were all laughing and sneering at me.

Abe said: You are a crazy man, Gene, but you are the best man and the greatest genius I've ever known.

March 13—

To Luchow's with Aline—at Luchow's Abe in, fleeing, he says, from justice. After lunch to see Perkins. Talked about Guggenheim. Then to see Mr. [*Henry Allen*] Moe—He made most generous proposals—can go to Europe in 2 or 3 installments—now, next year, any time. Went back to see Perkins. He goes to Key West Saturday. Then home. Abe Smith still there telephoning—Then Henry Volkening came. Then I worked.

The park in Union Square—walking across it *to feel the earth* again. Make something of this.

Mar. 14 at Mario's—on way to passport:

This I think: The little man I saw die in the subway night before last—if he had lived among toughs, in the worst slime, if he died by their bullets, smashed slugs, baseball bats—would he have come to more than this?

Can we come to more than this?

At 29 thus I had $14,000, no ties, and the ability to travel where I chose.

[*From the October Fair ledger*]

When Abe came in to hide the other day—calling up a lawyer named Rosenthal—Has New York begun to do this to him already?

Sat. M'ch 15th—

Met Perkins at 5:00 at Harv. Club. Went to 49th St. Grill for drinks—Then walked with him to Penn Station. He's going to Key West for 2 wks. with Hemingway. Talked of many things—He said— Mary Colum [15] says Americans cannot write love story. I say not so. People are born and die here. They also love here. Walked with him through the crowded sts. of 6 o'clock to Penn Station—*Gewirr! Gewirr!*

Girls and boys who work at Macy's leaving shop. Boys waiting on girls to come out "Satiddy Night"—Young Jews with packages— Newsdealer collecting bundle of yellow sheets on shoulder—7th Avenue sinuous and long running into smoky mad brilliance of Broadway Life like a censer fuming—Penn Hotel—*Gewirr* of taxis—Jew in front of bare store rented for purpose strewn with cheap neckties, women's hose, underwear, shaving sets, brushes, clocks, etc. yelling ironically "Selling out, folks" in hard kidding Eastside Jewpeddler's way—Two girls in front of cheap shoe shop 34th St.—"No, no. It's this way. Tight fitting shirt with Russian boots. You know what I mean?"

Young men conspiring at office entrance of building. "Sure, I know what I'm talking about . . . 200 dollars—come on inside."

"There it is, John! Up there. 11th story. They're still there! Do you see it?"

1) Esther	1) David Hawke
2) Alma	2) Lincoln Weisman
3) Lulu Burke	3) Stephen Hooke
4) Dorothy Midaster	4) Fritz Jacobs
5) The Lowenthal Sisters	5) David Burke
6) Amy Parker (Al. Baker)	6) Ike Cabot
7) Edith Isaacs	7) Roy Croly
8) Leah Bellamy	8) Mr. Sulzheimer
9) Sonia Jones	9) Gorewitz
10) Mrs. Funk	10) Joel Pierce
11) Trapp	11) Millbrook
	12) Mr. Rosen

Part I The Fast Express
Part II Faust and Helen
    Chapter I—Another Ship
    Chapter II—The Loft
    Chapter III—Early Spring

15. Mrs. Padraic Colum, a literary critic and a frequent contributor to *Scribner's* and other periodicals. Since she was born in Ireland, she looked with the perspective of a naturalized citizen upon the American scene.

Chapter IV—Summer—Love Voyage
Chapter V—Exile
Chapter VI—Return
Chapter VII—The Loft
Chapter VIII—A Voyage
Part III Antaeus
Part IV The October Fair
Part V Telemachus.

Part I The Fast Express—	12 hours.
Part II Faust and Helen—	2 years.
Part III Antaeus	one year.
Part IV The October Fair	6 mos.
Part V Telemachus	one year and half.

Very Brief Sketch of the Action: Book starts with "The Fast Express"—a thing of terrific movement and passion—really an essence —a *concrete* abstraction of whole book—The Real Narrative Action begins with "Faust and Helen"—Lyrical beginnings culminating with idyllic love scene at Chartres—Passion deeps and darkens on return. By beginning of "Antaeus," it has grown dark and bloody, full of madness; from this time on it marches up to an insane [*page missing*]

Sunday, March 16—
Aline called early on way to country—Then Mina, to give me useless advice—Sauvez Aline! Sauve qui peut! Sauve qui peut! I must go away, says Mina, as if this is not the thing I have been raving about for three months—I called Mina later—Aline, very clever about people, I said; could do what she liked with me; but we can not be clever about the fundamental structure of life—that settles itself and us— Now eating at McAllisters; a swart-faced N.Y.U. teacher sits opposite with his dull woman discussing me and my book—The fat boy face, full of ignoble righteousness—the other sparse blonde hair—The faces at McAllister's—the calf-faces of young men, full of Columbia University smugness.

But always he remembered the great rivers that girdled the city; he heard horns baying in the gulph of night. He remembered great bridges and the barges far below.

The swine-man and his girl know of me and feast here on me and 30 cents worth of coffee and chocolate cake. It has become a contest to see which one will leave first. Shall I? Such contests as these are childish—especially for me now—but they are also human.

I called for the boy Williams here—he came—a nice shy grinning coon—said he was getting along very well at university—Has changed English class.

The man and his woman are making love—an afternoon at Alice's for fifty cents—verbal fornication in the Shoppe.

Being born, living, dying—and we waste ourselves on petty squabbles—I am now in such mood that the little things possess and harrow my soul—the small imbecile triumphs of other people give me pain, and my own, no pleasure at all. This is courage: to screw and rivet every jerking nerve together by the supremest effort of the will, to conquer the nausea around the heart, the weakness in the bowels, and to strike hardest when most afraid. This is courage—and we must learn to do it—men like me—to beat life to this extent unless we are to let it beat us entirely—The blow in one's own kidney hurts cruelly but *the other one* has kidneys, too. This too is courage: to know when one is beaten for the moment or for good, and still be ready *to fight again.*

To endure, this is the greatest courage: patience makes of our life a battlefield, but however bitter, in the end it is good.

Men are for the most part childish and foolish—and this is more true here in this childlike nation than elsewhere. We are all damned together—all of our strife and swinking get us nowhere finally; the little man who died so abjectly, so dismally in the subway, is no better off than we.

There is no balm in Gilead—there is heaving of the breath and weariness.

Now, keep hold: strike hard—keep your breath cool and calm, and endure. Do all that can be done with calmness and with decency —if you are forced to leave, leave because you are forced by things outside your control—and leave without fear or shame—Do not bluff —endure—and remember constant victory has no meaning.

[March 20–21 (3:05)—
Trying to sleep—have taken bromide Aline gave me—It has no effect yet—Must go to dentist tomorrow for extraction of two teeth. "Toothless Kinch the Superman." [16]]

16. This is the name Buck Mulligan calls Stephen Dedalus in Joyce's *Ulysses.*

Sunday March 23—after last night at Sullivan's—writing this on I.R.T. Union Sq. uptown to meet Jack Wheelock—now passing 28th St.

O April cruel and flower wise.

[*From the October Fair ledger*]

Sunday–Monday—M'ch 23–24:
Today with Wheelock on walk through Park. Later to eat with him at A. F. McDougall's on 57th St. and to Harvard Club. Then home; bought papers with news of Guggenheim appointments. Then H. Stevens to see me, drunk and insulting. Gave him drink, took him home, where I quarreled with him and cursed him.
Away! Away!

You should have known Daddy. He was the only person I have ever known who was as grand as you. He had the wild thing in him, that's what killed him. He had the most beautiful smile, the corners of his mouth and his whole face seemed to turn up and it was just as if someone had turned on a light. He was always making a joke to make people feel good: he said the funniest things, you never knew anything like it in your life; I know one time when Jessie Huge and I were going to art school together she got awfully blue because she couldn't finish the drawing she was working on. She came home with me one day and cried as if her heart would break. Daddy came in and put his arms about her and said "What's the matter?" Jessie said, "I can't draw." Daddy said "Ah, my dear but you can *attract*." I remember he got us both to laughing so we forgot all about the drawing. He was always doing things like that.
I guess I was staying at Auntie Girt's then, no I wasn't I was staying at Nana's—no, perhaps it *was* Auntie Girt's. I get it all mixed up because I changed around so.

Born where Macy's now stands—Phil M[*oeller*] born next door —then went to living on 8th or 9th Streets where Mother and Nana owned 3 or 4 houses—Then to England—First with Auntie on 32 S. Weymouth St.—Mama and Nana in Paris—Then back here and with another aunt now dead on W. 44th St.—then to house just behind on W. 45th St.—Board fence between knocked out for tennis court—then Mama died (sick two years)—Nana kept house—Nana goes from bad to worse—gets married, house sold and furniture at auction—We all went to old Hotel Bristol corner 5th Ave and 42th St.—Nana got worse—got little house in country in N.J.—stayed out there one winter—Daddy died—then went to live with Auntie Girt at 68th St. between Pk. and Columbus Avenue—magnificent house—She took all our money—then with Papa's sister Aunt Mary for few months—then got married—18 years old.

Mario's—March 25—

 O bitterly bitterly Boston one time more.[17]
 The boys are here without the girls, O God strike me dead! [18]
 A long chapter instead of a book, called "A Woman's Life."

 No, but you shouldn't—why don't you—well lissen, Charlie, you can go to the house—yes, you can.

 Trouble is it's a relief—y'know it is—I go up to one of those big places west and live—.

 I was *comin* out one day (brighter) about 3 weeks ago, I was comin out—.

 Well, that's just the way I felt—on the level—.

 I know my expression wasn't changed—It don't bother me at all —I've seen it all—It never bothered me—Over there—they don't bother me—y'know.

 What do you go over there for?

 D'ya think so? D'ya think so?

 I think he's just kiddin' y' along.

 Tha's terrible t' say, George.

 D'ya remember tho' las' year he was goin' t' see that girl Madeline.

 Well, I think she was sensible.

 All she was thinkin' about was Madeline—Summer School—.

 Summer school she used to wear sport close all the time, y'know somethin made her look very young.

 He says, I'm comin over, y'know. Are y' goin t' be in?

 Y'know, she looked very young—y'know the reason I thot she was very young was Girard—.

 Lissen—.

17. Wolfe uses this line as a thematic motif associated with Bostonian repression. It appears in OT&R, pp. 863–64 and elsewhere.
 18. This line eventually turns up as part of the drunken chant of Dexter Briggs, W&R, p. 270.

Every one was a knockout.
Joe was awful crazy about her. Well, I told Joe—.

I wanted to find her lapped in harlotry in Harlem (or else-where). I dreamed of finding her quilted and paired with her daughter in evil lusts in places thick with smoke and drink and drugs and gone through double door to find.

Dear Mr. Moe:
I accept most gratefully my appointment as a fellow of the Guggenheim Foundation. I should like to see you and talk to you within the next week, and if I call your secretary perhaps she could suggest a time for me to meet you. Please accept again my sincerest thanks to you and the committee for my appointment.

Faithfully yours,
Thomas Wolfe
27 West 15th Street
N.Y.C.

Dentist—Dr. George Babbitt—40 East 49th—3 o'clock.

Warm glut, warm hissing glut.

"Anything they say is perfectly allright—isn't it—y'know I think there auta be a law."

Today Aline, I was in bed, then lunch, nurses home behind University on side, then newspaper stand, cigar stand at 14th Street, boys coming from lunch to school—Then Gramercy square and book-shop—workmen—subway—Then uptown—Then dentist's—Then walk downtown to next stop—Then G'd Central—Then Harvard Club —Then telephoning Aline, then this place here.

For life is more savage than any war: it is not for the million men who are slain in a battle that we should grieve, but for the hundred million men around us who are daily slain by living, and for whom, soon or late, the earth is waiting. I do not grieve that service-men die in battle: I simply grieve that all men die—with all our hunger unappeased, with all purpose gone amort.

Defoe—*The Secret History of The October Club.*
The Young Lady's Cabinet of Gems—a choice collection of pieces in poetry and prose—by Virginia De Forest, New York, 1860.

[*From the October Fair ledger*]

Sunday night—March 30–31, 1930—
The cycle has swung back. I find myself at the same depth of fruitless and sterile exhaustion as I had reached two years ago. I am unable to create, unable to concentrate, and I am filled with fever, with bitter and restless anger against the world; and I am beginning to feel this against Aline. This must be the end! the end! the end!
Went to the Public Library today—the Jews pushing in and out, the hideous clicking of the trains, the sound like the sounds of Grand Central Station.
The prints and drawings of old New York in the corridors—1836, 1837, 1840—the forest of slender masts along the wharves, the warehousey looking buildings—O how peaceful it all looked.
Had lunch in Child's at 5th Avenue—the woman with good legs and the sly dry long face who looked at me—"Drink your good Child's coffee, dearie."
Last night on the streets (6th Avenue) after theater—hell and confusion—the crowds—"pull the wool over his eyes"—the 8 young Jews horseplaying, hitting swiftly at each other with hard fists, thudding *en passant*, doubling, redoubling—"Let's cross over here."
In the Public Libe a woman thinking over the index at Catherine di Medici.
The window full of false faces one flight up at corner of 6th Ave. and the 40's.

O, but by all means, save yourself. This heart, this heart, 'tis a tender thing—it bleeds too bloodily: now have fair words hereafter, be full of talk of love—but never feel it. She will come wailing to your doorstep. *Don't let her in!* Say you are sorry, that your own sorrow is greater than you can bear, but that neither of you must be *selfish.* Speak of the beauty of resignation and forbearance: say you have concluded it is not right, it is not fair, it is not *honorable* to go on: repulse her gently with sad sorrowful bastard's face: then go in and enjoy your god-damned dinner like a man.
Don't let her in! No more! No more! Don't let them through the house doors of your heart, they'll sneak, they'll idle in. They'll peer

round corners with their asking flower face: they'll mouse and nuzzle up, and purr like cats along the corridors. They'll steal like perfume into every crack and corner—until they're in your house, my boy. They're settled there, bag and baggage, and then just try to get them out! *Don't let them in!*

They'll weep, they'll sob, they'll moan! Where? Upon your bed, my boy. They'll sob upon your bed with swelling silken tail proposed in amorous sorrow. O g-lub, g-lub, g-lub! That it should come to this, etc.! O Lord, what am I going to do? How can I go on living without you, etc.?

And you? You'll melt like butter, you clabberhead. Don't! Please don't, dear. Don't cry, dear. There, there—it's all right—You'll say with great originality, first stroking at the brow and then, with great originality, the silken swelling tail.

Delighted you're coming Ocean grand but other beverage scarce Verbum sap Also bring latest issue New Freeman Let me know time of your arrival

Love TOM

Front window—Steel Pier—Atlantic City:

Chompingly, with mush-mouthed chomp, the blind newspaper man just outside Nedick's, chomps upon an apple. His face is lifted in a rapt fat pucker as he chomps rolling with sensual rumination the apple mash upon his tongue.

Chop Suey and Chow Mein above.

An old well-to-do with cane, a cap, a coat, spats, a red groomed surly dog's face and his two old women gaunt cracked and with clumsy butts—Niggery niggers plod by in wheel chairs and one sees many glass-eyed faces of Pure American women—the Snodgrasses, the Simpsons, the Whites and Browns, some with four sterilized glass-eyed mugs of 35; others with petulant hangdogginess, the queasy irritable pouts with drooping sallow mouthbags of 50 or 55.

Young leggy, butty American girls—"may I touch your,"—"You may touch my"—O but lightly, etc.—with long cloaks wrapped about it.

Some of the blackest niggers here I ever saw.

The bluntfaced Lithuanian woman with rich clothes buying lavishly of junk at the little auction Booth.

"There's a lady that knows a piece of tapestry when she sees it" etc.

[*From the October Fair ledger*]

Atlantic City—Sunday night, April 6—

"There was a roaring in the wind all night." The wind is blowing with a steady heavy drone, and the waves are piling, ceaselessly on the beach. The rain is blowing in hard fine driving sheets—I walked along North Carolina Street until I came to the Atlantic Ocean —the ocean rolls in with a vast grey loneliness—today full of wet grey sparkle and long white caps—it boils up the beach with scummy hiss and washes into estuaries leaving thick foamy eight inch suds—Heinz 57 Varieties burns over tremendous swell—and sea slop—6 miles of immense hotels, bead shops, salt water taffy, auction places and wheel chairs—the immense cheapness of the resort and the roaring wind, the infinite, inexhaustible wetness of the sea.

The sea boils in across these miles of sand and meets—what things?

Greenberg, a young Jew, with cigar tilted upward from his hard mouth-corners: for the rest, a sporty camel's-hair coat, spats [*page missing*]

Meditation of gentleman in subway on the subject of Death: "Well, I don't know—he may be lucky at that."

"Could I reveal eggs-ac-ly what I *feel*" [19]

The ruined winter earth from which such lovely things may grow.

The immense brown winter's earth; the tough brown winter grasses.

Tiles and laths and hollow clayey tubes at track's side.

The level densities of stunt scrub pine.

O early April cruel and flower wise.

19. A line from a popular song of the time.

Small trees are smoky with small tender green and yellow—.
The seared leaves of autumn hang on stunted trees.
This is the lonely land.

I see bright glints of water, ponds and lakes with cool steel waves forever lapping—and green level wastes around of the small pine. It is the sea, the sea perhaps, but I think of ecstasy and New England cool white thighs in summer shades and quilted love at night.

Fat chickens clucking in American yards and women pinning clothes up on string lines.

Do you know any more good jokes, etc.
How you makin' out?

Early October is the time I sing, when leaves are burning and you see bright sprigs of flame among dry grasses.
Bleak moaning in bare winter trees.
In the bleak land the willow trees are green and feathery.

Upon this ancient earth there are few builded places that match the permanence of the soil. Atlantic City. The outskirts of great cities (and yet one finds new places "Coatesville, Pa." with surprise)— But the old German Towns—Not the Riviera. And the German great fat permanent fellows who drink in ancient buildings and say the ancient things to one another.

[*From the October Fair ledger*]

"Monday, April 14/15—
Today a sobbing hell with A_____.
The inner ache, the wild sterile regret.
What new monsters? Seductive air washed round the midges on Sixth Avenue.
What rapes and murders? The beads that bought the island boom like cannon balls.
Fat legs flesh-hosed marched down the stairs of 14th St. subways at 5:30. Above, the overripe lips of Jewish girls 3 abreast. The unending and sterile fecundity of nature here.
Four thugs at midnight sit in Child's—their inch of brow and bearsgrease hair—Crude laughter widens over gappy teeth—Dark I curse and speak of Jack the Ripper and of a murder for $25.

Mr. Simonson [20] in H. Club tophatted—a boy killed himself here 2 days ago.

Nestlé's Chocolate:

 Now when the man comes up you have him dig here.

 We'll go right up to Harlem tonight—right up to this smoke joint.

 Now listen that isent a bit nice—what did you say?

 Do you want to know really?

 Honest.

 Absolutely.

 Well, we got to get girls.

 Do you mean that? etc.

 They got girls up there.

 High yellow—H_____ K_____ she's a beautiful girl.

 There's someone I been lookin for—someone who doesn't like Harlem.

 It's marvelous—for the *incentive.*

 You're right.

 I'm damned glad it aint my fault.

 Never mind—I'm hungry—well, you finish your drink—I want to eat.

 Right now we're goin' to eat and goin' to Harlem.

 Are we goin to Harlem?

 Lissen, Joe, Lissen, you take that one, you take that one.

 No, I take my own jus' as is—drink with my foot on the bar.

 Now that my boss is gone let's drink.

 (These are 3 business men with the whore [leading?] on business men.)

 As far as my boss is concerned its bizness only, an' as far as Mr. Ladd is concerned it's my own bizness an' after 5 oclock I'm my own boss.

 At the same time there's the psychological side.[21]

20. Lee Simonson, an outstanding theatrical designer, a director of the Theatre Guild, and a friend of Mrs. Bernstein's.

21. Wolfe made use of this material for the "tones of lady-like refinement," OT&R, pp. 417–18.

After the Sullivan's—Second Time—
Complaint, complaint, the nightingale's complaint.
Dry bones, the barren land.
Lives the old poison; old love dead.
If not old love, to waken in me the old fear—complaint, complaint.
Who tills the barren earth? The dry bones, the dry land. Who sows the barren Land? That look? It's worth a thousand pains. What's death?

Check and double check.
He aint worth the dirt under her little finger.
I wouldn't put it past him.
A million chances I had.
They lay there all naked, etc.
Holy Jesus.
You know what she'd do with me? She'd get cock-eyed drunk an' strip rite in front of me (a man of 70).
He was there cockeyed drunk with his jock out ([whisper] tryin' to do it t' the wife, see) an' the husban' was passed out cold. An' the wife was there "Thinly clad"—an' the guy had his jock out when Redman came by.
And Redman hit him one rite under the chin an' then agin f'r luck. "Gee," said Redman, "I was so mad I hit him agin fer luck—an' over the back o' the head goin' downstairs—I was so sore at him."
Now the guy'll never try it again.
An' she was a decent respec'able woman.

So I says that prick, that friend of yours owes me $150.00, when's he goin to pay me? [22]
So Johnny Sheehan says to me, he says, Any Goddamned thing you want I'll do, he says.
So I says, Thass all rite.
So he says, Can you reach Bill Griffin?
So he says, Yess—What did I start to tell you? Oh, I know—So he says to me one night, so he says to me, Do you know a fellow named Mike Martz?
So I looks at the Son of a Bitch and I says, Sure. So I says to him—.

22. Wolfe adapted this for the Voice of "pugnacious recollection," OT&R, p. 417.

So he got into Lindy's an' he stayed there at Lindy's crap game till daylight.

Well, I think I'm going to beat it.

[*From the October Fair ledger*]

Monday, April 28—

Got passage on *Volendam* today—Went to dentist's first—Then to Harv. Club to write letter—Then to Scrib. and to station with Mr. Perkins—Made arrangements with Kazenberger over phone for man to help me pack—Called Mr. Van Doren tonight—he called me back—Dining with him and brother in pent house tomorrow night—Then special delivery from Aline—said she was in torture—then sent her telegram saying lunch at Tenbrink place tomorrow at one—then to Mario's—4 cocktails—then Alice McAllister's—steak—and mocked woman.

Then took resolve to go to end of Manhattan by subway—and did so—getting off right across river at 225, drinking milky-sweety-paley-sickening coffee in back room & walking back to Dyckman street where egg sandwich & coffee in Coffee Pot—so home from Dyckman street with frayed whores; young Italian thugs with rolled out battered lips and thick necks, with pale tough fighterfaces; young Irishman; Jews; sporty nigger men with thin black asheny faces; a young kid in a polo shirt on his first hobo trip, etc.—Home at 2 o'clock.

Add—the early morning trucks moving in to New York; Sheffield Farms electric sign across the river at 225th—the heavy powerful swinging rumble of the subway-become-elevated; the dark gleaming sweep of rails along Harlem river with the high signal—semaphores burning red—the great humming powerhouse—"Drake Court" elevator apartments—a whore getting out of a cab and entering a 207th st. ap't house fumbling for keys—the night-time rabble of toughs, whores, and taxis at Dyckman St.

In Coffee Pots the taxi men, the night workers, the men with dirty stained aprons smacking wet hamburgers on greasy black frying slabs—the coffee cakes—the thick sugar rings on doughnuts.

The long lines of streetcars coming across town at 5:30—Union Square.

The Police Parade.

The station on W. 47th where I went with Abe Smith and girl to retrieve taxi.

The street cars at 225 St. in Bronx coming lonelily in at 1 A.M.

—180 St. cross town, White Plains Ave. etc. The slow yet rapid emptying of car between 125–200th St.

"Are you gonna see the ball game tomorrow?" A big red-faced young man with a grey felt hat and a leather jacket in a Coffee Pot with smaller companions.

A nigger in a cap; a cop; a taxi man.

A young Jewess—a face of perfect regular ripe coarseness—almost delicate—too regular.

An old woman with a sagging American old woman's face—petulant jowled with horrible corpsiness, false toothed, spectacled, powdered, rouged, a haggis of frail bones and dry corruptness smiling horribly.

A young man giving directions with forward New Yorkness—"I'll show you—Follow me—get off at 96th, etc."

Baker Freed.

Football Middleburg Sept. 28.

This Week at Capitol.

Pep at 6 or 60—Shell Gasoline.

The stabled streetcars—the all night garages with hoses on concrete floors.

"C'mon, swellhead, sit wit' us."

He had the bitter sensitivity of young people for what other people said about him; he disliked and felt contempt for many of the instructors, yet it angered him to think any of them might dislike him. However, he was not vindictive; he only wanted to be free from them, from having ever again to see them.

Greene sat much of the time in moody rumination in his chair, with his poisonous eyes moving venomously about the room.

Utility Cultures, Inc. (Dramatis Personae).[23]
Crackenthorpe (McCullough)
Ella May Maird
Plato P. Hoak
O'Hara
Varnish
Whelpe
Oscar J. Teddy.

23. This is Wolfe's first reference to the School for Utility Cultures, which was to be his satiric reflection on New York University. McCullough refers to Bruce McCullough, one of Wolfe's colleagues who was in charge of the Freshman Composition program.

April 30th:

Aren't you the playful old thing? (Woman with ha-ha-ha-ha laughter.)

Noo-o—I was just tryin to get my money back.

And then all of a sudden—You get yourself in such a condition that you're not fit to do anything, you know.

(And then one girl looked and looked and looked at me and said nothing.)

Get me.

It's a toss up, etc.

"Bianco." "Bianco."—at Louis Martin's Bianco means martini cocktail.

The October Fair.

In English: Shakespeare
    Oxford Book
    Of Human Bondage
    Tom Jones
    Bleak House
    Lady Chatterly
    Ulysses
    Donne

In American: Moby Dick
    Memoirs Davy Crockett
    Mark Twain
    Young Wild West
    The Scarlet Letter
    Whitman
    Franklin, Edwards, Mather

In German—Goethe, Kleist, Rilke, Oktobertag.

War and Peace, 6×400, 2400.

All this at Louis Martin's:

. . . I mean, I mean . . . I mean, after all (the sonsofbitches who say this are all sonsofbitches)

I remember once when I was a kid—I thought "Well, if this will make me strong as an ox"—etc.

Chairs were scattered in such a way I could hardly walk myself so I persuaded a woman (This was the fellow with the deep deep voice that I disliked—he was full of sex and impertinence).

What I shall Do:

I shall get on a great ship.

I shall eat fine food and drink red rich wines and splendid beers and liquors.

I shall try to fuck beautiful woman.

[*From the October Fair ledger*]

April 30–May 1—

Cold, chilly tonight—the remote and dying rumble of the 6th Ave. L—whistles of boats and steamers in river.

Up in an elevator—what floors please—Down alone—"O I hate hot weather I simply loathe it, etc." says dentist's assistant—Down alone—Italian elevator man burlesks grand opera.

Packed books today with Campbell-sent packer—Dentist early —preparing for inlays & tooth—To lunch with Laura Powers[24]— Home—Aline came in, feeling better she says, has had medicine—Then alone later—called Doctor—the landlord—He agreed to $3 a day until my boat sails—Aline called me at 8 o'clock to advise this—really I think to see if I was in & if she could go out. I called later, she had gone somewhere—Then to 49th St. Grill where notes on talk—In came 4 y'g men one of whom says he is Allen (?) Priest—old friend of K. Raisbeck now at Metropolitan—So to H. Club and home.

[*A long list follows: of New York streets, landmarks, characteristic people in the street, places Wolfe has visited in the last four days, and so on.*]

May 1—May Day—

Seven o'clock Daylight Savings (D.S. began week ago about). Just back from walk to Union Square—an air of completion over the completed battlefield—Police patrol watchfully—the loitering remnants discuss in groups, gesticulate.[25]

The soft thunderous air full of its brooding wait. The deep purple clouds and the heavy delicious omen that stirs the loins with pleasant qualms.

24. Mrs. Laura Powers Peirce, a friend from Bristol, Rhode Island.

25. The Communist Party had celebrated May Day with a parade and had run into opposition from Veterans groups.

The summer street cars out, filled with heavy-legged people.

The bombardment begins: the purple-clouded sky is split with enormous jags of lightning. Like a blast of artillery the thunder smash and rattle comes.

The big drops fall—then heavy rain. I run home by the hospital and see a child crying bitterly on its cot—its back strapped up.

When you see the first pure green of a tree in New York in Spring, a cry bursts from your throat. Spring here more poignant than in the country.

May 3d—8:20 at evening—

Darkness just coming to the full—a sliver of crescent moon in the pure delicate sky—Today was the most delicious day of Spring—Yesterday too hot—but today was full of ecstasy, of cool and warmth, and of bitter joy.

O bitter and lovely life, the old cry wakens on my lips, and I fling my arms out for ecstasy and loss. O lovely and impalpable promise, you waken qualms along my loins, you stab my heart with glory and the hauntings of brief days.

The horns are baying in the river (the river was pure and lovely said Aline this morning when she came from seeing Terry [*Helburn*] off to Europe)—the horns are baying in the river and great boats with bright red funnels are putting out to sea—A brooding quietness and the faint rumble of the elevated rests over this immense city, and our eyes are filled with tenderness and love, and music comes from open windows—from pianos, radios, and talking machines.

The quiet side streets of New York in the pure dark and distant vistas of Union Square in peace after a week of riots, of crowds gone home from work.

May 3d—

Had luncheon with Aline at her house—magnificent lunch: old-fashioned whiskey cocktail, chicken broth, a tender thick steak with new string beans, potatoes, and peas, tomato salad and baked banana for dessert.

May 4, Sunday—late at night—

Up for luncheon with Marjorie Fairbanks [26]—Talked all afternoon with her—Heard of her trouble with Sidney, divorce, his new

26. Marjorie Fairbanks, Helen Harding, and Kenneth Raisbeck accompanied Wolfe on a tour of Paris and the surrounding countryside in 1925. Wolfe made use of this experience in "Jason's Voyage," OT&R, pp. 680–794, in the adventures of Eugene Gant with Elinor, Ann, and Starwick.

wife, child, etc. Also scandal and gossip of Cambridge—[*Conrad*] Aiken, [*Robert*] Hillyer, *et al*. Also K. Raisbeck. Also Helen Harding has become old maid, says Marjorie, living with another woman—a mess all around, it seems.

Then to Harvard Club where wrote letters, then H. Volkening came and to dinner at Luchow's with him. Then home with him to see Natalie and talked until 1:30 almost. So home.

Another glorious day—the pure sweet green of the budding trees brings a cry to the throat & tears to the eyes. Here to be caught only for a few days. Henry and I talked together in the twilight.

Marjorie that I thought so cruel and clever 5 years ago seemed pathetic today. I felt a great pity for them all—yet four years ago I could not have talked to any of them without pain. What hath time wrought!

Monday, May 5—
Now in the wood, the wood, the dear Spring wood at home the angel stands; and all of the dogwood bloom is flowered out.

May 6, 10 at night—
Took suit to tailor's; Aline came for lunch; went to 48th St. place; then to Melville Cane's—made will and got advice on M. Boyd;[27] then to Mr. Moe in Frick Bldg.; then to Scribner's Book Shop where Aline was waiting—bought books—then left her—to H. Club, wrote letters—then to Hoboken by tube—then to see boat—vast empty pier, etc.—then to Hofbrau House where met with man named Hansen—then back with him on ferry to 23rd St.—then walked across to 9th Ave—down to 14th St. across town to home.

May 7, 12:15—
Out to take suit to tailor's, watch to jeweller's—Child's with Aline for breakfast—to bank for money—802 in bank—Frank's Tours not in—a very hot day—the heat mist over New York—the great funnels of boats blurred by heat-wave over the top of the piers—A great parade of airplanes over New York—at least a dozen squadrons cleaving through the hot blue in triangles, squares, wedges, spears, etc. —at different heights—along 14th St. Jews come from their stores, small children look wonderingly up, the workmen stop on subways and buildings.

27. Wolfe's first will declared that his estate should be divided equally between Mrs. Bernstein and his mother. Since Wolfe disliked and distrusted Madeleine Boyd, he no longer wanted her to act as his literary agent.

"Those guys must be cool up there," says one.

"Ah, how do you know?" says another. "It may be hotter than down here."

Thursday, May 8—At Child's 11. A.M.

Go to Bank and get express checks.

Get pr. of shoes.

Take remaining laundry out.

Continue packing.

Go to dentist.

Meet [*Dan*] Howard.

See Mr. Perkins.

Get suit from tailor.

Buy wing collars for dress suits, black socks, (and shirts?)

Call up or visit Watt and Munn.

Pay Harvard Club Dues. pd. House charges.

Buy ledger for writing.

Buy Strap for trunk.

Aline's Books:

Sets of Shaw, Dickens, Scott, Wells, Thack., Saki, Wilde, James, Dorothy Richardson, Geo. Gissing, Wasserman, Beerbohm, T. Mann, Borrow, Proust, Rabelais, DeMorgan, Huxley, May Sinclair, George Moore, *Die Mode*, Ferrario—*Costume Ant. et Mod.*, Ramet—*Le Costume Historique*, Hottenroth—*Le Costume*, Biedermeier Book, *Shakespeare's England*, *Masques et Bouffons* by Maurice Sand, *Historic Wallpapers* by Nancy McClelland, Balzac, Thomas Hardy, Numerous plays, *The Elizabethan Stage*—Chambers, Mantzius—*Hist. of Theatrical Art*, Complete vols. of *The Mask*—Gordon Craig, Edgar Wallace, *Tapisserie Gothique*—Demotte, Sam'l Butler, Encyclopaedia Brittanica, Willa Cather, James Stephens, *Old People and The Things That Pass*—Couperus, Hergesheimer, *Costume of the Ancients*—T. Hope, *Ancient Egyptian, Assyrian and Persian Costume, Rajput Painting*—Ananda Coomaraswamy, *Colonial Furniture in America*—Lockwood, *History of Art*—Elie Faure.

Books on Lautrec, Goya, Breughel, Picasso, Hogarth, Holbein, Grünewald, Blake, Fra Angelico, Books on glass, Furniture, Tapestry.

Poems by Keats, Shelley.

You don't want a shoe that's too big fer yuh.

Natcherly—your foot was wet—it's dryin' out now.

[*In Mrs. Bernstein's hand:*]
Aline Bernstein, Armonk, New York, U.S.A.
Armonk Village 434.
270 Park Ave.
My dearest love.

[*From the October Fair ledger*]
May 14 (Wed.) At sea! At sea!
Mid-afternoon—the ship hums tranquilly with slow leathery croakings of the woodwork, a low soothing dynamic whine.
The top of the water near the ship—the watery scum is *marmoreal*—i.e. it gets streaky like marbled columns.

Since leaving New York:
Last day in New York [*May 9*]—in afternoon after finishing all other business, went home—Aline there packing. We got packed for cleaners—went out bought shirt, collars, etc. had coffee at Child's—Aline had previously bought at Hearn's underwear, socks, neckties—then home and finished rest of packing—then to Mario's—many people, many costumes. Terribly moved, horribly nervous—old jealous suspicion that she was flirting, etc.—Mario's wife, drunk and tragic, embraced me and gave me a bottle of sparkling champagne for going-away present. Bar full of drunks—then we walked to Sixth Avenue and got taxi—Last look at 14th and Fifth Avenue—then upstairs to finish packing—over in 5 minutes—then in taxi to 23d St. Ferry, over to Hoboken by ferry—Aline and I stood out on front of boat going over—the marvelous cool wet coddy sea smell after hot day in New York—smell of the ferry slip—like old warm wood—the tugs with strange lights up and wet cool water wash surge by. Then the piers, the parked cars, the people.
We go to stateroom and drink champagne. We unpack, she gives me old medal to wear that Marsden Hartley [28] gave her. We talk some more, we go on deck, we kiss again tenderly, tenderly, on eyes, lips, mouth—the staring people, the shouting people on pier and boat—She goes down gangway and walks away weeping—the shouting people on pier and deck—the foolish shoutings back and forth.
Then out into harbor—the tugs nose her out into the river—we slide down by New York—Blazing milky moonlight—The tugs are backing and now receding, backing away—the steady hum of the

28. An American expressionistic painter. Mrs. Bernstein probably knew him in the early 1900's, when Hartley was working in New York.

engines—the end of the island—Great boats with twinkling jewel lights go sea-wards—Battery—the great buildings—the Staten Island ferry boats—the cool blowing seaward air—Brooklyn—the flashing finger of searchlight—Liberty, a dim torch, Staten Island—The Narrows—the Coney Island and Long Island lights—the open sea—the pilot comes down darkly hatted—"Well, good night, folks"—the rowboat comes in deftly from pilot boat—he drops into it, grasps light standing, one of the oarsmen takes little canvas bundle from hook—they're off—so are we—Europewards. Blazing but milky moonlight which obscured sharp lines of lower New York.

First day out [*May 10*]—Saturday—Absolutely placid sea, blue cloudless sky—elysian voyage.

2nd day out [*May 11*]—Sunday—Sea a little rougher but calm.

3d day out [*May 12*]—Monday—Part cloudy and bright—a roll to the ship—my bowels running off—beer and wine I think—at night I dress up and dance—Faces already familiar-looking to me—quite cold —Full moon.

4th day out [*May 13*]—Tuesday—Gulf stream weather—a gentle heavy roll to the ship—sun and cloud—mostly cloud—at night magnificent moon in and out of cloud—at top of boat again with Kahn, his daughter, the German girl.

5th day out [*May 14*]—Wednesday—Gulf stream weather—mild, delightful—shine and cloud—mostly shine—I am a little nervous and tired of some of boat's people.

Volendam, May 17:

8 days at sea—The thing you feel at sea is time—I go back to May 8? 9? 3? in this book—it is like dreams, coral hauntings, unrent marble.

Sunday, May 18—Lunchtime up the channel—bright sparkling whipping windy day—The wheeling soaring gulls—The sea full of emerald green—of manifold tints—the coast of England old, worn, incredibly touching earth.

O bitterly bitterly Boston one time more.

The foaming sea, the broken spring.

O will you ever come back to it, ever come back to the marvellous hills of home?

The dry bones, the bitter earth; the dry, the bitter bones in barren earth.

Sunday, May 18—going up the Channel at 10:30 after leaving Plymouth—"England lighted for an eternal feast"—says Conrad—The lights along the shore, the deep velvet sky, star encrusted. In the smokeroom the remaining passengers are playing bridge.

"I can't play cards tonight."

"It's a quarter of eleven clear, that right?"

"I'll be right back up, I'll meet you right here."

"Are you satisfied with it?"

"Queens."

"No hearts."

"You can't play it" etc.

This voyage: The Beekman Jews; the French couple Mrs. and Mr. Merlier—the old Austrian; the two American ladies; the German girl.

The enormous gossip—the boat buzzing with whisperings, etc.

The two old-American young couples from Mass.—the Sperry boys rugged and plainspoken but O so Yale.

"O Don't worry about *tha-a-t*."

The man with the big dark wife who carried on the flirtation with the pert 16-year-old girl—He lights a cigarette—or tries to—the girl pertly blows out match, the wife sits quietly, suffering—her back bowed below the girl. We feast upon her grief. The man's nasal unpleasant voice.

Seven mos. ago today my book was published.

Pocket Notebook 14
May 20, 1930, to August 12, 1930

The Guggenheim year was the big test, and Wolfe was rather shaky when he went into it. He had to prove himself to his mentors at Scribner's and to reviewers who had likened him to Melville and Dostoievski. Although plans for "The October Fair" were still scattered, two clusters of ideas remained constant. The book would tell the story of David Hawke's love for Esther Jacobs, a middle-aged married woman, and reflect all the intensity and anguish of Wolfe's own affair with Mrs. Bernstein. It would also embody the consciousness of being an American and thus would aspire to be a national epic in prose.

This notebook shows Wolfe suffering fully the ordeal of "second book trouble." He had enormous difficulty getting started, and he tended to blame much of his own uncertainty on others for distracting him. Still, his loneliness was very real, and his emotional disturbance, as a result of his break with Mrs. Bernstein, was as great as what he had gone through in order to shake loose from his mother. The notebook, which begins with his arrival in Paris, records a variety of emotional states, only some of which are channeled into creative activity. But it does afford some of the best glimpses of Wolfe at work: his playing with thematic phrases and returning again and again to chew them over, his jotting down of a mixture of memories and current observations, his ritualistic listing of titles and chapter headings, his statistical recording and categorizing of a bewildering assortment of facts about his life. Besides this, the notebook gives us, once again, Wolfe the American tourist, alert, sensitive, roaming about and preserving impressions for future use.

[Enclosed in the endpapers are
  1) A clipping from the Paris Herald, *"Life in Paris," with a list of restaurants and bars.*
  2) A sheet of stationery from the Hotel Mondial, 5 Cité Bergère, Grands Boulevards, Paris, with the following list of reminders that Wolfe made out upon arrival in Paris:]

Tuesday, May 20, 1930:

1) Go to Guaranty Trust Co. Find out about letter of credit, etc.
2) Take Watch to Jeweller—63 Hausmann.
3) Have suit of clothes made—Jackson & Poisson—Ask for suit within 4 days time.
4) Get room in hotel—ask at G.T. Co. of hotels in Etoile quarter—visit Hotel Vignon (?) & Hotel Burgundy.
5) Write Aline—also letters to Mr. Darrow, & home; Dr. Kang [1]—etc.
6) Send laundry out.
7) Find out about ways of getting to
    (1) Valley of the Chevreuse; (2) North Coast of Brittany; (3) Rouen.
8) Buy big ledgers & begin to write.

O bitterly bitterly Boston one time more: the flying leaf, the broken cloud.

At Guar. Trust Co.:

Found letters from Darrow with dentist's bill; Mrs. Gorman; [2] Hilda; also cable from Aline.[3]

Wrote Mr. Darrow telling him not to pay dentist.[4]

[*In a letter to Aline Bernstein, May 20, Wolfe describes his surroundings:* "I am staying for a few days in what is for me a new part

1. Younghill Kang had been a colleague of Wolfe's in the English department at New York University. Wolfe encouraged him in writing the story of his Korean boyhood, *The Grass Roof,* and introduced him to Perkins, who accepted the book for publication in 1931.

2. Jean Gorman, the wife of Herbert Gorman, the biographer of James Joyce. She wrote Wolfe on May 7, asking him to visit them in England. During the next two months she continued to write him letters of invitation. She even mentioned to him that the Joyces were coming to London and that John Galsworthy had once owned the flat the Gormans were staying in.

3. Wolfe said to Aline Bernstein of this cable: "Two or three words from you of any sort give me a much greater thrill than a letter from anyone else." Letter, May 20, 1930.

4. Dr. H. M. Babbitt had done dental work for the Bernstein family, and Mrs. Bernstein had given Wolfe his name. Before leaving for Europe, Wolfe had some serious dental work done involving the treatment of a diseased tooth and the pulling of some others. Dr. Babbitt was now sending a bill for $285.00; his assistant, "who did most of the work," said Wolfe, "demands $250." "With the $60 which the toothpuller charged for butchering me, this makes about $600," Wolfe raged (Letter to Aline Bernstein, May 20, 1930), and he was willing to pay only what he thought was reasonable—$200.00. Over the months, Dr. Babbitt tried through Scribner's and through Mrs. Bernstein to get the account settled, and in his notebook Wolfe scribbled furious letters, which he never sent.

of Paris. This is a little hotel right off the Grand Boulevards and a noisy all-night street, full of cafés and cabarets called the Rue Faubourg du Montmarte. It sounds very noisy but this is really one of the quietest places I have found in Paris—it is a 'cité': i.e. a group of old buildings having its own street and entrance. There are gates and arches at each end of the street: at night the gates are shut, and if you are out you ring a bell and an old man lets you in."]

[*The entries in the notebook itself begin.*]

Bought in Paris on Tuesday May 20, 1930, the day after my arrival there.
Tues. May 20:
Eating at Café Madrid on Grand Boulevard—later to Palace Music Hall—Raquel Meller.[5]
For Wednesday May 21:
Mail letter to Aline.
Get another hotel.
Write S. Fitzgerald.[6]

Proud potent whores who walk the streets at night.
Must we *forever* walk the million streets?
Paris-Soir.

Possession was the law of his soul: what he wanted he wanted wholly to possess, and if he could not, he got sick.
What we do not own with our spirit is not worth a roasted fart to us or anyone else.

To Dr. Babbitt:
Before I pay you a penny we shall wait and see how the work you did serves and whether you have destroyed any more teeth besides those you had pulled out. I felt that you were a swine—a large hog-faced swine—when I saw you; but your swinishness is greater than I thought, it passes understanding.

Today Wed. May 21—Up at 11—finished letter to Aline—Mailed it at hotel—Went to Café Madrid for picon-citron; took taxi to Marguery; dined there filet of sole and Chablis; took taxi to Guaranty

5. Raquel Meller was the star of the Palace Music Hall and later of the Folies-Bergère.
6. Maxwell Perkins always liked for the Scribner authors to know each other, and he had asked Wolfe to look up Fitzgerald in Europe.

Trust Co; wrote letters to Holliday [7] and Scott Fitzgerald; got addresses of hotels; then to American Express Co; took taxi to Quai Augustins; looked at hotel; walked along Quai, looking at books; then up St. Michel to St. Germain; had aperitif there; took taxi to Boulevard Garibaldi; walked around that district and Tour Eiffel; across Pont de l'Alma; ate there; took taxi back to hotel; got overcoat; then to Folies Bergère (I write this next day at Wepler's) Here I broke off because the most delicious choucroute I ever tasted arrived—pommes soufflés over sausages, ham, & sauerkraut (Brasserie Graff Montmartre—it was called); then to Café G'd Boulevard where I had little liqueur for stomach then walked to Place Republique; then taxi to Montmartre.

Six years ago I was teaching my first year at N.Y.U.

A rich scream [8]—David by the river in the dark—the terrific pageant of 10 years sweeps through him—his membranes swell, his muscles harden for a terrible effort—a terrible goat-scream bursts from his throat, tears spurt from his eyes—he screams again, again, again— The memory of Paris, cafés, Vienna, New York, 50th Street, the university, London, the steamer at Plymouth, München, North Carolina, the book quays, the art exhibits, the leg-crossed cunts, Budapest, Atlantic City, the farm land around Lancaster—etc.

How different is Wepler's from 49th St. Grill—the men playing billiards in front of me, the soft European romanticky café-music playing, the laughter & talk everywhere, the Frenchman aged with not-too-young mistress; the sprouting moustache-ends—the waiters.

On the train: Esther waking at morning, the city awake also— Coming in hickety hickety hack—*tell the whole thing* as her rich body is prepared for the day.

The elevator men, the flunkies, the etc. in a great ap't house as hubby comes home just after lover leaves.

60 Mos.—	4 yrs, in New York
Hotel Albert—9—(N.Y.U.)	
8th St.—8—(no N.Y.U.)	

7. Terence Holliday, owner of the Holliday Book Shop in New York, was just returning to America after a European vacation.

8. Wolfe uses the "goat-cry" of his autobiographical hero to stand for exuberance in life. Although it appears in Wolfe's first two novels, it figures more significantly in *The Web and the Rock*. This notebook entry is later developed into the episode in which George Webber regains his equilibrium when he returns to Europe (pp. 631-33).

11th St.—9—(N.Y.U.)
15th St.—16—(½ N.Y.U.)
Hotel [Dalaes?]—4
Chelsea—2
Oxford—1½
Asheville—1½
Munich—1½
Vienna—1½
Maine, Canada, Budapest, Lake District, Italy.

During last sixteen months—Canada, Maine, Boston, Rhinebeck, Atlantic City, Philadelphia, New York, Asheville, Anderson [*S.C.*], Lancaster [*Pa.*], Glen Ridge N.J.

A Chapter to be called "The Arithmetic of the Soul."

The music deepened like a passion.

All of our hearts are fulfilled of you, all of our souls are growing warm with you, all of our lives are beating out their breath for you, and the strange feel of our pulses is playing through our blood for you, immortal and unending living.[9]

This above was written yesterday, Thursday May 22—I write this at the Taverne Royale 10:50 after dinner, Friday May 23.

Friday, May 23—Home at 2:30 last night—Letter to Frere Reeves[10]—To bed—Up at 12:30 today after distressed and living dreams—Packed—Copied letter to Reeves—Descended—Paid bill—left hotel—Came to Hotel Burgundy—Top floor *installé*—Forgot lunch—cocktails Adega—lunch at Restaurant Alsacienne—20 Fr.—[vin?] non compris—then Guaranty Trust—Letter Emily Davies—Answered—Got money—talked with man about hotel—Came to Weber's for coffee—then to Harry's bar—Then to coiffeur for shave and massage, had everything—then to hotel—then opened trunk for list of maisons in old *Sourire*—then slept—Then here to Taverne Royale.

How things go: at 4:10 A.M. the street lights of Paris go off (May 23–24). I sit at all night cafe on G'd Boulevard opposite Rue

9. Beginning here, Wolfe tore several pages from this notebook to use for Eugene Gant's notes in Paris. The three entries above appear in OT&R, p. 676.

10. Wolfe tells Reeves how lonely he is and that "you have no idea how much comfort I get from knowing you are so near at hand, and that I can go to see you." He expects to go to London soon and would like to rent a little cottage and hire a cook. *Letters*, p. 229.

Faubourg du Mortmarte and watch light *widen* across the sky. At first a wide strip of blue-grey—a strip of violet light. You see the line of the two clear and sharp. The paper trucks of Hachette, Le Petit Parisien, etc. go by. In the bar a rattling of hole-y money—taxi drivers drinking cafe rhum. A fellow sweetly tongue-licking his whore and making with loud laughter cutey, kissy, wetty talkie. A morning rattle of cans and ashes on the pavement. (I took the little dark fellow home from Harry's short time ago.) With rich jingle, jangle, and hollow clitter-clatter a Paris milkman passes. A skreak of brakes all over the world, a skreak of brakes and racing, starting motors.

Dear Dr. Babbitt:
  You have destroyed my teeth and my health. You will get no money out of me, but if possible I shall force you to pay for the damage you have done me.

  [*There are several pages missing here, but Wolfe's activities for the next few days are recorded in some entries in the October Fair ledger and in a letter.*]

Paris Sat. May 24 Late at Night—Hotel Burgundy:
  The girl was no good. She was not bad: she was simply no good.

  Today—Home at 7:30 A.M.—to bed—terribly tired—saw day break on Paris, Bourse in early morning, the *Gewirr* of street, little bars, with women in ratty clothes and shirt-sleeved barmen giving workmen drinks, etc.—The vast *Gewirr* of Paris, the early wagons—
  Telephone from Emily, letter from her, finally her maid climbed stairs for me, went to lunch at her apt.—Rue Montalivet—Her gigolo and head bed-fellow there—Later Griffes and the Hollidays—the Hollidays on way back to America today from visit to O'Neills. Then with Emily to book shop, leather shop, etc.—then back to apt.—then to tailor for fitting—then to Cité Bergère for laundry—then back to hotel —slept till 10 o'clock—then to Weber's for dinner where met Florence Luckheim, husband and family. Then to Harry's, and so home to bed —Dreadfully tired now, air cold and fresh—very calm here in my garret—O blessed sleep.

  [*From an unfinished letter to Aline Bernstein, May 24, 1930.*]

  [*Emily*] asked me to come to lunch and I went. Now I must go again to lunch tomorrow with her & Mr. Griffes (you remember him), and she is calling up bookstores, literary friends, etc. to cart me around next week. Further she is not doing it out of love and friendship—she knew I was trying to get away from all that, and she is taking advantage of the fact that being alone all of a sudden is like being doused in freezing water: it is very hard for me being alone now, and I shall try not to lie about it. I would be grateful for companionship from almost anyone now, but I had rather stay alone and have fits of depression than be dragged around again: I shall not see her any more after lunch tomorrow . . . .

It is my own fault—I should not have answered her note, but I got a warm and happy feeling when she wrote me; I was grateful and felt that I had a friend near at hand. You say I condemn people, but I think there is a good deal of charity in me: what I think now is that nobody is bad, but that only a very few people are good. The people who are good invariably have something in them on which they can rely—When they have nothing in them on which to rely and go lazily about from place to place relying on things and people, then they are no good. That is the trouble with Emily.

Monday night May 26: I saw Emily yesterday—Mr. Griffes had us to lunch: she came by and got me at the hotel, then drove me to the Crillon where Griffes stayed; we had a cocktail, then we all went to L'Écrevisse for lunch. Previously Emily called me up: she was in a hysterical condition and asked me what to do, that Raymonde had disappeared, that she had not seen him since 3:30 A.M., etc. As it was only about mid-day it seemed to me she had no cause for alarm, and I got quite angry because I had to listen to this rot, and listen to some more of these histories that I thought I was leaving behind in New York.

I forgot to tell you that this Raymonde is a young man she has picked up over here and is now supporting—he wears riding boots and trousers and a creamy white shirt which he wears open at the throat. He has black sheiky hair plastered down with 8 ounces of vaseline: he is like a bad edition of the late Rudolph Valentino and he can stand on his hands and cut flips, and pick your pocket without your knowing it. He also jumps from one airplane to another, so she says, and hangs down by one foot: he can also do the hoochy-koochy and sing American nigger songs in French. Emily said he was "a genius" and that we both had much in common, and that we were both to be brothers. This was during luncheon: I got violently sick, and could eat no more, and had to rush into the restaurant to vomit.

I was supposed to go back to her place last night for dinner with her, the sheik, and two or three of her other friends, but I did not go, and I sent no message. I hope this ends it, and I think it ought to. Emily explained to me that she had a terrible night the night before and had got very sick—she said she had been smoking opium: I sup[*pose*] she wants me to try it with her, since I think she has some silly idea in her head she is a terrible "destructer-ess" who wrecks men's lives, etc; I don't think she's ever going to wreck anything, not even herself. There is nothing to wreck—she'll be banging around this way 20 years from now, trying to fill up her own emptiness with other folks' richness; she will have to hire gigolos in earnest then—she will keep coming to Europe and that will be all there is to it. [*Breaks off*] [11]

Monday, May 26—

It is no good denying it—I am sick at my heart for home, for a sight of that immense and terrible land. I must live out my exile here, I must conquer or keep down the sadness in my heart, above all I must work, and perhaps the answer to it all will be there.

Perhaps it is true that we have no native earth, but when it is midnight here I keep remembering that people at home are sitting down to dinner and my flesh is one long dull ache from throat to belly.

He tried to forget her but it was no use; it would never be any use. The flower-face was there to go haunting through his brain and heart forever.

Tues. May 27—

Today up at 10:30—Nordoff [12] called—dressed—out to Guaranty Trust Co—then to Weber's for aperitif—then to tailor's—then by taxi to Eiffel Tower—lunched there and stayed about 2 hours—Then back to tailor's—got suit—then back to hotel where note from Emily —answered her—Then to Louvre—writing this from Régence.

I-I-I-I-I hardly know just how-how-how-how-I-I-I-I-shall begin. David and Esther were . . . I-I-I-I-you know what I mean . . . were . . . lovers. Oh, of course, I know it sounds silly, but I mean— you know . . . lovers. I-I-I-I-mean!

11. This is one of three letters which Wolfe started to write to Mrs. Bernstein in the next few weeks—none of which he finished.
12. Paul Nordoff, a young song writer associated with the Theatre Guild. His song "Put It Away Till Spring" was used in the *Garrick Gaieties*, third edition.

Tues. May 27:

I therefore will begin:

David and Esther were lovers, and in their lives they were lovely, and in their deaths they shall not be desolate.[13]

Wed. May 28—

Look for lost letters.

Go to Guaranty Trust.

Go to Carnavalet, Cluny, or take motor trip or go to Rouen.

William Troy

Hotel des Balcons

Rue Casimir Delavigne [*written in Troy's hand*].

An American type: he is "going to run down to Spain next month to do a little writing" (Osborn).[14]

(Avenue D'opera at night—part of the lights erotic pinkish—saw this long ago.)

[*These are paintings in the Louvre.*]

Giotto—St. Francis of Assisi receiving the stigmata—the bird-like Christ.[15]

The big Veronese—"Les Noces de Cana" [*The Marriage at Cana*].

The G't Picture: "La Vierge Aux Anges" [*by Cimabue*].

Murillo—"La Cuisine des Anges" (The Kitchen of the Angels).

Rose-butted Rubens—flesh-tunned Rubens.

Man is a measure, *the* measure, not of all things, but of himself. He may quest far, and the scope and depth of his apprehension, the amount of his knowledge can be enormous. But he cannot know all,

13. As part of the warm-up before getting down to "The October Fair," Wolfe had been steeping himself in Old Testament stories. Note how this statement echoes the lament over Saul and Jonathan: "Saul and Jonathan were lovely and pleasant in their lives, and in their death they were not divided," II Sam. 1:23.

14. This probably refers to the same person whose name Wolfe jotted in his October Fair ledger: "Frederick Osborn 73rd Street."

15. An altarpiece with three small compositions at the bottom depicting episodes in the life of St. Francis. In the large composition, Christ with outstretched wings hovers over the kneeling St. Francis.

nor see all. The only infinite, the only insatiable thing in man is hunger and desire. That is unending and everlasting, and it steeps him in his deepest hell. But it is also the greatest thing in him: it is the demon that can possess him, and that may destroy him.

Love is the only triumph over life and death and living; over hunger and desire. Love begins as madness and disease: it can end as health and beauty.

The eternal coward is with us yet, is with us always. It is necessary to affirm rather than to deny, and love is the supreme belief, the final affirmation. Nor is it wisdom to call at all times for a definition.

[*From the October Fair ledger*]

Thurs. night–Fri. morning, Paris:

Wed. May 29 Assumption Day. Returned from movie at Gaumont Palace and dinner and wrote this:

There was the dream where you fell and the one where you soared, and the one where you stepped through walls, and the one where you were black as night and were in the wind and went hawking through the world full of a dark and terrible glee.

Lost words! Lost faces! why did they reappear so suddenly: why did whole canvasses of forgotten memory reappear to mock at time, to haunt men with the briefness of their days, as when, on going through a door we have not entered for twenty years, we find the landlord there in the same old place: he says "Good day, sir"—and the dreadful years are blotted out, and we hear our boy's voice saying "Good day," the while our mad eyes stare into the mirror behind him and see—no more the boy's face, but the yellowed skin, the veinous vinous eyes, the blackened teeth, and the smeared crooked nose, broken in a brawl. Good day! Good day!

The lost words; the forgotten faces—no, no: not lost, and never forgotten—but ghosts that might walk forth at any hour to haunt us.

I love my Chile Bon Bon, My Chile Bon Bon loves me—"It's really a great song, you know, a very great song"—the voice of Francis Strudwick,[16] the smell of Paris, the smell of the cafés, of roasting chestnuts, of the black bitter chicoried coffee, and of the winter's fog.

---

16. See OT&R, p. 701, for Wolfe's treatment of Francis Starwick and his favorite song.

A name that will evoke an entire past:

Theda Bara, John Bunny, the old Galax Theater on the Square.

The fact that Esther's early life belonged to all this gave it an unreality when he thought of it. There was a picture that had been painted when she was 25 and at the full height of her loveliness—she was very fashionably dressed in the picture with her hands thrust into a rich little muff, and with a funny little hat that stuck somewhat comically off her head. Below it her lovely child's-woman's face was blooming like a small dark flower: the face was lovely and innocent, full of eagerness and desire; he felt, with a bitter pang of jealousy the rich young body, seductive, small, voluptuously rounded, and wondered what powerful and brilliant men had panted after her, to which and to how many she had given herself. He stared, pierced first by this bitter pang, and then with sadness and inescapable grief. She stood looking at it with him, then said in a voice that was happy but anxious:

"I don't think I've changed much since then. Do you?"

"No," he said, roughly and indifferently. "No. You haven't changed at all."

She seemed entirely satisfied with his dull answer.

"I think so, too. I was looking at one of my pictures the other day made when I was a little girl. I'm the same as I always was."

The innocent satisfaction with which she spoke the words suddenly pierced him cruelly: he wanted to cry out loudly. And he wanted to cry out because what she said was really true—the lovely child's soul, full of its strong and eager faith, that bloomed forth darkly in the painting, was radiant also in her face: she was the child, the maiden and the woman with an indelible oneness, an everlasting youth of spirit—and her hair was getting quite grey, there were deep markings underneath her eyes.

His eyes grew hot with tears; he seized her suddenly and pressed her against him:

"You're just the same! The same! The same! You'll always be the same, my dear, my darling! Only more lovely, only more beautiful!"

She knew at once what was in his heart and what he could not utter save by a cry: the cruel haunting of time and our brief days to which there are no answers. She said: "God, if only I were that age again! Nothing in the world would keep me from you! I'd come to you and live with you whether you wanted me to or not! I'd never let you get away from me!"

He seized with a harsh joy a release in bitter words: "Big talk! You know damned well you'd never look at me if you were twenty-five." [17]

On May 31 in Paris on Saturday, after many letters to me, Mrs. Emily Davies Vanderbilt Thayer conspired that I be insulted at her ap't 6 Rue Montalivet. [18]

At Rouen 11:25 Monday June 2:
For in this pulling of his teeth, he saw the victory of living over flesh, the victory of time and death—the victory of love and women. He had lost four teeth since meeting her: at times he cursed her and said she had taken them from him—had drawn marrow from his spine, the core of his bones, his bowels, his loins.

Immortal love, forever living and forever young.

October is the richest of the seasons; there is the harvest in, the granaries are full. October is the richest of the seasons: all of the blood and meat of living is plumped full.
The breast hangs over like a sheaf of golden grain.
And in America the chinquapins are falling. The corn sticks out in hard and yellow rows upon dried ears, fit for a winter's barn and the big yellowed teeth of crunching horses, and the leaves are turning, turning up in Maine. [19]

17. Wolfe later developed this material for the episode in "The Party at Jack's" in which Stephen Hooks and others look at Esther's portrait. See YCGHA, pp. 250–54.
18. Just what the insult was is not known. Wolfe later told Henry Volkening that he felt he was being "paraded before a crowd of worthless people, palmed off as someone who was madly in love with her," and generally exhibited as a higher grade edition of Raymonde. As an outlet for his resentment he soon began to sketch out in his ledger plans for a satiric fictional portrait: "*Amy Van Leer:* Beneath her covering of kindliness and generosity, her heart was proud and insolent, as the heart of a rich person who has forgotten how his money came, most often is. She pretended to despise money and love art, but her spirit really worshiped money and despised art. The law of her soul was vile possession: being rich and having beauty, she was yet mean and covetous in her heart, for she could boast, as some village Casanova boasts of his seductiveness, that she could 'have' whom she desired; and if there was someone another woman loved, this woman wanted him, not out of love, but out of vanity: she was like those rich people we have read of in many parables, who have a thousand vineyards, and yet covet the little garden of poor people; or having rich flocks, contrive to steal a neighbor's ewe."
19. These notes were developed into Wolfe's rhythmic paean to autumn in America. Later they became part of Eugene Gant's meditations on the season when he returns home after his Harvard studies, OT&R, pp. 330–34.

Rouen, June 3—Tuesday:

The soft air that entered in easy flows into his lungs heavied and drowsed him; they recalled to him 200 other reeking days in Europe—200 days upon that soft wet continent—he missed the sharp burning oxygen of America.

Around the tower of Jeanne D'Arc the light green grass of France was growing—the sight of that kept nature so old, so clergy-staked filled him with sadness and despair—he wanted the old piercing hope and agony of Spring in his native land.

Rouen, June 3—Eating at old Opera Restaurant—vast room full of creamy yellowed baroque of 1890s.

She had done for today what is being done for today—she visited her husband and his new wife declaring she was "most awfully fond" of both of them. They were modern.

ON THE JEWS

He now remembered often the little Jew who ran the tailor shop on 15th Street; and he thought of the man with warmth and tenderness, of the plaintive Jew's rhythm of his voice—"Iss not de little voman who comes in here your vi-eff?"

EXILE

He was alone with his sorrow—with early sorrow, unanswered and lasting, that drinks the joy and sparkle of our youth away.

But we do not "get over it" We do not forget it. We do not get used to it. We accept it, and we live with it forever.

There is nothing to be afraid of—except fear.

THE OCTOBER FAIR

by
Thomas Wolfe

"I am a little world made cunningly
Of elements and an angelike sprite"

to

Maxwell Evarts Perkins

"The moment that his face I see
I know the man that must hear me
To him my tale I teach"

THE OCTOBER FAIR

Part I

The Fast Express

Part II

Faust and Helen

Part III

Antaeus

Part IV

The October Fair

Part V

Telemachus or The Native Land

THE FAST EXPRESS

Chapter I

Antaeus

I.

Of wandering forever and the earth again.[20]

---

20. This is the first line of the proem, which stated an important thematic conflict in "The October Fair." Later Wolfe placed the proem at the beginning of *Of Time and the River*. Commenting on its significance, he explained to Perkins: "By 'the earth again' I mean simply the everlasting earth, a home, a place for the heart to come to, and earthly mortal love, the love of a woman, who, it seems to me belongs to the earth and is a force opposed to that other great force that makes men wander, that makes them search, that makes them lonely, and that makes them both love and hate their loneliness." *Letters,* p. 239.

2.

October is the richest of the seasons

3.

All of the Wienerwald was turning yellow [21]

4.

Great moons are hanging at the pine trees' tip: the level moon is barred against the pines.

Chapter I	Antaeus
Chapter II	The Ship.
Chapter III	The Letter
Chapter IV	Street and Stone
Chapter V	Night! Night!
Chapter VI	The Train
Chapter VII	K 19 (K 14)
Chapter VIII	The Fast Express
Chapter IX	America (Virginia) By Moonlight
Chapter X	Sleep and Some of the Sleepers
Chapter XI	A Woman's Life
Chapter XII	The Horses of Sleep

O softly, softly, the great dark horses of sleep are galloping over the land.

I cast my eyes among the spaces of the stars, and the horses of sleep, the great dark horses of sleep are galloping among them.[22]

Chapter IV

Will crawl now, dark has come, up to the sill's grimmed edge, and hear loud mocking tongues.

[*Wolfe planned to include the story of Esther's early life as part of "The October Fair." When he left for Europe, he asked her to write*

21. Wolfe had in mind a scene he had described to Mrs. Bernstein two years before:

"All of the Wiener Wald is growing yellow; I went through Grinzing the other day, and the pickers were among the grapes, and the branches of pine hung out before the wine shops, where the new wine is drunk, and on the Kobenzl hill, and on the lovely hills around, all of the Wiener Wald was turning yellow. And today at Schönbrunn, the paths and lawns going from the palace to the carriage house—where we were—were covered by yellow leaves. The sun was thin and red, the ghost of the moon was already over Vienna—and Vienna has reached its autumn too. This life, the glorious city is in its yellow leaf." Letter, October 25, 1928.

22. Wolfe's dithyrambic chant of the horses of sleep was written during this summer. He also carried it in his head for the next couple of years: William Tindall remembers Wolfe striding across the Brooklyn Bridge at night reciting his set piece about the horses of sleep. At length they galloped into his short novel "Death the Proud Brother" in 1933.

down some reminiscences of her childhood and youth, and eventually she did send him a batch of material. Wolfe referred to this story as "A Woman's Life" and later gave it the title "The Good Child's River." The thematic opening statement was, "Long, long into the night I lay awake thinking how I should tell my story," as Esther lay listening to the clock strike in the night. Mrs. Bernstein describes her efforts in the first letter she wrote to him in Europe, May 23, 1930: "I have been writing the events of my life for you, but find it very hard to make it simple. I keep putting down all kinds of extraneous things, first thing you know it will turn into a novel and then I'll have to use it myself. It goes slowly and I tear up a great deal of what I write because I find myself going off into descriptions of things we had to eat, (showing the influence of Thomas Wolfe, early period). Also I keep remembering all our servant girls, who seemed to play an important part in my childhood. Long long into the night I lay awake trying to think how best to tell my story. Only it is reversed, I get sleepy about 10 o'clock or somewhat later, go to bed and wake up about four A.M."

Wolfe worked on "The Good Child's River" off and on over the next few years. The bulk of it appears in the chapter "Penelope's Web" in The Web and the Rock *and in the story "In the Park" in* From Death to Morning. *Mrs. Bernstein later used some of her own sketches in her book,* An Actor's Daughter.]

"Oh-u-n-c-e! ounce!
Pee-u-a-r-t! Kwart! [23]

A Woman's Life
"Long, long into the night I lay thinking how I should begin my story."

For Wednesday June 4:
(1) Get up; pack; pay hotel bill; find out about boat to Le Havre and train to Mont St. Michel
(2) Go to Mont St. Michel.

Northward and Southward, to inward and outward the wilderness stretches away.
Shall a dead foot waken the memory of a desert's silence?

23. This refers to Esther's anecdote about overhearing her daughter Alma earnestly going through her spelling exercises. See W&R, p. 431.

The dry bones, the barren land? The living wilderness, the silent waste?

Immortal love, alone and aching in the wilderness we cried to you. You were not absent from our loneliness.[24]

Of Today—France:

Gide, Valery, Cocteau, Bernanos.

Delteil, Kessel, Morand, La Rochelle, Lacretelle, Constantin-Weyer, Marchard, Jouhandeau, Soupault, Istrati, Desnos, Maurois, Larbaud,

Colette, Bourget, Regnier, Noailles, Hermant, Proust, Margueritte, Duvernois, Bordeaux, Estaunié, Mauriac, Benoit, Hirsch, Barbusse, Leon Daudet, Maurras.

Chal. Etienne, Champsaur, Dekobra, Derennes.[25]

At Paris 2 p.m. Wed.–Thurs. 4–5 June:

I came to France to stay in Paris "a week or two"—I stayed 10 days. I came to France saying I would go to Rouen—I went—stayed 3 days. I came to France saying I would go to Brittany—? Or to Switzerland—? Or to Mont St. Michel—?

There is also, Belgium, Holland, Germany, Austria, Italy, Spain, Scandinavia, Switzerland, England. Tomorrow I think I shall go to Switzerland?

Les Deux Baisers—(one the kiss of love, one the kiss of money? or of pure love and of lust? Or of uncorporeal love and corporeal love? Or the spirit and the flesh?)

The tarantula goes crawling through the oak (the tarantula lies sleeping on the rock?)

For lovely April, cruel and flowerful, will tease us with sharp joy, with wordless unfulfilled desire. Spring has no language but a cry.

24. These jottings show Wolfe groping for phrasing in passages about the American earth (a chapter he later projected as "The Immortal Earth"). Note that some of them appear in Eugene's cry of affirmation countering Bascom Pentland's defeated vitality in OT&R, pp. 148–49. The last one became the final line of Wolfe's proem to OT&R.

25. Although lists of this sort seem meaningless, one like this is the germ of Eugene's fantasy about the Parisian literary scene in OT&R, which begins: "Their names were Octave Feuillet, Alfred Capus, and Maurice Donney; their names were Hermant, Courteline, and René Bazin . . . ." pp. 655–60.

June 5, 1930—Thursday—Another Day—Midnight—Montmartre—3 o'clock—took cab to Sebastopol—went into Moulin #8 (?) Rue Blondel—Sat with a negress—was threatened by drunken thugs—went to bed with negress—left at 4:05—walked along G'd Boulevard to Rue Faubourg De Montmartre—had cognac there—bought paper—bought soap, lotion, toothbrush at pharmacy—home by broad day—awakened by loud bawling servants—discontented at me—went by Bank—met Geo. Seldes,[26] had lunch-breakfast with him, met Gollomb,[27] was invited to party in Montparnasse with him, then to bank to find out about hotels, then found hotel for myself, then to Cook's where [lonesome?] women, then packed and paid, then to new hotel [*Hotel Pfeiffer*], then wrote, then out for cocktails (2) and dinner in little restaurant behind Madeleine—Now at Café Royale drinking coffee.

12 Books to Take Out of France:
    Anthology Mod. French Prose
    Le Rouge et Le Noir
    A Dirty Book
    Sous Le Soleil de Satan
    La Rochefoucauld
    One of Zola

Friday June 6—
    Up at 11:30—Frere Reeves came by for me at 12:20—he had flown over from London this morning—we went to Café de la Paix for a drink—then to Ritz where met Michael Arlen and had drink—Then to Guaranty Trust where letter from Miss Susan Hyde[28]—Answered her—Then to lunch at Taverne Royale—oeuf à la gelée, grilled salmon, and bottle of Barsac—then to my tailor's for repairs, then back to hotel where wrote & left watch, then to Trois Quartiers for big book—writing this from sidewalk—Café de la Madeleine—drinking lemonade—

26. George Seldes, journalist and later editor of the left-wing sheet *In Fact*, is best known for his book *The Lords of the Press*, 1938. Wolfe probably met him through Mrs. Bernstein's circle.
    27. Joseph Gollomb, journalist and novelist, who specialized in detective and spy stories.
    28. Susan Hyde had met Wolfe in New York shortly before he sailed. She was now traveling in Europe with her brother, Robert Hyde, and two other friends.

then to Amexco for—nothing—then back to hotel—then ordered bath
—found lost overcoat—gave watch to Mlle. for *reparations*—then took
suit to tailor's—then home bathed wrote slept—then Mlle. with note
—pneumatic—from Miss Hyde—then dressed sent answer to Miss
Susan Hyde—went to Weber's—2 picons—took taxi to Place D'Italie
—sat in café there—then taxi to Lipp's—ate there—then walked back
by book shops in Rue des Saints Pères through Louvre and am writing
this at Régence.

[*From the October Fair ledger*]

This book started in Paris, June 6, 1930, from notes and fragments which have been collecting for two years. Now I hope with all
my heart for courage and strength enough to see it through to its end,
on paper as it is in my spirit, to make it as good as I can, and to do it
day by day no matter where I am, no matter what despair or loneliness
I may feel, and at no matter what cost of flesh or blood or spirit.

THE OCTOBER FAIR

By
Thomas Wolfe

"I am a little world made cunningly
Of elements and an angelike spirite"

To
Maxwell Evarts Perkins

"And though that he were worthy, he was wys,
And of his port as meke as is a mayde
He never yet no vileinye ne sayde
In all his lyf, unto no maner wight.
He was a verray parfit gentil knight"

[*The last quotation is crossed out, and the following is sub-
stituted:*]

"And ever and anon	I pass, like night, from land to land;
throughout his future	I have strange power of speech
life an agony con-	The moment that his face I see,
straineth him to tra-	I know the man that must hear me:
vel from land to land	To him my tale I teach"
. . . .	

I knew David. We were both born in Altamont, and we had known each other since childhood.

The "vitality" words:
    rip—ripping—ripped
    drove
    tore
    bombed
    shot
    swung
    she coasted swiftly with easy knees (a bicycle)
    dangled
    His arm swung bonily.

"denizens of the underworld who have not been seen around their old haunts for at least a week"

"Discovery of the bullet-ridden body of Eugene 'Red' McLaughlin, notorious gangster"

"four of his lieutenants"

"outbreak of gang warfare"

"Chief Inspector Pat Roche is certain the canal holds the *secret of their fate.*"

"the cold blooded slaughter of 3 members of the Terry Duggin gang"

"freely discussed in gang circles"

But in the night, in the dark, I heard an army marching on the land, and in the night Lee gallopped through Virginia on his great white horse (O softly softly the great dark horses of sleep are galloping over the land).

In the night, in the dark I heard an army marching and below the moon the rebel hordes marched past—the starved ghost-glimmer of their faces in the moon.

(For Virginia lay dreaming in the moonlight, moonlight, Virginia lay dreaming in the moonlight).[29]

[*From the October Fair ledger*]

Whit Monday, June 9 (10 or 11?)—Slept *15* hours—from 9 last night to 12 today—then up—weak no food yesterday except omlette for lunch at L'Écrevisse with Hyde, sister, and Mrs. Londes—up, went to Weber's for lunch—then to see Aldingtons [30]—with them until midnight—then with young Patmore [31] at café—then to Weber's again —and so home.

Talk with Patmore—or rather Patmore's diatribe against American women, American men, American sex, etc.

The Apes of God—Wyndham Lewis
Ash Wednesday—T. S. Eliot
A Dream of the Luxembourg—Aldington
Death of a Hero (52 days)—[*Aldington*].

Do you think there will be here no pains and labor? What earth, then, was ever free of its pain? (at Boeuf à la Mode—Paris June 11, 1930—Very hot—Going home to see if work is in me now. A Sauterne; a raie with beurre noir and a cold quarter of chicken salad and coffee for lunch—55).

[*From the October Fair ledger*]

June 11, 4:15 afternoon:
Antaeus
1. Of wandering forever
2. Invocation

29. These jottings show work on the section "The Fast Express," in which the young man passes through Virginia by night on the train. At length it appeared in OT&R, pp. 68–76.

30. When Frere Reeves had come to Paris, he had introduced Wolfe to Richard Aldington, the English poet and critic, known principally for his association with the Imagist movement. His wife, Hilda Doolittle, the Imagist poet, was with him. Aldington liked Wolfe's work and later wrote a highly favorable review of LHA for the *Times Literary Supplement.*

31. Derek Patmore, journalist, art critic, and man of letters, was the greatgrandson of the Victorian poet Coventry Patmore. Patmore was very proud of his ancestors and their long association with literary figures since the days of Charles Lamb and his circle, but Wolfe thought this was insufficient ground for Patmore's attitudes toward America.

3. Whoever comes—etc. (the roots of David Hawke) [32]
4. The barren land (Make this elaborate—"Hath not a Yank" etc.) [33]
5. Now October had come again
The vast low stammer of the night.
The nights are cold, and lovers draw close in their beds—this and the rains of spring.
The college boys are waiting for their first—
People drive back from the country with cut autumn flowers.

CHAPTER—?

The evil in this world is immense and everlasting, but it is not personal: it controls men, but it is not controlled by them. We do evil and we do not know how we do it.

The boys with the tough voices that swagger up to the little 14 year old bitches on 9th avenue, with nastiness in their hard loose faces —were those boys evil in their cradle?

The college boys, the Princeton "pricks."

The shyster lawyers by the Washington courts.

Van Vechten.

The Frenchmen sneering after you.

No, it is as true now as it was when Plato said it that we desire for ourselves what is good, we do not desire what is bad.

If you can still live in the sun, if the pure green of the country, and the glint of water can make some music in you, if food melts in your mouth, and your eyes can still take on the sparkle of good wine, for God's sake play the man, and say so, and fear no more the mocking of some cheap imbecile.

My dear Frere: Thanks very much for your nice letter. I assure you that nothing that happened the other night could alter in any way

32. This refers to the medley of voices of David Hawke's dead ancestors speaking out of their burial places. It finally appeared in *Of Time and the River*, summarizing the heritage which Eugene Gant brings to the city. See the passage beginning, "Whoever builds a bridge across this earth . . . ," pp. 413–16.

33. This is one of the products of Wolfe's national consciousness during the summer of 1930. It found its place, at length, in Eugene Gant's dream of time and longing for home in OT&R. The English voice has spoken with gentle deprecation: "Of co'se, I know you couldn't undahstand my feelin'—faw aftah all, you ah a Yank—but thöh you ah! Sorry!" and Wolfe's bardic American voice takes up a long reply: "Hath not a Yank ears? . . . ." See pp. 864–70.

my feeling about you; you are my friend, I trust and respect you, and I am proud to know you. At the present time, I am very bloody and beaten inside me—fools and cowards sense this and rush in to triumph over me.[34]

Scatter his dust among the gorges.
Clean salads tasting of the loamy earth and morning.
The foods of home.

Tues. June 17—1930:
In the last 10 or 11 days I have made few or no entries in this book—the most important thing is that I have got to work—I am eating at Wepler's at 11:15 after having worked 5 hours.

Fights
I've never seen a good one—there has been talk and threats of fights galore—but the only good fights I've ever seen were in the movies and one I started and ended myself.
For *Early October*—Last prizefights in the Yankee Stadium (Young Dempsey whickered at the lips and leaped)

Thin in the ankles, small-boned as a cage.
The flesh is mottled on the thighs below my gripe—the amber neck is soft, and hollowed for the pulse, then the great breasts droop down.
The silken butt.

—Jai dite m'seer vouley vouz donnez—(the cigarette butt downwards in the holder—the I-am-right-he-is-a-fool tone—the all-the-world-are-fools-but-me tone—etc.)

Saturday Night June 21—
At Café de Madrid drinking Perrier—weather very hot and sticky—I worked from 5–9 o'clock this afternoon—up at 11:30—to bank for mail—there was none—Cassis at Taverne Royale—then to Casenave for lunch—Seldes there with young woman—then to Marche St. Honoré for bottle of 50 yr cognac—then to bookstore where bought *L'Assommoir* [*by Emile Zola*]—then home—read *L'Assom-*

34. A draft of a letter apologizing for his volatile behavior the evening that Frere Reeves had introduced him to "Michael Arlen and some of the Left Bank people." If Wolfe ever sent it, the letter is now lost.

moir—worked 4 or 5 hours—then out to Nigger Morgan's—Rue Duphot—food not very good—then along crowded Sat. night boulevards to Madrid—observing bookstalls, etc.—Pneumatique from Miss Susan Hyde assuring me of eternal friendship, etc.

A feeling, particularly with part of Paris (near Faubourg Montmartre) of dreadful depression—the way they hold their cigarettes with a curious inimitable sneer—the cheap strong tobacco burning in acrid fumes from a Frenchman's twisted lips—at night—in hot stickiness—among the young French, by the filthy brawl and welter of the café terraces—I tremble lest my head be broken, my nose smashed again. The hardness of the French women—hard-eyed and vulgar-mouthed.

The Girl from Tours:
  "O of course, I'm really much more French than American."— etc.

Sunday, June 22—
  Up at noon—after working to 3 o'clock—*chocolat* at 9:30— Sunday Herald Trib—up at noon—bathed—r'd D'ly Mail—out to Brasserie Universelle for pressé-citron—American men and women there—women already beginning to soften up for cock—The hot tarred wooden pavements—a hot blazing but rather nice day—Now after good meal at Cigogne—cold consommé—Boeuf en goulash en Mode de pays—crêpe à la Mirabelle et café—writing this.
  Ah oui—Ah non.
  The French are themselves—we are us—to *know* them is not to be a buttery, slimy imitation but to know them from outside—*always* —We *must*—we are like Admetus,[35] gods forced to serve in another world—*here* this is TRUE.

  Soleil repercussions in the brain.

  [*In the following entries Wolfe appears to be working out a series of David's memories of Boston. Outstanding are suggestions of his fantasy about being taken up as the lover of a wealthy lady whose purse he has found lying in the Fenway. This fantasy was published*

---

35. Wolfe uses the wrong name. He means "like Apollo," who for punishment was forced to serve in the house of a mortal, King Admetus.

finally as Chapter 16 , "Alone," in The Web and the Rock, *and the locale was changed to New York.*]

Bitterly bitterly Boston one time more.

[Argue?] me to weather-in with books and gentle (?) luxury —to have in winter glorious foods and ladies dear—the crackling fire, soft lamp but no dull lumpish weariness of flesh or soul—mad stirrings of the loins as we hear the winds.

(It grows, it waxes greater—"Wot'll I do-oo-oo").

As David heard her voice the old lives came to him—

Perhaps here the fantasy of richness and seduction in Boston—y'rs before (red book).[36] O bitterly bitterly Boston one time more: the flying leaf, the broken cloud!

(then)

Play me a tune on an unbroken spinet—and let the bells ring! let the bells ring! [37]

Then Hilda's confessions.[38]

Sunday, June 22, 1930 up at noon, bathed, etc. (see notes before) lunch at Casenave's—went to Delacroix at Louvre—something overrich and bloody about it.—Note how French stare with fascination at pictures with blood in them—also how they love to paint blood (Delacroix)—then along Seine book stalls—found only junk—then to Lipp's for beer and cervelas—then back to hotel where worked from 6:30–10:30—Then out to eat at Taverne Royale—walk back through Vendome and and Rue St. Honoré—read a little and worked from *one* to 3:00—6 hours today.[39]

[*From the October Fair ledger*]

The Wanderers: Bacchus; Esther's father; George Richards (H. Stevens); Jim Swain; Dan Regan (Harry's New York Bar); the

36. Wolfe had written this fantasy in a big red ledger in 1926 as part of Eugene Gant's life at Harvard, although none of the material was used in LHA.

37. A thematic motif which Wolfe used in dealing with concepts of time. Note how frequently it appears in "Kronos and Rhea: The Dream of Time," in OT&R, pp. 853–99.

38. Probably Hilda Bottomley's unpublished novel, which Wolfe had read and now intended to draw on.

39. Another entry which Wolfe used for Eugene Gant's Parisian notes, OT&R, pp. 676–77.

Sailors; the "Asheville Boys;" Howard, the railroad man; the Bums; the Carnival man; Captain Bob; the Duke; Uncle Andy's Son; Percy.

ANTAEUS

I	The Ship * (in part)
II	The Song of David * (in part)
III	Early October * (in part)
IV	The Letter *
V	The River
VI	Pioneers, O Pioneers
VII	Perty Little Gal When I'm Lonesome
VIII	Virginia, Virginia!
IX	The Return of the Native * (in part)
X	The Bums at Sunset
XI	Two on a Tour
XII	Congo
XIII	The Girl from Tours

To die so many deaths is the hope and the memory of his thousand births.

The Americans have not built great ships but more than any other people they have used them.

Group them this way:

America	*Europe*
Pioneers, O Pioneers	Art Pilgrimage #31
The Bums at Sunset	Girl from Tours
The River	Bitterly, bitterly Boston
Two on a Tour	New York Bar
Congo	Opera
On the Rail	

Rainbow
A Woman's Life
The Horses of Sleep [40]

40. This is representative of Wolfe's outlines when he was combining the American and European scenes. A good commentary on it appears in his letter to John Hall Wheelock, June 24, 1930:
"I've just finished the first section of the first part—it is called *Antaeus*, and

Mon.–Tues. June 23–24—

Up at 11:45—out to Guaranty Trust—several letters—two from Aline, one Reeves, one Henry Hart, one K. Day [41]—wrote Reeves but didn't mail it—Then to Prunier's for lunch—Then to Smith's where spent much time looking for book—Bought D. H. Lawrence *Boy in the Bush*—Then bought cakes and candy on Rue St. Honoré—Then home, read Lawrence, took nap—worked 7–10:00— out about 10:45 to Chez Marianne—ate—watched American sailors brawling in cafés—walked down to Madeleine (bought two books— Gautier & Daudet in Montmartre)—then liqueur at Madeleine—so home—worked from 2–4:00—4½ today.

---

it is as if I had become a voice for the experience of a race . . . . In *Antaeus*, in a dozen short scenes, told in their own language, we see people of all sorts *constantly in movement* . . . .

"Well there are these scenes: a woman talking of the river, the ever-moving river, coming through the levee at night, and of the crippled girl clinging to the limb of the oak, and of how she feels the house break loose and go with the tide, then of living on the roof-top with Furman and the children . . . . Then the pioneer telling of 'the perty little gal' he liked, but moving on because the wilderness was getting too crowded; then the hoboes waiting quietly at evening by the water tower for the coming of the fast express; then a rich American girl moving on from husband to husband, from drink to dope to opium, from white lovers to black ones, from New York to Paris to California; then the engineer at the throttle of the fast train. Then a modest poor little couple from 123RD St . . . cruising in their cheap little car through Virginia and Kentucky in autumn—all filled with details of motor camps, where you can get a shack for $1.00 a night, and of 'lovely meals' out of cans—whole cost $0.36—etc. Then a school teacher from Ohio taking University Art Pilgrimage No. 36, writing back home '—didn't get your letter till we got to Florence . . . stayed in Prague 3 days but rained the whole time we were there, so didn't get to see much, etc.' Then Lee coming through Virginia in the night on his great white horse; then the skull of a pioneer in the desert, a rusted gun stock and a horse's skull; then a Harry's New York Bar American saying 'Jesus! What a country! I been back one time in seven years. That was enough . . . . Me, I'm a Frenchman. See?' But talking, talking, cursing until he drinks himself into a stupor. Then a bum, a natural wanderer who has been everywhere; then a Boston woman and her husband who have come to France to live—'Francis always felt he wanted to do a little writing . . . we felt the atmosphere is so much better here for that kind of thing;' then a Jew named Greenberg, who made his pile in France having changed his name to Montvert, and of course feels no homesickness at all, save what is natural to 4000 years of wandering. And more, and more, and more!" *Letters*, pp. 234–35.

These materials were later scattered in several of Wolfe's works, but much of it appears in "Kronos and Rhea: The Dream of Time," in OT&R.

41. Henry Hart was a young man Wolfe had met at Harvard, who was just finishing law school. He was later instrumental in helping Wolfe get proper medical diagnosis at the time of his fatal illness in Seattle. Katherine Day was the wife of Clarence Day, whom Wolfe had met in New York after the publication of his novel.

Whom do I know best?

Mama, Mabel, Fred, Aline, Perkins, Coates, Polk.

Last ten years:

Aline, Perkins, Wheelock, Baker, Olin, Raisbeck, P. Grant, Abe, M. Eggleston, W. Meyer, G. Wallace, Uncle Henry, Hilda, Elaine, [*Fritz*] Day. White—If you knew him years you would not know him better; he had become a microbe.

The vast wild breathing of the earth.

Aline's culture: Dickens, Chekov, Gilbert, James, Shaw, Shakespeare, Carroll, Joyce, Browning, V. Woolf, D. Richardson, May Sinclair.

He did not know whether at some "party" in the past someone had said "O but Dickens is perfectly swell, you know"—had done it or not. During this time that he knew her his reading declined—he returned to his poets. She, however, had always been a voracious reader especially of novels—Moreover, her people were rich—they walked into Brentano's and ordered twelve or 15 books—$40 or $50 worth at a time.

Those patient dogs that wait the world's abuse.

THE OCT. FAIR

Part I   The Fast Express
          Book One   Antaeus
          Book Two   Heracles [*"Street and Stone" crossed out*]
          Book Three   The Train
Part II   Faust and Helen
Part III The October Fair
          Book One   The Voyage Out
          Book Two   In the Dark Forest
          Book Three   Oktoberfest
          Book Four   Telemachus

FAUST AND HELEN

Chap I   Chance
Chap II   Another Ship
Chap III   Beginning
Chap IV   Early Autumn

2 yrs. 8 mos.

Hawke needed grand apartments and regal service—he lived mentally on a romantic scale of grandeur—he visited the house of Victor Hugo in the Place de Vosges and was amazed to see the princely, the lavish apartments in which Hugo had lived as early as his 31st year.

Thursday, June 26—
Up at one after working to 5 o'clock this morning. Dining at Drouant's—very rich restaurant filled with business men talking of Les Anglais, Les Americains, and "cinq cent mille francs"—at Drouant's a cold consommé, a rumsteck grillé avec du pommes soufflés, a fond d'artichaut mornay (a cheese and cream dressing and the ends of artichokes—delicious), a coffee, and half a bottle of Graves Domaine de la Grauere—couvert 4 fr.—total 44 frs.

At one table 3 Frenchmen of 50 or more—one of 40—one with black beard—coal black neatly trimmed naked around jaws—another a heavy distinguished man—grey beard pompadoured—grey close-cropped moustache—high colored—nervous grey eyes shot with red—hands which beat and tap constantly while the face smiles—talks politely—another red gnarled satanic face—fierce with rich foods and wines—smooth shaven—and the youngest—black hair, a black moustache—a quiet smiling well fleshed type—the high rich color—red shot with richness the satanic yet not unpleasant cast of face—the cropped brown moustache—and slick pompadoured brownish hair—a Gallic type.

Later: Seated at the café in front of Magasin du Louvre & Palais Royal—Heard a high even monotone that tickles the ear like a dynamo sometimes sounds. It made me think of great locomotives in the yards at Salisbury or Greensboro—steam shut off (perhaps) and this high small ear-tickling noise they make.[42]

42. Another entry which Wolfe used for Eugene Gant's Parisian notes, OT&R, p. 662. Besides altering the date to November 27, 1924, he allowed Eugene a different wine, Nuits St. Georges.

Let's go! Let's go! Let's go! Let's go places! Oh comalong, comalong, comalong, comalong! Comalong, comalong, comalong,. comalong. Let's go, Let's go, Let's go!

Go to Swiss Railroad—find out about ticket—hours of trains to Dijon—Leave tomorrow if possible.

Go home, pack.

The rush and glare of the interminable hours.[43]
O wounded bitterly.

A woman working in her garden—Eliza, Esther [44]

Scott Fitzgerald, Hotel Righi-Vaudois, Glion-Sur-Montreux.[45]
The bums at sunset tread the antic hay.
Jim Boyd, Hotel Lincoln 24 Rue Bayard at 7 o'clock.[46]

The Old Songs:
There's a lit-tul bit of bad in e-v-ry good lit-tul girl—
They're *awl* the same.

He had to get under, get out an' get under.

Oh Ev-lyn, Oh Ev-lyn

43. Quoted from Matthew Arnold's "The Buried Life," one of Wolfe's favorite poems and one from which he drew the subtitle for *Look Homeward, Angel: A Story of the Buried Life.*
44. Mrs. Bernstein had been writing to Wolfe from her summer home in Armonk, New York, and had been describing her work in the garden.
45. Wolfe and Fitzgerald had spent an evening roistering together in Paris. "Mr. F. had had me to his sumptuous apartment near the Bois for lunch," Wolfe wrote Henry Volkening, "and three or four gallons of wine, cognac, whiskey, etc. I finally departed from his company at ten that night in the Ritz bar where he was entirely surrounded by Princeton boys, all nineteen years old, all drunk, and all half-raw; he was carrying on a spirited conversation with them about why Joe Zinzendorff did not get taken in to the Triple-Gazzaza Club: I heard one of the lads say 'Joe's a good guy, Scotty, but you know he's a fellow that ain't got much background—' I though it was time for Wolfe to depart and I did." *Letters,* p. 263.
    Wolfe was to see Fitzgerald again this summer in Montreux and in Geneva, though they did not get on well in these meetings. Fitzgerald thought Wolfe's feeling for the American earth was sentimental corn, and Wolfe thought Fitzgerald something of a snob and a social climber (especially when he displayed a lively interest in Emily Thayer).
46. James Boyd met Wolfe for lunch in Paris in June. "We went to a nice café," Wolfe told Perkins, "and drank beer and talked over the American soil and what we were going to do for literature." *Letters,* p. 238.

In the dark, in the park

O how I wishegan
I was in Michigan
Down awn the farm.

You'r going *up-p*
   Boom boom bee boom bee bah.

After I'm gawn . . . O babe, what are you doo-in?

Esther was like crisp carrots and the morning. Minna and Ava loved her and were jealous of her love. They fought. Yet no one who saw this crisp face like dew and morning, and like blooming roses, would have called Esther a Lesbian.

Yet he watched Potts rub her face—Is there any man he thought whom I would allow to do that to me?

But women are more beautiful than God. They are the last the greatest and the loveliest of the flowers of the earth. Get for your love the women who have worked in gardens.

Sunday, July 6—
   Eating for first time at hotel—pretty depressing—a man at table opposite me drinking lemonade and eating vegetables, 40 chews to the swallow. A lovely ripe subdued young woman with tender arms and a big old woman with an underslung jaw—they leave with another woman spectacled & underslung.
   Meeting the pretty Jewess Rita Vale at 3 o'clock—more later.

This for the book: You pass a place in New York where you have loved a woman. It is being demolished—Where was the bed on which you had your love 200 times—By the right wall? By the left wall? You weep.

Tuesday, July 8—
   Eating at Trois Faisans [*in Dijon*] after a ride down from Paris through the rich land of Burgundy—the fellow with an eye-glass and his girl.

Silence! Silence! Silence!
   Do not let them see you! Do not let them spy on you! Go to the wilderness and live alone in silence, silence, silence! Do things that they

can not share in or be a part of! Live a life that they cannot feed upon! When they ask you lie! Say other things! Deal out your honest heart in tricks and keep silence, silence, silence!

The death of Charles Winthrop—

When Esther spoke to him over the phone he caught the accursed sounds of drama, the accursed sounds that haunt our voices and our lives, and that make us conscious of playing a grand part and moved by our playing and aye! convinced in our playing—believing, believing, believing!

He took her hand—she spoke formally, briefly, coldly—a great woman meeting a great grief. The other woman sat formally in a chair, full of cold and wellbred grief, Esther and Mona embraced, Esther weeping gently, and from the nearby room the hoarse and unbelievable breathing of Winthrop Charles told plainly that he was dying, dying, dying. He wanted to bare his face to the immense and cruel sky and laugh, laugh, laugh—Mr. Winthrop Charles was formerly a backdrop to this immense, this glorious act!

[*Wolfe is here jotting possibilities for various side trips in Switzerland. Many of them are splended mountain prospects:*]

Go to Berne—Oberhofer on Lac de Thonne
Go to Sierre then to Zinal
Gstaad
[*Les*] Diablerets
Champéry
Saas Fee near Zinal
Mürren
Rochers de Naye
To Interlaken about 4 hours
In the Engadine.

Montreux—First night July 11 in a café—*a mountainous rain*— hard, steady, soaking, fecund—the rains of the great hills of home— Moonlight on the broken waters of a mountain stream (moonlight in the tramp scene).

Book—Give me the book, and let me hold the book! What is not held in you, book? Aye! What is *not* held in you, book—Can you recall one moment of lost time, one vanished hour—

When that he was and a tiny little boy, he saw the books.

Build up until you get the old man in lodging house in Cambridge (Napoleon),[47] and the old woman in the Ulloi Ut in Budapest.

Willa Cather:
  My Ántonia
  Youth and the Bright Medusa
  A Lost Lady
  The Professor's House
  My Mortal Enemy

July 14—Monday—

Early dinner at Hotel in Montreux—went to Champéry this afternoon—the inevitable mountains—a steepness, a depth, an eternity that is indescribable. Why is it that the vastness of nature never humiliates one, but the vastness of a city does? This is true.

The Swiss peasants in the little inn drinking wine—all men that you would turn and look after in New York—their talk—how much they had been paid for potatoes—etc.—the farm women, red as beets and, grinning, waved huge bunches of carrots at us—The young fellows working in the fields—the rich valley of the Rhone—haytime.

"I know I'm awfully old fashioned but I don't smoke."

[*The following entries show Wolfe working on the material about the ocean voyage during which David and Esther meet and fall in love. In fact,* October Fair Ledger 1 *contains the full manuscript of Chapter I, "The Ship" (also called* "The Voyage Home"), *beginning:* "Towards sundown on a day near the end of 1926, a ship was approaching the North American continent at her full speed of twenty knots an hour. She was the Vesuvia, a vessel of thirty thousand tons, of Italian registry, and this was her first voyage." *It continues with the material published in Chapter 17 of* The Web and the Rock *and includes the entire passage "What is Man?" which Edward Aswell revised and placed in* You Can't Go Home Again.]

Caged in each little round of skull was some dear memory of the everlasting and beloved earth, which has betrayed no one. These Italians were stricken out of volubility.

47. An old man in one of the rooming houses Wolfe lived in near Harvard had a collection of 3,000 books on Napoleon—so Wolfe says in "Passage to England."

The ship as much alone there as a man was.

We do not feel that the ship has triumphed—there is no triumph over the sea. Our hearts are fastened [*breaks off*]

The sea—the wine-dark sea—as fast as the thought of a man can leap. The earth is our garden, in thousands of years it has yielded to our care—the sea never.

[*From the October Fair ledger*]

For Thurs. July 17—Up at 9:30—Dress—go for walk—work till lunch—after lunch sleep—work till dinner—write letters.

Ships

There are the painters, the polishers, the soapers and scrubbers, the wipers.

How gloriously man inhabits this ruined tenement of his flesh.

The smoky gold (Montreux, Geneva after a day of rain and dreary grey—the clouds breaking open in the west and all the rainy mists and mountain veils and floating wisps and cerements of clouds turn old gold).

Ships

The men who paint her all day long: new paint on the bow, the mast, the lifting booms, the rails (already rust had touched her—men were retouching her with paint all day long). The neat-bearded stewards, good at stowing things in ship-shape fashion. The men who get her ready for the sea—who take in great ropes and heave them out again.

The bells that ring out time upon the sea: the suggestion that a passenger always gets that he does not count—that there is only the ship—that the crew has its quiet understanding. The food that wearies one after several days. The orchestra making music—dull music— against the sea. Christmas on the ocean, Mass in the chapel.

There was a sense of sharp excitement, of constant expectancy on that ship. Sometimes, in some lower deck a door would open suddenly and big men with dungarees would come up—They belonged to the hidden side of the ship—to her buried heart: they were those grave-faced Ajax on whom this whole gleaming upper world of grills, marble baths, chapels, Pompeian and Japanese rooms rested. They moved by rapidly turning their big thick bodies as they passed. Their faces had the dignity, the stern benevolence that you would find in the faces of great enginedrivers everywhere.

At night the crews who drag great hose along the decks playing a heavy shot of water against all dirt, scrubbing until at morning the decks have a whitened gleam.

Women have no morals: they have only the sense of fashion. If the fashion is for adultery: they will adulterate openly; if the fashion says niggers are better than white men, they will have niggers, if the fashion says niggers are loathesome, they will loathe niggers; if the fashion is for art and beauty, they love art and beauty; if the fashion is for poetry, they swear they will live and die for poetry, if the fashion says a book is good they love the book and its author, if the fashion changes the next week and says the book is bad, they hate both book and author.

This is man: a foul, wretched, abominable little creature. This is man, a pocket of decay, a bundle of degenerating tissues, a creature that gets old and hairless, and has a foul breath. This is man, the would-be warrior with the paunchy belly, the great romantic with the barren loins. This is man, for the post part, a coward, with moments of heroism.

I have sought for my father in a foreign land. Is he here? Is he there?

Your father lies among the hills of home.

Full fathom five thy father lies.

Oh Absalom, my son, my son.

Will he come to me as I sprawl beaten, bleeding in the stews? Will he strike terror to my enemies?

A Woman's Life
The Faithful Heart
The Earth Flower
The True Pansy
The Good Pansy
The Good True Child
The Good Child

The True Child
The Good Child's River
The Good Child's Vision

THE GOOD CHILD'S RIVER

The Story of a Woman's Life

By
Thomas Wolfe

THE GOOD CHILD'S RIVER

The Story of a True Woman

By
Thomas Wolfe [48]

O sweeter than the berry, and redder than the cherry! [49]

Sunday, July 27:

I have made no entries in this book for about two weeks—I have written a great deal during that time, and I believe the book will go now. My life here is very quiet—It has rained terribly—It rained for a solid week or more—yesterday however it turned off hot and fine—I go out in the mornings to look for mail; I go out at night to the Casino, later to the café terrace—So home work and bed.

I went to see Scott Fitzgerald over at Vevey.

THE G C'S R

"I suppose that's some more of the elegant refined expressions that you learned down there. If you ever say a word against Alma I'll

---

48. Wolfe now returned to work on "The Good Child's River." On July 21 he received a letter from Aline Bernstein, in which she told him: "I have been writing my story for you and nearly finished it. It was a painful operation for me, and I hope will be of service to you. I want you to let me know if you really want it before I send it on, as no one else in the world must see it. You must promise to return it to me, as I know your careless habit and would be angry to have your new friends [i.e., Perkins and Wheelock] see it."

49. Lines from John Gay's *Acis and Galatea:* "O ruddier than the cherry! O sweeter than the berry!"

smash you in the face you low, coarse fellow. You've never been used to anyone like us before, that's the reason."

Thursday, July 31 (about 1:30 in the morning—)

Frere-Reeves sent me great batch of clippings today, said book was selling well—I wrote Perkins long letter, sent him 2 or 3 clippings and went to Lausanne. Back about 12:30 tonight—Beautiful night sown thickly with stars. Lake very calm. Some drunken young people (Americans I think—boys and girls—fooling with rowboats on lake—I [*heard*] the oars and drunken voices).

Aug. 1—

Dinner Time at Hotel Lorius—a hot magnificent day with a sky like deep drenched blinding violet—after lunch coming back from Cook's and met Mr. Horace Coon, a young man in retinue of Madeleine Boyd. Don't know if he's been sent here to spy or not. He came this morning he tells me and is staying above Montreux 20 or 30 mins. up by mountain train—He stayed with me on my balcony during afternoon, we talked and drank whiskey and soda. I also read Duhamel's *Scènes de la Vie Future*, a foolish book about America. Now in dining room they are making me suffer for my lateness—Soup comes cold after a half hour, get charged 3 francs extra for my own bottle of Beaune. The doctor with the steaks for his fat little girl, governess and smug-faced wife next to me—

Aug. 1—continued—on Monday (today is Friday) *on Monday* —July 28 I sent *Aline Bernstein*, my former mistress, a cablegram, in response to repeated letters and cablegrams of *hers*, in the last *cablegram* of which she *said:* "Are you all right: Answer at once, otherwise I am sailing to find you at once" [50]—I had not written this woman since 2 or 3 days after my arrival in France (May 23) but in answer to these threatening letters & cables I sent the following message: Aline Bernstein, Armonk, New York—Am well living Montreux—Tom Wolfe" —I had no answer during interim but today Mr. Horace Coon (O quite by accident, of course, showed up)—This woman, of course, is behind it: she wrecked me, maddened me, and betrayed my love constantly, but she will not leave me alone now. I hope the whore dies immediately and horribly, I would rejoice at news of this vile woman's death.

Aug. 5 (?) Tuesday:

Letter yesterday from Aline—says she is about to die etc. What is the matter. She is almost mad with anxiety, etc.—It's too bad, but I think she will live and love again (Ha! Ha! Ha!)

50. An accurate paraphrase of Aline Bernstein's cablegram, July 25, 1930.

Write.

[*Aline Bernstein's letters to Wolfe during the summer had been increasingly full of unhappiness, and her most recent one, written in mid-July, had been genuinely distressful. She repeatedly cried out over the pain of their separation; she upbraided him for his failure to communicate in any way; she reminded him of their many happy times in the past and of what he had inscribed in her copy of* Look Homeward, Angel; *she accused him of deserting her for his new book.*

On August 11, she cabled just three words: HELP ME TOM. *The drafts of his reply are below. When sent, the cable read:* LETS HELP EACH OTHER BE FAIR REMEMBER I'M ALONE LETTER FOLLOWS HOTEL BELLEVUE GENEVA THREE DAYS PARIS ADDRESS THEREAFTER.]

Let's help each other Remember I'm alone in strange land. I love you dearly. You have never had to endure exile and loneliness.

Remember I'm alone You have never had to endure exile Letter follows Be fair I love you Address Paris hereafter.

TOM

I love you dearly How can I help
I love you dearly Will write Address Guaranty Trust hereafter.

[*Wolfe to Aline Bernstein, unfinished letter, August, 1930*]

Grand Hotel Bellevue
Genève

Dear Aline:
I cabled you this afternoon and said that I would write, but I am unable to say very much to you. I have tried to write you, but the letter I started had too much bitterness in it about our life together, and about your friends. So I destroyed it. I no longer want to say these things to you because they do no good, and most of them have been said before.

We have known each other for five years, I can never forget you, and I know that nothing else to equal my feeling for you in intensity and passion will ever happen to me. But we are now at the end of the rope. My life has been smashed by this thing, but I am going to see if I can get back on my feet again. There is just one thing ahead of me:—work. It remains to be seen if I still have it in me to do it. If I have not, then I am lost.

You have your work, you have your children, you have your friends and family. If you feel the agony about me that you say you feel in your letters and cables, I can only say that you should give yourself completely to those things you have. A letter as short as this one is bound to seem harsh and brutal, but you know what I feel and that I gave everything in me to my love for you. [*End of fragment*]

Geneva Aug. 12, 1930:
   Who hates life but will not leave it is [*breaks off*] [51]

The wild dove flying.
The burnished sky, the ruined corn, the wild dove flying.

Shall he feel rivers in his blood that glut the sleeping land?
   The arrows rattle through the laurel leaf or on the old plank road the smell of pine woods and the turpentine. The springs are bitter on their lips, they see the cities and they are not there.

   Roger Williams
   Winthrop
   The Maypole
   "Drive down to the beach"
   —Go up to the mountains
   That night he went on westward, it was hot, the fans were droning.
   In red oak wilderness at break of day long hunters wait for bear.
   He awakes at morning in a foreign land and he thinks of home.[52]
   They came home to the small cape towns with hard tarred hands, their eyes were grey, and they put money in the banks. They lived in Salem in the lovely houses; and occasionally had apes and

---

51. This refers to a long passage which Wolfe cut from his sequence about the ship and the sea and man. It begins at the end of the "What is Man?" material: "Who hates life must die; who hates life has died already. There is nothing living on this earth but life, there is no faith except it live and except it love; and man is faith, he is life, the light and glory of this world. Neither is there any generation which has ever been 'lost,' nor any generation which will ever be found; but there are ten thousand generations and all are lost, and one follows another, and each is lost; and there is only the living and immortal earth which receives our flesh, and which endures forever." This continues for several pages.

52. This statement becomes a thematic refrain which is used to introduce nostalgic thoughts about the American scene and the American past. Wolfe eventually used it to intensify Eugene Gant's homesick yearnings for America in OT&R, pp. 859–70.

monkeys there. O often there were spice and tattered fans in those old houses.

    "When we get back it won't be so hot"— [53]

I had 30 francs
And then the rain came (the great drought)
The railroad accidents
The football teams
The road gangs
The soldiers
The outlaws
The murderers
Van Bibber
W. D. Howells (the wedding trip)
The hot trucks sweat and fume in powdered dust.[54]

What pulse beats for the father and the nation?
    New England, Virginia, The South, Louisiana, The Middle West, The Far West.

53. In one portion of Wolfe's writing about America he discourses for several pages on the heat of summer in the American land. Here is a sample: "The cows stand to their briskets in hot daisy fields; at noon the black snake drops his lazy length down seven feet of road and coils and stretches in the sun's fierce glare; there is a smell of new pine lumber and across the fields the sound of the carpenter's nail and hammer, vast drowsy fumings of earth smells, and broken tinklings of belled and ruminative cows. The sky would be a fierce bright blazing blue, or else a fierce blue massed with piles of tumultous clouds, all drenched with blinding light."

54. Another list that has to do with the theme of wandering. The Howells item refers to his first novel, *Their Wedding Journey* (1872).

Pocket Notebook 15

August 14, 1930, to February 14, 1931

This black-covered, firmly stitched notebook is one of the fullest in Wolfe's collection and covers an intensely creative period of his life. The notes reflect thought or work on materials that form important sections of his next three novels and several of his short stories. At the beginning, when he is in Switzerland, he is still distracted, but he soon cuts off communication with everyone in the United States and retreats into his lonely wandering about Europe. Finally, he settles down to a steady routine for ten weeks in London.

But the whole period is one of creative strength and variety. Wolfe developed the most complex and appealing character of his later career, Esther Jack, and he began to supply materials about her family, especially her remarkable father, Joe. For his own alter ego, David Hawke, Wolfe trumped up a new literary disguise. He gave him the nickname Monkey and a suitable gorilla-like appearance. He brought the old Emerson Pentland material out of cold storage and put him into the Hawke family as David's Uncle Bascom. He pumped more blood into him by giving him a new series of adventures. Other notes appear to be seedlings to be nursed along over the years for later growth into incidents or passages of the ever-extending autobiographical narrative.

Bought & began this book today—Thursday, Aug. 14 (?) 1930—Wrote this in Bar of Kursaal—The unutterably dull sows fill the bar looking in by droves at the dance room just beyond—If this is a sample of Swiss-French gayety!!! At the hotel some queer ruins—two terrible lustful women of 50 or more who look at me with horrible leers—Pert precocious children—a feeble old Italian and his young scowling discontented wife—Some English women scattered in among this crowd here—the dull grey stockings—the red dull faces—the dull tasteless dresses—the light lemonish greyish hats—the light dull raincoats.

[489]

Theodore Bernstein
Hirsch, Lilienthal
Brokers
New York City
Order your wife to send me no more letters or cables.

THOMAS WOLFE [1]

Friday, Aug. 15—

At Geneva—other side of lake at night brightly lighted café—music with program and hundreds of numbers—Last was #437—O. Straus.

Is it possible to live in Suisse without becoming dull?

Walked across bridge here at lake head where river begins—the pure green-emerald water.

Went to Montreux today—got baggage—mail at Cook's—left forwarding address—returned here—A valise full of dirty laundry—Letters & clippings from Frere Reeves—one by Frank Swinnerton who panned my book.

The dull wines of Switzerland climbing the great slopes in minute rows and terraces around Geneva.

The old American maid at my hotel—the carroty mass of hair—the sagging folded carroty face.

"Do you like it here?"
"O, it's beautiful."
"Do you like Swiss food?"
"Yes, I like it better than French food."

In the broad precise [way?]: "I have been here 8 weeks & before that I was in Paris for 7 weeks."

Dear Mr. Perkins:

I have decided not to write any more. It is therefore necessary for me to make plans for the future. Will you please have Mr. Darrow send me a statement of how much my book earned and how much is coming to me?

I send you and your firm my thanks for your favors to me.

Yours,

T. WOLFE

My address will continue to be The Guaranty Trust Co., Paris. [2]

1. A draft of a cable which Wolfe probably never sent.
2. Wolfe's first reaction to the bad review from England was a melo-dramatic gesture. This draft of the letter to Perkins is the last of four, all similar in tone, which Wolfe has in his notebook. For the letter he actually sent, see *Letters*, p. 258.

Just before I left America I was packing up some of my books one night and I came across *The Idiot.* I opened it and read the first line I saw: the line was from a scene toward the end of the book when one of the characters was departing. I'll call the character, without much originality, "Uncle Vanya." At any rate, the line was somewhat as follows: "Uncle Vanya is good, Uncle Vanya is kind, he is beautiful," the children cried as they danced around him.

That simple line, so true and beautiful, has lived in my memory ever since. I don't suppose children, even Russian children, ever talked just like that.

[*The following outline is for a story on which Wolfe was then working and which he intended at times as a chapter in "The October Fair" and at other times as a separate book. The plot concerns a young man who was brought up on a dairy farm, earned a Ph.D. in English at Cornell, and then taught in a large urban university. He first developed diabetes, then tuberculosis, and later died. The young man, who bears various names (Hugh Crawford, Ernest with a variety of surnames, Stephen, or Hugh Desmond), was based on Wolfe's friend and colleague Desmond Powell. Wolfe never finished the story, but he later gathered several fragments of it, written at different times, entitled them "The Diabetic," and included them in the rough outline for his last book. Edward Aswell, however, never used the story in the posthumous novels, and it remains unpublished.*

By the title "Hunger" Wolfe meant much more than simply a desire for food. In describing the boy's return after having delivered milk to the nearby town, he wrote: "For Ernest, this return each morning to the farm was not only marked by a ravenous physical hunger, but by a hundred strange desires, a thousand hopes and promises."]

HUNGER

Scene I   The Faculty Room at the University—Late at night —Weariness and sterility—Hugh Crawford.

Scene II   The walk home—the square brilliantly lighted—the buzzing taxi cabs—the food shops on 6th Avenue.

Scene III   Home on 11th Street—Food—The shelves and the ice box.

Scene IV   Hugh Crawford's home—the dinner cooking—the test-tubes neatly boiling with colored urine—the little poems, etc.

Scene V   Interim—The search of the food shops—the meals together.
Scene VI   The news of death.
Scene VII   Eleventh Street Again.
Scene VIII   Speakeasy and Departure.

And they began the fast drunken ride—the ride that so many young men in New York have taken—the ride over the hard gleaming pavements.

Hugh had paused for a moment. David turned to find him and found him attempting to light a cigarette but in such a state of uncontrollable excitement that his cupped hands could hardly hold the match.

A few weeks later when he was preparing to go to Europe he got this letter from her: "Hugh died on Tuesday."

1. The Class Room
2. The Faculty Room
3. The Walk Home and the Food
4. At Hugh Crawford's
5. Interval and Bad News (The Girl)
6. At David's and The Speakeasy
7. At David's Again
8. Conclusion

[*Wolfe was distressed by two English reviews of* Look Homeward, Angel, *angered by letters and cables from Mrs. Bernstein, and irked with F. Scott Fitzgerald, whom he blamed for Mrs. Bernstein's learning of his whereabouts. With an aimless impulse to escape, he determined to leave Geneva at once and took his first plane flight— from Geneva to Lyons.*]

Flying	30 S. francs
Geneva	12:45
Lyons	1:35
15 kilos	
13:10 for Marseilles	
15:55 arrive Marseilles	

Rise—go to Amexco—Buy ticket to fly go Lyons—Return to hotel—pack—Leave all unnecessary baggage at consigne at station—go to flying field.

Lyons—Place Bellecour—at a café—on terrace—11 o'clock at night—trams with trailers rattling by—Sweet Trees around [place?] in middle—Trams crisscrossing to all parts of this 800,000 city—a cool breeze flowing—one or two electric lamps advertising flashing on and off—cars with their funny little honks—A Sign *Dentiste*—electric bulbs—but grimed with dirt and not burning—A little car with wire wheels outside café terrace just across—belonging to young French sport—Two young French sports next to me—A man selling L'Ami du Peuple before me—a man selling peanuts—cap but no collar, heavy— Two whores talking over business vigorously over at other café— waiter *slapping* cups and glasses on tray as he cleans up with disinterested look on face—A Frenchman in plus fours and Beret—A Lyonnais bourgeois, with his hard thirsty face and its curious *reddish* French moustache, chewing on cheap cigar—Frenchmen holding cigarettes with curious little twist in mouth—people standing around waiting for cars to go home—little compact French private cars with superior-snooty bourgeois inside—trunks on back—little roaring cycle affairs also—and get a feeling of quiet—of stagnancy over all—one lusts for the life behind shutters—one thinks of whorehouses. Near here— perhaps in that massive-looking building across the street Aline's cousin lived—married to the French silk merchant—and they had 19 big rooms to their apt.

[*In the following entries Wolfe is making another of his attempts to write verse. He picked out some of the thematic phrases he had already worked into passages of rhythmic prose and others that he would develop later.*]

THE OCTOBER FAIR

Now October had come again,
   Had come again!
The sharp, the frosty months had come again,
   Had come again!
Cooled & a dusky glow the red sun slips.
All through the night lone star,
   Lone star!
O forested and far,
Through all the waste and lone immensity of night,
   Return! Return!

He wakes at morning in a foreign land,
    And he thinks of home.
Where are the footfalls of a million streets?
And where is the crickety stitch of mid-day now?

The adder lisps against the breast, cups fall.
Call for the robin! Call! Call! Call!
And the copperhead is crawling through the oak.

Long, long into the night I lay awake.

The dry bones and the barren earth.
The living wilderness.
The branches in the wood were dying, dying.
The fields were shorn and the sheaves were lying.

The engineer was pulling at the throttle,
He sadly smiled and opened up the bottle.

Lyons. STORIES (if I write them)

Hunger (The Diabetic, etc.) about 25,000 words
Early Sorrow (written) about 8,000 words
The River (written)—4,000 words
The October Fair (only the last part of it—a short novel)—
70,000
    The Good Child's River (a novel) 100,000
    The Swiss Hotel
    The New Store (Bergdorf Goodman)

Project For The October Fair (Poem).

I am all broken up in fragments myself at present and all that I
can write is fragments. The man is his work: if the work is whole, the
man must be whole.

Mara kept on talking in his absurd, irritating voice: Hawke got
very nervous and annoyed, and began to dislike him. Suddenly he
looked up and caught Mara's glance: he looked into the eyes of a boy,
hurt, brave, slightly tearful. Instantly he forgot the mannered tone, the
heavy circumlocutions, "to whom am I indebted for this mark of
esteem," etc.

He had gone abroad in a cattle boat, and then bought a high silk hat in London.

As he began to tell the history of his grievances his face smouldered with a beety glow, his eyes were shot with wild tears: at that moment there was no one in that city of seven millions but himself and a monster called Hobbs and his private woe.

(Hugh) His little place was a miracle of neatness and orderly precision but it was very evident that this order did not come from any finicking or spinsterly quality in him, but from a love of comfort, a love of living, a delight in all the movements and objects of life, great and small.

"What do you think of that chair?" he asked eagerly.

"Why, it's a good chair," David said. "It's a fine chair." He threw himself back in it with an expression of the greatest ease and luxurious relaxation.

"By God!" he said, "I can certainly stretch out in this one."

Stephen was looking at him with eyes that simply sparkled with pleasure and glee.

"You like it?" he said. "You really like it?"

"Why yes, of course I like it," David said. "Why?"

"I made it," Stephen said. He laughed gleefully at David's expression of unbelief. "Yes, that's right," he said, "I made it myself."

"The hell you did?" David said.

Stephen was fairly rubbing his hands together with joy. Suddenly he picked up one of his pipes and began loading it with tobacco. He affected a somewhat ridiculous air of indifference and casualness.

"O there's nothing much to it," he said. "I have the knack, that's all. It's a cinch to make a chair like that."

David looked at the test tubes with their brilliant vivid colors with insatiable curiosity.

"O it's nothing but a little urine test," Stephen said modestly, "I make it every day." [3]

[A list of possible names for the young diabetic:]

Stephen; Gilbert; Philip; Ernest; Edward.

Ernest Walker; Pond; Parks; Carter; Collins; Coates; Poole; Howard; Martin; Meadows.

3. On the flyleaf of his ledger Wolfe indicated the reason for David's surprise: "Use for suspense the fact that Crawford conceals his *diabetes* for professional reasons—'he doesn't want Watt to know about it' etc." October Fair Ledger 2.

Roy; Carl; Fred; Joseph; Robert; William; John; James; Matthew; Louis; Frank; Walter; Bruce; Homer; Nathaniel; Lee; George; Daniel.

Ernest Parker; Porter; Peebles; Groves; Meadows; Adkins; Booth; Cosgrove; Dale; Eakins; Flitcroft; Greenleaf; Hyde; Igoe; Jarvis; Kopp; Lawrence; Morris; Norwood; Oakes; Poteat; Robbins; Simpson; Thompson; Updyke; Vance; Williams; Yeager.

Knowles; Jordan; Harper; Ernest Jordan; Ernest Reeves; Graham Reeves.

The Old Home Town [4]
Captain Bob of the Nat'l Guard
Tim Cocke

The Gifted and New England

Uncle Emerson [5]	North Carolina
Hilda—childless	Harvard
Elaine—2	The Middle West
Carl—2	New Jersey
Harold—childless	North Carolina
	Melrose
3 yrs.	Medford Boston
	Reading

The Season of The October Fair Was Now Approaching.

The best people in America still come from Virginia. Magnificent people come from North Carolina—and they usually *come;* they don't stay.

The most interesting family that has ever lived in America is named Westall: its branches are scattered far and wide, but the seat of the family is in Asheville, North Carolina, or in the regions thereabout. This however is another story, a great many other stories.

4. Monkey Hawke's hometown. Captain Bob and Tim Cocke were to be characters from Monkey's boyhood. Captain Bob is sometimes called Captain Dick, and in one draft he is Monkey's uncle. October Fair Ledger 2.

5. The four names listed under "Uncle Emerson" are the real names of Henry Westall's children. The column on the right lists the places in which he had lived.

Ernest's history was not remarkable for variety. He had come from a town in the upper part of New York State: his people were farming folk, and a good part of his family's income was derived from a dairy. (Here work in the story of the tubercular cows and its effect on the family—His father's reaction to it, etc.)

His story was full of all those homely little stories that make such vivid markings in the history of American youth—of how he "got his first piece of tail"; of "the city girl" from New York who was staying at the farm for the summer, and of what he did to her in the barn one day; of the two whores at college; etc.

His father felt that some personal stigma attached to him because of the loss of the cows.

It seemed to Hawke that this memory of the early morning and of the drives into town in all kinds of weather had done more than anything else to stamp the love and memory of his native earth into Ernest's heart.

"God, it was wonderful!" he said. "All dark and cool, the way it gets just before dawn, and the stars were out—"

"They weren't out all the time, were they?" Hawke said. "There must have been times when you had no stars at all, or when it was raining or snowing. I should think that there were times when it was mighty damn hard to roll out of that good warm bed. I'll bet it gets cold up there, too, doesn't it?"

"Cold!" Ernest said, "It would freeze the balls off a brass monkey—that's how cold it gets."

A good part of his father's total capital had been invested in a herd of cows—they had over eighty: the income they derived from their dairy was considerable.

The veterinary inspectors had adjudged all but a dozen or so of the animals tubercular, and condemned them to be destroyed.

The grief that this loss caused the family was immense: men feel a sorrow over the loss of a fine animal that is in some respects deeper, because less selfish, than the emotion they feel over the death of a person.

A small epidemic of typhoid fever among the children of the town where Ernest took his milk for delivery resulted in the discovery that the milk was tainted.

Lyons, Aug. 21—
Today for an immense tour of town in bus—Began with slaughter house—Ended with Fourvière, the pilgrims' church on hill.

For The Deep River
Scenes: The Maternity Hospital.

[*A list of possible titles:*]

Joy and Hunger	The First Hunger
The Deep Hunger	Ponderous
Ernest Adams	The True Faith

Early Harvest
The Faithful
Delicate Death
The Deep River
Call For The Robin

"Wo wird einst des Wandermüden
Letzte Ruhestätte Sein." [6]

Ernest Rand—Can't use the name Ernest Graham (initials are the same as Eugene Gant).

Stories and Novels To Be Written:
The Early Harvest
The Good Child's River
The October Fair
Faust and Helen
The Immortal Earth

Aug. 23—Lyons—hot sticky day.
This is a note on what happens in France during a single summer's day—(Aug.). The heat and enervation of Paris, the moving catlike people, Montmartre at night, Gare du Lyon; trains reeling in across country; people in the rich countryside looking out windows; men working in fields; people sitting on terraces of cafés in Lyons,

---

6. "Where will the last resting place of the weary wanderer be?" These lines are from Heinrich Heine's *Buch der Lieder* and are carved on his gravestone in the Cimetière de Montmartre. Wolfe eventually worked this quotation into the proem of OT&R.

Marseilles, Paris; airplanes roaring over country; papers that get to Lyons at 5 o'clock in the afternoon; etc.

Lyons, Sunday, Aug. 24—

Eating at La Mère Guy's—on banks of Saone outside of town.[7]

La Mère [Brazier?], La Mère Fillioux, Sorret, Jean's, La Mère Guy; all excellent restaurants.

Sunday in Lyons—a deserted looking day—Bare streets—Very hot and bright sun today.

La Mère Guy's is magnificent: Melon, Matelote (explanation of this), Poulet, Raisin (very sweet and mellowed by the sun), Coffee, A Bottle of Beaujolais, (50 francs for the whole meal).

The point of going into oblivion and exile as I have done is, of course, not to brood or wonder what they're thinking or who will write and how often when one returns—the point is solely and simply to get *a piece of work* done at the rate of *1000 or 1500* words a day. If you do that—then brood, grieve, mourn, curse God, the world, everyone, and everything all you please. *But get the work done!*

At La Mère Guy's: The garden—The Chestnut trees with broad cool leaves above—the gravel below one—The cool, plaster wall with shrubs hanging over it—The shrubs with broad leaves—The French voices talking argumentatively—The bright hot river outside —The freight cars on other side of river—the hot bright river banks— the green trees beyond—The hills behind with greenery, trees, grass, flowers, terraces, villas.

Problem: A young man who lives life intensely discovers that he has diabetes—Three years later he develops tuberculosis—Question: Does he try to prolong this life in the hope of an almost impossible cure, or does he live freely and fully until death ends it?

Chapter—The Maternity Hospital
Chapter—Madison Square Garden
Chapter—The Speakeasy, The Subway

Persons: Ernest, David, Sturgeon, Black, The Girl.

[*The outline below is one of the fullest that Wolfe compiled for his projected book. It follows the actual events in Mrs. Bernstein's life*

7. For an appreciative description of this restaurant and the fictional account of Wolfe's visit to Lyons, see OT&R, pp. 879–80.

rather closely. *Item 8 was the first episode that Wolfe brought to a finished state, in a story entitled* "In the Park." *It was rejected by* Scribner's Magazine *but was later published in* Harper's Bazaar *and is included in* From Death to Morning. *Item 3, Esther's meeting with Wilkie Collins, occurs in* The Web and the Rock, *p. 409. Item 24 became Chapter XXVII of* The Web and the Rock.

Morgenstern is Wolfe's usual name for characters based on the wealthy Lewisohn sisters, who sponsored the Neighborhood Playhouse. Item 30 lists three plays produced by the Neighborhood Playhouse for which Mrs. Bernstein had designed both the costumes and the sets. The full title of The Follies *is* The Grand Street Follies.]

THE GOOD CHILD'S RIVER

The Early Grief

1. Policeman in The Park
2. Child's Voyage (2 yrs.)
3. Wilkie Collins, etc.
4. Mama, Daddy, Nana
5. Mama's Death—Nana, Daddy
6. Auntie Kate—(2 yrs.)
7. School, Jessie (3 yrs.)
8. Daddy, the two priests, the auto
9. Daddy's Death, Nana, Mackay
10. Uncle John and Uncle Fred
11. Auntie Kate, Uncle George—Miss Gunn
12. Fritz—Marriage—etc.
13. Birth of young Fritz
14. Alma
15. Art school—George Mallows
16. Trip to Germany to Fritz's people
17. Suffragism—Movements
18. The Theatre
19. The Morgenstern Girls
20. A trip to Europe with Fritz and the children—etc.
21. "One of them was a lawyer"
22. The War
23. Young Fritz's sickness (the day they got him)—The old doctor—on the roof in blazing sunshine
24. How Edith got her job at Stein and Rosen's
25. Lily's Husband, etc.

26. A summer at Gloucester
27. A summer at Saranac, etc.
28. The miracle (got right up—with painters, he scoffed—stayed in town and worked all that summer: Reinhardt, Lady Diana, Gest, Belasco, Bel Geddes)
29. Edith's Love Affair (Her underwear)
30. The Dybbuk, The Clay Cart, The Follies—etc.

The Twenty Years In Between

10 years working at theatre
2 years nursing young Fritz
Birth of two children, nursing, weaning, etc.—5 years
The War—4 years
Love Affairs, etc. (?)

God! Steve Hook when he gets to spouting about Mallows[8] makes me tired! Mallows in one breath and Pieter Breughel in the next! God, that fellow wasn't fit to clean Breughel's brushes. And all that gaff about wanting to be a professional bicycle racer instead of a painter. It makes me tired. And how he "didn't know much about painting—he was a real primitive—" God! Henry was about as much of a primitive as Oscar Wilde eating a crepe suzette—as for having no tricks, he had nothing else but tricks: he knew more about the styles of painting than anyone they ever had in this country. The greatest painter they ever had in this country was John Singleton Copley: he is one of the greatest portrait painters that ever lived.

Wednesday—Marseilles—Flew here yesterday from Lyons—A hot day—a cloudless August sky—smoky blue—a little humid at the edges—To tell the story of this flight is impossible—we roared right off (I was the only passenger) without turning—the great machine bumped over the ground—bounded heavily—was in the air—we circled the field—almost immediately when you take off the ground seems 100's of ft. below you—it has that minimized look as if a man would be 2 inches high—Then we roar far up over the hangars and see the little dots there—Then over the great Rhone valley—The tens of thousands of farms below—the minute cultivation of everything—the

8. Henry Mallows, who is briefly mentioned in YCGHA as the artist who painted Esther Jack's portrait, is based on George Bellows, the great American realistic painter. Thomas Beer, the model for Stephen Hook, was quite interested in Bellows and wrote the biographical sketch for the book *Geo. W. Bellows: His Lithographs* (1927).

bright rich clayey looking strips (perfectly neat) and the strips of green—the poplars—the hedges—the roads straight were they can be like white chalky arteries—and curving elsewhere—over all the enormous fruitful rolling countryside groups of villages—dots of farms —sometimes big towns—the fat rich green reaches right up, is cloven right to, is seen right on the massed *clean edges* of the rich woods— sometimes below us—sometimes far away the winding snake—the hot, light, silver snake of the Rhone that is drinking France down—Then the Alps march in to the left, the East—then other mountains to the West and valleys below—then the calcareous sub-alps—the chalky buttes and tables with their mass of runt pines, etc.—the rich clay land gets grey and chalky—we still have rich valleys but the color of the land has changed—A sickening lurch and tilt around the corner at Avignon—one pilot pumps furiously—the land rushes toward us at a slant—I think I'm done and see a race course, 1000's of little dots of people, and big stands below—Then we right ourselves and go on down a valley—Almost before I know it, the great hot water of the sea—the chalky buttes—the blasted runt calcareous mountains—We fly over them, see a little bit, and then land on the grey aridity of Marignane.

This is the season of the ripe melons—the great big peaches— the big yellowy sugary grapes—A blazing hot day—I am writing this in the night coolness from open air restaurant of hotel on Mediterranean—It is blazing, dusty, plastery hot in day—I came here from town this afternoon after a nightmarish night in Old Port hotel—with taxis tooting—trains coming by—people singing or talking in streets.

I hope he doesn't find out about that young negro fellow she's had. God! the way he is with his suspicious mind, coming from the South the way he does, he'd raise hell. Don't you dare say a word about my little Alma, you low fellow. O, what does it matter the way people are outside? I know what she's like inside. God! if women only told the things they really thought! Yes, really did. I think you would go crazy for a fact.

Marseilles. For K 19—People: [9]
    George Corpening (the negro porter)
    Walt Hill

9. Wolfe spent a considerable amount of time drawing up potential lists of passengers for car K 19 of "The Fast Express." Some of the characters are ones he has already written about, some were developed later, and others never pro-

George Albert Cecil Thorncroft
Henry Ford's nephew

"She's got a half, I guess," said Mr. Goldberg knowingly. "Yeh, she's got a good half, all right. Boy, you don't have to worry about anything. You're fixed."

David stared drunkenly around at Jim Swain, a burble of idiot laughter bursting from his throat.

"Yeh, he's fixed all right," said Tim McCoy. "He's fixed the same way they fix the god-damned turkey the day before Christmas."

They burst into a roar of laughter—a great moon had come up over the state of Virginia: it lay like a silence over the immortal earth. David flattened his face against the window and looked out.

"Land, Land!" he cried.

"Do you see land, Captain?" said Jim Swain.

"Land, Land! The earth, the earth!" cried David over again.

"The boy must be seeing things," said Tim McCoy. "First he sees land, then he sees the earth."

"Land, land, land!" cried David over again. "And not a real-estate man in sight."

"Don't you worry about that!" said Jim. "They're there all right. They're behind all the bushes. They're hiding behind all the trees."

(Pieces which are either written in part or in whole, and which I can complete.)
*K 19 (part of The Fast Express)
Early Sorrow (completed)
The River (completed)
*The Native Earth
*Antaeus
*The Good Child's River
*The October Fair

---

gressed beyond names on the lists. From this list, for example, the Negro porter appears, unnamed, in OT&R and YCGHA. Walt Hill had already appeared in LHA, pp. 187–88, as Walter Creech, the butcher who had a trace of Negro ancestry. George Albert Cecil Thorncroft later becomes one of the train passengers in the Orestes section of OT&R, where Wolfe gives him the name John Macpherson Marriott. He has four names because Wolfe modeled his character on John Francis Amherst Cecil, the first husband of Cornelia Vanderbilt. "Henry Ford's nephew" later appears in the Telemachus section of OT&R as Emmet Blake, one of the young men whom Eugene accompanies on the drunken ride which ends in jail.

What would be a typical "Altamont" group in K 19?
The Porter
Dreyfus
Wallace Davis
Mrs. Pitman
Jim Swain

At this moment Gerald Malone [10] entered the room and advanced to meet Edith. David had watched him on several occasions as he entered rooms, and although he despised the man, he was impressed by the assurance with which he made his appearance. He advanced with a proud, birdy carriage of his slight figure, with the little strutting movements of a pouter pigeon, with delicate and luxurious little struts, touched by the sensual languor and the spoiled boredom of a little whore. His face always bore traces of too much powdering, and his thin, corrupt mouth was touched by a smile that was indefinably loose and vulgar.

What did it matter if one such as this was exterminated—there would always be others to follow—there would always be rich women like the Morgenstern sisters, like Edith, like Alma, and there would always be the eternal trifler and vulgarian like Gerald Malone who would be honored and applauded by every other trifler he met.

"The-nigger-is-better-than-the-white-man" people; "the-homosexual-is-better-than-all-other-men" people.

Airplane—360 francs to Geneva from Marseilles.

Marseilles—The Old Quarter—a fecund squalor—The filth passes understanding—it reaches the dignity of evil—it does not seem to be the result of casual accumulation—it seems to be the result of some malignant intelligence which has steeped people in subtle combinations of filth so long and for so many centuries that they have come to love it—old cobbled lanes that are streets a few feet broad filled with a foul coolness—littered with sewage, bits of rotting vegetables, the smell of urine, child's excrements—a cool wet foulness from rotting walls that lean onto each other—the wet drippings of strung wash—Then the Grande Rue—women flatfootedly truckling through the crowd with clumsy bundles in which one sees greasy half-filled bottles of wine, pieces of rotting fish, bits of broken bread—workers in blue denim jackets and overalls, surprisingly clean undershirts—niggers of unbe-

10. A sketch of a character type Wolfe usually labeled "the eternal trifler." Edith is Esther's sister.

lievable blackness—women with dirty hands fingering and cutting strips off fly-eaten fish—meat weltering in the sun—ruined grapes rotting into ooze—aubergine, melons cut open and crawling with flies —little bars filled with workingmen and sailors—The stench of France, one of the great stinks of Europe—The worst districts of the East side are beds of roses by comparison.

Ate at Pascal—a Provençal Restaurant—Bouillabaise—quite good—Boeuf Sauce piquante—fair, but cheap—white wine ordinary —waiter—old portly fellow very intelligent, tells me there is no unemployment in France—20,000 for whole country—a mason earns an average of 45 frs. a day, a mason's helper (unskilled labor) 28 frs.

Europe is now (for past several days) suffering from its first "heat wave" of the summer—91 day before yesterday in Paris—it must have been 100 or more here—it has been terribly hot—The French sports with their open-at-the-collar shirts—the women with their bare tanned arms—some of them quite handsome—The Monkey bar on the quay of The Old Port (where I saw the American sailors reel in and out 6 yrs. ago)—Last night the whore waitresses who pull up their dresses to snap the garters of their heavy legs—the freshskinned young Dutch sailor with his rough sailor's gesture reaching for her tits and shoving his brown, stiffened hand into her crut.

The number of people you see in Marseilles with scars and knife wounds on their face.

At terrace of big café—on Cannebière—The Frenchmen swarming up and down on sidewalk—the chatter of voices on terrace —the café orchestra playing old mahogany music inside—two Englishmen and an American at next table—American looks like young ship's officer—hard red satin face, white flannels, a rakish panama turned up —the waiter nervous and annoyed and showing his French insolence and dislike, which they do not notice at all—An elderly Frenchman with his wife & another man & his wife—old boy good looking fellow and knows it—white Hapsburg whiskers—cigarette stuck out of mouth—erect figure—well cut clothes—insolent Gallic assurance.

"You must be sure to come, my boy, Ruth McCracken Livermore is going to be there," or "Don't miss it, my boy, Henrietta Seymour Terwhilliger will be present."

What this gentleman's accomplishments were no one seemed to know. He wrote occasional letters to *The New Republic* and he contributed reviews to *The Squire and The Fox*, the review of which Miss Mona's brother, with the aid of some 20,000 dollars a year, was editor. But he had the magic name of La Vallière [11]—any one with such a name must be a literary person; nay, a literary person of the most delicate refinement.

The crash in the stock market came in November and December of that year. By the middle of December it was evident that Jacobs was pretty well "cleaned out." He had possessed reserves of 1400 thousand dollars in his firm: this amount was almost entirely erased; he had hoped eventually within the legendary "two or three years" that always marks the period necessary for recovery in any boom, even though the real time may more likely be ten, fifteen, or twenty years, to recover about 200,000 dollars. At the present time he was faced with ruin and in a state of moral and physical collapse.

On December 28, therefore, about 9:30 in the morning, Miss Alma received a telephone call from Trowbridge. His voice was rapid and excited, he stammered a little. He said he was "all shot to pieces," that "something had happened," that "he must see her at once," that "he had had a terrible night."

Perhaps the facts are incredible. The facts are often incredible. Perhaps in the tense atmosphere of those days, with the drama, the deeds of courtesy and gallantry, the brave men, the faithful women, the true hearts, etc., the facts did not emerge so baldly as we have them here. But the perfume of those roses has vanished. These are the facts.

Thus K 19 came at length to rest—She had crossed 6 great states of the union with a population of almost 40 millions—one third of the nation's people.

Now, although this immense and smiling negro could make this trip both ways only twice a week, and the chance of travelling on his train was as one to three, David on every trip he had ever made into the South since he had come North, with two exceptions, had found this negro waiting for him at the train.

K 19 (sketch)

The Story Elements:
    The Station (the people rushing about—Time)—2,000 words
    The Race outside Elizabeth, N.J.—1,500 words
    The Bums at Sunset—3,000 words
    The Approaches of Evening—1,000 words
    Baltimore—Washington

11. Wolfe probably had Louis Galantiere in mind.

The South—People who get on Train at Washington:
George Albert Fortescue Traill
James Vance Swain
Robert Montgomery Evans (Henry Stevens—New York)
In the Engine (The Fast Express) 2,000 words
The Personal Histories:
Robert Evans
George Albert Traill
Samuel Schwartzberg
Wallis Teague
Harry Bryant

GENEVIEVE VAN LEER [12]

Genevieve was a nice girl. She had grown up tall and lanky, and rather sickly: she had a long, bony face and stick-out teeth. Everyone who had ever met them said that "they were very democratic." They were pleasant and kindly-spoken people: they had not "put on airs," they had been as other men are.

It had never occurred to the awed and grateful townsfolk that there was no valid reason why a gentleman whose grandfather had done drunken Indians out of their furs and turned the tables on some of the shrewdest criminals who ever inhabited Wall Street by methods no more scrupulous than their own should not be "democratic."

She turned out to be a generous and warm-hearted girl.

"You haven't got anything a bit stronger, have you?" he said with a wink.

"Why, of course," the girl said, "What would you like?"

They existed for three quarters of the year for David in a golden mist—they were absent from their great estate, they were "abroad," they were at their place in Newport, they were in their chateau in France, they were in their castle in Scotland.

Jim Swain (a murderous tenderness: "Are they trying to abuse you, Dave?" he said. "Nobody's going to abuse this boy," he said. "There's no son-of-a-bitch living going to abuse a friend of mine.")

Tim Reeves.

12. This is the beginning of a sketch based on Cornelia Vanderbilt, daughter of George W. Vanderbilt, who owned the palatial Biltmore Estate near Asheville. The people of Asheville were greatly awed by the Vanderbilts' manner of living.

U zun uv ah bidge! (Ay-ay—ay—ee—aye—aye—ee ay ee!) Gummon! Awe! (Then a rift of pure light broke upon the chaos of his brain—the heavy clouds roll back—he sees the moonlight painted on the earth like silence—old songs haunt him—The moonlight burned more brightly still but it was green—his mind lived clearly in another world.)

> Lean death and pale pity
> Rode out for to take
> A city, a city awake.

Robert: Robert was the only child of Judge and Mrs. Robert Evans.[13] In his mother's family there had been a streak of madness. Robert's childhood had been carefully guarded. He was a nervous and sensitive child and his nervousness was probably increased by the solicitude of his parents. They watched over him with hawk-eyes. He could learn anything; he learned without difficulty. His mind had neither slowness nor profundity; he had an incredible memory: he would read his lesson over twice, and he would have it committed word for word.

The Judge had continued in his gentle, grave, Southern states-man's voice, with its rhetorical pauses, its twos and threes of things together: "I want you to be a gre-e-at and noble man, Robert, an ornament to your profession, and a credit to your name.

> S. A. Lynch
> "Goat" Redmond
> Robert Evans (to awaken ever the smell of autumn in the South)
> George Albert Traill
> Wallace Tyndale
> Tim McCoy
> Walt Ball (Creech)
> Sam Schwartzberg
> Jim Swain

Marseilles—Brasserie de Strasbourg—12:50 at night—

Tomorrow I leave Marseilles and the South of France—I am flying back to Geneva—It has been almost a month since I spoke to anyone I knew—namely F. S. Fitzgerald—but who is there left for me

13. Robert Evans later became Robert Weaver, the madcap playboy of OT&R.

to know?—I have been reading *Robinson Crusoe*—why not a book on Robinson in the modern world—the Crusoe in the desert island of this world—It would be hard to do.[14]

It has been terrifically hot down here—a town in Provence on an August day, Marseilles on an August day—the sweat oozing from every pore—when you try to sleep it runs down into your ears and splashes about in puddles there—the incredible messiness and untidiness of the crowds—the heat and the dust and the filth—the people pawing over the junk before Galeries Lafayette—the "Museum of Art"—this is the South, the happy land, the good-hearted happy people—Sailors in Marseilles—American sailors—British and Scotties determined not to be "done."

I have started three books and written twenty or thirty thousand words on each—I *must* finish one.[15] Which?

The True Child's River
K 19
Fatal Earth
The October Fair
Antaeus
Faust and Helen
Telemachus

Marseilles—Last night there.

Garritus, Paris
Send all mail on hand Amexco, Geneva, immediately. Hold future mail.

THOMAS WOLFE

Early Morning	The Delicate Dawn
Delicate Death	The Delicate Day
The Young River	Early Glory

14. Wolfe explored this idea briefly, though, and linked it with the search-for-a-father theme: "For every man is born a Crusoe: he carries his own solitude within him, the desert island of this earth is in the million streets of life, and the hope, beyond all human hopes or dreams of love and fortune, the hope that makes us wanderers and for which we wander, is that someday we shall find in the wilderness the print of our father's foot." October Fair Ledger 3.
15. Wolfe has in mind three bodies of material rather than specific titles: the love story of David and Esther, Esther's early life, and the trip on the train.

Early River	Delicate Time
Early Bells	Delicate Bells
Early Time	Delicate Joy
Early Chariots	Delicate Morning
Early Joy	
Call For The Robin	

DELICATE TIME

"Long, long into the night I lay"—*One*, two, three are bells, and that is time! "Long, long, into the night I lay." One, *Two!* Strange Time, Strange tragic time! *Three*, Four! Strange time, strange tragic time, that hangs over our heads in lovely bells! Thinking, I thought (*one*, two, three, four!) how I should tell my story! "Long, long into the night I lay awake, thinking how I should tell my story."

Strange time, strange tragic time. (O, now I hear the whistles on the river.) Strange time, strange time, dark time. (O, now the boats are going down the river, great boats are going out to sea) and that is time! time! time! (one, *two*, three, four) strange tragic time, forever flowing like the river.

I want you to take me—to a factory where something is made. (At 12:30—Geneva—Lac—Café—whiskey 2—at other side of lake the sign *Longines* (in the pink purple sign A's husband invested in)—But —*I want you to take me to a factory where something is made.* (America—supposedly the land of factories—have any of our people (writing) been there—I must go.)

Culture
The Shoe Factory (New England)
The Cotton Mill (The South)
The Iron Foundry (Pittsburg)
Charley Brown's Father shoeing a horse
One of the things I remember is Charley Brown's father shoeing a horse. There was nothing remarkable about the horse or about Charley Brown's father. There was a searing sound when you put the hot thing to the foot and a smell of burnt horse hoof.

A Book Called: I Remember, I Remember.

(In France since I arrived 1/100 part of my life.)

I will tell you a little story:

There was once a young man who came to have a feeling of great trust and devotion for an older man. He thought that this older man had created liberty and hope for him. He thought that this older man was brave and loyal. Then he found that this older man had sent him to a drunken and malicious fellow, who tried to injure and hurt his work in every way possible. He found moreover that this older man had sent him to this drunk in order to get the drunk's "opinion" of him. That is the real end of this story.[16]

What have they here? O, well, I suppose they have a little of this and a little of that: they go to the cafés and have these little drinks —they look at the servants suspiciously, where are those two eggs I put here yesterday, you are using too much butter, etc.

And on one side of it was this young man with his arm outstretched and his long body and I said he looked like you, and on the other side was this lovely horse with the thin legs and there were some words written down below, and I was dying to know what they mean and I asked you if you knew and you said yes, they meant "the beautiful young man," "the fine horse." And I said how lovely, how grand that was; if I was a writer I should like to write like that.

She was always getting up on a chair to make a speech, she was a horrible woman but there was something very powerful about her.

Blauen—near Badenweiler.[17]

Phone from Freiburg.

10 YEARS

1920–1923—at Harvard
1924–1924—New York U.
1924–1925—Europe
1925–1926—N.Y.U. (met A.)
1926–Jan. 1, 1927—Europe
1927–1927—(writing)—Europe in Summer
1927–1928—Finished Book—N.Y.U.
1928–Jan. 1, 1929—Europe

16. Wolfe has Perkins and Scott Fitzgerald in mind.
17. Blauen is a mountain, one of the highest points in the Black Forest.

1929, Jan. 1–1930 (May 10—New York—Revised Book—Got it Published—had success—Taught 1 yr. at N.Y.U.)

May 10, 1930–until tonight, Sept. 8—In Europe sweating blood, loneliness, and trying to do new book.

The Big Stories
Auntie Kate, Nana, Uncle Fred & Uncle John, etc.
Daddy & The Automobile Ride.

Incidents:
"As for me I am noted for muh torso."
Wertheim and the peacocks [18]
"In the Dark Forest"
Fritz's family—the kitchen—the food
The Egg [19]
Mr. Wilkie Collins.

Where are you now and in what place and at what time? In the Dark Forest now.

Lees little Jew-baby.[20]

[*On August 18, 1930, Mrs. Bernstein wrote Wolfe and thanked him for a cable. Her letter is more restrained and less pleading than the previous ones. She said that she was going to continue her work with the Neighborhood Playhouse. Indicating that she could now restrain her tears over her loss of Wolfe's love, she quoted Shakespeare, "Time hath, my lord, a wallet on [at] his back." Wolfe jotted the quotation, which is from* Troilus and Cressida, *into his notebook, changing the word order, and proceeded to write a passage in which Esther discusses a costume for Romeo.*]

18. An anecdote related to Wolfe by Mrs. Bernstein about Maurice Wertheim, New York investment banker and Theatre Guild director.

19. In 1928 Mrs. Bernstein and Theresa Helburn took a three-week "hunger cure" at Carlsbad, Czechoslovakia, which consisted mainly of drinking water from the mineral springs. As Wolfe relates the incident in the October Fair London ledger, the first day after the rigorous diet the two women could eat only a boiled egg. They decided to eat it in style, however, and rented a Rolls Royce and went to the best restaurant. The egg was served in a silver cup. Esther could not finish hers. This incident is included in YCGHA, pp. 239–40.

20. S. Whitlock Lipinsky, an Asheville friend of Wolfe's, had changed his surname from Lipinsky to Lees.

Time hath a wallet on his back, my lord.

Romeo shall have a doublet of that lovely plum-color that you can get only off the backs of these French chocolates I buy. I wanted to dress him in something darker at first and let the lovely words talk for him, but God! that fellow McDougal! I told Amy his face was just like a slice of cold ham and she almost had a fit, but that's exactly what it's like. They might as well get Calvin Coolidge to play the part. I know he would get more passion into it.

[*Wolfe, who had been worried by the consequences of his first venture into autobiographical fiction, now began to think of ways he could make the hero of "The October Fair" quite different from Tom Wolfe. He gave David the nickname "Monkey" Hawke and added more details about his simian body structure. Further, he decided to endow Monkey Hawke with natural, versatile athletic ability—a quality which Wolfe himself most certainly did not possess. Monkey was to excel in every sport and was eventually to become a circus acrobat. At this time Wolfe began to experiment with first-person narrative and have Monkey Hawke tell his own story.*]

Here I must relate a circumstance, or rather a fact of physical nature, about which I would prefer to be silent altogether, but which I can no more conceal in these pages than I have been able to conceal it in my life: it is a fact that will color almost every word that I write just as it has influenced all my actions, and been present in all my thoughts. As a child the earliest name I remember being called by children my own age was "Monkey" Hawke. Later on, as I grew older, this name was changed to "Jocko."

While idly observing the practice of the varsity football team at Soldiers' Field one day, and seeing how few of the kicks of the punters went over forty yards, and were indeed fortunate to go so far, I observed to my companion: "None of these men know how to kick." One of the assistant coaches who was standing nearby heard the remark, and was annoyed by it.

"Perhaps," he said, "you could do better."

"Perhaps," I remarked calmly, "I could."

"Perhaps," he said, "you might show us how it's done." With that he tossed a football to me and stood, hands on hips, regarding me with a sarcastic smile.

Without a word I stepped out onto the field with the ball and punted into the wind for eighty yards.

Early Youth: The Military School, Climbing Trees, My Uncle in South Carolina, My friend.

Freiburg, Sunday, Sept. 14:
Ich hab hier 3 tage gewesen.
Today is the great election day in Germany—19 parties—papers filled with bitter exhortations—the sun however shines upon the Black Forest—the immortal earth endures—I sit in the hotel dance hall & drink black coffee—A whore with black oiled hair—A German's whore genteely plays piano.

The fat corrupt faces all over Germany—Has any German ever protested against it—In the papers "Vote List 6—Save the Deutsche Geist"—A cafe 89 of my steps from end to end—the air heavy to go through—the steaming smell of cookery—the people all around—suddenly above a great peal of bells—deeptoned, musical and yet almost without plan—from moment to moment you wait for a great harmony to break forth—The gothic earth—The head of a German before me turns into a Wild Schweinskotelett [*pork chop*]—Bells Bells Bells— The moon is rising over the Black Forest—A young German and his girl are lying on a mountain meadow—He lies on top of her—I hear her laughter—The sheep were filled with strong drunkenness.

A map of Europe; then a map of each country; then a map of each quarter; the shading for high places; the blinding numerousness of the placenames; the rivers; forests; etc.

"O, Albert!" he said in his insolent and effeminate voice. "He is looking for his father; do we know his father, Albert?"
"O, I'm sure we know his father," said Albert with his corrupt smile. He came a step closer, his soft corrupted body pressed against me. "I'm sure your father is an awfully nice man," he said.

People with abnormal physical traits, if their mental power is of average strength, very often are interesting people. All lonely people have something that the world desires, and that they themselves would willingly lose.

Maxwell Perkins
Chas. Scribner's
New York City
Working again. Excuse letter. Writing you.

TOM WOLFE

[*Wolfe's exact height is disputed, but it is frequently given as six inches above six feet. In converting his height from the English to the metric system he gives it here as six feet five inches.*]

$6 \times 12 = 72$

$\underline{5}$

$\overline{77}$ inches.

Ein meter ist 39 inches.

$\overline{2}$

Zwei meter ist $\overline{78}$ inches.

Ich bin 77.

Captain Dick of the National Guard—How he gets me to climb buildings as the villain in the piece—Captain Dick of the National Guard—A picture of the town from the rooftops.

"I saw three of my grandfather's cadets down below."

(I was "Gorilla" Pete—the police take me—"they shall not touch a hair of that boy's head," Dick said. But when the time came to pay the fine, my grandfather paid it.)

How I could climb trees.

How I hated Shoes (they could not fit me—a small town Shoe store).

How I would prowl barefoot through the woods at night.

5 yrs. ago—60 mos.
of which: 6 mos. in Europe
          2½ mos. in Europe
          7 mos. in   "   (including Asheville)
          4½ mos. in   "
           —————
          20 mos.
40 months with Mrs.
1200 days   "   "

German "Unendlichkeit" [*Endlessness*]:

Cities.

Ponderous smoke-and-beer-filled cafés (the bells ring over them).

Books (30,000 a year but at times it seems like 30 million).

Black Forests.

Men with shaven heads, fat decayed faces, necks.
Women with broad bottoms and ugly Saxon faces.
Boys with blonde hair on their faces.
Food.
Alte Stadt—the bewilderment of endless Gothic—Ponderous
towers with great painted figures on them.
Newspapers.
Professors.
Students with sword cuts on their faces.
Older [*Breaks off*]

The Germans: There is no way of really liking them. There is a
ponderous craftiness.

I was mad at the waiter for not taking my order—he explained
that he had been outside watching the police—end of a fight—(This is
Election Day)—and two men in a "Workers Beerhall" next here
stabbed and shot each other.

"His arm was all gerisst [*torn*] and ausschnitten [*cut*]," the
waiter said, "from here to here, and he had a deep cut over his right
eye and cheek-bone."

They make America the land of the flesh but America is really
the land of the spirit.

I was born on the sixth day of February 1894, about three miles
northwest of the town of Belmont, the beautiful hill district in one of
the middle Southern states that lies not above a day's journey from
New York. By birth I can boast of connections with one of the finest
families of the old Southern aristocracy: My mother was a member of
the famous Dinwood family which had its origins in Virginia (its
American origin, that is, because the family was known in England as
early as the time of the Norman invasion and played a prominent part
in the wars of Lancaster and York) and my grandmother, the wife of
old Colonel Dinwood who plays some part in this story, was a member
of the great Beauclerk family of Louisiana.

It got its plantations in America through the royal grant; and
the head of the Virginia branch of the family (James Dinwood,
Canterbury Hall) still lives in the family seat in the magnificent
Shenandoah valley.

I can remember him when I was a very small boy—certainly I
was not over five or six—he used to visit grandfather for a month or
two in August; and in the cool austere room that served as my

grandfather's study and living room—his fierce straggling moustaches, his thin, sinister, and yet somehow jolly face, lit by a kind of diabolic humor that somehow, when I think of it now, always suggests the Presbyterian Church—they came there for their picnic every Sunday.

Mr. Hollins and his thin hairy arms with his starched cuffs rolled up making lemonade in fruit tubs—the trestles under the trees—the glut of the river down below—the magnificent mountains.[21]

Mr. Hollins' speech: We will now have an exhibition of acrobatics and contortionism by Mr. David Hawke; immediately a great cry went up from the children—"Monkey" Hawke, "Monkey" Hawke.

The Real Things You Wanted:
  To Be a Great Athlete (Baseball, Football, Boxing, etc.)
  To Rescue Beautiful Women
  To Be Desired by Rich Men's Wives
  To Be An Engineer
  To Be A Soldier
  To Be Famous
  To Discover Gold
  To Lie With Miss Lindquist
  To Be A Hobo
  To Save People from Fires
  To Run a Restaurant ("Monkey" Hawke's place)
  To Go with a circus
  To make money out of hot dogs, etc.

Book Shop: Frank Thiess—a novelist; the Art Books; Max Brod; the Tauchnitz; Travel Books; Thomas Mann; S. Lewis; Dreiser; Freytag.

"Monkey" Hawke: How Wild leaped from the airplane—the look on his face—etc.[22]

Playing Baseball with "Goat" Redmond.[23]

21. An outline on the back flyleaf of the October Fair London ledger indicates that an early chapter was to be "The Sunday School Picnic." This is a note for the picnic scene.

22. Young Wild West was to be a colorful circus character and a friend of "Monkey" Hawke.

23. A note for the character who, after many changes, was to emerge in the posthumous novels as Nebraska Crane, the baseball star.

Making moving pictures in the mountains.

How I liked all men that were a little beyond nature:
"Goat" Redmond
Wayne Mears (He was the riding master—Colonel didn't know whether to keep him—amount of talk—things he could do with horses —the burning of the stables—the way he fought to get in there.)

The Harvard Years:
    Uncle Emerson (my father's brother and his family)
    The Ginter Bros. Restaurant
    The Rich and Beautiful Young Woman
Then the Circus
The Wandering Years
The Years Abroad—The October Fair

The Strange Life and Adventures of Mr. David "Monkey" Hawke, a gentleman of good family, of his early youth, of his wanderings in America and Europe, and of his remarkable search to find his father, and how he found him.
    As Compiled from the original manuscripts and edited by
               Thomas Wolfe

Episodes around School:
    The Picnic
    The Fire In The Stables (Claude Mears)
    The Dairy
    "Goat" Redmond (Baseball team, etc.)
    Dick Gudger (Capt. Dick)

The death of animals has always had a horror for me that the death of humans hasn't.

"Here comes that awful Monkey boy."
    Mr. Dinwood Carter of Norfolk, Virginia, and of what befell in Baltimore, Md.
    Sunday (going to church—the little boys trotting to bring up the rear.)
    "Nigger Dick"—the coon who is hunted by the posse.[24]

---

24. A note on the character who eventually became Dick Prosser in "The Child by Tiger," Wolfe's powerful short story which appeared in the *Saturday Evening Post*, September 11, 1937, and was included in W&R.

For my part, I would far rather be a real giant—one of those eight or nine foot Leviathans that one occasionally sees in a circus—than a man who is only very tall, than a man who is, let us say, six feet and six inches tall. I had certainly rather be a real dwarf than a man who has only been stunted in his growth, who is, perhaps, 4 feet 10, or five feet one. During the years I spent with the circus, I remember that the society of freaks was a particularly happy one, and I want also to say, a very sane and healthy one.

The Circus Smells—The Animals—The Food—The Trains.

Letters:

Dear Mr. Perkins:
I got your letter in Basel, Switzerland.

Yours,

TOM WOLFE

Dear Emily:
I got your note in Geneva, Switzerland.

Yours Truely,

TOM WOLFE

Dear Jack:
I got your letter the other day. It is a fine letter. I wish I could answer it. I am all right now and will write you later.

TOM WOLFE

Dear Mama:
I died in Marseilles on Aug. 22. I am buried in a good Christian Churchyard there and I hope you will come to see me.

TOM WOLFE

Dear Mr. Haeckschatz:
Thanks for your letter of Aug. 3rd.

Y'rs Tr'ly,

TOM WOLFE

To Mr. Ezra P'd
Dear Mr. P'd:
I r'd a p'm of y'rs once. K.M.R.A.A.[25]

Y'rs Tr'ly,

TOM WOLFE

25. The initials, which vary slightly from those Joyce used in the "Cave of the Winds" episode in *Ulysses*, stand for "Kiss My Royal American Arse."

Paris: Men on backends of buses; [Topaze?] from Café Madrid; The Cité Bergère; Bookshop from station; the city's bewildering angularity, etc; Marguery's; the crowd in old part opposite it; the taxi men in street middle; Hotel St. Anne; Miss Emily; Mr. Tytus; Viking's; on Bridge with Fritz [*Dashiell*]; Bois at morning; The whorehouses; The Guaranty Trust; The Paris Fair; The Rue de L'Université; Weber's; etc., etc., etc.

Le Bercy on summer evening—Coming from subway at Boul. Capucines at 5 o'clock—The little square behind Bibliothèque Nationale, etc.

Esther's story—people:

Irish maids	Actors
Jewish tailors	Actresses
Italian masons	Buyers
German relatives	Designers
Painters	Writers
Teachers	Playwrights

Some of the most interesting people I have known:

Uncle Emerson and Aunt May
Esther Jacobs
Robert Weaver (H. S.)
Grosbeak

FIRST ACT

Scene: A rocky seacoast during a heavy storm. The ship [*of*] Daland (a Norwegian sailor) is anchored here and the crew is resting. The ship of the flying Dutchman enters the harbor and anchors opposite Daland's ship. The exhausted Sea-Farer (the Dutchman) comes ashore and begins his song. After seven years wandering on the sea he is going to see whether he can find on the Earth a wife who through her love and faith can free him from his terrible fate. Daland sees the strange ship, and comes up to the stranger who is leaning on a rock. Upon being questioned about his name and business the Dutchman answers that for countless years he has sailed every sea without finding the land of his desire, his real home, and he asks Daland to take him as a guest in his house. When Daland answers the question whether he has a daughter, with "yes," the Dutchman promises him all the treasure that his ship holds if Daland will give him this daughter for a wife.

The talk with Christus: [26]
"You will exguze me," he said rapidly, and with just a trace of the gutteral tone, "but I have been very busy baking today. That is why I have had to geep you waiting. Yes? You are going back to München, behaps? I think it will perhaps be besser for you there. Unterpfalzheim does not have the gumforts of a great city, and the bad weather is now beginnink."

The face of the man who now sat opposite me might be likened to the heads of a million men in Germany: the noble intelligence of the brow, the swinish hunger of the body.

The "preventive" box which instructs one to wash his privates with urine.

I was afraid to enter far into the country; for a long time I hung upon its borders. I visited the cities along the Rhein; I came to Freiburg; I went to Bavaria. During all the time I had been in Germany I had always been placed so that freedom and escape lay not over four hours away by train. Then one day I flew to Berlin.

Strasbourg (Sept. 20—First night there):
I sweated out great drops of agony; at night in Europe I tossed upon a thousand distressful beds; I slept, yet through the night I heard the thousand sad and tortured sounds of time; I slept, and during all my sleep, I knew that I was sleeping; I slept, and yet I heard the hollow footfalls of old Gothic streets; I heard the ponderous bells peal sweetly over ancient cities; the ten million movements of my life were moving in my sleep in tortured restlessness and all the time I knew that she was living in the world.

[*The next thirteen pages are loose, and most of them have writing on both sides. Wolfe tore these pages out of his notebook and*

26. When Wolfe visited Oberammergau in 1928 he met Anton Lang, who played the part of Christ in the Passion Play, in Lang's pottery shop. In this passage Wolfe attempts to recapture Lang's accent from memory. Unterpfalzheim is a fictional name for Oberammergau.

used much of the material for Eugene's notebook in Of Time and the River, *pp. 674–76.*]

Go to Colmar.

Buy Books By:

Giraudoux	Cami
Cendrars	Marchard
Istrati	Dekobra
Morand	Montherlant
Chamson	Bernanos
Lacretelle	Pourrat
Duhamel	Thérive [27]

In The Station at Strasbourg waiting to go to Colmar:
I was sick with my love; I did not believe that I was the only one who had ever loved, but I believed that my love was greater than the love of most people; and I believed it was certainly greater than the love of any one I had ever known.

The chatter of the psycho-analytic people—that wretched little chatter of the apes which I had heard so often on the lips of people in New York.

Characters Around Esther
The Comic ones
Uncle Fred and Uncle John
Margaret Gunn
Mr. Schultzheimer (Take avay the scenery and vat haf you got) [28]
Katie Hogan
Gorewitz
Martin Janicek
Alice Morgenstern

27. Wolfe has checked four names on this list: Morand, Chamson, Lacretelle, and Duhamel. His library, now in the Wisdom Collection, contains one book by Morand, *Lewis et Irène;* one by Lacretelle, *Amour nuptial;* and two by Duhamel, *L'oeuvre des athlètes* and *Scènes de la vie future.*

28. Mr. Schultzheimer is a friend of Esther's whom she encounters, in one draft, on board ship returning from Europe. The line of dialogue is his reply to her complimenting his English-tailored suits. Wolfe later used the line as a compliment on Esther's ability as a set designer.

Alice Crump
Amy Van Leer

When one looked into the face of Miss Alice Morgenstern one knew that one was looking at a woman who had suffered. She was rich, but she was humble. Her physical stature was small but her soul was great. Some people may have passed her by lightly without noting her; others, if they had noticed her, might have thought her a small and rather ugly woman; but the sensitive few, the people who really, really know, would have seen at once that she was very, very beautiful.

Written on The Spot: Colmar, Alsace-Lorraine.
    The Isentheimer Altar of Mathias Grünewald in the Cloisters of the Unterlinden (Schongauer) Museum at Colmar: [29]
    There is nothing like it in the world. I have spent over 4 mos. getting here—it is much more wonderful than one imagines it will be. The altar is set up *not in one piece* but in three sections in a big room with groined ceilings, a long groined room like a Dominikaner Cloister.
    The first two "volets" of the Altar—Everything is distorted and out of perspective. The figure of the Christ is twice as big as the other figures—the pointing finger of Saint Antoine is much too big for his body—but everything in this figure points along the joints and elbows of that arm and ends in the pointing finger.
    The lamb with its straight brisk feet, its dainty right foreleg bent delicately about the Cross, and rich blood spurting from its imperturable heart into a goblet of rich gold, is a masterpiece of symbolic emotion that strikes far beyond intelligence.
    The body of Christ and its agony is indescribable. The hands and the feet are enlarged to meet the agony—the hands are tendons of agony, the feet are not feet but lengths of twisted tendons, driven through by a bolt and ending in bent, broken, bleeding toes. A supernatural light falls upon the immense twisted length of the body (a grey-white-green and yet *completely solid* light)—you can count the ribs, the muscles—the head falling to the right is full of brutal agony —it is crowned with long thorns and rusty blood—it droops over, it is too big, Christ is dead.
    The great figure of the woman in white comes up and breaks backward at the middle and is caught in the red arms of the pitiful Saint. The fingers of the Magdalen are bent in eloquent supplication.
    The blackness of hell's night behind—the unearthly greenish

29. Wolfe has two errors in his description: first, the spelling should be Isenheim; second, the saint who is pointing the finger is John the Baptist.

supernatural light upon the figures—on Christ's dead, sinewed, tortured, riven, gigantic body and on the living flesh of the other figures.

It is the greatest and also the most "modern" picture I have ever seen.

The sly face of the Virgin in the wing of The Annunciation—the eyes slanting up under lowered lids in a sly leer—the fat loose sensual mouth half open with the tongue visible—a look of sly bawdiness on all.

The enormous and demonic intelligence that illuminates the faces in Grünewald's Altar—The angels playing instruments in *La Vierge Glorifiée par les Anges*—the faces have *a sinister golden light* —an almost unholy glee. You can hear *mad heavenly music*. This is not true with Italians—syrup and sugar.

> To T. Beer Esq.
> Dear Beer:
> I believe you are interested in Mathias Grünewald. I have just come here from Colmar; I spent all day looking at the Isentheimer Altar. It is a great deal more wonderful than I thought; you can not imagine how magnificent it is until you see it. And I am writing you this from one of the best restaurants in Europe—Valentin Sorg's in Strasbourg.

Paris—	5	
Mars.—	1	
Rouen—	200	
Dijon—	100	
Lyons—	700	
Strasbourg—	200	
Colmar—	60	
Arles—	20	
Boulogne—	100	
	8,000,000	⅕ of France

The approaches to Paris through the Valley of The Marne—autumn—The magnificent rainbow—the rocking clacketing train.

The suburbs of Paris—Dark—The little double-deckers rattling past loaded with people—The weary approaches to a great city—Endless repetition—monotonous endlessness—The sadness of seeing people pass you in a lighted train or subway. Why is this?

Paris—There is nothing that I do not know about Paris—that sounds like the foolishest boast but that is true—I am sitting on the

Terrace of The Taverne Royale—Rue Royale—It is autumn, it is cool, but it is the same—to the one hand the Madeleine—to the other the Place de la Concorde—to the right of the Champs-Elysées—the Arc—the Bois—the fashionable quarters—the whorehouses of that district—the rue—the Troc—the Tower—the Champs de Mars—the Montparnasse section—the Latin quarter—the book stalls—the cafés—the Ecole —the Institute—the St. Mich—the Ile—the Notre Dame—the Old Houses—the Rue de Rivoli—the Tour St. Jacques—the Carnavalet—the Hugo—Vosges—the Bastille—the Gare de Lyon—the Gare de l'Est—du Nord—the Montmartre—the Butte—the cafés—houses—the Rue Lepic—the Porte Clignancourt—the La Villette—the Monceau—the Bois.

But unannealed by water the gaunt days sloped into the grots of time.

Paris, Sat. night—

Today has been a horrible one—I was able to sleep only the most diseased and distressed sleep (the worst sort of American-in-Europe sleep) last night after leaving Mary Caumartin.[30]

I was sick with my loss (the loss of the picture Aline sent me and of several letters—but really the *picture*) and I got up sick and with the *shakes* this morning—I came to the Adega bar—I went to the Guaranty Trust Co.—I went to Wepler's in Montmartre—At each place, as I knew they would, with mean and servile regret cut by mocking, they were sorry, sorry, sorry.[31]

The day was of the most horrible European sort—something that passes understanding—the wet heavy air that deadens the soul, puts a lump of indigestible lead in the solar plexus, depresses and fatigues the flesh, until one seems to lift himself leadenly through the thick wet steaming air—With this a kind of terrible fear—an excitement that is without hope, that awaits only the news of some further grief, failure, humiliation, and torture. There is a lassitude that enters the folds and lappings of the brain that makes one hope for better things and better work tomorrow, but hope without belief or conviction.

The grey depression of the wet buildings—the horrible nervous pettiness of the French, swarming, honking, tooting along the narrow streets and the two-foot sidewalks while the heavy buses hurtle past.

30. An Englishwoman Wolfe met in Paris.

31. This passage illustrates Wolfe's editing for OT&R, p. 676: Mary Caumartin and Aline are given the names of characters suitable to Eugene Gant's Parisian adventures, "Mrs. Morton" and "Helen," and the Guaranty Trust Co. becomes the "American Express Co."

A chapter called *Paris* or So You're Going to "Paris"? (Perhaps a Piece For *Scribner's* In This.)

The fear always of the corners—you are coming out into the open, they will be waiting to thrust at you, etc. The heavy grinding buses—the irritation of the horns.

Weber's at midnight:
The waiters in Weber's standing in a group in their black coats and white boiled shirts—all around the great mirrors reflecting them—for a moment a *strange* picture I thought of *time!*

The horrible monotony of the French—Weber's at midnight—Some Frenchmen in evening dress—the heavy eyelids—the dangling legs—the look of weary vitality. Then in came some "Parisiennes"—God! God! All sizes and shapes and all the same—Unfit for anything else in the world, and not good for what they are—The texture of enamelled tinted skin, the hard avaricious noses, the chic style of coats, hair, eyebrows, etc.

[*End of the loose pages*]

"Parisians"
Mernoz—wife and hub
The concierge at St. Anne and Burgundy
The little bald-headed American who delivers mail at the Amexco
The boy behind the bar at Chez Marianne
The barman at Harry's New York Bar
The elegant young Parisienne with the big beaklike nose—the thin lips
The coarse look about the mouths of the women

Silence! Silence! And Patience!

Things to write a half-page on:
(1) A train coming into Paris—Evening—the double deckers clacking past to the suburbs filled with workers
(2) Grinzing [*Austria*] at night

My life is bitter with your loveliness: you slay me and my senses burn.

In 10 seconds I will be 30 years old! (Hotel Russell—Blooms-bury Square—Midnight—First day in London—the lounge.)

Things of the Most Intense Interest:
    (1) A Great Ship Approaching America
    (2) Nick's Grill
    (3) An American Nearing The Coast of Europe (England) for the first time
    (4) An American Railway Train—A Station—Time (K 19)
    (5) A Food Shop
    (6) A Fire on Park Avenue
    (7) The Maternity Hospital
    (8) Death In The Subway

    (1) The Ship
    (2) The Letter
    (3) The Street
    (4) Afternoon
    (5) Night (Abe)

Some of the feats which Monkey's father could perform and of which they still tell: Throw a baseball farther than any man who ever lived—Jump six feet and four inches—Stand on one foot.

[*After early October, Wolfe made no further entries in his notebook until late December. By October 14 he was comfortably situated in a flat at 75 Ebury Street, which Frere-Reeves had located for him. He settled into a steady regime of writing, and during the autumn and winter filled several large ledgers with material he intended for "The October Fair."*
    Sometimes he jotted a note in his ledger on his surroundings: "In London—Ebury St.—the whistle of the paper boy upon his wheel—the smell of dawn, crisp and smoky—People silent and fast on bicycles." *For, wherever he was, Wolfe surveyed the scene around him with the never-slumbering eye of the artist. He was interested in the Russian physician Dr. Belilovsky, whose office was below his flat; and the charwoman they shared, Mrs. Lavis, was to become the unforgettable Daisy Purvis in* You Can't Go Home Again. *But for the most part*

he turned his thoughts homeward. Among the passages he wrote at this time were: Old Catawba, the meeting with Esther, much of Esther's dialogue describing people and experiences in the theatre, many of the love scenes between David and Esther, the genealogy of the Hawke family, some of the Jerry Alsop story (where Alsop is called "Fat Jack Harvey"), "The Names of the Nation," a story of the 1916 Asheville flood, and many other scenes.

Only occasionally, however, did Wolfe date the material in his ledgers. A loose page in the October Fair Ledger 2 bears the note: "Eureka!!! Sunday morning, Nov. 16. In the chant (the Song of David now beginning) intersperse at the appropriate moments—" and he gives a list of statements. In the London ledger, at the end of a draft of "The Ship" (the meeting with Esther), he affixed the note: "Written Dec. 16—Two ½ mos. in London—1930."

During this time, in spite of his hard work, Wolfe's social life was not lacking. Frere-Reeves served as his social sponsor. He met Donald and Catherine Carswell and through their Hampstead Heath circle a number of interesting people. He wrote his mother on November 11 that he had more invitations than he could accept, including two for Christmas.

Wolfe's greatest unhappiness during this period stemmed from the financial troubles suffered by his family as the depression spread in America. He appealed to Perkins to help them, sent $500.00 himself, and continued writing. All in all, it was a rather pleasant time for Wolfe and one in which his "work moved forward."]

Sunday—December 21, 1930—London—10: 30 at night—
The Coventry Restaurant in Soho—Ritz—too late for drink (Sunday)—Pea Soup—mixed grill and chop—potatoes on way—Somewhat foggy as always tonight—but brighter and colder.

Mr. Perkins:
I suppose you think I have been plainspoken enough—too plainspoken for your taste—but I have not begun yet. On the contrary, I have always had a partial reserve in speaking to you, I have hinted at things, and got at them indirectly.

6 hrs. a day for 6 wks.—250 hrs.

[Just after Christmas, on December 27, Wolfe went to Paris to spend New Year's. He felt weary and in need of a short vacation, but he carried his ledgers with him.]

Jan. 2, 1931—

Paris 2:35 P.M. day of departure back for London—La Cigogne on Rue Duphot—Two elderly but robust old Frenchmen—two Frenchwomen—naturally with the [lignes?] & hard features (not too hard but calculating)—a waiter trying to get rest—Ahah! Aheh! (to the cashier)—The infinite repetitiousness of this scene (C'est pas possible, says one of the women).

Places I've seen this time:
Paris—	5	[*weeks*]
Switz.—	6	
London—	10	
Black Forest—	2	
Provence—	2	
Marseilles—	1	
	25	⅒ of the business

What of the names of Balzac, Zola, Dr. Cabanis,[32] Proust, Verlaine, Baudelaire—What of them?

There are also 4 million other books in the Bib. Nat.—There are 4,200,000 in the Congress—Isn't this perfectly wonderful?

Dear Susy: [33]

Your nice note and Christmas card reached me here today—I have been here 5 days for New Yr's.—1st vacation in 3 mos., but I have just missed train back to London (by 4 minutes!) and feel very dissolute and debauched in consequence. If it is true, as you say, that I have any friends in New York who will be glad to see me, I have a feeling of joy and glory in my bowels because of it. You said in your note that it was a day in New York that would have rejoiced such "patriots" as I am. Well, dear old Susy, I am not much of a patriot, but all I was trying to say to you last summer was that we are each of us the first ten or twenty or thirty million moments of our lives, and we can't forget them, whatever people say or say they think, and the old country (I mean the Bronx & Brooklyn & the suburbs of Boston & all those wild places) is incredibly beautiful and magnificent to me. And I don't give a damn for Hoover or Coolidge or the Rotarians or the

32. J. P. G. Cabanis (1757–1808), a physician and scientific writer.
33. An unfinished draft of a letter to Susan Hyde. The handwriting and the general levity of the letter indicate that Wolfe had been drinking.

Constitution but I think they will always have the Mississippi River and the Great Smokies in No. Car. and that is America.

The wife of the Soviet Commissar wanted to be beaten with straps (But not beat "O, no, O *whip*, O whip," she said) across her bottom.[34] Whale Spawn of the Skyldings, Skoal! What about [part?] wheat? Those men of foretimes were those men of those times. [*The passage becomes more incoherent and illegible.*]

Scornmaker's pride.

Feb. 5—10 at night—
Simpson's—cleaning up—mutton—Beaune—corona—coffee—cheese—cabbage—potatoes.
Rouse murder case
Blazing car mystery
The Evening Standard

Red Lewis—Georgian House—I've seen him! [35]

Tomorrow letter of credit starts again—Went to bed at 11:30 this morning—worked all night—Mrs. Lavis—[Walter?]—scrambled eggs on toast—Mrs. Lavis's husband's family—"Ah! they wanted 'im to marry money!"
Got up at 6 today—Major Proctor's old actor friend to see if there was Book-of-Month.[36]

Europa—Feb. 26—25 £—Tourist Third—Arrives New York —March 3.

Chinese Restaurant in Glasshouse Street, Piccadilly—People rave about it here, but not so good as many in N.Y.—Looking out over Piccadilly—The constant roar and passage of the red buses, old hearse-like taxis with the brass-rimmed radiators, and the foggy flowing of people—a foggy night—Lights flaring up through fog of lower Regent

34. The handwriting here shows that Wolfe was further in his cups when he wrote this. In a list of people he had met in London, the last person on the list is: "An English woman, wife of a Soviet Commissar—she wants to to be beaten." October Fair Ledger 3.
35. For Wolfe's fictional account of his meeting with Sinclair Lewis, see "Enter Mr. Lloyd McHarg," Chapter 33, YCGHA.
36. Wolfe subleased the flat from Major Proctor.

Street—Nancy Carrol in Laughter (Electric)—*Plaza* in Neon lights [37]
—The bit of the world here.

8:15—Liverpool—2nd Class to Amsterdam—2 £ 6s 10d.

[*At this point, in one of his periodic inventories, Wolfe lists thirteen women with whom he has had sexual relations in the last sixteen months.*]

Scene with Joe: [38]
  1. The Bridge
  2. Enter Daughter of Desolation
  3. The Ride In The Park
  4. Late at Night—the Bedroom—Richard III
  5. On The Ship, England, Uncle John & Fred

Scene with Nana:
  1. Going to Harvard
  2. Meeting At Night on Broadway
  3. Uncle Fred, John, and Nana

[*Wolfe's Guggenheim year was drawing to a close. Before he sailed for home at the end of February he visited Holland. He arrived in Amsterdam on February 11, 1931.*]

The man who asks: "Vair vere you last night, eh?"
"Oh, I went to a café."
"So. Dit you go to La Gaîté?" (He mentions the only gay cabaret of the town.)
"Yes, I was there."
"There were many people there?"
"A good many, Yes."

37. Wolfe was looking at the Plaza cinema on the corner of Regent and Jermyn Streets.
38. This "Scene with Joe" (and the following "Scene with Nana") was intended for "The Good Child's River." Joe is Esther's father, Nana is her aunt, and the items are all associated with her early life. Wolfe later wrote most of this projected material, and some of it appeared in his posthumous novels. The first item, for example, Esther's visit with her father to the builder of the Brooklyn Bridge, appears in "Penelope's Web," W&R, pp. 410–14.

Amsterdam—Old Goudschmidt [39]—rich, delicate—The rich and delicate houses on canals—the broad high streets of gleaming windows, the view within, yet the withdrawn and secretive richness—"They have money here but they are hanging on to it—these Dutch."

To Mrs. B.

You wrong me grievously when you accuse me of deserting you in my days of prosperity, and of ingratitude. No indeed! No, no, no! My bowels are moved with love and tenderness whenever I think of you. My gratitude is so great that I should adore to see you disembowelled publicly, quartered alive, and nailed up to the door of the nearest shit house.

[*The unfinished letter directed to Mrs. Bernstein which Wolfe has above in his notebook is another example of venting his spleen by drafting a letter he never mails. This intemperate outburst is the culmination of the grief and the rage built up during Wolfe's almost year-long struggle to break with Mrs. Bernstein.*

She had bitterly opposed his going to Europe. During his entire stay abroad she had bombarded him with letters and cables which alternated between pleas to return to her and threats of what would happen if he did not. The intensity of emotions revealed in these letters is very great; the letter she sent him for his birthday is signed with a drop of her blood. After a lull in the autumn, she began the flow of cables anew in the middle of December. This fresh onslaught so disturbed Wolfe that he wanted to transfer some of the burden over to the new authority figure in his life, Maxwell Perkins. He wrote Perkins a long letter on January 19, 1931, in which he went over the whole history of his relationship with Mrs. Bernstein. A large portion of this letter is quoted by Miss Nowell in her biography of Wolfe, pp. 189–91.

Wolfe attempted in his calmer moments to reply to Mrs. Bernstein. An unfinished letter to her that was never mailed explains his feelings toward her at this time better than the fragmentary one in his notebook, and it is also included here.]

39. Esther's grandfather. As Wolfe described him: "A Dutch Jew named Goudschmidt, a member of a wealthy and cultivated family of Jews, which had been established in Holland for a long time, came to New York to seek his fortune in 1831. Cornelius Goudschmidt, or Goldsmith, . . . held a degree in law from the University of Leyden, . . . and he had himself practiced with his brother in Amsterdam for some time before coming to America." October Fair Ledger 4.

London
January (?) 1931
Aline:

I got your note today. If you wrote me two letters and destroyed them, I understand that: I tried to write you this summer but could not—I had said everything a thousand times before. But for nine months now you have sent me first letters, then cables saying that you could not go on living, that life without me was impossible, that I was killing you and was I willing to take the responsibility. I did not think you would carry out these threats and injure yourself, but I thought that they meant you were in the greatest distress and suffering, and I was afraid that some terrible calamity might occur. I would get sick as I went for the mail—if there was news it was bad, and if there was no news it was bad. Then, after one of these terrible cables, when I was afraid to pick up a paper for fear of reading of some tragedy, I read that you had made a great success in the theatre. As recently as the first of the year you sent me cables saying you were desperate, why had I deserted you, your pain was too great to bear, you could not go on living, everybody, your family included, knew how you loved me. Ten days later your sister wrote me and came to see me here in London. She said you had never been happier, healthier, more successful and contented in your life than this year. Another person, a man who is your own relative, told me at Christmas that he had seen you at one of the New York wild parties a few weeks before. Other people have told me about your new and old love affairs. Yet, for nine months, while you were rich, successful, and in full pursuit of sensuality, you write me letters and cables which have destroyed my work, my peace, and my health. You have driven me from France to Switzerland to Germany to England and now you are driving me from here. The horrible pain and suffering these messages have caused me is past belief —they have made me so ill I have vomited and had to stay in bed for two days. [*breaks off*]

Amsterdam—Eating at La Réserve—The potent unforgettable indescribable taste of Liebfraumilch—Ate—6 oysters (tiny) with lemon —Sweetbreads—lettuce salad—fried potatoes (strips)—Crêpes Suzette—nuts—coffee—(2 bottles—½—Liebfraumilch)—The sound of a piano remote & rich downstairs.

Do you understand English?
Sprechen sie Deutsch?
Parlez Vous?

[*On the back flyleaf:*]

The American States—What I Know About
North Carolina—Everything
New York—A good deal
Mass.—A good deal
South Car.—A good deal
Florida—A good deal
Texas—Little
California—Something
Ohio—Something
Illinois—Something
Kentucky—Something
Arkansas—Something
Colorado—A little
Louisiana—Something
Miss.—Something
Maine—Something
Connecticut—Something
Wisconsin—Little
Minnesota—Little
Kansas—Little

[*Although Wolfe had left a few blank pages scattered through his notebook, he now had it filled to the back cover, and he made his next entry in October Fair ledger 4. It is included here as the final entry made during the time span covered by this notebook.*]

Amsterdam, Sat. Feb. 14, 1931:
 Have been here since Wed. morning—That means 4 days out of 365, 4 days out of 3650—1/900th part in living of last ten yrs.—in population about one million (or 800,000).
 What do people do in Amsterdam?—They ride bicycles by thousands, they go to cafés at night, they read papers at a paper table in café center—they go to cafés on Rembrandt's plein which is one solid mass of cafés—They go out into wet streets at 10 o'clock and the police eye them—The streets are full of whores and riff raff masculinity —A man was shot within 6 ft. of me the other night—the whole crowd set out in immediate pursuit as if they had expected it.
 A winter's night—Amsterdam—Suddenly a woman's sigh in streets, high, full, loose, yielding—to some man.

World Events: Depression everywhere, grey skies, grey air in Europe; beautiful Jewesses in Amsterdam, fat delicate but unpleasant Dutch faces; London an endless wet rot of houses going on for thousands of dingy miles, Cadbury chocolates, and cross streets with houses and wet dingy pavements below; a bank clerk steals bonds in N.Y.; measures for relief before Hoover and Congress; Big Bill the Builder says English Rum Fleet cause of depression; the canal streets and delicate yet opulent houses of Amsterdam—the clatter of feet in the Kalverstraat—principal shopping district—no wheels or motors, only tens of thousands of feet, bewildering multiplicity of small crowded shops.

Pocket Notebook 16
February 16, 1931, to September, 1931

Still at work on his story of David and Esther, Wolfe gathered his ledgers together and sailed for home on the Europa *at the end of February. His notebook entries cease to be regular, but the intermittent jottings over the months reflect that he was spending time mainly on "The Good Child's River." His emotional life still seethed with ambiguous feelings about Aline Bernstein. The climactic period of his breaking away from her occurred in March, when she had a breakdown which put her in the hospital and brought about a temporary reconciliation between them.*

Perhaps as a way of avoiding thought about the more painful episodes of the love story he was writing, Wolfe turned back to the childhood of Esther and the life of her father Joe (an actor, who is given various surnames including Barrett and Lindau). Most of the entries in the notebook show Wolfe pursuing a kind of research into old newspapers and magazines and looking at early photographs of New York. Clearly he was establishing "a sense of fact" to support his composition of "The Good Child's River." The order of the material in this notebook is not chronologically reliable. Wolfe made entries beginning at both ends of the notebook, and he probably made his jottings in the same way the Lilliputians broke their eggs—at the convenient end.

Amsterdam, Mon. Feb. 16, 1931, 4:30 P.M.—

A grey wet wintry day full of rain-spume and wetness—Coffee in Bodega at top of Kalver Straat (the main shopping street)—It is a small tortuous continental street crowded with shops and people— Here there are no motors but people wheel bicycles, and there is the single solid strangely lonely sound of thousands and thousands of men and women walking—the sound of shoe leather. Watched the great motor barges in canals—piled with fat filled sacks—children coming from school like children coming from school the world over—their bright shrill noises—the people go by under wet skies, many bear umbrellas, it is the 16th day of Feb. 1931 and now this is lost forever. Bought collars in store on Kalver St. from handsome Jewess.

Went into bookshop to buy this notebook—Shelves of the cheap English yellowbacks—the Oppenheims, Ruby Ayres, Mulfords, etc.—

Ibsen in Dutch, Dickens and Vautel also—Elsewhere a window full of dirty books—The German *Feile Weib, Uppige Weib, Grausame Weib,* etc.[1]—French and Dutch books on flagellation, etc.

The familiar sluggishness and heaviness of European weather rests upon me. No more will I waste myself here. At theatre nearby John Gilbert in "Resurrection"—an old film.

Away!

To the Hague tonight!

At Station in Amsterdam—going to Hague—electric train— large wet flakes of snow falling—fuming of engines in Stations.

To be a stranger; always to be a stranger.

Den Haag—Arrived at night—Hotel Terminus—the hotels are very clean and comfortable—Two beautiful Jewesses on train between Amsterdam and Haarlem.

Paris—a record of his dreams during these periods abroad would have formed a vivid and terrible picture of a world in which all the elements of reality had been enhanced and intensified, and formed into —who can say?—a horrible world of nightmare, or really into a world more real, more vivid, and more unmasked than the one we know. Here the suspicion of his mistress' betrayals became certainties; he walked directly to the places, into the rooms, where she was consummating her unfaithfulness and he found her there in the bed and in the embrace of _____ (by daylight he could not utter their names—but of these men he knew and whom his soul hated).

One of the most curious examples of this, which was perhaps without any significance but which at the time it happened struck him with the force of a physical blow, occurred on one grey drizzling day of February in Paris. He had come from Holland the night before, over a flat crowded landscape, the part of Europe which was sheeted with snow. He had retired early and during the night he had had a peculiarly vivid and terrible dream. In this dream he was passing, always in that dark light of no-time, that strange tragic light of death

1. *Woman For Sale, Voluptuous Woman, Cruel Woman.*

and memory, along a street when he came to a crowd gathered before one of the rich little shops of European towns. The shop window blazed with light and was crowded with objects; with a sudden feeling of nausea he realized that the things in the window were candies, glaced fruits, sweet meats, and rich little pastries oozing with whipped cream. He did not know why the sight of these delicacies should have made him sick, but thrusting in among the crowd now, he saw extended on the pavement the sight he had suspected and dreaded. A man lay dead there, but such a man as only a madman might dream of: the man lay dead of madness—his face and head seemed to have exploded from madness, some horrible explosion seemed to have burst within him, and to have torn him to pieces: now his face and head had a huge hydrocephalic appearance. As one looked at this horror one saw yet the glint and ruin of a handsome and lovable person—the horror one felt was akin to the horror one feels when a medical student takes him to the museum where the relics of aborted and unnatural births are kept in jars.

For the youth who began his manhood about 1920 the ten years that followed must have been a tortured and tormented time.

To do this it is only necessary to mention some of the horrible movements and multiplications of the world.

The Rue de Rivoli in its cheaper quarters at five o'clock in the afternoon.

Camden town about 6 o'clock in the evening.

The Victoria Station at pub-closing time at night.

The Charing Cross Road at 5 o'clock.

The bookstalls along the Seine Quay.

Tooting Town and the Stations of South London by night.

Times Square during the subway rush hour.

Broadway at 2 o'clock in the afternoon.

Mr. M. L.—Proud, wet, spermatazoic, juicily greasy, his flesh shoved back.

Will um with his great juicy large whip fill nize leddy's whangpus with joye? O yez.

His wet yearning eyes gazed with ham fairness out of his little theatrical face. His neck was soft and white and round, yet stable; good grease was there; also he had been circumcized.

Wet warmsquish with bright globules of warm loving there!

The Ladies of the Board:

Was this the Big Stick that served them well?

ON A THEATRE

Why did the ladies have a theatre? For what reasons were they interested in a theatre? Why should anybody run a theatre? Why should anyone be interested in a theatre?

Did they love the theatre? No; they loved the sound of hundreds of hands being clapped together; they loved people saying "Darling, you were just wonderful." They loved reading pieces all about it in the New York papers by these wonderful critics who write so well that often one reads a column and a half without understanding a word save that it is very beautiful.

[*The number of names and addresses which fill several pages of the notebook indicate that Wolfe had returned from Europe and was looking for an apartment in Brooklyn. He finally settled at 40 Verandah Place in a house owned by Marjorie Dorman. The next significant entry is a draft of an episode in the story of David and Esther that Wolfe had been working on when he arrived. Esther, in a fit of jealousy over David's wandering eye, mocks the treatment another woman would give him. This material finally appeared in Chapter 41, "The Weaver at Work Again," in* The Web and the Rock.]

I know now what she'll give you: oxtail soup out of a can with all the ox left out of it, picked-up codfish with a gob of that horrible white gooey Christian sauce, a slice of gluten bread, acidophilus milk, and a piece of stale angel-food cake that the little bitch picked up at a bakery on her way home from Roxy's.

Come Davey-darling! Be a nice boy now, you haven't eaten any of your boiled spinach, dear. It's good for you, pet, it's full of nice healthy iron. (Healthy iron, your granny. In three month's time he'll turn green with bellyache and dyspepsia! I hope to God he writhes with acute indigestion, I'll bet he thinks of me every time he takes another bite.)

No, you bad boy you, you can't have any more creamed beef, you've already had meat 3 times this month and its very bad for you, you've had 63 ounces of meat in the last three weeks, dear, you'll be getting uric acid before you know it. If you're a good boy I'll let you have a nice burned-up lamb chop week after next, I've got the most delicious menu all fixed up for the next two weeks, I read about it in Mary Sloppem's colum in the Daily Mistake. O yum! yum! yum! your mouth will water all right when you see what I've prepared for you, Dave, dear (Yes, and if I know him his eyes will water, too).

Next week is going to be Fish Week, Dave dear, We're going to have *nothing* but fish, pet, won't that be nice (O yes! that will be just too god-dam nice for words). Mary says fish is good for you, darling, the Body needs lots of fish, it's Brain Food, pet, and if my big boy is going to use that Great Big Wonderful Brain of His and Think All Those Beautiful Thoughts, he's going to be a Good Boy and eat lots of Fish like Momma tells him to.

You bad boy! I don't like to see my big boy's beautiful face all *wrinkled* up by that ugly old frown. Open your moufy, now, and swallow down this nice big spoonful of stewed prune juice. There! Now doesn't he feel better—it's good for my darling's bowels—O! You'll wake up in the morning feeling Just Wonderful.

Only last week my darling used the most dreadful word, I didn't know what it meant, it began with an F. I was never so shocked in my life. If my darling is going to have Beautiful Thoughts and put them in books, he must put all those Evil Thoughts out of his mind, he should think only Clean and Lovely Things that will elevate people, and Have a Great Big Pure Mind like Lindberg and Bruce Barton. My boy must have run around with some Low Company before his momma came to *wescue* him.

And I wish my darling would[*n't*] scratch himself you-know-where when company come to see us. And he mustn't fling his clothes around and leave his shirts and you-know-what right in the middle of the floor.

And if my darling is going to write of all those things in his books, I want him to be refined about it, he mustn't come right out in a vulgar way; he must say "After eleven o'clock at night their lives pursued separate courses." You know what I mean.

[*Shortly after he returned, Wolfe discovered that Aline Bernstein had suffered an emotional collapse and was in the hospital.*[2] *Since*

2. There has been some question as to just what happened to Mrs. Bernstein at this time. Because of the extreme desperation expressed in letters and cables to Wolfe, and because it is known that Mrs. Bernstein once took an overdose of sleeping tablets, biographers have assumed that this was the occasion of her attempted suicide.

Mrs. Bernstein's letters make clear, however, that this was not a suicide attempt. She wrote to Wolfe in April, 1931, and explained that she had been having fainting spells: once at Carnegie Hall, again while working on stage at the Playhouse, and yet again while shopping. In addition, she had suffered severe sinus headaches. Recently she had been confined to bed for two weeks, and in her weakened state the news of Wolfe's arrival in the United States was too much for her. She fainted dead away and was hospitalized, for she felt as if her heart had burst.

*he made no entries in his notebook about this event, we include here a
letter he wrote to Mrs. Bernstein. He had just received a note from
her written at the Doctor's Hospital, East End Avenue at 87th Street,
saying that when she read the news of his return in the paper, she
keeled over and was now in a hospital bed with two nurses in attendance. She found it impossible to face her daily life and blamed it all on
Wolfe's indifference to her love. He replied immediately:*]

[*March, 1931*]
Dear Aline:
    I found your letter at the Harvard Club last night—it was the
first news I had had about your illness; I called up the hospital at once
and asked about you. Then I wrote this letter which I was going to
send by a Western Union messenger, but it was late, and I was excited,
and I thought of our friend Abe Smith—I wanted him to bring it to
you himself and to talk to you, and to tell you the things I have told
him; we called up your doctor and he has promised to let Abe see you
tonight. I have written this by way of explanation.
    Now about your letter: I want to say this first of all as a first
answer to everything—Aline, I love you more dearly than anyone or
anything in the world. I will love you all my life, and it will never
change—there are so many people in this world who hate life and love
barrenness and they would mock at such a statement—but it is true,
and the way I feel about you will never change. If your present trouble
and illness is in any way due to me, I want to tell you that I would
rather shed my own blood than cause you any pain. Your letters and
cables to me abroad have caused me the most horrible pain and worry
of my life. I did not answer them because I could not answer them—I
tried to answer them, but I could not, I had said all I could say, by
word and letter, thousands of times, and there was nothing more to
say . . . .
    Then your sister came to see me in London in January and she
said you had never been healthier, happier, more full of joy and
contentment and success in your life than you have been in this last
year. I then asked your sister why, if this was true, you had sent me
these terrible messages saying that you were desperate, could not go on
living, were desperate, and that I was responsible. Your sister then said
that you were an emotional and impulsive woman who might think she
believed a message like this during the few minutes it takes to send one,
but that you then promptly forgot it, and were happy and full of
health again . . . . But if you were in this distress, your sister was
wrong, and I am sorry. You cabled me that everyone, including your

family, knew you loved me, and of your trouble, but your sister denied knowing anything about this . . . .

I will love you, by God, as long as I live, and it will never change. But *do not* misunderstand me, or try to break me with threats, or make me begin something that is ended—that is the way of madness and death, I will never yield, I will endure loneliness and physical death before I do.

Aline, do you understand what I am saying plainly to you here? Will you be my friend and love me as my friend? If so tell your friends and tell your family and tell the earth without fear or evasion that you love me, and that I love you, but that we are not physical lovers. Let us no longer have any tricks or evasions, I am ashamed of nothing, and tricks and concealments drive me mad.

Finally, I want to say this: I could never write a word about you or about my love for you in print that was not full of that love I bear you—no matter what little things we have said, I remember what was glorious and magnificent and lovely, and I remember all that was beautiful and grand in you: all of my hope now and for the future is that I can wreak out of pain, hunger, and love a living memorial for you: I can not think of other men or reputation. I am living alone with little money, and have forgotten the literary world—but if ever I put down what is in my heart, what I have known and felt, and the glory and magnificence I have known through you—then men all over this earth will be moved by it, and will know that it is true . . . .

Surely, you must know and see and understand what I have written here—it is dashed down in a few minutes, but my heart is in it. As for me, I shall love you all the days of my life, and when I die, if they cut me open they will find one name written on my brain and on my heart. It will be yours. I have spoken the living truth here, and I sign my name for anyone to see.

TOM WOLFE

[*Mrs. Bernstein was back in action in a few days. She wrote him on March 26 that she was traveling to Wilmington for the try-out of a theatrical production. Wolfe's letter, she said, brought her back into the world of the living. She wanted to see him soon, for he was branded into her heart and soul.*]

[*Wolfe's mother visited him in April. A couple of loose ledger sheets are the only remaining records of this event.*]

Tues. April 14 [*1931*]:

Today up, breakfast at home, then with Mama to see New York —Went across Bridge on street car, saw lower N.Y., Wall Street, Trinity, Battery, Aquarium—met ex-student Palmer in Trinity churchyard—took st. car with Mama back up B'dway—across to Wash Sq.—Saw Univ., Hot. Albert, old place on 8th St.—Then on 7th Avenue Bus uptown to Grant's Tomb—across to Columbia—look out over Morningside Hts. and Harlem Flats—then back by subway to Clark St.—walked home bringing groceries, we ate here, she cooked. Had drinks of gin, and talked late into night—until 3 o'clock.

April 18, 1931:

A magnificent day of Spring—In the last few days everything has begun to burst out of the earth. You can see it grow—brooding and sudden growth—a musical rich chatter of birds—a light pattern of children's voices in the air—In my basement at Brooklyn I hear this—5 o'clock.

April, 1931—City Hall Sq.—The Bums:

The parade to W.C.—Hey gimme a smack o' dat.

The one who weeps and tells of his skill with multiplying fractions.

I bet you I got de best seat in dis God-dam park.

[*In his search back into the "lost time" of Aline Bernstein and her father Joseph Frankau, Wolfe consulted old issues of the* New York Times. *A sample of his notes from this reading is given below.*]

Jacob Hess—story Feb. or March 1886 [3]

Mingo Jack—Lynching in New Jersey—March of 1886—Times —Bloody Story.

Kweet-kweet-kweet-kweet-kweet.

Chirra-urrup, pwee, pwee, pwee! [4]

3. Jacob Hess was a well-known Republican politician and the Commissioner of Electric Subways in New York. In the later part of his life, Joseph Frankau took a job as secretary to Jacob Hess.

4. This representation of a bird's song indicates that Wolfe was working on "In the Park," a story about Esther and her father and their first ride in an automobile in Central Park. The first fruits of his year's labor, Wolfe submitted it to Perkins for publication in *Scribner's Magazine*. It was rejected, however, and Wolfe went into one of his deep states of despair.

Times Dec. 23, 1884—p.5:

A young man with electric bulb in scarf-pin "newest thing from Paris."

Slush rain and fog—congested traffic—rivers of slush in gutters —liners held up at Sandy Hook—din of foghorns and bells in harbor.

Union Square Theatre

3 Wives to 1 Husband.

Times Dec. 24, 1884:

Bijou Opera House B'dway at 30th—Henry E. Dixey in Adonis.[5]

Koster and Bials [6]—Ill-fed Dora.

101 Waverly Place—Single Rooms $7 with board.

A Gentleman going to Europe wants to sell his horses; sixteen hands high—stylish blacks, long tails, good and mild in every way— also a Brewster landau and harness.

A bill poster—May 17, 1873—Union Square Theater—Frou-Frou—Miss Agnes Ethel.[7]

Dion Boucicault—Daddy O'Dowd—Booth's Theatre.

Sothern in Lord Dundreary—Walleck's [8]

Aline Bernstein

Armonk Village 434

P.O.—Armonk N.Y.

[*During the spring Wolfe reluctantly renewed his association with Mrs. Bernstein, and she occasionally crossed town to visit him. But their relationship had undergone a change, and she knew that he had won partial freedom from her. She wrote on May 30 indicating that she was resigned to this change. She enclosed Milton's lines, Eve to Adam in* Paradise Lost, "*With thee conversing I forget all time,*" *as a "decoration" for Decoration Day. She went on to say that although she wanted his companionship more than anything else in life, she did not want to be a burden to him. She told him how much she enjoyed her recent visit to his apartment and being able to cook for him. She*

5. *Adonis* was a very successful musical extravaganza which ran for 603 performances in New York alone. Its star, Henry Dixey, became a matinée idol. For an example of how Wolfe intended to bring him briefly into "The Good Child's River," see footnote 12 below.

6. A large "opera house" on 23rd Street near 6th Avenue which specialized in musical revues, ministrel shows, and variety acts.

7. *Frou-Frou* was one of Augustin Daly's adaptions from the French. Miss Ethel, an inexperienced actress, rose to stardom in this piece.

8. Edward Sothern created his most famous role as Lord Dundreary in Tom Taylor's *Our American Cousin* in 1856. He continued to play it over the years.

offered to prove her love by preparing meals for him frequently and by being his devoted friend.

The remaining entries begin at the back of the notebook and continue upside down toward the front.]

Scenes:
1. Mr. Wilkie Collins
2. The Bridge
3. Clothes—the tailors, old women in Eng. and Boston etc.— things that are lovely
4. As for me I am noted—
5. Enter Daughter of Desolation—etc.
6. Auntie Kate and the money
7. Bella
8. Uncle John and Uncle Fred
9. Boy at Harvard [9]

The things that are lovely: [*it*] is the cloth on tables; it is great ships where you find your love upon the sea.

"Have you any milk for me there?" he says. "No," I say, "No." "If you were any good, if you loved me, if you cared anything for me, you would have milk for me." "I love you, I adore you, I am faithful unto death to you, but I have no milk for you." "Ah, but you have milk for the others," he will say. "I have no milk for no one: if I had milk for anyone it would be for you: I love you, I am full of blood for you, I will give my blood for you, I will give my life for you."

"You liar and you bitch, you trick, betray, deceive, and whore me every day."

Eat me like honey: let me be consumed—I will be in you, I will be devoured by you.

A rose-lip thing, proud of her muff; a darling, a dear, a sweet kid—have I known hunger? Yes: but was there not the glory and the loveliness; did not all things cry out to me?—I saw the empty shoe. I

9. This series of scenes planned for "The Good Child's River" includes the episode of the cruel aunt Kate who accuses Esther of stealing money and the episode of Esther's grief over the death of the young Harvard student whom she loved.

filled it with dead people. I felt the life in all things like this, I knew joy and all the glory.

Yes! Monkey Hawke, that men thought mad, I saw the angel in him, and I fed his hunger.

Look for your father, if you like: in foreign lands look for your darling and your dear. I hope you find him, and may it bring you joy: but remember who your friend was in the bad years, remember who stood by you when you had no friends: who came and fed you, who cooked your steaks, who loved you, and took care of you.

Look for your father in the foreign fairs, but no more broken noses and fractured skulls if you please.

[*The following fragment was written as Wolfe drafted a letter to his brother Fred in April or May, 1931. Wolfe was concerned at this time over his sister Effie and his brother-in-law Fred Gambrell, who were about to lose their home in Anderson, South Carolina.*]

I do not think Fred G. is entirely to blame for what happened in Anderson years ago. I haven't got much sympathy or respect for a man like Harrison who paid a man 50 or 75 dollars a month for 12 hours daily drudgery and expected him to stay honest and support a wife and 7 children on it. It seems to me this is dishonesty on the part of the employer to begin with, for if we expect people we employ to be honest and fair with us we must begin with honesty and fairness to them.

But since Harrison held a whip hand and would be considered right as long as [*he*] had money and could employ other men, and since the feeling in a little town is what we know it to be, I think Fred G. was wrong in not taking his family away from Anderson years ago. I do not know whether any great effort can be expected from Fred G. now, but all of the children have their lives before them, they can be saved by saving themselves, and they must be made to understand this. I suppose Effie could say to us that we have never had children and know nothing about it, and that it is not up to us to give advice, but I didn't think she would be foolish enough to say that all is well, and that she does not want things to be better. Things can be made a hell of a lot better if she can only act with firmness and decision now. I think she has been a good mother and loved her children, but [*breaks off*]

[*From Good Child's River Ledger 1*]
4:50 A.M. Sunday Morning, June 18(?), 1931:
First bright light just breaking—outside my windows on Veran-

dah Place—low voices of several men in shirt sleeves pleading with woman to get up. Woman, fat, Irish looking, has befouled herself.

Get up now. Come on, get up. You ain't actin' like a lady, that's the trouble wit' you.

O le' me go home.

Not until you start actin' like a lady. Come on now (low persuasive voice). Get up. Start actin' like a lady.

To hell wit' you! Lemme go home. O lemme go home.

Start actin' like a lady. Get up. Get up.

To hell wit' you. I wanna go home.

Two other men: Aw, why can't you get a cab and take her home?

Not until she starts actin' like a lady. I don't wanna take her home till she starts actin' like a lady.

To hell wit' you. Lemme go home.

Don't talk like that. Start actin' like a lady.[10]

4:55 o'clock

First light—first bird—wind in leaves—yesterday, a scorching 93° heat struck—today prob. the same.

Chapters to Follow

1) The Three Sisters
2) My Father's Family
3) Bella (Dr. Bunine—His Day—His Woman Patients—His Xmas stories, etc.—How E. drank morphine) etc.
4) The Trip Abroad—England—my aunt—Wilkie Collins—Mrs. Daisy Pace—
5) Home Again—My Grandfather, etc.
6) Aunt Mary's Boarding House (The Doctor has died, killed himself during our trip abroad)—The People There (Father was starting immediately on tour—we went there)
7) Difficulties—Poverty—Grandfather, etc.
8) The Street and Our Neighbors—My friends
9) School—Miss Lavinia Brill etc.
10) The Library
11) The Mother's Death
12) The Bridge
13) Bella's Pink Tea

10. Wolfe later used this incident as one of the mock-nostalgic memories of the author in "No Door." See FDTM, p. 10.

14) Uncle John and Uncle Fred—Bella's Second Marriage
15) Mrs. Daisy Pace—Her Story

[*Wolfe jotted these notes about time from encyclopedias. Later, in 1934, he tore them out of his notebook, redated them* "Tuesday, Dec. 23, 1924," *and used them for Eugene Gant's Parisian notebook in* Of Time and the River, *pp. 670–71. He then added at the beginning,* "The mystery explained! Today at the American library, found out what it is:"]

"Time—that dimension of the world which we express in terms of before and after."

"the temporal sequence pervades mind and matter alike."

Time, the form of the internal sense, and space, the form of the external sense.

Theory of Relativity . . . the true units of both time and space are neither points nor moments, but moments-in-the-history-of-a-point.

W. James—within a definite limited interval of duration, known as the specious present, there is a direct perception of the temporal relations. After an event has passed beyond the specious present, it can only enter into consciousness by reproductive memory.

James—"the object of memory is only an object imagined in the past to which the emotion of belief adheres."

Temporal experience divided into three qualitatively distinct intervals: the remembered past, the perceived specious present, and the anticipated future—By means of this tripartite division we are able to orient our present selves in the stream of our own experience.

By arrangement of temporal orders of past with temporal orders of future, we can construct a secondary temporal order of our specious presents and their contents. Thus time has its roots in experience and yet [*appears*] to be a dimension in which experiences and their contents are arranged.

Thus the stuff from which time is made is of the nature of experience-data.

The Zenonian paradoxes: Achilles cannot catch up with the slowest hare save by occupying an infinity of positions. A flying arrow cannot remain where it is nor where it is not. These things do not deal with space or time but with the properties of infinite assemblages and dense series (Americana).[11]

---

11. Notes from the unsigned article "Time" in the *Encyclopedia Americana*, 1920, and also in some later editions. It does not appear in the most recent editions.

Britannica—measurement of Time—has this difficulty—nothing similar or simple to compare it with.

Duration, permanence, existence—all presuppose the lapse of time—*fact* upon which all these ideas are based is possibility of repetition of experience.

Thus psychological history of construction of [*our*] world.

Pulse beats, alterations of day and night, artificial instruments such as the balance watch and pendulum clock.

Time simpler than space—"has only one dimension." [12]

For this relief much thanks; tis bitter cold and I am sick at heart.
Well said, old mole! Canst work i' the earth so fast?
Wild and whirling words, my lord! [13]

[*A long sequence of entries, omitted here, show that Wolfe looked up Theodore Bernstein in every volume of the New York City Directory from 1901 to 1923. He took note of his rise from clerk, to cashier, to broker, to member of the firm of Hirsch, Lilienthal Co. He wrote down the changes in the address of his residence from year to year. Then Wolfe followed Joseph Frankau through the directories from 1873 to 1900. He was not only attempting to retrieve the past years in feeling, he was also finding addresses he could look up and draw on for realistic detail. The entries are very simple, like this sample.*]

Vol. 108   1894–95
    Frankau, Jos.   actor
    218 W. 45   "Bella's."

12. Notes from the article "Time Measurement," by Ralph Allen Samson, in the fourteenth edition of the *Encyclopaedia Britannia*. It does not appear in the recent issues of the fourteenth edition.

Aside from his general preoccupation with time, Wolfe apparently planned to work into Esther's monologues a fascination with time. In the Good Child's River Ledger 2, Wolfe has a dictionary definition of time followed by a sketchy draft of Esther speaking:

"Tomorrow and tomorrow and tomorrow—to the last syllable of recorded time (one, two, three, four, etc.)

"That time of year (when you went away that time you said you were only going to be gone six months: I was reading your letter over only the other day.)

"Time! God, I saw Mr. Dixey on the street the other day: the poor old fellow was looking awfully old and feeble, I spoke to him, I didn't think he would recognize me but he knew me at once. Gee! There was something awfully sad about it, I thought of all the times I used to see him when he was well known, and I kept thinking of Daddy: the poor old fellow kept shaking me by the hand, he wouldn't let go! 'Well, well,' he said. 'Esther, you haven't changed a bit,' he said. 'You look exactly the same as you did when you were a little girl.'"

13. Wolfe probably added this series of quotations from *Hamlet* in 1934; thus they would represent Eugene Gant's ironic comment on the information about time.

[*Another part of Wolfe's research into the life of Joseph Frankau was his looking into Percy MacKaye's two-volume biography of his father, Steele MacKaye. Joseph Frankau's most successful role was that of "Met" in* Hazel Kirke, *a part which Steele MacKaye wrote into the play especially for Frankau when he was reworking the play from its earlier version,* An Iron Will. Hazel Kirke *had one of the most phenomenal successes in the history of the American theatre: it was performed more frequently than any other play except* Uncle Tom's Cabin. *A few notes from MacKaye's book follow.*]

Epoch by [*Percy*] MacKaye.

On June 30, 1881 Wm. Winter wrote to him (Steele MacKaye) (referring also to Moulinet in Rose Michel):

My dear MacKaye:

Miss Couglan for Lady Teazle . . . .

Don't forget to speak to Mr. Frankau about Moulinet (for an actor's benefit).[14]

Feb. 4, 1880—

Hazel Kirke opens New Madison Square Theatre.

Joseph Frankau was *Met* in original cast.[15]

Also Effie Ellsler and Mr. and Mrs. Thomas Whiffen.

"The wonderful elevator stage"—one of the wonders of the century.[16]

14. One character in *Rose Michel*, by Steele MacKaye, was a comic servant named "Moulinet," a role especially suited to Frankau's talents.

15. Wolfe later brought into Esther's story a great deal about *Hazel Kirke* and its cast. He supplied this as background for the episode about Esther's birth. It begins in the Good Child's River Ledger 1, p. 243: "At this time my father was appearing in a play called Hazel Kirke [crossed out and "Esther Craig" is substituted]: it was one of the most famous plays of the time, it had run for years and broken records for performances . . . . My father did not have the hero's part in this play. He took the part of Pittacus Green.

"Pittacus Green was the comic figure in Hazel Kirke. I do not think he was strictly essential to the action of the play. All of the great events of the drama could have occurred without him. And yet, I think he was perhaps the most important figure in the play. He acted as a chorus, an interpreter of events, as a confidant and as a comic force to relieve the tension of tragedy, and to give the whole play the ease and belief of laughter."

16. This is a reference to Steele MacKaye's inventive genius in designing the New Madison Square Theater. Wolfe later worked all this into "The Good Child's River," too, in a chapter entitled "The Theatre": "For a brief period the theatre was almost a national monument, an object in which a people that measured itself pugnaciously against other peoples in terms of size and modernity of its possessions could take pride and comfort. The newspapers when they described the theatre assured their readers that there was 'nothing in Europe to touch it.' From cellar to roof every fixture and device represented what was most up-to-

Burning of curtain at professional benefit in Feb.—actors piece together a new one—terrific applause—play beautifully—later Mac-Kaye takes them to supper at Pimlico.

MacKaye left theatre in Jan. 1881 in state of brawl with Mallory's.

On March 30, 1881, Dominick Murray writes to MacKaye who has opened in Phil. in Won at Last: "Frankau and I are greatly consoled by hearing of your success, which Dan Frohman has told us about. More power to you! I trust this does not sound like treachery to the devout brothers!" [17]

[*The next entries show Wolfe, perhaps in the New York Public Library, looking over several issues of* Life, *in the days when it was a comic weekly like* Punch, *and later examining a series of old photographs. He was searching especially for a picture of New York in 1881, the year Aline Bernstein was born, and for one of the surroundings of the Frankau house at 133 W. 34th Street, a site now occupied by Macy's Department Store.*]

Life—June 9, 1904:
Picture—Light of Asia, showing Russian Bears fleeing away from Japanese sun.

June 2—Last character notice of season—Successes of year:
Maxine Elliot in Her Own Way
Wister's The Virginian
[*Barrie's*] Admirable Crichton

---

date in theatrical construction, and there were, in addition, several notable improvements which no other theatre had ever possessed. There was a balcony, cunningly suspended in mid-air, from which a hidden orchestra discoursed aerial music to an enchanted audience which said, 'Where? Where?'; there were sliding and adjustable seats, calculated to give the spectator the comfort almost of his own bed (this device had to be abolished); there was a courteous and capable staff that refused tips and dispensed free ice water during the intermissions (this lavishness was noticed in columns of print); and finally there was the wonderful elevator stage which could sink swiftly and noiselessly into a vast basement, where it could be instantly detached with its whole freight of scenery, rolled off along a track and dismantled while another stage, already set for the next scene, rose swiftly into place behind the footlights."

17. The Mallory brothers, editors of the *Churchman,* were the financial backers of the theater and the play. They were very slick businessmen and arranged a contract with MacKaye whereby he drew a modest salary while they made thousands on *Hazel Kirke* and its touring companies. Wolfe combines them into a single character, Prince, in "The Good Child's River" and assigns to the character a series of anecdotes which combine rascality and hypocrisy.

Belasco's Bellairs
Thomas' The Other Girl
Zangwill's Merely Mary Ann
Musical
Three Little Maids
Babes in Toyland
The Girl from Kay's
Babette
The Yankee Consul
Piff, Puff, Pouf

Hackett, Belasco, Fiske, the threatened Trust, etc.[18]
Men with white vests, wide cuffs, widebrimmed straw hats.
Women with stick-out busts—long-lined skirts

June 30—1904:
Indignant editorial over burning of *General Slocum* in East
River. Burning with Sunday School picnic aboard—rattled captain,
rotten life preservers, 800 lives lost, not enough boats.
Talk about Russia.

Broadway at 34th St. 1880—Details of photograph:
The house on 34th St. 4 stories and basement—top story has
Mansard roof—with outside windows—Elevated with little engine—
plume of smoke shown at stack.[19]
Tower of Broadway Tabernacle at right—*cable* cars on Broadway—dreary dingy blackened Residence Houses on 34th St begin
about two or three from corner apparently—On N.W. corner a dingy
3 story building—sign Siegel and Cooper Co.—On S.W. corner a
dingy 4 story building with various signs *Massage Operators, Trained
Nurses*—On roof a stick-up sign on iron framework.
Koster and Bials.

18. These notes are from an article which attacks James K. Hackett for
surrendering to the Theatrical Syndicate, which is denounced as a trust more
vicious than the Standard Oil Trust.

19. Notes of this sort eventually led Wolfe to write drafts about the birth
of Esther which he felt had authentic details. One of them, in the Good Child's
River Ledger 1, p. 52, begins: "A few nights before the Christmas of 1881, there
was subdued but very intense excitement in the house of Joseph Barrett, an actor.
The house was one of a block of brownstone dwellings on the north side of
Thirty-fourth Street, a few doors west of Broadway, and was in no respect different from its neighbors, or few thousands of other houses of other streets which,
block by block, duplicated one another with an insane precision of detail. The
house where Joseph Barrett lived was four stories tall, it had a high stone stoop,
three tall windows on each floor, and a small basement court to the left of the
stoop . . . ."

N.Y. Herald Bldg.—much as now at intersection—island up B'dway—a ragged line of buildings of three or four stories broken by six or eight story hotels—Hotel Normandie.

Broadway at 36th 1882:

N.E. corner from B'way to Sixth Ave where Greenwich savings bank now is—on corner cheap 3 story Bldg.—Broadway Dental Parlors —above huge hand poster "Slaves of Gold"—Black eyes painted sign one door down toward 6th Avenue—Herald Square Storage Warehouse a 4 story Bldg.—Dramatic News 1364—2 story bldg.—a wagon, closed, with white horse clopping on cobbles—granite lanes across the cobbles—a cable car in full view—an open wagon with tin cans—a horse with a waterproof closed wagon—people with umbrellas.

[*The remaining material in the notebook is made up entirely of more notes from old issues of the* New York Times. *A generous sample is given here to show the variety of news stories that caught Wolfe's eye.*]

Dec. 27 [*1881*]

Clara Morris—to open in The New Magdalen at Union Sq. Theater.

Christmas celebrated on Monday—Dancing Bands of ragamuffins tooting fifes in street—Christmas in missions, Newsboys' lodging houses, etc.—Mrs. John Jacob Astor and Andrew Carnegie—Crowds of carriages on Fifth Avenue.

Dec. 23, 1881:

Booth's Theater sold—to be made Dry Goods Store—price $550 000—opened Feb. 1869—Booth as Romeo.

Also Lawrence Barrett, E. L. Davenport, et al.

Gilsey house appears frequently in news.

Costumes of the season—Sun. Dec. 25, 1881:

"Many fresh capotes are to be seen. The newest among these are of feathers. They are very small, with flat crowns covered with royal pheasants or 'lophophore.' On the brim is a full plush or velvet ruching harmonizing with the general coloring of feathers."

Dec. 20 [*1881*]:

Death of Siro Delmonico.

Died Mon. Dec. 19 between 1 and two in morning at nephew Charles' house—

On Sunday evening at Fifth Avenue and 26th St. Delmonico with party of friends—Later went to Brown's restaurant at midnight for supper—smoked 100 cigars a day.

Rich. Mansfield collection—Mrs. Mansfield as Tessie Tagrag in Ten Thousand a Year, from novel by Sam'l Warren.

Dec. 25 [*1881*]

"Guiteau's Insulting Ways"—Disgraceful Scenes in the Assassin's Trial.[20]

"You have a mouth like an old catfish"—to Porter, prosecutor —argument as to difference between delusion of "inspiration" and insanity.

As court broke up, handcuffs are put on prisoner—he says "Tomorrow is Christmas. I wish the court, the jury, the American people, and everybody else a happy Xmas. I am happy."

New York Times Dec. 27, 1881—Tuesday:

A Noble Porker's Death.

Christmas Hog-Guessing at Gabe Case's Club House (a saloon) "a string of carriages formed under the horse sheds."

"leaning over mahogany bar."

Guesses cost $1 apiece—Stoop of Hoboken Turtle Club House covered with spectators—an Italian 4-piece band playing away for dear life.

The band played "I'm going home to die no more" as pig died. As Gabe Case awards prize (coming around corner) band plays "See the conquering hero comes." Case followed by judges, James Casey, Clerk of the Gentlemen's Driving Ass'n, and Sam Sniffen—won by Frederick A. Ridaboch, the W. 54th St. Liveryman.

Martin B. Brown guessed 591 lbs. Harry McCoon, Mrs. Ellis, W. H. Davis, D. Kelley, Justice Ambrose Monell, and F. W. Quimby & Co. guessed 595 lbs. Ridaboch dropped off carcase to Lang, butcher on W. 52nd Street for $74.12.

N.Y. Times. Dec. 26, 1881

Mark Twain's speech in Philadelphia on the Pilgrims—Scenes of N.E. dinner—Fine.

20. The trial of Charles J. Guiteau, a strange and probably insane lawyer who shot President Garfield on July 2, 1881, was reported in great detail during December and January.

Guiteau—assassin of Garfield—Christmas in Jail in Washington —Eats Hearty Dinner.

Births in week before Christmas 515 (Bureau of Records) 189 marriages, 762 deaths—Police made 1321 arrests.

During that week 5115 immigrants land at Castle Island—Rhynland of Antwerp brought 781 (Dec. 24)—Devon from Bremen 435—Russian exiles.

Jacob Schaefer and Wm Sexton to play Billiard Match in Tammany Hall Thurs. Dec. 29—600 pts. up for stake of $5000.

Dec. 25, 1881:

Fayetteville N.C. Morally bankrupt.[21]

Dec. 22, [*1881*]

The Standard—8:15—Patience.
Also The Casino 8:15—Patience.
Union Sq. Theatre at 8—Lights of London.
Grand Opera House at 8—M'Liss.
Booth's Theatre at 8—The Vokes Family.
Academy of Music at 8—Macbeth.
Abbey's New Park Theatre: 8:30—Mother In Law.

Dec. 21 [*1881*]:

George G. Sickles 81—marries his mistress Mrs. Mary Sawyer 48—had three illegitimate children by her.

Census
Population 1880
50,155,783
N.Y. 5,082,871

Times Dec. 22, 1881:

General Mention (Theatrical)

Mr. McCullough repeated his performance of Othello at Fifth Avenue Theatre last night.

Mme. Patti's first performance in Philadelphia Tuesday night—receipts $9820—immense enthusiasm.

Miss Kate Claxton at Booth's next Monday—The Two Orphans.

21. A news story reporting that the municipal government of Fayetteville had repudiated its debts.

Mrs. J. H. Hackett to give her performance as Lady Macbeth tonight.

Wreck of the exploring vessel, Jeannette.
Average temp. for Dec. 21, 41–5/8—cloudy & rainy weather.
Prohibition in Kansas—overwhelmingly "dry."

[*During the late spring and summer Wolfe had a brief love affair with a school teacher who had an apartment on the upper East Side of Manhattan. At length he broke it off, and the following fragment of a letter to her indicates why the relationship ended. It also reflects Wolfe's attitude toward women in general and his feeling about Aline Bernstein in particular:*]

"Last night I saw you in the way—with the tone, the look, the manner— that I fear in women. For there seems to be some terrible chemistry at work in them—we remember their deep tenderness, their lovely and beautiful ways, their gaiety and humour, but when they become angry at us we see the other thing in them—the formidable and repulsive enemy that we are always at war with. Their voices tremble and grow loud, words of abuse pour from them—we feel that they will use any means to get the best of us—every sort of horrible suspicion crosses the mind, as we look at their inflamed and violent faces—they will rush to the doors or the windows shouting they have been attacked, they will scream abuse and lies at one so everyone can hear—in a moment the lovely creature who made a music for us just by coming near has turned to a horrible monster, and we remember all our former contact with her with loathing. Our flesh turns sick, we could not touch her, we want to get away and forget about it . . . .

"I believe you are made of the best stuff on earth, and I want you to have the best there is—I cannot give it to you, but if you found someone who could, I would cheer loud, hard as it would be to see you go. You said at one time last night that I am 'a fine person.' I'm not. I am ugly, cruel, and mad in a way you know nothing about: if anyone loves me I torture them, curse and revile them, and try to drive them away. The best friend, the only person who ever loved me with all her heart, I treated in this way. I have committed crimes of this sort for which I would burn in hell for a million years, if there were a hell: instead I have burned ten million years in a hell of my own. If I loved you, and you loved me I would treat you the same way.

But there is another part of me that is all right—the best there is. It is as good as anything on earth. I eagerly welcome your offer to be my friend. You say you can be counted on if for any reason I ever need you.—I need you, I need you all the time. I hope you will be my friend forever. If I could give you the utmost and final love of my heart and spirit I would give it to you, whether you could return it or not. But I can not. I only felt that way toward one person, and I will not feel that way to any person again, because it has been given [*end of page*]

[*From Good Child's River Ledger 2*]

America:
The yellers, the whoopers and hollerers—was it only some national loudness, something they had been taught, something they thought smart?
The rebel yell, and the yells of the Western miners, the yells of drunken mountaineers as they stamped their feet, there were the numberless yells of the college boys, the yells of the camp evangelists.

Professions and Trades

A Scene Designer from New York
A Grocery Clerk in South Carolina
A Machinery Salesman in North Carolina
A Radio Writer from Iowa
A "Conveyancer" and ex-minister in Boston
An Advertising Man from Michigan
A Tennis Champion from California
A Prize Fighter from Philadelphia
A Hotel Bookeeper and actor from the South
A Newspaper Woman from Brooklyn
An Aesthete from Indiana
A Schoolteacher from Wyoming
A syphilitic lawyer from Norfolk
A Diabetic from New York State

America—perhaps a book of ten thousand pages to describe it; perhaps the description of an old brick wall will do it.

The city man-swarm—"The locusts have no king"

Hatred on an island—Orr's Island,[22] for example—the reason why Englishmen when they begin to hate their country hate it with such an intense and bitter hatred.

Traits:

Some parts of the country definitely marked by traits of character and manner—others were levelled out.

1) New Englander—sharply and often unpleasantly marked—viz. tartness of speech, reticence after a certain point, wintry and sparse quality—a mean prim surliness—examples:

"This is a nice town you've got here"—"Tain't mine: I ain't got it."

"Are these checks all I need?"—"Well, it may not be all ye need, but it's all we're goin' to give ye."

"Have I got time to eat here"—"Cain't say. Don't know how much time it takes you to eat."—etc.

The suspicious chip-on-the-shoulder we're-as-good-as-anyone attitude.

Meanness of down-easter with money—Mrs. Fides.

The "Some folks I know" kind of allusiveness—the female eye-glasses—the prim pursed parsley and boiled scrod faces—the lack of "temper" or "nature" in the women—even in the pictures of Mr. & Mrs. Wadsworth T. Coolidge's daughters in yachting togs at Marblehead one feels this.

2) Southerner—the hearty insistence, the false effusiveness, the belly laughter, the drawling pleasantness.

3) Iowa—corn-fed absoluteness—want to be one big family—to have a "crowd"—our "crowd" etc.—their "crowd."

But with places like New Jersey—Philadelphia—upper New York State—even parts of Connecticut—it is harder to see plain and definite markings—When one says "Maine," "South Carolina," "Iowa," the "East Side" to me, I see things much more clearly.

The People in the Orr's Island Boarding House:

Dr. and Mrs. Burns

The schoolteacher waitresses

Mr. and Mrs. Fides

Dwight Mansfield

22. In late August, 1931, Wolfe took a brief vacation to Orr's Island, Maine, in Casco Bay. These notes reflect his rather dour outlook at the time.

The New England Spinstresses

The New Englander who had gone west to Colorado and rarely spoke with others.

Mrs. Ida Lubee—husband a fisherman, son a Coast Guardsman.

THE HATRED ON THE ISLAND

The hatred on an island is worse than the hatred in any other place. It swelters in the hearts of men, and they can nowhere flee it. At night they come up to the fringes of the sea: they go down across the springy turf of pine-warm woodlands, they clamber over rocks, they walk along the hard sliding mast of salty sea-warm beaches and the sea confronts them with the glut of full warm tides—level, salty, unspeakably exultant, and illimitable—the sea confronts them and they cannot escape their hatred.

And yet the island is beautiful. If there were only one man on the island there would be no hate.

Pocket Notebook 17

September, 1931, to December, 1931

During the fall Wolfe occupied himself with further work on the early life of Esther and her father Joe, although he turned aside frequently to begin more episodes about the early life of Fritz Jacobs and about Hawke's experiences in the city, his travels, and his memories of childhood. Wolfe had lost, or continually changed, any structural plans he had had for "The October Fair." He was writing steadily but not moving toward an end. He was also running out of money, so in December he looked among his manuscripts to see what he could put together to sell to Scribner's Magazine. *He worked with what he had written over the years about "Uncle Emerson," and finally came up with the short novel "A Portrait of Bascom Hawke."*

Very little of this literary activity is reflected in the notebook. It is filled mostly with names and addresses—many of them entered when Wolfe was apartment-hunting—and with notations from his researches at the Public Library.

[*The first five leaves are missing.*]

. . . this photo—shows back of Pabst Hotel—and a 4 story bldg. on Times island—at left *The New York Burlesque Ballet and Vanities* (electric sign)—Rector's Restaurant—Hotel Cadillac (Barrett House)—Criterion Theater next to The New York Criterion—sign John Hare in "The Gay Lord Quex" (identify).

For New York—sign Grand Opening Wed. Evening, Oct. 31.

Horsecars coming up out of 7th Avenue—white horses jingle-jaunty with their potent weary assurance, their friendly and sorrowful box-heads together nodding—Two powerful black horses with white marks on forehead and gleaming harness spanking up strongly with a carriage (?)—gig (?) with two derby hatted men in front and one behind—a helmeted white man with a long handled tray pushing together long dark hedges of dung.

Sign—The Pabst Hotel—Restaurant Rathskeller James B. Regan Prop.—Several hansoms with their queer jaunty backward view.

Two or three four-wheelers—several high gleaming grocer's wagons—odorous musty "Delicacies and Fruits." The cab drivers with their battered high hats and double-breasted brass buttons—a wheeled clean-up can—a common sight—a driver of a grocer's wagon with a long white apron.

This is certainly before *1904*—(Times Bldg.) four lines of women, late nineties or early 1900's—Broadway cars may be street cars —7th Ave. cars horse cars—tracks seem to have middle slot.

The Broken ragged appearance of B'dwy and 7th Ave. The 44th St. corner at right with brownstone blvds. gives only unity.

(Note—"The Gay Lord Quex" played by John Hare's Company in New York in Fall of 1900.)

Herald and Greeley Squares 1878 (from 35th St.) shows Esther's corner 34th (looking south) Horse car going down B'dway—Elevated coming in station on near 34th St. corner (Now Macy's)—a 3 story bldg. of brick-steel-work—a sign above—United States Express Co. (1313 B'dway)—Below—Business College—Ground floor sign *Choice Imported Cigars* cigar store—on other corner—4 story brick bldgs.—mass of signs—*Family Machines*—W. Klauser Photographer Trusses—Brunswick Pharmacy Trusses—P. H. Schmidt and Son— Surgical Instruments and Trusses—The Palais Royal Cigar Stand—Removed Inside the Drug Store [*sketch of "The Hand"*] M. Kolfin— Finest Brands Imported Cigars—Telephone poles—hanging awning with ten crossbars.

Cobbled sts. with stone cross steps for pedestrians—sidewalk sign—Bijou—open—on front side of SW corner 34th—Trained Nurses.

Portraits (very center of sign) in Crayon, Oil, and India Ink— The back of a four-wheeler—back of a furniture van.

Part of 1st brownstone house next to S.W. corner of 34th St. 3 stories and basement (or entrance floor)—can't make out if there is stoop—looks as if there's not—balcony under 1st (?) 2nd (?) story windows.

Men in wagon—with poles and slotted sides—in short sleeves with straw hats—woman with parasol—men with unpressed pants— some with straw hats—some with derbies—one with long Prince Albert (?) coat—again the ragged lumpy look of B'dway.

All very familiar and near—The potent and living message of the street.

Leaving Grand Central 4:04 Arrives Greendale 7:35 Catskill about Eight I think.

WOLFE [1]

Faces—The faces of 1895 and those of 1931.

1931—Faces most familiar to people:
   Politics—Hoover, Coolidge, Smith, Jimmy Walker, Roosevelt.
   Business—Ford, Rockefeller.
   Sport—Babe Ruth, Dempsey, Carnera, Tilden, Jones.

Oct. 2, 1931—11:15 P.M.—

In 45 minutes I will be *31* years old. I have made these comments before—I know now there is no sense in pretentiousness—I have done little—finished and published one book—know not where I am on the other—Three days ago K. Raisbeck either killed himself, died, or was murdered. That ends one of the clinging threads—Have written this in The Blue Ribbon.

[*In October, Wolfe moved to an apartment at 111 Columbia Heights in Brooklyn overlooking the New York harbor. The next several pages of the notebook are filled with names, addresses, and rental charges that he set down while looking for his new apartment.*]

With goat's milk on round cusps of barren hills among coarse bunch grass of white blasted earth their shepherds moved.
Against white walls, in livid sun-glare of 5000 years.

And there they killed the poor Jewsbody of our God.

THE CHILDHOOD OF MONKEY HAWKE

Chap. I
   1) The Doctor, the horses, the feet
   2) The picnic—"Monkey" Hawke
   3) New York—actors, the circus
Joe In The Streets of Life.
Esther—The Streets of Life.

Monkey Hawke
Rebecca

1. At the end of September Wolfe spent a few days in the Catskills at the estate of some friends, Mr. and Mrs. L. Effingham De Forest.

Bella
Dr. Belogrovsky
Esther Hawke
Edith
Rebecca Goldsmith
Mrs. Daisy Pace
Frederick Jacobs
Big Jake Dietz
Auntie Kate
Brandell—(the good actor)
Latimer Street
Mrs. Fairchild

THE YOUTH OF M.H.

1) Physical Remoteness—observations

[*The notes that follow about the lives of the four American presidents were taken from the* Encyclopaedia Britannica. *Although Wolfe was gathering this information for the background of Joe Barrett (or Lindau), he used it principally for an evocation of his own father's years in "The Four Lost Men."*]

Garfield, Jas. Abram (1831–1881).
B. log cabin frontier town, Orange, Cuyahoga County, Ohio.
Walks across country to Cleveland aet. 16—works on lake schooner for canal boatmen.
Works way through school as teacher, carpenter, farmer—studies at West. Reserve Eclectic Inst. at Hiram—Goes to Williams—returns to Hiram as principal, enters political life, anti-slavery man—enlists—lt. colonel—then, Brigadier—then maj. gen'l—gallantry at Shiloh and Chickamauga.
Year 1874—one of trouble—Reconstruction, Credit Mobilier, Salary Grab, Greenback issue.
On July 2, 1881 on way to Wms. College commencement shot in Wash. rwy. station by Guiteau.

Arthur, Chester Alan (1830–1886).
B. Fairfield, Vt.—Oct. 5, 1830—son of an Irishman who came to Vt. from Canada.
Enters Union College in 1848 as Soph.—1853 enters law office NY City.

Known as defender of glaring negro cases—1855 gets decision that negroes entitled to ride as whites on st. r'ways.

Quartermaster Gen'l of N.Y. state troops in War—1862 resumes practice—1871 appointed collector of customs for port of NY by Pres. Grant—Office noted for abuse of "spoils systems"—Gen. Arthur makes no reforms.

In 1877 Hayes tries to oust him—In 1878 he is removed—Becomes V. Pres. and Pres. on death of Garfield.

In spite of public fear makes honest pres.—vetoes spoils appropriation of 18 mills. for bigger over little states (1882).

North. Pacific, South. Pac., Atch. Top. & St. Fe completed in his admin.

Wash. Monument—Feb. 21, 1885, dies 1886.

Hayes (1822–1893).
B. in Delaware, Ohio Oct. 4, 1822.

Goes to Harvard Law School practices in Cincinnati—enlists—becomes brig. & maj. gen'l.

Goes to Congress—in 1868 becomes gov. of Ohio—to 1872. In 1875 again elected. 1876 becomes cand. for pres. against Tilden. Hayes declared elected 8 to 7 by commission.

Policy of pacification in South—Ends carpetbag govts. withdraws troops.

Attempts civil service reforms, able and honest.

Suddenly, his own life, central to the most portentious, colorful and dramatic events on earth, seemed to him only a minute, a millionth part of the earth's daily story—he thought of all these people that he had that day seen at the game, and he knew each had his central story. The effect of this was to make Joe's own character story suddenly turn stale, weary, sterile, and indifferent—the multiplication of light color on the earth had made all things gray and weary.

Horace (on the Gks.—study them) Vos exemplaria Graeca nocturne versate manu, versate diurna.[2]

Harrison, Benj. (1833–1901).
B. North Bend near Cincinnati, Ohio—log school house—Miami University—studies law in law office—aet. 21 goes to Indianapolis, soon leading lawyer.

Enlists in Civil War, breveted brig. gen'l.

2. "Study the Greek models day and night." Horace, *Ars Poetica*, ll. 268–69.

Then resumes legal profession—elected U.S. Senator 1881—nominated for pres. 1888—defeats Grov. Cleveland.

Passage of McKinley Tariff Bill and Sherman Silver Bill of 1890—

Suppression of Louisiana Lottery—enlargement of navy—civil service reform—arbitration of Bering Sea fur trade with Britain.

Revival of trade—defeated by Cleve. 1892 because of strikes—labor unions against Tariff party.

Mon. Nov. 16—

People I have talked to since return from Catskill's Oct. 1:

L. Stallings	Y. Kang	Mrs. A. Smith
Mrs. Stallings	Mrs. Kang	Francis
Meade	Gessner	His Friend (name?)
N.Y. Sun Man	W. Meyer	Man in St. George
Mrs. Peterkin	W. Demen	Drug Store
Mrs. Clark	Kieran	M. Benson
Mr. Clark	The Princetonian Editor	H. Hoppe
The Clark Boy	The Mg. Editor	Her mother
H. Loeb	F. Dashiell	Her father
May Spencer	C. Dashiell	The maid
Vera Schuyler	Mrs. Freeman	H. Volkening
Dan Young	Mr. Freeman	The Knickerbocker
Bill _____?	L. Deforest	family
M. Dorman	Ann Deforest	Chowdray (?)
Roberta Dorman	Aline	Daniels
Mr. Dorman	H. Arthur	M. Perkins
Elinor Dorman	M. Fairbanks	H. Hart
C. Greenwood	Webbels	
Bill Robinson	Olin D.	
Lacy Meredith	A. Smith	

Life—[*Sept. 2*] 1886—The hind legs of a heifer [3]—Dixey—Irving can't do it—

Making the eagle scream.

Mr. John L. Sullivan from Boston in N.Y.—Humanum est errare—the classic shades of Boston.

3. A cartoon entitled "The Pleasures of Summer Bathing" shows the waves bringing dead animals and other refuse up to a group of bathers.

Adv. Old Crow Rye H. B. Kirk & Co: No other house can furnish Old Crow Rye—Honest Madeira $3.50 per gal. good value—

Sour Mash Whiskies 5 years old—$4 per gal. 1158 Bdway cor. 27th St.

From "*Life*" Sept. 2, 1886:

"Moral indifference and social contempt are the dominant qualities in that school of fiction writers of which Mr. Howells is the head. These realists are in doubt as to what is wholly admirable in life because like many people in this transition period they are giving up the old forms of faith, and have not grasped the significance and responsibility of the new."

1886—Eden Musée—23d St. between 5th & 6 Ave.

Gifford and Street.

Street: Giff, have you ever noticed how many questions that fellow asks about figures? If you say you've played in Pittsburgh, then the first thing he asks is, how big is Pittsburgh? How many people has it got? How many miles is it from New York? How the hell should I know? There's a screw loose somewhere!

"Yes," said Gifford, "and sometimes when he gets a few drinks in him he can think up the queerest things to say of any man I ever knew. God! You'd a'laughed yourself sick one night if you could have seen Joe while Pat Healey was trying to tell a story. It was all about a shooting scrape he saw out west and one man gets killed, and you have his girl screaming and roaring and the sheriff, and all the rest of them! Christ! I thought Healey would go crazy before Joe got through with him, 'In four minutes,' Pat says, 'everyone in town was there: you never knew where they all came from.' "

" 'How big was the town?' Joe says. 'How many people did it have?' 'How the hell should I know how many people it's got!' says Pat. 'What d'ye expect me to do—count them!' "

Life, Jan. 1883:

"Put up or shut up"

"a high old time"

Jokes about Boston—ice in her bath.

The natives reading Browning.

The American money aristocracy—is it raining in London, mister?

Why does he use a riding crop in Central Park? (cartoon).

Possible conversation—Bitterness of "old-timers" against imported English actors.

Complaints—can't hear them—absurdity of accent, etc.

Healy (bitterly): Yes, they fought to make men free—Englishmen free: free to come over here and take our jobs away from us.

(See *Life*—Jan 4, 1883) Burlesque on Boucicault's "Old Heads and Young Hearts" at Wallack's, "will be performed by Mr. Wallack's Imported Company of English Comedians."

Poem to Eighty Three, welcome to Bartholdi's Statue—"Wiggins Cyclone" What was this?—The Bloody Shirt—Ben Butler becomes Gov. of Mass. (New Years Day 83).

Life Jan. 1883, "The Romance of A Parisian Young Man"—Mansfield makes big hit—

Old man, "I have seen him act before—up at the Standard—in comic opera."

—Look here, Joe: I remember when Brandell was acting comic opera at the Standard. Everyone said he couldn't do it.

Wed. Dec. 16 (?) 1931–333 Fifth Ave—

Went inside the Church—said "It is open" (I was drunk, coming from Bill Robertson's) Man said, Yes, sir, it is open—then went to pew and said to man "Hey, buddy, you can't sleep here."—whether became mistrustful of me or of man—cant decide. Outside the bare 5th Ave.—the hurry of autos—the bright rows of Christmas lights—the passing taxis (a paper stand on st.—Two men pass, collared, with the wind—the approaching *thirl* of a taxi).[4]

The easiest thing in the world to paint is flight. All of us can do it (with a pair of wings) [*Birds drawn all over the page*]

[*A list follows of "N.Y. Homes"—of Wolfe's friends and acquaintances.*]

Uncle Bascom
1—The Office—15 000
2—The House—15 000
3—The Streets of Life—15 000
4— Resurrection—.

4. Since the writing in this entry is a very wobbly scrawl, the editors have had to guess at several words and phrases.

[*From loose sheets of typing paper:*]
Jan. 1, 1932:

Yesterday was the last day of one of the unhappiest, dreariest years in the nation's history. The "depression," so-called, has a strong and oppressive physical quality. Just how one feels this I don't know, but we breathe it in the air, and we get it in a harassed and weary feeling which people have: the terrible thing in America now, however, is not the material bankruptcy but the spiritual one. Instead of revolution—which is a coherent and living act of the spirit—one feels the presence of something worse—a mindless chaos, and millions of people blundering about without a belief in anything, without hope, with apathy and cynicism. We seem to be lost. The faces of the people in the subway are sometimes horrible in their lack of sensitivity and intelligence—they ruminate mechanically at wads of gum, the skins are horrible blends of the sallow, the pustulate, the greasy: and the smell that comes from them is acrid, foul and weary. They are all going home into that immensity of mindless sprawling horror and ugliness which is known as Brooklyn.

Last night—New Year's Eve—I went to the Dashiell's: many people were there drinking egg-nogg—of whom I knew Fritz and Conny, Mr. and Mrs. Ross, the Deforests, Wallace Meyer, H. Ferguson, Bill White, the Dexters, as well as a number of Princeton friends —wives and husbands—whom I did not know. There is a kind of warfare—of smiling hatred—being waged between Cornelia and Ann Deforest—and I seem to be one of the trophies—that is, they want to get the best of each other—and, as for myself, I won't be the goat: I piss upon it. The hatred that exists between so-called friends in this world is horrible—and yet if they were faced with it, they would deny it and say they had been misunderstood. Fritz, I believe, is a good man caught in the trap of his wife's provincial venom and his own Princeton associations—I have now picked up enough scraps of envenomed and onerous feeling between the Deforests, the Dexters, and Conny to reveal a picture of life so black and poisonous that I wonder they don't choke in their own venom. And yet they are all "friends" of all the people I knew at all well there. The one with the best, deepest, and kindest spirit is Wallace Meyer. Fritz is also a good man, with much that is affectionate, loyal, and true—he is not subtle or penetrating, and he is somewhat on the make: in his friendships there is always a kind of calculation—he wants to get ahead.

Had a long talk with Wallace and told him frankly of my distress, confusion and doubt about the book. Came away with Bill

White—his "girl," Charlotte, has given him the go-by for the present
—we went to Thompson's lunch and discussed American bitchdom, in
all its phases of involved and cunty bitchiness.

Had drunk much—a bottle of gin before going—so got up late
today—New Year's—a raw, rainy, foggy day—and heard reports of
the Tulane–U.S.C. game in Los Angeles—U.S.C. won 21–12—Tulane
for the most part outplaying them.

Tonight, to see _____ _____ and wife. She, a hot little bitch
who wants to be seen in bed, let her gown come open, etc.—and have
her husband's friends around to enjoy in all the lustful indiscretions of
hot Jewish wenches. Oi! Vat a time she'll hev tonight when she tinks
of me, and he tinks of her. Little does he reck that I'm the Holy Ghost.

Mama is in Wash. with Mabel—Aline went to see them both.

[*Page missing*] at the car barn and asked them to describe the
old cable cars to me, saw a white woman carried out unconscious from
drink from a night-club in the arms of a negro man, saw a fat ragged
negro boy of eighteen with a banjo fall down on the pavement and
have a convulsive fit, saw a huge negro policeman force a spoon into
his mouth, bend his fingers backward, carry him into a drug store and
finally take him away in taxi, when ambulance did not come, saw a
white man with one side of his face smashed in from falling on the curb
—also unconscious though drunk—talked with some negro whores and
their escort in lunch room—escort, with purply yellow face, boasted to
me he had "white woman on Park Ave. who gave him ten dollars every
time"—saw negro and policeman putting drunken white man with
small grip into taxi saying "Where do you live huh—Doncha know
where you live," walked down Lenox to 110th St. and Central Park
where was stopped by two men driving motor hearse with coffin
behind; they asked me how to get on to Lower Seventh Avenue and I
told them to drive through Park—walked up 110th to west side of
town and had milk toast and coffee in Child's rest. at 112th St—walked
to 79th St. where took subway to Brooklyn and am writing this at
home Sunday morning Jan. 3 at 6:45.

Such is a very brief outline of things I saw in a single evening—
but to describe the smell, the shape, the sound, the color of things, as
well as the conversation of all those people which I remember word for
word as well as the terrible shapes of horror, cruelty, and fear which
are evoked out of these immense and terrible skies of America, from
the swarming pavement, and the angular streets of brown, dark brown
—even to illustrate this would be a formidable work. Saturday night in

America—a shambles of drunkenness, raucous and mirthless laughter, cheapness, tawdriness, and the smell of vomit, brains and blood upon the pavement! As it was in the beginning.

Jan. 3 [*1932*] Sunday:

   Slept until two o'clock—Then Bronson came at 3 o'clock and typed until eight o'clock—We went to Joe's for dinner, and he returned, but we talked and got no more typing done. Must finish this book before autumn. If can write the equivalent of 25 typed pages every week will finish—But must do it conscientiously.

PART FIVE ~

DROWNING
IN BROOKLYN

Pocket Notebook 18
January, 1932, to August, 1932

At this time Wolfe began to follow a pattern of creative activity that he pursued for the rest of his career. He began to write novellas or short novels. Actually, they were parts of the larger structure, which he was unable to master, but they were parts that would capture his interest for a month or two and could stand by themselves as units. He began to write them because he needed money, and publication was the only way he could get it. But he was also eager to get his work before the public—to demonstrate to himself and especially to Perkins that he could bring work to completion.

This notebook reflects Wolfe's work of various kinds with five short novels: 1) the proofreading of "A Portrait of Bascom Hawke," which appeared in Scribner's *in April; 2) the composition of "The Web of Earth," which appeared in* Scribner's *in August; 3) the composition of "K 19," which Scribner's announced for book publication in the fall but which Perkins later advised against publishing; 4) the development of "Death the Proud Brother," which appeared in* Scribner's *the following year; and 5) the development of "A Vision of Death in April," most of which appeared finally in Book IV of* The Web and the Rock.

Wolfe was calling his central character John Hawke now, and he was writing in the first person. Thus it is sometimes difficult to distinguish between his personal entries in the notebook and those which are a part of the fictional projection of himself.

[In January, Wolfe's mother visited him in his apartment on Columbia Heights. With her characteristic phrasing still ringing in his ears, he set to work on Delia Hawke's monologue, "The Web of Earth," as soon as she left.]

She didn't say to me, She said to Mr. Mack, she said, You know, she said, she didn't say, she said, but then she started talking about some other girl, she said, Vee-na makes a wonderful appearance, you know, she said, so when she said that to the man—

[573]

Mother Earth [1]

1. The Spanish Fort—The Platter—"all stewed down to about the size of a squirrel."
2. Ella Hill.
3. The Raleigh Days.
4. Ed Wray—The night before "it came."

[*The next two pages are too badly smeared to be legible, but they contain more of Delia Hawke's talk. The entries then conclude as follows:*] What is that! What say!—Pshaw, boy, those boats out in the harbor got me all confused.

How did you come here? What ever possessed you to live in such a place?

Why, yes, when I heard it, I said, Well, that's him. Why yes—say! here! don't I remember—didn't I tell you—Why, yes! . . . long years after that, boy, it was just a few years before he died . . . reckon you were at the university . . . why, pshaw *you* remember, boy! . . . the time all of us went to Johns Hopkins with him.

[*During Mrs. Wolfe's visit Aline Bernstein appeared at the apartment one afternoon. A terrible scene developed in which Mrs. Bernstein said that Mrs. Wolfe knew nothing at all about real love and Mrs. Wolfe said that Mrs. Bernstein spoke only of "licentious" love and really ought to be at home with her husband and children. It was the last time Mrs. Bernstein saw Wolfe until 1934. In a letter of January 14, 1932, written just after the blow-up, she revealed the depth of the humiliation she had felt at their hands when they had forced her out of the apartment. She defended her life, declaring that it should concern no one if she had no sexual life with her husband, for she had carried out her domestic responsibilities and she could not be bound by the opinions of society—her life was her own to live. She regretted that she and Wolfe had bowed to public opinion and kept their affair secret, for this shadowy behavior had troubled their relationship. She regretted that she had not left her home and come to live with Wolfe when he had proposed it. She declared that she had given Wolfe all of her being but now was forced to recall her soul from the place where it was no longer wanted. Nevertheless, her love for him was timeless even though they were now to go separate ways into the unknown waters of the future.*]

1. An early title for "The Web of Earth."

135 lines of small type to cut out.[2]

Ship—1 week
The City—2 weeks
The Boom Town—3 weeks
The City Again—1 week
October—4 weeks
The Fall—3 mos.
The Winter—3 mos.
The Spring—3 mos.
Voyage—1 week
The Trip Together
Alone
Return
That Winter
The Voyage Again
Together.

The Fall
The Winter
Hunger
Madness
Apart
The Fall.

[*Unable to come through for Scribner's with his long-promised novel, Wolfe decided to take the materials about "The Fast Express" and draw them together as a separate book. Thus he worked most of the spring on a unit entitled "K 19" about a group of Southerners on a train trip from New York to the South.*]

And here we were, the ten of us, out of the core of the nation, with the history of all our wanderings and the million lives our own had in some way touched, now imprisoned in a projectile of roaring steel hurtling across the continent under the immense and lonely skies that bend above America.

1. Gerald Rogers
2. Jim Swain

2. When a story or an article in *Scribner's* was continued in the back pages, the type size was reduced.

3. Goat McCall
4. Mrs. Buckley
5. Henry Woodsend
6. Mason Bruce
7. Ike Lichenfels
8. Arthur Groyer George William de Chevy Wynant
9. Curtis Wright
10. Fate Radiker
11. Monty Bellamy
12. Dick Pegram (Ingram, Plemmons, etc.)

Arthur Ambler, Ted Folsom, J. Y. Jordan, Jimmy Howell, Billy Sullivan, Tim Cocke, Sanford Brown, Brigham McKee, Percy Grant, Robert Bunn, Robert R. Reynolds.[3]

In those days among the million images and fantasies that swarmed and coursed across my mind, the following picture recurred to me again and again: the engineer of a powerful train had for twenty years driven his engine over the same route, and at the same time, every day, during all that time as his great locomotive begins to sway and rattle across the switch points [*he starts*] to pick up speed with a powerful stroking movement and short explosive thunders of its funnel.

On rising land just outside of town, there is a bend: for twenty years as the man has passed this place he has blown the whistle and a woman and a child have come out on the back porch of the place and waved to him. He has seen the woman grow from youth to middle age and the child to her young womanhood.[4]

The cheap smug party faces.

Written:

Look Homeward Angel
Portrait of Bascom Hawke
The Web of Earth
Robert Weaver.[5]

3. These are the names of Asheville people whom Wolfe was considering for his group of passengers on K 19.
4. This situation formed the basis for Wolfe's story "The Far and the Near," later published in FDTM.
5. A large portion of the material in "K 19" was a section entitled "The Man on the Wheel," the story of one of the passengers, Robert "Weaver." Wolfe later made use of some of it in OT&R.

To Be Written:
>The October Fair
>The Death of the Enemy.

1920–1932

1920 1921 1922 1923	Harvard—Raisbeck, Baker, Carlton, Geo. Wallace, *Hilda, Elaine, Uncle Henry, Aunt Laura.*
1924	New York—Margaret, Mabel Eggleston, Watt, Munn, Abe Smith, *Terry, Meredith.*
1924 1925	Europe—*Raisbeck*, Helen, Marjorie, Mrs. Weldon, the Countess, the Liverpool Jewesses, Jack Hardesty, Roger, The Whores of Paris, The Calverts.
1925 1926	*Aline, Mina Kirstein, The Neighborhood Playhouse,* etc.

The City
Sometimes the city stirred me to a leaping certitude and joy: I walked the pavements with a victor's stride, my legs bestrode the island.

I took it in my hands and felt its beamed weight, I ate it, devoured it, loved it—

Again I was a mote—a thing crawling in the dust, a stricken atom full of humour.

City Night: In the city at night a clean spare certitude pierced my soul.

Why can not one remember faces?

The subway.

Esther's face—the certitude of love.

The light I liked—the pallid sweet pure light of dawn—the buildings seemed to have been just discovered.

The light I hated—The light thickened with the million feet of men, marked with dust, movement, footfalls, thousand strewings.

The horrible monotony of the Jewish faces—Esther's face triumphant.

NEW YORK

Feb. 1924 Sept.	}	8 mos. Hotel Albert
Sept. 1925 June 1926	}	9 mos. Hotel Albert
Jan. 1927 July 1927	}	7 mos. 8th St. Garret
Sept. 1927 June 1928	}	9 mos. 8th St. Garret 11th St.
Jan. 1929 May 1930	}	15 mos. 15th St.
March 1931 April 1932	}	13 mos. Brooklyn

EUROPE

Oct. 1924 Sept. 1925	}	11 mos.
June 1926 Jan. 1927	}	6 mos.
July 1927 Sept. 1927	}	2½ mos.
June 1928 Jan. 1929	}	6 mos.
May 1930 March 1931	}	10 mos.
		_____
		3 years

Let us for once attempt to tell the truth about it. The day mama
and Mabel and Fred and I went down to the station. The hurled fistful
of clean gravel rattling at a wall or shutters. The dawning sun-warm
earth.

The memory of my father's great ghost.

Robert coming up to us—the way mama took his hand—the old
common great woman took his hand.

Mabel plucking at her chin.

Luke—the prized whah-whah-what—then running along the
track.

The stroke of the North was felt among them; the shining cities.

In the dawning fragrant air the train coming gripped at their entrails with its sense of joy.

The house at night.
The teeth.

The River—The bridge was different—only a concrete road—but the river was still the same.

Ruby Tennant, a football player, a good natured thing, played football, made chemical stunts, went to Petersburg Va. Heard no more of him since.

Robert Weaver, son of a lawyer, a madman, a snob, a wanderer, a drunkard, a lost man.

Dandy Victor Roncey and his proud eyes his dark face sneering as I passed on Oak Street.

[*At this point, there is another list of thirty-eight passengers for* "K 19."]

The girl with drawers on the high school swing—The girl at Norfolk on the swing.

A woman with piled-hair at a movie theatre in Boston—the shades that went up.

A girl in Norfolk who almost ran me down—her smile.

An old negro woman who stood naked in her door to get her paper.

A young negro woman who stood likewise.

A tall Jewess who smiled at me in New York the morning I took ship for France.

A Year's Chronicle—April 18, 1932:
March 4–March 11—St. Geo. Hotel, New York.
March 11–Nov. 1 Marjorie Dorman's house, Verandah Place, Brooklyn.
Nov. 1–April 18 111 Columbia Heights, B'klyn.

In Between:
April—Washington to visit with Mama.
July—Boston, Maine.
November—Thanksgiving—Washington.
Jan—Montreal.
Also trips to Princeton, Harmon, etc.

K 19
Esther's Childhood
    Youth
    Womanhood
The Early Pentlands
The Trips Abroad
My Years in New York
My Mother's Life
What Happened to Me As a Young Author
The Death of the Enemy
Oktoberfest.

David Cohn, 2 Beekman Place.[6]

He could sit right down and write some stories: doin' light work like that wouldn't hurt him.

I know I was tellin' your Uncle Bascom when I was up there—"Why, Bascom," I said, "What on earth do you mean at your age"—here he was, you know, goin' out there an' choppin' down birch trees for wood because the man that owned—

Lord! my nasturtiums, and geraniums and lilies and lilac and roses and fuchsia and tulips and jonquils—the prettiest flowers you ever saw.

Lord! I've had five thousand of 'em in my house, I reckon: I've seen 'em come an' go—from all parts and all over (pshaw! that woman was no more a widow than I was)—As we sat on the porch of summer nights and hear[d] you children at the corner—those carbon lights that winked and the moths and bugs aflying round it.

(Make it go with a rush—start with a rush).

Shake your little foot out Nancy Ann—And here he told me about it for the first time on our weddin' trip (to Philadelphia about Ella Hill).

First electric lights in Harrisburg—and the second, sir, the second place in this country to have 'em (that's what they said all right)—I know I remarked to a gentleman standin' beside me here last Spring in Washington at the Smithsonian Institute—.

O why should the spirit of mortal be proud half a league onward.

6. Stringfellow Barr had long wanted to meet Wolfe. A meeting was finally arranged at David Cohn's apartment while Barr was in New York in April.

The Pains of
The Pleasures of [7]

Sat.–Sunday, May 8—
Went to David Cohn's place for dinner—2 Beekman Place—
New Orleans Jewess and husband—literary curiosity seekers, taunters,
gibers there—On way home a man in crawling rags—his body covered
with sores—scratching himself unashamedly—bleeding—[like my
leg?]

K 19

Prolog
The Station
The Madness of Love
Abraham Jones
The Train
The Passengers
Now Death Goodbye.

[*Mrs. Bernstein had continued to write and to telephone Wolfe,
which annoyed and upset him. On the back of one of her letters (May
or June, 1932), he wrote the following message, but he did not send it:*
To Theodore Bernstein, Jr:
I have to say this to you: if you are a man with a shred of pride
or decency left in you, you will see to it that your mother no longer
disgraces herself and her family by wilfully running after and doing
the utmost in her power to wreck the life of someone twenty-five
years younger than she is. I here and now demand, having exhausted
every other means long ago, that you see to it that your mother no
longer tries to see me or communicate with me in any way.]

The Book of The Dead.
Alma—the prizefight in Paris [8]—a series of cruel physical images

7. Wolfe had admired Thomas De Quincey's *Confessions of an English
Opium Eater* for a long time. He was now preparing to use De Quincey's pattern
of contrast for his love story.
8. Wolfe has many drafts of an episode which he felt represented the corruption and cruelty of wealthy city-dwellers. It was a story Esther told Eugene
about a private boxing match that was arranged for a wealthy group of viewers,
all of whom came dressed in formal evening wear. One detail present in all of
the drafts is the fact that the blood of the boxers spatters the stiff, white shirt-
fronts of the spectators.

almost intolerable in their memories of pain—then their correspondence of ever intense cruelty, in the life of these dead people.

Had *they* purposely baited me with this woman with her rose-leaf face, her roselipt health and wholesomeness?

Again, when she stared at me with her rosy red indignant protesting face "I dont know anything about it. What are you going for me for?" etc.—would it be possible that she was ignorant of the filth that surrounded her? Must I really be duped by this masterly counterfeit of rosy innocence when every element of her experience proved her to be a mature, capable and experienced woman of the world, the associate of the "moderns" in painting, music, and writing, the mistress of Henry Mallows, the leader of one of the modern schools of painting (what she had said of Mallows etc., of young Vinson, etc.)—and the woman who had so deftly and with such understanding designed some tale of bawdry for the theatre—some comedy of an adulterous love, some gay jesting of a woman's whoredom and a man's cuckoldry.

Moreover when Jacobs went to the theatre to see these plays—when his neck swelled and grew pale with laughter as he saw some story of adultery enacted, did he laugh because it was real to him or unreal—did he roar with laughter because he saw himself there or for an even more contemptible reason because he saw whoredom now made fashionable and he felt he too could now accept what other men had anointed with their sanction. As I looked at the faces of the dead and hated them [*breaks off*]

THE BOOK OF THE DEAD (Possible Arrangement)

A Description of Death-In-Life.
(Perhaps for a title: The Nightmare Death-In-Life).
An Analysis of Love Madness & its causes.
A description of physical death.
The Death In the Subway.
The Man Who Fell from a building.
A description of birth.
A description of the death of love.

The Cancer of Jealousy is Rooted in Good Health—only a living man is jealous, a corpse is jealous of nothing.
"The Lord Thy God is a Jealous God."

In Tolstoy's great romance *Anna Karenina* there are some profound and moving passages that lead up to the scene where Anna ends her life by throwing herself under the wheels of an approaching train. These passages describe the fatal color of life in the eyes of this doomed woman for whom the world has now gone dead, rotten and hateful. In her railway compartment she has as fellow travelers a man and his wife and their appearance, their conversation, their affectations, their dress—everything about them seems hateful to her: she looks at them and suddenly they seem ugly, base, dull, cruel, and loathsome.

This is death. And yet it is also truth: if the dead could still be dead and yet return to visit life again it is not likely that the eyes of a dead man would brighten with joy at what he saw, or burn with desire to be part of it again.

During these years of ceaseless and ravenous hunger, I have often thought that if the end of all my fury could for a moment be satisfied—if for a moment I could be omnipotent and all-seeing and in an instant look into a million cells of life, and see the acts and hear the words of ten million people, I should go mad with horror—Or, is horror just the focal moment of a single experience: viz.—the night I saw the boy slapped in the face by the Irish policeman; the day I came back to Leopold and saw a man with head exploded in the pavement, his brains [*page torn out*]

Alcohol: its action on the love-mad man.

It is not a *stimulant* it is rather a *depressant*, it releases all that burns and smoulders—instead of a leaping and vibrant flame a convulsive and murderous passion begins to smoulder dully and doggedly in me again with an almost literal and visual sensation of a mass of dully glowing coals in a brazier of blackened bronze.

Love and madness in the spring—the knife of jealousy pierces most deeply at the sight [*of*] a tree of slender and incredible green—the thought of a woman's falseness at this season becomes most intolerable—because there seems no medicine for pain, no cure for treachery; it seems that they must betray and love at one and the same moment as inevitably as the earth renews itself again—they are as insatiable as a river, as indifferent as the earth—fields to be sowed by all man's grain. They are the whores of nature—but the fact is too colossal for man's understanding, too stupefying for his wisdom, too grand in its cruelty for his heart to hold.

The rich man's wives and daughters—There is in Boccaccio a story of a wise and learned monk who sends his serving girl to town upon an errand. The girl "goes out a maid but never a maid returns." When she comes back she is no longer virginal. Now, although she enters meekly and modestly, as is her wont, the old monk with scarcely a look at her knows she has sinned and drives her from the house—a conviction that the wives and daughters of the rich men lay with their young lovers not at night but at some moment of the furious day, and further that the time of day at which the moment of infidelity reached its literal and physical consummation was at some period during the afternoon and usually between the hours of three and five o'clock— Now, I remembered Boccaccio's story of the wise monk's intuition and extending the limits of perception immeasurably, it seemed to me that these rich men who had their business in the lower city must know instantly the exact moment at which their wives betrayed them. At such a moment, I thought, a knife of betrayal would be driven through their hearts—horrible vision of fat brokers reeling backwards.

They reel backwards, mouths agape like gasping fish, with fat hands clenched above their hearts.

Visions of joy—how they had changed in tone and quality since my childhood—from the fantastic to the real.

The things I wanted as a child (to be fabulously rich—to be famous—to be a crack-shot—to have a movie woman—a society girl, etc.).

The things I wanted as a youth (The Boston vision).

The things I wanted now—the fantasies now:

    —a large blonde travelling with her brother and his wife abroad.

    —a woman standing in a doorway in the West.

    —a woman at night time in the middle west (off the train).

    —a woman in a little German town at night.

    —a girl in Norfolk.

    —memories of a woman who passed by me in a train.

    —of a tall, witch-haired Jewess with a thin and tender smile in New York the day the boat sailed.

    —of two girls in a pension in Naples.

The dreams—of the tender and corrupt children—of their clinging lips—of incestuous horror—of having slept with one's teacher's wife, of returning to a place and being received quietly and without smiles and to find the houses closed the streets bare—nothing but shame and silence.

    —of the houses at night—of their grave homely intelligence.

—of lean good faces from the old life who grinned at me and grinned at one another and said "It's all right."

—of getting off the train in the west and feeling the earth spring like rubber below my feet—the ground paved with fruits and vegetables—of saying to a man there—and saying "Where are we, Illinois?" and he said without surprise "No, son, you're in Nebraska."

The years flow by like water and one day it is Spring again.

Shall we ever ride out of the gates of the day again, sons of men?

—the sense that drugged in some foul magic I had gone far and had grown old and had returned too late—and of looking into the sad and worn faces of men and women that I had known in my youth and crying to them, "Jim! Jim! You've grown old," and how I heard their voices quiet and sorrowful, "Why did you wait so long? You've grown old, John."

—and then I would hear my father's voice again and see my brother prowling by the facades of the square through all the thousand minutes of lost time.

The sense of time gone time wasted—in the night a horror of having missed my classes, of having let all my work go undone.[9]

In Europe—the dream of having crossed the sea and having come back again—the sense of irrevocable time, of years which had passed like water, of a life which was gone, a youth which was wasted, as I lay drugged in some dark and fatal magic.

—Finally, of seeing Esther again at some fatal and final moment of ruinous discovery—the scene at the theater.

I believe that my life, as much as the life of any man I know, has been lived alone. For a period of fifteen years, since my thirteenth year I lived in an almost complete physical isolation.[10]

Death In The Subway
Birth In The Hospital
Death In The City
The Death of The Falling Workman
Death In The Subway
Death of the Smith Boy

9. Although this material was planned for the story of the love affair with Esther, Wolfe eventually used the nightmares about the return home and about the neglect of his teachng duties in SN, pp. 64–71.

10. This is the opening of the first section of the short novel "No Door." This section is set in David Cohn's penthouse apartment on Beekman Place.

Death In The Apartment House
Unseen Deaths
Mr. Gibbs at The Hotel
(Try To Insert a Scene Where a policeman blows a man's brains out.)

Shame
1) A Kid Slapped In The Face before his girl.
2) A Manly-looking Man Humiliated Before His Mistress.
3) The Man In the North Station at Boston.
4) The Fight at the Dance.
5) The National Guard Kid in his uniform.
6) The Jew on the Boat.
7) The Sailors on the Subway Car.
8) The woman and her lover at Nick's Grill.

The Man who Hit My Father In The Eye When He Was Drunk.

For a Boy there is no more terrible thing than to see that his father is afraid before another—Uncle Will and Fred at Riverside Park.

I had noticed how some men who saw a street fight (or a street-car fight) develop at once an uneasy pugnacity—Thus, in near-street-fights (as between taxi drivers) one would see men (with women) turn away with hard sneering faces, looks of lashed and whipped-up pugnacity, saying "Hell! they're not going to fight."

(Esther did this one night on B'dway—below—the street—steaming like a censer in a pollenated million-light) "they had a fist-fight."

The pale feeble looking man that Allport threatened (how Benton told about it) and how I was disgusted and felt pity for him later—his good-looking wife.

The Times I have felt fear:
When the Girl Drew Her Hatpin on Me In Paris.
When the Policeman Drew His Pistol On Me.

Thurs. May 19:
Magnificent day—Lunch with Younghill Kang in Chinatown—walked back across Bklyn Bridge—Slept part of afternoon—Miss Martin taking day off—a lovely day—at night—about 10 o'clock—went

out to eat—on Willow (?) St. opposite Towers Hotel—a man in 1st Floor Apt. beating screaming woman—"Oh Henry! Henry! Don't Oh Henry Don't!" she screamed—a couple watching—woman saying, "Someone ought to call a cop. Honest, they ought! Oh! Will you lookat that" (somewhat gloating) "Oh its terrible! He's beatin' her all over the room"—We watched—the woman ran across & up stairs to peer in—I went over too—Man came to window woman ran back, I came back hastily. Then man went over and I went after, then janitor (Filipino!) came out of bldg. to side went up—man got scared when he saw us & walked toward back.

Filipino said to us, "Sh. It's all right she's quieting. She's drunk."

I went back saying, "You hate to mix up in other people's business." Woman says "Yuh can't do it. They don't thank yuh for it. It only makes trouble"—went on.

Was woman a ?

Also (May 19—same night) went to Louis' (123 Schermerhorn) —no one knew H. Hoppe [11]—went to Lido, got pt. gin—went to Joe's, ate, walked to Atlantic Ave.—Rode to 4th Ave. on st. car—came back to Clark St. on Subway—drunk woman crying and weeping and accusing man of beating her—negro elevator boy says to cop above "Dere's a fight downstairs. A man's beatin on a woman." Cop runs into booth—gets (gun?) and goes down.

Horror! Horror! Horror!

Smell of tarred roofs, coffee, and old boards from Bklyn. Bridge.

Of Shame, Fear, and Death.

The shame and fear that men have felt are the things they hardly ever speak of—that they speak of with the most reluctance . . . and usually our silence is not honorable or creditable.

The boastful and threatening voices of New York and the whole country—the product of fear and shame.

Shame in the family—the feeling of wetness, nastiness, meanness, and discomfort.

(For The Web of Earth)

My apple tree is full of all the birds there are in June, and your flower-tree you planted as a child is blooming by the window where you planted it (for the very end—the final paragraph).

11. Harriet Hoppe, who worked for the Brooklyn *Eagle*, was a friend of the Dorman family.

In the Spring—the falseness of women, the death of one's brother, the loss of a friend.

Well, what t' hell, den? Whatcha arguin about?

I'll beetcha two t' one. At de end of de day I'll have twice as much as you have. Yes, sir, I'll beetcha two t' one.

Funny thing, y'know, about dat guy—.

(Yeh he said a mouthful).

It was a good one, I said, Jesus, he got a sandwitch, a ham sandwitch, was it a sandwitch! Ho—oh Jesus, I said.

I was standing by 'm, dat's what I'm tellin' yuh. Yeh, I was standin by 'm, Graham McNamee, S'help me God.

Well, you'd be surprised how many *does* come in. Sure!

5,500 graduate or get diplomas at Columbia.

A family of poor New York Jews (Abe's family).
A family of rich New York Jews (Aline's family).[12]

Youth, Death, and Love, in May.

Perhaps her age, the end of her youth, the coming of old age to Esther heightened and sharpened, in obscure ways of which I was not conscious, these feelings.

The green of May and the sense of time.

The high health and sanity of noon—the madness of night— The dull smouldering blood-smeared madness of the nights in February—the leaping madness of night in May—touched with the smell of the sun, the odor of the earth.

The party in house opposite Mr. Brissey's house in Anderson.

The madness of night in May—the young green—thoughts of the mistress with some sensitive youth—at the estate of a rich friend in the country—the only reality their accursed wealth and power could touch was this reality of pain, this corrupt inverted joy of spring (Did they sicken the green with their naked flesh at night—mother and daughter?). What place was left in those years for the youth whose heart was like the vine, whose heart beat fast with joy and hate. Did the accursed dead make way for him with grace, or did they mock him with monsters—wrestlers and prizefighters in the beds of love, or the obscene mincings of bright precious boys?

12. Wolfe developed this comparison into a passage in which Stephen Hook wishes that he were a Jew because he admires the enormous vigor of their lives. W&R, p. 476.

Have I eaten you into me only to get madness and the accursed darkness of the east into my blood?

Will it ever come back to me, ever again, the summertime, the singing, and the land, the music in the flesh.

A young man is like an ignorant and insolent fighter who has never yet been hurt.

The forms the madness took—the rivals—Starwick.

After she had gone the sight of something she had left behind— the uncooked food—a handkerchief—or one of her costume drawings —the coat—the arm well turned—the strong, delicate and jaunty lines in which not only her talent but her strong jolly competent life was visible—pierced me like a knife.

Her friends—Roberta—upflung and uprooted into proud glittering air, soar in the man-swarm, unstricken, unperplexed among ten thousand million glittering night time faces.

Lilly—arrogant with power the sweat of five thousand Irish and Jewish slaves had given her.

I was stricken down beneath their obscene wealth & power. I could no longer see them save as the glittering excrescences of a stupefying and brutal power—It was the time when the rich felt like Romans.

When she was my dear mistress cooking my lunch it seemed that I had known and possessed her always but when she would mention casually having seen a friend of the family, a rich Jew, lose forty thousand dollars in fifteen minutes at roulette in a Paris gaming house, when she spoke of ten thousand dollar necklaces for her daughter and of household and personal expenditures of more than 88 thousand dollars in a single year in a family of five people, even though there was no hint of boastfulness in those statements, I lost her at once as a person.

> Death In The City
> The End of Death In April
> Death in April
> The Death of The Evening
> A Confession of Death In April.

June 1, 1931,[13] Green-seeming June.

---

13. Either Wolfe is referring to the previous June, or he has made a mistake in putting down the year.

Possible Arrangement:
1. The Nightmare Life-in-Death
2. The Dreams and Visions
3. The Book of the Dead
4. Death in April
5. A Day in June
6. Goodbye to Death
7. A Vision of Death in April

Use The Circus Scene of Last Year In the Dreams and Visions.

A Vision of Death in April   21 letters
Look Homeward, Angel   17
Death Comes For The Archbishop   26
A Portrait of The Artist As A Young Man   30
My Heart And My Flesh   17
The Rhyme of The Ancient Mariner   27

A Vision of Death in April

by

Thomas Wolfe

Outline for today:
The power of Spring and of the color *green.*
The magical properties of green—its effect on time (temporal effect—contrast this with autumn).
Its power of synthesis.
Its power to waken the bitter ache of jealousy.
Its poignancy of love and death (Esther as a false mistress and as a woman growing old).
Finally its synthesis over the whole scope of life—the image of the house—the people walking in it—a man in a darkened room upstairs—His face at the window.

Today, Thurs. June 8:
The falseness of women in springtime—and the vision of the house.
The way a score of grey nameless people came to life that spring—the tailor, the grocer, the laundry man.

Robert Raynolds [14]
Ridgefield 478 Ring 1–2.

Of Late, while winds passed singing in the Thracian Gulf, we heard two voices speaking of the times of old.

The hoof thuds hard upon the sea worn beach.

For who has heard the trumpet calling in the night, the great bell broken in the wind, the voices of the flame haired men?

Beyond the gastanks when the world was young did not miles of blue glass explode around us and the cat creep trembling in the shame of noon?

[*On August 1, Wolfe moved to another apartment at 101 Columbia Heights. The next few pages are filled with notations about apartments and rental costs.*]

The snake of the night, the fog of the dark, the tongue of fire. [15]

Dintcha getcha potty?
No I dint.
Oh'm sawry ah'll connetcha up again.
Hello!
Hello!—Is this extension 312?
That's it. You got it.
Now, I was speaking to you a few minutes ago about a parcel.
Oh! *You're* the one! Dincha get that fellah?
No I dint.
Someone musta cutcha off I guess.
Yes someone musta.
Well, you hold the wyeh I'll go gettum for yuh.

Greensleeves was all my joy,
Greensleeves was my delight,
Greensleeves was my heart of gold,
Oh who but Lady Greensleeves—

14. Robert Raynolds, a novelist, had written a very favorable review of LHA in *Scribner's*, December, 1929. He came to know Wolfe in 1932 because he wrote Wolfe a letter on March 31 praising "A Portrait of Bascom Hawke." Later he recorded his association with Wolfe in *Thomas Wolfe: Memoir of a Friendship* (Austin, Texas, 1965).

15. Wolfe is playing with one of his rhythmic series. It finally formed the opening words of "Death the Proud Brother": "The face of the night, the heart of the dark, the tongue of the flame."

Comfortless April
April's Ending
Death in April
Harvest April
Time and The River
April late April
From Death To Morning
April
April Late April
Fatal April
April the Knife
Cruel April
Lost April

[Inserted in the endpapers are a sheet tabulating the votes in the Democratic national convention and a postcard concerning the Pop Concerts of August 17 and 31.]

Pocket Notebook 19

ca. *September, 1932, to January, 1933*

During this period Wolfe was using his notebook very little. A few jottings, however, reveal the usual kind of scattered work: a hasty draft for the concusion of "Death the Proud Brother," notes for Esther's morning scene which eventually became part of "The Party at Jack's," drafts and outlines of scenes and memories of home. Actually, most of this smudged and torn notebook is taken up with notes from overheard conversations and from newspapers of late April and early May, 1928, which Wolfe read through in order to refresh his "sense of fact" and thus strengthen his powers while finishing "A Vision of Death in April." A sampling of this material is included here.

Boston Yanks Divide Day
Ruth Hits His First.

Editorial—Already a crisis—If we could wildly imagine our being plunged into a gigantic war before the middle of June, that would furnish the sufficient excuse for nominating the President against his express wishes. But neither that nor any natural or formal emergency is at all likely to present itself . . . . At present it is evident that the sole great emergency is one that terrifies politicians only.

Fearing that they cannot find a man with whom to defeat the nomination of Secretary Hoover the Republican best minds are now hoping to beat him with an abstention. They call it an "emergency."

. . . . But Pres. Coolidge himself has a pretty keen eye to distinguish between a genuine and a trumped up emergency.

Sanctuaries for Migratory Birds.

100000 Homeless in Bulgarian Earthquake.

N.Y. Times Wed May 2, 19[*28*]: [1]

Max 67, Min 52 weather clear—(Before that cloudy).

3600 Hail Bremen Crew At County Dinner All Rose In Silent Tribute To Bennett.

Lindbergh May Fly To Paris Via Arctic.

1. By mistake Wolfe had written 1932.

[593]

May Day Observed By World's Workers Blood-Shed in Poland.

Gov. Smith Is Victorious In California Primary; Reed Next, Walsh Last.

How Much Do You Think This Coat Is Worth—It's Smart To Be Thrifty—Macy's.

Delineator Joins The Two Million Club.

Giving the public what it wants is still the secret of successful publishing.

It is *hydrolysis* that causes so many men to dread shaving—Because in Squibbs Shaving Cream *hydrolysis* is controlled—your face is left smooth and supple . . . Try it tomorrow morning . . . There are thousands of men, etc.

Ruth's Fifth Sends Yankees Marching On.

Coolidge Goes To Circus To Study Sea Elephant.

Lv. Gd. Central at 11:50 (standard) Gets Albany at 4 o'clock.[2]

[*At this point Wolfe sets down a tabulation of the number of times he has had sexual relations since his return from Europe. He arrives at a total of "57 in about 75 weeks."*]

(Somewhat with the Highuh casualness.)

Scandal (Young artistic Jew and Jewess):

"Sounds like one of those trite sitch-u-ations," he said with a little chuckling laugh.

"You'll die—eh—when you hear it."

"She was an awfulleh nice pers-on—but I didn't care for him at aw-ull."

"Which one was he—the one with the hay-uh?"

"Nah. *You* know—the one who came in when the rest of us were—."

"Art Student's League—This year I don't just know what I'm going to do."

"If you put them in a glass jah I think you'll find they'll keep quite niceleh—a glass jah or a glass bottle. We used all the gin bottles we had."

(The man) "She must be very na-ive—yuh know what I mean."

For Daybreak:

You're the cre-e-em in my caw-haw-haw-*fee*.

You're the lamb in my stee-ew!

2. Wolfe took a brief trip to Montreal over the Labor Day weekend.

You spell out for me *per*-son-al-it-*tee*.
I'm just mad about *yew*.[3]

Time. There was a time when meadow lake and stream.[4]

A fly in a glue bottle.
I was amused the other day with reading in Tertullian that spirits or demons dilate and contract themselves, and wiggle about like worms—Ambrin's similes.

Diya evah see dose old movie shots—say ya know I gotta great laugh outa that—de hats dey wo-eh.
You've been sayin' I was wrong—who tuh hell told yuh I was wrong.
John's a shark—not only is but was one then.
But can yuh i-*maj*-ine—Ira's twice as big as me-e—an' arrestin' me f'r assault.
I let it be known quite frankly—.
Say! I'da put him—I was *pac*-ified—He got outa town till—Oh ya never heard dat story didya? Ben knows all about it, she knows all about it, Herb knows all about it.

Said the Bishop of Bristol
To the Abbot of Bath,
"Don't finger your pistol
T'will awaken God's wrath."
"Away with your wistful
Complaints, I've a fistful
And he conquers who hath,"
Thus to the Bishop of Bristol
Spake the Abbot of Bath.

Esther.
Oh isn't that beautiful? Her face flushing and flaring—I would swell with laughter, want to kiss her, then remember her "evil" city surroundings.
As if it was part of their victory that his love, his hatred, the frenzy and anguish of his spirit had been evoked and lavished on a race of sawdust dolls.

3. A slightly inaccurate rendering of lines from a popular song. "Daybreak" was an early title for the "morning scenes" in the Jacobs household.
4. A line from Wordsworth's "Immortality Ode," one of Wolfe's favorite poems.

—and to *think*," my mother cried, "to *think* that you would do a thing like that."

At this moment, my brother entered the room.[5]

He teetered . . . and stammered about in his huge unhappy way, his harassed and driven eyes going back and forth at us in a large unhappy way. "Well, folks" he cried out drearily in a rich stammering voice, "What do you say? Let's go for a ride!" . . . and then with his too-muchness added nervously. "F-f-f-frankly," said he, "I think we ought to! F-f-f-frankly," said he, "I think we need it! It would do us all good."

"Why, yes!" my mother cried instantly and briskly, "that's the very thing"—then the ride—the collision it causes.

Whatcha goin' t' take (awdeh)?
Whatjalikethave?

In old houses time gnaws with its ratsmall tooth. The house of darkness where doors creak rustily. In old houses, brushing afoot on beds of needled pain.

Aus meinen jugend

The City:
    The Trolley Car
    The Circus
    Mamie Flenner
    The Alger Book.

Proud death! Proud death! that sits so grandly on the brows of little man. To you, proud death. Whatever have you touched that you have not given your grandeur, death? Not for the glory that you added to the glory of the kin[g], proud death, nor for the beauty you have [added to the] dignities of the great, proud death, nor for the beauty you have given to the lips of genius but because you come so gloriously to us who never yet knew glory, death, because you touch the atoms of the earth with grandeur, death, and because, death, on the city's iron breast you have made given glory to a nameless people, death, and this has made the towers of the earth bow down before a shabby atom.[6]

5. A draft of the material about the Gant family and the automobile ride, OT&R, pp. 338–53.
    6. The first draft of a passage for "Death the Proud Brother," FDTM, p. 68.

[*In October Wolfe made a brief voyage to Bermuda. The fact that it is the only journey he ever made which was a disappointment to him reveals his disturbed state at this time. The only records in the notebook are some jottings of expenses. Among other papers, however, was found a single sheet which preserves a fragmentary account of his arrival:*]

First Day in Bermuda
Oct 20 [*1932*]:
Landed Hamilton between 3 and 4 o'clock in the afternoon. A rainy squally day—laving shores—Summer Tour man told me to go to Royal Prince hotel—Went there—got room with bath for $2.00 day —Slept and bathed—Went to Hamilton hotel—where drank one Manhattan, several whiskey sours—whiskey at lunchroom—also at Royal Prince—In room again—Priest and boy, Johnson, called on me, walked with them—ate with them (they not eating) in lunchroom—Left them —Back to hotel. Hired bicycle—back to hotel—slept till 11:30—awakened by old woman next door making obscene grunts and sounds— Rode the bicycle—turned it in—Back to hotel about midnight—In lobby found young woman in evening dress telephoning. She couldn't find party she wanted—Asked her if she knew where nightclub was— wanted to get beer—She said too late for beer but drinks always at Hamilton hotel—Asked her to go with me—She consented—was in fact too too eager to go to Hamilton.

Went to Hamilton with girl—She was brooding with some insult her lover had given her and kept speaking about it—at same time claiming she cared nothing about it or him—I understood strangely yet obscurely that her beau or persons she wanted to "show" was at Hamilton—but allowed myself to go with her—We danced—and she maneuvered me constantly in front of table I later knew was her sweetheart's—Later we sat at table and drank whiskey—He approached was courteous enough—She sprang up and started to leave— Then he left us—also politely enough and apologizing—A young man she said was in her office approached—Sat with us—Then her sweetheart—She sprang up—I told him I was with the girl and bid him to leave—But she insisted on going having had her feeble triumph—Scene of leaving proudly with people staring at us somewhat horrible—Later we sat in lounge outside cafe drinking—Her lover came by said "Hello Wolfe" insolently as he went by—then began to say to hired help that I was a "big shot" and a "big yellow Jew" I thought it over for a moment—excused myself [*the remainder is missing*]

[A fragment of a letter to an unknown correspondent.]

. . . is too terrible to contemplate—I'll vote for Roosevelt and hope to see the 18th Amendment repealed. It is the first time in my life I have ever been deeply interested in politics, and I am sorry there is no party or candidate in this country in which I have belief or confidence. But if we go through four more years like the last two we may not need parties any more—we may have not only a new party but a new government. Stranger things have happened. I don't think it will happen in the next four years, but I do think far worse times than any we have known are ahead of us.

Jacobs, Esther, Hawke, Alma, Edith, Freddy.

Monty Bellamy, The University Instructors: Tisdall, Burdick, O'Mara, Barney.

Old Man Wakefield, The Characters of the Night: Nick, Leo, Some Actors, The Bald Waiter, A Taxi Driver, The Police, A dead man.

One voice there with a hateful sneering assurance: "My dear, I know it, I know it. I could ab-so-*lu-u-tely* swEar it—unless her husband is a *Sap*—of course.

"—and whoever he is he must be a *Very* Exceptional Ma-a-a-n."

Bacchus [7]

    The Negroes
    The Bakery Wagon
    Dr. Ballard
    Bacchus
    His Life
      Early Years
      The Civil War
      Death of Billy W.
      Bacchus's Message
      The Trip West
    Armageddon

Bacchus—the purity and beauty of his countenance—the strong revolting odor of his body, But—

7. This is an outline of the beginning of the unfinished novel "The Hills Beyond Pentland." Most of the material eventually appeared in the early chapters of W&R.

"Whew-w!" my mother cried when she came back to the kitchen "that odor—that awful odor."

Three In A City.
From Death to Morning.
Mag Whittaker.
The Death of the Enemy.
The Hills Beyond Pentland.
Fury.
The Return of Two Brothers.
Clara Harper.

End of Mrs. J's conversation with maid—her life—deceiving—her round and open indignation—Maid's Revenge—a friend of yours called up last night—Departure of maid.

Alone—the mistress—Looks about room—Looks out window "out at life"—(connect this with maid somehow)—But love is real—"Now I shall see him in four hours," she thought.

Description of her room—Oh, I'm stuck to you, I'm stuck to you—an exultant music—are you my lass, he will say—Yes—are you my delicate damned darling and my dear?

Then, she looks out the window and sees the people swarming in the street below—the city like a ship—a trembling in the walls about her—Oh you great city that are like a ship, she thought—flowing southward, southward to the sea.

Each day we see them going to their million destinations but which one goes to glory, power, and love or which to ruin, death, and madness, what man knows.

"Well, you poor thing," she thought. "You've had your revenge. Do you feel better for it now?"

"Hail, light" her spirit cried with jubilance and song, "Hail, potent and oriental light that . . . and you great city that is masted to its lips, packed to its edges with the weight of all these men—."

[*The notes above indicate Wolfe's work on material about a morning in the Jacobs household. An outline found on a manila envelope describes what the sequence and extent of the material was:*

MORNING: THREE IN A CITY

I Jacobs—German background—Schoolboy scene.
II Jacobs Awake.

III Esther and the Maid
IV Jacobs and Esther (pages to be retyped here about "Gristo-
pher Golumbus" etc.)
(25000–30000 words).

[*Four years later, Wolfe blended the material into his third and
final version of "The Party at Jack's." Edward Aswell's cutting of the
manuscript when he published it in* You Can't Go Home Again *consid-
erably reduced Wolfe's characterization of Frederick Jack (Jacobs).
We are including here Mr. Jacobs' dream of his childhood in Germany
and of the anti-Semitism that colored his early days because it is an
excellent example of Wolfe's imaginative projection.*]

MORNING

I

"Hartmann!"
"Hier, Herr Professor."
"Das wort fur *Garten*."
"*Hortus*, Herr Professor."
"Deklination?"
"Zweite."
"Geschlecht [*gender*]?"
"Maskulinum, Herr Professor."
"Deklinieren!"

Hartmann stiffened his shoulders slightly, drew a deep breath,
and, looking straight before him with a wooden expression, rapidly
recited in an expressionless sing-song tone:

"Hortus, horti, horto, hortum, horte, horto; horti, hortorum,
hortis, hortos, horti, hortis."

"So. Sitzen Sie, Hartmann."

Hartmann sat down blowing slightly at the corners of his thick
mouth. For a moment he held his rigid posture, then he relaxed warily,
his little eyes wavered craftily from side to side, he stole a look of triumph and of satisfaction at his comrades.

He was only a child in years, but his limbs and features held in
miniature the mature lineaments of a man. He seemed never to have
been young or child-like. His face was tough, sallow and colorless: the
skin looked as thick and rough as a man's and it was covered unpleasantly with thick white hair which was not visible until one came close
to him. His eyes were small, red, and watery looking and thickly lashed

and browed with the same silken, unpleasantly white, hair. His features were small, blunted, and brutal: the nose small and turned up and flattened at the tip, so that the nostrils had a wide flaring appearance, the mouth was coarse, blurred and indefinite, and the cheekbones also had a blunted flattened-out appearance.

Hartmann's head was shaved, a bluish stubble of hair covered it evenly, and the structure of the skull was ugly, mean, and somehow repellant: it seemed to slant forward and downward from the bony cage at the back of the brain to a pinched and painful brow. Finally Hartmann's body was meagre and stringy looking, but immensely tough, his hands were disproportionately large and raw, and dangled crudely and clumsily at his sides. Brutal in mind and body, neither his person nor his character was pleasing, and Frederick hated him. And this hatred Hartmann returned on him with cordial measure.

"Jacobs!"

Frederick did not hear that word of harsh command. His dark eye brooded into vacancy, his mind was fixed and lost in stellar distances, his spirit was soaring far away across the surging blue, the immense and shiny wink of an ocean that washed the shores of all the earth. And a channel of bright water led him straight to the goal of all his dreaming. Upon the decks of clean white river-steamers he went down the river Rhine. He went from Koblenz on to Bonn, from Bonn to Köln, from Köln to Dusseldorf, and then through Holland to the sea. And then he put out to sea upon another mightier ship. The sea was blue and shining, but there was also gold upon it: it was never grey. The great ship foamed and lifted with a lordly prancing motion, like a horse, he felt the rock and swell, the infinite plangent undulence of the sea beneath that foaming keel, and the great ship rushed onward day by day into the west.

And now, after many days, Frederick saw before him the outposts of the land. He smelled the brave familiar fragrance of the land, the spermy sea-wrack and the warmth of earth, and he saw before him first pale streaks of sand, a low coast, and then faint pallid greens, and little towns and houses. Now, the ship entered the narrow gateways of the harbor, and now Frederick saw before him a great harbor busy with the play and traffic of a thousand boats. And he saw before him, at the harbor's base, a fabulous city, built upon an island. It swept upward from an opalescent cloud, from which it seemed to grow, on which it was upborne lightly, and as magical as a vision, and yet it was real and shining, and as solid as the rock on which it had been founded. And by the city flowed a river—"ein Fluss viel schöner als der Rhein [*a river more beautiful than the Rhine*]"—a thing almost incredible, and yet it must be so, for Uncle Max had seen it, and sworn just the night before that it was true. Beyond the city was an immense, fertile, and enchanted land—"ein Land von umbegrenzten Möglichkeiten [*a land of limitless possibility*]," Uncle Max had sworn, and surely Uncle Max had known, for he had come back from that country speaking its strange nasal accents, wearing its strange garments, rich with the tribute of its enormous bounty. And he had said that some day he would come and take Frederick back with him, and Frederick, dreaming of the wealth, the gold, the glory and the magic of that far shining city that floated upward from its cloud of mist hoped for this more than for anything on earth.

"Jacobs! Jacobs! Ist Friedrich Jacobs hier?"

He came to with a sharp start of confusion as that harsh and choleric voice broke in upon his revery, and the class whose attention had been riveted for some seconds on his dreaming face burst into a sharp and sudden yelp of glee as he scrambled frantically to his feet, straightened his shoulders, and stammered out confusedly,

"Hier, bitte. Ja. Ich bin hier."

That high and hateful face, hairless, skull-like, seamed and parchment-dry, scarred hideously upon one sallow cheek, with its livid scorpion of saber wounds, and with thin convulsive lips drawn back above a row of big yellow teeth, now peered at him above its glasses with a stare of wall-eyed fury. In a moment the stringy tendons of the neck craned hideously above the choker collar, and the harsh voice rasped with fury as old Kugel's ramrod form bowed with a slightly ironic courtesy in its frock coat sheathing of funereal black.

"Wenn Sie sind fertig, Excellenz [*if you are ready, your excellency*]," he said.

"Ja—Ja—fertig," Frederick stammered foolishly and incoherently, wondering desperately what the question was, and if it had already been asked. The class tittered with expectancy, and already unnerved by his shock and confusion, Frederick blurted out with no sense at all of what he was saying: "Ich meine—Ich bin fertig—Onkel!"

A sickening wave of shame and mortification swept over him the moment that he spoke the words, and as the instant roar of the class brought to him the knowledge of his hideous blunder. Onkel! Would he ever hear the end of this? And how could he have been such a fool as to identify, even in a moment of forgetfulness, this cruel and ugly old ape with the princely and heroic figure of his Uncle Max. Tears of shame welled in his eyes, he stammered out incoherent apologies and explanations that went unheard in the furious uproar of the class, but he could have bitten his tongue out for rage and mortification.

As for Kugel, he stood stock still, his eyes staring with horror, like a man who had just received a paralytic stroke. In a moment, recovering his powers of speech, and torn with fury between the roaring class and the culprit who stood trembling before him, he snatched up a heavy book, lifted it high above his head in two dry, freckled hands, and smashed it down upon the table with terrific force.

"Schweig [*silence*]!" he yelled. "Schweigen Sie!" a command that was no longer necessary, since all of them had subsided instantly into a stunned cowed silence.

He tried to speak but could not find the words he wanted. In a moment, pointing a parched trembling finger at Frederick, he said in a small choked whisper of a voice:

"Das Wort . . . das Wort . . . fur Bauer [*farmer*]." He craned convulsively above his collar as if he was strangling.

Frederick gulped, opened his mouth and gasped wordlessly.

"Was [*what*]?" screamed Kugel taking a step toward him.

"Ag—ag—ag!" he stuttered like a miserable idiot.

"Was!"

He had known the word a moment before—he knew it still, he tried frantically to recall it, but now, his fright, shame, and confusion were so great that he could not have pronounced it if he had had it written out before him on a piece of paper.

Desperately he tried again.

"Ag—ag—ag," but at the titter of laughter that began to run across the class again, he subsided helplessly, completely disorganized and unable to continue.

Kugel stared at him a moment over the rims of his thick glasses, his yellow bulging eyeballs fixed in an expression of hatred and contempt.

"Ag—ag—ag!" he sneered, with hateful mimicry. "Erst es war *Onkel*—und jetzt musst er den Schlucken haben [*first it was uncle—and now he has to have the hiccoughs*]!"

He regarded Frederick a moment longer with cold hate, and then dismissed him.

"Schafskopf [*sheepshead*]! Setzen Sie," he said.

Frederick sat down.

That day as the children were going away from school, he heard steps pounding after him and a voice calling to him, a word of command and warning, raucous, surly, hoarse. He knew it was Albert

Hartmann, and he did not stop. He quickened his step a little and walked on doggedly. Hartmann called again, this time with menace in his voice.

"Hey—Jacobs!" Frederick did not pause. "Excellenz! Onkel!" it cried with a jeering note.

"Ag—ag! Schafskopf!" At the last word, Frederick stopped abruptly and turned, his face flushed with anger. He was a small neat figure of a boy, well-kept, round-featured, with straight black hair and the dark liquid eyes of his race. His somewhat chubby face was ruddy and fresh colored, his neat blue jacket and his flat student's cap were of far better cut and quality than Albert Hartmann's, which were poorly made and of mean material, and his firm plump features had in them a touch of the worldly assurance and scornful complacency, the sense of material appraisal that the children of wealthy merchants sometimes have.

Hartmann pounded up, breathing thickly and noisily through the corners of his blunt ugly mouth. Then he seized Frederick roughly by the sleeve, and said:

"Well, Ag—ag, do you think you'll know the word next time he asks you? Have you learned your lesson? Hey?"

Frederick detached his sleeve from Albert Hartmann's grasp, and surveyed him coldly. He did not answer him. At this moment, Walter Grauschmidt, another of the boys in the class, came up and joined them. Albert Hartmann turned and spoke to him with an ugly grin.

"I was asking Ag—Ag here if he'd know the word for farmer the next time Kugel calls on him," he said.

"No. He'll never know the word for farmer," Walter Grauschmidt answered calmly, and with assurance. "He'll know the word for money. He'll know the word for cash. He'll know the word for interest and loan in every language in the world. But he'll never know the word for farmer."

"Why?" said Albert Hartmann looking at his more gifted and intelligent companion with a stupid stare.

"Why," said Walter Grauschmidt deliberately, "because he is a Jew, that's why. A farmer has to work hard with his hands. And there never was a Jew who would work hard with his hands if he could help it. He lets the others do that sort of work, while he sits back and takes the money in. They are a race of pawnbrokers and money lenders. My father told me." He turned to Frederick and spoke quietly and insultingly to him. "That's right, isn't it?" You don't deny it, do you?"

"Ja! Ja!" cried Albert Hartmann excitedly, now furnished with the words and reasons he had not wit enough to contrive himself. "That's it! That's the way it is! A Jew! That's what you are!" he cried to Frederick. "You never worked with your hands in your life! You wouldn't know a farmer if you saw one!"

Frederick looked at them both silently, and with contempt. Then he turned and walked away from them.

"Yah! Pawnbroker! Your people got their start by cheating other people out of money! Yah!"

The hoarse and inept jibes followed him until he turned the corner of the street in which he lived. It was a narrow cobbled street of ancient gabled houses, some of which hung out with such a crazy Gothic overhang that they almost touched each other across the street. But the street was always neat and tidy. The houses were painted with bright rich colors and there were little shops with faded Gothic signs above them. The old irregular cobbles had a clean swept appearance, and the old houses were spotless in their appearance. The stones and brasses seemed always to have been freshly scrubbed and polished, the windows glittered like flat polished mirrors, and the curtains in the windows were always crisp, fresh and dainty looking. In spring and summer, the window ledges were gay with flower boxes of bright geraniums.

In an old four-story house half way down this little street, Frederick lived with his mother, a sister, his uncle and his aunt. His father had died several years before, and had left his family a comfortable, although not a great, inheritance. And now his uncle carried on the family business.

They were a firm of private bankers and they had always borne a respected name. Beginning with Frederick's grandfather, over sixty years before, the firm had carried on its business in the town of Koblenz. And it had always been assumed, without discussion, that Frederick also would go into the firm when he had finished school.

Frederick went along the pleasant ancient street until he came to the old house where he lived. In this house, members of his family had lived for eighty years. His bedroom was on the top floor of the house. It was a little gabled room below the eaves and at night before he went to sleep he could hear the voices of people passing in the street, sometimes a woman's laughter suddenly, and sometimes nothing but footsteps which approached, passed, and faded with a lonely echoing sound.

The street ended in a broad tree-shaded promenade that crossed it at right angles and which was one of the leading thoroughfares of the town.

Beyond that was the river Rhine.

Mrs. Ad Schulberg [8]
Taft Bldg. Hollywood

The great trains were steaming in and out of the enormous station. People swarmed back and forth. It seemed to me there was a smell of coffee in the air.

Dinwiddie Scott—Baltimore—my brother and father—Dinwiddie's wife.

Later Boston—the station—the Park Street Station—The Fury.
The Books.
The Food.
Uncle Emerson & family.
Professor Butcher & his classes.
Home—arrest—disgrace—flight.
The first year in the city.
I was now twenty-five years old.

8. "I had lunch finally today with a very elegant, highly perfumed and fancy talking lady, an agent out there." Letter to Robert Raynolds, January 25, 1933. Mrs. Schulberg, the mother of novelist Budd Schulberg, was trying to persuade Wolfe to come to Hollywood to be a script-writer, but she had no contract or financial arrangement of any kind to offer him.

Pocket Notebook 20

ca. March, 1933, to October, 1933

Since Wolfe made very few entries in his pocket notebook during these months, we have included here some relevant documents from his papers which reflect his lurching progress and accumulating self-doubt. During the year he published three pieces in Scribner's: *"Death the Proud Brother," "The Train and the City," and the short-novel version of "No Door."*

SCENES TO FOLLOW [1]

1. Policeman & Robert in cellroom.
   Kitchen and Rest of us.
2. My Brother—Release—Farewell to companions—The Restaurant—Arrest Again.
3. On the Road—Feeling toward my brother—My Sister.
4. Home again—my mother—my sister—etc.
5. The Ride Together—The Restaurant.
6. Departure—The Station—The Train—Nighttime in Virginia.

Dr. Ballard.
The Nigger Killer.
The Arrest in Greenville.
Lora French.
Maid—the S.C. Girl.
Effie's family—Fred G. behind the flour sacks.
Fred on the Road (make something out of this).
Papa and the Furniture Shop.[2]

1. This material has to do with the sequence about the young man's arrest for drunkenness in South Carolina. It appears in OT&R, pp. 361–98.
2. Mr. Wolfe had once bought a small used furniture business, only to discover that it was a front for a usurious money-lending operation. Thomas Wolfe used this in YCGHA and made Judge Rumford Bland the money-squeezer. See The Hound of Darkness ledger for a draft of "The Furniture Business That Gant Bought."

My Sister Helen and her husband.

My Sister Helen: Mrs. Jarvis—the "natural" Southern woman —the adderous reptile's eyes "ah-hah! ah-hah!"

[*In March, Wolfe traveled to Washington to see the inaugura- tion of Franklin D. Roosevelt.*]
The trashy young people in the Washington rooming house— without aim or purpose—a society of soda jerkers, government clerks, etc.—My sister likes them—(Suddenly I understand what had hap- pened to my sister's question that my mother avoided).

On the train, as soon as I had left them—conscious of a feeling of sorrow and wild resolve. "What wonderful and good people they are!" I thought—and my throat was tight and ached with a feeling of love and affection—and at the same time my heart was swelling with a feeling of wild exulting and joy, saying: "O God! O God! I am alone —alone—alone—again!"

The green, warm, slightly stale smell of the pullman filled me with an intolerable joy.

Don't I get nuthin', he says. Sure, I says, you get duh air.
Gimme a pimento cheese sandwitch wit' Russian dressin' & a cup o' cawfee, I says, to 'm.
I'll give ya a sock in duh jaw, he says—Gee he was rich.

Chee! Sadie's in trouble.
What's a matteh?
She got to goin' wit' a guy an she let him slip her duh woiks.
Chee!
I tol' her she was a fool t' let 'em. I neveh let 'em get that far. I kid 'em along, y' know—I let 'em cop a feel but dat's as far as it gets.

I saw your friend last night.
Who's that?
Joe Kelly.
That bastard's no friend of mine.
I t'ought you and him was friends.
Naw—we uster be.

Where'd ya git the fool chair, [*he*] says to her. What's it to ya, she says. Gee she was sore. Gee you'd a laffed t' heah him—Honest I couldn't keep from laffin' right out.

You know, I says, they are passin' perls out wit' cigarette coopons. Not real ones at any rate. They're real all right, she says.

The Southern Bitch.
The Policemen.
The Cafeteria Waitresses.

Brooklyn:
M. Dorman
Roberta
The Old Man
Harriet

DIRGE [3]

Why are we unhappy?

. . . I have no need to envy this man's fortune nor skill to cloak myself in that man's manner. I am only as naked now as sorrow, pain, and weariness . . . and all I ask is why are we unhappy?

Why are we unhappy? In my father's country there are yet men with quiet eyes and slow, fond, kindly faces.

The Unhappy Scenes
1—The Men In Brooklyn (now is duh mont' of March, duh mont' of March).[4]
2—Hello dee-e-rie, this is Ha-a-ariet.[5]
3—Get me into the Town Hall Club.[6]
4—Nick's Grill.
5—The City People.
6—My Brother on the Road.

3. Wolfe developed a series of observations on modern city life which carried the refrain, "Why are we unhappy?" Some of this material finally appeared in W&R, pp. 275–78.
4. This chant, the spring song of the lost men in Brooklyn, appears in YCGHA, pp. 429–30.
5. This became a short story entitled "This is A-a-adelaide." See Notebook 21 for Wolfe's notations about getting it ready for publication.
6. This became the sequence in which one of the "lion hunters" asks George Webber to use his influence to get her a membership in the Cosmopolis Club, YCGHA, pp. 349–50.

Night scene:
> Down in Stygian dregs corner row.
> Prowl-puss alley at night.
> Whisper lane.

[*In the middle of April, Wolfe gave Perkins a huge stack of manuscript to read. He attached the following "Note," which explained his current conception of the book he was wrestling with.*]

NOTE

The concluding scenes of Antaeus which are to follow will require one or two weeks work to include them in the manuscript. This whole manuscript is a first draft. There are still many things to be woven into it as it is and is intended to be a web of a man's memory of the past, but I hope its final purpose and relation to the Proteus section which follows may be evident from this first copy.

The plan for these remaining scenes that end this book and that lead directly into the book which follows which is called *Proteus: The City*, the opening scenes of which I am including with this manuscript, are as follows:

1. There is a scene in which the narrator describes the life and movement on the road by day and some of the people that his brother meets along the road, and the life that flows around them in the towns they go to. There is a scene that describes the return home into the hills again by night.

2. There are the final scenes at home, the night before departure, a family party in a restaurant, the streets of the town by night and then a scene similar to the scene about October at the beginning of the book.

The purpose of all these concluding scenes whether in the panorama of furious movement and human unrest over the earth or in the streets of passing towns or in the scenes after the return home is to emphasize and complete the ideas already described in this book. These ideas are:

1. The frenzied dissonance and the tortured unrest in the lives of people from which the strong figure of the father has been removed and who no longer have any great image to which they can unite their power and energy or any central and direct unity to gather and control them and who are being driven like leaves across the earth in a fury of

wild unrest and longing without a door to enter or any goal or summit to attain.

2. The impulse drives the narrator to flight from home and wandering. When having returned home again and found his father dead he finds that now he can inhabit this life which he has known only as a phantom or as someone walking in a dream who sees, feels and remembers and experiences all things with a blazing vividness but who is unable to touch them, live in them or make them a part of him again.

The final scene begins at the moment of departure with the going of the train and concerns the journey of the train through the night and ends at morning as the train nears the city. This scene makes use of rhythms, memories and visions of time, the recurrent theme of wandering forever and the earth again, and the ideas concerning the eternity of the earth outside the train and the movement, unrest, and brevity of the lives of men who are being hurled across the earth in darkness which the movement of the train induces of which I already have the notes and to which I have already given the title—K–19.

This scene and the end of this section ends at morning as the train begins to enter the tunnel to the city underneath the river, the first scene in *Proteus: The City* is about the river and the city and follows immediately upon this scene.

Finally, I want to give you the following information about the whole book. I have called this first section—*Antaeus: Earth Again* because Antaeus was a giant whose mother was the earth and who wrestled with Hercules. In my use of this fable I understand Hercules to be the million-visaged shape of time and memory, and it is with this figure that the narrator is contending in this whole section. According to the fable Hercules discovered when he threw Antaeus to the earth that his antagonist redoubled his strength each time he touched the earth and accordingly Hercules held him in his arms above the earth and conquered him that way. Accordingly, this part of my book is about a man who is conquered by the million shapes of time and memory which come to life around him with every step he takes and every breath he draws, the life which was once his own, but which now he can no longer make his own no more than if he were a ghost.

In the beginning of the book the feeling is expressed that when a man's father dies the man must then discover a new earth for himself and make a life for himself other than the life his father gave to him or die himself. Therefore, the final words of Antaeus spoken just as the train which is taking him to the city nears the tunnel are these:

"Antaeus, Antaeus, there are new lands. Child, Child, go find the earth again." That new land, new life and new earth is the city, and *Proteus: The City* follows immediately after, and just as Antaeus is revisiting and going back into the life of time and memory and just as I want, much more than I have ever in this first draught, to loot my life clean, if possible, of every memory which a buried life and the thousand faces of forgotten time could awaken and to weave it into *Antaeus* like a great densely woven web, so has *Proteus* a forward going movement into time and is filled with all the thousand protean shapes of life in the city going on around him. I am giving you here the first part of *Proteus* which concerns the first year of a young man's vision of the city. The remainder of *Proteus* which you have not seen is written either in whole or in part.

The third part of the book I have called for the present *Faust and Helen,* and of that third part you have already seen most of the concluding section, which deals with springtime in the city. The first part of *Faust and Helen* is only partly written; it begins on a ship and introduces the figure of the woman.

The fourth and concluding part of the book which will be called either *Oktoberfest* or *October Fair* will occur entirely upon the continent of Europe. For this part I have made notes but have written almost nothing. Its purpose is to conclude the fury of movement, unrest and wandering that drives men across the earth and to show that whether any final peace or assuagement can be given to people who have ever felt the Faustian hunger to drink and eat the earth, they cannot find the peace and certitude they sought by wandering or beneath a foreign sky.

Finally the last book deals with the impulse in men's lives to return, to find a dwelling place at home and a door that they can enter and it includes the general movement of the book which is stated in the words "of wandering forever and the earth again."

Therefore, of these four books you have now seen in the first draft almost all of *Antaeus,* part of *Proteus* and the concluding part of *Faust and Helen.* The fourth part of *October Fair,* as I say, is still, save for notes, drafts and scenes, unwritten.

It is now my desire to call the whole book *Time And The River* instead of *October Fair* as I think that *Time And The River* better describes the intention of the whole book. By the time you have read this new manuscript and this note you should be able, with what you have seen of the whole, to judge if the project is feasible or just a mad delusion on my part.

I myself believe it is feasible and believe now that after all the despair and suffering of the last three years that I have not been chasing a phantom or deluding myself with the fragments of a disordered intelligence. I believe, on the contrary, that it is possible for me to complete this book and have a coherent legend of the savage hunger and unrest that drives men back and forth upon this earth and the great antagonists of fixity [*and*] everlasting change, of wandering and returning, that make war in our souls. If this is incoherent it does not seem so to me now; that the book if completed would be one of the longest books ever written I have no doubt, but that so far as I am concerned, is no valid objection to its being done and if it is worth being done it seems to me that it is the publisher and the world of practical mechanics and salesmanship that must somehow adapt itself and not the world of the creator.

You know that I am so desperately anxious to get this great weight off my soul, that I will yield to you on any point that can be yielded, and solicit and be grateful for any help of editing and cutting that you can give me, but what I want you to do now, and what is desperately important to me is that you be able to get from the manuscript which I have given you some coherent idea of what I intend, and just tell me with naked frankness if what I intend is worth intending and worth doing and whether I shall continue.

I ask you to bear in mind that I am in a desperate frenzy to get something finally accomplished. I have written in less than three months time over 300,000 words and this present manuscript which I am giving you now has been done in the last five weeks and has I believe something like 150,000 words in it. As a man works with this frenzied haste he cannot give the best and the utmost that is in him; he is tortured by the constant memory of all the things he can and should do to improve it and all the power and richness that long and painstaking effort will sometimes give to a piece of writing. But I earnestly hope that if I have lost some of this I have gained something by the very frenzy with which I have gone ahead and that whatever has been lost enough has been left to show that the thing *could* be done if it is worth doing at all.

Now finally it is up to you to tell me whether you understand what I am trying to do. Whether it is worth doing and if I shall go ahead and for God's Sake do it without delay and with merciful even if brutal honesty.

Finally look at this outline once again:

Book 1—Antaeus: Earth Again (given to you here in rough draft with much left out that I want to put in, only the final three or four scenes lacking to make it a complete draft)

Book 2—Proteus: The City—given to you here in its first part and with most of the remainder written but still to be included in the manuscript.

Book 3—Faust and Helen—The final part of which you have read, of which you are printing two sections [7] this spring in *Scribner's Magazine;* the first part of which is mainly written either in full or in scenes and sections, still to be included.

Book 4—The October Fair—unwritten save for notes and rough drafts.

---

10 Years:
     5 trips South.
     5 trips Europe.
     2 trips Canada.
     4 trips Washington.
     2 trips Pennsylvania.
     10 trips Boston.
     1 trip Bermuda.
     3 trips Troy and Albany.
     2 trips Maine.
     2 trips New Hampshire.

Oxford Scene [8]
1—The Family at the Inn.
2—The Streets, the Dinner, and the Food.
3—The House.
4—The Rhodes Scholars.

Sunday, May 21:
    Loneliness [9]—Today's Schedule
    1. The Greatest Works on Loneliness—Job—Ecclesiastes—Everyman—The Old Testament is the supreme expression of Loneliness—The New Testament is Love—yet Christ one of the most lonely men that ever lived.

7. "Death the Proud Brother" and Part IV of "No Door." Although the pieces had been accepted by *Scribner's,* they did not appear until the summer issues.

8. This entry outlines the material that eventually appeared in OT&R, pp. 601–55.

9. This material was shifted about in various manuscripts. Edward Aswell finally published it as an essay entitled "God's Lonely Man," in the collection HB.

2. Shakespeare writes greatly about loneliness—Wordsworth, the world is too much with us—Emerson—things are in the saddle and are riding us.

Sat. 3:50 on the subway. My watch is gone. Hard to believe it is at home. Maybe left it on gold hall table.

Sunday, June 3:

Today—Get in bit about Wilson's Mill [10]—No more! No more! —the rebels fall back through the mountains—the immense and lonely earth preserved them once again—yet the battlefield was not level— Hot steep rocky—My father and his mother [walking?] over the muddy roads. Farmers standing in another road.

My father's world (continued)—the days in Baltimore—Jeff Streeter's Hotel.

1) Germany—October Fair Fight
            Hospital
            Departure
2) England— The Lakes
            London
            Oxford
3) France— The Three Friends
            Orleans
4) Switzerland
Holland—The Man who was Shot—The Dream.
Italy
Austria
Hungary
Belgium.

Barren Winter (The Clairvoyants).
Professor Ayers and his wife—The Keeblers and the Glenn boy —The consumptive cousin—Sudden departure of Ayers and wife— Then Professor Edwards.

High Jinks
The Sunshine of Your Smile
Dreaming
Senora

10. This material about Wolfe's father's memories of the Battle of Gettysburg found its way into "The Four Lost Men."

The Happy Farmer
We Were Sailing Along on Moonlight Bay
Because
Sylvia
The Chocolate Soldier
Peg of my Heart
In the Shade of the Old Apple Tree.

At the end—the very end—nothing but silence—there will be silence, lonely silence in the end.

Silence, received us as a king gives pardon, a lord gives bounty, and a king gives grace.

[*In September, Wolfe moved to 5 Montague Terrace, another apartment overlooking the harbor. Most of the remaining space in the notebook is taken up with names, addresses, and notes on apartments.*]

Blind as the darkness
Blind as birth
Blind as these years, Ben,
Is the earth.
Up on the mountain
Down in the field
Long, long in the hill
 Cold, cold, cold.

O bitter and beautiful,
 Seek no more.
Deep, deep in the earth, Ben,
 Was the door.

For
Benjamin Harrison Wolfe
Oct. 26, 1892–Oct. 19, 1918.[11]

Se Hemat Engel.[12]

[*Not since 1931 had Wolfe replied to any of the letters which Mrs. Bernstein wrote occasionally either accusing him of deserting her*

11. Perkins planned to issue the short novel "No Door" in book form in the fall of 1933, but later he decided against it. Wolfe was going to dedicate the book to his brother Ben. The dates should be October 27 and October 20.
12. *Look Homeward, Angel* was published in Sweden in 1932.

or attempting to bring about a reconciliation. On September 28, Mrs.
Bernstein wrote once again to wish him a happy birthday, October 3.
Wolfe struggled very hard to reply, as the number of drafts and
fragments show. But his feelings about her, combined with his own
distress about his uncompleted book, worked him into a hysterical
digressiveness. The following item is the latest draft of the letter,
which apparently has not survived.]

Dear Aline:

    I have tried to answer your birthday letter twice, in the last few
days, and I have failed to finish it each time, after writing many pages.
There is something that I want to say to you now, but there is a great
deal which, it seems to me, does not need to be said. It is two years
since I have seen you or written to you and I may never see you or
write to you again, and it seems to me it is better now to try to say
what is in my heart than to try to conceal it. You say you don't know
how many years it is since we met. Well, I can tell you. It is eight. The
day I met you in front of the library was my twenty-fifth birthday and
I am thirty-three now. When I met you I was a boy with the faith,
passion, pride, ignorance and good constitution of a boy. Now I am a
man alone, first youth has gone, the boy's face and figure is gone, I am
a gross, heavy figure of a man and I am getting bald. When I met you I
was lonely and obscure and penniless, and bitterly resolved to justify
my life and make it prevail. Now, after eight years, I am in the same
boat: I am lonely and obscure and penniless and although I have lost
the faith and hope of youth I have something left. I have despair—and
men have managed to live by that before.

    What I want to say to you especially is this: when I met you
you were the only person who had ever had faith in me, you were the
only one who believed in me, and I think you were the only woman
that ever loved me. My family did not think I was any good or that I
would ever amount to anything, and later out in the world I found that
the workshoppers, the Neighborhooders, the precious people put their
faith in other precious people and had no word of comfort or belief for
me. My life before I met you was lonely and full of bitter self doubt
and agony. It was as solitary and desperate a youth as any man has ever
had. When I met you it was as if I had discovered a new world—although perhaps I didn't know it at the time. But for the first time in
my life I found a world more fortunate and happy than any I had ever
known, and from another person I had love and warmth and joy.

    It is this that I wanted to tell you. I want you to know that now
I know how to value it and that I will remember and treasure it as long

as I live. I want to tell you also that no matter what else you did, or what anguish, madness and despair I knew, that that woman who came to my room day after day for years was beyond every standard of comparison, the greatest, loveliest, and most beautiful woman I have ever known. And I also want to tell you that I now know I loved that woman with my life, that she is mixed into my blood, and that I shall love her forever. I want to tell you this because there are some things that can now be said, and it would be shameful not to say them. Now you are an old woman and I am a middle aged man and what has happened was inevitable and right, but there are a thousand things I bitterly regret and would undo them if I could. I did them when I was mad of mind and full of agony and desperation in my heart, and for all that was wrong and bad in what I did and said I would like you to know I am sorry. And I hope you can find in your own heart now some charity to admit that there was wrong upon your side as well. I hope vanity and pride is not so strong in you that you can now see nothing but right in everything you did.

It was for this reason I could not finish the two letters I began to you. Too many bitter thoughts and memories came back and I see no reason now for speaking them. It seems to me now that a stranger and an enemy maked [*sic*] in the image of someone that I loved did those things. Aline, if you—I will not call her you but this stranger is your mask—could have known [*what*] my childhood and boyhood was like, how desperate and wretchedly lonely my life was, how I had to go on alone in a world whose people, even my own family, had no idea what I was or what I wished to do, and where I had no one to believe in me and no way of knowing whether I had any of the artist's power in me, or was just another of those wretched, yearning, impotent young people one sees everywhere, who try to make of art the basis of their life without talent, energy, or creative power of any sort to see it through—if that stranger who looked like you could have known this, I don't think even she could have found it in her to strike the coward traitor's blow at the heart of life as she did. At the very moment when after all that black and wretched time of self-doubt, groping bewilderment, and despair I had for the first time won a position that promised me some sort of security, honor, dignity, and esteem in life—some entrance into the world of brightness, warmth, and fellowship other men have had—that woman mad with vanity and pride treacherously and deliberately destroyed what I had gained.

But I think even she would not have dared to do this thing had she known how much I needed that entrance into the warmth and fellowship of life, the artist's place of dignity and honor, the beautiful good life of work and certitude and high esteem. I do not think even that woman could have done as she did had she lived alone as I have, and known what loneliness and despair is like. It is all over now, but when I think of it the hideous viper thoughts and memories come back. I remembered all those things I would forget if I could—the memory of which is like weariness and hell now, so that words do no good to tell about them. I remember all the cables, letters, threats of suicide, warnings of death, bitter reproaches, falsehoods, last words written from hospitals, taunts, jeers, and the constant purlings of a morbid [hounding?], hideous and unwholesome hysteria—the attack that never let up when I was living abroad and trying to get something done and went on after I had got back here. Finally I remember the bitter letters I have had during the last two or three years here in Brooklyn—the letters telling me how bad and vile my life was, how none of my work was any good any more, and how people were talking and laughing about me behind my back, and how the reason for this decay in my life, my work, my future, was because I had deserted the source of my imagination, my guide, critic, and the one who was responsible for all good in me, and how nothing could come of my life and work now since I had done this—.

I am taking this letter up again after having carried it around for several days and I am resolved to finish it this time and send it to you. During the last few days I have moved again—the tenth or eleventh place I have lived in since coming to New York ten years ago—but the best and happiest places were the garret on Eighth street and the place on Eleventh street.

What is life and what is it for? Ten rooms, ten different places in ten years, in each of them all of the hope, hunger, joy, magic, fury, pain and sorrow that the world can know. Ten years, ten rooms, ten thousand sheets of paper in each of them covered with ten million words that I have written. Waking, eating, sleeping, rushing out on the streets where a million people are swarming past, staring in their faces and listening to what they are saying, trying to find out where they are going with all this fury and what is driving them on forever and what it is they hope to find—and finding nothing but fury in the end. Is there nothing but fury in the world—fury uncoiling in the streets and moving, fury driving, mounting, savage, overwhelming in the streets at noon, fury in the driven eyes and tortured faces of the people as they thrust, curse, jostle, jeer, threaten, call one another fools, liars, cheats, cowards, tricksters, thieves, fury in the lives of the poor, fury in the lives of millions of wretched, stinking, terrified, superstitious, ignorant, and submissive people crowding into subways, swarming out again, swarming drearily at night towards the barren glitter of Broadway, trying to regale their jaudiced lives on brutal and sterile pleasures that are lower than the pleasures of a dog, swarming around the place where there has been a brawl, a shooting, an accident, or a suicide, staring with their grey faces, and dead fascinated eyes at the blood of a young man out of work whose brains have exploded on the pavement after a 20 story jump as if you had shot his brains out of a compression hose, being thrust and forced back brutally by the police, shuffling, jesting, swarming around and then going on again to the brutal, idiot repetitions of ten thousand days of fury?

And in the lives of the rich and fashionable is it not the same? Is it not even true that their lives instead of being better than the lives of poor people, since their lives do not know the ugly poverty and despair that give the lives of poor people a little tenacity and courage, are empty, barren and brutal as the lives of the poor without knowing grim reality? Look about you at the people that you know, Aline, and tell me if this is not true? How many of them are better, wiser, greater people than they were ten years ago? Year in, year out, they drive furiously after a barren, feverish, and empty life, which has all the glitter and shine of a thousand varieties but which is really false, empty, sterile, and monotonous as hell. They go to see the latest plays and talk about them later round the dinner table. They read the latest books that have been praised by the critics and rave about them, or say they "hate" them or "dislike" them, but really what they saw, read, or heard that they loved, hated, or disliked, they can not remember from one season to another. Now it is Joyce, now Proust, now Gertrude Stein, now D. H. Lawrence, Faulkner, Hemingway, or someone else, now Picasso, Matisse, Rivera, Sert, or someone else, now plays about how gaily and lightly we frig in Vienna and now plays about we the people, now "Alice in Wonderland," and now plays about lesbians and pederasts—

I will not answer this letter to you with bitter words, because it was not to revile you that I wrote it. I wrote it to tell you of the memory of love and happiness I have when I think of the woman that I loved, who came to see me every day for years. I wrote it to tell you how much I now value her love and goodness, how bitterly I regret what I did that was wrong. But to get back to that woman that I loved I have to go around the ugly figure of that other woman—the stranger who came in and used every rotten and despicable means she knew to destroy me.

Well, she got everything I had gained—reputation, security, the belief of the people in my work—but she did not get me. I am 33 years old and I have nothing left, but I can begin again. My father, who was a stone cutter, began a new life when he was just my age, when it seemed to him that everything was lost; in that year he came up into the mountains, a stranger and an outcast, with nothing but ruin behind him—and he began a new life—the best part of his life—and his life was a strange and wonderful one. What he did, I can do. There is just one person in the world today who believes I will ever come to anything, that person is Maxwell Perkins, but that man's belief means more to me than anything on earth, and the knowledge that I have it far outweighs the disbelief of everyone else. In your letter you say you wish that you could help me, that you have faith in my "greatness" and my "genius" and that you pray for my success. If you do, you may have become again the great woman that I loved, but what you say belies everything you have said and done for four years, and men must love and prove themselves by deeds not words.

Aline, the time for your helping me is past. There is nothing you have now that I want. It is no good to write about the beautiful life you have achieved or about your flight of pigeons, threads of gold, and clear designs. It is no good for you to talk about "the great creature that lies dormant in me" and to hope that someday it will awaken and free itself from the chains that bind it. The woman who writes that [*page missing*]

If I ever win release, it will not be flights of pigeons or threads of gold or fine art theatre sentiments that do it. It will be because I am the son of a stone cutter and have known the same kind of fury, anguish, shame, drunkenness, regret, and suffering that my father knew. If there is any great creature dormant in me he will have to come out not because I am different from other men but because I am compounded of the same sweaty stinking clay of toil and agony as every mother's son of them—and the only difference is that I have more of that stinking sweaty clay.

[*On envelope postmarked November 13, 1933.*]

The Happy and Unhappy
1. Darrow—Driving ahead with hope all the time, furiously active, miserable as soon as he stops driving.
2. Perkins—The best life I know about—but not happy.

3. Wheelock—Unhappy.

4. Wallie Meyer—Unhappy.

5. The Garveys—Bklyn janitor—no light, no air, no joy—bitter, and fiercely unhappy.

6. Harriet Hoppe—Lost, gabbling forever, unhappy.

7. Carlton—Unhappy.

8. Mabel Carlton—Unhappy.

9. Manley—very unhappy.

10. The N.Y.U. Instructors—White, Varney, McCullough, Miss Walton, Troy, Gottlieb, Vardis Fisher—embittered, jealous, malicious and unhappy.

11. Mrs. Perkins—embittered and unhappy.

12. Darrow's wife—embittered and unhappy.

13. The Bums down in the Subway—one beating in another's face, the other sits quietly at stool, his bleared face quietly, stupidly receiving the blows.

14. The Jews and Jewesses in the Greenwich Village restaurants —the people in Brooklyn—the young men sitting in cheap lunchrooms and cafeterias late at night—The Policeman and the Boy in the Hoboken Saloon—a [*paper torn*] in the hospital [*paper torn*] woman's voice screaming "let me die, let me die."

[*In May, Wolfe had signed a contract for "Time and the River," as he now called the book. The contract stated: "It is desirable that the said work should be published in the Fall of 1933, and said author agrees to deliver to said Publishers a copy of the manuscript complete and ready for the press not later than August 1, 1933." By Thanksgiving Wolfe was still floundering, and he turned to Perkins for help. Perkins told him that he was really finished and asked him for the manuscript in its present state. Wolfe spent a couple of weeks putting it in sequence and drew up a detailed outline and statement of intentions to go along with it. For the first time he was able to see his work as a whole. This is the typescript that accompanied his manuscript or was drawn up shortly after he delivered it to Perkins.*]

SECTION ONE
OCTOBER 1920

I Written:

1. Old Catawba: Description of Old Catawba and its people (with the last part still to be written).

2. The Train (Flight Before Fury—Complete save for revision and closer weaving together).

II *Yet to Be Written:*

1. Very little except conclusion of Old Catawba scene and its people.

2. A brief scene showing boy (John) saying good-bye to his people, at the station on his way out to the city and the world for first time.

III *Purpose of Scene:*

1. To give the background of the story with all its weavings back into the past of his own life and the life of his people.

2. To set the theme of flight and fury, the great dream of the city which a young man has and what it means to him, and the homelessness and unrest of Americans with the cause of it.

3. The reason why men wander: The longing of youth for security, place and certitude, and the belief that they shall find it in their furious search for it.

4. This introduces the theme of man searching for his father which runs through the book—the search for the father is the search for an outer image of certitude, strength and wisdom to which he can confide his life and which he is certain he will one day find in the streets of life.

5. The wandering, homeless, furious restlessness of man is set against the eternity of the earth (time and the river, the eternal and the momentary, the father and son theme again).

6. This scene ends with the end of Flight Before Fury,—the faint light breaking across the old earth of Virginia in the morning as the train rushes over it, "fixed in unsilent silence, moveless movement, changeless change."

SECTION TWO
OCTOBER 1920—BALTIMORE

I *Written:*

1. This section begins with the passage about America and the things that happen there.

2. The dying old man on the hospital porch. His meeting with his two sons described. The father theme again: A man's real father and the father he is seeking (Scene incomplete).

3. The meeting with the blind man, Dinwood Bland (scene incomplete).

4. The scene in the disreputable hotel between Dinwood Bland and his divorced wife (scene incomplete).

II Yet to Be Written:

The conclusion of foregoing scenes and

1. A brief scene describing the great house of death—the hospital.

2. A scene at night in the negro quarters of the city with the blind man Bland and his mulatto mistress.

3. A brief scene of parting between the son and his father.

III Purpose of Scene:

1. To show in the meeting between the old dying man and his son the feeling that they are strangers to each other and the phantasmal dream-enchantment of time. The boy cannot believe this old dying spectre was ever his father or had anything to do with the life of his childhood and which now seems stranger than a dream. For this reason, he looks upon the old dying man as a ghost, an impostor of his real father, and in his heart he loathes him and wants to escape from him and the spell of black horror and unreality he casts upon him.

2. To show in the description of the great hospital the conflict between the energies of life and death and its effect on youth: the young internes who have already been infected by the fatal, morbid, almost reckless gayety of death. A brief description (already written but not typed) of the stimulation of the great drug of death upon the young internes (whom the boy has known previously) and his own revulsion and loathing of it. His desire to escape into life towards his vision of the shining city, the fortunate, good and always happy life that has no death in it.

SECTION THREE
OCTOBER 1920

I Written:

1. The Hudson River meets the Harbor (etc.).

II Yet to Be Written: (Already in MSS.)

1. A brief scene describing a young man's first vision of the city —the kaleidoscopic strangeness of the first impression—its dream-like quality when he remembers it in later years and passes by the places he saw on his first brief visit.

III Purpose of Scene:

Already described in the foregoing sections:—to express the phantasmal legendary *Time* in which the city-people live, the legend of Now and Forever, the movement of the river which changes always and is forever the same—the legend of *Time and The River* (already expressed) and its phantasmal strangeness to a youth who sees it for the first time.

SECTION FOUR
THE BEGINNING OF THE FURY—BOSTON: 1920–1923

I Written:

1. The description of the Fury. The desire to read all the books, to eat all the food, to visit all the States, to know all the people, etc. (already used in the second part of NO DOOR and included here).
2. Sunday in Boston. Visit to his uncle's house. The son-and-father theme again.
3. The Boston Irish in a rooming house.
4. The fury of numbers, faces, places, etc.

II Yet to Be Written:

1. A scene describing the moment in which fury first came to him and entered him:

a. First when he gets off in the tremendous smoking old South Station and sees the great engines steaming all around him, smells the acrid smoke, and sees and smells for the first time the narrow twisted old streets of Boston with their eternal smell of fresh ground coffee.

b. He sees a lusty Irish girl passing in the manswarm outside the Park Street Station—suddenly conscious of the million-footed manswarm, is drowning in it, feeling of joy and desolation, mad hunger seizes him to eat the earth and he plunges forward into crowd.

c. The first coming of the snow at night—the numb ominous feeling of the air—waking suddenly in dark night to know the secret, numb and all-engulfing snow is all around him, to rise and rush out in the storm with wild joy and fury in his heart.

2. A scene that tells of the dream-strange passing of time while this fury possesses and devours him—he has come here for *one* year and *three* years go by him like a dream. The lives and faces of his father, his people, and the county he comes from seem lost, sunken and buried like a city at the bottom of the sea. Suddenly a message comes to him telling him his father is dying. He rushes down across America by night and awakes to find the marvellous hills of home around him. His father dies suddenly and horribly a few hours after his arrival, emptying his life out instantly in a great pool of blood upon the bed. For a brief instant the old life of home and of his people possesses him with its reality—then he is back in the North (in Boston) and the dream of time again. In this way three years pass by him like a dream. Suddenly, he wakes one day and thinks of home again. A wild longing to see his home and his people comes to him. He goes home in October (most of this is already written in type or in manuscript and a good deal of it is here included).

III   *Purpose of Scene:*

Already described for the most part in the foregoing:—to describe the Beginning of Fury, and its causes; the Faustean soul of man with its desire to possess the earth; the mystery of dark time and its million shifting faces—the present passing all around him with a furious intensity of actuality while the great river of time floats quietly around him and his life is passing onward like a dream—and finally, the first description of man's loneliness: the savage hunger and unceasing belief that he will find the fortunate and wonderful life, while he prowls ten thousand barren streets; the huge promise of the city, of abundance, love, joy, and certitude, and the terrible actuality as he goes by ten thousand doors at night and finds none open to him.

SECTION FIVE
THE RETURN HOME ENDING WITH HIS FLIGHT FROM HOME
OCTOBER–NOVEMBER 1923

I   Written: The enormous section of 180,000 words tentatively called Flight from Home:
1. "October had come again"—etc. (already used in NO DOOR).

2. His feeling of loss and emptiness now that he has come home again and found his father dead. He cannot believe his father dead and he thinks he will find him everywhere. At night he lies in the darkness in his bed and cannot realize his father is dead and that October has come back again (all this previously used in NO DOOR).

3. Description of the family and the effect the death of his father has had on them. Suddenly he realizes that his father is dead, and that all the life he has known in his childhood is lost and broken as a dream.

4. Day by day he is waiting, as ten million other boys have waited, for a letter to come from the city which will bring him fortune, fame and triumph instantly. It is a letter telling him his play has been accepted by a great theatre and that his fame is made. At last the letter comes rejecting the play.

5. In black despair now at his failure, thinking his life is lost, he lashes out blindly all around him: on this wild, lashing impulse, without knowing why, he starts out across the mountains into South Carolina where one of his sisters is living. On the way down the mountain he falls in with three boyhood companions from his town, and gets into their car with them. They get drunk upon corn liquor, and suddenly all the joy and power and victory of life return to him—he hears a train wailing in the mountains and thinks with triumph now of the great city. When they reach South Carolina, they are all roaring drunk, they stop among the cotton fields, they rip crazily along the road in their careening car: when they get into town the police have been warned and are waiting for them.

6. Description of the arrest, the jail, the shame and horror that he feels now over his act as he sits in his cell, the way time passes during drunkenness.

7. His brother hears of his arrest and comes to pay the fines and get them out. An hour later he and his brother get into a fight with the police because of his first arrest, and both are put in jail again. This time a friend comes and pays them out.

8. On the road now with his brother—hurtling along the road for three days now with his brother with the feeling of shame and horror in him—the conviction that all is lost for him at home—that he must leave forever now because of his disgrace.

9. His brother's life—its goodness, its frenzied dissonance, fury and unrest that communicates itself to everything he says, does, or touches—even to the tortured, stammering little car he drives. His brother's frenzied, aimless life, with all its fury, dissonance and tortured hunger, a microcosm of the lives everywhere about him in America. What is it? What are we looking for? Why are we so

unhappy? His brother and his father: his brother's dependence on his father, his brother's loss and hopeless bewilderment now that his father has gone. Is that the reason for our vast unhappiness? Is every man looking for his father? What are we seeking in America? "The Locusts Have No King."

10. The unending pageant of the roads as his brother hurtles onward in the car—the thousand sudden, instantly lost and lonely faces of America, his brother's desperate wish to talk to everyone—his hunger and his homelessness.

11. The Return Home into the Mountains, and the Final Departure to the City.

II Yet to Be Written:

Nothing except the last section above, describing the actual departure from his people, and the coming of the train (This has already been written in MSS).

III Purpose of Scene:

The purpose of the scene has already been pretty completely described: the desperate longing of the wanderer for return to the place he came from (the theme of "wandering forever and the earth again"); the man, looking for his father and not believing he is dead, and sure that some day he will find him; the bitter discovery of the wanderer that the life he has returned to is stranger than a dream, that he can no longer live in it; the frenzied unrest and homelessness of his spirit (which now becomes the unrest and homelessness of his brother and of the whole nation, that madness that is consuming everyone) and his final flight to the great city again, with the desperate resolve to justify his life, to find the fortunate and happy life he wants, to meet his father.

(All of this written save one short concluding section.)

SECTION SIX
THE FIRST YEAR IN THE CITY: NOVEMBER 1923—OCTOBER 1924

I Written:

1. The Great City University with its dark, swarming faces, the furious tempo of its life.

2. His desperate fear of failure (motivated by the disgrace at home which still weighs on him and the determination to succeed or die); his feeling of abysmal ignorance as he stands before his noisy classes, his fear and loathing of his work at first, fear of exposure and dismissal, etc. The instructors and their poisonous and petty lives, the dark tides of swarming, noisy students, the age and evil that has never known innocence in them, and yet is still young, charming, attractive and naive.

3. Abraham Jones:—an East Side Jew—the first manswarm atom of the city that he comes to know—his first entrance into the great wall of the city's life—the history of Abe Jones, his family, and the life he represents.

3A. Two other city people who weave into his life and the pattern of that first year in the city.

a. Monty Bellamy—a hotel clerk from the South, who thinks he is a great actor and weeps bitterly as he tells the youth of the bitter frustration of his hopes: the evil sterile glamour of the theatre and its ruinous effect upon the lives of millions of young people.

b. Hugh Desmond—a university instructor: he is a diabetic who loves life with a ravenous hunger—who wants food, drink, women, pleasure—and who is still brave and true to life when everything is lost for him. The horror of his death, the courage with which he meets it, his farewell to the narrator, and the image of man's deathless courage and loneliness he leaves behind him.

4. The One and the Many: Man's struggle against the million-footed monster of the crowd. The first year of a young man in the city —its loneliness, fear, and desperate hunger—the feeling of drowning in the man-swarm horror, of being dwarfed beneath the gigantic architectures, the hatred of the little cell in which he lives, the cheap hotel in which he lives with all its grimy and yet wonderful lives, his loathing of his little room and constant desire to rush out into the streets, his horror and sense of drowning in the grey atomic desolation of the lives and faces, retreating to his room again, shuddering and defeated by the crowd, then out into the streets again.

5. Why are we so unhappy? What are all the people in the swarming streets looking for? Why do they hurry on forever with the look of furious and desperate unrest in their eyes? What is that great magnetic force in life which draws us every night out of our little cells into the furious streets? What are we looking for and why is it that we never lose hope that we will find it? What is this undying hunger for joy, love, pleasure, and excitement in people? Swarming, swarming, swarming, ten million feet, five million faces on the city streets at

night, the barren sterile lights burn lividly upon their feverish faces—
one hundred million lights, one hundred stoney buildings, and not a
single door that we can enter, not one single room of comfort, love,
and peace that we can find. Why? Which brings us to—

6. The Million-visaged City and the Tantalus-Frustration of our
Hopes: The bitter enigma in the life of the American, the frenzy, fury,
hunger and unrest that drives us on (not only the city myriads but his
brother hurtling down a dark road in the South). What is it? The
contrast between the city of his boyhood vision—the fabulous, time-
enchanted city with its heroic men and lovely women, its fortunate
good and happy life—and this city of his real experience. The thousand
lights and weathers of New York. The spell of time it casts upon its
people. At once the gayest of great cities, and the city of the most
terrific age: the age of twenty thousand furious and innumerable days
and nights, of countless lives and deaths, of a sea-time horror of
sensation. Its thousand lights and weathers beneath which the visage of
the city is forever changing: the horrible barrenness, sterility, and
nameless fear of a night in February—the barren streets, the hard and
cruel glitter of the lights, the inhuman ice-hard architectures, soaring
into frozen and star-blazing skies—horror, loss, the sense of cruelty and
death—and suddenly spring again, the first fine days in May, the
feathery green of a young tree in a city street, the rebirth of the hated,
dying, grey faces into life and hope and joy, a thousand harmonies of
life and color everywhere—and suddenly the glorious women bursting
like great flowers from the pavement. Where have they come from?—
A magic and a miracle of city time.

(All this is either written in whole or in part, and included in
entirety, or suggested here).

II   Yet to Be Written:

1. A scene entitled TROY—which summarizes all of the city's
cruel enigma—its promise of love, abundance, glory, joy, and peace,
and end of loneliness everywhere, a million doors reaching to welcome
and receive the youth—and its damnable tantalus-like irony of what it
lets a young man have—a barren little cell in a cheap hotel, the
ceaseless prowling of the accursed streets, the looking into a million
faces to find one that is his own—and never finding it, returning to the
cell again, fighting the manswarm struggle day by day.

The youth has come to the city to find all his heart has visioned
there and now in fury, drunkenness and despair, he lashes out across
the country in great trains at night. A dozen times that year he gets on

trains and goes wherever they may take him—Boston—Washington—Pennsylvania—Montreal—Coming back from Montreal in the middle of a snow-white winter's night, he wakens suddenly from his sleep and with the near unreality of a dream he sees the station bricks and brothels of a place called TROY, a boy standing just below him outside of one of the brothels, as he has often done, with chattering lips, trying to make up his mind to enter. The train moves slowly away, the boy runs swiftly up the brothel steps below him, the door opens and a woman takes him in.

Returning to the city, the vision haunts him. Spring comes, he is tortured by the city's tantalus promises and finds nothing, a dozen times that spring he takes the train across the dark earth of America and goes to Troy to get there what he cannot find in all the million-footed myriad-doored promise of the city.

2. A scene describing the passing of the first year, the coming of brutal summer, two women in the hotel that he knows casually, his growing hatred, despair, and frenzy with the city's life and his growing determination to escape now to another kind of illusion—to find the fortunate and wonderful life where all the young men of the [*new*] life are looking for it—in "Europe," "Paris." The old delusion tortures him again that he can "change his soul if he can only change his skies"—he resolves to go abroad in October when his work is done.

3. The first half of the book closes with the end of the first year in the city—the vision of the mighty ships—the great towers receding in the distance—the everlasting question of the wanderer—"And now the voyage out? Where?"

III *Purpose of Scene:*

The purpose of this section has been thoroughly described in the foregoing passages.

(This marks the end of the first half of THE OCTOBER FAIR October 1920–October 1924) [13]

13. There was still a good bit of see-sawing about the title of the book. As late as March 8, 1934, Wolfe explained in an unpublished letter to Katherine Gauss, who wrote a news column about contributors in *Scribner's*, that Perkins had in his hands the manuscript of the first book of a series to be called "Time and the River," and that Perkins wanted the first book to be called that too, rather than "The October Fair." The second book of the series would be "The Hills Beyond Pentland," and what the third book would be called "or what, indeed, its size and design will be I do not know at present since all I have for this are some notes and a few scenes."

SECTION SEVEN
THE FIRST VOYAGE—OCTOBER 1924–SEPTEMBER 1925

I Written:

1. The Expatriots
2. The Ship: Meeting with Esther.

II Yet to Be Written:

1. An episode in Paris which introduces Starwick, a character who appears in Boston scenes and will reappear later, and two Boston women.

2. A brief variation on the homelessness of the American—the strange magnetic attraction that Europe has for them—what they hope to find there and their bitter disillusion. The reasons for this: Americans a homeless people haunted constantly by almost-captured memories of their father's country. This necessary because of what happens in later voyages in book and in the German sections.

III Purpose of Scene:

1. Because this is a story of man's wandering and the reason for it—to describe an American's first year in Europe, his homelessness and unrest, and what he thinks about and longs for when he thinks of home (all of this written in mss but not typed yet).

2. Also, an episode with one of the Boston women, to show the effect of Paris on young Americans, who use it as a romantic background for their lives and are sure they suffer, love, etc., when what they are really doing is being Americans in Paris.

3. To prepare the way for the meeting with Esther and the real love episodes which are to follow.

(This section largely untyped and unwritten but must be included in the book).

SECTION EIGHT
OCTOBER 1925—JUNE 1926

I Written:

1. The City Again: Meeting with Esther, Esther's House, Beginnings of Love Episodes.

2. Esther's life and former history told in her own dialog.

3. Scenes of their life together in an Eighth Street garret.

4. The coming of spring to a man in love: the feeling of wild power and joy and happiness it gives him, his desire to embrace all life, and his feeling that he will find some wonderful good fortune at every corner: The Train and the City.

5. His sudden wild longings for home in all this happiness—man shown in his conflict as lover and wanderer, his sudden longing to see his home again—the return home—the realization that he is homeless now and can not live here—his departure: All this known here as The Boom Town.

II   *Yet to Be Written:*

1. A narrative scene describing the swift progress of the man's feeling for the woman, from desire to love during the first months of their intimacy: the design of their daily lives briefly described.

III   *Purpose of Scene:*

1. To show the transforming alchemistry of love upon man's life—the way it transforms the city all around him—the way it banishes the old feelings of homelessness and loneliness, the way it makes him want to embrace all life into his love.

2. To show the conflict between the lover and the wanderer, between the loneliness of man and the duality of woman—between Faust and Helen—and the beginnings of the struggle between them— the reappearance from time to time of the old unrest—the desire for new skies—the longing for home again as shown in THE BOOM TOWN.

3. The final purpose of this section is to show the happiness and health of love and its magic transformation of all life—just as later on the madness and disease of love with its fatal, black, distorted interpretations of all the life around it will be shown.

SECTION NINE

JULY 1926–JANUARY 1927: EUROPE AGAIN

I   *Written:*

1. Passages about Time—Time is a fable and a mystery.

2. The Oxford Scenes from NO DOOR (including those which were cut out of magazine version).

3. The first visit to the land of his father's people (Germany), his instant recognition and familiarity with everything—its haunting dream-like effect on him—the fascination, horror, attraction and repulsion that it has for him—the son and the father theme again: The German Train.

II *Yet to Be Written:*

A scene describing the earlier part of the summer in France and England with Esther, his decision to stay when she returns home, the beginning of the open conflict between them.

III *Purpose of Scene:*

To show man, the wanderer, looking for his home, his father's land again—to show the growing conflict between the lover and the wanderer, loneliness and love.

SECTION TEN

JANUARY 1927–JULY 1927: THE CITY AGAIN

I *Written:*

1. The beginning of the madness of love—the nature of jealousy and its physical effect—the struggle of attraction and repulsion—the desire to leave the woman and to possess her in bondage, excluding everyone and everything else from her—the effect of this developing madness upon his vision of the life of the million-visaged city all around him—the curative power of work in which he now for the first time utterly loses himself.

II *Yet to Be Written:*

Not so much to be written, but the whole to be reshaped, revised and rewritten.

III *Purpose of Scene:*

1. The developing conflict between love and wandering, and the growing madness of love with its distortions of all the life around him, previously explained—also,

2. To show here for the first time that man, the furious, famished wanderer may find the home for which he is looking in his work.

I   Written:

Very little except notes.

II   Yet to Be Written:

A brief account of the voyage, the second visit to Germany described, with its growing fascination for him, the bitter growing struggle with the woman.

III   Purpose of Scene:

To emphasize his growing restlessness and desire to escape, the haunting fascination which the forests and cities of Germany have come to have for him; and the struggle with the woman which has now grown naked, brutal, desperate.

SECTION TWELVE
OCTOBER 1927–JULY 1928

The Last Year in the City with Esther, the end of love, the coming on of the catastrophe of madness, which now begins to dominate all his life.

I   Written:

1. The nature of the madness and fury which has now filled his life—the sense of impending catastrophe all around him—life, the great traitor, in its conspiracy against him—the madness and disease of love here contrasted in all its evil distortions of hate upon the city-world about him, just as previously the health of love was described with all its transforming magic of health upon the life around it.

2. The savage conflict between two people day by day—scenes between the man and the woman—the bitter quarrels, curses, hatreds,

the strangling tenacity of the struggle—he to leave her, she to hold him —together with the bitter, inexpiable regret and anguish, the moments of deep love, the bitter enigma of the love and hate in whose toils he is now caught.

3. The dreams of time—the visions of nameless shame and desolation which haunt his sleep at night—the dreams of inexpiable guilt and self-loathing, without knowing what his crime is—the horrible time-dreams in which his life has passed away without his knowing how it has gone, in which he has left some great work undone, with which he had been entrusted, and not knowing how it happened—the terrible dream of the naked snake-haired woman, etc.

4. The coming of spring and its effect upon the madness of love: the union of joy and pain—the fusion of madness and sanity in his mind: how his mind keeps watch like an impassive witness at the madness and jealousy that invades it, yet is powerless to check it—the evocative power of the first green of the year in a city upon man's memory, etc.

5. Esther Present and Esther Away. Love by day and madness by night—the tenderness, fierceness and health of love still present when she is with him in the daytime—the sanity of noon—the hour of hope, faith, love, invincible belief—Esther Away: he can no longer remember her face or how she looked at noon—the cruelty, sweetness, madness of night in April—he sees her now at night, her face smouldering like an opulent and drowsy flower, impregnably fixed and secure in a corrupt, baleful, glittering night-time world of the sinister, secret city—quilted in darkness and the green of April somewhere in the embraces of soft youth—a million images of death, madness, jealousy and despair surge through him—every laugh, whisper, or fugitive word out in the street he takes now as a reference to himself and his betrayal, he rushes out into the streets of night, a madman, to curse and fight with life everywhere, seeing nothing but Death and hatred all around him.

6. From Death to Morning: A Passage of Eighty Thousand words that describes the life of the city from midnight until nine o'clock the next morning. It includes:

a. "The Locusts Have No King"—a series of twelve swift scenes describing the night-time life of people all over the city, of which two or three only are included here.

b. "Death the Proud Brother" (already used in Scribner's Magazine).

c. Morning: The long scene which describes (1) Jacobs Awake; (2) Esther and the Maid; (3) Esther and Jacobs; (4) The

Station—in which, after a night of madness and distorted shapes, the narrator recovers sanity again.

    7. The final scenes of separation with Esther:
        a. The Man In The Window (used previously in NO DOOR).

II *Yet to Be Written:*

Mainly revision, re-arrangement, and weaving together.

III *Purpose of Scene:*

To describe the final separation between the lovers, the madness of love in its vision of the city life around it, the final triumph of the lonely man, the wanderer, over man the lover, and to set the stage for the catastrophe of the concluding section.

SECTION THIRTEEN
JUNE 1928

A very short section not yet written.

Purpose of Scene:

To show man's homeless and intolerable longing for home. Before going abroad again, he leaves the city one day on a sudden impulse and goes back to the country of his father's birth (in Pennsylvania) for the first time since he was twelve years old. Hunts for traces of his father's life —on a drowsy rutted old country road he finds the ruins of the little house in which his father was born—nothing but a few mouldering bricks in a field beside the road—the bricks all overgrown with a tangle of bramble bushes and some wild strange leaves—nothing around but the fertile nobly swelling earth of America—a great red barn set nobly on an upswell of the earth in the distance—the drowsy humming in the roadside hedges—the drowsy crickety stitch of afternoon—an intolerable loneliness as he thinks of his father's vanished life, and all the men who now lie buried in the great earth of America—an intolerable sudden loneliness and a sense of haunting memory—a wild longing to see again the time-enchanted forests of Germany.

    (The scene would have a few people in it—members of his father's family—but this is the substance of it).

SECTION FOURTEEN
THE OCTOBER FAIR

I Written:

1. The Scene at the Fair.
2. The Hospital.

II Yet to Be Written:

1. A scene to be called either *The Dream of Time* or *In The Dark Forest*—which describes the dreamlike passing of a summer's time in Germany, the old swarm-haunted mind of man, the sense of recognition, strangeness and familiarity, fascination and loathing in everything he sees—the overwhelming feeling he will hear there in the dark forest a step, a word, or hear his father's voice again.

2. The scenes at the October Fair—the final bursting of the fury—the bloody fight—the sense of drowning in the blood, the mud, the darkness of the old barbaric forest.

3. Then the scenes at the hospital, part of which is already written, and finally

4. As he lies there in the hospital room at night and hears the steady ceaseless dripping of the rain upon the fallen leaves in the hospital garden, a monody on Silence, beginning:

"Silence receives us as the earth takes rain—" and weaving his life back now out of the fury which for ten years has devoured it and finally exploded it, into silence, peace, repose, the beginnings of his life in childhood—from which will begin the next book of the series to be called THE HILLS BEYOND PENTLAND.

(This is the end of THE OCTOBER FAIR.)

PART SIX~

RESCUE OPERATION

Pocket Notebook 21
ca. *January, 1934, to April, 1934*

After Wolfe turned his manuscript over to Perkins, one of the first decisions they agreed on was to concentrate on the first portion of the hero's adventures and to postpone the love story for development in a later volume. Further, John Hawke got back his real name, Eugene Gant, and the book was planned as a continuation of Eugene's adventures. During this period Wolfe met with Perkins almost every afternoon to cut the manuscript, and he worked every night filling in gaps. This concentration on chunks and pieces made him aware of units within the manuscript that he could sell for publication in Scribner's Magazine. *The notebook records these sales, plus the income from foreign publishers, which was barely enough to keep him going as he moved slowly toward the formation of his book. A reference to the sale of "Boom Town" to the* American Mercury *reflects Wolfe's first association with Elizabeth Nowell, a lively young Bryn Mawr graduate who became his literary agent for sales to periodicals and who also became an important force in his literary development. Wolfe had spent more time than he wished painfully cutting and revising "Boom Town," but Miss Nowell's persistence and encouragement were well worth it—"Boom Town" was selected, later in the year, for inclusion in* O. Henry Memorial Award: Prize Stories of 1934.

This notebook does not contain much more than the previous two (and has a similar number of lunchroom and barroom conversations), but it is a little more difficult to present because the entries were made at each end of the notebook and probably were not made chronologically. Besides omitting most of the tap-room trivia, we have excluded some of the outlines and tabulations of progress which are repetitious.

SECTIONS

I From Altamont to Baltimore and Parting with Father. Incomplete: Dinwood Bland

II   Boston: From Baltimore to Coming Back Home.
    Incomplete: Butcher's Workshop
                Starwick
                Professor Butcher
                Introduction
                Gant's Death
III   Return and Flight from Home.
    Incomplete: Last dinner of family together
IV   1st Year in City.
    Incomplete: Hotel Leopold
                Troy
                The Instructors
                The Diabetic
                The Southerners
V   First Year Abroad From Leaving City to Return Again.
    Incomplete: Ship in harbor river England
                1st Mo. in Paris
                Starwick, Elinor, Helen
                Remainder of 1st year abroad scenes
                Ship.

Tuesday, March 13, 1934:

    42nd St.—opp. Grand Central. Leighton. Bought hat there. Probably lost brief case there.

	$250
	50
Mod. Libe.[1]	300
Peasants [2]	300
Boom Town	192.50
Germany L.H.A.	80
Web of Earth	40
Czechoslovakia L.H.A.	100.00
England (Time and the River)	500.00

Trips in America
1—St. Louis.
1—New Orleans.

    1. Wolfe had sold reprint rights for LHA to the Modern Library, and it became one of the new series of Modern Library Giants. The extra $50.00 was apparently for a preface which Wolfe supplied but which the reprint publishers did not use.

    2. "The Sun and the Rain," a short sketch about riding in a train with French peasants. It was later included in OT&R, pp. 787–802.

1—Hot Springs, Arkansas.
2—Jacksonville, Fla.
1—St Pete, Tampa, [Bradenton?] etc.
1—Daytona, Palm Beach, etc.
2—Atlanta, Ga.
3—Richmond, Newport News, etc.
1—Charleston, S.C.
1—Columbia, S.C.
6—Anderson, S.C., Greenville, etc.
3—Gettysburg, York Springs, Harrisburg, Pa.
[*10*]—Boston, Cambridge, etc.
3—New Hampshire.
2—Vermont.
8—Connecticut.

A story about the man who *Must Write A Book*—the letters, the publisher, the people who know him, etc.

[*At this point there is a mostly illegible entry which is possibly a parody of an operatic aria or duet. Repeated phrases are "In old Arkansas" and "I want some pussy."*
This is followed by several pages in drink-wobbly writing which apparently describe the contents of the windows of an A&P grocery store in Brooklyn and then record the presence of the other stores on both sides of the street.]

To Be finished:
    1) End of first year in City scenes.
    2) End of Starwick, Elinor, Helen Episodes.
    3) End of 1st year abroad stuff.
    4) A Woman's Life, etc.
    5) 1st part of 1st trip abroad with Esther, etc.
    6) The Year of Labor.
    7) Summer abroad with Esther.
    8) Last Year with Esther—Madness and Jealousy, etc.
    9) October Fair Scenes—1st part of summer abroad, etc.

What Will Certainly Get Published This Year:
The Four Lost Men
The Web of Earth [3]

3. "The Web of Earth" was reprinted in Alfred Dashiell's *Editor's Choice* (New York, 1934).

The Peasants	3
Boom Town	12
House of the Far and Lost	15
Dark In the Forest	5
	40

Probably:

This is A-a-adelaide [4]	3
Dark October [5]	12
	55

Bascom Hawke	30
Train and City	10
Death the Proud Brother	20
No Door	20
	80

135000 [*words*]

Stories:

Gilmer
Mad Mag
The Death of the Enemy
Barton
Still Vex'd Bermoothes
Horton (Happy Pair) [6]

What I Have Sold Since Jan. 1:

Peasants
House of Far and Lost

4. A short story, never published, about a woman who keeps calling the young man on the telephone. It is an uncharacteristic piece, made up mostly of Adelaide's monologues over the telephone, and it is not an interesting or successful work.

5. A longer version of Chapter 49 of W&R, in which Esther mourns for her lover who has left her. It also contained some of the material which Edward Aswell placed in YCGHA, pp. 12–14, about Esther's question, "Will you go on loving me forever?"

6. Most of these projected stories got no farther than notes or fragments, except "Barton," which eventually became "The Company." "Gilmer" was to characterize a boarder at the Old Kentucky Home. "Mad Mag" was probably an extension of the sketch about "Mad Maude Whittaker." "Still Vex'd Bermoothes" was to satirize Bermuda and its tourists. "Horton" was to feature character sketches of Wolfe's friends from Harvard and New York University, Henry Carlton and William Manley, who became a team of radio script-writers.

Boom Town
Modern Library and Preface
The Web of Earth (in book edition)

Scenes from beginning to end—First five years:
  1. Robert Weaver
  2. End of Dinwood Bland Scenes
  3. Introduction to Boston Scenes
  4. Professor Butcher—"Modern"
  5. Death of Gant
  6. First Dinner at Home
  7. Troy
  8. Hotel Leopold
  9. Going Abroad (Joel Pierce)
  10. England Ship
  11. 1st Mo. in Paris
  12. End of Starwick Scenes
  13. End of Europe Scenes
  14. End of Ship Esther Scenes

BOSTON (Present Material)

Professor Butcher's class
Miss Darling
Uncle Bascom
Food
Alcohol
Conversation with Starwick
Leaving Boston

New York Nights (2000):
  Joe's Place—Brooklyn   100 (or more)
  N.Y.U. (night class)   180 (or more)
  8th St.   250 (or more)
  Hotel Albert   150 (or more)
  11th St.   150 (or more)
  15th St.   150 (or more)
  49th St. Grill   100 (or more)
  Steve's   100 (or more)

On Big Time, Bright Boys Who Came To The City: Carlton, Geo. Denny, B. Carmichael, W. Blount, N. Mobley, Clell Greenwood, John Terry, Henry Stevens.

Thursday—a Coffee Pot on Montague St. In Brooklyn—March 22, 1934:

A *Character*—A Counterman—A *Swede*—who says Huh?—after every statement, question, or utterance—Like this: Hey—Steve —the milk is out will ya tell him we need ten gallons—huh? They've only got three million people in whole country—huh? When you want a girl all you gotta do is tell the taxi man—huh? He'll bring her without charging *you* a cent—huh? etc.

New York at Dawn—(Day Starts)—The Awful Stillness—The Shapes of things (The Awful Stillness and Loneliness is Interrupted— The Milk Wagons—taxis—etc.) But the awful stillness of streets, pavements, lampposts, fire hydrants, curbs, bldgs. all shut, bldgs. staring.

Diary of a Brooklyn Pepys—

Home after five A.M. of a cold morning after evening at Joe's restaurant with Lieut. [Canby?], Lido and in a Coffee Potte on Montague St.—and so to bed. Lay late (till 4:35 as a matter of fact) called Me 77212 and found 'twas too late to catch Boston boat—so up to bathe and back to bed again where slept till 8:51—so up and to subway to Beefsteak Charlie's on 50th St. where dined on beefsteak—and so to Translux theatre—then down B'way, across to 44th where found Blue Ribbon closing—then back along Broadway up 45th and to Child's Restaurant at 43rd St. near Grand Central where this is written.

Coffee Pot, Montague Street, Brooklyn, March 31, 3:00 A.M.:

The Two College Boys (the one with thick, soft features, eyeglasses and a thick soft college-affectation of speech)—the other sharp-visaged and sharp-nosed, etc. "I'm sufficiently egotistical to think that here is the point . . . You and I are sufficiently well thought of to be considered a catch" (the familiar affected college tone—a young fellow with thick soft features, eyeglasses, and dull eyes—the college prick in mere cosmos).

"Well, you weren't drunk—I mean, you weren't drunk."

"I mean but *after* all—you've got to admit that I can drink."

(Thick, soft): "But I mean, the point is, you and I had quite a set-up—and we had enough to drown—. We drank a quart of rye, a half quart of gin, a quart of sherry, a half quart of creme de menthe—I mean, after all, that's a lot of drink when you're seeing a doll who wants watching."

"Yes, after *all*, we had a bunch of stupid dolls along—say, where the hell does that doll live?"

"She lives one block past, etc." (Brooklyn Heights).

"I mean, after all, here's the point, Bob—I started out with 30 bucks—I spent 8.40 plus 1.68 actual fare—which makes 10.45—I spent 5.45—(after we got there). I spent fourteen dollars and sixty cents, and etc.—for that evening, etc."

(Soft—dull—thick): . . . "dinner tomorrow?"

"Well—look—if I tell Mother I am going to Long Island I can get the Rolls . . ."

The Coffee Pot, Montague and Henry (from 3 A.M. to 6:30 A.M., Tuesday, April 3, 1934):

1) Went in—conversation between Pete (Czech) and Karl (Swede) about healthy European climate—Pete contending people didn't have appendicitis, toothache, etc. over there—Karl, laughing tolerantly, contending contrary.

2) Hold-up man comes in—they disarm him—Whatcha think a that, eh! says Pete to customer (hands on hip)—Discussion of hold-up in general between Karl and Pete.

3) More conversation about 4th Avenue and 18th St. where Pete used to have lunchroom—and of gunmen there.

4) Two Drunken college boys.

5) More conversation—Talk about Russia between Pete and Karl, etc. Pete's rent, large amt. Losses, etc.

6) Two tough whores come in.

7) A little blackhaired fellow to whom Pete gives cartridges. Blackhaired fellow throws them carefully down sewer.

9) A rather good-looking redhaired whore (morning sunlight now). Men coming in restaurant on way to work—Russian shows picture in paper of first Russian ship to enter port of New York.[7] (Full morning, underway, departure then homeward.)

Stories without me: Gilmer, Mary Caumartin.

So then I found he spoke out of his turn so I stopped talking to him.

7. The *SS Kim*, which displayed a banner in her clubroom: "Ahead to World Revolution."

People don't know who he is when they give him money.

You know I usta talk to dis guy who usta panhandle down in Prospect Park so then I heard he was a little queery so I stopped talkin' to him—he had funny ideas—he talked funny.

The Cop and the Taxi Man:

Is zat what it was all about?

Yeh—15 cents—an' yah . . . give dat—.

He puts in a call—.

Someone puts in a call an' we gotta come down. *You* know how it is—We gotta come down.

I met a cop an' two detectives. "*I* don't know," they say,—a little trouble in duh cohneh house.

Seated in coffee pot. Cop at lower end. A worker in kitchen of coffee pot and two taxi men.

Cop: So he says t' me—whut's d' chance a playin' it. I says play duh line—.

Bust up—So instead a' bustin' up, I says, Back, back—So I says where t' hell is dis guy goin'?

The First Episode

Prolog	500 words
Old Catawba	5000 words
The Platform	5000 words
The Train	15,000 words
Baltimore	5000 words

Fill *the train* with "exultancy and joy."

Pocket Notebook 22

April, 1934, to August, 1934

Wolfe continued to work closely under Perkins' supervision. His writing during this period was directed toward completing unfinished scenes and supplying the missing scenes in Books III, IV, and V of Of Time and the River. Because what Wolfe wrote was sometimes longer than what was needed, Perkins would cut it down. This procedure gave Wolfe a sense of futility: a feeling that what he created in the labors of the night would be thrown out by Perkins the next day. The long sequence "The Death of Stoneman Gant" was one of these disproportionate additions, but Perkins had the good sense to let it stand in its fullness.

This notebook is largely filled with outlines which show both progress and shifts in order or plan. We have omitted about half of them in order to avoid excessive repetition. The first entry is a chapter outline of the whole book, but the first two pages are missing. The items marked with an asterisk were apparently still not written.

Chapter XXI The City; The Hudson River
Chapter XXII The Southern Boys; Monty Bellamy, Jack
        Harvey *
Chapter XXIII The University
Chapter XXIV The Hotel Leopold
Chapter XXV Abraham Jones
Chapter XXVI Starwick, Joel Peirce; The River People
Chapter XXVII Conclusion of 1st year in city; Departure *
Chapter XXVIII Europe; Smoke Gold by Day, etc.
Chapter XXIX The Rhodes Scholars
Chapter XXX The House of the Far and Lost
Chapter XXXI The Three Friends
Chapter XXXII The Countess and La Marquise
Chapter XXXIII Tours; The Names of the Nation
Chapter XXXIV Riviera—Italy—The thinking of home, etc.*
Chapter XXXV England; The Lakes *
Chapter XXXVI The Ship; *Meeting with Esther

FINIS

So Far—States Used in Scenes
3 N.C.—A great deal
3 Va.
2 S.C.
2 Fla.—Web of Earth, et al.
3 Ga.—a little
2 Louisiana
3 Tenn.—a little
1½ Maryland—Gant, etc.
½ D.C.
10 Pennsylvania—Gant again
2 Arkansas—Eliza
12 New York—Death the Pd. Brother, etc.
4 Mass.—Bascom Hawke
——
48

THE DEATH OF (THE STONEMAN GANT)

Ernest Pegram: The sweet lay of the yard, the old house, and the oaks.

Mr. Campbell: something lacking, a bald frame house in a common place above the r'way yards.

Eliza's house: had in it that deftly compact character of the [sultry?] South—Women with shrill powdered faces saying "Yeah . . . Well I certainly do hope!! etc.

—dredged out of the James, the Hensleys, the Ingrams, Winstons and Reynoldses of all eternity—coarse as a chick weed (dull as a chick weed)—wondrous as the earth, drawling, murderous, savage, old.

London River
The Whore house in le rue Blondel?
In the thick yellow fog there was the creaking wheeling sound of gulls.

[*Sketch of man's head*] An Irishman who runs a diner here up st. near Luchow's. This makes him look innocent—he's really pretty rotten, much fatter, "naggier" than I have drawn him.

THE DEATH OF GANT

Things To Be Done

1. Revision of McGuire Scene.
2. Completion of working men in Gant's room scenes.
3. The Completion of Death Scenes.

It was a little after the middle of June. Spring had never been finer than it was that year. The windows of the dying man's room were open, the curtains stirring gently in the cool flowing air of mountain night, and it seemed to Helen that he could not die, that death was inconceivable. She felt an inexpressible happiness and peace.

The stunned feeble mind of the little city cipher saying "Well, it's like anything else—you know how it is."

Since Jan. 1, 1933:
    Death the Proud Brother ⎫
    The Train and The City   ⎬   70000
    No Door (Finished in Feb.) ⎭

Feb. to April 1933:
    Return Home, Flight from Home, etc.   200,000
       (200,000 words)
    The Four Lost Men ⎫
    Dark in the Forest, etc. ⎬   25,000
    Flight Before Fury   80,000
    Boston   ⎫
    Starwick ⎪
    The Names of the Nation ⎬   300,000
    The Death of Gant ⎪
    Etc. etc. etc.   ⎭
        Between seven and eight hundred thousand words

March 1931—Returned from England.
March to October 1931—Marj. Dorman's, etc.:
    (Much writing: results later—Death the Proud Brother, etc.)
Nov. 1931–Jan. 1932:
    Bascom Hawke
Jan.–March: The Web of Earth.
April, May, June, etc.: The Man on the Wheel.

Sept.–October: May in the City, etc. (trip to Bermuda, etc.)
November, December, Jan., 1933:
    Death
    Beginning of river and city, etc.

Amt. Published:

Bascom Hawke	
Web of Earth	
Train	70
Death	
No Door	
The Four Lost Men	50
Boom Town	
Dark in the Forest	
Sun and Rain	43
The House of the Far	
	163,000 words

Written Since Jan. 1, 1934—250,000.
Between Jan. 1, 1933 and Jan. 1, 1934:

The Train and the City	
Death T.P.B.	70,000
No Door	
Return and Flight from Home	200,000
Morning, Jacobs, Esther etc.	40,000
	310,000
	250,000
	500,000

    Over 600,000 words.

A man with a grey hat looking in a plate glass window in America.

DEATH OF THE STONEMAN GANT

Outline
1. How long Gant had been _____.
2. Scene with McGuire and Helen.*
3. Gant begins to bleed.

4. ¶ through day up to evening; Gant accepts death.*
5. McGuire comes: McGuire in Hospital.
6. The Pentlands and the workingmen.
7. The workingmen in Gant's chamber.*
8. Helen and others, Gant asleep.*
9. Gant's Dream.*
10. Gant's Death.

His Death had gone back through so many deaths of winter in a little town when there is nothing at night but the moving of wind among the bare boughs of a barren street, the creak and stealthy flicker of the corner lamps, something that moves in the wind. And the death had had its wintry way of horror through her soul.

How can we sun our flesh here in America?

Marjorie Marsh
The tunnels of New York—Down in the tunnels, April above and song, down in the tunnels of New York fear, venom, cruelty, filth and sweat.

Deaths: Gant's, McGuire's, A Man in the Street's.
Births: an unknown child's.
Fights, Brawls, Cuttings, etc.: Fight with police in Blackstone.
Whores, etc.: Whores in Boston, New York, Troy, England, France.

[*A list of the names of his typists and the number of words each one typed.*]

The members of Professor Hatcher's celebrated course in play-writing were as follows:

1) Mr. Carson: a y'g man with a withered left hand and a penchant for acting; his father was a prominent Chatauqua leader from one of the richer Pennsylvania colleges. Mr. Carson was bohemian.

2) Mr. Waters (Taylor): He was a young man with dark dead hair, pompadourized but in a dead dark fashion, with a dead face, dead eyes, a dead moustache, a dead body, and dead limbs. He sneered.

The Death of Gant
The Tunnel
The Death at the Leopold
The Southerners

Starwick, Joel Pierce, etc.
End of Starwick Scenes Abroad
End of Ship and Meeting with Esther
End of Leopold Scenes
Troy.

1) *Helen:* a woman who lives her *life* in the *death* of her father.

2) *Eliza:* a woman who has had a dozen lives—who is always looking ahead.

3) *Luke:* a man dissonant and broken, an American—not dead but lost since his father is gone.

4) *Eugene:* in search of his father.

5) *Starwick* the almost-artist—destroyed by the thing that should have made him.

6) The Dark Helen: a New England woman unable to come through.

7) *Esther:* The woman of power.

[*Wolfe and Aline Bernstein had not seen each other for over two years. Suddenly they were brought together once more in near tragic circumstances. Mrs. Bernstein tried to commit suicide with an overdose of sleeping pills at her summer home in Armonk. The only record among the Wolfe papers is an account jotted down by Edward Aswell when he interviewed her many years later:* "Mrs. Bernstein told me that when Wolfe finally left her, she felt that her life had come to an end, and that she attempted suicide. 'And I died, you know,' she said. 'I was completely gone for three days, but they worked over me and brought me back.' She said she was in a hospital in White Plains for the better part of a summer following this event, because as an aftermath of her suicide attempt, she had pneumonia and pleurisy. She said that Wolfe visited her in the hospital."

Whether Wolfe's two-year absence was the sole cause or not is uncertain. However, she did write him a letter at this time from Smoky Hollow Lodge in Washington, Connecticut, on June 8, 1934, in which she told Wolfe that she had gone to a sanitarium where she would be able to break down and weep to express the grief of her life and not have to go through the pretense of happiness for the sake of people around her. She declared that she had gone through a terrible emotional ordeal since they had parted and that she had lost all her beauty.

Wolfe did not reply.]

[*A list of European and American cities and their populations, with the heading:* "Where have I been?"]

[*A list of American states and European countries (and their populations) which the wandering hero visits in* Of Time and the River.]

[*A long list of "Boston Scenes" in* Of Time and the River.]

Girls

"Hello—How are yuh, dear," she would say in a low, husky, somewhat hoarse voice: "Where yuh been keepin' yerself?" etc.—her [clever?] bubbs would touch his hands and he would be mad with lust to have her.

What is it that we feel when riding in a train—it is that thing we feel when we are driving through Pennsylvania in May; the thing that we feel when we are coming back at evening through Western Maryland, the thing we feel when we hear the sigh of the [elm?] tops in the street in leafy June; the thing we felt when we remembered Memphis, a train that rumbled around the Mississippi, and the green lights at night on wharves sunk low in swamps. And what is that thing: it is the ungraspable joy; the unknown lyre, the nameless joy.

It is literal and immortal and intense; it means that when we hear the lovely woman down below stir in silken drowsy warmth her sensual legs—it means that somehow in a [forest?] we will be with her.

Taylor: He had the look that one sometimes sees in young men who have moustaches, and are dead, and in a coffin. His brown-blue-black hair had a late full look of death and his hands were small and phthisique.

Concede now and confess: What is the look of maidens that we're looking for?

Complete
1) Starwick, Joel, River People—Going abroad scenes.
2) Conclusion of Starwick-Helen-Elinor scenes in Paris.

   3) Lake District Scenes.
     In Part: Hotel Leopold.

Tonight, Thursday, June 14:
   Go home. Get notebooks ready for typing.
   Material that can be used.
     1) Notes on Loose Paper
     2) Notes in Ledgers
     3) Notes in Notebooks
   Tonight. Get notes on loose paper ready.

THE RIVER PEOPLE

1. The Ride Up the River

2. Joel meets him at station
3. The Estate and the House
4. The River People
5. Lunch at "Granny's"
6. Fourth of July at Astor's.

What Is Now Ready for Proof:
   Coming of the Train
   The Train
   Baltimore
   The Faustian Life
   Meeting with Mr. Bascom Pentland
   Starwick
   The Playwriting Classes
   Professor Hatcher
   Sunday at Bascom's
   Food
   Drink
   Miss Darling: Oswald Ten Eyck
   Spring in Boston: Bascom
   The Boston Irish
   Death and Time
   The Death of Gant
   A Conversation with Starwick
   Return Home.

All Possible Necessary Scenes: [1]

Baltimore:	Hospital
	Dinwood Bland
En Route:	The Guy
	The Great City—First Impression
Boston:	The Southerners
	Bascom's Children
Return Home:	Barton and Day
The City:	The River People
	End of Leopold
	The Instructors
	The Southerners
Abroad:	London River
	London
	The Riviera
	The Lakes
	End of Voyage

Between here and subway—June 20:

Children playing on Remsen Street. Perhaps some friends saying goodbye on steps of brownstone house. Taxis coming by up Henry and taxis driving past down Clinton. A woman with a severe, hostile face living in basement area of brownstone house. A young Jew and Jewess sauntering along [young Jewishly?]. Brooklyn nondescripts going down Henry-Clinton towards South Brooklyn—small, nondescript looking Italians, or nondescript looking Armenians. Jews standing around corner of Joralemon and Clinton at drug store. Young Jews and Jewesses sitting, standing, sprawling outside school there. Subway ins and outs and Borough Hall bums—old men broken, rough, pale.

NEW YORK

The University
The Leopold
Abe Jones
Troy
Starwick
The River People
Voyage

1. It is not clear what Wolfe means, but most of the scenes do not appear in OT&R.

EUROPE

Oxford
The Rhodes Scholars
The House
Starwick and Elinor and Helen
The Restaurants
The Countess
The Names of the Nation
The Lakes
The Ship

1) October.
2) Eliza's Talk about writing; Eliza's motor car.
3) Quarrel with Helen and Eliza about writing; letter comes.
4) Ride down mountain; arrest and fight with police.
5) Scene in cell: Conversation with Robert and Ernest Blake—Luke comes to release them.
6) Out in street: Scene in cafeteria with Luke.
7) On the road: unrest in Luke's life.
8) Trip back into mountains.

[*At this point Wolfe lists the names of seventy-one "New Characters" who appear in his book.*]

The Way They Had of Talking:
  Steubens to 7th Ave.
  "But then, I mean, there's *nothing* you can *do-o* about it."
  "But naturally! But of course!" etc.
  Why did they run one another down so—with each new person —with this air of great sincerity, candour, and directness? And if they ran each other down in this way to each acquaintance or newcomer, why should he, too, not feel that he would not be run down, sneered at, lied about, and betrayed with this appearance of sincerity, candour, and honest, frank and open directness?
  "It was *wonderful*." "He wants to sho-o-ow that."
  What made the young people so false, cheap, spurious and vindictive in America at this time?
  But that's—that's the tragedy of the thing, I mean there's nothing you can do-o about it!" etc.

Elizabeth Lemmon, Welbourne, Middleburg, Va.[2]

Steubens to 7th Ave.

To left of Steubens—Mayfair Coffee Shoppe—A man with a burned blistered or stuck out horrible lip inside—a wall of green—A platinum whore coming by the end light.

Radio—a taxi in front of Steubens playing violently.

Several night-time men in front of Coffee Potte—one with battered nose, blue denim, and ah-f'r-Chris'-sake manner—another with little weasel-rat face and white canvas shoes.

"You know . . . duh girls dat would . . . call up duh guy." etc.

The Brass Rail 48–49 Broadway—The night time faces—a thick young waiter of Italian (Jew) face with rolled swarthy lips, large dark corrupted eyes, grease-hair curly parted in middle—thick lines.

"What is dat? . . . creme de coco. . . . Whuts duh mattuh . . . is duh rice puddin' out?"

Behind bar young German waiter—Amer.—soft young face by right arm—blonde—high-hatted him.

THE CITY

1) Prolog: The Hudson River
2) The University
3) The Hotel Leopold
4) Abe Jones
5) The City
6) Troy
7) The River People
8) Starwick: Jason's Voyage
9) Conclusion.

[*At this point Wolfe sets down a list of the women with whom he has had sexual relations in the United States and the states in which they were born.*]

2. Elizabeth Lemmon, a friend of Maxwell Perkins, invited Wolfe to visit her estate, "Welbourne," in Virginia. He stopped off there in the fall on the way back from a trip to Chicago. Later he included a scene at "Malbourne" among his nighttime sketches for "The Hound of Darkness."

The People: How d'you get to Columbus Street? Hello, Eddy. Whatya say, man?

To Be Written:
1. Revision of Train
2. Conclusion of Dinwood Bland
3. The Hospital Corridor
4. The Guy
5. First View of the City
6. Boston: Rooms
7. The Hunger—waitress—Day by Day
8. The Playwriters—Taylor, Dodd, Wallace, Ferry
9. Professor Hatcher and Starwick
10. Starwick
11. Bascom's Children
12. The City; The Southerners
13. End of Leopold
14. The Instructors
15. The River People
16. The Voyage Out
17. London; River; Fog
18. The Channel; Train to Paris, Rhodes Scholars
19. First month in Paris, Thirst and Hunger.

One night on Subway going to Brooklyn (Temp 90° today—3 o'clock in morning).

1) A huge pot-bellied fat-assed German of 40 or 45—seen several times—cheap blue shirt—a pair of incredibly greasy trousers (looks like he did live in them when he walks) face of a great beer-bloated body.

2) An old man with long face and straight blade nose, a big face [smaller?] in the front—pale wasted chin—eyes lightly blue—a straight slit mouth with its look of humble petition.

3) A Jew with reddish hair—fat—red face—young—spectacles —thick fat lips—fat hands—picks nose, reads papers—white shoes and socks—a sort of light machine made trouser with lighter stripe.

4) A girl—Swede—thick face asleep adrool—with bunch of blonde hair.

Pocket Notebook 23

October, 1934, to November, 1934

Wolfe made almost no entries in his notebook during the fall. In fact, most of the pages are blank, and he probably replaced it because it began to fall apart. The last portions of Of Time and the River *had been sent to the printer while he was off on a two-week excursion to the Chicago World's Fair at the end of September, and he was now doing no writing. He was just recovering from fatigue and from the emotional stress of letting the book out of his hands. The only look forward which appears in the notebook is the projection of a sketch about an interchange with someone pretending to be a newspaper reporter and one about a trip to Pennsylvania to visit his father's birthplace at York Springs which he had made in October, 1932.*[1]

---

1) When you told me we were finished I didn't know what to do, etc.

2) What I did.

3) Got on the train—Trip to Harrisburg—the lights of night in America looked spare and lonely and my head began to clear and I began to get peace—the peace that comes from the powerful motion of a train, etc.—conductor on the train etc.

4) Meeting Jim[2] at paper office—trip to Brant's Mill, etc.

5) The Pow-Wow.

6) Charley Wolf's death.[3]

The next day the notice Scribner's had sent out appeared in the papers and the telephone began to ring. The first call was from a man named Ellis Winteringham DeKaye.

"Did you see what Sinclair Lewis said about you in the Herald Tribune?" said Ellis Winteringham DeKaye.

He told me that he was a reporter on the World-Telegram and the story certainly sounded all right, except that he was one of the

1. Wolfe describes this trip in detail in a letter to his mother, January 11, 1933, LTM, pp. 192–93.

2. Nickname of Wolfe's cousin, Edgar Wolf, son of his uncle Gilbert Wolf.

3. Wolfe's cousin Charles, son of his uncle George Wolf, who lived in Dellsburg near York Springs, died a day or two after Wolfe's arrival.

most respectably and well dressed reporters I ever saw. Later, however, I learned that he had been a bootlegger on the Heights for the past six years and that he was now a salesman in the liquor store and that this World-Telegram story was one that he told to strangers when he was drunk.

Saturday night
Departure.
The Trip to the West.
Dramatis Personae:
  Willis DeKaye
  The Liquor Salesman
  The Greek at Eton Grill
  Joe the waiter at the Lobster
  The Hollywood writer
  The men in Steuben's
  The waiters along B'way
  The men unloading pigs
  Steve and Paul.

The Trip
The conductor on way to Harrisburg
Jim, Aunt Mary, Dorothy [4]
The Pow-Wow
The Death of Geo. Wolf.

[*A tabulation of the women with whom Wolfe had had sexual relations* "since coming back 3½ years ago."]

George was a young man who was very smug, very smart and very assured. Every day he ate his lunch at a cheap little restaurant in the Boulevard St. Germain where for 6f50 one got a meal from soup to nuts and a very small carafe of sour red wine. George was not in any sense of the word passion's slave. He was not one of the young men of that time who got drunk at the Dome or the Rotonde or hit gendarmes on the nose or riotously ejected. George was sure of himself. He did not make a fool of himself. If he had [*breaks off*]

[*During the year Mrs. Bernstein continued to write letters to Wolfe. On August 13, she had written from her summer home in*

4. Aunt Mary was Gilbert Wolf's widow; Dorothy was their daughter.

*Armonk that her money was gone—she was down to $8.11. The
Bernsteins were at the time trying to sell their summer home. On
November 4, she wrote Wolfe from her apartment in the Hotel
Gotham that she was going to California with Aline McMahon. The
following draft in Wolfe's notebook was probably written in response
to the November letter, but he did not send her any message at this
time.*

Once or twice I have read that you were assisting a successful
B'way playwright in the production of plays full of indignation over
the oppression of the worker by his capitalist exploiters—When I hear
that you or your playwright friend have experienced real hardships or
known hunger or cold I may be convinced by your sincerity—You put
up a poor whining mouth in your letters about being "broke" and
having lost your money—Well, being broke in the understanding of
most of us does not mean apartments at the Gotham Hotel and buying
homes in Westchester County and trips to California—My own people
fought in the wars of this country and helped settle it and have
endured all its poverty and danger and suffering. You and your kind
who belong to an alien and disloyal race have fought in none of our
wars and done none of the building or working or pioneer work that
made the country. I have often heard you and your kind sneer at this
country and at its people—my own people—and talk of our ignorance
and crudity and babbittry—Well, if it had not been for us there would
have been no rich pickings for smooth soft-handed German Jews who
were able to exploit simple ignorant people through dishonest speculations and by so doing keep their wives and daughters in Park Avenue
apartments and able to entertain select gatherings of Lesbians, pederasts, and other vicious people that are spawned out of the theatre.]

Pocket Notebook 24

ca. November, 1934, to ca. February, 1935

Toward the end of the year Wolfe struggled without success to correct proofs. He simply did not want to let the book go and insisted that he needed another six months to add sections which would clarify his intentions. Finally, John Hall Wheelock had to be called in to complete the proof-reading, and the only concession to Wolfe's insistence on further writing came when Perkins agreed that some sense of conclusion and connection with the subsequent volume was needed. It was in this way that Wolfe created Book VII, "Kronos and Rhea: The Dream of Time," [1] *and the scene in which Eugene first sees Esther on board ship at Cherbourg. Wolfe's other activity of the period was more mechanical: he tinkered with the manuscript, he played with chapter headings and a dedication, and he spent time with Elizabeth Nowell revising rejected eposodes so that they might be used for magazine publication. He also wrote a long introduction about how the book came into being, which Scribner's did not use and which later formed the basis of* The Story of a Novel.

Since he was still not using his notebook for regular entries, Pocket Notebook 24 is almost as sparse as the previous one.

August 1903—Saluda Mt'n

June 1904—Pantry in St. Louis—Forest

Feb. 1908—[*page torn*] Alabama—en route to New Orleans—the *haunted forest*.

Moving the fall, the winter, the spring of the years 1906, 07, 08, 09, 10—The tolling bell of the Plum St. School.

Earth in the month of March (1907)—the fall of the house of [Pertny?] and Ollie Mercle, the big strong brute—bully of the neighborhood running beside it twisting his big hands like a demented thing and crying O papa—O papa, papa, papa—O papa, papa, papa.

1. In place of "Kronos and Rhea," the proof sheets show a Book VII entitled "Faustus and Helen." Wolfe took material from the end of Book VI, expanded it, and wove into it two separate thematic word fugues about time. This recasting makes the episode of Eugene's recapture of lost time more truly climactic.

November 1904—Knoxville, Tennessee—Papa and mama on the platform following the coffin.

O America, America.

[*Some pages missing here.*]

. . . was in an affectionate mood he waved his napkin in the air and put one hand on the back of my chair and said intimately: "Listen, Mr. Wolfe—you have your drink. You sit here as long as you like, and if you're here until two o'clock it doesn't matter, if you're here until three o'clock, it doesn't matter. We'll stay open until you're ready to go, and if you're here all night it doesn't matter."

Sitting beneath trees in Arles—Marseilles sees Starwick.[2]
St. Raphael—"Each day he had lunch" etc.
Venice—Englishman from Java.
Milano—the abbey by moonlight.
Switzerland—The Englishman—The man in the café.
Dijon—He thinks of home.[3]
Paris—(?)
London.
The Lakes.

An extraordinary thing happened. He suffered from one of those astonishing suspensions of the will which were to be frequent in his life, and which were common in the life of most men but which had never before held such a sway and mastery, or for so long a period in his life. For six weeks he found himself powerless to do a single act which would release him from the limbo of this terrible inaction in which his life was held. The year had ended—the Harvard year that was to have been the limit of his mother's gift. Now he found himself unable to move or eat.

Why could he not go home? His shoes in ragged soles and tatters.

A feeling of horrible insecurity.

The two old maids who fed him.

The Irish negress.

He was at that time of man's youth when the very fierceness of his desire will make a history.

2. This material was developed to become OT&R, pp. 881–87.
3. This is the scene in which Eugene hears the bells of Dijon and achieves his transcendence of time.

TO

MAXWELL EVARTS PERKINS

A great editor, and a brave and honest man, who stuck to the writer of this book through times of utter hopelessness and doubt and would not let him give in to his own despair, the dedication of a work to be known as *Of Time and the River* is offered with the hope that it may be in some part worthy of the devotion, skill, the loyal and unshaken friendship that was given to it, and without which it could never have been written, with the hope that all of it may be in some part worthy of the loyal faith, the skill, the patience and devotion, without which none of it could ever have been written, and which were given to it always by a great editor and a brave and honest man.

> Look Homeward, Angel
> Of Time
> Book of Stories
> The October Fair
> The Hills Beyond Pentland
> The Death of the Enemy
> Book of Stories
> Far Pacific
> Book of the Night.[4]

I believe that a work that causes a tremendous expenditure of man's spiritual and mental energy may cause temporarily a powerful derangement in his nervous and physical self as well. This happened to me. The reason for this would seem to me to be apparent. The creation of a work in art demands depth and fertility in experience, largeness and wholeness of conception, and profundity of scope. But in execution, it demands the intensest concentration, the most absolute expenditure of energy that life knows. The artist in his perception may be a man of the greatest and most compassionate understanding, but the artist at work may be a kind of maniac.

Like the Ancient Mariner—am wracked with a woeful agony.

These five books which are to be known successively as **Of Time and the River, The October Fair, The Hills Beyond Pentland,**

---

4. This list represents Wolfe's view of his publications over the next few years.

The Death of the Enemy, and The Far Pacific, of which the first three have now been written, and of which the present volume is the first—.

[*Two drafts of the Perkins dedication have been omitted.*]

The reason I have published this piece anonymously is not that I am ashamed or afraid of anything that is here contained or would wish to change it—since here, as often in a piece written at such speed, I do not speak with the force, the eloquence, or the passionate perfection which a writer wishes to achieve. Nor am I particularly concerned lest any reader recognize the writer of this piece. I should still prefer to write it as I have, believing that it gains in force by anonymity—that its general truth is more important than its particular and that what happened to me is typical of the experience of a million.

[*The next entry is the first outline or plan of an important fictional project, entitled "The Book of the Night" or "The Hound of Darkness," which Wolfe worked on intermittently over the next few years. The basic idea was to present a series of scenes representative of the variety of American life, scenes which take place simultaneously all over the country. Sometimes it is a night in the 1930's and sometimes it is 1912. This material underwent various changes and remained incomplete at Wolfe's death. Only one part of it, "Prologue to America," was published in his lifetime.*]

AMERICA 1934

A lodging house in Washington.
A Communist editor in Greenwich Village.
A woman with seven children in a South Carolina town.
A German professor's family on the outskirts of Chicago.
A plantation in Virginia.
A Farmhouse in Vermont.
A Milkman in Brooklyn at 3:30 in morning.
Seven whores at Troy, New York.
The conductor of a train going across Indiana.
An all night Coffee Pot in Brooklyn.
A Junction town in Ohio.
A witches' pow-pow in Pennsylvania.
An old woman in North Carolina.
The Cop in the hot dog stand in Boston.

The freezing moonlit ice-glazed grade coming across New Jersey.

You could not say along the road the sea was there.

This is A-a-a—delaide.

Night Piece.

$$\begin{array}{r} 365 \\ 44 \\ \hline 1460 \\ 1460 \\ \hline 16060 \end{array}$$ [5]

30 The Web of Earth
8 The Four Lost men
3 One of the Girls
5 The German Train
8 In the Park
5 The Circus
10 The Locusts Have No King.[6]

Saturday Night.[7]

Feb.—1935
Sept.—1935
Feb.—1936
Feb.—1937.[8]

TO

MAXWELL EVARTS PERKINS

A loyal and unshaken friend and a brave and honest man who stuck to the writer of this book through times of utter hopelessness and

---

5. Wolfe was here calculating the number of days Mrs. Bernstein had lived when he met her in 1925, or the number of days Maxwell Perkins had lived when he met him in 1929.

6. The significance of this list of Wolfe's works and the number of thousand words in each is not clear. He may have been beginning a tentative list of short pieces to include in his planned "Book of Stories," which was scheduled for publication in the fall of 1935. "The German Train" refers to "Dark in the Forest, Strange as Time." "The Locusts Have No King" is a title Wolfe gave to several different portions of manuscript over the years, most of which had to do with life in Brooklyn. See Richard S. Kennedy, *The Window of Memory*, p. 428, for identification of these various pieces.

7. "Saturday Night in America" was another title for "The Book of Night."

8. A tentative schedule of publication for Wolfe's projected works.

doubt and would not let him give in to his own despair, a work to be known as *Of Time and the River* is dedicated, with the hope that all of it may be in some manner worthy of the devotion, skill and patient care which a great editor gave to each part of it [*and*] without which none of it could have been written.

Mrs. Jelliffe [9]
Typewriter
East 59th St. 2nd or 3rd block Underwood Portable.

Hamilton Basso [10]
403 W 21 St.

People in 5 Years since L.H.A.:
Scribners: Max, Jack, Dashiell, Darrow, Wally, Weber, Charley, Scheffler, Georgie, Mrs. Dewey, Cross, Young Georgie, Old C.S.S., Arthur, Will Howe, Coney.
Europe: Frere, Manx, Old Man Roberts, Daisy Lavis, Boleslovsky [*Belilovsky*], Mrs. Elstob, Mrs. Litvanoff, Mrs. Carswell, Carswell, Son, Tom McGreevy, Aldington & Wife, Scott, Julian Van Cortlandt.
Brooklyn: M. Dorman, Old Man Dorman, Roberta, The Mother, The Nephew, H. Hoppe.
Mabel's Washington: Hardin, Salline, Mrs. Price (everywoman), Chaput

Minor Figures:
101 Columbia Heights: Clark, His Wife, His Son, Wakefield.
111 Columbia Heights: The Janitor, His Wife.
5 Montague: Old Bradford, His Daughter, Gunther, His Wife,

9. Belinda Jelliffe, the beautiful and vivacious wife of the psychiatrist Dr. Smith Ely Jelliffe, came to know Wolfe simply by writing him a letter praising his work. She was working on an autobiographical novel based on her early years in the Southern Appalachians, *For Dear Life* (New York, 1936). Wolfe helped her to place the book with Scribner's by introducing her to Perkins. In the Wisdom Collection there is a copy inscribed to Wolfe: "Most grateful for your friendship and encouragement." The address in this notebook entry indicates the occasion on which she offered to give him a typewriter.

10. Basso, the New Orleans newspaperman and novelist, first met Wolfe in the Scribner's office in the spring of 1935. Their friendship developed, however, after Basso wrote "Thomas Wolfe: A Portrait," an article which appeared in the *New Republic,* June 24, 1936, and which praised Wolfe's work highly as "legendary autobiography."

The Bum, His Wife, Severson, His Wife, The Norwegian, His Wife, Their "Niece."

Steve's Place: Steve, Carl, "Schnabel Redshirt," Taxi Men.

York Springs: Jim, Aunt Mary, Dorothy, Mrs. Charley Wolf, Harry, The Schoolteacher, The Old Witch, Her Husband, Her Son, Old Mrs. Jacobs.

PART SEVEN

ANOTHER LOOK AT EUROPE

Pocket Notebook 25
March, 1935

Of Time and the River *was scheduled for publication on March 8. But since Wolfe felt that his book was really an unfinished product, he feared that reviewers might hold him up to public ridicule. It was an assembly of chunks, uneven in quality but with magnificent narrative and declamatory material scattered throughout. Its astonishing variety —in subject matter, in tone, in form—gave it an encyclopedic nature, placing it in that area of fiction which Northrop Frye has labeled "anatomy" or perhaps establishing by its uniqueness a new fictional genre. Since there had never been anything quite like it in English or American literature, Wolfe was really risking his literary reputation, and the tension drove him to make plans to sail to Europe on March 2.*

But the book was unfinished in another way too: at the end, the narrative was left hanging. To ward off criticism on this point, Wolfe placed an announcement opposite the half title that the book was part of a larger whole:

"This novel is the second in a series of six of which the first four have now been written and the first two published. The title of the whole work, when complete, will be the same as that of the present book, 'Of Time and the River.' The titles of the six books, in the order of their appearance, together with the time plan which each follows, are:

Look Homeward, Angel (1884–1920).
Of Time and the River (1920–1925).
The October Fair (1925–1928).
The Hills Beyond Pentland (1838–1926).
The Death of the Enemy (1928–1933).
Pacific End (1791–1884)."

Just before Wolfe left New York he sent a prepublication copy to Aline Bernstein. He marked for her the passage on page 911 in which Eugene sees Esther on the ship: "He turned, and saw her then, and so finding her, was lost, and so losing self, was found, and so seeing her, saw for a fading moment only the pleasant image of the woman that perhaps she was, and that life saw. He never knew: he only knew that from that moment his spirit was impaled upon the knife of love," *and he wrote beside it simply* "my dear."

> *This notebook begins in Paris on March 11 and ends in London near the end of the month. The handwriting in this notebook is scarcely decipherable, for Wolfe was drinking heavily day after day to subdue his anxiety over the critical reception of his book.*

Mimi, 2me aire, 16—pass. Rue Blondel.

Sunday–Monday morning [*March 10–11*] (3:50 A.M.):
Written in my room in Rue St. Honoré—outside all quiet as death save for small incessant dripping of the rain—arrived Paris, St. Lazare, Friday night [*March 8*] about 7:40—Terrific tumult at station —porters charging back and forth—frantic efforts to get taxi etc.— Porter who tripped over my baggage and got nasty fall—sympathetic cries and ejaculations of French women whose baggage he was carry- ing—then in taxi here to hotel—First experiences of great crowded Paris after 4 yrs.—the changeless change of Paris and the French— Back of buses with people hanging over—looking out on life with Gallic snarls—Cafés—eternal figure of the waiter with his long white apron—the eternal whore sitting within—the eternal people meeting —swift kaleidoscope of streets—got me mixed up—saw back of Made- leine, thought it was front—all unfamiliar—then suddenly Rue Royale and Rue St. Honoré—the curious *smell* of Paris—at once seductive, enervating, langorous—somehow filled with something dark and cruel and terrible.
Friday night—left hotel and "went the rounds" to see if places were still there—went to Adega—the smooth slick [French?] and whore begged in ribaldry—4 cocktails—Grand Vatel—one—Mont- marte in taxi looking for Marianne's—couldn't find it—Had Chou- croute at Graff's—Harry's New York bar—cashed checks (2 I think)— Place Louvois in taxi—went to swell whorehouse but departed after haggling over price—then to whorehouse Rue du Moulins—lay with big blonde—then home.
Sat. [*March 9*] slept until 3'oclock—went to Weber's for Per- nod on terrace—talkative waiter who kept exclaiming over cold—later to Taverne-Royale where ate—then to American Express—got there too late—then to Wetzel's—then to Café de la Paix—then to Rue Blondel—went in but did nothing—then for a walk through quarter— out on boulevard again—then to Montparnasse—walked Select, Dome, etc.—then save for interlude at New York Bar all goes blank—can't remember eating or how I got home.
Today [*March 10*]—Up at four terribly shaky—bathed, shaved,

dressed—out to Weber's terrace for picon—then to Taverne-Royale for fines à leaux then to Brasserie Universelle—then to look in Brentano's window—then to terrace of Café de la Paix for fines à leaux— then to La Cigogne for first food I can remember since Saturday at Taverne-Royale—wonderful dinner of snails, chicken, white Alsacian wine, tart with cream and quetsch—but took up all my remaining money—over 60 francs—so home down Rue Duphot—along Rue St. Honoré—and now in bed.

Have $710 in checks left—Have used up $70 in checks since I left N.Y. 9 days ago—this includes tips to stewards on boat, railway fare 2nd class from Havre (103 francs), taxi fares, porters' tips, etc.

A wet grey dreary rain-drippy day—*wetness* has a peculiar deadly penetration—explains perhaps the caution of people here—not sitting on Café terrace etc.—the cold, *stealthy* and *insidious*. The ground still swaying below me like a ship—not over rocking of the boat yet although 2½ days have passed—March coming—something about the changelessness of the French—the incredibly beautiful and varied tapestry of earth between Le Havre and Rouen—then the approach to a great city—the lights of Paris.

Monday [*March 11*]—Vetzel's Cafe opp. left side of Opera 3:50 P.M.:
A night of dream-projected realities—horror and madness— awoke bathed in cold *grease-sweat*—left hotel at 2:00—so up Rue St. Honoré and up cross street in Opera—cashed $10.00 check at Banque Americale du Nord (?) 149 fr.—then to Brasserie Universelle—one pernod—2 fines à leaux—walked here across [strange?] Place de l' Opera and now here at Vetzel's with another fine à leau—no lunch— no breakfast—facing "grand test" at the American Express Co. a few minutes now—and if the news is horribly *bad?*—and if there is no news —*nothing?*

[*What he found was a cable from Perkins: "Magnificent reviews, somewhat critical in ways expected, full of greatest praise." But he brooded over that second phrase for two days and finally cabled desparately for further word.*]

Dear Max:
I can can face blunt fact better than damnable incertitude. You are the best and truest friend I have. Give me the straight plain truth. Let me have it.

TOM

Wed.–Thur. March 13–14:

The deadly little place—I am here at one o'clock in the morning (or more) at Café near the Régence (next, I think, to it, in front)— Today one of the strangest and most terrible days of my life—My head reels—I think from *ship*—perhaps from *drink* (although I have not drunk near as much as in New York)—the count is about as follows—Arose at one o'clock—(1) whiskey at Adega Bar (13F) at 2–3:00—Two or Three amer picons at Régence—3:30–4:20—2 (or 3?) fines at Café de la Paix at 5:30—(?)—(Resolved to take nothing more) —got taxi and went to Mrs. Beach [1] (had impulse to take drink before seeing her)—saw her, did take drink—Went to Mrs. Massey's (who had called at 10 or 11—I was in strange, ship (?)-dizzy state and arrived foolishly)—Drove from there to Lipp, had cervelas and (1) beer—from there to Prunier's (oysters and (1) glass Cognac)—from there to hotel where slept 3 hrs.—and now out to Régence and next place—where (3) fines.

Later (written at 5 A.M. in morning in my hotel room in Rue St. Honoré)—(Grande street)—went to Harry's New York Bar—drank only beer—told them (Bob—"Mr. Allen"—Roy-etc.) that I was sorry for last night—this upon recollection that I called someone ("Mr. Allen" or Roy) a son of a bitch—and that Bob said, "Now you're out of order—that's the only time you ever have been out of order but you are now"—so I apologized for what I had said—I can remember little of what happened last night—I wanted to fight "Mr. Allen"—and suspect there was something objectionable about him—Bob said it was all right and all over—They all seemed good enough—but I have a big bruise toward right front hip bone—It is like something a drunk man would get knocking into handle or some other hard object—can not remember being hit or where I got it. Bob said, "Nothing ever happens to you in here"—Feeling of ship-dizziness continues—a little less drinking today—Heart beating at high speed—Do not go back to New York Bar.

[*Perkins' reassuring cable was sent March 14: "Grand excited reception in reviews, talked of everywhere as truly great book, all comparisons with greatest writers, enjoy yourself with light heart."*]

Thursday–Friday, March 14–15—2:55 A.M.:

Today the grand wonderful beautiful news came—had dinner with Mrs. Massey—left around midnight—walked to Place St. Michel

---

1. Sylvia Beach's bookshop, Shakespeare and Co., at 12 Rue de l'Odéon, had been a gathering place for writers and intellectuals since the early 1920's. She was best known, however, as the publisher of Joyce's *Ulysses*.

and by taxi here—already feel better and believe I'll be quieted down and all right in day or two—*Rixe* [*fight*] in bistro at Place St. Michel —How cleverly they got the little man's hat and coat away from him and held it for 3 fr. bill—and threw him out—remember bistro man going over bar—Madame calling out in a shrill voice, etc.

Sunday, March 17—

Think I am on my feet today—Friday called up Eleanor Fitzgerald (Miss Whiting at Harvard) [2]—made engagement for dinner—met her at her hotel (Raphael in Avenue Kleber) she took me to fine Alsacian Rest. in Avenue Victor Hugo—had big dinner—still feeling rocky—took her to Weber's later—then back to her hotel where she gave me sleeping medicine—so walked home—drank castor oil I had bought—took some of her sleeping medicine—could not meet her for lunch the next day.

Saturday (as I had promised) called her up and told her so—still nauseated a little with castor oil—began to perk up in afternoon—about 5 o'clock out—to Régence—choucroute, Brioche, etc.—then to café on Capucines for 3 vermouths—then to Taverne-Royale for dinner—soup, échaudé, salad, ½ bottle Pommard—so home to bed.

Monday, March 18:

I was alone on Terrace of Closerie des Lilas—3 fines à leaux—knocked on window for addicion—waiter just around corner to right by semi-concealed door. *Point—I don't say he was watching me but here in France it would be hard to get away*—et puis alors—le cochon m'a eu en observance—C'est maintenant 1:27 [3]—heel taps of little dame drab clad (comme tous les autres) [4] [strangish?] person—et wooden table—chairs—rattling—nearby unending pick up of waiter.

        2me classe
          Berlin—400
          Vienna—575
          London—250
          Moscow—1000
          Copehagen—525
                      ——————
                      4000

2. Eleanor Whiting, who was enrolled in the 47 Workshop at Radcliffe, 1922–23.
3. Well, then, the pig had been watching me. It is now 1:27.
4. Like all (*toutes*) the others.

[*In the long description following, the handwriting is such a bad scrawl that many of the words we use to transcribe it are only reasonable guesses.*]

7 o'clock in the morning—Rue de Provence:

A great green motor truck half covered, with open space [*sketch*].

An ice wagon with two great wheels—one loose [*sketch*].

A "wain" with hoofs clopping, bells jingling—a-ooo-ga of taxi horn—clatter of ash cans—sweep of horns—old white long street—café—bar—smell of country—yard-long bread—new coffee—clatter of feet on street—motorcycle pump-pump by—old doors—fermé, fermé—now open—voices far—toot toot of taxi horns—an open window suddenly—an iron railing—a rubber plant—inside, sleep.

The old and the new: café—bar—new brass—silver—heavy bar—plate glass—then old hanging lines—white old blackened shutters falling nearby giant walls—woman spilling water bucket over it—front of long narrow sidewalk entrances—Pâtisserie—Glace—corner—yellowing-golding glass—weird old women—work-wrecked—shapeless, bereted—silent, saboted—going through streets with wicker baskets, bags of trash—others aproned, carrying trays of crusty croissants, brioches, etc.—[corner?] boys in denim wheeling bicycles delivering things—the great strange leather purse at side—Rue de Mogador—Rue de Provence—au coin [*on the corner*].

Behind Opera big green buses gathering (7:07 now)—Plaisance—Porte de la Villette (Boul. Haussmann et Rue Scribe)—Bus marked, Partir et au delà, another Le Bourget, another Jardin des Plantes.

The queer smoky bright light of Paris in morning—young Frogg in leather coat [belted?] pumps past on motorcycle—old man with whiskers bearing bottle—another old man caped and capped (pocket with leather bag beneath)—boy pumps by on tricycle piled with great wicker baskets—buses beginning now in all directions—men walking past—[(how many notice with a limp—is more definite)?] two fellows here aproned, dragging carts [*sketch*]—big horses—Denigrets Laversey (?)—workers going by—little solid Frenchman bandy legged—cap—white scarf—heavy suit—*worker*—where—Some well dressed men—workers also—others (workers) in denim earnestly pedaling bikes—stump cigar holding in mouth.

This last in front of Amexco—Rue Auber et Rue Scribe et Place Charles Garnier—Great, smoke dingy, black thing—mass of Opera—with gold figures outside—busts and [*illegible*] Frogg with wide black hat—black whiskers—thick blunt body—paper held behind and birds going past.

Tuesday evening, March 19, 6:30:

Sitting on terrace of Café de la Paix—away from the Opera—after being up all night—awoke at 4—out of hotel about 5—then along Rue St. Honoré to Régence for Vermouth cassis—then to Amexco—no cable—found out about baggage—German Tourist checks—and so here.

The dense life of evening is passing by upon the boulevards—2 Frenchmen with faces of vultures—one with corded face of a snake in front of me—telling a story—snuffling with laughter of how an Englishman was robbed, tricked and beaten—mixture of hate, fear, and triumph. [*Sketch of man with derby and beard, with the comment:* "This does not get him."]

Suite de Tuesday, March 19 (But written in Graff's, Montmartre, M'ch 20–21, Wed.–Thurs. morning, really Thursday, at 4:23¼ AM which is 11:23¼ N.Y.) When I came in to room at 6?&7?—plastered un peu? [*a little*]—in Rue St. Honoré was going to tell all about it—but this is what happened (now skip to page marked AB).

AB Tues.–Wed. (19–20?) After leaving Café de la Paix went to Jean Casenave's in Rue Boissy D'Anglas where ate—had good dinner composed of—a good thick soup (I forget which) a turbot poché—(a la "English" but swimming in fine butter with beautiful little potatoes) —after, chicken with yellow thick sauce and rice—an apple tarte with cream—and coffee—Proprietor, waiters, all beautifully solicitous (came to 31 f?)—asked proprietor where Jean Casenave with beard was. "Il est mort, monsieur. Je suis son frère—Le vieux Jean—n'est-ce-pas?" [5]—walked to Boul. Malesherbes—near Madeleine—took taxi to Rue Faub. du Montmartre, coin des Italiens (had previously called for telephone amanach [*almanach*] at Casenave's to find L'Alcazar (the old Palace)—called waiters in consultation—one finally said—Ah-h, c'est à côté de L'Auto (which turned out to be a not very impressive bistro-café—bar-café).

Frere Reeves—Heinemann's, London.

Dear Frere:

Is England cheaper than France—money melting fast here would like to come over for week or two if possible—address Amexco Paris.

TOM WOLFE

Café de la Régence, Wednesday afternoon, March 20—about 3:30:

Two men seated two tables away talking books—either French [*sic*]—or French talking English remarkably well—one of them men-

5. He is dead, sir. I am his brother—the old Jean—all right?

tions my name, I think says my book has been getting "rather good notices" and claims to know me—acts like agent.

[*Another section of hardly legible notes:*]
Café de la Paix—6:30 (Wed. March 20):

The tide is at its full (how noble that sounds). Well, the tide is composed of a wasp-like swarm of little taxis (they've made them change their notes now from the imitating New Year's blast)—now they go hink-honk-hink and hink-honk-honk—the heavy insistent grinding of the great green buses—and in the street the people swarming by—faces of well-pleased pleasers ogling in through the glass screens of the Café de la Paix to see what they can see and find—cigarettes down-slanting in twisted mouths—dark cynic's way—jaded mouth—whores—well groomed—much care in the face—about now —old worn cynic's faces of the waiters—[wearing?] boiled shirts—half round aprons—faces somehow good—young clerky clerk-desk *quartier* chaps with pomaded hair—[and manly?] too—on café terrace —elderly women two by two—Fresh once, old and worldly—everyone is old and worldly and they know nothing—Boy hoarse Parisvoiced comes by Intrans—Intrans—Par-*ree* So-o-o-ir—Some crying [feud *formidable?*] involving perfidious Albion, perfidious Allemagne —perfidious everyone else except perfidious France.[6]

Difference between French whore and French respectable woman—whore with whore's furs and finery—respectable woman with deliberate drab dress, hat, shoes, clothing, [furs?]—but in faces of both the same large proud avarice—the "ah mais *non!*—mais c'est formidable!" pug prickly look.

Evening now—black—tainted—Frogg whiskerandoes rushing past—every now and then country—Touraine—stocky red-faced—little red-brown moustaches—full of wine and blood and choleric juice —from Tours comes by—and then of course the drab, the draggled, very beaten and obscure of life.

Characteristic gesture of well-pleased, somewhat elder, pleaser —hands behind back—cigarette gripped in firm taut lips—face of full blood—*pervertie* Gallic faint mirth and scorn.

Frere, Sunlocks, London
Taking 10:30 Sunday Train Visit Entirely Friendly and Recreational I never read a book nor heard of one and don't want to
Best wishes—TOM.

---

6. The Paris newsboy selling "L'Intransigeant" (Intrans), calling out the latest evening news—something about perfidious England and Germany.

Impressions since I Came to France (12 days ago):

1) The denimed Frenchmen waiting on quay at Havre as ship was brought to—how did she get there—suggestion of classical Frenchman with twist lips again [*some pages missing*]

(Notes in Graff)—a whore (not bad)—with "fat electric light face"—blond—marcelled—clean—millions of little ringlets colored but with bleach blond—not, I say, bad (sit sideways).

Today [*March 21*]—3:30 on:

Régence (food)—Amexco—Café de la Paix—La Cigogne—Bourse (telegraphed Frere)—walk back to Café de la Paix—Café (Italiens)—petit café (per Weber)—Donares (whorehouse)—Bistro Lazare et ici.

At my mothers' house:

Mrs. Stone.

An unknown woman with her mother.

Mrs. "Smith" (but in a way she made me pay—poetry—hah!)

[*At this point, a list of Wolfe's love affairs, 1925–35.*]

Montmartre, Pl. Blanche, 6:00 A.M. in morning—

A pearl grey light—deliberately rose expanded before me—*et* before me the Place Blanche and I suppose the Rue Blanche going down—the old houses and the chimney pots—a little broken by new tones—descending—taxis without *at wait*—and green top-flattened cylinders of Paris street-washing motors—Inside the bar—variety of night time leavings—whores—taxi drivers—still going—still wandering —work-boys in blue denim—a whore with broad black hat and face of one of Rops' women—drunk—kicking various men in ass—while others look on with disapproving. Quietly—let—us—leave—this—ai. But morning—morning!

"Ah-hah-hah-hah," he cried, shaking his finger roguishly; "I am a leetle beet late. Did you think I had forgot?" he cried and collapsed for the rest of the night upon a sofa (Café de la Paix—6:50—Thursday, March 21).

Thurs.–Fri. (March 21–22):

The Most Brief Itemage: Rose 4:00—bathed—out, Café de la Régence 5:40—Amexco (Taxi) 5:50–6:00. Café de la Paix,

6:00–6:55—(taxi) Mrs. Massey (7:20?)—et Miss Pantland (Irish-English-[Embassy person?]—Henriette, 8:00–9:30—Miss Pantland's (?) (9:30–11:00)—with Mrs. Massey to Edgar Quinet (11?) to look at old studio—there to Dome to 11:(?)–12:30—then with Mrs. Massey home—here at Miss Pantland's (1:30) (The moon is burning up here in the skies—Miss Pantland's place—Rue du 4 Septembre (Café de la Paix) etc.

A brasserie—Place du Gare Montparnasse—a drunken party going [*the remainder is illegible*]

[*Wolfe traveled to London on March 24 and stayed there until the end of April.*]

Scribners—23 Bedford Square—Museum 0730 [7]
St George's Court—corner of Hanover Square and George St. [8]

Millet Cigarette machine corner of Strand and Southhampton on Strand—put in shilling for Gold Flakes—it did not return and did not get money back—Yellow machine, patenter and mfr. The Harper Cartmaker Machine Manufacturing Co. London.

[*The notebook ends with a long list of numbers of American Express traveler's checks.*]

7. Mr. and Mrs. Charles Scribner, III, were visiting in London at this time.
8. This is the address of the flat in which Wolfe lived during his three-week stay in London.

Pocket Notebook 26

April 2, 1935, to April 29, 1935

Although Wolfe arrived in England on March 24, he made no entries in this notebook until April 2. His continued anxiety about the reception of Of Time and the River *caused him to drink heavily and seek solace in an active social life. He renewed acquaintances made during his Guggenheim stay in London five years before, and he made new ones.*

Meanwhile, the critical reception given Of Time and the River *was overwhelmingly favorable, and the mounting excitement about the book made it a best seller. Despite the fact that Wolfe still reacted sharply to any negative criticism, he was heartened by the general recognition of his achievement and the appreciation of his gifts, and some of his tension relaxed. He began to think of his next project and to jot down suggestions for future writing. As it became clear to him that his new book would establish him as a celebrity, he hit upon the idea of writing up his trip and publishing it "under some such title as "The Busman's Holiday.'" Consequently, he wrote from memory an account of his first ten days in England, and he began to keep full notes of his daily activities and random thoughts.*

Though Wolfe wrote from both ends of his notebook, we have rearranged the material in chronological order and have placed the few undated notes at the end. The handwriting in this notebook is very difficult to read because Wolfe not only continued his heavy drinking but also followed the practice of writing in bed.

Tuesday, April 2, 1935:
    (Exactly one month since leaving New York (–2 hrs)—it is now about 3 o'clock in Garrick Hotel pub restaurant—ergo 10 o'clock at New York).

[683]

THE SHIP

People I Remember (rapidly)

(*on boat*)

1. Dr. Pescosolidis (?)—Lithuanian Jewish—Worcester, Mass. Doctor.

2. Mr. G. McDonald—Young charmed in the eyes—rather sweet—melancholy—isn't-England-wonderful illustrator—for English-imitation-American film mags (takes long walks in English countryside).

3. Little French Steward at table with goatlike body and tufty hair on bald head—red vital Frog's face—standing alean with waiter gainst pitch and roll of ship.

4. The three sisters—one young with smug meaty-sensual-beautiful face—grim sisters of death they were—walking the decks towards sunset in the evening—(all reading their books).

5. The Holy Father—Hairy-red-sensual face—also walking towards sunset at a nook of deck—reading his book.

6. The Vienna Childs' Choir and their leaders—little shouting raspy voices of castrated boys—leader with thick, lank, pompadoured hair.

7. A Jewish flax-expert—look of the vulture and the reptile mixed with kindness in his face.

PARIS

(Friday, March 8–Sunday, March 24)—

(1) Elderly American-French (!) woman I talked to coming up in train—she had microscopic sets—plants, bulbs, and flowers, and lived next to Etoile station.

(2) French porter at St. Lazare who stumbled over my baggage and hurt himself.

(3) Little boy who showed me hotel rooms in Hotel St. James.

(4) The well-pleased pleasers in Adega bar—like time and forever—and the vital-but-worn young whore with them.

(5) Mr. Allen in New York Bar.

(6) Big Blonde in Rue des Moulins.

(7) Waiter on terrace of Weber's who kept looking at mercury and mulling—Ah, oui quatre degrés—Fait froid—Br-r-r! etc.

(8) Miss Sylvia Beach—with vivid concentration of white front teeth.

(9) Elmo K. Budes at American Express.

(10) Great bloated fat old humble toad of a woman with flattened nose (face of a horribly bloated and corrupt Thackeray) at Bistro corner of Fauboug Montmartre & Boul. des Italiens.

Since Jan 1, 1935—new people I can remember well:
Mrs. Jellife ⎱
Dr. Jellife ⎰ America
The Cockney waitress woman in Garrick hotel
Pat, Frere Reeves' wife
Mrs. Jellife's beautiful woman friend
Mrs. Massey

Ivy and Irving, 6 Fitzroy Square, Flat 5—Top Back—7:30 Wednesday.[1]

Between Last April and This—
10 Dingman's Ferry—May (Pennsylvania)
10 Albany—Troy—During Summer (New York)
4½ Chicago—September (Illinois)
2 Virginia—October (Virginia)
½ Washington—Christmas (D.C.)
5 France—March
10 England—April
5 Germany—April
5 Russia—May [2]

A note—10:25—Wed, April 3:
Things done to-day—up—breakfast—bath—wrote in note book —took taxi Hanover Square to meet Charles Scribner—Carlton— Scribner—his wife—their friend—American-Englishman—Hutchinson —drinks—lunch—with Chas. Scribner to Heinemann—saw Frere Reeves—old man Roberts (Re Hugh Walpole)—back with Roberts [3] to Piccadily Circus—thence to Amexco for additional *New York Times* literary ads. and "best seller" reports Time and River—then to

1. Friends whom Wolfe had met in 1930. Irving Davis operated a bookshop in Bloomsbury.
2. Wolfe's plans to visit Russia did not materialize. At this point he intended going "to Russia in time for the May Day celebrations."
3. Henry Chalmers Roberts, who was born in Texas, was for a long time editor of the London magazine, *The World's Work,* and Director of Heinemann Holdings Ltd.

Stone's Bar for Scotches—thence to various stationery stores Leicester Square district for *New Yorker*—found one with review finally—then to Soho pub for Scotches and now at Escargot Bienvenu on Greek Street.

London, Wednesday, April 3, 1935:

Have been in this country ten days—A quick summary of what I have done since coming here:—

Landed, Folkestone, about 3:30 o'clock in afternoon of Sunday, March 24—Frere Reeves waiting for me at boat Quay—Got through customs, packed baggage in his car and was driven by him through Folkestone, Hythe, etc. until we came to his house at Aldington overlooking Romney Marshes—Passed on road an actress in walking pyjamas named Jeanne de Casalis with young man whose name I do not recall and stopped and talked to them—Found Frere's wife Pat (daughter of Edgar Wallace) waiting for us outside house—went in, had tea, and then went for a walk in woods and fields below house—Fine bright day with many flowers appearing and signs of Spring everywhere—primroses out, and violets, weeding thistles from the ground—Returned to house, sat around fire in living room, had sherry, and went in to good dinner—soup, good roast beef, potatoes and green vegetable (cabbage or peas) and salad—Then a great rhubarb tart with thick cream—coffee—red wine with cheeses—went back and sat around fire and talked together until 9:30 or 10:00 and then started for London—very sleepy for first time in days—and nodded and dozed all the way up—going through Maidstone—Lewisham—Camberwell—etc.

Got up to London around midnight—they took me to Regent Palace hotel—Frere went in and got me room 9s6d bed and breakfast —Said it would be on order of "Hotel Pennsylvania, Commodore sort of thing"—but he was wrong—A gaudy, glittery, and, I thought, horribly uncomfortable place filled with Nottingham butchers and their wives or Stenographers—and Leeds, or Birmingham, or Manchester 'Erbs and Alfs and Charlies down for a bit of a spree, y'now, with baggy flannel trousers, and brown tweed coats, and very snooty, bored, casual ways—blimey, now almost as good as a bloody bleeding Camebridge bloke—The fixed pitiable deep-rooted snobbery of lower class England—But the bed room, which after all was what I had come to this glittery hostlery to find, was small, cold, miserable, cramped and cheerless—there was no heat—save that provided by a minute electric heater tucked snugly away between the bureau and the wash stand—it could provide only a small and feeble radius of heat, and when I turned it on it did not provide it—But I was dog-tired—fell asleep with my clothes on—rose presently and undressed and had the best night's sleep in weeks—So ended the first day.

Monday, March 25:
    Up and down to good breakfast in "Louis XVI room"—back to cold little bed room—talked to Pat and arranged to meet her—went to Amexco—got money but no news—met Pat at Albany—two pansy like young men—one with extraordinary face like some strange bird came in—stayed a few minutes ("Oh, no—not at all—I believe engine drivers pinch her on the bottom—that sort of thing" etc.)—they left—then good looking young woman named Mary Leveson (admiral's daughter, Pat said) and Pat's young brother—a gentle and soft-spoken youth who is an ardent worshiper Sir Oswald Mosley and Fascist dictatorship—Took them all to lunch at Escargot Bienvenu—then all out to look for flat for me—went to Duke St., Jermyn St., etc., finally to Hanover Square—Miss Leveson left us—drove back to Albany with Pat and brother—talked and had tea—then left—went back to hotel—called up Mrs. [*Catherine*] Carswell—found her out—had coat repaired—was invited to Hampstead by Mrs. Carswell—had dinner at Stone's—steak, old ale, Stilton, cabbage, etc.—then to Hampstead by bus—saw Mrs. Carswell, Donald, and son John, now a tall young man of 17—sombre Russian looking young woman with passionate, smouldering face and strange accent who sat by fire and poked it, and turned out to be Scotch—talked of Russia—"*Lor-rence*" etc.—in kind of tone and weathering of their life, a "we are betrayed" attitude—a precious-Hampsteady-aesthetey-defeatism—"Ah, the same old crowd, eh, Tom—now with your success you'll do so-and-so"—and so home by taxi down from Hampstead at 12:30—Had two drinks in gilt-gold-splendor lounge of Regent Palace—eagerness of Nottingham butchers, etc. with broad bottomed wives in evening clothes—great elegance going gradually to vulgarity—"the gentleman's very eloquent and very charming address"—etc.—descending to "You don't know who Epstein is."
    "Of course I now 'oo Epstein is."
    "Nah yer down't—Yer been talkin 'ere all night about 'is theory of relativity an' you can't tell us what 'is theory o' relativity *is*"—etc.
    Meanwhile, one woman taunting her husband with screams of laughter—"Look at 'is fyce!"—cruel-woman's-business—when he is goaded too far and says too much—" 'Ere! 'Ere! Mind what yer syein," —etc.

"Relativity—I'll tell yer what it is—Relativity!—I know a *proper* man when I sees one—Now some folks lookin' at yer head, my friend, my think that yer was *bald*—but *me? Nah-h!* When I looks at yer head I sees a fine 'ead o' 'air—*That's* relativity."

" 'Ere! 'Ere! Mind wot yer syein!" etc.—It got painful to watch —so to bed—Thus ended *Second* day.

Notes for Diary

March 21—Today got a letter from Max and a large number of typed excerpts from the reviews—I suspect in the interests of my general peace and serenity he has kept out some things that would get me into murderous condition—but I can see from the tenor of these excerpts—and they are wonderfully good—what some of the criticism may be—God knows, I could be helped by criticism as much as any man alive—but how much more critical am I, who am generally supposed to be so totally lacking in the critical faculty, than my critics —Every intelligent artist, I believe, as he grows older, wishes to profit and learn and grow through the persuasions of a wise critique—but how rare—how damnably rare—how much rarer even than the great master-works of art itself such criticism is!

I think I can see from these excerpts what the main trend of criticism will be—and how wrong it is!—It is one thing to profit by criticism, but no reasonable man can hope to profit by being torn limb from limb by 27 different people all pulling him apart in different directions—Before I left New York, for example, I saw an advance note of my book by one of the w.k. lady reviewers [4]—The upshot of this was that all my people were monsters of the species—giants seven feet tall whose gentlest whisper was a bellow—It was all interesting enough she said, but would it be so interesting—would the high-brow critics be so impressed by it—without the value of his language—and his method, his adjectives to denote violence, altitude, size, immensity, etc.—Well, having got away to a good start by taking away my adjectives, why not do a really good job and take away my nouns, pronouns, participles, verbs, adverbs, conjunctives, and parts of speech whatever—furnish me with a vocabulary of her own choosing—culled no doubt from the delicate works of one of her own pet authors— Monsieur Robert Nathan, for example—forbid to write any more about "myself" or any people or experience I have managed to see or know in my thirty-four years—lock me up in a cell and thrusting the

4. In "Turns with a Bookworm," a column by Isabel M. Paterson in the New York *Herald Tribune Books,* Feb. 24, 1935, p. 18.

approved vocabulary and a sheaf of paper in my hands, hiss venomously: "Here damn you—Use these! And mind you write about something you know nothing at all about! We'll see if you can *really* write,
you dog!"

Tuesday, March 26, 1935:
        Pat called me at 10:30—arranged to meet her 12:30—to buy
clothes etc.—went down—had breakfast hotel—went to Amexco—got
money—back to pub at top of Haymarket for drink—usual crowd of
English [routine?] josh-the-bargirl jokers—back to hotel to pack—
called Pat saying it was too late to meet her—brought baggage downstairs—left in baggage-room—paid bill (one armed porter—red-haired
snippy cashier girl who made me sign things)—got taxi—went to
Russell street to meet Frere—Charley Evans—old man Roberts there
—rode in old man Roberts' car to Garrick Hotel—where 3 of us—
Roberts, Frere, myself, had drink in bar—then with Frere into dining
room where old cockney woman waited on us—ancient ale, grilled
herring, rumpsteak, greens, cheese, coffee, and brandy—then Frere
with me back to hotel where collected baggage and with Frere to
Hanover Square where I moved in—Frere inspected apartment and he
left me—So there an hour or two—then to call on Scribners, Bedford
Sq.—talk with old man Kingsford—dry, cold, grey man—then to see
Ivy Elstob and Irving Davis in bookshop Museum street—while there
Mrs. Carswell came in—so all of us to pub nearby for whiskies—Mrs C
leaving after drink—Davis and Ivy staying on—so left them around
seven—and going home to Hanover—and deciding not to go to literary party given by Gollancz at Claridge's—not wanting to go, and
evening suit I had sent out by Sykes [5] not having returned—so out late
to eat (Spanish restaurant I think) and so to Café Royal—crowded—
and so home with drink in me.
        Thus ended third day.

Wednesday, March 27, 1935:
        Up and to meet Pat to go for overcoat—walked down New
Bond Street and to Albany—Thence to Austin Reed's where selected
and chose material and was measured for coat—the smoothness of
clothes buying in England—thence back to Albany where had glass of
sherry, and Frere came in, and all three of us down Piccadilly of a
glorious sky day—Frere in great spirits—and greeting people all along
way—the Green Park filled with people sunning themselves—so to
Walpole's sumptuous flat for dinner—a delicious one—the three flun-

5. The valet who looked after Wolfe in the flat in Hanover Square.

kies—the art treasures—So left a little after three, Walpole inviting me to lunch on Saturday—so left Frere and Pat at Albany—went to see "Ruggles of Red Gap" [6]—then to Café Royal perhaps—and home—and can't think where I ate (Stone's perhaps).

So ended Fourth Day.

Thursday, March 28:—

No clear recollection of what happened this day—wrote letters in morning perhaps—went to Garrick perhaps for lunch—Amexco—bought notebook in Haymarket—map in Regent Street—came home and drank—Frere called asking me to come down at ten o'clock after dinner—went down and found several guests—Sir Somebody, Ronald Squire, the two Du Maurier ladies, man and woman who dropped in later—talked to Du Maurier gal—very lovely, I thought—was rude to Sir Somebody and told him of 18,000 war airplanes in Peru—talked of Ruggles of Red Gap [7] to young man—liked woman with him—Frere asked me to stay and I stayed when all had gone and acted badly toward Frere—was drunk—left in an atmosphere of tension—went to find something to eat—to Oddenino's—couldn't get it—finally ate at Lyons—fillets of fish etc.—and so home drunk and miserable.

So ended Fifth day.

Resuming Diary (From memory)

Friday, March 29:

Woke feeling very shaky and jittery after night before (at Frere's)—Frere called me at 10:30 and asked how I felt—I told him I was wearing a hair shirt and apologized for night before—Told him I wanted to send Pat a letter or some flowers and he said not to, it was all right—Sounded very tired, said he was on edge too, and going down to country at once—Asked me not to forget luncheon with Walpole next day and to call him up later—Do not remember exactly what I did rest of day but think I wrote & finished letters to John Terry, Lacy Meredith, Mann, et al.—went to Amexco—and at night went to Simpson's still feeling wobbly, but better after mutton, cheese and Beaujolais—then to little news-theatre just off Strand—(they're all over London now, by the way) then home to bed—

So ended Sixth Day.

6. The Paramount movie starring Charles Laughton.

7. Wolfe's nickname for his valet, who "would make Ruggles of Red Gap look like a blacksmith." For his oft-repeated anecdote about the valet, see *Time*, July 15, 1935, p. 45.

Saturday, March 30:

Up, breakfast, bath—out to American Express Co. for money —to Stone's for drink—to Austin Reed's for coat fitting—then by taxi down Piccadilly to Hugh Walpole's for lunch—He amiable as usual— excellent lunch—sherry wine, brandy, fine cigar—and so off with him in taxi to see *Henry IV, Part II* at Od Vic—Acting spotty and on whole not very good (Shallow, Mistress Quickly, Doll very good) but play magnificent—has everything in it—low life—grandeur—the nobility and care of kinghood—a universe of life—I have never been able to laugh heartily over Jack Falstaff—but he is a wonderful, rich character, and full of wisdom—so away with Walpole in taxi—left him at Athenaeum—said goodbye—he was going on a tour of Greece and said "look him up" in May—so walked home, bought bottle of whiskey —drank some of it—called Frere about 7:30—he said he had wanted me to come down but too late now—I told him what [had been?] paid —he said meet them for dinner at Escargot Sunday night at 9:00 o'clock—so drank some more and ate, I think, at Spanish restaurant off Regent Street and home to bed.

(So ended Sixth [*sic*] Day.)

Sunday, March 31:

Stayed in all day—great slab of petrified time—English Sunday —had breakfast and lunch in house—then read *Times* and Evelyn Waugh's *Vile Bodies*—a wonderfully clever and decayed rot of book —Then to meet Frere and Pat about 9:00—taxi man who said, "These foreign names, sir—etc."—Had good dinner with them—Vin Rosé, fish, chicken or beef, good salad, coffee, brandy—then Pat's older brother (in British movies) and her brother's wife, beautiful blonde young woman who works for *Daily Mail*, came over and sat with us—invited us to their flat—They started in their car—we followed— Frere driving me through Ebury Street and Pimlico—past my old dwelling and around corner to their flat—a nice place in charming little street—Liked Pat's brother, but on remarking that I might fly to Germany, Pat—or, she said, brother's wife—said, "Well, you'd better get rid of your big belly before you do"—I told both of them it was none of their damned business whether my belly weighed an ounce or a ton—and shortly thereafter the party broke up under a sense of constraint—So Frere drove me across Bridge into South London, back across Waterloo Bridge and left me at Swan and Edgar's corner, where I apologized to Pat for my conduct of two nights before, thanked her for all she had done, and told her I would not see her again—and stalked away again, feeling like a callow, over-sensitive, damned fool who had acted badly—went to Café Royal—later home.

(So ended first week in England—Think this gets in about everything except the girl I brought home with me—This must have been either on Tuesday or Wednesday night because I remember telling Frere about it Thursday).

(Notes on Week from Monday April 1–Monday April 8—by Memory) [*written on April 18 or 19*]:

April 1—Can remember little of day but suppose Am. Ex. Co. etc. came into it—Got home late, I was afraid, for engagement with Ivy, Irving, etc.—went in—found they weren't there—told maid to let them in if they came—went to pub around corner and got bottle of whiskey—came back—they came in sometime later with a Frenchman —a bookseller—He left first to go to hotel—we went to Ivy Restaurant where Frenchman joined us—good dinner, grilled herring, goulash, cheese, coffee, etc.—Tavel wine, then Nuits St. Georges—left Ivy, went in taxi to Café Royal—so parted later—Italian-Frenchman drove me home in taxi—and so to bed.

Tuesday—Charley Scribner called in morning—[*breaks off*]

Monday, April 8, 1935—Restaurant des Gourmets—about 9 o'clock at night—

I built better than I knew in "The House of the Far and Lost" [8]—Two of the horseneighing voices in front of me—having a good time neighing at each other running other people down—the young man neighs even more loudly than the young woman but they make a good pair.

"But what's he like?" (neigh).

"Oh it's fantastic—He's *exceedingly* (neigh) tall—he'll never be able to get near (naher) her."

Man: "You see (a high neigh)—she definitely belongs."

"But don't you find him *terribly* dull?"

"But now you see it's getting too late because she cahn't *marry* an undergraduate of New College . . . . But there aren't any—"

—"But you see, what's she going to do . . . She has no money to speak of . . . no lineage . . ."

"Oh yes . . . . it's good lineage . . . . good lineage . . . . I should regahd it as quite a good match."

8. "The House of the Far and Lost" was published in *Scribner's Magazine* for August, 1934, and was later included in OT&R, pp. 619–27 and 637–52. It was originally written as Part III, "October: 1926," of the short novel *No Door*.

"I don't think her parents are very worried about it . . . and I don't think she particularly cares."

Man: "I can't imagine" (starts with a high squeak goes up and down) "any of the awd'n'ry things happening to Mary—I mean a man's saying to her, (Come to lunch with me tomorrow)—etc."

Woman: ". . . . Yes, it's rather difficult—I *quite* agree with you."

odd (this word's used dozens of times)—". . . . still I mean he seems like such a *very* odd man."

Man: "Still I don't think we've got to worry about him at present"—

"I mean, if *Mary* (same sound as *very*) married him it would be quite awful."

"What's he like?"

"Oh,—*awful.*"

"Which one was that—the fat one?"

"Yes the fat one."

"Ow—him, yes."

"—architect"

"Yes, that's the one."

"I must say, I thought her family rather *awful.*"

Man: (neighing up and down) . . . . "I don't want to meet her . . . ."

"Now, now, now now now—"

"I mean it doesn't *excite* me enough."

"What's the new man like?"

"Odious."

"Yes"

"Oh, little Scotchman . . . . *frightfully* dull."

Man neighing: ". . . . I've heard him described as the stupidest man at New . . . . but then it was rahther a good yöh."

"St. Johns' Wood would be rahther decent—"

"Rahther expensive, I should think—"

"They saw something that was £20, I believe."

"Electric lights?"

"I believe—oh, now now now now now now—gas fittings—I believe."

Part of the Guildhall's glorious record:

Henry Howard, Earl of Surrey, A Poet, was tried for High Treason and Beheaded on Tower Hill in 1547; Aged 29.

Lady Jane Grey and Her Husband Lord Guildford Dudley were tried for high treason and beheaded on Tower Green 1554.

Archbishop Cranmer was sentenced to death for high treason in 1554—pardoned—sent to Oxford where he was burned 1556.

John Felton a Roman Catholic Layman was tried 1570 for high treason—Drawn on a hurdle to St. Paul's, Hanged, Beheaded & quartered.

Notes: a few modest and no-doubt elementary-Watson inquiries, etc.:

Talking to Mrs. C(arswell) the other night in Hampstead—she took me to task pretty smartly because I said I found the French pretty much the same as when I left them 4 years ago, and the fundamental structure of their life apparently unchanged, and that I now find a great deal of it depressing—e.g. the incessant talking about money: "vingt sous," "quatre francs," the arithmetic of greed, etc., with which their conversation was interminably studded.

Mrs. C. took me up somewhat sharply, saying how could I possibly know what was going on in France—since I had been there only for two or three weeks this last time—and that the most fundamental changes were probably going on underneath in the country which a mere foreigner like me could know nothing about.

Well, that's all right, and no doubt she's right—But the curious thing about the conversation was that just five minutes before, Mrs. C. was talking to me most brilliantly about her trip to Russia last fall when she spent all of ten days in the country—The extraordinary thing about it is that, although I, who have lived in France perhaps a year, and gone there perhaps a dozen times, and can read the language perfectly and speak it badly but sufficiently, and have been in practically every part of the country can really know nothing of what is going on, while this lady, who knows not a word of Russian, can discourse brilliantly on the economic, social and political condition of the country, what is going on, and where communism leads and where it lags—all on the basis of a week's visit.

Now all this is just for purposes of illustration and is not pique, and not a criticism of Mrs. C., whom I like, nor justification of myself —It is just that the situation I have described is a typical one and I want to know why.

Why is it that to people of this sort, France is a country that no-one—(except themselves)—can ever get to know nothing about— Dare to utter one word that is against their own cherished sentiments —or delusion—and they are buzzing at you like a hornets' nest—"How silly—how ridiculous—hold your tongue—you know nothing about the French—You're a foreigner—no foreigner ever gets to know them," etc.

On the other hand, a three days visit to Moscow, under the careful supervision of the Intourist organization, is amply sufficient to give you a complete knowledge of communism, its success or failure, and the lives and spirits of the Russian people—and one can return from such a trip amply provided with material for three books, a dozen magazine articles, and any number of lectures.—"one feels the atmosphere of hope."

(For The October Fair—Characters): Esther, Miss Lily Mandel, Laurence Hirsch, Miss Heilprinn, The Morgenstern Sisters, Miss Agnes Martin, Miss Helen Foster, Roy Malone, Edith Goldsmith, Alma, Aaronson, Phil Heller, Lorber, Jacobs, His Son, Stephen Hook, Alice Hook, Lula O'Toole, James O'Toole, Amelia Van Leer.

THE WAY MEN LIVE

(Being a few notes, as factual, concrete and uncontroversial as the writer can make them of people seen, observed, lived with, and known together with the actual physical state in which each lived in the United States of America between March 9, 1931 and March 2, 1935, during which period the author himself lived at various addresses in Brooklyn N.Y.)

1. My Brother Fred: at the present time aged 40—went to High School in his home town in N.C., later to Ga. School of Technology, Carnegie Tech, etc., education interrupted by war, and finally took degree in electrical engineering at Ga. Tech—For ten years or more between 1920–1930 a salesman of farm machinery, farm lighting equipment, etc.

Condition in which he lived during this time:—In a condition that was strained, perilous, and painfully uneasy, and that at one time—as I now know—just escaped actual want.

This was in 1933–1934 when, he told me, he had to limit his expenses for food to 75 cents to $1.00 a day.

Frame of The Hills Beyond Pentland

Chap. I—The Beast of The Night (America)—A lion in the mouth sulfurous, so in the maw ocherous—etc. (great medley of thoughts, scraps, chants, a child's impressions).

Chap. II—Three o'clock—

The trees of England—Mortlake [9] and the Duke's Meadows and the look of English trees—and how the noblest state for trees I know is Maryland but New England trees the suddenest, sweetest, and most full of Spring the sharp knife.

Mabel's address: 920 17th St N.W., Wash DC, U.S.A.

THE WAY MEN LIVE

(Notes on Life and Economics)

1. My Brother Fred: Formerly salesman of farm machinery, pumps, lighting equipment—now sells Ice Cream in the Piedmont of South Carolina.

2. My Cousin Jim—worked with his father as a stonecutter until father's death then worked as baker—now has job as rural delivery man for a Harrisburg paper—makes circuit of 100 miles twice a day—leaves him pretty tired and with little time for other activity.

3. The Dormans—Brooklyn—A good family gone to seed— Roberta rents apartments—Marjorie has done little or nothing in recent years except rent houses in Verandah Place.

4. The Clarks in Columbia Heights—Brooklyn—Clark chauffeur for a rich old woman—got $40 a week wages—rented home in Columbia Heights as side venture—appropriated rent and was ejected.

5. The Garveys—a pale sunless stricken lot—no sun, no air, no light in their lives—they look as if they have always lived in basements.

6. The Gunthers—Decent self-respecting people who find it hard to live on $25 a month their employer paid them, and who probably suffered from insufficient food and comfort.

7. The Holths—man formerly a sea-captain—now gets occasional jobs on tugs and barges—A queer lot.

8. The Gambrells (a South Carolina family—my oldest sister's) —Family composed of Father, aged 49, mother 47 or 48, and seven children—

    1. Father by occupation a grocery clerk—but for ten years or more employment has been sporadic—Recently has had part-time employment on gov't relief projects as time-keeper.

    2. William—oldest child—aged 26—Has never had regular

9. Site of the finish of the traditional Oxford-Cambridge crew race. Wolfe was among the half million who watched Cambridge defeat Oxford on April 6, 1935.

employment in his life—of an oversensitive, proud, finicky disposition, takes offense easily and gives up jobs, will not take jobs where he has to carry packages through street, etc.—Pretty self-centered—was about to take job in gov't conservation camp, but refused flat when he found that $25 of his $30 monthly wage would be sent home to his mother.

3. Miriam—oldest girl—aged 24 or 25—gets occasional employment at Christmas or week-end in stores, but for most part stays home and helps mother—was told by her mother that she was very beautiful and "must set her cap for a millionaire" and believed it—A young farmer with good cotton farm in the county began to pay her attentions and call at the house but was so ridiculed and mocked at by mother and rest of the family that at length he left her cold.

4. David—the best of the lot—is now 22 and has spent his life in working for the family—works in grocery store for $12 a week.

5. Virginia—aged 20 or 21—works in Nash. Department Store—gets about $15 a week and sends part of it home.

6. Frederica—About 17 or 18 now—Lives at home and gets occasional jobs in stores.

7. and 8. George and Edward—The two little ones.

IX. Steve and Carl (The lunch room men on Montague St., Bklyn).

X. My Sister Mabel and her husband Wheaton—Now Runs Lodging House in Washington.

XI. Mabel's Lodgers:

1. Jimmy Salline—a little Irishman with good deal of intelligence and a law degree—Has done good deal of reading and can talk about it intelligently—loves to display his knowledge—when drunk, as he is frequently, quite offensive, sentimental, maudlin, weepy, or violent.—now has job paying $2400 a year in gov't.

2. Mr. Hardin—a Dostoievskyan character—unquestionably insane—has small pension or income of some sort.

3. Eddie Chaput—a good steady little lodger, but quite effeminate, and with feelings easily hurt.

[4.] Felice—From New Orleans, aged 21, pretty and well kept as many a young American girl is—has job in gov't.—$100 a month—"puts it all on her back" as saying goes—goes playing golf on Saturday on Municipal Golf Links—has boy friends—thinks it all grand and does not want to go home.

Note—Eating in Stone's, Tuesday, April 9—3:00 P.M.—20 mins after ordering brandy:

"I suppose then you are out of brandy?"

"Oh, yes, sir, you see it's *gone* 3, sir; its ten minutes after 3."

"Yes, but I ordered it from Charles 20 minutes ago."

"Did you, sir—Then maybe they've *got it up*—I'll put him on lunch, sir." etc.

Note—National Gallery—Tuesday afternoon—4-5:00—April 9—

Wrote letters all morning—Clayton Hoagland,[10] Fritz Dashiell, long one with more corrections to Jack Wheelock [11]—then drove in taxi to Stone's—Panton Street—whiskey and soda in old wine colored bar—served by nice-looking, most intelligent barmaid—then back to dining room to eat—roast beef, Yorkshire, braised onion, mashed potato, rhubarb tart, cream, whiskey and soda, ½ pint old ale, brandy, coffee—then walked to Amexco—no mail—then to German consulate, Carlton Terrace, for visa to Germany (3s6d)—then along Mall where workmen erecting wooden stands for King's Jubilee—sound of hammer and saw and smell of lumber same the world over—then to post office off lower Regent Street to mail letters—then to Trafalgar Square and National Gallery where I write this.

First time I have looked at pictures in years—Looked for all the ones I used to like, and if I found their position changed it was a great and unpleasant shock—why is this?—Looked for "Hogarth's Servants," which used to hang on left side of door of big room at west end of gallery—It has been moved to another part of the gallery and this affected me unpleasantly, as I had thought of it as being just there a thousand times—The pictures I like—I may as well admit that on the whole I do not care for "old masters"—painters like Titian, Veronese bore me profoundly—I can see the magnificence of their composition —the richness of their color, etc.—and it leaves me cold—The pictures that mean something to me, that seem to speak in any way to me, are pictures that communicate in some way with my own sense of life—I mean Hogarth, Holbein, Breughel, John Bellini, Pietro Longhi, Manet, Renoir, and even Turner.

To illustrate:

But I am sitting now in a portion of the Nat'l Gallery I do not recall having seen before—It is the Sir Joseph Duveen Gallery and was

10. Clayton Hoagland, of the New York *Sun*, and his wife Kathleen (Kitty) were friends whose Irish awareness interested Wolfe greatly.

11. For the kind of corrections he wanted made in OT&R see *Letters*, pp. 445-46.

erected in 1929—Right before me in a magnificent gold frame—or rather a sort of shrine—is a picture called "The Virgin Enthroned with the Two SS. Catherine" by one Ambrogio Borgognone (aet. 1481 d. 1523—School of Milan)—It is quite a beautiful picture and it rouses me to a state of profound apathy.

The virgin enthroned is sitting on her throne wearing a rich blue robe with a kind of rich crimson underneath—Her pure, completely empty, face is turned a little to one side, eyes cast coyly downaway—She is supporting a fat, rather stupid-looking little boy with chubby legs and a short yellow dress, who stands on one knee—on her right hand is one S. Catherine wearing a crown, with long golden curly waved hair and a crimson dress—and on the other, another with a sad, dormant face, wearing a black and white dress and a hood—Beyond deep blue sky—It is a very fine picture, I am sure, and it means nothing to me—

But Manet's picture of the bar at the Folies Bergère in 1882 with the pretty *barmaid* and her banged hair—and shapely, corseted, bustled figure and all the bottles of red and rose wine, and Creme de Menthe, and tray of canapes—and the back of another barmaid with a well pleased pleaser on other side of counter with tall hat and little moustache—and men and women moving around, drinking, etc. in background—this gives me a wonderful feeling of pleasure and excitement and seems to speak directly to my life.

"The Virgin and Child Enthroned" by Carlo Crivelli—Same business with a dutiful looking monk on one side and St. Sebastian naked save for loin cloth at other side transfixed by 14 arrows which pierce him through bowels, neck, heart, legs, thighs, etc.—with a calm, patient, and rather reproachful look on his face—I say it moves me not, I don't believe it—

On other hand how good they were when they painted living people—Is anything better than their portraits of men—Portrait of a man by Andrea Solario—for example—how great and living a picture that is, or "Portrait of a Man" from School of Gentile Bellini or "A Mathematician" of same school.

"The Rout of San Romano"—was there ever a richer, more golden picture of a battle (Paolo Uccello—1397–1475). The warriors, the great deathlike forest and the raised lances—the merry-go-round hobby horse prancing upward—and yet how well everything is painted—and the men in the background—just a few—an archer stooped to load his cross bow—a spearman coming over a bridge—two knights—a man passing, etc.—field and wood and mtn.—the whole world all painted with the vague nearness and impression of a dream.

The Kind of Thing I mean that leaves me cold is represented by "Scorn"—an allegorical group of Paolo Veronese of the Venetian School, or for that matter "The Vision of St. Helena" by the same, or even A Family Group by Titian (called the Cornaro Titian)—Although the colors are rich, the people human looking, everyone wonderfully painted—but the spurious gestures (like St. Someone leading swine), the look of tranquil, sad placidity on the faces of everyone (children too)—it is a world I know not and means nothing to me—or "The Consecration of St. Nicholas" by Veronese—or "Happy Union" (an allegorical group)—an allegorical husband, wife, child and dog holding olive leaves, being crowned by a huge, fat and almost completely naked lady, who seems to be sitting on top of a large urn—are we not liars when we say that this has meaning to our life?

Rembrandt's "Night Watch" ("The Butchers" in Chicago).

"Two Bankers or Usurers" by Marinus van Reymerswael (1497–1567).

"Adoration of the Kings" by Pieter Brueghel—Faces of The Kings Are Superb masterpieces of comic [incident?]—the nigger king is rolling the whites of his eyes around in minstrel show fashion—and there is one fellow over in the corner with thick rimmed spectacles that's enough to make a monkey laugh—and yet the picture is a great one, and full of reverence and worship—why?

Note—made in lounge of Charles Grill near St. Martin's—Tuesday, April 9 at 7:30 P.M.—

It is a curious thing how people of every kind and condition, whether they know anything about anything or not, are instantly convinced that the proper thing to do with any piece of writing is to "cut"—"cut ruthlessly"—"be relentless"—"don't spare yourself" etc. —It seems to be taken as a fundamental axiom of artistic truth that any book which exceeds 300 pages should be "cut to the bone"—and the result will eventually be a marked improvement—Why is this?—So far as I know this conviction (about the necessity of "cutting") applies only to the art of writing.

A man who waded into the paintings of Turner, or to go to more fecund and enormous canvasses—those of Rubens, say, or Paolo Veronese—with a "blue pencil" and a pair of shears, saying "You don't need this, old boy—much too much of that"—slash!—"out she comes —I assure you, you'll be all the better for it in the end" etc.—such a man, I say, would be regarded as a maniac and a dangerous criminal, but when the same thing is done to a man's book—and, in God's name, what in art is more living than a book, what has more life and sinew than man's living language—when such a thing is done to a man's book,

I say, the act is regarded as one of noble virtue—and the only pity is he didn't do more of it, etc.—By an ironic circumstance (it has occurred to me) perhaps my greatest chance of success may come from the fact that the critics find so much in me to criticize, and may come to have a kind of affection for me in the end, because they can whack and thump at me to their heart's content.

Tuesday, April 9, 1935—at home in bed in Hanover Square 12:40—
      After leaving Nat'l Gallery at 6:30, around corner to bar of Garrick—had two Scotch and sodas, and watched bar fill up—curiously hard, dark, impenetrable nobility of barmaid serving me—very black hair and dark skin but English—"Thanky ah"—an impenetrable hard-as-agate courtesy.
      Then to Charles Grill—another Scotch—watched people—then to Simpson's for mutton, cabbage, cheese, and ale—curious tone-expression of head-waiter—Looking at him, suddenly remembered a conversation with him four years ago, about a son who was a waiter in New York, and calling to him I said "How is your son in New York?" The man—a stocky little man who suggests a tremendous vitality—bald—with a great hooked nose—"I'm A Sussex man"—curiously strong, comic, and yet noble face—almost threw his arms around me—and began to tell me about his son, how well he was doing, his job at the Plaza, the £5 he sent his mother Christmas, the prized job in Florida, his work at World's Fair—and the American girl he's in love with—" 'is Mary, 'e calls her, sir, 'e wrote in 'is last letter, sir,—I'll be back for a visit some dye an when I do I'll bring my Mary with me—that's the way 'e put it, sir—Oh, 'e knows languages, sir,—'e learned to speak French an 'e was steward on a South American boat, an 'e picked up the South American language, an' he fell in with some Italian chaps an' they taught him their language—'e wanted to chuck it all as a lad but I says to 'im—'Ere, you get along with it—it's what I should have done if I knew what I know now.' "
      There was something wonderfully moving about all this—and something wonderfully strange and sad—I thought of *time*—of those 4 years I had spent in all the rust of Brooklyn putting words on paper—and how we had both grown older—I more than he—because he is a man with a certain stocky, time-weathered quality that doesn't change much—but the way that face, that living moment of the lost past four years ago came back to me was dark as night, and strange as time.
      When I went out he had told all the other waiters and the men who serve the meat about my remembering and they all called out cheerful good nights to me as I went past—*People are all right.*
      Then went to Stoll's in Kingsway to see movie—Fred Astaire in

"The Gay Divorcee"—then along Kingsway to Holborn and so along Oxford Street to Regent Street and home.

Parts of London that depress me—why?—write this up tomorrow.

Wally Meyer saying after 40 like a camel I'll begin to live off hump—Is that happening to me now?—Am no longer so ravenously hungry for new sights, new experience as I was ten years ago—Have retraced many of my old tracks this trip—But is this bad? If I had not gone back to Simpson's tonight I should not have had the strange time-experience with waiter—(Finish and check this tomorrow).

Wednesday, April 10 (written 1:20 AM, Thursday, in bed in my flat—have been reading *Richard Mahoney*):

Day's log: Up with bad headache—last night's whiskey-ale-beer mixture at Simpson's I think—had breakfast, lay abed then till one o'clock—had bath—wrote letter to [*Whitney*] Darrow, P. Engle,[12] post cards to Perkins—took taxi to Escargot Bienvenu, Greek Street—good lunch with vin rosé, poulet du grain, salade d'endive, cheese, coffee—then walked to Amexco—no mail—mailed letters—then walked down Pall Mall into Mall past St. James Palace and Buckingham Palace into Ebury to my old house—rent signs all over—rang Belilovsky's bell—maid answered—went in and spoke to old Snuffy—toady green—could see him standing in dark—He came to the door and looking away said "They're all gone—they left last June—that I couldn't tell you" and closed door in face—walked away feeling sad, and to Victoria Station—got bus going to Saint Paul's—so there around about Piccadilly, Old Bond St., Oxford St., Holborn, Cheapside—went into wine tavern beside Paul's—so pleasant that I stayed till Paul's was closed—then into cheap bookshop beside Paul's—bought *Richard Mahoney*[13]—then into Paternoster Row looking at religious book stores—into pub on Paternoster Row for drink—(beauty of old scrubbed wood)—then along Paternoster Row into Fleet (?) or Ludgate Hill—got taxi—and to Fitzroy Square by Gray's Inn Lane (?) etc. through Bloomsbury across Tottenham Court road—There dinner with Irving Davis, Ivy Elstob and woman from California—after wine and talk of Russia, America, etc.—took California woman home to her place in Bloomsbury and so home to bed a little before midnight.

The [bright?] singing of birds in eaves of old St. Paul's.

The golden light of flowers in gardens round the Church—

12. Paul Engle, the Iowa poet, was then a Rhodes Scholar at Oxford.

13. *The Fortunes of Richard Mahoney*, by Henry Handel Richardson (pseud. for Henrietta Richardson), London, 1931.

Bloomsbury, Russell Square, the hearselike taxis, the Hotel Imperial, strange thoughts of Conan Doyle—the wonderful square of Bloomsbury and the private hotels—why the feeling of depression?

People in Last Five Years:
> France: Susy Hyde, Her Brother, Mary Caumartin, Miss Smith.
> Boat: Harold Loeb, Lewis's wife.
> Switzerland: Scott Fitz[*gerald*], Julian Van Cortlandt.
> Black Forest: A Waitress.
> London: Daisy Lavis [*checked*], Belilovsky [*checked*], Trixie, Mrs. Janes, The Girl In The Shaftesbury News Reel, Frere, Manx, Old Man Roberts, Ivy Elstob, Davis, Ivy Litvanoff, Catherine Carswell, Donald [*Carswell*], Old Man Green, His Wife; Red Lewis [*checked*], Bechhofer Roberts [*checked*].
> Oxford: Cowley Road—The Girl, Her Mother, The Three Englishmen [*all these crossed out*]; The Rhodes Scholars [*lined out*], Kirwan.

New York Again

> Brooklyn: Marjorie Dorman, Old Man Dorman, Mrs. Dorman, Roberta Dorman, Eleanor Dorman, The Nephew, Harriette Hoppe, [*all seven checked*]; Old Hoppe, Bertha, Her Mother.
> Manhattan: Clair Zyve, Dr. Smetana, His Wife.
> Washington: Mr. Hardin, Jimmy Salline, Eddie Chaput, Edwards (dipsomaniac from Tennessee), Alberta.
> York Springs: Jim Wolf, Aunt Mary, Dorothy, Charley Wolf's Wife, Henry, The Huge Brute Woman In Café, Her Wop Husband.
> The Typists: [*Jack*] Bronson, The Ex-Vaudeville Actor, Miss Rose Steinman, Miss Miller (from Michigan), Miss Edna Vincent, Miss Stribling, Miss Alladine Bell, Miss Eleanor Buckles.
> People at Scribner's: Max [*checked*], Jack [*Wheelock*], Whitney Darrow, Wally Meyer [*checked*], Dashiell, Cross, Miss Wyckoff, Miss [*Davey?*], Will Howe, Weber, Mr. C. S. Scribner [*checked*], Mr. Arthur Scribner, Bridges [*checked*], Chapin.

Note—Thursday, April 11—1:00 P.M.—looking out my window over Hanover Square—
> Bright April Sunshine that comes and goes with greater swiftness than we have at home—"April, April, Laugh thy girlish

laughter" [14]—Bright sunshine golden on old, foggy brick—making it mellow—ripe yellow—golden-rich—on old London yellow plaster first floor fronts and window facings—mellow on red brick—and bright and shining on casements, facings, solid wealthy battlements of fog-white wealthy stone—and Bright as April on new-painted green of iron fence encircling park—and on the lovely green of grass and plants within—and on all the laughing light of Primroses and people passing —houses—old hearselike taxis strangely rich, sedate looking as they are with baggage racks on top—and people passing, flowing, throb of motors, put-put of little cycles, of which they have so many—and people passing, flowing—bowler-hatted Englishmen—well dressed and prosperous—with neatly bound umbrella-cases, and men in dark, men in light trench-looking coats, and private chauffeurs uniformed with flat, black caps and shining visors—and little boys "in service" in blue uniforms, brass buttons—and the line of cars and taxis all around the square—and taxi drivers, cigarettes in mouths—and poor and rich and shop girls, office girls and fashionable women—a well dressed woman with good figure coming out of Worth's with hat box in her hand— and April smiling on the hair of girls, and blowing coats, and whipping hair—all of the daybright—morning gold—a boy that wheels a cart— another peddling a tricycle wagon—clip clop of pony hoofs, the distant roar of London and the clopping of a horse—and William Pitt in somber bronze looking down on all.

The painters in white coats apainting the park fence April-green —and the circle of old, stately trees with tiny-gold-green buds atremble in the wind.

Thursday, April 11—1:AM (Friday morning) in Flat—
Went to Amexco by taxi—no mail or papers—got $100 cashed to pay for clothes—went to Stone's—2 drinks—½ pint ale—steak kidney pudding—then to Strand and bus for St. Paul's—went in, heard service St. Paul's—then bought post cards bookshop—then down Cheapside to St. Mary le Bow—then to Guildhall—then back by bus to Oxford Circus—on foot to George Street to tailor's—found suit ready with few slight alterations—ready tomorrow—then down Regent Street to Austin Reed for shirts—got shirts—Regent Street thronging with buses, traffic, some very pretty women—then back to Hanover Square and around "lane-screw" to little pub "The Bunch of Grapes" —so here for 2 drinks—bought bunch of primroses from old woman —so home where found phone message from Charley Scribner inviting

14. The opening lines of the poem "April" by Sir William Watson.

me to tea with Briffault but had missed it—Called him & talked to him and Mrs. S.—so did on new shirt—and walked down Regent 9:30 or 10:00 into little dingy Soho—into pub—sodden, depressing, loud with sodden voices, clammy with body warmth and gas heat—then up Greek Street to Escargot Bienvenu where had good dinner of tripe en casserole, green beans, sauterne, endive salad, coffee, brandy—amusing conversation young waitress and proprietress about "it is better to give than receive" with madame craftily tallying up bills behind counter putting in word from time to time—so away and along Shaftesbury Avenue to Picadilly through theatre crowds—up Regent Street past theatre goers, long frocked women and the eternal whores and so home to Hanover Square to bed—a magnificent ravishing Spring day and tonight a halve of moon over London—old Spring London.

Mrs. C. and Mrs. E. kept coming back to "The atmosphere of hope"—"Yes, things are bad, but still there is the atmosphere of hope" —It seems I have heard those words before—Alas, my prophetic soul tells me that in our own misguided land there is more hope to the square inch than any other part of the inhabitable globe can produce to the square mile, and would to God we all were not so hopeful!—I have heard Communists I know in New York talk gloatingly about our people sodden with despair, muttering with revolution, long in a miserable degraded state of utter hopelessness—but by such foolishness they betray their ignorance, their feeble grasp, their failure to know anything about the country they are going to revolutionize—The American hope is fantastic, staggering, mad—

LOG

Friday, April 12, 1935 (written in bed 2:20 A.M. Sat. morning):
Up at 10—breakfast—fish (haddock?), poached eggs, tea, marmalade, etc.—*Times*—letter from Paul Engle inviting me to Somerset, etc.—Bathed, dressed, taxi to Frere Reeves, showed me letter and advertising folders from Max—letter said book outselling all but 2 cheap fictions—With Uncle Henry out then to Café Royal for lunch —melon, whitebait (tiny little minnows), scalloped chicken (delicious), rhubarb with cream, coffee, whiskey soda, two glasses hock— Then to Amexco—no mail—New York Papers—Sunday *Tribune*, March 31, gave me 3d on best seller lists—*Times*, Monday, Two firsts, three seconds, two thirds—a little down from week before, but *Tribune* up from 7th to 3d—Then from Amexco home—read Amer. papers

—took evening suit vest to Austin Reed Ltd., tailor's—suit ready—paid him bill £ 12: 4 s—with braces etc.—left vest for repairing—then by taxi to Heinemann's—found Uncle Henry there—talked to him—then walked with him down across Oxford Street through Shaftesbury Avenue etc. to Piccadilly—Jermyn entry through Piccadilly—I had two, three drinks with him—then home by taxi—found vest and required material waiting—put on evening clothes—by taxi then to Cornwall Gardens, Kensington, 15 minutes late but before Scribners— Drinks with Hughes and Scribners—Dinner—oysters—soup—chicken —ice cream—etc.—Tavel wine—liqueurs—left with Scribners 11:20 —drove with them to Carlton—went up for drinks and talk on God, Man, Faith, disillusion, belief—England, America until 1:20—then departed—walked home up Regent St. to Oxford Arms—2 Teas, [*illegible*]—Gold Flakes at lunch wagon—so home to Hanover Square and to bed—meeting Scribners for lunch with Briffault tomorrow— Sales April 3, 17,600.

Sat.—April 13, 1935—
   Up, breakfast, shave, bath, etc.—did on new suit, shirt, etc.—out to tailor's and ordered another suit—so by taxi to Amexco, no mail, got $20 cashed—so 12:30 to p.o. to mail post cards—[*Robert*] Cross, Mama, Fred, Effie, Mabel, etc.—to Stone's for one drink (Scotch)—so to Carlton—Chas. Scribner outside as I arrived lecturing chauffeur—So up to room—and presently Mrs. (?—friend of Scribners), Mr. Hutchinson—Mrs. S.—and later Mr. Briffault [15]—so drink in Charley's place, and down to big lunch—hors d'oerves—whitebait—asparagus—curry —hock—dessert—brandy—so upstairs—Charley, Mrs. S, Mrs. (?), Hutchinson, leaving to go chg.-buying—so talking with Mr. Briffault on great variety of things—chiefly America till 5:30—then with Mr. B to tea—Criterion—then left him—and by Piccadilly, Bond St. to Bunch of Grapes—a drink—and home—called up G. Macfarlane [16]— out again of rainy evening about 9:30 to Leicester square—where several Scotch's in Queen's Bar—and to Empire Movie at Leicester Square—S.S. Van Dine—Philo Vance—and so home by Regent Street about one o'clock.

Sunday, April 14, 1935—
   Up, breakfast, bath, etc.—shaved—dressed—out about 12:30 to lunch of Macfarlane's—fine Spring day—sunny and overcast by turns

15. Robert Briffault, English anthropologist and novelist.
16. George Gordon Macfarlane, a London architect, whom Wolfe met through Mrs. Carswell.

—but full of earth and flowers—by taxi to St. John's Wood—through Regent's Park—Park's great yellow Crescent magnificent—and Park glorious with flowers and grass and birds and people, gold and green and gold—so with Macfarlane and wife and little daughter Ann for lunch—then for walk through St. John's Wood, up Primrose Hill with Macfarlane—much interesting talk of London architecture and different style of architecture in St. John's Wood—most interesting—back to big tea—and more talk—left about 6:15 by taxi for Brown's hotel to meet Mr. Hutchinson—as he had asked me to do—but he not there— (People listening to speakers in Hyde Park at Marble Arch—red flag of communist—green striped one of something else)—so down Albemarle St. and up Piccadilly—magnificent Spring—sweet day—could feel and see Spring everywhere in London—in look and feel of Sunday crowds just "waking up"—so to newsreel theatre at Piccadilly circus until 7:45—then to various pubs off Regent Street until 9:30–10:00— then to Spanish restaurant for dinner—down Piccadilly and through little streets to Mayfair for walk—back and up Regent Street again to coffee stand Oxford circus for tea—and so home to bed.

Note: Mr. Robert Briffault
    Some of Mr. Briffault's remarks—That every country—or epoch of time—is given its dominant tone by the culture of some dominant country—and that this is an incontrovertible fact of history —That the culture of the 17th and 18th centuries, for example, were French—that of the 19th English—and that that of the 20th will be American and Russian—That England is a 19th century—a Victorian country—and her efforts to become a 20th century one are unavailing.

Note—Monday, April 15—4:30 PM Holbein room—British Museum—
    People seen, met, and talked to this time in England: Frere, Pat, Pat's Younger Brother, Miss Neveson [*sic*], Pat's Older Brother, Her Sister-In-Law, Two Pansy-like young men at Pat's, Catherine Carswell, Donald, John, The Scribners, Their friend Hutchinson, Robert Briffault, An American Lady, Miss Litchfield, Ivy Elstob, Irving, Old Man Roberts, Herschel Johnson, Kingsley, Mrs. Kingsley, Hugh Walpole, A Young Prostitute from Wales, The Waitress at Garrick, Gordon Macfarlane, Mrs. Macfarlane, Their little daughter Ann.

Monday, April 15—
    Nat'l Gallery—Turner's fine painting "Rain, Steam, and Speed" (1844—The Great Western Railway)—shows fiery monster of train

coming across bridge—the way bridge mass and arches is heavily, solidly defined—elsewhere arches of another bridge pretty well painted—shiny—blue pearl water—and all the rest a rainbow span of faery colour—of light—gold, sapphire—"Rain, Steam and Speed"—an exciting picture.

Monday, April 15—written at flat, Hanover Square, 8:25—(days are getting very long—it is now 8:30 and sky not wholly dark yet— weather mixture of Spring—April sunshine—gold and green—and rain and rain and damp and discomfort)—

Day's Log: Up, letting breakfast get cold as usual (Bkfast: Ham and eggs, tea, marmalade, etc.)—bath, shave, dress etc.—wrote letter regretting etc. to P. Engle—so out on foot—fine, golden-green morning down Jermyn, Bond, Piccadilly, Regents, Whitehall to Horse Guards where weather now grey ("a silver day" as Mr. McFarlane called it)—so G. McFarl. there—the Horseguards Nonsense and the gap-toothed, rotten-toothed populace onlooking—through the Horse-guards into St. James' Park—lovely green—flowers—gold-green flow-ers—people—so to Bridge with golden faery's lace down water and the playing ducks and an incredible vision of enchanted towers, minarets, towards Lord's grave-stone—miraculous Whitehall morning—a feeling of April, April, as if there were no war, and people passing, and a girl to smile, and London, London, as if there were no war—So then along St. James' Park and King's palace to Victoria Station and to Windsor Arms, Great Pub Macfarlane had [customed?]—and the grind of buses, smell of petrol, and the people passing—So into Windsor Arms, great lunch pub on rounded corner—"Shall we have a look at the Dove?"

So to Dove with Gordon's windows, arches, etc. buffet bars with beeves tongues etc. all looking better, I much fear, than they are, —so big meat-faced 'Ere-Sir man came up behind Gordon—was the mgr.—says—"May I 'ave the pleasure?"—set us up to drink—so on by lift to rest. (2d floor), a really expensive first class rest. sort of place with great chop-and-steak coal grill—Gordon explained his decorations —So good lunch of Scottish broth, [*peut?*] steak, f.f. potatoes, braised onions, fruit salad, cream, black coffee, a bottle of Sauterne—much talk with Gordon about Cathy [*Carswell*], (her first, coarse husband) and the general state of woman—Then gave him Am. addresses—hotels, names, etc. for his projected trip—then by bus along Victoria St. (solid Victorian depressing street, great fog-brick buildings) so to rich stone of old Westminster [stability?] so by Whitehall bus to Trafalgar Square.

So by foot to Amexco where a letter from Jack's paralytic girl —so to P.O. where mailed letter—so to Nat'l Gallery where some pictures (noted before) (stood on balcony looking at London-Trafalgar Sq. Pageant—buses—people—taxis—distant tower of Parliament etc. in fog-silver light)—so at ex for Nat'l Gallery out—the bells (fog-stone-green-white-old) of St. Martin's ringing strange and sweetly, ding, dinging, and the people passing, flowing, facing homewards with the flurry movements—so to Leicester Sq.—to Panton St—into the nice bar of Stone's where the pretty—not-so-good—new—Sweet—but cold-as-ice—new bar-lass, and all the voices—vices? did I say?—the See-höh-now—fairly good—see-höh-now voices—so a drink—and so to Jermyn Street—where found H. Johnson the young American diplomat,[17] a fop-dude—prissy with a twaddly movement called the baron, presently old Uncle Henry, late, with—"Where shall I take them?—I don't know if I'll have room enough for them here, and if the Prince of Wales comes, of course, there would not be room for him" etc.—The "Now I shall have cocktails here and then I shall take them to the Ritz—I think that's the only sensible thing to [*do*]"—H. Johnson (in a quiet, Southern, very gentle voice) "I think I'd take them to the Ritz for dinner, Jester—that's the thing to do" etc.

Jester (old man fumbling with trembling hands suddenly among papers) and Nancy Astor [18]—"now she's gone and gone off somewhere —no telling what she'll do—you see, Baron, what she says"—he gave him the letter—"I [telephoned?] to Sir-Somebody-Somebody—I said, do you think H.R.H. would come to dinner here on the 29th—He says, 'I'm sure he'd be delighted if he can, I'll ask him and find out what he's doing and let you know'—He called me later and said (note: put in casual transition words here) 'H.R.H. said he'd be delighted and will come in for a cocktail anyway and will come to dinner if he can etc.' " —So, a young man friend of the Baron's arrived, and I departed telling Uncle Henry I'll be glad to come Wed. to meet someone—American —American—Poor old man! It is pitiable, tragic and [revolting?]—and yet the old man has a good heart.

Later at home—2:15 AM (Tues., April 16 morning) out about 9:00 (after trying to find Ivy and Irving's number without success) to Shakespeare Pub behind Liberty's—several whiskeys there—so by Great Marlborough St. to Greek and Frith Sts.—found Crispino and

17. Herschel V. Johnson was then first secretary of the American Embassy in London. He had graduated from the University of North Carolina the year Wolfe entered.
18. The American-born wife of the second Viscount Astor, and the first woman elected to the House of Commons.

Isola Bella closed—So to Dickens' pub for drink—½ doz Whitstable oysters—2 drinks—so to Hungarian Restaurant for goulash—glass tokay—½ white Hungarian wine—apple strudel etc.—12s—so to Café Royal 12:15 closed—so up Regent St.—picked up nice looking woman —promised her 10s—went to coffee stand for cgs. bought her pack— took her here—paid her £ on [urging?]—then 10s more ("for being without letter") [19] then looking for money thought she had robbed me —she [making scene having but?] 10s—finally counted up and found she had not robbed me—paid her and put her out—So back, undressed *again,* washed privates, urinated, used préservatif carefully, found all pyjamas gone to laundry, now have on shirt bought in Vermont.

Tues., April 16, 1935 (in bed 2:AM—Wed. morning):

Short Log: Up, breakfast, bath, etc.—out to pub around corner —then by taxi to Bedford Square—then with Mr. [*Charles*] Kingsley on foot to Escargot on Greek St. for lunch—then back to office, got 50 £—then on foot to Y.M.C.A. on Great Russell St.—looked up G. McDonald—so with him and a friend of his to tavern on Gt. Russell St. —so by bus to Amexco—cable from Louise [*Mrs. Maxwell*] Perkins —answered cable—so to pub top of Haymarket—3 whiskies—so home by Piccadilly and Bond St.—so McDonald and friend at 7:30 for dinner—so to Shakespeare pub for sherry—to Restaurant des Gourmets for dinner—to Tatler (?) newsreel in Charing Cross road—wonderful picture about Gourmets with Julian Huxley talking—so with Mc. and friend to Oxford St. and Tottenham Court Rd.—said goodnight—so by Oxford St. to coffee stall at Oxford Circus for 3 cups tea & cigarettes—so home—wrote letter to Bill Weber [20]—so to bed.

Wapping Wall Station—by underground—The Prospect of Whitby—

The George and Vulture—Behind Royal Exchange & Bank.

Wed., April 17, 1935—at home in bed at 2:00 A.M. after very strenuous day—

Brief log—Up, breakfast, G. McDonald here at ten, sat for drawing 11:45—out to tailor's for fitting—then to Davis bookshop by taxi 12:30—met Davis, Ivy Elstob, her daughter Ianthe, and went to pub for drink, then to Café Royal for lunch in their car (I paid for lunch—very good and with two bottles white Corton)—then alone to Amexco—then on foot to Leicester Square, Strand, Aldwych to In-

19. In English slang a condom is called a "French letter."
20. William Weber was head of the publicity department at Scribner's.

tourist organization in Bush House—then along Kingsway, turned right into Lincoln's Inn Fields, New Square, Old Square, quietness, rattling of [bystanders opening of papers?]—then to little bookshop in Chancery Lane, where bought Sunday School sob-and-treacle special for 3d—then back through Lincoln's Inn, through recreation grounds where paused to sit and watch children playing, noble trees and monumental London all around—then into Kingsway, Holborn, Bloomsbury Square, Museum St.—there found Davis, Ivy, Ianthe waiting, said goodbye to Davis—then with Ivy and Ianthe in their car back through Holborn, Cheapside, Bank, Aldgate, etc., Tower, East London, away to Wharves and Docks of Wapping Wall—there to The Prospect of Whitby, a pub, publican fat red faced man, and men with caps on sitting on benches drinking bitter—and back on to verandah, and a view of Thames, The Pool of London, all of the barges and ships, (contrast with N.Y. harbor).

And so away and back through London to crowded Piccadilly, where left Ivy—said goodbye and went to old man Roberts' flat on Jermyn St. where found him, and old American-English internationable [*sic*] named Mrs. Bird, and presently an old alcoholic rabbit with a nervous giggle named Maurice Bing and a drink for all—and Bing leaving—with Uncle Henry and old Mrs. Bird to Apperodt's for dinner, which he gave—later with both of them to Piccadilly Circus (Eros) News Reel, and to see Elizabeth Bergner in "Escape Me Never" at Pavilion—actress good—but piece only part convincing, strained tragedy and theatricals—so put Mrs. Bird on bus at 11:30, said goodbye to Uncle Henry—paused and looked with thoughtful eyes at Café Royal, but passed it and its extended and unsavory midnight dinner—walked up Regent Street, had 2 Scotch at supper-house place near Oxford Circus, bought Gold Flakes there—and so home around the corner into Hanover Square and to bed, having seen much today and travelled far.

Notes—Impressions

"Nightingale Lane"—leading to Wapping Wall—Great walls of grimy brick to either side—slow footed horses with huge shaggy hoofs unhitched and clopping slowly from their work—no nightingales—good nature and good humour of the people—a bobby who looked at us when we came to a blind end—the people wanting to tell us how to go—the great humor and intelligence of the people, noticed many times before.

Thurs., April 18, 1935:

Up, b'kfast (sausages, etc.), wrote long letter to Louise Perkins [21] suggesting Max come over here—out to tailor's—took waistcoat for altering—tried on 2d new suit—paid him 11 £ 11s (11 gns.)—then on foot to Amexco—note from P. Engle—my dear Wolfe sort of thing—in training for Oxford 8s etc.—bought several N.Y. papers including Monday, April 8, N.Y. *Times* showing me leading in N.Y. and 1st, 2d, 3d in other places:

Of Time and the River

FIRST	SECOND	THIRD	FOURTH	FIFTH	SIXTH	SEVENTH
1 (New York)	2 (Philadelphia– Wash.)	3 (Boston, Atlanta, Chicago)	1 (St Louis)	0	1 (New Orleans)	

Ferber [*Come and Get It*]

2 (Wash San Fran)	4	1	1			1

—then to Stone's for Scotch (½) then to Café Royal—lunch Corton Blanc—then to Leicester Square—back to Amexco with round railway ticket Folkestone–London, which turned in—then to P.O. mailed letters S.S. Bothnia, Louise P. and Bill Weber—then by taxi to [Intourist?] —tailor—then on foot to Piccadilly, Jermyn St. etc. (now raining) intending go Westminster Abbey—so along Jermyn into [*Cavendish Hotel*] Rosie Lewis, and saw old Rosie—very red of face and drunk, propped up on sofa—also two whores fixing stockings—asked for Mr. Jackson Gregory knowing he had once been there—so did she, I think—said "Yes, he often stops here but is not here at present —Drop in again, dear" etc.—so to Criterion Rest. Piccadilly for tea—so to Plaza Cinema for Ann Harding in "The Fountain," [Cin. 99?] etc. (out 9:30).

So to Long Bar, Queen's Hotel, Leicester Square for whiskey (4) where a most [loathful?] old woman—trickster—came in kissing barmaid's hands etc.—and at length a horrible little tout—so-called [horseleader?]—a kind of decayed, more-corrupt Frank Swinnerton face with little sparse goatee, hairs over upper lip, rotten teeth and rotten soul, came siding up beside me—wrote me names of two 'osses "sure to win" tomorrow—said 'ow 'e loved Americans—worked in Pennsylvynia oil fields 'e did, says 'e, one time—I asked him whether it was near Des Moines or Sioux City, Pennsylvania—and he said it was

21. For this letter to Mrs. Perkins, see *Letters*, pp. 452–54.

Des Moines—asked for couple-a-bob guv-ner, pay yer back tomorrer
—when I refused—[taught?] him [that?]—he kept nudging closer—I
put him back—and after venomous looks, [hard pushings?]—I knows a
proper man when I sees one, you're a prize sport, sir, (trying to [wring
his beard in?] his horrible shining, cold, flabby hand)—with a venomous look of murderous hatred at me he departed—so at dining time to
Spanish restaurant in Regent St. where ate chicken—bean soup—nougat—quince honey—honey-almond—strong white Spanish wine—and
so up Regent St. to Hanover Square and bed.

Good Friday, April 19—written 1:AM at night in bed on Ebury St.—
    Up, breakfast, bathed, showered, put on new suit, wrote C.
Brett letter [22]—out to Shakespeare pub for drinks and to a late lunch in
Café Royal—bought *New Yorker* for April 6 Piccadilly—then down
Haymarket into Whitehall there saw the Horseguards at their spectac-
ular and gaudy nonsense, and hordes of people with their grey
[*illegible*] some most poor, ragged, dirty, starved ones too, gaping and
craning at it—then down to Westminster Abbey—which was crowded
with service and to be closed immediately after at 4:30 so couldn't get
in—so along noble houses of Parliament and looked at magnificent line
work of old time-grimed stone and all the rich old figures of old
knights and kings, and reflected how kind time and the English
weather had been to London and how much of her glory and magnificence owed to this—so down the stairs to quays at foot of Westminster Bridge and many people out and looking at the river, and walking
back and forth, and crowded pleasure boats coming in—and got some
cigarettes at underground Whitehall [way?] and back by "subway" to
quays and took seat in boat going down river and watched it fill, and
presently, sharp at four o'clock, we cast off swiftly turned and circled
and started down the river with cockney guide a-pointing out the
points of interest.
    And trip was grand—the great *monument* of London shone
magnificently—and presently came among the warehouses and shipping and those big grimy wharves and warehouses with the great dirty
river flowing silently past—was like a somber vision of old time and
silence that one sees in dreams and I know that I *have* dreamed—shall
dream upon this river of dark time—with these high sombre walls of
grimy brick and great monuments and spires and towers in the background—and the reason I think that one feels old time and silence here

22. Catherine Brett, Director of Brett's School (for retarded children) at
Dingman's Ferry, Pa. Miss Brett introduced Wolfe to the beauties of the Penn-
sylvania landscape by taking him on fall or spring drives through the Pocono
Mountains and the Delaware Water Gap Area.

as nowhere else on earth is because the warehouse walls come sheer down into the water and there are no docks out into the river—the river being not wide enough—even the ships—the tramps, the barges and the lighters being laid up flat against the warehouse walls of old fog-time-grimed brick—And one feels beneath these gloomy walls of brick—Curiously enough, God knows, the ancientness of London, and ten hundred cities and all her faces and all the houses that stood here in Queen Victoria's time—and when one passes the Haig whiskey warehouse on the Southern Shore and is told that Shakespeare's theatre was there, one knows it was, and feels it there and sees just what the London of that day was like.

So back again—up river—all the people on the boat—two girls next to me—and intelligent looking people too—a boy, a girl, two women and a man opposite—but all most starved and undernourished looking—and fat man with red face playing delightfully with his little fat blonde child, and many others—so back to Westminster a little before six, and the sun just coming out nicely now—but somewhat raw and cold upon the river—and into Lyons place in Whitehall for tea and scones—then up to Plaza in Regent St. for the W. C. Fields picture— but couldn't get in—so walked into Shaftesbury Avenue and stood on corner watching—and a high clear sky of mild, approaching Spring—a feeling of softness and peace and delight in the air—and not quite seven —so along Shaftesbury to Cambridge circus where looked at advertisements of David Copperfield picture and [freak?] notices—so down Charing Cross Road to little Square behind Nat'l Gallery where a dark-faced Latin-Nigger sort of man who called himself the Nat'l Health Food League harangued a gape-mouthed crowd of a hundred or two with vital, perky energies and utterly meaningless and disconnected "scientific data" about women's worries, knischen salts, beer cancer, God knows what else, but left before I found out what his gag was—seeing people same in London as Brooklyn or anywhere on earth—and ever ready to be fooled and hypnotized by sound and clamor.

So into Garrick Pub for drink and sat on leather cushions watching people there—so to Panton St. where found Stone's closed but entered another pub there for a drink—and woman with most lovely eyes and rather lovely face sat next to me with man and smoked, and had a drink and then both went on, and guess that she both fucked and worked somewhere, but we don't have just her kind, I think, at home—it takes an older country—and so back to Plaza where theatre was just emptying first performance and queues going in, and joined 3s 6d queue and got a seat—and marvelous picture of Bali (Java)—a travel picture made in a kind of fiction-love-story but girls beautiful with most beautiful breasts and bodies I ever saw—and all the customs and rituals strange and wonderful—and saw the "Mississippi" picture and liked Fields as I always did—the rest gluey, pseudo-Southern claptrap—so out at 11:30 and up Regent street (pubs being closed at 10) to supper place and back room, on upper Regent near Hanover Square, where had beef and tongue sandwich, glass of milk and on home.

ON ENGLISH SERVILITY, LOVE OF LIBERTY, ETC.

(written Good Friday, April 19—at midnight in my rooms in Hanover Square just after returning home from day out sightseeing and to see W. C. Fields in new film "Mississippi.")

(Notes)

Rousseau mistakenly but eloquently said that man was born free but you find him everywhere in chains. I have sometimes thought that Englishmen were born free but deliberately forged their own chains, because they preferred to wear them. All of my life I have heard of the English love of freedom, their respect for individual liberty, the independence of their minds and spirits. My own experience in England has not shown me these virtues to any striking degree.

It is a curious fact that the so-called democratic countries have not made anywhere near the use of that priceless heritage of democratic citizenship—the ballot—that some of the non-democratic countries have. In the autumn of 1930, for example, I was living in the Black Forest of Germany when a national election was held—the number of political parties competing in the election was staggering—2 dozen or more—and the total vote in a population of 65 millions was between forty and forty five million. I believe this figure tops our own greatest figure—in the Campaign of 1932 when Roosevelt was elected—and our own population is about twice that of Germany's. And I don't believe England has ever come anywhere near this figure.

Sat., April 20:
Ed Feeney [23]—[Foger Club?]—Greek Street—Right opposite Escargot Bienvenu.

23. An Irishman Wolfe met in London who gave County Kerry as his address.

Sat.—After Good Friday 1935—April 20th:

Up, ate, bathed it, and shave etc.—by taxi Amexco—bt. 3 H. Trib. newsp. N.Y. [*illegible*] etc.—letter C. Brett etc.—Stone's— Scotch [*illegible*]—on ft. to Café Royal—then Ed Feeney "Tom!" etc. etc.—and what he [*illegible*] 5 years ago etc.—out with E. Feeney after brandy to his place with girl [*remainder of passage, two and a half pages, is illegible*].

Sunday, April 21—

Awoke at 11 feeling very rocky after drinking of yesterday—no b'kfast—I called Sykes for tea—also called Feeney & made engagement for lunch—Sykes brought [Chu?] tea with lemon & aspirin—talked to him some time—expressed regret for conduct of night before—he very nice—then bathed—Feeney came while bathing—2 drinks with Feeney —then to Café Royal for lunch—good lunch with Johannesburger 12s each—then came to flat—most of the afternoon talking—Feeney's pitiable grotesque phoninees—then out at 6:30 with Feeney to Claridge's for cocktails—Hungarian & Viennese blonde played beautifully for us—3 cocktails—Feeney getting very drunk and very stagey— cheap imitation of stage Englishman—so away about 8:40 and by taxi to Mount Royal where Feeney ordered wine for dinner and left pound note—then up to room, ordered whiskey, left note for cousin—then down to dinner where now Feeney loud and drunken—they brought smoked salmon—"I'll tear up the fuckin' joint" etc.—so his physically very attractive, seductive Miss Pat Maloney found us—so up to room —Feeney very drunk now and discovering in fact he was just a Boston Irishman, and I know this bloody lot over here—Don't trust an Englishman etc.—and how the Prince of Wales would get out of bed to meet me—and don't pose—that's just a pose, old boy, etc.—so Pat left about 12:30—and I towards one—Feeney coming down stairs his face now thick and Irish and coarse with drink, his eyes inflamed and mad—so along Oxford Street to Oxford Circus coffee stand—3 cups of tea—a bit meat pie—a pack of Gold Flakes and all the nighttime people —whore—strange street gang—quietly ordering biscuits etc.—so home to bed.

Seen: Museums, Public Monuments, etc.: Nat'l Gallery 2, St. Paul's, Guild Hall, St. Mary le Bow, Westminster Abbey, Lincoln's Inn Fields.

Three Phonies: Deegan, Bob Foster, Ed Feeney.

Easter Monday—April 22, 1935, Oddenino's Café—10: PM—

Three people—two men and a woman—the men Jews—and American-looking—one with big extraordinary nose someone I know —or have seen before—Dark time—This place a new, modern-looking sort of place with modern chairs of nickel-like springs—sort of place Americans might patronize—Came here from old musty-fusty-browny-motley smelly pub—Think I like this better—

Today: up, bathed, let b'kfast get cold etc.—wrote letter Miss E. Nowell [24]—got times of trains to Cambridge—out in dead Sunday calm—to Shakespeare pub, 4 whiskey—bar-maid—Alf-Erbert sort of talk—then to Café Royal—good lunch (braised steak) still hungry as we haven't eaten dinner tonight—½ bottle white Burgundy 23 (Meursault)—then down Whitehall to Horseguards—a little before four—thousands of people to see less than a dozen men dressed up like monkeys go thru their hokus pokus—*the white damned faces of the English poor* (different from 14 St. N.Y. Jews)—underfeeding, ill-nourishing, rotten teeth—then down to Westminster Abbey and great crowds there, too, streaming in and out and so there till closing time 5:30—and by bus to Regent St.—and slept from 6:00–8:—not going away today—and out to Shakespeare pub again and down to Bodega and then to pub with snack bar nearby—and so here to Oddenino's.

Don't forget porters with pads on arm at Folkestone—[the brother pulling others?]

Continuation:—And leaving Oddenino's at closing time, they putting off lights until the lights burned violet, and bartender coming round saying "I must ahsk you for your glass please"—man I had seen, New York Jew with big nose, and his friend, and a woman there to end, but so departed—and I to Spanish Restaurant Regent St. (people on street waiting for bus with busy-closing-up feeling all around) and in Spanish restaurant—dry sherry, thick bean soup, meat balls, very good, a bottle of red Spanish wine, "the Selection," a slab of quince honey, another of nougat, one of honey and almond, coffee etc.—so up Regent to Oxford circus for 2 cups tea [*at*] coffee stall—Gold Flakes —and so home very full and tired to bed.

Tuesday, April 23, 1935 (written at Cambridge in room at University Arms hotel at 12:30 A.M.)—

Up at ten—b'kfast—egg—bacon—tea—marmalade etc.—wrote long letter to Mabel in answer to hers of other day—telling her too

24. For this letter, misdated April 23, see *Letters*, pp. 457–58.

much of Olmstead business [25] too little other news—read *Times*, bathed, shaved, etc.—out at 12:30—down George St. to Oddenino's, 4 dry martinis—talked to little waitress of night before—several good-looking women about—waitress has relatives in Chester, Pa. and told me an aunt was "drowned"—washed overboard from deck of ship when returning to Eng. to visit them—so through Piccadilly into Soho to Greek St. and Escargot—Frere's wife and other woman sitting near door but didn't see them till I passed, and didn't speak—Frere with another woman in back of rest. but didn't see him either till later.

So good lunch of filet, artichoke with butter sauce, coffee, Chablis, brandy—Frere came over to talk to me—he said, "What are you trying to do, old boy, avoid me? Didn't you see me when you came in?"—I said "No, just a minute ago"—I said, "What are your plans?"—He said they were going to publish in May—no further news from book club but go ahead without a con[*tract?*] etc.—I would have stirred you out old boy but thought you preferred to be alone etc. Why didn't you look us up—you could have come down over week end, etc.—told him I was going to Cambridge and so to Norfolk, Holland, Germany, etc.—"If you need anything call on us" etc. "Why don't you come back here when book comes out?"—so he left—I presently out—"Bon Jour, monsieur" old French host at door—so down to George's—where looked at *New Republic* [26]—made me tremble with despair and hopelessness and a feeling of "die, dog, die"—the world is to be made safe for the Cowleys, Josephsons, etcs. forever—so shout your God damned lungs out, Wolfe—Cowley and Josephson forever—

So to Amexco—no mail—so changed 2 × $20 Amexco checks in Eng. money—one $20 into German tourists marks—80—bought 3 N.Y. *Times*, April 11, 12, 13—nothing for me in them—so to French Line—will make transfer arrangements in Berlin—so back up Haymarket into Leicester Sq. to George's—bought *New Republic* which spoke of "smoke and fury" on "check Spring list" [27] etc.—so by taxi from Leicester Square to Hanover Square—So Sykes and I packed—I paid Sykes balance on bill, £16s 2d—and gave him one £2s (10s for Davis, 10s for Lansers, 2s for elevator boy) and 2s 6d extra for himself as I left —a perfectly magnificent, beautiful American woman fabulously

25. Stanley Olmstead, whose sister was a friend of Mabel's, had sent Wolfe a manuscript to read, and Wolfe had lost track of it. For the letter to Mabel, see *Letters*, pp. 454–57.

26. The March 20, 1935, issue contained a review by Malcolm Cowley, one of the most unfavorable the book received.

27. The April 10, 1935, issue had "A Check List of Spring Books" which included *Of Time and the River* with the comment: "A 912-page portrait of the American artist as a young man and as a myth of smoke and fury."

dressed with young Englishman or European—and picture of George St. and Hanover Sq. with kodak—so down Regent, Haymarket, to Embankment and along it—magnificent light along courts of Temple —into city by Victoria street—English lute very sweet with song, and all the faces of the people seen—farewell, and when will I be this way again—and so by bank and Royal Exchange and by Threadneedle Street and then into dense old London, rich grimed London and the streets of dense, rich shops, old grimed monumental stones—and all the weather, the drabness, the complexity, and suddenly the real complexity of the culture, the gewirr, gewirr of grinding traffic and the sudden perky pertness—Right you are, sir—baggage masters—Right O Jawge —Ticket windows.

"Number 2 for Cambridge"—then the great huge smoking sheds—the refreshment rooms loaded with people drinking "bitter"— and the musty fusty smell—smell of malt and tea and bitter and cigarette tobacco and the trains steaming—and the great news stand loaded with a thousand kinds of fiction, mags. etc.—and the Cambridge boys, the university people, the girls et al sitting on baggage, talking in doors etc.—then the ride up in late, high springtime—all of the filth of London—Bethnal Green—Hackney—Tottenham—miles and miles of chimney pots and grey-grimed brick—and rabbit hutches of brick rows of houses and the sudden green and then all of the sudden green of young fruit budding trees—the incredible green tapestry of the English earth—and the gentle, mild, the good and old and saxon sweep of wold and wood and field and slope and sky—and eating in dining car thick soup, meat loaf and rhubarb tart and wine and brandy and muddy-uddy-bittery-mud-coffee—and old beef-face with white mustaches beside me and "I'll take the rhubarb tart" briskly from woman up ahead and Cambridge presently and [instantly?]—going into baggage room to find my two big pieces and finding one and not the other —and presently a porter and *of course* the other—so out to taxi—so here to hotel—so out for walk through old, bending streets, past colleges—across a stream behind the backs, and so through college yards to streets again—and so to pub filled with beer-drinking natives and coarse laughter—so to another opposite hotel with publick—and a-little-effeminate, bright college boys—so to hotel to awful garish hotel—dismal—huge lobby—whiskey—and so up to read Pepys diary and to write this while old, sweet bells chime sweetly.

A Pub In Cambridge (Morley's)—Big high ceilinged room full of brown malt smell—long rounded bar—great stained kegs and casks behind—above a great kind of walnut screen with inscriptions in gold Elizabethan-shaped letters—a clock at top—above, "The shifting hour"

—Elsewhere below, "Dost thou love life? then do not squander time for that is the stuff life is made of"—Elsewhere, "Money lost, little lost —Honour lost, much lost—Pluck lost, all lost."

Wed., April 24, 1935—Written in bedroom at Royal Hotel, Norwich, at 12:25 A.M.

Up in Cambridge at University Arms at ten-thirty—so to late breakfast—tea, sausage, bacon, marmalade etc.—so wrote two letters to Miss Wyckoff and Miss Gwenneth Beam [28]—mailed them—out for walk through town to Magdalene—[magnificent?] gardens—the wizard-green of trees (with broad lines like backs) and the cool green water of the Cam between old red walls—the luxury of punts—so to little pub across from Magdalene where sat in pleasant, scrubbed, little mapled bar—light maple back—and pleasant view—mellow yellow coming through—and watching Cambridge students passing in their uniforms of flannel grey and plaid coats, brown or grey or checked— and had two whiskeys—read my guide and maps—so back over Bridge and by John's street (?) along by colleges and to Angel Pub just off the Market Hill, and huge fat gargantuan publican and workmen with their beers and "Aye, Jawge—that 'e did" etc.—and farmer talking of his crops and 'ow we should-a-had grahss last week in May—"it's got to come from seed."

"I blowed two ewes up that I been keepin lahst four year—I told my chaps" etc.—and old man with square derby hat and scraggly beard and face of a distinguished character in to drink his beer—'e couldn't drink Bass ale—no, when I ran a public 'ouse meself I allus found marl (barl?) beer was best—that's wot the draymen allus said an' they should know—and so on huge fat publican's advice to Bath inn for steak—and had whiskey first—then thick grilled steak in little peeweest room of house with voices of young Cambridge squirts and show-offs—one with beagle—all around me—one talking French, "C'est formidable" etc. to companion—and other men—perhaps not of the university, and each with a little of the vulgar would-be-loudly show-off in him—so at length back to Market Hill and through a line before an old book store—bought Thackeray's *Book of Snobs* and *Paris Sketch Book* on the 3d shelf—and so inside to pay and man inside at desk most courteous and concerned about the 6d—and the little shop was full of fine old books—great sets of Racine, Pope and Johnson in fine old bindings—so I left at length—a good, a pleasant place—and to King's Chapel—there in that wonderful vaulted make of stone we have

28. Miss Irma Wyckoff, Maxwell Perkins' secretary, typed letters and occasionally a manuscript for Wolfe. Miss Beam was also a typist for him. For the letter to Miss Wyckoff, see *Letters*, p. 458.

[*sic*]—so through King's Quad and to the college backs and green incredible married to carved lovely stone—and so across King's Bridge into the College backs and saw King's Chapel and Clare College and the college backs all riotous with an incredible Cranach-sewed-in tapestry of flowers—and the view of the great chapel—Clare, the bridges, and the backs, the noblest, calmest and most magnificent prospect I have ever seen in Europe—its loveliness is incredible and no wonder poets grew here.

So across Clare Bridge through Clare and so to the great quad of Trinity, then to lesser one, and Wren's great library, and the backs again—and wonder and magic loveliness can do no more—and beauty joins with beauty—so into St. John's, across the Bridge of Sighs into John's Second Court (vide Ruskin) and out on street and in to Caius for a moment—this, too, lovely—out by Senate—so by book store on the corner into Market Hill and by the old bank and rich shops of Petty Cury—oh, how rich and fine the shops are—and the butchers, with the lovely guinea hens and pigeons, the great York hams, and cheeses, and the smell of smoked ham—oh, how succulent and rich— and students and the townsmen passing—and a healthy and good looking woman (maybe don's wife) in the great delicious food store with the smell of cheese and eggs and great smoked hams about her, and all of her rosy flesh and golden hair of morning gold—so for a moment into Christ's on way back, then into Emmanuel—so to hotel where wrote 4 cards with pictures of colleges—had a drink—paid bill —packed up and left my baggage with porter—so to station by taxi with only my brief case—ticket 3d to Norwich—and a light, late golden evening of green England—so drink at station with gold late light streaming in pleasantly in faded, smoky, dingy old refreshment room.

Then train came in with casual intimacy of slammed and unslammed compartment doors of English train—a long, long train of little, sedate, rich-colored cars—uncoupled restaurant put at rear of train—I found a seat far forward in 3rd-class comp. with two men who talked rich Scots—and so with bright late gold astream and blinding on as we rattled through the yards and out of Cambridge—to either side a level, green, and lovely carpet of the land cut by calm streams that ran through sodded banks, green to the water's edge, and with a greening feather smoke of trees set sparsely, wonderfully across land—So Ely and a moment's glimpse of its cathedral—so the green flat carpet of the land again, calm cattle grazing, folded sheep—as we went northbound, land more barren with hints of sea—the yellow tufted marsh grass— waste demesnes of tiny stunted pine—and sometimes tall and lonely pine, wind shaped, sea shaped, and not unlike home—occasional roll and lift to land as well—a less calm and pastoral, and more wild and lonely scene.

It kept light almost into Norwich—so out assisting young woman on her way to Yarmouth—and with stream of people up the station platform past ticket taker into another town—and by taxi from the station past great line of houses uphill to the Royal Hotel, a large unvented, forbidding, cheerless hotel room in the Victorian tradition—a cheap chop in the grill (grilled over coals) and "chips" and cabbage and a drink and glass of old ale—a friendly would-be-helpful young waiter—so out and for a walk in vague direction of Cathedral and in a place with the grim name of Tombway (?) [*Tombland*] past a house in fake Elizabethan with great bands of neon light and sign that said the House of Samson and Hercules—Swimming Pool—Mixed Bathing, Adults ls Children 6d, Spectators 3d—how *can* we foretell things like this—so in the dark and shadowy half-emergence of new strange town down what seemed to be a rather cheerless street to Bridge —so turned, retraced my steps along the Tombway (?) to hotel—consulted pamphlet of Norwich which the porter loaned me (in Cambridge)—and so to bed where I have read in *Paris Sketch Book* and have written *this*.

Thurs., April 25, 1935 (Brief log—fill in tomorrow):

Up at 10:15—dressed, shaved etc.—down to breakfast—poached eggs, bacon, tea, toast, marmalade—sent telegram to Reeves for 10 £s —out to White Maid (?) [*Maid's Head*] hotel for whiskey—then to Barclay's bank to cash $20 check (only *one* left now)—by splendid new vault of bank—"what do you think of our bank, sir"—Down to pub on King Street filled with working men—for drink—listened to them talk of races—the long, keen, big nosed Norfolk face—the almost humiliated attention to civilities—"*Good* mornin', Jawge"—"*Good* mornin', *good* mornin'—I spoke w'en I come in I did" etc.—Face of Norfolk woman washing windows etc.—dark Huguenot look to some of 'em—then to pub down below of sweller rest.—the red faced publican—with spurious, sly, good nature—"Come on, now, drink up and 'ave a drink on me, sir"—yes, and gets *two* out of you before he does, and laughs about it to the lads as you go out, 'e does, and his sport —man all dressed up in checked plus fours and loud checked stockings, quite good-looking, and even crookeder looking than old man—so up to Central Hotel—a cold, chill place redolent of boarding house dining rooms the world over—and had the dinner of the cold, chill place— soup, slivers of beef, dumplings, carrots, canned peaches with gooey cultured cheese and crackers, and a glass of Bass—and traveling man chattered at next table to a maid—and a cold and dreary looking couple who looked as if they'd come from Ely for a little cold and dreary boarding house adultery.

So out and to Royal Hotel where found 10 £—so to Cathedral —there an hour or two and listened to the guide—a grey-bearded "proctor" or whatever you call him—quite pleasant and intelligent as he talked of screens and glass and Norman arches—and "we regret unfortunately" etc.—"which I regret to say was used as a jail"—"and I hope I have not bored you too much" with a modest yet somewhat complaisant air of a man who feels he has done pretty well—the place where the monks played marbles, etc.—and their [wading troughs?] —so out and all around Cathedral Close, past pleasant old houses of red brick and strange, flinty-agatey stone crushed, and so across river and along river for rear view of cathedral across green fields and trees dense and white with blossoms—apple and cherry I suppose—along street of rather cheery red-brick houses with square, big windows and two doorways to a house—ugly and depressing looking but still neat and solid compared to our like streets in Phil., Chicago, etc.—so along green, sweet, calm river to r'way station, and up hill again towards hotel, past silent sheltered shops (Thurs. early closing)—so up the hill to castle where four o'clock and so was closing—Market hill and square by castle empty, too, with all the non-paved storebacks of sheep and cattle market, I suppose—so around castle walls for view of town and quite spread out with low green hills—not unlike Eastern Pa.— then through country line-like shops near castle—business and shopping centre with good shops, too, and a bookseller named Goose and Son—and now the sun out, gold and pleasant on the plaster and old red brick—so back to hotel where paid bill and packed my brief case, left Berlin address, and so on foot to r'way station where arrived 6:45 with plenty of time before my train out 6:57.

So train to Yarmouth across a level, lovely carpet of green, fertile country with small calm rivers, great green fields full of grazing Cuypian cows, others full of fat thick-wooled sheep, and constantly more Dutch looking and windmill too—so at last to Yarmouth—and walked from station across town through old lanes not 4 ft. wide, with old houses leaning and melted down by age together and brown, old plasters, old red rotting brick, and crazily askew and gnarled with age—so out into main busy street and tents and canvasses of unopened carnival—"a Fair" that starts tomorrow—and throngs of people and hundreds of Navy boys and children—(made me think of deserted carnival at home 25 years ago, and how we ran the elevator all day long on Sunday).

And so across and through into never more solid looking streets of red-brick houses—some quite large and opening with many "board" and "hotel" signs—and presently out upon the Marine Parade with great piers, beaches and aquariums—and hotels and boarding houses on one side—all sparsely peopled now, depressing looking, raw and chill, too—a more sedate and solid, and more dull, edition of Atlantic City —and dull as all the places of this sort that I have ever seen in England —and somehow depressing picture theatre saying Doug Fairbanks tonight—and a third-rate music show from London—and presently Royal Hotel where a smootheyed Jew proprietor said yes sir—certainly sir, etc.—give me room and breakfast for 10s 6d—so up to see it —so down to drink—and found in bar a gathering of local sports including bar room wit and semi-drunk who insisted on buying gentleman a drink, which I refused, seeing insolence and lurking offense behind his manner.

So out after drink of my own to simple pub up the Parade and had two whiskies—and friendly proprietor, and red faced customer from Birmingham who said "aye," and wife who found things "nahss," and kiddie who stayed outside with ginger wine until pub owner said "Bring the kiddie in"—"There's three flats over there"—"Ah, no matter," said the other, "they're not noticing, bring her in"—Then big discussion about silliness of law—yet good thing too, it was, they used to bring the kiddies and keep them outside there rest o' the night—I don't mind tellin' you either I've had to tell 'em I thought it was time they was takin' their kid 'ome to bed"—"Aye—that they did—I've seen 'em"—"In the old days they'd come in 'ere and stay all day—I've seen 'em bring the old man's dinner to 'm many a time—saying, we couldn't get ye to come home to dinner so we brought it to you—hah! hah! hah! an' 'im a-playing cards an' not able to get on with it."

Then big discussion of hard drinking habits of the Scotch fishermen—"When they 'ad the money—aye, all night long, a double Scotch, neat, mind you—I never seen a Scotchman yet as mixed his spirits with water—they'd follow it up with beer as a chaser—just take the 'ead off the beer, y' see—not enough to spoil the taste of the whiskey"—and so on about a pub he had before the war when a big pint of beer was tuppence, 'alf pint a penny, spirits tuppence—an' coffeee and tea at either end of the bar—all you could drink of it free —I never charged 'em for it—cus' I used to take in my ten pound a day afore nine in the mornin, and the rest of the day everything I sold in flasks—a quatern of gin for six pence, etc."

Then another customer, and a technical discussion about football—[*illegible*]—"There's too much money in it" etc.—so presently all out, and after little more talk with man I too—and back to hotel—where went late for dinner I had ordered—but had it—soup, cod, a good steak, cauliflower, tart and cream, and ale, etc.—and bar-room sports, new lot still in bar—so out for walk along Parade, and into a large modern pub-saloon for brandy—so went along Parade, and back, and down on beach to sea—and so in before eleven—so write this in room—and so to bed—Don't forget swimming pool in Norwich— (also publican and Birmingham woman's statement that most working people can afford only one drink a week—at weekend)—(nahss—poor contorted young face—it was nahss, it was).

Friday, April 26, 1935 (written Saturday, April 27—11:15 at night in bed in room of a little inn called Anchor, Blakeney, Norfolk—Resumé of *yesterday, Friday, April 26,* as briefly as possible):

Up, 10 or 10:30, down to breakfast—kipper, eggs, bacon, tea, marmalade, etc.—wrote note to Frere Reeves acknowledging & thanking receipt of 10 £—then on porter's advice down Parade towards fishing wharves—stopped at new-looking, well-fitted-up pub at turning-in toward monument place—had drink—In comes man with ruddy face and gout—Discusses gout and swollen ankles with publican—a ruddy, curly haired, plump man named Riley—Riley opens window of pub when he leaves and shouts out to him (who is in car)—I say, Tom, cut out the cigarettes—an' go easy on the spirits—an' ahfter that you may as well shoot yourself.

Then in two men—one old and ruddy and jolly and assured of manner—about 75—and another with bowler hat and mustache and thin humorous mouth—they shake dice for drinks and old man wins, and man with bowler says to dice in humorous-tragical tone, "Curse you; roll off on the floor" etc.—Then Riley tells old man about late departed customer's gout—and about his own—and old man says, "It comes from laziness—If either of you worked for your living you'd never know what gout was—I'm 75 and I never had a touch of it" etc. —So very hastily and merrily out with other man and into car and away—and Riley and a working man in old, ragged, paint bespotted garments with mustaches, wide-fantastic-twisted, and waxed, with long points—begins telling me now about old man who just left—His name is Beacon (?)—he has been mayor of Yarmouth twice—he is the richest man in town—"he has his finger in everything" (so paint-bespotted man)—" 'e was a baker to begin with—an a gamblin' man—'e made 's money with the 'osses—I've seen 'em up at 5:30 kneadin the dough for the bread with 'is own 'ands—an' on the train for Epsom by nine o'clock—'e gave me 'is 'ole story once—beggin' yer pardon, George, Yuh don't mind my goin' on this way in front of the gentleman—but in me 'umble way I'm a bit of a journalist," etc.—(now waxed mustaches and explained)—" 'e says to me: if I 'ad any gift of words, I'd write it down meself—all the things I done—'e had a fleet of herring boats, sir," etc.—"an' I says to 'em—I kept the rekkid, Mr. Beacon, of the whole story—I'm goin' give it to the world someday—beggin yer pardon, sir, in me 'umble way I'm a bit of a journalist—an a painter, sir—"

He then asked me about things in America, sayin' "I can't 'elp bein interested—I'm a bit of a journalist, sir, an' I keep up with affairs in the paper—George, you don't mind my askin' the gentleman do you —I'm a bit of a journalist, an I'm interested in wots goin' on"—I gathered that George (Riley), a choleric and probably unread Irishman, was a bit jealous and resentful and apt to flare up with "You'd better be tendin' to yer job instead of marchin' about" etc.—We talked about the Germans and the French, and the "bit of a journalist" confided he had lived 3½ years among the French, and cos 'e knew their ways, all the whole lot of 'em are out to do you—

"I lived among 'em for 3½ years, sir, an I'm 'ere to tell you"—leaning forward, long waxed moustache tips quivering, eyes serious, most earnestly—"I'm 'ere to tell you, sir, the most that I saw 'em do was villainy"—no mistaking his earnestness—Bought them drinks and left finally with a "Cherio, old man—all the best" from Riley, and a handshake from other—"Pleasure to o've made your acquaintance, sir —As I say, in me 'umble way I'm a bit of a journalist myself" etc.—Then down past monument—past deserted fish sheds—quays—along by River Yare—the tethered tugs—(fishing boats?)—the tidy closed appearance of all—the brick walls coming sheer down to the neat, small-cobbled quays—the tidy, straightened-up appearance of everything in contrast to America's actual shambles of factory, rust, rubbish, slum, waste-land field or ash-heap—formless chaos—so at length to Town Hall—into Star Hotel for drink and lunch—and good lunch, too, late as it was—with scallops, plum, spring lamb, tart and cheese, and ale—so out, and walked about, and up Regent St. to Market Place, and cheap carnival going with thousands of people—I must have seen 10,000 pople, 10,000 Englishmen, 10,000 Yarmouth men—the greater part women and children, many children in perambulators, and the things I noticed were these:

1. The astonishing, noble and serene, healthy and rosy-featured beauty of the children—Calmly, like little lords of life and of the universe, they stared out at the world from their perambulators—and sweeter blue-eyed, more delicate, and ruddy, golden-headed children I have never seen—

2. As they got a little older—i.e. beyond 1 or 2 or 4 or 6—when they reached the schoolboy stage of 8 (?) or 9 or 10 or 12 etc.—they

got grubby, ratty, dirty, muddy, ill-complexioned, sometimes even meager and ill-fed looking—little English schoolboys—in their shabby little clothes (of the lower class) and little mottled fyces, etc.

3. The general "goodness," and yet a general look of "feebleness," among the people, viz.

4. Not to say I did not see strong and healthy people among them, for there were (strong, red-and-large-fyced fishermen), or even little Scots fishermen with strong, sturdy looking bodies, etc.

5. But generally a look of malnutrition—and not a malnutrition of their life, but of the last hundreds of years, so that one saw, for example, little, dwarf like figures, hands in pockets, caps on head, but as my mother would say "all stewed down to rabbits' size." [29]

6. No goodlooking women—no women with good teeth, tits, legs, buttocks, thighs, or bellies.

[*Monday, April 29*]

Cambridge—sitting in a railway carriage (3d class compt.— smoking) of L.N.E.R. train at the Cambridge Station 6:35—bright, late, English light of evening after a glorious day and ride across the sea-moor North of Norfolk and West Norfolk—On my right hand— the station gigs, and low, 6 inches above the ground, sit baggage trucks with yellow, strong, wrought box ("the English ry.") upon it—and to my right the rilewiye yards with three rows of tracks clumped with their smutty, grease-grimed, splendid, smooth sleepers—and then a train of polished oak—and walnut looking cars (coaches) with golden letters 3 and J and old stage coach rolling to the [even rhythm?]—of the big, high [*illegible*]—Little work trains rolling by now—Brick-end backs of dismal fog-white-yellow-gray—the muck and mist and grime —a "peaty" look and smell to everything and in between already patches of the sweet green grass—across to left now—newer places plastery—[villa?]—yellow—in rows along something—or around—and yet not bad—better than our New Jersey 50 mns. from New York "Tudorstein" streets—and oh, the sweet, flat, green of fields—all of the [marigold?] of little yellow flowers—the incredible, sweet, thick green of grass—and now the town coming—masses of solid brick—and yellow and white smoke—columns of trees—the spire of every church the great [*illegible*]—(and crazy thing—we are going the way I thought we wo'n't—Ely-wards)—the [*illegible*], not unpleasant red of new red-tiled roofs—rows of brick and yellow fog and new rowed houses —who lives here?—the butcher's chief ass't—how much better, finer, than our own—the long fields of sweet, high green—the hedges—a

29. Wolfe developed this note into a sketch of the wretched delivery boy in YCGHA, pp. 531–33.

windmill on a gentle rise—some trees now greening into May incredible—yet not really full yet—O the springtime, the pretty ringtime, hey ding a ding, ding.[30]

This morning being Weds.—the very shy, and gentle, tall young man with receding chin, brown silky moustache, and protruding stick-out teeth—¾ false—"I'm very sure of myself with the grahses but I'm still a trifle shy with the sedges"—and the other—little creature with shaved scalp naked, but hair that looked as if it were coming out again after typhoid fever.

"Yes, but the destitution is very bad" etc.

"She'll never do it, my dear fellow, until she sits down at a table and learns it—I know, I've been through the thing myself—She's come on amazingly well—she really has a very good [brain?]—but she's still weak on the grahses and the sedges."

(Here 6:59—Just stopped at place called Six Mile Bottom and lovely flowers by the little station—and every [*illegible*].

[*The following notes were apparently made sometime between April 19 and April 29.*]

NOTE: ON TRAVEL AND THE MODERN MAN

My own life:

aged 4 — St. Louis—home	1500	miles
aged 6 — Augusta, Ga.—home	500	"
aged 7 — New Orleans—home	1500	"
aged 8 — Hot Springs—back	1500	"
aged 9 — Jacksonville—St. Augustine	1500	"
aged 10 — Palm Beach, etc.—	1500	"
aged 11 — St. Petersburg, Tampa, etc.—	1800	"
aged 12 — Washington, etc.—	1000	"
aged 13 — Knoxville, etc.	500	"
aged 15 — Charleston, etc.	1000	"
aged 15–19 Chapel Hill—Asheville	5000	"
aged 17 Asheville—Norfolk, etc.	800	"
aged 15–20 Asheville—Anderson	1000	"
Miscellaneous	2500	"

20 or 25,000 by my 20th year

30. A snatch of the pages' song to Touchstone and Audrey in *As You Like It,* Act V, Scene iii.

20–23	Harvard	7 or 8000 miles
	Asheville	
	Baltimore	
	Madison, N.H.	
	etc.	

23–30	New York	Europe—	55000
	Asheville	N.Y. Asheville—	5600
	Europe	Other places	
	etc.	Maine	
		Philadelphia,	1000
		etc.	

$$61,600$$

30–34	25,000

Thus, I have travelled not less than 125–150,000 miles in my 34 years, and not without considerable scope and variety—I have seen a great deal of the life of about ⅔ of the states of the union, as well as something of Canada, Bermuda, England, France, Italy, Switzerland, Austria, Hungary, Czechoslovakia, Germany, Holland, Belgium, and Denmark.

THE LIFE OF SEAN O'FEAN

1st Scene Meeting him at Harvard in 1923—his acquaintance with Irish Taxi drivers, Harvard Square, etc.

2nd Meeting 1923 Christmas—Beacon Hill, with Mrs Mack, etc.

3rd Meeting N.Y. 1927—living on Eleventh St.—met him one night.

4th Meeting 1929—after *Look Homeward Angel.*

5th—Episode in N.Y. Times.

6th Meeting He calls up in New York with thick Oxford accent.

7th meeting Café Royal in London.

5th Episode I saw or heard nothing of Jim for eighteen months. In May, a few months after this last meeting, I went abroad, and was gone a year. The following [*breaks off*]

I have just recently found that a man who has reached my present age—which is thirty-four—is likely to make a very interesting and illuminating discovery. It is this: he has reached a stage of life which is certainly not old, but which has lost the shine and fire of his first youth, and although he may not yet—or ever—be old enough "to

730 / Another Look at Europe

see life clearly and to see it whole" [31]—he is yet old enough to have seen and felt a kind of dimension—to have experienced a sort of curve and demi-cycle by which he may perhaps, for the first time, estimate the *direction,* the *probable finality* of certain lives that he has known.

For the first time, at this period of a man's life, he begins to look at the lives of many people of his own age and generation and—sadly enough, perhaps—to realize there is not much doubt about the weft, the course, the [*breaks off*]

(Dedication for The Hills Beyond Pentland)
To the Honored Memory of His Brother
BENJAMIN HARRISON WOLFE
Oct, 1892–Oct, 1918

The writer dedicates a work to be known as The Hills Beyond Pentland, believing it of All His work Thus Far Published the one most worthy of such a dedication.

Faulkner 38 or 39
Hemingway 38 or 39
Fitzgerald 39
Caldwell 32 or 33
Myself 34

[*Written on an envelope inserted in the notebook:*]

Things I finished to the end:
Roberts School (until 16)
U.N.C. (4 yrs)
Harvard M.A. (3 yrs)
N.Y.U. (Teacher 5 years)
Look Homeward Angel (3 years)
Of Time and The River (4)
Book of Stories

31. A paraphrase of the line, "Who saw life steadily, and saw it whole," from Matthew Arnold's sonnet "To A Friend."

Pocket Notebook 27
April 29, 1935, to June 18, 1935

Wolfe continued his leisurely approach toward Berlin, making rather full notes on his journey. Although he was only taking a vacation and going for the purpose of spending German royalties (which he could not take out of the country), he soon found his Berlin visit a great personal triumph and one of the most exhilarating experiences of his entire life. His publisher, Ernst Rowohlt, had done well with Look Homeward, Angel *and was planning to bring out* Of Time and the River *as soon as it could be translated. Having learned of the book's success in America, Rowohlt determined to capitalize on Wolfe's visit. He gave Wolfe some of the lavish parties for which he was well known, arranged interviews with press and radio, and promoted Wolfe with all his considerable ability for publicity. His son, Heinz Ledig-Rowohlt, became Wolfe's constant companion and served as a German version of Frere-Reeves or Maxwell Perkins.*

In addition, the American ambassador, William E. Dodd (a native North Carolinian), and his family received Wolfe most kindly. His daughter Martha had been an enthusiastic admirer of Wolfe's work since the appearance of Look Homeward, Angel; *she also sponsored Wolfe through embassy parties and her contacts with the intellectuals in Berlin. Wolfe fell in love with her briefly, and romance added zest to his Berlin adventure.*

Wolfe's work was popular in Germany, and the German people responded warmly to his presence. After the long, lonely years in Brooklyn and the desperate struggle to "prove himself" with his second book, Thomas Wolfe suddenly found himself the reigning literary lion in Berlin.

The notebook ends with Wolfe in Copenhagen, where he made only a few entries. Once again, we have had great difficulty deciphering the handwriting, not only because of Wolfe's wobbly condition but because of the smudging of penciled notes. Also, we have had to make a slight rearrangement to place the material in chronological order.

Maid's Head Note:

The peculiar, raw, peaty, chill of an English bed room—chill and discomfort (and a smell of *peaty smoke*) and the morning's bacon, a sick belly, and a feeling: O God, now I'll have to go to that cold W.C. and sit on the clammy seat, and I hope to God the window's closed, I do.

Saturday, April 27 (?) 1935:

(Written in 2nd class Dining Room of Hook of Holland boat at 11:10 P.M.—From Memory.)

Got up (Maid's Head [*Hotel*], Norwich) about 10:00—breakfast in dining room—wrote a great number of postcards and comic postcards bought day before at Yarmouth—bought descriptive pamphlet of inn [1] from ladylike manageress—So out and went to pub-parlor across street for drinks—and a man with bowler and red face and pipe sitting at table talking to two girls and another man with two boxes of cheeping chickens which filled the parlor of the pub with Springtime—and one of the girls got up and, with a sideward glance at me, sat down on piano stool and began to thump with stiff drawn fingers a tune that presently became faintly recognizable as American popular tune—and other began to sing in a hoarse, winded, uncertain voice—and presently the men went, and a little later the girls too—and the pub-woman told me they were shoe factory girls, and Norwich was noted for the fine shoes it makes, and girls like that made £2 5s a week sometimes, they did—an' lived at 'ome some of 'em, too—and so talked a bit to her husband—alcoholic, good-natured, and quite fascinated by me too—an' 'e advised me, sir, to see the cattle market and to go to Central 'otel to eat an' say they sent me—we gets lots of travellers in 'ere, sir, an' they all say they like it there.

Sunday (April 28?):

Slept at Anchor at Blakeney—up and for 8 mile walk across dunes and sea marshes—and the day grey and chill but all the green of hedges and field and trees alive with birds—so back into Blakeney (by way of Minster) to White Hare pub—and young policeman from Norwich playing darts asked me my bet—and by his tone I knew he had made a bet—So he bought me drink and I bought whole house drinks then—it came to very little—and man with two, black, wonderful Labrador dogs (Mr. Stepney) bought me drink—and I explained to

---

1. An ancient hostelry that claimed existence from 1287 and showed its guests the room in which Queen Elizabeth I is supposed to have stayed in 1578.

all my wish to go to King's Lynn and young policeman [explained?] and [*illegible*] and long distance and had no way of getting there save by way of Norwich—Mr. Stepney said, "I'll drive you over to Wells and you can get bus there"—so after farewells to all this good crowd —and across road to Anchor to a fine lunch of soup, three chops, potatoes, cabbage, apple tart and cream, and cheese, and old ale—and Mr. Stepney joined me then and had a bottle of the ale with me—So we out into his little old car, and for a fine drive along sea to Sheringham, and back through Norfolk villages—and so to handsome, sumptuous tea at Anchor—and so talking for an hour or two (Mr. Stepney's life and character)—and so about seven—still light—to Wells—and then to hotel where had drinks in hotel-pub-parlor, and invited Mr. Stepney to dinner and he accepted—so cold Sunday night dinner beef, and ham, and salad, and cheese, and ale—so back to pub-parlor for a drink with Mr. Stepney—where he said good-bye with bright, birdlike face—and so left me feeling lonelier and the loser for his going—so talked with young hotel-pub-man (a trifle insignificant) for some ½ hour—and so up to bed—(Here all must be filled in about the beauty of the country, the walk across the dunes—a man calling to his dog—Mr. Stepney with his bright, fine, birdlike face—the men in pub —Mr. Stepney's account of life, etc.—How young policeman had his beard shaved, a little unpleasantly, with kind of narrow streaks to the skull).

Monday, April 29:
    Early up (at 8:30), dressed, shaved—had breakfast in George (?) hotel just over way, across court—then to railway station between old cobbled walls—missed station but came around by way just as train was pulling in—Two naturalists in train, little old fellow and young fellow—"Still a little shy with sedges"—got out at next station—Two little schoolboys—one still baby—and a nurse with them—young English girl with *very, very*, oh, simply *aw-w-ful* (down in the throat cool sort of voice)—so got out at Heacham—watched engine turn around like toy on turnstile at yard—out again—so presently train for King's Lynn—so in King's Lynn for two or three hours—drinks and lunch— went to old church and custom house, etc.—so away at 3:17—arrived in Cambridge 4:37—so inquired about train to Harwich—walked to hotel where wedding party just coming out—and the English populace standing around with their love of shows—two bridesmaids quite lovely in their big hats and long, pink, lacy dresses until they smiled and showed bad teeth—so to hotel and spoke to Porter—so into town —sent cable from P.O. to Scribner's for money—then into Market Hill

—bought *Oxford Book of English Prose*—students coming along in fine spring air (a glorious day)—so back along Petty Cury—saw some lovely girls—so collected baggage at hotel and off in taxi for station—so pulled out at 6:37 for Harwich—ride through late evening air with men in gardens working—changed at Bury St. Edmunds where, after 15 minutes wait and drink (girl lighting gas lamps in refreshment room), off on Continental Express for Harwich—where arrived about nine, and onto boat, and watched the uncanny deftness of great cranes loading—and the boats in long lines on either side, some dark and silent, waiting—so watched polished oak-and-walnut [king's?] coach —baggage cars ahead—so London train comes in with influx of hurrying passengers—some first, some second—"Them as goes second, straight across"—So without noise, and almost instantly, the boat sliding swiftly away, out the waterway, and then a complete turn around (the other boat for Belgium following)—so between beacon buoy lights and the big lights of shore, down the long, long road that leads to Harwich—and at length—ahead and past the last lights of land—(a great bracelet and blaze of lights—Felixstowe, I think)—the open sea, a smooth crossing, and the Hoek van Holland in the moon.

Note—the lovely day—the sweet estuary of the land—the glorious sea—with fields and moors and meadowlands of Norfolk—and every blade and leaf and flower alive with gold and green, and grass smell, and the singing of the birds—and quietness, and cows.

Tuesday, April 30:

Rapped on at door by steward (Cockney-[Highbrow?], dead, had sneery, very-good-sir fyce) at 6:00—did something to watch (set back 40 (?)) which made it 5:30 (?) about—had tea in cabin, etc.—dressed, repacked briefcase, etc.—out about 6:00 (Dutch time now) on deck—official to take landing card—thought he was porter—said "No, I don't need you"—he continued with Dutch girl—the [usual?] we-are-accustomed-to-this sort of air—"Thank you, this way, sir"—when gave over landing card—then across into customs shed where perfunctory examination—Have you any cigarettes, etc.—really weren't interested—made me open briefcase but soon through (finished)—so to change £ note—a little shocked to find only 7 guilders exchange (should have been a [way?])—so through on to train quay—porter signaled to me—train rather full, apparently—so they put me in 1st class compartment with 2 Englishmen—one, who later said he was a member of Stock Exchange, etc.—and other, a rather nice, 'ere-now, pleasant friend—m'f'r of "[gentry?] furniture" in Birmingham—with a-face-like someone-I-want-to-remember.

And so up from Hoek—and morning there now grey—and the almost incredible flatness of the land with water ditches quiet flowing all through it—and the cattle with tow-sack [*of*] wattles on their back —and windmills—in the distance canals, fields—and pretty landscape —little houses neat with gabled doors—tiled pitched roofs, not old, etc. —A man milking cow with look of Dutchman in a picture by a Dutchman milking cow—[*sic*]—[*illegible*] after all the morning gold of Norfolk and of England—foreign—and a little grim and [glowering?]—great spaces of almost interminable flatness that would be great space of almost interminable flatness if one did not know that Holland was a tiny country—then into town called Vlamingen(?) or Vlaringin(?) [*Vlaardingen*]—then heading back and out, etc.—and up again at angle *too*-wards Amsterdam—and all this says what a little backyard of a country it must be—Then enter town—the flatness of the green watery fields all between—good land [*illegible*] from Amsterdam—Schiedam—then the Haag—and an electric train on next track with new, varnished, 3rd class coaches—and men going to their work observing us intently (on the steamer-train: Aye: and was a steam train)—then the flowers!!!!

Arrived in Amsterdam, porter, got taxi, drove to Polen Hotel (which address Englishman from Birmingham gave me)—People just going to work—the flights and flocks of shining bicycles—more here, I believe, than anywhere in world—as we passed through Palace Square a band just tuning up to give a concert—and people looking on—at hotel I was informed it was the birthday of the Dutch princess, and the band, and all the flags flying (which could be seen on way up on train) were in celebration—So got room with breakfast for 3:50—went up and slept for two or three hours—and so down and out—almost noon —and to Amexco offices and was told by little, fidgety, Jewlike man that yes, there was a telegram with money for me, but I came too late, will I come please later, will I come back please at two o'clock—so changed my remaining English money 2 £ 3s 8d into Dutch, and went out looking for American Newspaper—Back for Dutch gins at De Gorte (?)—German Jews and Jewesses not far away—Dutch people to fore—Noticed again how like the *American* the Dutch *intonation* is —so back to Polen for lunch—(old white-grey-bald waiter) etc.

So in afternoon to sleep a little more—so into Carlton, found it crowded—so by foot to Leidse Plein—drinks at Café-Amer. there —began to notice women, women, lovely women—So to Realto (?) where had one or two more—so back to Kempinski's for dinner—so on foot to Rembrandt's Plein—the blaze of nighttime neons, etc.—So to Schiller—talk with waiter—look out for your money, substance of his remarks—so to Tuschinski's cabaret—so to various cafés—(drunk who tried to put arms around me, etc.)—so home to bed.

[*The following note is a curious revelation of the illogic of many of Wolfe's social and political positions and an indication of how personal experience and intuition were, for him, ultimate guides. The Negro boys in the Scottsboro case were accused of raping two white girls, but it later became known that the girls were prostitutes. Wolfe apparently thought the boys innocent because of his own observations of and feelings about black and white relationships where prostitutes were involved.*]

Note: I have never in my life known how to "get women." My ideas about getting them are primitive, crude, and plain. At college (in North Carolina) I used to go to the neighboring towns—Durham, Raleigh, Salisbury, etc.—and go to a whore house down in the nigger section or on the fringes of it, or in a cheap hotel, where I would pay the nigger porter—often an insolent one. My ideas on the Scottsboro case[2] are guided mainly by these experiences. As I remember these various Georges, Johns, etc., and their black and servile insolence, I am convinced now that some of them had intercourse with the whores who came to these hotels. I think there is no shade or doubt or possibility of mistake upon this point whatever.

Wednesday, May 1 (?) 1935:

Up at 9:00—Down to breakfast—Dutch breakfast—Coffee, brown glutinous bread, butter, jam, cheese, smoked ham, blood sausage —bought ticket for Volendam–Marken trip, etc. from porter—then by tram to Stationsplein—then young fellow at boat landing near station ("Yesh shir," etc.—guide in summer)—showed me Marken boat landing behind station—paid him 25 cents (Dutch)—and so soon off in little boat—a fine wonderful day but very dull—through canal locks (most interesting but foreseen)—through field of grazing cows— through a green land of watery and incredible flatness—So Broek (?) and Monnikendam—went to cheesery, etc.—spotless, made-up cleanliness of everything—so to eat as we went through country lanes—opposite Monica and Maude and Mona—three English ladies viewing their way through Europe—and "Have you heard the reel story about Lord Hyde's death?"—"Poor Jessie will be quite overwhelmed, etc."—

2. The U.S. Supreme Court had recently ordered a new trial for two defendants in the Scottsboro case on the grounds of Negro exclusion from jury rolls in Alabama. The case was followed closely in the European press.

"Shall I wipe out the glasses"—"Just the rims"—"I'd like to chuck it overboard (the bouillon)—it's so *greasy*"—etc.

So to Volendam and Marken and began to talk to two old American ladies, and one gave me a doll—and most pleasant time with them exchanging stories of N. England, etc.—and they had read L.H.A.—and knew my name, etc.—and waiter making change for me dropped one guilder overboard which I gave back to him—and he went away grumpily as if I'd done him a disfavor—one of old ladies saying "You should say thank you, you may not find anyone so generous as that next time"—So left them at quay and walked away around station and tried to get St. car, but couldn't make self understood—so walked and found Birmingham Englishman and Mr. Bendien in Polen Café and had two drinks with them of Holland Gin ("It makes you Bee." said Mr. Bendien very earnestly)—so upstairs—and later out to Carlton where had several cocktails, and lovely woman came in to meet man there—so to Saur's (which Mr. Bendien had recommended as the best for fish)—So had large sole, bottle of Rhine wine, etc.—so had only 2 or 3 guilders left, and to Rembrandt's Plein for coffee, brandy, etc.—and so home to bed.

Notes: Beauty of Dutch countryside and miraculous newness of boat—sodded earth 4 or 6 inches from the water—In distance great canals and spread of Amsterdam—In the evening the great harbor with big steamers lying in [to side?] for miles down—The wonderful beauty of the children—the incredible, leathery, tanned, great-nosed "character" of old men's faces in Volendam and Marken.

What shall we cry who stamp proud feet about the red, the yellow, crimson, and the rose?

Thursday, [*Amsterdam, May 2*]:

Up, and down for very late breakfast—to Rembrandts Plein for lunch at Schiller's Café—Calf liver, bacon, mixed fruit compote, pilsner beer—then down Kalverstraat to Palace Square where got into bus for tour of city—Five other people—two young men—one German, one I think Dutch—and two English women on Cook's tour eventually showed up, and the tour started—a very good and thorough tour it was —the old guide was a kind of man I have seen here in Holland several times doing work of this sort—a Dutchman of advanced years and degraded fortunes, a little embittered at his fate. We drove first down to great station, around the station on the harbor side where all the boats leave for Marken, Volendam, Friesland, etc.—then along west side of city along Singel, Herensgracht, Keizersgracht [*canals*], etc.

—stopped at old Catholic hostel—inside courts—then swing round by Keizersgracht to Eastern side of city—stopped at diamond factories—drove then through Jewish quarters—then down by station and out *east* again to newer quarters—by zoo, planetarium, etc.—swing around to South of town now, and the great, new apartment houses, Olympic stadia, tennis courts, etc.—beyond, the flat green land, etc.—through quarters of greatest richness and prosperity—then back towards center of town, stop at Rijks Museum for ¾ hour—then across Leidsche Plein through city in behind P.O. and out finally at Palace Square again—So back across the square—the flock and season and memory of great flights of bicycles—workers homeward sped—so into Kalverstraat and to Polen Café—had Holland gins here—watching people pass by in the street—Two English women came by—one was tall and had a jolly laugh and other not pretty was attractive.

Note: Friday, May 3, 1935:

3:30 in afternoon in Excelsior restaurant looking out at canal (Amstel—Rubens picture), Mint tower, Carlton, with flags flying across, etc.—canals meandering with infinite patient slowness—and all the dreary water—light upon the ceiling of rich restaurant—mixture of old and new—rich cream carpets—modern ceiling—pebbled plaster—modern lights—amber glass—radio—tables etc.—Before me at next table in next window—four prosperous men—European type—talking German—well dressed, bald or getting bald, one with paunch, pink and rosy with good living—must have eaten $40 worth of food—one rich dish after another—great bowls of golden asparagus followed by great trays of chicken, ham, veal, etc., brandy, cognac, the rich red wine in great glasses, liqueurs.

Note:

How to get through $15 a day in Holland with absolutely no difficulty whatever: ($5 is 7 guilders—$15 is 21 g).

Hotel (with Dutch breakfast)	3:50
2 drinks before lunch with tips to waiter	:75
Lunch	1:50
2 glasses wine with lunch	1:00
Coffee, Brandy, etc.	1:00
Tour of the city in afternoon	2:00
Tip to guide	:50
Drink before dinner	:50
Dinner, wine, coffee, etc.	2:50
Café or theatre afterward	2:00
	15:75

Friday, May 3, 1935:

Up late, and missing breakfast, dressed, and wrote post cards in great café room of Hotel Polen (under green lights)—so to Amexco, etc., and to Excelsior for best lunch I have had in Amsterdam—soup, poached turbot with [*sherry?*], dressing, wine, coffee, and brandy—(rich Germans ahead of me noting everything)—also Monica, Mona and Maude—("I hope you saw his thanks," said Maude)—the wonderful way bargemen manipulated boats to get them in under bridge, etc. under Munt plein—so left about 3:30 or 4:00 and by taxi to American Consulate (just to see what it was like)—and asked questions about my German marks from German publisher (if I got them), and talked to young man and he most pleasant and unhelpful, saying: "Go to Amexco, they'll tell you"—So back to Hotel—and to newspaper place near station for N.Y. papers—they had none—lots of German ones—and about 6:10 to get Haarlem st. car near P.O.—and past office corners outside shed—"Nay, Nay, it's around the building"—so missed one while I was buying cigarettes in tobacco store but got the next about 15 to 7 (6:45)—and big, fine, powerful [*tram?*]—like London—double-decked they were, and we crawled out of town—about 15 mns. to reach city limits and wide flat green fields—I could have walked it sooner—so hitting it up across flatlands until Haarlem—then changed to local street car for Heemstede—little *Greek* opposite me showed me the way and was going same way himself—most obliging—so through magnificent, luxurious suburbs—and finally out at Flora—down street—turn right—buy ticket—and in—and many people at the booth, in changing light, ablaze incredibly, and under shed the red, the crimson velvet, the [*striped?*] rose—white and velvet black, the great pink and rose, etc.—the most incredible flowers I ever saw or heard of—and the Dutch with quiet clear blue eyes [*alone?*] and looking at them—and I out at last in a clear, perfect, evening light, then blue—on terrace of great café—and had great [*illegible*] roast beef and beer—and watched people go by in the cool and perfect [*tint?*] of light—then into crowded and more homely place—and band playing and waiters dressed in boy Dutch costume and woman in Dutch bonnet conducting band—but plain Dutch people all around and several most attractive girls—so at length back to Haarlem—and into Amsterdam station—and so home about 12:30 or 1:00 and found them closing or closed—and with no dinner—so bought chocolate from night porter at hotel—and so up to bed.

Sat., May 4, 1935:

Up, having been rapped for, but slept late and missed the German train—So up, bathed, and to Amexco where got $20 more in tourist marks—20 dollars in guilders—and 20 dollars left in Express checks—so into Kalverstraat and into haberdashery shop where bought four ties for 95¢ (.8 guilder) thinking only *one* for that price—and girl who waited on me was a knockout—tall, blonde, slender, with lovely sweet face, good-natured, humorous, intelligent looking—so out and through Reguliersbreestraat (?) to Rembrandt's Plein where into Cook's for names of hotels in Hanover and Berlin—so to café terrace nearby (Heck's, I think it was) for 2 sherry wines—and place crowded —and to one side of me Jewess with Indian—the high-boned, courtesan's face who looked as if she were angry and two were with her— man with little girl on other side—so out and over bridge to Excelsior where had martini and lunch—day very warm and hot light shining on *viscid* canal water in shimmering glory and [explained work?]—so home to hotel from there—and could not get suit pressed, it being Sat. afternoon—so upstairs and had nap—so out six o'clock to station and took tram for Haarlem—so there in fifteen minutes, and by street car out to Heemstede—for a walk just at or after seven in garden of glorious flowers—so watched all the people—and walked up hill among gardens of all kinds of flowers.

And so climbed tower and looked out over all the countryside at young, thick woods just greening at May, and in the distance at Haarlem, Amsterdam, and many other towns—and thought what hath time wrought—the tall, thin spires of 16th century churches and the round drums of oil tanks, the skeletons of great cranes, etc.—so down off hill, and around through flower fields again, and the scent at times overpowering—and back by exposition buildings again—and many, many people, and a man borne past, lying on stretcher, by uniformed red-cross bearers at sedate step in hushed evening light—and the man's eyes were closed, his face waxen, his nostrils seemed to have been stuffed with gauze or cotton, which was stained with blood, and his folded hands held neatly, gently, like a flower, a piece of cloth stained with a deeper crimson than even the great tulips knew—so he was borne sedately past, and people turned and looked a moment, so all the same as before—and looked at people, and most most ugly and [underfed?] looking, now and then a lovely girl—and presently left fields and walking to car line—sat at table before little café there and had 2 brandies—and people came and stood in line, and the lines grew and grew, the trams coming too slowly to take the flux of them, until it seemed to me that all of Holland had passed before me, and I thought the most orderly, good tempered, and obedient crowd I ever saw, and one policeman there, but nothing for him to do.

So presently, the crowd thinning, got in line myself and soon on car, standing—a good looking young girl beside me with a young man with a pale, dark, sullen face, full of quiet wit and cynicism—so back to station, and had some gin at one restaurant there, and hamburger steak and a glass of wine at another (Heck's)—so into station, and waited 15 minutes for tram—so back to Amsterdam by 12:15 and town quiet looking, and for walk through town from station to Rembrandts Plein and found the cafés closing and crowds of sinister looking, little Jewish men standing around in crowds, and the crowds would flurry, eddy, suddenly with Jewlike excitement as if there was about to be a fight, and one little dapper Jew would jerk his head to another (as they do on B'dway) and with an air of disgust as if to say "F'r Chris' sake whatsa matteh with ya—are ya crazy?"—they would back away a few feet and confer and wait with ostentatious secrecy—so had drink at Schiller's (the men in street happened later) & they closed the place on me, and stood over me waiting for glass—closing was strict here too.

So out and watched the groups of men in darkening square—the whores walking back and forth, trying for eleventh hour trade—so presently away, and picked up little girl near Munt and went home with her, and gave her five guilders, and she determined both to be and not to be a whore—the whole thing unreal and fantastic—voices laughing and whispering in next room, and seeing a crevice in next room pulled out nail and opened door on cupboard with rows all over of glittering cups and saucers, china, etc.—and so left presently amidst excited whispering and laughter—and so home to bed—and left call for eight o'clock and wrote post cards—so to bed.

Hanover, Sunday night, May 5, Wiener Café: [3]
Miles travelled in Europe thus far—[*followed by a list of cities and distances which total "1200–1300 miles"*].

[*List of "characters" met on the trip thus far.*]

"Thoughts Written in Dejection"
Note:
I came away "abroad" to be alone, but what I am really tired of, what I am sick to death of, what I am exhausted and sickened and fed up to the roots of my soul with—is being *alone*. I am tired of myself, I am tired of being with myself, I am surfeited. I have too good a mind. In times past, I have often said to people that I did not have a good

---

3. H. M. Ledig-Rowohlt later reported that Wolfe explained this stop in Hanover as "pursuing some amorous adventure."

mind, but this was a lie and I knew it. It was a form of that boasting that people have been guilty of so often in the last fifteen or twenty years: I think I got into the habit from my mistress, who used to put a very earnest, puzzled look upon her jolly, rosy, little face and say, "You know I haven't got any sense. I get at it some other way, but I've got no brains at all."

Wiener Café (1:10 A.M. Monday, May 6):

How often I have seen Spring come and in how many places?

Once in St. Louis as a child, of which I can remember little, save that the barn behind the house was red and the smell of an old mattress with the sun upon it—A great many times, 18 or 19, in North Carolina, in the mountains where I was born, and at Chapel Hill where I went to school—three times in New England, once in Pennsylvania, six or eight times in New York and Brooklyn, once in the South of France, once in the North, this year in England, and now in Holland, in Germany—work this into "They flee me who aforetime did me seek with delicate pays there within my chamber" [4]—O where now? Where now? (List of "Where Nows?").

Sunday, May 5, 1935 (written in Berlin, room in hotel, Tues.–Wed., May 7–8, about 3:00 or 3:30 A.M.):

Up at 8:20—bathed, shaved, etc.—packed and closed up big trunk—where went down and had breakfast of bad coffee, Dutch cheese, black stale bread, jam, etc.—paid bill and when I got through had about 5 guilders left—went to station in taxi cab—by the time I got through paying taxi and porters—who showed a spirit of French avarice, looking at their palms, asking for more, etc.—which the Germans do not—I had about 3 guilders or so left—some argument with train conductor about my baggage—but big case was finally left in corridor in a corner where it took up little room—So the train out and away—a magnificent, cloudless day in May—and through the morning across the Western part of Holland, which after the tiny microcosm of Amsterdam, Haarlem, Leiden, etc.—and surprised at the width and extent of Holland, finding it not near so tiny as I had supposed, although small enough for all that—also how *new* and *sensible* the building is—the ablest architects now living in the world I think—and the Dutch have no respect for a thing just because it's old—They tear it down and their new city and suburban architecture, with the tiled

4. A paraphrase of two lines from an untitled poem by Sir Thomas Wyatt: "They fle from me that sometyme did me seke/ With naked fote stalking in my chambre."

roofs and the flat brick [services?] seems to me to be able, competent, and comely—no rival to Athens—it is true, but very good and to the point.

Magnificent day with Sunday-sunlight painted like peace and stillness in everything—all the passing stations and the cows in the field seemed to know it was Sunday—So we went lolloping along across Holland at a leisurely rate, stopping at times at good sized towns like Deventer, Amersfoort, etc.—the country at first flat and fat and green and fertile with great herds of Sunday Cuypian cows—but growing wilder and more waste as we went on—wide stretches of grassy, marshy looking country covered with grassy straw grass stuff, growths of scrub pine, and scrub growth of other sizes, and some barish spots, and looking as if the sea was near—so finally, about two o'clock, we came up to the frontiers and crossed into Germany at Bentheim, Germany.

[*Wolfe arrived in Berlin on May 7. He was immediately swept up into the busy social life that Herr Rowohlt had planned for him and unfortunately made very few notes of these exciting weeks. The first entries are a page of names and Berlin addresses in handwriting other than Wolfe's. One is that of Hans Schiebelhuth, whose masterly translation of* Look Homeward, Angel *and later of* Of Time and the River *enhanced Wolfe's reputation in Germany.*]

Coubière-Kurfurstenstr.—Taverne.[5]

Herr Rowohlt—Rankestrasse 24—7 o'clock.[6]

St. Pauli [*bar on Rankestrasse*].
Mildred Harnack, *Continental Post.*[7]

"Good ones" I have heard about: N.Y. Daily Times, N.Y. Sunday Times, Sunday Herald Tribune, Daily Herald Tribune, Har-

5. A night spot at the corner of Kürfursten and Coubière streets that was a favorite with foreign journalists and was the place to which the Berlin intelligentsia went when all the other cafés closed.
6. A party for Wolfe at the private apartment of Ernst Rowohlt.
7. Mildred Fish Harnack, a native of Milwaukee and former English teacher at the University of Wisconsin, was married to an official in the German Ministry of Economics. A translator and intermediary for American literature, she was beheaded by the Nazis on Feb. 16, 1943, for her participation in the underground.

per's Magazine, The Forum, Time Magazine, Literary Digest, Vanity Fair, Current History, Sat. Review of Literature, N.Y. Evening Post, N.Y. American, New Yorker Magazine, N.Y. Sun, Life.[8]

Thursday–Friday night, May 16–17:
(Written in room in Hotel Am Zoo in Berlin—I have made no notations in this book of any sort for almost two weeks and this must be here annotated briefly and expanded from memory since coming in Hanover.)

Hanover, Sunday evening and night, May 5, 1935—
Arrived Hanover about 6:40—went to Kasten's Hotel—got room—rested a little—Borrowed 10 marks Hotel porter—went out on street and had drinks in open gardens Kröpcke's great café—back to hotel for dinner—so to Wiener Café for drinks and music—later for walk—so home to hotel and bed.

Hanover, Monday, May 6, 1935—
Rose late—went to Garten of Kröpcke's Café—fine, flashing, sunny day of shell-fragile blue—went to Kröpcke's Garden for drinks —many people there including some good looking women—then to Knickmeyer's for lunch—huge, oaken Germanic, Bürgerbräu place with heavy Wotans—food to match—great ships' models hanging from ceiling—young aviators, special table, and the waiters' obsequious hast to serve them—then to Dresdner bank for registered marks— where man with bulge on neck and bandages cashed—then for Grieben's Guide (did this before bank because bookseller told me where bank was)—and after leaving bookseller and bank and going back to hotel discovered that my Grieben's for Hanover had got mixed up with Breslau one and was half Breslau—I took it back to bookseller, a pleasant, blonde, middle-aged man, and pointed out the error. He looked intently for a moment, then burst into hearty laughter—"Just a moment please—I will get you another—but hah! hah! hah! hah! hah! —you must excuse me for laughing, but it is so *comical:*—Hah! Hah! Hah! Hah! Hah!—You come in and ask for a guide of Hanover, and when you open it up—Hah! Hah! Hah! Hah! Hah!—You must excuse me, but it's very comical—you find you have a guide for Breslau!— Just a moment, sir, I will get you another"—He took the faulty guide and went into another room where he could be heard still chuckling to himself—In a minute or so he returned with the proper guide, and

8. Reviews of *Of Time and the River*. The entire list is heavily marked through.

giving it to me, said: "Excuse me for laughing, sir—but when I think what the expression of your face must have been—how you must have looked—When you opened the Hanover guide and found Breslau— hah! hah! hah! hah! hah!—you must excuse me, but it is very comical!"—so left him—he with a pleasant smile, a kindly auf Wiedersehen —and I with the kindly feeling these people give me—and so to study the guide and then for a walk through town according to the guide— and again the old quarter of an old German town that haunts the soul of man with Gothic magic—the incredible design and facades of old houses, warped and leaned together like old crones, and yet still wondrous.

In the Knochenhauer Strasse a sign said Herrenhausen bier—and Frederick Wolfe proprietor—so in I went to see my 197th cousin on the job, and a filthier damned hole I never saw before or since—I opened a door—and was immediately greeted by such a slough of filth and fetid odors, and stupid and corrupted faces that my heart recoiled, then braving in I went—a narrow, dark, and filthy room with a bar at one end and some tables along the wall—an old man all hair and eyes and yellowed whiskers of the kind one sometime sees in New York shambling along the streets and picking up God knows what and dropping it into the cavernous bags of their rags—well, he was sitting at one of the tables slobbing up some mess out of a plate into his whiskers—various other people, men and women, sat around with mugs of beer, and at the door, just as I entered, a toothless, drunken, and most foully besotted hag I ever saw—she reminded me of such- like hags you used to see in moving pictures of *Les Miserables* or *The Two Orphans*—except, by God, this was no moving picture—was seated there at the door with a man who wore a working man's cap—she looked up at me with a humble, toothless, leer and muttered something, all the other people stopped talking, eating and drinking, and stared at me with a look of stupid astonishment and mistrust— which was so strong and palpable in fact that I halted there in the door and stammered something about "Bier—Bier bitte—I should like a glass of beer"—turning finally to the man who was sitting with the hag—he looked at me sullenly and stupidly, wrinkling his inch of brow in painful and suspicious perplexity—and his eyes as he looked at me just got horribly sooty, all of a sudden with the most stupid, bestial glance I have ever seen—and suddenly I thought of France *and* Germany and how wars are made—"Was?" he said, harshly and stupidly, still staring at me with his sooty, sullen look—"Was?"—I muttered my little piece about bier again, and he sat there just looking at me, his eyes getting rottener all the time—"Bier," I said more loudly, "Bier"—"Ach—

bier!"—Someone now cried with an air of sudden enlightenment, "Its bier he wants"—"Ja, Ja."—I stumbled between the tables away from soot-eye—that horrible, toothless hag who had now begun to leer and grimace at me horribly—and sat down at a table next to the bar [*breaks off*]

Scene:
    An operating room in the College of Surgeons and Critics, New York City. Gathered in conference, and prepared for the bloody task before them are the following physicians: the Messrs. Fadiman, Chamberlain, Soskin, Hansen, Rascoe, [*breaks off*]

    The directors of *Die Dame* [9] have asked me to say something [*breaks off*]

    [*The telephone numbers of Martha Dodd and Lisa Hasait.*]

    [*Wolfe wrote part of the following passage in his notebook. Then he wrote the whole passage and tore the leaf out of the notebook. It is addressed to Mrs. Bernstein, but whether it is a draft of a letter to her or not is uncertain.*]

deep and country green of one small tree in May, and the cat that trembling crept upon the ridges on the fence in June—you are my "more than moone" [10]—I love you old false woman that you are—and the worst thing of all that I knew of you—was this—that (when I first knew you) you said you wanted to die in four or five years more—that was evil and against the real life and without honor, faith, or courage —simply a sensual woman from the elegant world who couldn't take it —Emily, Raisbeck, Henry Stevens—where are they now? And Ethel, Edla, Carroll, Hart, Wasson, Mina, Alice Lewisohn, and yourself?

Wed. Morning, 5 A.M., May 22 (?), 1935:
    Written in room in Hotel Am Zoo—Have just returned from American Embassy—beautiful green purity of Tiergarten at 4 o'clock in the morning—incredibly early light here in Berlin—incredibly

    9. Wolfe described *Die Dame* to Perkins as "a German magazine that corresponds to *Vanity Fair.*" For an account of the article he wrote, see *Letters*, p. 466 n.
    10. The creeping cat is a recurring symbol in Wolfe's writing. This passage was eventually worked into "April, Late April," *W&R*, p. 444. The quotation is the first line of the final stanza of Donne's "A Valediction: Of Weeping."

lovely flowers and flower-beds in Tiergarten and ponds of dark green lovely water—So picked up taxi on Tiergarten Strasse finally—the splendid, luxurious houses facing the Tiergarten with their great lawns and gardens around them—a wagon approaching with swift-trotting horse—same the whole world over—a man on bicycle, etc.—and the beauty, purity and stillness of an incredible lovely May morning—So by taxi through Hitzig Strasse passing Bill [*William E., Jr., son of the ambassador*] Dodd's parked car—Bill and Dela locked in embrace inside—across bridge across canal and down towards Gedächtnis Kirche and around it into Kurfürstendamm—the great cafés, restaurants, konditorei, etc. closed—a couple of whores standing rather forlornly in front of [*sketch*] tall, cylindrical cigarette or chocolate turret—so paid taxi 1 m. + 25 pf. (tip) and so in and to bed—buying orange and apple, and telling old man not to send telephone calls up before 11 o'clock (since newspaper articles appeared day before yesterday—have had no peace)—Martha is to call me at 11 and we will go to Weimar if she does not change mind.

Last night (Tuesday) Herr Hitler's speech to Reichstag—Martha met me at Schlichter's restaurant at 3:30—we left about 5:30—went to Amexco—got there too late—went to Hotel Adlon where I got shave and had hair slicked down—then drinks with Martha—and so home just in time to hear Herr Hitler's speech over radio—he spoke 2 hours 20 minutes [11]—radio broke down upstairs and we went downstairs to servants' quarters where all of them were sitting around drinking it in—(Remember noting solid magnificence of house—even in porter's quarters—and the green trees of yards outside fading into last light)—Then radio fixed upstairs and so went up again—Martha and I finally ate at mother's urging while Der Fuehrer talked and filled all rooms with voice—Bill came in and helped translate parts of speech —then Bill left to go to Taverne—then Mr. Dodd returned almost immediately after speech ended and his homely, dry, and pungent remarks about the way the Jap looked "the Englishman," the "Frenchman," etc., and what he said to the "Dutchman" etc. was very homely, plain, and amusing—Also what he said to "the Dutchman" on their way out—"Good speech—but not entirely historical," etc.—and Mrs. D— "Was the Englishman [*Sir Eric Phipps*] there?"—"Yes, he was there"— "How'd he seem to like it?" etc.—wonderfully plain, practical, and amusing—Then Mr. and Mrs. Dodd upstairs to bed—Martha and I talking and quarreling, and I was just leaving when Bill arrived with

11. A major address before the Reichstag, with the entire diplomatic corps in attendance, in which Hitler outlined the "thirteen points" of Germany's foreign policy.

Dela—he asked me to come up for drink—so up again—and Martha and I friends again—and so together rest of time until I came home while ago.

Have been in Berlin two weeks last night—and this is first time I've been able to make an entry in this book since I got here—A wild, fantastic, incredible whirl of parties, teas, dinners, all night drinking bouts, newspaper interviews, radio proposals, photographers, etc.—and dozens of people chief among them Martha and the Dodds, Rowohlt, Ledig, Lisa [*Hasait*], Mrs. Harnack, Carlla, Elinora, Dela [*Behren*], the Feuers, Grunen Zweig, etc.—May never do it again but it was interesting and worth seeing, and people told me startling things—must reconstruct from memory—viz:—[*breaks off*]

Three weeks ago I had an experience that can not happen to me often now. It was my experience again to enter for the first time one of the great capital cities of the world. This time the city was—Berlin [*breaks off*]

Sunday, June 9:

Kurfürstendamm 8:50 in the evening by gold figured clock on the Gedächtnis Kirche—just leaned over geranium hedge on second floor of Weisz Czardas [12] to read it—not yet dark—the half—helve of a moon—bright yellow-silver in the sky—a cloudless, blue-fragile sky above the sweet green trees of the Kurfürstendamm—below, the play of life—the somewhat-slow movement of the people passing—taxis open and most pleasant—parked, glittering cars beside the railroad-car tram track in middle—on each side—café—café-terrace restaurants—Strumpf's—Czardas—Mampe's Klause—Alte Klause—Russische Eier—Kranzler—Burgkeller, Fensterkeller—etc.—and people people people, slow-flowing Berlin people going past—Record today:

(Yest., Sat.)

Up, Amexco—Perkins cable—don't let Rowohlt in yet—sold continental rights in America, etc.—*Die Dame*—signed release—no money yet—taxi hotel—Ledig—lunch here on terrace of Czardas with Ledig—goulash—wine, etc.—good—a dreamy summer's afternoon—the lovely dreamy shimmer of the trees in the Kurfürstendamm—the lovely girls—in spring summery dresses—alley-like-crossing—strawberry ripe ripe ripe 1 M etc.—left Ledig 5:30—[_____] called—asked her to hotel (2 times)—noticed disquieting penil symptoms—but all right—so to Martha Dodd's in taxi at 8:00 o'clock—said good bye to

12. A popular Hungarian restaurant that was a favorite with Wolfe.

[_____]—sent her home—so to dine with Dodds—later alone with
Martha talking, fighting, crying—so to Romanisches Cafe with Martha
at 2: A M—few people there—so 2 drinks on terrace (weinbrand u.s.w.
[*cognac etc.*]) watching light pale the western skies behind Gedächtnis Kirche—so at closing of café to Taverne—there after closing hours
by invitation—so there hearing Austrian music until 4:30 or 5—so
home to embassy by cab—so looted icebox in great kitchen—so to
library—ate sandwiches—left then—so to bed in Bill's room.

So up at 1—bathed, dressed—lunch with Dodds—so with Martha talking all afternoon—3 or 4 drinks (whiskies) so Delhock came—
so talking about Death until 7:20—so away to Hotel promising to
return by 8:00 for dinner—so called Martha saying I was busy talking
to people most important—so shaved—looked at penis—used prophy-
laxis—dressed in grey, rough Tweed—so out on streets—and so here to
Czardas where write this on balcony with helve of moon up in the sky
and fine Farbentopf before me and the sweet trees of the Kurfürstendamm—the cars—the busses—the people flowing past—and the Germans and night—now night.

Housecleaning: [13]
    Still Vex'd Bermoothes
    Wind from the West
    A Letter to Catawba
    A Busman's Journey

[*When Wolfe returned to Berlin on May 26 after a trip to
Weimar and the Wartburg with Martha Dodd, he first learned of
Madeleine Boyd's threatened suit against him. This news took some of
the bloom off his Berlin adventure and he left in mid-June, weary and
depressed. His plans to visit Russia were abandoned, and he went
instead to Copenhagen. Exhausted by his high living in Germany, he
became ill and spent two weeks under the care of a physician.*]

Dear Max:
    I am ill and must stay here until cured. Address Amexco Copen-
hagen.

                                     TOM

[*On June 18, Wolfe was interviewed by C. H. Clemmensen and
Hakon Stangerup, literary critic of the* Dagens Nyheder.]

---

13. Ideas for stories, the first two of which he had had for a long time.

SCRIBNERS, NEW YORK

MUST HAVE HUNDRED AT ONCE AMEXCO COPENHAGEN

WOLFE

I went out on the bridge and leaned across and looked down into the water. Some children were playing in one of the old narrow streets, and in one of the high old houses a woman was leaning out the window and looking down, as I. And below us, between old masoned walls, between the high old houses whose foundations went straight down into the water, the river flowed a channel swift and dark and narrow, forcing, rushing, curiously silent, and as strange as time. I kept thinking of the girl Wachter [14] all the time, and of the old ancient house she lived in, and of all the vanished life that had passed through these narrow ways, that had crowded these huge, strange and marvelous old tenements. And then I thought of my own life and how I had been born thirty-four years ago in a little American town that had been not even an Indian trail-blaze in the wilderness when this great ancient town was in its prime.

[*The following entries begin at the end of the notebook and come forward to this point.*]

Esther

The world of which she was a member was unquestionably a world abnormally marked by corrupt and tainted elements, and there can be no doubt that Esther, mature and knowledgeable woman of the world as she indubitably was, was aware of this.

Notes:

The two naturalists coming from Wells in Norfolk—the one who said he was fairly sure of himself with the grahsses but rather shy with the sedges, and the other older one.

—The older man was a little almost wizened man whose head and scrawny neck seemed to wiggle on his body and gave him a somewhat vertebresque appearance—He was dingily, almost shabbily dressed—was wearing an old shabby black-grey overcoat, no hat, and beside him had a large tin box of the sort the English used to pack

14. "Hannover: Wachter" is included in a list of people Wolfe met from 1935 to 1938. See PN 33.

biscuits in—In fact this seemed to have the vestiges of trade label still on—and I found it as holding God knows what litter—a fragment of bread and cheese, an old rusty razor, a pair of socks, etc.—His face was covered by a scraggly beard, his face also was covered by a scraggly beard [*sic*]—a thin scraggly growth of "new" hair, cut very close but not Germanic, but giving him almost the unpleasant look of just coming from a hospital after a long attack of typhoid fever—At first sight he looked like a cross between Dusty Rhodes, the cartoonists' tramp, and Blowemupski the cartoonists' bomb-throwing anarchist— No! that hasn't got it yet—he looked like a kind of decayed, unkempt, and unenervated *Lenin*—and that gets him pretty well.

To the Honorable Memory of His Brother
BENJAMIN HARRISON WOLFE
Oct. 24, 1892—Oct. 19, 1918

The writer dedicates a work to be known as The Hills Beyond Pentland, deeming it of all his work thus far published the one worthiest of such dedication.

Work Completed:

Look Homeward, Angel	150
Of Time and the River	150
A Book of Stories	100

Work Already Laid Down:
    A Book of Stories (completed)
    The October Fair (in Draft)
    The Hills Beyond Pentland (in Draft)

Stories:

The Still Vex'd Bermoothes	3 weeks
The Wind From the West	2
The Return of the Bondsman Paul	

Books:
    The Death of the Enemy
    Pacific End
    The Book of the Night

PART EIGHT

A SENSE OF
THE AMERICAN CONTINENT

Pocket Notebook 28
June, 1935, to September, 1935

Wolfe left Denmark at the end of June and returned to New York on July 4. Fame awaited him at the dock, where newspaper reporters interviewed him, and in the Scribner's office, where a stack of fan mail had accumulated. He was soon preparing to leave for Boulder, Colorado, however, where he was scheduled to join the Sixth Annual Writers' Conference sponsored by the University of Colorado. Before he returned East in September he had stopped over in Denver, Greeley, Colorado Springs, Santa Fe, Taos, Grand Canyon, Hollywood, San Francisco, Reno, Salt Lake City, and finally St. Louis, where he made a solemn pilgrimage to the house in which he had lived at the age of three, during the summer of the World's Fair, the house in which his brother Grover had died of typhoid fever.

Only a small portion of Wolfe's ranging from Copenhagen to the Pacific Ocean is reflected in this notebook. Most of the pages are blank, and many others are filled with names and addresses. Wolfe was apparently too busy or too overwhelmed after his return to the United States and during his travels through the West to record his activities.

HOMAGE TO DENMARK

1.

A man named Hugh Malone [1] first told me about Denmark. A great many people knew Hugh Malone. He was a drunken Irishman and he wore a red beard which made him look like an embittered Jesus Christ. He came to America about the time of the World War and for some time he had quite a success there. Hugh Malone's great stock in trade was his reputation for colossal erudition. It was rumored that he spoke seventeen languages without a trace of accent and was a

1. Wolfe later developed this portion of his story into the character sketch "Mr. Malone," which appeared first in the *New Yorker*, May 29, 1937, and later in W&R, pp. 525–36.

specialist in several dozen literatures. In fact he wrote a book entitled "Studies in Twelve Literatures" and when the critics panned him for it he grew infuriated and came right back with a book entitled Studies in Fourteen Literatures. He could never write anything unless he was infuriated. He took any question of his divine authority as a personal insult. And he thought that he had had a rank rotten deal in life, had never got the recognition his talents deserved, and that people who couldn't hold a candle to him were being praised and elevated all around him. For this reason his remarks about the books and writers and current reputations was one stream of vituperative abuse which could continue all through an evening as he clutched feverishly at one scotch and soda after another, and which would reach its apogee about two o'clock with a kind of strangled snarl that twisted his pale red lips about in his beard with a frenzied snarl, shot his thin knees out sideward in a kind of mad and uncontrollable devil's jig, and drew from him the last wrung, panting, and exhausted screech of all his pent up bitterness and hate:

"It's all swill!" he would screech "It's *all* swill—but if you found four words that aren't swill—Why, then" he would say in a choking tone—"*Print* it. *Print* it" and with these words he would throw his arms up in the air with a gesture full of strangling despair, fall back in his chair panting with exhaustion, gradually his knees would stop their devil's jig, his claw like hand would grope out for the whisky glass, and as he became calmer, nothing could be heard for several moments but his panting breath, and a few gurgles indicative of alcoholic appeasement.

2.

Coming up in *train*, would go out of compartment and look at it.

3.

Arrival at hotel—meet young Oxford Movementer in lobby—go to Hotel D'Angleterre—"God attends to all that—the economy of God"—etc.

4.

Next morning—Editor Clemmensen arrives.

5.

Lunch with Editor Clemmensen and the Danish Babbitt—But why should you pay, they say?

6.

That night went Bergsen. Elsa, Mrs. Fisher, Clemmensen at Bergsen's place. Sleep with Elsa.

6.

Next day meet at D'Angleterre bar—why should you pay—Go to [Autre's?] and sleep with her—then to Italian restaurant—why should you pay? etc.—then alone with Elsa to Arena—then home with her.

7.

Next day Elsa meets me at Franati, then to Valencia where I very drunk and (so she says) accuse her of taking one of my Express checks—and she leaves me—so home somehow.

Scribner's, New York
Sailing Bremen Friday Cable Fifty Reichhof Hamburg Immediately

WOLFE

Thursday, [*June*] 27: [2]

Last day in Hamburg—Things I need to buy today: toothpaste, toothbrush, pencils, perhaps another notebook, socks, perhaps some handkerchiefs.

Bremen 9:34 from central station—11:04 arrive in Bremen.

What shall they do when the winds give over who so obeyed the tides increase?

Something has spoken to me in the night, and told me to lift up my heart again and have no fear, and told me I shall live and work and draw my breath in quietness again and told me I shall die, I know not where.

Autumn was kind to us, winter entombed us, but in April late April no birds sang. Summer surprised us coming up from the Starnberger sea.

George Fox Horne	Richard Reagan
New York Times	Herald Tribune
229 W. 43rd St. **N.Y.C.**	West 40th Str. N.Y.C.[3]

2. In his haste and confusion Wolfe wrote "May 27."
3. The names of reporters who interviewed Wolfe when he disembarked from the *Bremen*.

Cornelius von Erden Mitchell
350 Madison Avenue, 21st floor
Mitchell and Mitchell [4]

Palace Hotel, San Francisco. Order *"Crab Louis"* with Toasted Rolls.

July 12, 1933, $2,050.[5]

1. The Ship
2. Going to meet woman at House
3. Meeting at Library.
4.
5. Spring came that year
6. "Each day at noon"
7. The Voyage—London, Oxford—Working alone
8. Meet again
9. Working together.

Mario, copy of book, 140 West 13th Street.

Nowell
114 East 56th.[6]

[*A great many addresses appear at this point—of people in New York and all over the Midwest and Far West.*]

[*Alfred Dashiell had arranged for Wolfe to be invited to participate in the Writers' Conference at Boulder, Colorado, July 22 to*

---

4. Wolfe went to the law firm retained by Charles Scribner's Sons for defense in a law suit brought against him by Madeleine Boyd. Wolfe had dismissed Mrs. Boyd as his agent when she mishandled his funds. Now she was claiming agent's fees for OT&R because it had been announced as part of a series including LHA (on which she was still legally drawing ten percent of Wolfe's royalties). The case was settled the following year: Mrs. Boyd relinquished all claims for $500.00; Wolfe generously threw in another $150.00 in memory of the initial contract with Scribner's that launched his public career.

5. Wolfe probably meant to write "1935." The $2050.00 is the amount of money to Wolfe's credit on the Scribner's books. OT&R (plus a spurt of sales for LHA) had not only earned this amount but had also wiped out a debt of $1234.00 which Wolfe had built up at Scribner's by the time of the February 1 royalty report and had paid for Wolfe's European vacation.

6. The address of Miss Nowell's office, where Wolfe occasionally worked during the next three years. He also used it as his business address from September, 1937, to June, 1938.

August 7. Soon after his return from Europe, he began making notes for the lecture he would have to deliver:]

Suggestions for Talks
1. Some problems of a writer
2. The Artist In America

Some Problems of Writing or What Shall I Write About.
Some Problems of a Writer
1) The Florida doctor who wrote me that he had a story that would make me a million dollars and would I please give him $25,000. Notes: a few general misconceptions—"I've got a story that would make someone a million dollars—if I only knew how to write it, I'd write it myself," etc. Well, this is usually worthless—the statement "make someone a million dollars" indicates the nature of the difficulty —it would not make anyone a million dollars; neither, what is more important, would it be of any particular value to anyone.
2) Or the waiters, bartenders, etc. who say, on being told you are going abroad "I suppose you're going abroad to gather material."
Material Gathering. I think writers may almost be divided into two classes—those who gather material and those whose material is of value to them only after they have forgotten it—In a way, almost every writer will in the course of his career be both kinds of writers— Dickens as an example of this—Scott Fitzgerald's statement that every man has in him two books which he can write out of his own experience—I suppose the most mature and best method may be conceived as a fusion of these two—Tolstoy's *War and Peace* as an Example of this—Projected Experience and the Autobiographical novel —Coleridge's "Ancient Mariner" and the artist's use of his material.

Why do we write?
Why are we here?
What is a novel?
You can not fix the form of a novel as the form of a sonnet is fixed—a novel is *War and Peace* and *Moby Dick* and *David Copperfield* and *The Pickwick Papers*—But it is also *Pride and Prejudice, The Red Badge of Courage, Ulysses,* and *The Nigger of the Narcissus.*

[*This first-draft passage for Wolfe's lecture, which was found among his papers, reveals a personal and mythical consideration of his position as a Southern writer. He has been saying that he had felt some*

apprehension about the reception of his first book "at home and in my
native state":]

And the reason for this apprehensive consciousness was this: I
was a Southerner, by birth, by training, and inheritance, and I think I
realized as well as any man alive what thousands of other men and
women in the South have realized, which is this: there has been
something wounded in the South. There is something in the South that
is twisted, dark, and full of pain, which we have known with our lives,
and which is rooted in our souls beyond all contradiction, but of which
no one has dared to write, of which no one has spoken yet. I can not
tell you here in this brief narrative just what the nature and the source
of our great hurt may be; it came somewhat, I think, from our old war,
and the huge ruin of our great defeat, and its degraded aftermath; it
came somewhat, perhaps, from causes yet more ancient—from the evil
of man's slavery and the hurt and shame of human conscience in its
struggle with the fierce desire to own; it came too, perhaps, from all
the hot and fierce desire of the hot South, tormented and repressed
below the harsh and outward patterns of a bigot and intolerant theol-
ogy, yet prowling, stirring always, stealthy, hushed and secret as the
thickets of swamp-darkness; and most of all, I think, it came out of the
weather of our lives, the forms that shaped us and the food that fed,
from the unknown terrors of the skies that bent above us, the pineland
barrens and the haunting sorrow, from the whole shape and substance
of the dark, mysterious and unknown South.

Wherever it had come from it was there in all our lives—that
bitter, wounded, twisted hurt with all its pain, its terror, its lacerated
pride, its fear and cruelty, its sweltered secrecies, its explosive and
insane desires, as much a part of all our life as was the warmth, the
humour, the rich character, and gentle kindliness that were its more
benevolent possessions—and we *knew* it, we knew it with out lives, our
hearts, our spirits, and we did not dare to look upon that bitter and
tormented hurt, we did not dare to probe that raw wound to its naked
sources—fear held our spirit in subjection, and we did not dare to
speak. For these reasons too, I think, it came about that in the South,
more than in any other section of the land, we became makers of
myths about our lives, makers of myths about all living, and these
myths did not often have the core of truth or beauty that a great myth
had, but were more often spurious, sweet, and shoddy, and behind
their florid phrases dwelt forever the shame and silence of our fear.

I have said so much as this by way of preface because I now
propose to offer my own explanation of the terrible virulence of

anguish, hate, and bitterness which my book engendered among the people of my native town. In recent months I have read a good many estimates and appraisals of my work by various critics, but I do not remember to have read this one, and I offer it, and I offer it honestly and humbly just for what it's worth: I think I may be the only young writer in my generation who has written about the life he knew there with the kind of naked intensity I have attempted to describe, and for that reason, I believe, I could no longer live at home. I have read in recent years that I am compelled to "live in exile" from the South because of that first book, I have heard that I could not come home, and more recently, I have heard that now I could return if I desired, that "all has been forgiven," and that the bitterest assailants of four years ago, are now my warmest friends.

Well, I have lived out my exile, and I do not think I shall go back. And the reason that I feel this way is not because of what I *did* but because of what I have to do. Perhaps I am mistaken, but I do not believe that any man who writes as I write, who has to write as I must write, with the special necessity that my writing has to have, can live there in the South and get his writing done. And I say this with no bitterness—for I am from the South and think of it as home—and with no spirit of vainglorious assertion, because I do not think I know the way to write, because I do not think my way of writing is the one and only way, but because the way I write is the way that I *must* write— and my plain conviction is that I cannot write that way at home.

I do not think they cried out against that book of mine for what it said—seen now, without surprise, that years have passed, they see it now for what it was: the story of a family and a town—not *theirs* alone, and not with scorn and ridicule their own, but if the truth was in the book, then [*of*] all men's living—as true of Denmark as it was of home. I think the reason that they cried out as they did was not for what they thought it said, but for what they thought, they feared it might imply: that life so seen, with this intensity, held sunwards burning like a shining sword—would turn and shrink from nothing— not even the terror of our selves, not even the last bitter probing of our wound.

[*Other notes and drafts enlarge the criticism and the awareness to national proportions:*]

Here in America, as well, we have been wounded cruelly—and we cannot bear to look upon our scars.

We fear, we hate, we loathe, we execrate America—and some-how—oh, impossibly—we love her!

We must not look alone at the instances of defeat and shame and failure in the nation's life, but at the central core and heart of the defeat and shame and failure in our own lives, which has brought this ruin to pass; we must not look alone on the overwhelming evidences of ugliness, savagery, violence and injustice in the life around us, we must look straight into the ugliness in our own lives and spirits which created them. We must, in short, probe to the bottom of our dark and twisted wound; as men, as artists, as Americans, we can no longer cringe away and lie.

And why must we do this? Because we *are* Americans, there is no escape: we are all warmed by the same sun, frozen by the same cold, tempered by the same weather, and shone on by the same lights of time and terror, by the same immense and immutable skies of time—and of America—that bend above us all; we are all damned together, tarred by the same stick, scarred by the same wound, and there is no escape.

"To see life steadily and to see it whole"—yes, that is what as men and artists we should like to do, but if we ever see America in this way, she will not come to us in the radiant image of a classic and untarnished perfection.

I could, therefore, it seems to me, here state one of my faiths— one of my first convictions as an artist—in this way: that here, that here above all other lands and places, here in America, we are and must be desperate men, and must strive desperately—though not in utter des- peration—if as men and artists we are not to fail. Here, too, it seems to me, not only from the beauty, wealth and joy, the immortal promise of America, not only from the health and hope and life of her, but from the death, the horror, and the filth of her as well, must we make our truth, our substance, and our loneliness—from our despair so to con- ceive immortal faith, from our defeat so to achieve a victory that shall not die, so from the deep remorseless probing of our dark and secret wound to make the health, the triumph, and the glory that shall last forever—from the lion's mouth, honey; from the bush, a flame!

So, too, have I, born of this earth and shaped out of her clay, found here, from that hard lesson of my youth and my first book this stern and bitter faith—so, too, have I been here compelled to utter it in this language of essential violence—itself American!—so, too, upon this rock may I henceforth find strength to take my stand.

For if, it seems to me, we turn away from this hard fact, if we deny that here, above all other lands and places, we must turn or shrink from nothing—must, if we have to, take the lid off hell's pot, and ladle to the depths—if this hard fact will stick there in our craw, if we turn away and are too nice and dainty to accept it—if, avoiding the hard way, we continue to let Stylish Steve, Aesthetic Sal, and Sneering Sue take the play, make the rules and set the brief and easy styles for us—then, let mock the mockers and let gibe the snobs!—but, by God, we'll get no more than what we had or have, and we'll deserve none!

[*The following three paragraphs are the opening remarks of Wolfe's lecture at the Writers' Conference. The typescript is seventy-four pages long.*]

It has been suggested to me that I talk to you upon the subject, "The Making of a Book," and I am delighted to attempt a talk upon this subject because it has a pertinence and a direct relation to my own experience which topics of a critic[*al*] or academic sort do not have.

A very great editor, who is also a very good friend of mine, told me about six months ago that he was sorry he had not kept a diary—a kind of daily journal—about the work that both of us were doing, the transaction that occurred, the whole stroke and catch, the flow, the stop, the cut, the molding, the whole ten thousand meetings, gratings, changings, surrenders, triumphs, and agreeings that went into the making of the book. This man, this editor that I have spoken of, remarked to me when all was over that some of it was fantastic and incredible, and he was also generous and kind enough to remark that the whole experience was the most interesting that he had known during the almost thirty years he had been a member of the publishing business.

I propose to tell you about this experience. I believe that if anything I can say to you may have value or interest, it will be somehow related to the facts of this experience. I am not really a professional writer. I do not feel that I can talk to you about the trends in the modern novel or attempt to tell you what the modern novelist is doing or attempt an analysis of what he has done the last five or ten years or what he will do in the five or ten which are to come. I cannot tell you how to write books; I cannot attempt to give you rules and suggestions whereby you will be enabled to get your books published by publishers or your stories accepted by popular and high paying magazines. Yet all these things have happened to me. I have had my books accepted by a publisher and recently some of my stories were accepted by popular and high priced magazines, but I do not know any rules for telling you how this can be accomplished. I am not a professional writer; I am not even a skilled writer; I am just a writer who is on the way to learning his profession and to discovering the line, the structure, and the articulation of the language which I must discover if I do the work I want to do. It is for just this reason, because I blunder, because my life and every energy of my life and talent are still involved in this process of discovery, this need for an assured and final articulation, this constant search for the discovery of a language which every man must find out for himself that I am talking to you as I talk to you tonight. I am going to tell you, so far as I can in the special time that is given to me and as truthfully as I can remember, the way in which I wrote a book. It will be intensely personal. It came out of the substance of my life. It was the greatest and most intense part of my life for several years. It cost me the most intense effort, sweat, doubt, and suffering that I ever knew. There is nothing very literary about my story. It is a story of sweat and pain and despair and partial achievement. I did not achieve what I wanted to achieve; I failed in a way, which only I know about, and I came through, too. I don't know how to write a story yet. I don't know how to write a novel yet. Of all the people here in this audience, I am the last, the worst, the least prepared to tell anyone how to write a story in such a way that it will sell to anything, no matter what. But I have learned something about myself and about the work of writing, and if I can, I am going to try to tell you what it is. It takes me a long time to tell things. A good many friendly critics have told me this, and I know that it is true. Sometimes it takes me a good long time to get started. All of these things are true; a great many penetrating and sympathetic people have told me so; I know it; I realize it, and I am going to try to learn and do better, but right now I will have to tell you about this thing in my own way, and to tell you in that way, I will have to go back not only to what was perhaps the beginning of the book, but before the beginning of the book.

[*In December, 1934, Wolfe had signed a contract with Scribner's for a volume of short stories which he planned to call* From Death to Morning, *a title which conveyed a progression of mood through the volume. Perkins was now getting the book ready for publication. Wolfe intended to dedicate it as a memorial to his brother Ben.*]

To
The Honorable Memory of His Brother
BENJAMIN HARRISON WOLFE
(Oct.————, 1893—Oct.————, 1918)

and to the proud and bitter briefness of his days, the brave integrity of a life to which nothing could be given but fulfillment, from which nothing could be taken but the generous, noble, and inviolate radiance of a scornful and lonely soul, the writer dedicates this book believing that it may contain of all his work that has yet been published, the matter worthiest of such commemoration.

Up on the mountain, down in the valley, long, long in the hill, Ben, cold, cold, cold.

Roosevelt Hotel, Hollywood Blvd.

Hollywood—Sat. Aug. 31, 1935, 11:45 in Morning—

Got here day before yesterday—called up Sayres [7] and in evening went with Mrs. S. to Trocadero, Beverly Brown Derby, back to Trocadero, dining until 2 or 3 o'clock—so home to Sayre apt.—met S. —talked till daylight—home to hotel—talked to old woman with fishing rod on st.—she said wonderful things about Utah—but forget what—so home to bed—Gertrude Sayre phoned promptly at 12 o'clock to remind me of date at M.G.M.—with Oppenheimer [8]—so up bathed, dressed, by taxi to Studio of M.G.M.—had lunch with Oppenheimer—met Miss T. Schlesinger—so with Oppenheimer and Sam Marx around lot—sets of Western mining towns, French Villages, ancient fortresses, ships, small town streets, villages in Greece, etc. saw Warner Baxter and Frank Morgan making pictures, saw Tarzan of the Apes set, met Clark Gable and Miss Jean Harlow, Miss Una Merkle, various directors, writers, etc.—met Humphrey Cobb, so back to Oppenheimer's office—and with Gertrude in her car to Dorthy Parker's home in Beverly Hills—so drinking with Miss Parker, her husband, Allen, and a beautiful young woman named Muriel King—scene designer from N.Y.—Joel Sayre came in—and finally late departed for Gloria Stuart's and husband's house—Sayre had made some remarks so I offered to fight him—good-naturedly but willingly enough—so dinner at Miss Stuart's—Sayre and I still half friendly but truculent—so departed with Gertrude Sayre and Joel Sayre in their car along shore road above Santa Monica—singing—and Sayre fell asleep so home to hotel—good night and to bed—Sat. A.M.—am on my way to R.K.O. studios to lunch with Joel Sayre—he phoned me about 45 mins. ago.

7. Joel Sayre was a writer at the RKO motion picture studio.
8. George Oppenheimer, an executive at the MGM studio.

Seen in America

(Since my return July 4, 1935)

1. Western N.Y.—Syracuse, Buffalo, Detroit, Michigan at day light, etc.

2. Iowa on a hot Sunday afternoon at end of July.

3. Omaha by dark.

4. The Western plain: Nebraska and Colorado in the morning.

5. Greeley Col.—Boulder, the foothills of the Rockies, Estes Park, Denver, Central City, Colorado Springs, Buffalo Park etc.

6. Southern Colorado, the beginnings of desert country and the earth formations—Pueblo, Col.—Trinidad,—the beginnings of Indian–Mexican life—the Raton Pass—the New Mexican desert—Las Vegas, Santa Fe, Taos, the Tesuque country, New Mexico.

7. Arizona: The Grand Canyon.

New States Seen or entered:

Michigan, Iowa, Nebraska, Colorado, New Mexico, Arizona, California,—(Sept. 12 Reno), Nevada, Utah, Kansas.

[*The remaining pages are taken up with addresses and telephone numbers, some of which indicate Wolfe's search for an apartment in Manhattan before he settled into one at 865 First Avenue in September.*]

The Hound of Darkness Ledger
Fall, 1935

*Since Wolfe kept almost no record of his thoughts in a pocket
notebook during the fall, it seems appropriate to include at this point
some excerpts from the big ledger which was the principal workbook
for outlines, drafts, and new ideas during the next six months or more.
The following notes represent new literary activity from September to
about December, 1935. This period also included the publication of
such earlier material as* From Death to Morning *in November and the
serial publication of* The Story of a Novel *in December.*

*When Wolfe settled down to complete his six-volume series in
October, he turned back naturally to "The October Fair."* [1] *But the
emotional wrenching that underlay his turbulent love story apparently
made it very difficult to control this material. Another obstacle had
arisen too: Mrs. Bernstein had told Perkins that she was ready to sue
Wolfe if he published a book about her. These dissuasions made it very
easy for Wolfe to turn his attention soon to what he really wanted to
work on, the memories of childhood and the ancestral stories which
were to make up "The Hills Beyond Pentland." "For that," he told
Martha Dodd, "I am saving the best of everything I have in me."*

*But his recurring wish to write about nighttime in America
presented another temptation. The trip across the United States had
stimulated his imagination with scenes that he hoped to include. As a
result of this creative urge, Wolfe went from jotting ideas and notes to
writing episodes for "The Hound of Darkness," which was at times a
single book and at other times a long introductory section of "The
Hills beyond Pentland." Later during the winter, he developed the
material into a series of cinematographic scenes 200,000 words long.*

*Other excerpts from this ledger have been placed where they fit
chronologically among entries in Pocket Notebook 29.*

---

1. An outline for "The October Fair" is set down on the back of a telegram from Ernst Rowohlt dated October 8, 1935.

CHAPTER OUTLINE

THE HILLS BEYOND PENTLAND
PART I

CHAPTER I

The Hound of Darkness

(The Night of Wednesday June 18, 1913)

(Boy) . . . Is it a lion in the mouth sulfurous, a fox in the eye
humorous, a cat in the paw felonious, that prowls and breathes and stirs
round night's great wall forever, and will not let us sleep? Does the
beast spring to find the mountain, will the cat plunge to find the flood,
must we forever wait and watch and listen in the hives of darkness for
the great beast who comes and stirs and prowls upon the portals of our
conscience and who will not speak?

Who are you who keep silence in these watches of deep night?
Who are you, tell me what you are and how you came? In the rustle of
leaves along these nighttime streets of pleasant summer now or in the
hillside's thicket growth, in all the little winking eyes of night, thrum,
stir and flutter in the million-noted jungle depths of night, I feel, see,
hear and know your vast pervasive presence and I know that you are
there.

The Hound—I am the beast that comes—

The Hound: . . . a halter of light the town encloses, fabric of
houses, pattern of streets—

The Hound: I'll show him rivers—he's bound to want them—
I'll give him plains for his hill-born heart—fat farms and fields for the
mountain valleys—I'll give him his nation—part by part.

The Boy: Where? O Where?

The Hound: Up and away!

THE HOUND OF DARKNESS

(The night of Wednesday, June 18, 1913:—a Full Moon)

Scene:

A night of dazzling light above America. As the action begins,
the body and bones of the American continent are revealed from East
to West. The vision at first is governed only by immortal silence and
the still light of the blazing moon. The view in this first instant is
appalling—it seems crater-blasted, lifeless and inhuman, like the design
and fabric of a prehistoric world.

The spectator to this giant panorama sees at once and instantly
the whole dimension of the nation, spread out in the essential lineaments of a gigantic map. At first nothing seems to move or live or stir
upon this surface: it seems to be a desert region, lifeless, crater-blasted
as the moon. And yet one knows at once that life is here. The place is
burning with terrific instancy, and suddenly one knows it is alive and
swarming with the tremendous energies of forever and of now.

Steeped in this moon-bright stillness of essential time, the vision
sweeps the planetary distance of the continent: southward from Maine,
around the thumb of Florida, up and around the belly of the Gulf,
southward again along the curve of Mexico and up and out again
towards Oregon along the tremendous outward slope and surge of the
Pacific shore.

The huge wink of the all-surrounding seas is held there steady
in the silence of the moon: so too, the contour of the nation is defined.
Rising from Piedmont swell and coastal plain, the ancient ramified
embankment of the Appalachian range extends for 1500 miles from
New England into Georgia. On its western slopes the land swells
downward toward the inland plains, dividing which, the forked threads
of the Mississippi and Missouri rivers drink the continent, and burn like
strings of steady silver in unchanging time.

Westward again, forever west, the plain slants with tremendous
lift a thousand miles against the abrupt and basal ramparts of the Rocky
mountains. Row beyond row, their hackled peaks blaze down south-

westward through America, and beyond them is the desert, the fiendish convolutions of the blasted land, and this embankment too is blazing in the moon. It blazes there like silence and forever, it rises there like a still madness in the moon, and beyond it still there are the high Sierras, the last long dip and sweep through the Sequoias westward, down to the slopes of many-visioned California, the deeps of Oregon, the Pacific shore.

The vision nears and deepens with the speed of light: The million smaller shapes and contours of the earth appear. And now, for the first time, through that steep silence of the moon, a sound is heard. Vast, low and murmurous and like a sigh that breathes forever at the ledges of eternity, it is the sea, that feathers constantly upon the shores of time and darkness—and America. It is the sea, the sea that boils against the tortured granite of New England, it is the sea, the sea that roars upon the sandy shelf of long white beach from Long Island down to Florida. It is the sea that lashes to a cruel welter around Hatteras, and it is the sea that rises with its lazy, vast, deceptive swell against the coast of California. It is the sea that foams forever at twelve thousand miles of coast, and the sound of its vast low sigh is like the sound of time and silence and forever—and the sea!

PERSONAE

The Boy
The Hound
W. O. Gant
Ben
Tom Cline
A Train Going West
Bacchus
J. M. Pentland
W. H. Pentland
Eliza Pentland Gant
The Boarders (Come on out, Mrs. Gant)
Judge Sondley Webster
Molly Earle
Miss Jessie Rimmer
Old Man Helm
Willie Goff
Count Onions
Cornelius Willetts

George Spangler (The Bridge Builder) (Something has whispered to me in the night—and told me I must die, I know not where)

The Voices of the Summer Women are heard mixed with the rustling of the summer leaves

Eagle Crescent: Elizabeth and the Judge.

I The Hound Speaking—then the body and bones of the American continent.

II The Boy (In Bed)—"Is it a lion in the mouth sulfurous?" etc.

III

THE FURNITURE BUSINESS THAT GANT BOUGHT

The business masked a form of usury which at that time was prevalent throughout the South. The machinery of the enterprise was murderously simple and it worked as follows: A negro in urgent need of a small sum of money would come to the dealer, and negotiate a "loan"—the amounts ranged from ten to fifty dollars—and would be required to offer as security his furniture, household belongings, whatever personal property he had. Then, until he was able to repay the whole sum, he was required to make small weekly payments of interest at a usurious rate.

The Negro Woman

"How much does I owe?" she said, "I been a-payin' and a-payin' since I don't know when. Seems lak I ought to be gittin' paid up some day." Meanwhile she had been fumbling with the string that was tied around the cardboard box, and now she opened it.

"What have you got there?" he asked.

"I don' know what you calls 'em—re-ceeps, de man say," she answered sullenly. "I got de whole box chuck-full o'dem—I have been a payin' for de *mostes'* time—an all I got is dese little bits o' papuh."

He took the box and looked into it. She had told the truth. It was about full with the receipts—dozens, scores of those little slips of infamy. He saw at once that she had paid her original loan—a ten dollar one—ten times over—and as he turned away with a sick heart, the sight of the woman fumbling with her thick black fingers at a little purse, fishing into it for a few greasy coins, was more than he could bear.

THE WINTER'S TALE

Synopsis: The coming of Bascom, Louise, and their daughter Cornelia to Altamont—First sight of Bascom (Use *Street of Day* here) in front room at Eliza's house (and memories it evokes—how the Pentlands had always spoken of his "peculiar ways"—and a kind of malice when they spoke of him—the story of how he had told the man in church, "he was ashamed to tell him where he came from—Catawba"—and how the man said he "didn't believe he ever did hear of anyone coming from there who amounted to anything." What did it mean? Where did it come from?—this half-concealed antagonism and resentment of the Pentlands toward their brother—"an educated fool," etc. In this phrase there was something sneering and hateful.)

1913 THE BODY AND SOUL OF ALTAMONT

Its Body

Of the fifteen or twenty thousand people who composed the population of the town of Altamont, it is probably no exaggeration to say that half of them lived in conditions of poverty, filth, want, and squalor that was a foul and infamous insult to human life, and unworthy the dignity of a race of pigs. From what evidences are these figures derived? Well, in the first place, an approximate third of the population was composed of Negroes, living in settlements variously known as Niggertown, Stumptown, South Side, Cherry Hollow, and so on. The boy, from his work on the morning paper, knew every road and alleyway and turning in the shambles of these various settlements: he had been into hundreds of the negro shacks, had seen their filth and squalor, and had smelled the smell of them—so thick and foul and sickening, it could have been cut with an axe.

1) The Corn Blades Rustling in Illinois.
2) A Road in Maine (The Sea: It is the sea, the sea).
3) Thunder and lightning over two Drunken Mexicans in a smashed car near Santa Fe—the sound of coyotes howling.
4) Before a drug store in a Southern town.
5) A lunch room in Troy, New York—a policeman and an effeminate youth.

6) The estate at Malbourne—Margaret Meadesmith—I mustn't listen—I told myself I'd never listen (the moon swarms down among the sycamores)—O God! I wonder what is doing in the world tonight! (Then—the Boy and the Girl scene).

Bacchus.

A Brooklyn Alleyway (feet pass the window running).

A Hotel in Chicago—then the Stock Yards.

The Living Room in the residence of Mr. Ambrose Saltonstall, Louisburg Square, Beacon Hill: Mr. Saltonstall discovered reading the literary columns of the Boston Evening Transcript to Mrs. Saltonstall. Mr. Saltonstall (with a short grim laugh of satisfaction, rattling the pages with a decisive movement): "Ah, my dear, just as I thought—hem! Will you listen to this for a moment? hem!—takes the whole business off to a T—Ah-h (laughs grimly again with satisfaction)—a capital thing this! hem! absolutely capital! A voice (unmistakably Irish) passes below the window bawling lustily:

Has anybody here seen Kelly,

K—E—Double L—Y?

Has anybody here seen Kelly,

You can tell him by his smile—

Mrs. Saltonstall: Ambrose, don't you think you'd better shut the window? Mr. Saltonstall rises and does so.

Two Women in Gettysburg. First: They're only here for three, four days and by the time you're through with all your work and bother and charging around it's not worth the trouble that you go to.

Fourteen miles away two old women are sitting in the kitchen of a tiny little farm-house.

Augusta: Mother!

The Widow Gant: Hey-y?

Augusta (more loudly) Mother! I have a letter here from Oliver!

Augusta, clamping her powerful old gnarled hands, raising her eyes imploringly and crying out in powerful tones of resignation and despair: O Lord God! Lord God! What shall I do! She's gone and messed herself again.

The Train: Ho-Idaho! Idaho-ho! Ho-Idaho-ho-ho-ho-ho! (And across the Western plain her cry wails back; her firebox glares on walls of golden wheat).

New York—Mrs. Jacobs—the studio of Henry Mallows, a painter.

New York—Mrs. Jacobs going home—meets Bella.

The Bums on the Bowery—How do you like dat stuff, I'll give you some more of dat stuff.

An Irish Family around a Kitchen Table Drinking Beer.

A motor car, rushing along a country road in Western Illinois: in the moonlight the road stretches away as white and straight as a string, the acetylene lamps of the automobile add nothing but the ghosts of brightness to the dazzling light of the moon, the car bounds like a rabbit on the unpaved dusty road, level on either side in level rows stretch far away immense and level stands of young green corn. The corn blades stir and lightly clash as the car rushes past.

The Corn Blades (rustling with young bladed clash): Ah, sweet and coarse, ah sweet and coarse, America.

[*From a few of the jottings, it is clear that Wolfe hoped to work out some scenes or voices that would reflect the sexual seething of nighttime America—that is, if Perkins would not prevent him. The following are representative:*]

Mrs. Dan Sevier: But he fucked me till my very soul cried out for joy—and so I married him.

1913 (An Amusement Park—Dusty Summer—a big red-faced man swings a child of two in a rope swing)

How do you like that, son? (catches the child on back-swing, holds him for a moment, then chokes with high fat laughter) What do you think of that? (some as before).

The Hot Mysterious Desires: Let us go for a ride in the Hudson Super Six—Down by the river—Ooooh, let us fu-u-u-u-ck!

A GIRL AND A BOY

Boy: Say it!

Girl: I won't . . . Take your hand away!

Boy: Say it! Say it!

Girl: I won't! I won't! . . . You've got to take your hand away.

Boy: I'll take it away if you'll say it.

Girl: I told you—(a moment's silence while they struggle) I won't say it.

Boy: Say it and I'll take my hand away.

Girl (hesitantly): Well—

The Leaves (softly): Say it, say it, say it, say it, say it.

Girl: Will you promise—

The Leaves (whispering): Promise, promise, promise, promise, promise.

A Street

The Eagle Crescent district in the town of Altamont:

A short semi-circular street, situated on the high slope above the western edge of Niggertown, on the southern fringes of the town's business and market districts. The northern side of the street is walled in for almost its entire length by the back of the Altamont Supply and Foundry Co.—a sheer brick brutal flank, set high with grimy windows glazed with factory glass, through which a few machine-shop lamps of night are burning dismally. The southern side of the street is occupied by a half-dozen old frame houses, the porches of which are screened with a lattice work and set flush with the street. From this point however the earth falls sharply down and away, so that the backs of the old houses are two floors deeper than the fronts.

Beyond, towards the East, may be dimly descried, etched out the nocturnal and ramshackle world of Niggertown. Far off in that nocturnal censer from the vast jungle depths of night there wells up from the vat of darkness the dirge-like jungle wails of Africa, the sound of negroes singing in a church.

At first, the street is empty, then from the darkness comes a dark low whistle, rising, falling, rising, mournful, long and low.

The Voices of the Whores (calling softly):

Here! Oh Here! . . . Number Eleven! . . . Ask for Lily!

The whistle is heard again, louder, more insistent.

The Voices of the Whores (sharp, low, breathless):

Now, now! Now's the time! Go now, quick!

One of the latticed doors is opened stealthily: in a moment a man comes out, glances quickly left and right and then, head lowered, hat pulled down, walks swiftly away and turns the corner.

SCENES

1) A blazing moonlight above America
2) A nearer view—the Sea

3) Nearer—the Corn in Illinois—a negro on a country road down South—screen doors slamming, street cars—the leaves—a seaside resort in New England.

4) The Pelt of America
    a) The Mexicans near Santa Fe
    b) Before a Drugstore in the South
    c) Mr. Saltonstall reading the Transcript
    d) The Sailors In the Tunnel under the River
    e) A Train going across Indiana—the Brakeman talking
    f) Nigger bootblacks In a Tobacco Town
    g) The Whores in New Orleans
    h) The little fairy back room boy in Troy, N.Y.
    i) The House at Malbourne in Virginia
    j) A Boy and a Girl
    k) Grandma Gant and Augusta
    l) The Coal Crew—Altoona, Pa.
    m) (perhaps this should be the last) Bacchus in a day coach
    n) A Boy in a Bar in Hoboken.

SCENE

The house at Malbourne in the hunting district of Virginia. The house in its general design is not unlike the one at Mount Vernon, save that it is situated in a hollow rather than on a hill and, lacking somewhat the delicate austerity and precise design of its more famous neighbor, it yet surpasses it in warmth and naturalness. An air of ease and homely comfort has pervaded every line; and even the somewhat rambling and haphazard changes and additions of a century of use have served only to enhance the noble dignity of the old house. The place is warm with life, and grandly, instantly familiar the moment that a stranger enters it. It seems that he has known it forever, it speaks to him at once like a familiar voice, and the voice it speaks with is not only warm with present life and friendship but haunted by the sense of life dead and gone, by all the scenes and people who have lived here and vanished. It is a tragic house.

The action opens in one of the smaller living rooms or "front parlours," which extend the whole way across the house. It is an old high-ceilinged room with great cornice doors of dark polished wood: the room has the same air of homely comfort, sadness, noble dignity that the whole house has. The furnishings of the room represent almost every style and period of the past century and a half. There are several chairs and tables of the purest and most delicate Colonial pattern, a couple of huge old walnut bookcases with cumbersome glass doors that suggest the heavy and gloomy styles of the Victorian fifties, one or two upholstered chairs and a long upholstered "davenport" of recent make, and a long and cumbersome horsehair sofa of the late Victorian period. It is apparent that each succeeding generation that has lived here has left in this room two or three pieces of furniture as token that it has been here, and whatever the fault in taste and harmony thus produced, the gain in the sense of life and naturalness is tremendous.

On the wall are several paintings, portraits, evidently, of fore-bears of the family: one, a man dressed in the uniform of an English officer of the pre-Revolutionary period; another, a lady, probably his wife, of the same period, stiff in brocades, hair powdered and brushed tightly back, a kind of Copley shrewdness to the face; a third, a handsome man with a black beard, dressed in the uniform of an officer of the Confederate army.

. . . .

As the action starts four people are discovered in the room. Seated at the right end of the long davenport, which faces the fireplace, is Mrs. Latimer, the mistress and owner of the estate. Near her, on her right, in an easy chair, Mr. Edward Hawkins, a visitor from New England; facing Mr. Hawkins, seated in another similar chair, Mr. Andrew Latimer, and against the wall to the right, seated at one end of the long horsehair sofa, and a little withdrawn from the group, Margaret Meadesmith, Mrs. Latimer's younger sister.

. . . .

While Mrs. Latimer *talks* Mr. Hawkins *listens:* [2] nothing could more completely and more briefly illustrate the difference between them. Nothing could be more apparent to any one with half an eye to see but that Mr. Hawkins is a listener. Unfortunately, many people have no eye at all for seeing, and to such as these it might easily appear that Mr. Hawkins has no gift at all for listening, that, in fact, he *listens* to nothing. The reason for this is that the man is partly deaf, inimicably reticent, extremely—although not painfully—shy (one of the most salient features of his character is his utter self-possession)—and wholly New England.

American Dream: ". . . a little child that lightly draws its breath—what shall it know of death?"

Alone by afternoon there in your father's house and so desiring perfect glory in America.

2. This is Wolfe's earliest characterization based on Maxwell Perkins.

Two sections: 1) The Unknown North (to supplement His Father's Earth) 2) The West Unvisited.

The quality of joy is a remembered thing: it is the nature of remorseless time that men seldom know when they are happy.

In his father's imprecations against nature—against the weather —there was a kind of bitter and tormented justice. Gant's complaint was really man's everlasting complaint against life—there was really not enough good weather in the world—and there really *isn't*.

The Bartons had not always lived in their present straitened circumstances. They belonged, in fact, to that social class known as "nice people," and Mrs. Barton was grimly, formidably determined that no matter what economic disasters had befallen them, they would relinquish not an atom for their class distinction. The result of their loss of fortune, indeed, had only served to strengthen the emphasis the mother put upon their social inheritance. They lived now, from necessity, in "a poor section" of the town. The district was a shabby one, inhabited largely by workers at the factory, and the Bartons had no friends here. All of their friends, as Mrs. Barton frequently asserted, lived "on the other side of town." Further, even if either of the children had wanted to make friendships among the people of their neighborhood, it is unlikely that their mother would have permitted it. Hugh, in fact, feeling the natural desire of youth for companionship, had begun an acquaintance with another youth at the factory which threatened to develop into an undesirable familiarity, but Mrs. Barton had promptly put an end to it.

"My dear boy," she had said to him in her powerful deliberate way, "you can-not do it. I tell you here and now you can-not af-ford to as-sociate with that class of people."

"But, mother," he said quietly, "he's doing exactly the same kind of work as I'm doing, and his father is foreman of the whole casing room—and—and—that's a pretty good job."

But even before he had finished speaking, she had begun to wag her head slowly from side to side in a gesture of obdurate dismissal.

"I do not care"—(the slight paralysis of her tongue had thickened her pronunciation a trifle, so that she almost seemed to say, "I do *nod* care")—"I do *not* care *what* they do, or how good their job is, they are nothing but working people and, Hugh, if you as-sociate with that class of people, *nice* people will have noth-ing to do with you."

Books: The October Fair
   The Hills Beyond Pentland
Stories: 1) The Lost Boy
    2) Crazy Nigger
    3) The Life and Death of Hugh Barton
    4) April, April.[3]

---

3. Wolfe wrote and published all of these stories. They became "The Lost Boy," "The Child by Tiger," "The Company," "April, Late April."

Pocket Notebook 29

Winter, 1935, to Spring, 1936

These months were full of literary events for Wolfe. From
Death to Morning *was published on November 14.* The Story of a
Novel *appeared in serial form in the* Saturday Review of Literature,
*December 14, 21, and 28, and the fuller version in book form on April
21, 1936. But he still made no progress on the six-volume series which
he had announced the previous spring. In fact, he had begun to discuss
with Perkins his wish to write a new kind of work, not autobiographical, and one which would have as its theme that everything in life
turns out to be different from what was expected. Perkins urged him to
follow his creative inclination, and Wolfe began work in the middle of
March on "The Ordeal of the Bondsman Paul" or "The Vision of
Spangler's Paul." He was made even more ready to give himself to this
task as reviews of his recent work grew critical of his hyperbolic tone
and of his methods of composition. "I have a hunch the well known
'reaction' has set in against me," he wrote in Henry Volkening's copy
of* From Death to Morning, *and he saw his hunch become a staggering
reality when Bernard De Voto's powerful attack "Genius Is Not
Enough" appeared in the* Saturday Review of Literature, *April 25.*

*But since his creativity was always associated with autobiogra-
phy, this undertaking was soon swallowing up material developed or
planned for "The Hills beyond Pentland" and "The October Fair."* [1]
*Although he did not know it, Wolfe was moving now in a direction
that was to lead him away from his six-volume series altogether and
toward a new autobiographical chronicle that became* The Web and
the Rock.

---

1. For a detailed discussion of the merging of Wolfe's projects, see Richard S. Kennedy, "How Eugene Gant Became Paul Spangler," Chapter 20, *The
Window of Memory.*

THE COST OF A LIFE

The First 15 years and then the next 20 years.

$$15 \times \$\ 300 = \$\ \ 4500$$
$$4 \times \$1000 = \$\ \ 4000$$
$$3 \times \$1500 = \$\ \ 5000$$
$$6 \times \$2500 = \$\ 15000$$
$$6 \times \$3000 = \$\ 18000$$
$$\overline{\$\ 46,500}$$

Penance More "quoth he, the man hath penance done." [2]
Discovery and Pursuit
Search and Voyage
The First Voyage
Sailing For Home
The Story of a Man's Apprenticeship
The Apprentice Years
An (my) Apprenticeship
An Artist in America
An Apprentice Speaks
The Story of an Apprentice
A Man and His Book
The Story of A Man's Apprenticeship
Life and Letters
Embarkation
A Young Man's Life and Letters.

[*From the Hound of Darkness ledger:*
To Charles Scribner's Sons
597 Fifth Avenue
New York City
Deliver one thousand and fifty dollars to my apartment 865 1st Ave. by eleven o'clock.

THOMAS WOLFE

Sent at 4:00 A.M. *Friday* Dec. 13, 1935.[3]]

2. The quotation is from Coleridge, "The Rime of the Ancient Mariner." The list reflects Wolfe's search for an appropriate title for the published version of his Colorado lecture.

3. This draft of a telegram, the result of a quarrel with Perkins, marks the point at which Wolfe established his own bank account and stopped drawing money, ten and fifteen dollars at a time, from his royalty account at Scribner's.

[*Wolfe overheard the following conversation of printers or typesetters and planned to make use of it for the Press Room scene in* "*The Hound of Darkness.*"]

I have to go over to Newark.

Well, I'll tell you what I'll do. I'll give you a price.

Now then, I told Lennie to go ahead, and I told my printer to go ahead—[Stokely?] 10 points straight for [*illegible*].

I want to tell George. $9267.

You didn't make up the amount today, did you Lee?

Where the hell do you think all the stationery is coming from?

Did you check up your cash in the drawer?

Do you mean the check money?

Yes, there.

Yes, it's O.K.

(For the typesetter)

Christ, I set the ten pages (pages, etc. I says).

But all right we can't run ten pages.

I says, you figured 15 dollars. Lissen Al, I says. Lissen Al, we gotta have this thing out.

(Nervous—a fellow named Willy) We had it on the press—He says, Jesus, that's a great job. I says, you fellows don't want to do it. All right, it'll go right over to Newark. No, no, he says (nervous)—we don't want it to go to Newark.

LHA at $1.50 wholesale.
$$
\begin{array}{r}
25000 \\
92000 \\
\underline{7500} \\
124500 \\
\underline{1000} \\
150,000
\end{array}
$$

Does this pen write well? I don't know—I'm just afther tryin' it outh nowh.

Sylvia Marcher
Can run off *Informer* Friday night.[4]

4. Wolfe was deeply impressed by John Ford's film *The Informer.*

[*The following list includes Wolfe's Christmas shopping:*]
1) Get cleaning woman (McCutcheon).
2) Present for Miss Wyckoff.
   (84—Miss [_____?] Black velvet Rhinestone—$12.00)
3) Book for Aline ⁵
4) Send Mama money.
5) Telegrams to various people.

Mama—money
Mabel—telegram
Effie—telegram
Jack Wheelock—telegram
Mrs. Perkins—flowers
Mrs. Jelliffe—flowers
Betsy Hill— ⁶

Andy Jackson, 17 East 97th.⁷

Steaks (Washington)
1) Occidental—next to Willard.
2) O'Donnell's (also Pennsylvania Ave.)

Fish
McGregor's (on the Dock's)
Hotel Shoreham (for nice evening)
Old Ebbet—8th St. opposite Wash. Hotel (buffet food).

[*This is a draft of an informal after-dinner speech found among Wolfe's papers. He said he had been "wangled into speaking" against his wishes.*⁸]

5. Since the publication of OT&R, Wolfe had warily allowed a friendly relationship with Mrs. Bernstein to grow, and, in her motherly way, she helped him furnish his apartment. She even supervised the purchase of an extra-long bed for him.

6. Betsy Hatch Hill, a friend who worked in Macy's Department Store.

7. Wolfe had come to know Katherine Gauss Jackson through her position on the editorial staff at Scribner's and later had become friends with her husband, Andrew Jackson. Through Katherine, Wolfe also met Christian Gauss, the distinguished humanist and Dean of the Liberal Arts College at Princeton University.

8. Letter to V. F. Calverton, April 3, 1936. *Letters*, p. 497.

Ladies and Gentlemen, as some of you may know I am not often accused of a lack of words—wish I could think of a few of the adjectives, nouns, adverbs, pronouns, and other parts of speech the critics—.

—another reason for my present confusion is that I'm supposed to be anonymous—I thought I was going to be anonymous—My friend, Whitney Darrow of Scribner's, told me a month or two ago that I was going to be anonymous—and now look at me!

—tell about the Old Lady in Denver, Colorado this summer: the thing I liked about Denver was that I was anonymous—all that anyone knew about me was that I was a Visiting Author—they didn't know whether I'd written King Lear or The Face on the Barroom Floor—and they didn't care! It's a grand town, Denver—the only literary discussion I had while there was with an old lady (tell the story of the little old lady).

I can't tell you how I write novels, because I don't know enough about writing them yet—I hope to improve my knowledge as time goes on, and believe I shall—but even if I knew far more about the subject than I know now, there are so many other people who know more, and who are more competent to speak about it, that it would not be proper for me to make the attempt—

But I do want to say this to you before I sit down: I don't know why a man writes books—what it is that makes him want to write a book—but I suppose he does it because there is some need or force in him that has to write, and when that need or force grows strong enough, he has to write. And I suppose if that need or force *is* strong enough, a man will write under the hardest and most adverse conditions—will endure about any kind of failure, defeat, or indifference—and will still somehow find the power and belief in himself to do the thing he has to do—that has happened to men before this in the world, and will happen again—but I think we can all understand what a bitter hard experience it is—and I know furthermore that everyone who has ever done a piece of writing knows the joy and pride and gratitude a writer feels over the knowledge that anything he has written has meant something to a reader. It seems to me that this is one of the greatest rewards for which a writer lives and works—the thing that makes almost any hardship worthwhile—and it would be foolish and untruthful of me if I should attempt to deny that the warm and generous reception many people have given my work this past year has given me some of the greatest happiness of my life.

—I have begun again on a new piece of work, etc.

[*On the backs of the pages of his speech notes Wolfe has listed "Characters of Last Year." After listing the principal people whom he met in Europe in 1935, he continues with those he met on the return journey:*]

The Ship: [*Dr.*] Russel Lee, Ecklin, Ziegenbein.

New York: The Reporters, Perkins, Miss Maw, Mr. Cornelius Mitchell.

The West, Colorado—Boulder and Denver: [9] Cross, Davison, Mrs. Davison, [*Robert Penn*] Red Warren, Robert Frost, Tom Ferril, Helen, Olga Cosgriff, Marie Malcolm, the [Sebofroth's?], Four Men in Auto Smash, Jim Meyers and wife.

Colorado Springs: Des Powell [10] and wife.

Sante Fe: Alan True, Harriet Long, Esther Owens, Sally Saunders, The Smiths, Dr. and Mrs. Alexander, Spud Johnson, People at Party in Taos.

The Grand Canyon: People from St. Louis.

Hollywood: The Sayres, Dorothy Parker, Oppenheimer, Owen Francis, the [Bessoniere?] girl, actors, actresses, directors, etc.

San Francisco: Genevieve Saiz, A Communist and His Wife, A Swedish Girl, Anina's father.

Palo Alto: Mrs. [*Russel*] Lee,[11] Hugh Wylie, the Pausons, Kathleen and Charles Norris, A Whore.

Reno: A whore, a sheep herder, a Bartender, Miss (?), old red-haired girl.

Salt Lake City: Unitarian Minister, Mrs. Walsh, The Three Girls.

St. Louis: J. Lesser Goldman, Womack, Girl named Carmen—convent girl.

A Man the Train hit outside Terre Haute

New York: Louise Jackson, Dorothy Jackson, Mrs. Jelliffe,

9. Professor Edward Davison was the chairman of the Colorado Writers' Conference. Wolfe had joined Robert Penn Warren and Robert Frost in a Round Table Conference discussing "Poetry and Intelligibility" on July 31. Later he was associated with Warren in discussing the topic "Social Responsibility and the Modern Author." The Western poet, Thomas Hornsby Ferril, had driven Wolfe up through the highest peaks of the Rockies and then to the old mining town of Central City.

10. Desmond Powell had arranged to have Wolfe speak at the faculty club of Colorado College at Colorado Springs on August 13 and then had driven him through the Raton Pass down to Santa Fe.

11. Wolfe had met Dr. Russel Lee on the return voyage from Europe and then visited him in Palo Alto. Later, just before his death, he was planning to visit him again during his convalescence from pneumonia.

Dorothy Gardner, The Canbys, The Colums, Mrs. Colby's Party, Edgar Lee Masters, Hemingway,[12] Mrs. Sterner, The Arthurs, Lenore Cotten, Weinberger, The Masons, The Southern Crowd, the Perkinses, Miss Nowell, John Terry, Lacy Meredith & wife, the Munsons, Elizabeth Lemmon, [Clifford] Odets & Harris, Dos Passos & wife,[13] A. MacLeish & wife, Ina Lowthorp, Mrs. Leavitt, Mrs. Arnie Cabot, Mrs. B[ernstein], The Girl from Plainfield, the Gausses, Herschel Brickell & wife.

[The following notes may have been in preparation for a meeting with May Cameron, who wanted to interview him for the New York Post. In the end, Wolfe wrote the interview himself, except for the opening paragraphs. It appeared on March 14, 1936, and was later collected in Press Time: A Book of Post Classics (New York, 1936).]

Wolfe, Thomas Clayton
Born Asheville, N.C. Oct. 3, 1900.—son of Oliver and Julia Elizabeth (Westall) Wolfe—His father was a stonecutter, his mother ran a boarding house. In the first 12 years of his life he was taken on various trips by his parents and was thus enabled to see a picture of his country: viz.—
1904—St. Louis: The World's Fair.
1907–1912—a series of trips that took him to Florida (3 times)
New Orleans (1)
Hot Springs, Ark. (1)
Augusta, Ga. (1)
Anderson, S.C. (1)
Atlanta, Ga. (2)
Washington, D.C. (1)
1912–1916—few trips but one to Charleston, S.C.—some (?) to Anderson, S.C. etc.
1916—was sent to college to State University at Chapel Hill, N.C.
1916—Trip to Raleigh, Richmond, Va. etc.
1918—Trip to Norfolk and Newport News, Va.

12. Perkins had gotten Wolfe and Hemingway together for lunch. Rivals for fame that they were, they had a wary literary conversation.
13. John Dos Passos had met Wolfe at Perkins' house. The two of them had wandered around nighttime New York together and ended up drinking coffee in a little place on the East Side. "He was just the man to walk about the streets with. Appreciative." Letter from John Dos Passos to Myra Champion, November 22, 1951, in the Pack Memorial Library, Asheville.

1920—(First trip to North—Baltimore, New York City, Boston, Mass, New England)

1920–1923 (Harvard), Trips to New Hampshire, New York City, Baltimore, North Carolina, etc.

1923–1924—The South, New York, New England, New York, The Hudson River, etc. Asheville.

Oct. 1924–Aug. 1925—(First trip abroad) England, France, Italy, Switzerland, France, England, America.

Aug.–Sept. 1925—Asheville.

Dec. 1925—Asheville.

June 1926–Jan. 1, 1927—France, England, Scotland, Belgium, France, Germany, Switzerland, France, America.

June or July–Sept. 1927—France, Germany, Austria, Czechoslovakia, Germany, France, America.

June 1928–Jan. 1, 1929—France, Belgium, Germany, Austria, Italy, America.

        10000—1st 20 years.
         5000—next 3 years.
        15000—next 6 years.
        20000—next 6 years.
        ─────
        $50000

[*Wolfe then figures up his earnings to balance against the cost of his life:*]

        $ 1200—1st 20 years.
         8800—L.H.A.
         3550—Stories
        23000—[*Of Time and The River*]
         2500—[*Guggenheim fellowship?*]
        ─────
        $40000
         5000—[*From Death to Morning*]
        ─────
        $45000

         37.50 [14]
         17000
        ──────
        26250000
         3750
        ──────
         6375
         1000 Mod. [Library]
        ─────
        $7375

14. Wolfe made a 15 percent royalty on LHA, which sold for $2.50 per copy. He earned $37.50 for every hundred copies sold.

50¢ dinner
Bonat 330 West 31st St.

Claire Myers Spotswood [15] St 9–5063.
March 4—Night:
Mrs. Lee [16] called and met me—Came about 6:25—to Passy
about 7:50 or 8:00—home about 9:00—she left at 10:30½.

The History of Boob (also known as "Jock" or "Monk")
McNutt.[17]

[*The remaining pages contain several addresses, including those
of James B. Munn and Marjorie Fairbanks Crocker in the Boston area.
This reflects Wolfe's quick trip to Boston in March, from which he
wired Perkins on St. Patrick's Day:* "Wrote book beginning, goes
wonderfully, full of hope."
The Hound of Darkness ledger contains this first start on "The
Vision of Spangler's Paul," *plus other notes and drafts. In many of
them the narrator is a lawyer, Edward Mason. The following pages
offer a sample of this material.*]

THE INTRODUCTION [18]

In the course of a long and reasonably varied life, I think it is
not the least strange of my experiences to find myself writing these
lines in my present capacity. At any rate, I do not recall having heard
before of an elderly Southerner of legal training and conventional
habits—and certainly, in matters of literary preference my tastes have
generally been conventional enough—being called upon in his sixty-
sixth year to write an introduction to the work of a man more than
thirty years his junior.

And particularly at the present moment, less than a year after

---

15. A novelist, author of *The Unpredictable Adventure* (New York, 1935).
Wolfe was attracted to her Southern cooking, especially the way she cooked
string beans seasoned with bacon.

16. Mrs. Watson Lee, an acquaintance from New Canaan, Connecticut.

17. The Wisdom Collection contains one outline of material with this
title. In his groping for a new central character to carry his narrative, Wolfe
wavered between that of a misunderstood artist and that of a literary gull.

18. There is little doubt that this is the "beginning" Wolfe referred to in
his telegram, for on the previous page in the ledger appears the address of Marjorie Fairbanks Crocker in Cambridge, Massachusetts.

George [19] Spangler's death—or disappearance—when the critical air is still humming with the controversy which his work has excited among his defenders or detractors—my unfitness for the task which circumstance has thus compelled me to, would seem to be marked.

But I have observed, over the route of a life-time, that a man is likely to find himself doing—and with surprising willingness, too—a good many things which his prophetic soul could scarcely have reckoned within the scope of probability. One time, for example, not many years ago, while sitting in the middle of a hot and crowded summer session, my judicial contemplations in the matter of one Gus Williams versus the Southern Railway Company were rudely interrupted by the announcement that the athletes of the local baseball club had been left brutally stranded in the town of Knoxville, Tennessee, that their amiable manager had absconded with all ready cash, and that I had been elected, by unanimous consent, his successor. And I did it too—even though my previous connections with the celebrated sport had been merely those of an ardent and elderly contributor. And we came out third that year! and wiped out the deficit!—and the new park, I jubilantly acknowledge, bears my name!

Nor was that the most improbable of the situations with which even an elderly jurist may be confronted—but I will not delay the reader with a description of the other ones. In this present one, at least, I have the comforting knowledge that I have been vested with editorial authority by the persons most competent to bestow it, and this knowledge—with one or two other considerations which I shall mention later—have decided me to take the work in hand.

I suppose the last words that George Spangler wrote—they are, at any rate, the last of which I have any knowledge—took the form of a communication which he sent to me with the manuscript of this book:

"Here it is," he wrote, "my latest—and perhaps my last. It is the book I told you I should someday write—and not at all the book they thought that I would do—and now that it is done I leave the rest to you:—I make you, as the one most fit to weigh and judge events and characters, its executor—yours to publish or with-hold. Stay with me now—Yours ever—George."

By such authority then—and also by the invitation of his publishers—I have been persuaded to the task.

It may well be asked—and I am sure that if George were here, he would himself be the first to ask it—why write an introduction at

19. In the draft the name is Charles. Wolfe changed it to George when he had the material typed.

all. I know very well the author's own opinion of the subject: he expressed it to me often, vigorously, and sometimes profanely, as in the following letter, written in a characteristically explosive moment following the publication of his second book: "A book is written to be read," he said, "and not to be *introduced*. When I was a kid—some years ago, in fact—I was forever on the point of *commencing* to *start* to *prepare* to *get ready* to *begin* my book. As a result, with my first two books, it was necessary to cut away one hundred thousand words or more—chapter after chapter of commencing—to begin—just to get to the place where the real beginning was. In addition to this, I was forever wanting to write an *introduction* explaining my meaning to the reader, just in case it should not be wholly clear in the eight or nine hundred pages that were to follow. My first book, in fact, was dedicated to a man who had helped me enormously in the matter of editing, cutting, and suggesting possible revisions; and so passionate was my desire to make public acknowledgement of my debt—and also to let the gentle public in on all the nuances, anguishes, toils, and misconceptions of creation—that my dedication took the form of a sixty page dedicatory epistle—something that has not been known on the earth, I guess, since the eighteenth century—and not often then! The sum total of my effort was that my criticizing and editing friend promptly and ruthlessly cut the precious item right out of the manuscript, with the blunt observation that the public buys a book to read the book, and not to read twenty thousand words about how the writer wrote the book, the various styles of creation and who helped him to edit or condense it. He also remarked, very cynically, I thought at that time, that the last and least-to-be-hoped-for miracle of writing was for the artist successfully to explain the intention and the process of his art to the reader—that not one reader in a thousand would understand him anyway, no matter how long or desperately he strove, and that not one reader in a hundred really cared to know. I was so embittered at the time by this merciless destruction of what I considered a perfect masterpiece of explanation and perseverance—to say nothing of my wounded feelings at having my fervent dedication so cruelly rejected —that I went stomping and storming out of my friend's office, yelling imprecations, and swearing never to return—and in fact I went to Boston and was seen no more about the place for a week or two. But since then I have learned, along with a great many other hard and thorny facts, that the man was right—and more than right. I was to learn not only that not one reader in a hundred would understand, or care to understand the meaning of an introduction such as mine, in which I tried to explain the purpose and intention of my writing, but that I was very fortunate if, out of all the thousands of people that one meets nowadays—these Holy Rollers of the Arts—the "Have-You-Read-This," the "You-Must-See-This," "You've-Got-to-Go-and-Hear-That," "My-Dear-You-Simply-Must"—out of all these thousands and thousands of impassioned zealots who go sighing, wheezing, panting, belching, and ecstatically grunting their way through life in a state of perpetual exaltation over anything that has not the moment's crown of fashion, the accolade of critical acclaim—you will be damned lucky, and more than lucky, if out of all those thousands, you find a dozen who will really read your book through to the end and understand it, or give a damn for it one way or another! More than that, you finally give up hoping that most of them will understand anything—even a simple declarative sentence. I suppose this sounds bitter and extravagant but I've been through the whole experience too often now, and the evidence to support all that I have said is overwhelming and soul-sickening . . . So explain me no explanations, persuade me no persuasions, introduce me no introductions: let them take my books the way they are, or not at all."

This was George, of course—and George in a characteristic outburst. I think it was George also in a moment of extravagant excess, and yet the truth is there in what he writes, too. For my own part, I should readily and sympathetically agree with what he says—about introductions—if it were not that certain very pertinent facts did not alter the rule with this present volume.

[*The sequence goes on about the publication of Spangler's novel "Home to Our Mountains" and its reception in the home town, material that appeared in "Man Creating and Man Alive," Chapter 24 of* You Can't Go Home Again. *Edward Mason then goes on to describe how he told George Spangler what the town of Libya Hill used to be like and what early memories he had of George's father.*]

A POSSIBLE BEGINNING

When I was a boy I remember hearing my father say more than once that he had cases argued before him every day by "worse lawyers than Wes [20] Spangler" and that if Mr. Spangler had been "an educated man" he could "have gone far in the world"—a statement which he

20. The name in the manuscript is George. Wolfe changed it to Wes in the typescript. This is the earliest characterization of John Webber as he appears in Wolfe's posthumous fiction.

rarely failed to conclude most emphatically with these words: "He would have made a fine lawyer."

I heard my father say these words the first time more than fifty years ago and the reason I have been thus scrupulous in recording them here is that it strikes me as a very curious and significant that I should remember them at all. Ordinarily, a boy of twelve (and I certainly could have been no more than this when Wes Spangler came to our town to live) is not very much concerned with the respective or prospective merits of the gentlemen who adorn the legal profession—even when one's father *is* a lawyer and a judge of the circuit court, to boot. And unless my memory has gone gravely wrong in its picture of the fellow that I was about that time, my feeling towards the law when I was twelve might be best described as one of profound apathy. I was interested in a great number of things at that time but the law was not one of them: as I recall it now I had seen my first circus just a year or two before—a very modest version of Barnum's Mammoth Circus and Combined Shows: the railroad had not yet reached town and they had brought the whole thing in by wagon across the mountains all the way from Millerton: they even had an elephant named Jumbo and they had marched him up across the Blue Ridge, too—just like Hannibal crossing the Alps—and as I remember now, one of the things I wanted to be at that time, and for a long time afterwards, was the man who sat on Jumbo's skull and rode him up across the mountain—and if I could not be that man, then I was willing to be that man's man—or his boy or his apprentice—or his valet—or his valet's man—or take any office, however humble, that the retinue of such a princely officer could furnish—and then, of course, work my way up from there.

[*The sequence goes on to describe Mr. Spangler pulling the circus wagons out of the mud with his team of mules, material which appears in* The Hills Beyond, *Chapter 7, "A Stranger Whose Sermon Was Brick."*]

"General Mason," Mr. Spangler was saying as I came down the steps, "you must make up your own mind, of course, but if I were building *anything—anything!*" he repeated, his voice rising steeply, and with a sweeping sideways gesture of his hand "—I'd use just about as little wood as possible."

I don't know what would be the proper word to describe Mr. Spangler's activities: I think if I had to choose any I'd have to call him "a master builder." Certainly, the phrase "jack of all trades and good at none of them" did not apply to him: if he was a jack of all trades, he was good at everything he did—as my father said "He can do anything." He was a skilled brick layer and plasterer, an expert carpenter; and in his own way he was a better architect than many who practiced that profession.

THE RETURN OF THE BONDSMAN GEORGE [21]

The Story of His Birth, His Life,
and What Befell Him on the Earth;
His Vision Also of the Lost, the
Never-Found, the Ever-Real America

With An Introduction
By
A Friend

"Prince Andrey looked up at the stars and sighed deeply: everything was so different from what he thought it was going to be"
—War and Peace

I know my soul hath power to know all things,
Yet she is blind and ignorant in all:
I know I'm one of Nature's little kings,
Yet to the least and vilest things am thrall.

I know my life's a pain and but a span;
I know my sense is mocked in everything;
And, to conclude, I know myself a Man—
Which is a proud and yet a wretched thing.[22]

Summary: THE RETURN OF THE BONDSMAN PAUL

1. How Paul Got Born and What It Cost.
2. The Little Monkey (Paul's Father).
3. Childhood: Paul and the Other Boys (Their Names were etc.)
4. School: The Military School—Paul's Great Uncle—Colonel, etc.)
5. The University: [The Fizz, the Fizz, the Fizz Fizz?]
6. National Arts Associated: Paul meets Pangleek—Pangleek in all his phases.

21. The name George replaces the name Paul, which replaces the name Oake, as Wolfe scratched out one after the other.
22. Lines from Sir John Davies' poem "The Vanity of Human Learning."

7. Out in the World: Utility Cultures, Inc.

8. The Trip Abroad: Paris, London, Still Vex'd Bermoothes, etc.

9. Mrs. Feitlebaum and her Circle: Amy Van Leer.

10. Oktoberfest.

11. Success in the City.

12. Return of the Bondsman Paul.

"Child," Paul's mother used to say to him, "you were the youngest, and you've had all the opportunities the others never got. . . . Yes, and what's more, it cost more to get you *born* than it cost for all the others: when the other children were getting born your papa used to take Dr. Cardiac aside and slip ten dollars in his hand—yes, sir! —that's the way it was! That's all it cost—ten dollars apiece for Arthur, Edward, Mamie, Jim and Nell—why yes! pshaw! if I'm not mistaken Mamie only cost him five! But you!—why, you came later—long after all the others—and your papa, I reckon, was more prosperous or at *least* he felt that way. I know he'd just sold that house on Montana Street an' made a profit on it—and I reckon he felt *good* about it—but you cost *fifteen*—Yes, sir! I remember I was layin' there in bed and I saw him take old Dr. Cardiac aside—pshaw, I knew exactly what he meant to do—I'd seen him do it too many times before —and he gave him *fifteen* dollars! Yes, sir!—a *ten* and a *five*—for I saw the bills!

A TOWN ANALYSIS (1913)

The Square—South Side:

Brown's Hardware Store; outside Miller's Shoe Shine parlors: little Miller, tubby little Jew, negro boys, an air of cheerfulness, snapping rags, smell of polish, leather; associations of young sports Sat. night: clocked socks, pressed clothes, new hair-cut, etc.; above Heywood Parker's offices; Bourne and Adams, etc.; Public Library, Miss May Erwin, mannish woman, her friend, going in and out (friend of Reeves girls); old Major Waddell outside, high cracked voice of obscenity; downstairs Claude Willis, Batterham, etc.; above library, old man Avery; New Legal Building: the Bank, Wallace Davis, Russel Davis; Upstairs—Sinclair, Evans, etc.; Lawyers Tom Jones, Morton, Rollins, Wright, Purefoy; Below—Mark Brown's Bldg., Mark Brown et al; next door Sluder; next door, papa, Whiteside, Jannadeau, Old Man Grushard.

East Side:

City Hall: Chief Lyerly, Mayor Rankin; Police Court Judge Phil Cocke; Tax Collector Bartlett; Assistant Wilson, City Plumber Ernest Pegram; City Doctor ___?___; Sanitation Expert ___?___; Policemen: Big Bill Messler, Mr. Bailey (anachronism); Mr. Williams; City Solicitor: Robert Reynolds.

Bakery next market entrance (forget who) Stradley and Luther's Grocery (the Stradley boy); next a front store; next usually vacant store on corner College St. and Sq.

City Market (underneath City Hall): Manley's meat stall (Mr. Manley); Penland's meat stall (Mr. Penland); Kubler's meat stall (Mr. Kubler); Whitehead's meat stall; Hill's meat stall (Dan, Walt, and Frank); Jackson's vegetable stall; Shepherd's; Sorrel, the Fish and Oyster Man.

[*The catalogue continues recording places on the North and West sides of the Square, places on the Northwest side, the street car lines and the names of the "people who used the street cars," the places on both sides of Patton Avenue, Haywood Street, Church Street, College Street, and from Pack Square to Spruce Street.*]

SATURDAY NIGHT AND SUNDAY MORNING

The Presbyterian Church: Because that decayed and dying system of institutions comprised by the Protestant Church In North America is not yet utterly extinct, it may be useful here to enquire into some of the causes of its dissolution, its loss of function, its waning power. Twenty five years ago—even in the most backward provinces of the Church-bound South—the disintegration of the Protestant Church had begun, and was well under way.

Books to be Read in America:
Poems of Emily Dickinson

Books "the world could not do without":
Don Quixote
Faust
War and Peace

The Inferno
Leaves of Grass
The Works of Shakespeare.

[*The two following entries in the ledger indicate that Wolfe
was at work on the episode in which Edward Mason discovers that his
father is a war hero. It was published in the* American Mercury *in
August as "The Bell Remembered" and later became Chapters 8, 9, and
10 of* The Hills Beyond.]

MY FATHER

I understood, of course, even then that my father had been in
the war, but so unprepossessing—at least from my *own* glamorous
point of view at the ripe age of twelve—so *unmilitary* was this stocky,
red-faced, bald-headed man who walked with a limp, and whose
speech on all matters, and particularly on the matter of the war, was as
sparse and blunt as speech could be, that no-one could have seemed
more un-romantically un-warlike. And yet, as I continued to read
books about the war, I began to run across my father's name with
increasing frequency. I can still remember the queer stunned jolt of
surprise I got when I saw his name for the first time—and in a book by
a *Yankee* general, at that—the kind of feverish, heart-thundering concentration as I read the passage over again and again until I had satisfied
myself beyond a doubt that it really was *my* father that the man was
writing about.

Father had been a young man in his thirties when the war
began, already married and engaged in the practice of law here at
home. I suppose we were at that time "the leading family" of the
community: my grandfather had been governor of the State, and I
imagine people hereabouts instinctively looked to our family to supply
leadership when the occasion rose. At any rate, my father took out the
first regiment of volunteers to go from this part of the country—this
was the well-known fourteenth—and a month later he was commis-
sioned colonel in the Army of Virginia. He commanded this regiment
—and very ably too—during the first years of the war: in May, 1863,
after Chancellorsville, during the reorganization of command that had
been made necessary by Jackson's death, he was appointed brigadier by
General Lee, and in that capacity, led his command for the first time at
Gettysburg in Ewell's division.

THREE O'CLOCK

Each day at three o'clock the court-house bell would boom out solidly three full strokes, and yet he always knew beforehand when three o'clock was there.

[*In April, Wolfe was very annoyed at V. F. (George) Calverton, the editor of the* Modern Monthly, *a Communist (Trotskyite) publication, because he had agreed to attend the twelfth anniversary dinner and then discovered that Calverton had listed him among the speakers. He wanted to back out entirely but finally consented to appear when Calverton pled that the announcements had already been sent out. He sketched out the following remarks, which were delivered on April 17 at the Roger E. Smith Grill.*]

Ladies and Gentlemen:

First of all I would like to say how genuinely and sincerely glad I am to be invited to the Modern Monthly dinner and now I suppose I may as well confess that although I have been expecting the present moment for sometime now, I have not exactly been looking forward to it. I was wondering before I came here tonight, whether I was going to talk first and eat afterwards, or eat first and talk afterwards. The loss of good food is one thing that worries me. At any rate something tells me I am going to give the child's menu a good workout when this show is over. I think the thing that got me going, that set my heart to pounding and my pulse to racing a few days ago was when I read in the N.Y. Times that I was going to make "my first public address" at this dinner. Up to that time I had thought of what I was going to do, as what is called "make a talk" and George Calverton told me that was all I had to do. In fact he added in a very comforting manner that if all I did was to get up for a minute and say how glad I was to meet you and be here or something of that sort, it would be all right. I don't know what there is about the word "address" that has such a formidable and depressing sound to it, but ever since I read in the paper that I was coming here to make an address and the first one I had ever made to boot—I have been reaching for the aspirin bottle from time to time. Then the telephone would ring and people would say "see by the paper where you are going to make your first address" and I would tell them, "no, no," it is not really going to be an address, it is just going to be a talk. But they would answer, very stubbornly and grimly I thought, that it was going to be an address, because the N.Y. Times said so, and that I would have to go ahead and make one whether I wanted to or not. Then I kept thinking about the word address, and began to call up friends of mine to see if they knew what an address was or what they thought it was. The first man I called up was a friend of mine, in the publishing business, an editor who ought to understand all sorts of words and he told me that he thought he did know what an address was and that it certainly was different from a talk, because he said a talk was meant to be informal, but an address, according to his understanding was a set speech which varied in length from one to three hours, and was usually delivered by some authority on a political, religious or economic subject. I called up other people and some of them were even less encouraging than the first man had been. Then I looked the word up in the dictionary and although that may have helped a little, it certainly did not cheer me up. The first definition I found in the dictionary was: Address, to prepare one's self. That did not say to prepare oneself for the slaughter, but the way I felt at the moment, it might as well have. And then it said to—apply one's skill or energies, and then it said,—act of addressing one's self or one's words, —and then it said, attention in the way of courtship—suit—skillful management, dexterity, adroitness. Well, I won't give you all of them, but anyway the farther I went on the worse the definitions got. Well, I am not here to make an address to you. I don't know how to begin if I wanted to, but I do feel that I am here to help you celebrate a kind of birthday party—a kind of birthday party for the Modern Monthly and I believe you will all join me in congratulating the Modern Monthly on its birthday. I don't know how many birthdays the Modern Monthly has had, but I do know that I hope it continues to have them and have a great many of them and grow and flourish all the time and live to enjoy a good and influential old age.

I have no speech to make to you on any formal subject and at the present moment at least, no political suggestions to make or no social theories to propose or object to, but as a writer or as a man writer [*sic*], who is trying to learn how to write and who wants to make the writer's life his own, I think I can say sincerely what a genuine and deep value it seems to me any publication has which not only has its own deep and special convictions in policy and in ideas, but which also has enough breadth of tolerance and taste to publish creative work that ought to be published but for which unfortunately in spite of all the hundreds of publications which glut the market, there is not always an outlet.

From my own point of view it seems to me, that such a magazine serves a very vital and valuable function and I believe, [*sic*] I spoke of other writing people to whom I say that such a publication is essentially the ally and friend of people whose work and its essence is not primarily commercial or popular or aimed at a commercial market. I therefore should like to add my own congratulations to those of all the other people here to attend the Modern Monthly dinner, my best wishes for their continued success, and thank all of you for giving me the opportunity of being here tonight.

[*The following excerpts from Wolfe's manuscript sheets show that he had gone beyond the "Introduction" and was converting some of the material from "The Hills Beyond Pentland" into his new book. A typist dated one of the sheets May 22, 1936. This material is an early draft of what ultimately became Chapter 2, "Three O'Clock," in* The Web and the Rock.]

THE VISION OF SPANGLER'S PAUL

PART I
The Child Caliban

CHAPTER I
Three O'Clock [*crossed out*]
The Names of the Bondsman Monk [*crossed out*]
The Boy-Names of the Caliban Monk

"Child, child!—where are you, child?"—So did he always know that she was there!

"Son, son!—where are you, son?"—Too far for finding and too near to seek!

"Boy, boy!—where *is* that boy?"—Where *you*, at any rate, or any other of your apron-skirted kind, can never come.

"Confound that boy! . . . You can't take your eye off him a minute"—Keep your eye *on* then; it will do no good.

"The moment when your back is turned, he's up and gone"—and out and off and far away from *you*, no matter if your back is turned or not.

". . . I can never find him when I need him . . . ." Need me no needs, sweet dame; when I need you, you shall be so informed!"

". . . But he can *eat*, all right . . . . He's Johnny-on-the-spot when it is time to eat . . . ."

And, pray, what is there so remarkable in *that?* Of course, he eats—more power to his eating, too: was Hercules a daffodil; did Adam toy with water-cress; did Falstaff wax fat eating lettuces; was Dr. Johnson surfeited on shredded wheat; or Chaucer on a hand-full of parched corn? No. What is more, were campaigns fought and waged on empty bellies; was Kubla Khan a vegetarian; did Washington have prunes for breakfast, radishes for lunch; was John L. Sullivan the slave of Holland Rusk, or President Taft the easy prey of lady-fingers? No, more—who drove the traffic of swift-thronging noon, perched high above the hauling rumps of horses, who sat above the piston-wheels of furious day, who hurled a ribbon of steel rails into the west, who dug, who clove through gulches, sweated grades or bored through tunnels, whose old gloved hands were gripped on the hand throttles, who bore the hammer, and who dealt the stroke—did such of these grow faint with longing when they thought of the full gluttony of peanut butter and a ginger snap?

[*The sequence continues through the boy's meditations while lying on the grass before his father's house, and the Negro boys come riding by on their bicycles, calling, "Yo' name is Paul!"*]

Pocket Notebook 30

June 7, 1936, to August 1, 1936

As this notebook begins, Wolfe was in the midst of a creative drive that had begun in the middle of May. He was doing a series of character sketches about a publishing house very much like Scribner's, "James Rodney and Company," [1] *including all the material about Foxhall Edwards, his Maxwell Perkins figure. He was also at work rounding out the character of Nebraska Crane, the aging baseball player.*

The new perspective with which he saw his central character, Mr. Spangler, allowed a satiric view of his adventures. But Wolfe was also writing the satiric sketches about the publishing house because he wanted to leave Scribner's, and he was unconsciously searching for a pretext: he knew Perkins would object. During the spring, Wolfe had been outraged when Bernard De Voto declared in his review of The Story of a Novel *that Wolfe, dependent on Scribner's for editorial aid, was inadequate as an artist. Wolfe's need to prove the charge untrue brought him, by July, to consider finding a new publisher.*

As if fleeing from such a thought, he suddenly decided on a trip to Berlin at the end of July, to attend the Olympic Games. In Berlin, too, he could resavor the taste of fame he had found the previous year.

[The following is a sample of Wolfe's sketch "Old Man Rivers," [2] *drawn from Robert Bridges, the editor of* Scribner's Magazine *from 1914 to 1930.]*

When Old Man Rivers woke up in the morning, among the first objects that his eyes beheld were two large and very splendid photographs that faced each other on the top of his tall chiffonier dresser,

1. Wolfe's typist dated her daily work. The dates begin May 23, when she typed the chapter "The Lion and the Fox" (most of which later appeared as "The Lion at Morning" in HB); go on to May 27, when she began the material about the Fox (YCGHA, pp. 438–59) and his reading of the suicide of C. Green (YCGHA, pp. 461); and continue until June 12, when she began the sketch "Old Man Rivers," and June 18, when she started the final sketch, "No More Rivers."

2. Although this story was withheld from publication until after the death of Robert Bridges, it was finally published in the *Atlantic Monthly*, December, 1947.

and that were divided by the heavy, silver-mounted brush and comb that lay between them. It was a good arrangement: each of the two splendid photographs commanded its own half of the dresser like a bull in his own pasture, and the rich dull solidity of the brush and comb seemed to give each just the kind of "frame," the kind of proud division to which it was entitled. In a way, the two splendid photographs seemed to regard each other with the bellicose defiance of a snorting bull: if anyone of this present generation can remember the Bull Durham advertisements of twenty years ago, he may get the idea —three rails of fence, the pasture, the proud bull dominant with the great neck raised, the eyes flashing fire, and the proud rage of his magnificent possession simply *smoking* from his nostrils, and saying plainer than any words could do: "Here I am and here I mean to stay! This side of the fence is mine! Keep out of here!"

Old Man Rivers more *sensed* than *saw* these things when he opened his old eyes. He didn't see things clearly any more. Things didn't come to him in the morning as they used to come. He didn't wake up easily, he didn't wake up at once, "all over," as he used to do; rather his old, tired, faded, somewhat rheumy eyes opened slowly, gluily, and for a moment surveyed the phenomena of the material universe around him with an expression that was tired, old, sad, vague and unremembering.

Presently he roused himself and got up; he got up slowly, with a heavy sigh, and bent to find his slippers with a painful grunt; he was a heavy old figure of a man—a man who had been a big man, big-maned, big-handed, big-shouldered, and big-muscled, and whose bigness had now shrunk and dwindled to a baggy, sagging heaviness; round baggy shoulders, thin legs, sagging paunch—a big man grown old. It took him a long time to bathe, a long time to look at the sad old face reflected in the mirror, the face with the high cheek-bones, the slanting sockets of the eyes, the long wispy moustache, and the scraggly wispy beard, which, with the sensually full red lips and the old tired, yellowed, weary eyes gave Mr. Rivers a certain distinction of appearance—an appearance not unlike that of a Chinese Mandarin.

It took him a long time to shave, too—to do all the delicate work required about the edges of that long, straggling moustache, and that wispy Mandarin-like beard to which he owed a good part of the distinction of his personal appearance. He shaved with a straight razor, of course; as he often said he wouldn't use one-of-these-confounded-safety-razor-contraptions if they gave him the *whole* factory. But, really, he had become afraid of his old straight razor, which had once been such a friend to him; his old hands shook with palsy now, he had cut himself badly on more than one occasion, shaving had become a slow and perilous affair.

But he felt better after shaving and four fingers of sound rye:— none of your bromo seltzers, aspirins, or soda-tablets, or any of your other quack remedies for *him;* after a night of old-fashioned cocktails and champagne there was nothing like a good stiff drink of *whiskey* the next morning to set a fellow up.

Warmed by the liquor, and with a sparkle in his eyes for the first time, Mr. Rivers finished dressing without great difficulty. He grunted his way into his heavy woolen drawers, and undershirt, fumbled with shaky fingers to put cuff links and collar buttons in a clean shirt, grunted as he bent over to pull his socks on, got into his trousers without much effort, but had a hard time with his shoes—confound it, it came hard to have to bend and tie the laces, but he wasn't going to let any fellow tie his shoes for *him!* By George, as long as he could move a muscle he'd have none of that!

The worst was over now; fully attired, save for his coat and vest and collar, he stood before the chiffonier, buttoned the wing-collar, and with trembling fingers fumbled carefully with the knot of his cravat. Then he combed his sparse hair with the heavy silver comb, brushed it with the heavy silver brush, and—looked with satisfaction at the two splendid photographs.

The one on the left was really bull-like; the square face was packed with a savage concentration of energy and power, the moustache curved around two rows of horse teeth bared with tigerish joy; behind the spectacles the eyes looked out upon the world with fighter's glance. Everything about the photograph spoke the brutal eloquence of energy and power, its joyful satisfaction in itself, its delight with life, adventure, friendship, love or hate, its instant readiness for everything. Everything about the picture said: "Here I am boys! I feel bully!"—and this bully-feeling, brutal, savage, joyful, ready-for-fight-or-fun picture was autographed as follows: "To dear old Ned with heartiest and most affectionate regards from—Theodore!"

The other face, no less the fighter's face, was colder, leaner, more controlled. A long, lean face, a little horse-like in its bony structure, horse-like, too, in its big teeth, touched coldly, stiffly round the powerful thin mouth with the sparse smile of the school-teacher; the whole long face borne outward by the powerful long jaw, relentless, arrogant, and undershot,—face of school-teacher marking papers, Presbyterian face, to fleshpots hostile, to wine, women, belly-warmth, exuberance, and life's fluidity, unskilled, opposed, and all unknowledgable, but face of cold high passion, too, fire-glacial face, and face of

will unbreakable, no common, cheap, contriving, all-agreeing, all-con-
ceding, compromising, and all-promising face of the ignoble politician,
but face of purpose, faith, and fortitude—face of arrogance, perhaps,
but face, too, of a captain of the earth, a man inviolable, a high
man—and signed: "To Edward Rivers—with sincerest good wishes
and, may I say, affectionate regards—Cordially yours—Woodrow
Wilson."

Old Man Rivers' tired old eyes and haggard face really had the
warm glow of life and interest in them now. As he struggled into his
vest and coat, he looked at the two photographs, wagged his head with
satisfaction, and chuckled:

Good old Ted! Dear old Tommy! I tell you what those—those
fellows were—were *just bully!* He just wished everyone in the world
could have known *both* of them the way *he* had known them! Why,
the minute Ted walked in a room and flung down his hat, the place
was his. The minute he met you, and shook hands with you—why, he
made you his friend forever! By George, there was something about
that fellow—just the way he had of coming in a room, or flinging his
hat down, or jumping up to shake your hand, and saying, 'Delighted'
—there—there was just something about everything that fellow *did* that
warmed you up all over!

And Tommy? As Mr. Rivers' old tired eyes surveyed the long
prim face of Tommy, his expression, if anything, became a little softer,
a little more suffused with mellowness than when he had surveyed the
vigorous countenance of Ted . . . . Tommy! By George, there was a
great follow! He just wished everyone could have known Tommy as
he had known him!—Why, confound these fellows, anyway (a kind of
indignant and impatient mutter rattled in the old man's throat)—writing and saying all this stuff about Tommy being cold, unfriendly, not
able to warm up to people. By George, *he'd* like to tell 'em what he
knew! He'd known Tommy almost fifty years, from the time they
were at Princeton right up to Tommy's death, and there never was a
man on earth who had a warmer 'human side' than Tommy had! By
George, no! Ask anyone who knew him, ask any of Tommy's friends
whether he was cold and unable to warm up—By George, *they'd* tell
you pretty quick how cold he was! Confound these fellows, he'd just
like to tell them about some of the great times *he'd* had with Tommy
—some of the things they'd done at college—yes! And even later—
he'd just like to tell them about that time when Tommy had all the
fellows in the class come and visit him—that was in 1917, right when
he was in the middle of all that trouble, but you'd never have known it
from the way he acted, invited the whole class to come and stay two

days and all the fellows who could come *came,* too—and, by George, that *was* a celebration!

Sunday, June 7, 1936:
    Diary: Was wakened at ten o'clock by telephone call from Mrs. Clarence Day. Tells me she is in Lenox Hill hospital and has had an operation. I am to go there at four o'clock. Read *Tribune, Times* and O'Brien collection of short stories.[3] Drank Tom Collinses, a glass of vermouth and went to Mont D'Or for lunch (or rather dinner)—tomato juice, jellied madrilène, fresh sea food, chicken cocotte en casserole, camembert cheese, coffee, cigar, and whiskey and soda (now four o'clock).

MR. SPANGLER YEAR BY YEAR

    1904:—Back from St. Louis with mother—Lyerly's porch, the sputtering corner lights, the Vance St. corner.
    1905:—
    1906:—Orange St. School: the fall of Revell's house, Mr. Revell borne by on shutter, a sheet, blood—Hosley and Moule's Book Store —Mr. Owenby.
    1907—
    1914: The Hogwart Heights Military Academy.
    1920–25—Cousin Ellen, Cousin Bert; Beefsteak Charlie's (late at night); the School for Useful Cultures.
    1925–1929—Mrs. Feitlebaum.[4]
    1929–31: First Glory—(Day at Rodney's)
    1931–35 Brooklyn: The Whittakers; "This is Ha-a-riet"; Steve's Coffee Pot; Still Vex'd Bermoothes; Wind from the West.
    1935–36: Fame (1½ years)—Girl in Hanover; Berlin, the Ambassador's Daughter; The Magic Rock (Wartburg) Copenhagen; Return to Glory (4th July); the Great West; Fame Exploding in the City (Oct.–June—1936).

Possible Routes:
    From Here to New Orleans by rail—then to Texas.
    From here to Chicago by the Erie R.R.

    3. Wolfe's story "Only the Dead Know Brooklyn" had been selected for inclusion in *The Best Short Stories, 1936,* ed. Edward J. O'Brien.
    4. Wolfe's new fictional name for Aline Bernstein was Rebecca Feitlebaum.

From Chicago to N.W. by the Northwestern.
From here to Kentucky then by river boat.

Train Trips:

1) Age 3—St. Louis—by way of Knoxville, Cincinnati, etc.

2) Age 4—St. Louis to Asheville—How I don't know but by Knoxville.

3) Age 5—out through W.N.C. to Robbinsville—Effie teach school there.

4) Age 6 or 7—To Augusta, Georgia with Papa to see Effie.

5) Age 7 or 8—to New Orleans—Mardi Gras.

6) Age 8 or 9—to Florida with Mama—St. Petersburg—Back to Anderson, S.C. To see Effie.

7) To Jacksonville, St. Augustine—time I studied with little cripple in St. Aug.

8) To Daytona, Palm Beach etc.

9) a). To Knoxville, Tenn. etc.
    b). To Knoxville, Tenn. again.

10) (Age 12) To see Woodrow Wilson inaugurated (1913).

1915 (Autumn—age 15) to Charleston, S.C.

1916—(Aged 15–16) To Chapel Hill, To Durham, To Raleigh, To Richmond.

1916–17—To Chapel Hill, To South Carolina.

1917–1918—To Chapel Hill, To Richmond, To Norfolk and Newport News, To Asheville, To Chapel Hill.

1918–1919—To Chapel Hill, To Asheville (Ben's Death), To Chapel Hill, To Asheville (Xmas), To Chapel Hill (Xmas), To Asheville (In Asheville that summer).

1919–1920 To Chapel Hill, To Asheville (Xmas).

1920 To Chapel Hill.

1920 To Asheville.

1920 To Balsam.

1920 To Baltimore, N.Y., Boston.

1921 To Baltimore (Papa)

1922 To Asheville (Papa's death)

1922–23—To Boston.

1923—To Madison, N.H.

1923—To N.Y. (Wallace).

1923—To N.Y. and Asheville.

1923—To S.C. (Greenville).

1923—N.Y. (Graham Memorial), Boston.

1924 To N.Y.U.

1924 To Asheville.

1924 To England (etc.)

1925 To Asheville, To N.Y., To Asheville.

1926 (New Year's) To N.Y.

1926–1927—England, etc. (L.H.A. Begun).

1927—France, Germany, etc.

1928—France, Germany, Austria, Hungary, Italy, etc.

1929 Asheville (Sept. 1929).

1930–1931 France, Switzerland, Germany, England, etc.

1931–1932—N.Y. (Brooklyn), Maine, Bermudas, Canada, etc.

1932–1933—Washington, York Springs, Boston, Canada, etc.

1933–1934—Washington, Vermont, Washington, Washington, Chicago, Virginia.

1934–1935—Troy, Albany, Canada, France, England, Holland, Germany, Denmark.

1935—N.Y., Chicago, Colorado, N. Mexico, California, Nevada, Missouri, N.Y.

1935–1936—Washington, Boston, York Springs, Easton, Dingman's [*Ferry*], etc.

Friday June 26, 1936:

(Day of Democratic Convention in Philadelphia—Night of Roosevelt's nomination—phone call from Perkins 10 o'clock—answer from Los Angeles in Dooher matter [5]—called [Milman?]—Dictated letter to B. Polk and corrected MSS.—went to [Milman's?] office—dictated material to story for 3 hours—home (at 4:30) wrote for two hours—then listened to convention—so to Waldorf—and now at Park Ave.

[*The following excerpt is a sample of Wolfe's story "No More Rivers," the work which was the center of the conflict between him and Perkins. Based to some extent on the character of Scribner's editor Wallace Meyer, it was the story of a sensitive, perceptive literary editor, George Hauser, who withdrew from life and its emotional*

5. Wolfe had become involved in another legal tangle when Murdach Dooher, young brother of his friend Mrs. Kitty Hoagland, had become his agent for selling manuscripts to rare book dealers. When Wolfe became dissatisfied with the arrangement and discharged Dooher, the boy refused to return the manuscripts and sent Wolfe a bill for $1000.00 for services rendered as his agent. Wolfe began legal proceedings to recover his property. One of the manuscripts was in the hands of a Los Angeles dealer.

stresses because of an unhappy love affair. Sprinkled liberally throughout were little episodes about the publishing house of James Rodney and Company. When Wolfe finished it at the end of June, he asked Miss Nowell to show it to Perkins to get his reaction.

Perkins, very upset, muttered to Miss Nowell that he would have to resign from Scribner's if Wolfe began writing up the stories and gossip Perkins had relayed to him over the years. However, Wolfe was never able to sell the story. It was too long, and it attempted a characterization that he could not really get hold of. Although he cut and revised the story twice, he could never make a successful blend of Wallace Meyer's reticent manner and the inner vitality of Thomas Wolfe.

The passage which follows does not reflect any of the trivial Scribner's anecdotage that Perkins objected to. Rather, we have selected a passage which reflects the Wolfean side of George Hauser, for Wolfe tried to make him a man who was very conscious of his American identity and one who puzzled over the dualities of American life—the combination of beauty and ugliness, of light and darkness. At this point in the story, Hauser, who is a Minnesotean now living in a New York apartment, looks out the window at the East River:]

For a moment, George stood looking quietly out upon the river. A cool breath of morning, sea-fresh, and tide-laden, curiously half-rotten, flowed over his calm features: that living river and its smell, he understood, was like all life. That marvellous river, veined with the hundred cross-wise patterns of its moving tides, was at once corrupt and rotten, yet laden with the breath of morning and of life. The river was a flood of tidal filth, a flowing sewer surging back and forth to the recession of the tides, and bearing in its tainted flood the excremental dumpings of six million men. And yet the river was a tide of flashing life, marked delicately in a hundred places with the silvery veining of a hundred currents, and pungent with the vital, aqueous, full salt-laden freshness of the sea.

The tide was coming in upon the full; George stood there, watching quietly, and saw it come. It was a steady, flowing, crawling and impulsive surge—it kept coming on without recession, with the suggestion of an immense and sourceless plangency, a welling flood that would come on forever and that knew no limit to the invasion of its unfathomed power. The river was not quiet; the tide was ruffled, wind-roughened by the breath of morning into a million scallop-shells of winking light—rose, golden, silver, sapphire, pink—the whole polychrome of morning was reflected in the stream,—a million scallop-shells winked into life, and within the channel of the river's life, the tide came on.

Morning, shining morning, filled the river, and transformed the town. Across the river the tormented visage of Long Island City had also been transformed; that grin of wilderness of cement and brick, that forest of smokestacks, chimneys, enormous stamped-out factory moulds, million-windowed ware-houses, gas tanks and refineries, wharves, derricks, tug-boats, cranes and docks, and strings of box cars on rails of floating barges, was magically translated by the alchemic wizardy of every hue that morning knows.

. . . .

And—oh, hard and thorny paradox!—as is almost always the fact in America, the astounding beauty of the thing was derived from its gigantic ugliness. George had seen and pondered on the miracle a hundred times, the truth of it if found, he knew, would be somewhere near the heart of our unfathomed mystery: it was like coming into Pittsburgh after dark, which is like coming into Hell at night, when Hell is going at full blast, arrayed in the full panoplies of all its Hellish magnificence—the train wheels pounding steadily along the night-dark waters of the Styx (or call it if you will Monongahela)—the Hell fires flaring everywhere, bursting out with sombre terrifying glares through Hell-light auras of Hell-smoke, flaming upon the blasted hills, shooting upward suddenly in a fierce column in the smoking Hell-works there across the stream (the works of Bessemer)—the Hell-beauty of the Hell-city flaming, flaring, smoking everywhere around you—astounding, thrilling in its beauty. And the beauty of this scene, now bright with morning, was also of the nature of this mystery, an image too of this hard paradox.

What was it, then? As he looked, a tug set neatly in between two barges, each loaded with twin rows of box-cars divided by the long platform of a station shed, backed out into the stream and quartered slowly, steadily, with its enormous freight, then started head-on up the stream. Thick water foamed against the blunt snouts of the barges, the little tug between them, neatly forged ahead with its great cargo without a sense of effort, with a sense of limitless power, and with astonishing speed. The tug came out into the full light of the stream, the young cool light of morning fell flat and cleanly on the rusty sides of the old freight cars on the barges: everything began to blaze with thrilling color. The excitement, the beauty, the feelings of wonder and recognition which all the powerful associations of the scene evolved, was intoxicating. The harsh raw colors—themselves derived from the vast pigments of America—(at least, they can not be found in any other place)—now blazed there in the cool young light in a composition that was at the same instant marked by a delicacy, a purity, a transparent clarity, and an evanescent loveliness that was fragile as a shell, and by a brutal strength, a harsh and angular decisiveness, a sense of smashing power and hurtling speed and crushing weight that was as savagely exultant in its brutal thrill as the slamming roar of a locomotive. Moreover it was not *just* the composition of the scene itself—the harsh and powerful design of the great barges, the crude and thrilling shapes of the old box-cars, foaming up in the shining stream in the cool polychrome of morning; the thing that made it wonderful was that nothing was closed within itself, nothing finite, nothing ended by its frame. The thrilling beauty, the magic, and the intoxication of the thing—the thing that made the heart beat faster, and the throat get tight, and something stab as swift and instant as a knife—was not the familiar spectacle of a little tug clamped in between two enormous barges and long strings of rusty cars as it bore swiftly up the stream. No, it was more than this—the beauty was not so much the beauty and the wonder of the thing as the beauty and the wonder which the thing evoked, the little tug was not just a little tug that plied about the waters of Manhattan.

No, the little tug was sliding lights at night—red, yellow, green, as hard and perfect as cut gems, as poignant, small, and lonely as the hearts of men. The little tug was like all our lights at night, which burn so brightly and so bravely, but with such a small and lonely isolation in the immense and silent darkness, the attentive waiting of our enormous dark. The little tug was not merely like the lights of night, it was like the lights of darkness in America, which do not merge, which do not burn into each other, but which are poignant, small and lonely as a beacon—which stretch across the continent like strung beads, which burn and wink along our coasts like points in an enormous chain of which the links may not be seen, which are so brave, so small, so lonely in that huge unuttered vacancy of the attentive and eternal dark. The tug was like the lights that move and slide upon dark waters in the night, and like great ships that bay at night-times from the harbor's mouth. The tug was like dark waters of the night, the small and poignant lights that slide there in the viewless dark, down past the huge cliff of the sleeping, silent, and terrific city, the eyes of the unnumbered windows, the huge heart of the city, and the small and beating hearts of sleep. The little tug was like the evocation of those things.

. . . .

The harsh enormous barges with their blunt old snouts were like these things, as well. In all their thrilling evocations they spoke, as did the tugs, of the huge traffic of the harbor, of docks and piers and loading, of the great raw use and labor of America. The barges, though, spoke less of night-time than the tugs: the huge barges belonged to morning, loads of gravel, sand, cement, freight-cars, day-time, and the daily work of men. But more than anything else the barges belonged to sun-set; they belonged to the great hush of evening, the tranquil light, the long last slants of fading light, the old-gold of the setting sun that burns the fiery and intolerable fierce-glow of its last radiance in one pane of glass high up in the great splinter of a sky scraper, or in one pane of glass there in a ware-house or a factory of Long Island City. The barges, then, belonged to evening and to sunset in America. They belonged to the sense of vast completion, the sense of mighty labor ended, the huge and quiet respiration of the tired earth. The barges belonged to all the men who lean upon the sills of evening in America, and regard with quiet eyes, and know that night is coming, labor done. The barges belong to all the quiet waters of the evening, to the vast empty hush and quietude of piers, to quiet waters that come in with quiet glut, to slap against old crusted pilings of pier wharves, to slap against the sides of rusty barges, tethered there, to rock them gently, and to bump their rusty sides together, stiffly to rock the high poles of the derrick-booms. The old barges belonged to these things, to sunset and the end of work, and to the long last fading slants of light here in America that will fall, like loneliness, sorrow, and an unknown joy, upon the old red brick of houses, so to lie there briefly like the ghost of light, from which all the energy and heat of day has gone and so to fade, to wane, to die there, knowing night has come.

As for the freight cars, they were companion to these things, and they belonged to all the rest of it as well. Even their crude raw color—a color of dried ox-blood, grimed and darkened to the degree and variation of their age—seemed to have been derived from some essential pigment of America, somehow to resumé and to express the whole weather of her life. George looked at them and saw their faded lettering: he could not read it, but he knew that if he could he would find the names of most of the great lines of the nation—the Pennsylvania, the New York Central, the Erie, Lackawanna and New Haven, the Baltimore and Ohio, the Southern, the U.P., the Santa Fe, the Canadian Pacific, the Northwestern.

He knew that those iron wheels had pounded back and forth along almost every mile of rail whose giant web covered the country. He knew that those harsh ox-blood frames of wood and steel had been exposed to every degree, every change, every climate, every season, and every violence of weather the continent knows. He knew that they had broiled in train-yards out in Kansas, all through the sweltering afternoons of mid-July, when the temperature stood at 107°. He knew that they had been beaten upon with torrential rain, frozen over in a six-inch sheath of ice and snow; he knew that in the night-time they had toiled their way, behind the thundering bellows of a "double header," up through the sinuous grades and curves of the Appalachians, or pounded their way by day, straight as a string across the plains of Western Kansas. They had crossed the Mississippi and the Rio Grande; they had known the lonely barren pine lands of the South, as well as the towering forests of the great Northwest; they had known the cornlands, crossed the plains, gone round or through the Rocky Mountains, they had crossed the blasted fiend-world of Nevada, and they had sought and found the Pacific Shore. They had known the green loveliness of New England, the magic of the Hudson River, all of the homely freshness of the good green East, all of the solar space, the blazing color and magnificence of New Mexico and Arizona, the South-West.

They had lain for weeks in the vast train-yards of the great cities of the nation—somewhere in the smoky brute-sprawl of Chicago, in one of her countless train-yards, lost somewhere in the jungle of the freight cars, in the vast spreading flare of unnumbered miles of rail. They had lain for weeks in the great train-yards of the Jersey flats, in the smoky train-yards of Philadelphia, Pittsburgh, Cleveland, Buffalo, Atlanta, Omaha and New Orleans. And they had lain in the smaller yards as well; in towns like Harrisburg and Springfield; in smaller towns like Easton, Pa., Danville, Va., Salisbury, N.C., Mansfield, Ohio, and Davenport, Iowa. They had lain in great jungle strings of freight, uncountable and innumerable, in the gigantic yards of the great cities, and in the smaller yards of smaller towns. And singly and detached, they had lain on a spur of rusty siding at the loading platform of some little factory—some smaller flour mill, some packing place, some little one-horse works. He had thundered past unending strings of them, lined up across the midlands of the country, and he had seen them for a fleeting instant, from the windows of a speeding train, curved back upon a spur of rusty track in lonely pine lands of the South, at red and waning sunset in the month of March, empty, open and deserted, yet curiously and indefinably thrilling, filled somehow with all the wildness, loneliness, the promise of unknown joy, the message of enormous distance, that is America.

[*Wolfe took a train trip to Chicago in late June or early July. His trip apparently set in motion his cataloguing faculty, for he began*

*to tabulate aspects of the United States within his travel experience. He
began with a list of the states he had not visited:*]

Oregon, Washington, Idaho, N. Dakota, S. Dakota, Minnesota,
Wisconsin, Oklahoma, Texas

[*At this point appears a list titled "The States," which includes
cities he has visited in each state. He goes on to list natural phenomena
he has seen in the United States:*]

N.C.

Craggy
The Pink Beds
Pisgah
The Great Smokies

Seen:
    The Smokies
    The Mississippi
    The Appalachians
    The Rocky Mountains
    The Royal Gorge
    The Grand Canyon
    The Santa Clara Valley (Russ. Lee and family.)

Peter Jack, 52 W 9th.[6]

Paul Kollen (Eastman Room, Congress Hotel, Chicago) Told
me about Eagle River, Wis., Jack O'Lantern Lodge. (This fellow—a
fine looking boy—was from Wis.—said his father was a doctor.)

[*Here we have omitted a list of all the Midwestern states with
their populations, followed by a list of the Northeastern states and
their populations.*]

6. Peter Munro Jack, who was on the literary staff of the New York
Times, came to know Wolfe because of his perceptive and appreciative reviews
of OT&R, FDTM, and SN.

Here at Fort Wayne [*Indiana*] (Rt. Hand Side).

R'way yards and tracks—cinders (three lines of tracks)—then embankment runs down—[wrecked?] district of 20–30 yds. with caboose (Wabash), concrete wall—then other tracks.

On other side (left) more tracks—station group—everything grey—blistered on side—several train men in blue overalls and other fellows (one red neck and heavy face wide eyes) [*the rest illegible*]

[*Sketch*] This kind of house, grey, blistered—brick things—concrete things, etc.

[*Sketch*] Fort Wayne to the left as train stops.

[*Sketch*] Fort Wayne. Everything—even houses blistered, no color—concrete stack [*illegible*] a weed grown track between factory walls—all the weed growth just growing in between—concrete again weed growth—the cindered trackway—the weed growth going down from right of way—the landscape mixed with barns or houses or the houses mixed with landscape—which is which.

Freight cars by track—weed growth—track by track of freights and gondolas—trees above—a wood now (in Indiana) undistinguished trees but green—fields casual and unplanned.

[*Many crude sketches follow, some marked with a word or two:* "fields," "woods," "all flat," "hay wagon," "alone in a field," *etc.*]

Straight roads and the dark—heat opaque—American houses.

Barns (often painted red) the brightest spot on it all.

At evening—night comes down up[*on*] gaunt hills where no oak is.

At evening—a farmer with straw hat—tan baked—big barns and the [tracks?] of the hay rakes moving.

It is hard to keep the design of things at 60 miles an hour.

Evening—the light still bright but sunlight fading—beside the track—tall grasses (green but with yellow wheat-tips) lumpish nards of earth (perhaps a gully or ditch beyond the scene) a wire fence—rows of corn—a great width of agricultural distance—open, yet interspersed with trees—houses (tree surrounded or shade often)—barns, etc.—road going straight away—then blistered little towns at sunset—a main street—station with trucks—garbage trucks—blistered houses—some brick ones—weed growth—cars parked on streets—then country again—stuff by track bed—corn fields—now interspersed woodland—good but indefinite trees (the whole almost Dutch-flat).

[*More crude sketches follow with comments such as:* "a landscape of great flatness," "a road straight away clouded with white dust," "rounded barn ends."]

Olympic Try-outs, Sat.–Sun. July 11–12, 1936, Randall's Island, N.Y. [*The achievements in the various events are then recorded.*]

[*The following two items from Wolfe's manuscript sheets were dated by the typist July 2 and July 3, 1936.*]

Nebraska was battering the ball-fences of the nation. As often happens with the great player who has "passed his peak," his energies and skill had gone through a brilliant and temporary revival—he was enjoying one of the greatest seasons of his career.

When Spangler saw him, however, he was curiously unexcited over his success: like his father, like himself—like the Cherokee that tinct his veins—and like most veteran ball-players at the end of their career—he was calmly, quietly fatalistic:

"Yes, Georgius," he said, in answer to the other's warm felicitations—I've been havin' a good year . . . But, boy!"—he shook his head suddenly, and grinned—"Do the old dogs *feel* it!" He was silent a moment filling his pipe, then, as he lighted it, he went on quietly: "When you've been up there shaggin' flies as long as I have, you may lose count but you don't need to—your legs'll tell you.[7]

Mr. Spangler had not been back in his native land for many hours before he informed himself of the fortunes of his favorite athlete. That night, in fact, at midnight seated in a Lexington Avenue Child's Restaurant with smoking wheat cakes, coffee, and an ink-fresh copy of next morning's *Tribune* before him, he read of Mr. Drake.[8] The experience, certainly a familiar one in Spangler's life, suddenly attained an intensity, a clarification of interest in Spangler's life that it had never had before. His mind worked on it with a kind of quiet, yet furious, relish, a kind of absorbed and extravagant obsession of pleasure which these discoveries always gave him. Spangler's mind, in fact, was a remarkable instrument: he had already been accused of lack of judgment, of a lack of reasoning power, of a lack of "ideas." He was accused of getting at things with his emotions, rather than with his brain, of being intellectually confused.

As a matter of fact, none of these charges were true. Or, if they had truth in them, it was only the kind of lifeless half-truth which the "intellectual" mind is subject to—a truth without lustre, without

7. This goes on to include the material in YCGHA, pp. 57–67, although it has been rearranged and adapted.
8. At this stage, Wolfe called his character Nebraska Drake. The opening sentences appear in YCGHA p. 57. Aswell placed the remainder about the "intellectual" in another context, pp. 409–10.

warmth, without life, without breath, without reality—and accordingly, worse than no truth at all. Mr. Spangler had been accused of blindly stubborn prejudice, instinctive hostility, towards the process of the intellect, the intellectual, the "intellectual point-of-view." But the trouble, he had found, with the ordinary "process of the intellect" had been that there was too much process and too little intellect. His objection to most of the "intellectuals" he had met, was that they were not intellectual enough, and to the intellectual point-of-view, that there had been no point of view, but only many points of view, disparate, arbitrary, sporadic, and confused.

To be an "intellectual" was, it seemed, a vastly different thing from being intelligent. A dog's nose would usually lead him toward what he wished to find, or away from what he wished to avoid: this was intelligent. That is, the dog had the sense of reality in his nose. But the "intellectual" usually had no nose, and was lacking in the sense of reality. The most striking difference between Spangler's mind and the mind of the average "intellectual" was that Spangler absorbed experience like a sponge, and made use of everything that he absorbed. He really learned constantly from experience. But the "intellectuals" of his acquaintance seemed to learn nothing. They had no capacity for rumination and digestion. They could not reflect.

[*A loose sheet which apparently comes from the summer of 1936 lists a whole series of possible episodes for Spangler's adventures —as if he were the hero of a dime-novel series. The numbers in parenthesis indicate Wolfe's age when the incidents occurred.*]

    1) Mr. Spangler and the Girl from Durham (16)
    2) Mr. Spangler Meets Duh Guy (20) [*This occurred on his trip North, when he stopped at Baltimore.*]
    3) Mr. Spangler and the Blind Man—Dinwood Martin (20)
    4) Mr. Spangler and the Wind from the West (33)
    5) Mr. Spangler and the First Autos (12)
    6) Mr. Spangler and the First Movies (Ira Martin) (13)
    7) Mr. Spangler and the Still Vex'd Bermoothes
    8) Mr. Spangler and the Girls Who Worked For Him
    9) Mr. Spangler and His Father Visit His Father's Country

(13)
    9) Mr. Spangler and the Nigger Killer Dick (7 or 8)
   10) Mr. Spangler and the Girl From Hannover (34)
   11) Mr. Spangler and the Nobel Prize Winner (30)
   12) Mr. Spangler and Mrs. Ellen Lavis

13) Mr. Spangler and the Rooms He Lived In
14) Mr. Spangler and the House on 11th St. (27–28)
15) Mr. Spangler and the Milk-man (33)
16) Mr. Spangler and Steve's Coffee Pot on Henry St. (32–34).

[*The following draft of a letter is the first indication in Wolfe's notebook that he was considering leaving Scribner's.*]

Gentlemen:

I am the author of four published books of which two are novels, one a volume of short stories, and one a very short book—about 100 pages—about the experiences of a beginning writer. I am at present engaged in the writing of another long book. As I have no obligations of any sort at present with any publisher, whether personal, financial, or contractual, I am writing to you and to several other publishers to inquire if you are interested in the publication of any forthcoming books, and if so, upon what terms. I am going abroad within ten days and should appreciate it if you could reply to me within that time.

In all fairness, I should state that I think my physical resources, which have been generous, are at the present moment depleted, that the kind of vital concentration which has at times in the past attended the art of creation is diffused. But I think things may come back, and that there is a possibility I will do better work than I have yet done. That, of course, is my hope; and despite this present depletion of my energies I am of cheerful mind and resolute temper, and I have strong hopes that the energy and power of such talents as I have will return.

Finally—with no disparagement of any connection I have had —I feel the need of a new beginning in my creative life.

San Fran: Miss Saiz, [*Russel*] Lee's wife, His children, His cook, Hugh Wylie, the Consumptive Girl, Mrs. [*Kathleen*] Norris, [*Charles*] Norris, the Bohemian Club, etc., The Consumptive (Friend of Lee's), The Communist (and his wife), The Whore.

Reno: The Bartender, The Sheepherder, the whore, "Miss" Brown.

Salt Lake: Fen Dolby, Mrs. McMorrow, the Minister, the Walshes.

Colorado and the East: A taxi man near Pueblo, Some Harvard-Groton Boys and Girls, Their mother, A Man from Kansas, A Bitter Girl from Denver, A Woman Who Showed Me How Gratis, Goldman, Womack, A Girl, Hynds.

Back to New York: The Man We Killed, The Baseball Players, The Negro Porter (Is This Friday?)

Dear Fred—Letter follows[9]—I'm terribly sorry about whole thing and for causing you so much trouble. Everything's all right—I just had [*to*] blow up about things you and no one else in family had anything to do with. I wouldn't take a penny from any of you at present time—I don't need it—You don't owe me a cent—please be generous and [*breaks off*]

1) Toilet articles
2) Bank—Marks—American Express
3) Hat
4) Telephone Bill
5) Lunch with Mr. Mitchell
6) Dentist.

Chase Bank
Westall
48 Street Branch, New York
    Cable Me Two Hundred Dollars Amexco Berlin.

THOMAS WOLFE.

[*Using his blocked German royalties as an excuse for the trip, Wolfe sailed abroad the* Europa *on July 23 and went straight to Berlin. The enthusiastic welcome he received surpassed even that of the previous year. Rowohlt had bought out* Of Time and the River *in April, and its critical reception was the greatest success ever accorded any of Wolfe's books by any country. New admirers vied with his old friends to entertain him, and Wolfe was so caught up in a whirl of social activities, playing the role of literary lion, and attending the Olympic Games that he made no further entries in this notebook except names and addresses.*

One of the reporters who interviewed him was accompanied by a woman artist, Thea Voelcker, who made a drawing of Wolfe. The interview, "Wir sprachen Thomas Wolfe," and the sketch appeared in the Berliner Tageblatt *on August 5. Wolfe was furious about the drawing, which he said made him look "piglike," but he could not forget the strikingly attractive artist. He later sought her out, fell in love with her, and persuaded her to go to the Austrian Tyrol with him after the conclusion of the Olympic Games.*]

9. In a telephone conversation with his brother, Wolfe, who was upset about his relationship with Perkins, had quarreled with Fred about the $500.00 he had sent for Effie in 1930. The letter was sent July 23 (*Letters*, pp. 538-39).

PART NINE ~

CITIZEN OF
A DARKENING WORLD

Pocket Notebook 31
August 20, 1936, to Late September, 1936

This notebook begins with Wolfe in Innsbruck, Austria, await-ing the arrival of Thea Voelcker and covers the remainder of his stay in Europe and his return to New York. He reflects on the Olympic games, is concerned with practical matters of publication in Germany, and continues to jot down ideas for "The Vision of Spangler's Paul." But all the while there was going on in his mind an ideological debate on the pros and cons of Hitler's Germany.

During the previous year Wolfe had been too busy savoring the fruits of fame and romantically living in the reflected glory of the great German heritage to see much beneath the veneer of contempo-rary Germany. This time, however, his eyes were opened to the increasing terrorism. His friends tried to tell him the true state of affairs, but this resulted in a temporary restraint on his acceptance of their views. Wolfe was so constituted that, when anyone sought to urge him to take a position, he would frequently take the opposite for purposes of evaluation. He had to think things through for himself and make up his own mind. His efforts to evaluate objectively the situation in Germany are reflected here. His own debate was resolved with finality when, on the Paris train, he witnessed the arrest of a Jew who was trying to escape over the German border. The incident resulted in his powerful novella, "I Have a Thing to Tell You," the genesis of which is recorded in notes jotted down soon after the event occurred.

The arrangement of this notebook is chaotic. Wolfe began on the same day at both ends and evidently proceeded to write wherever the notebook fell open. Consecutive passages are sometimes upside down in relation to each other, adjacent entries were written in differ-ent cities, and creative passages and blank pages are interspersed. We have arranged the dated passages chronologically and placed the others in what seems to be the probable order. There is no certainty, though, that every one of them was written at the time or place indicated.

[Martha Dodd's telephone number is written on the flyleaf.]

[821]

Horses Are Happy in Germany.[1]

Innsbruck—Thurs., Aug. 20:

There can be no doubt about the validity of the German victory—Since the end of the games I have read and heard certain American sneers to the effect that in the future Olympics "freak" events and "phoney" competitions should be banned, that America considers the Games as a track and field contest with a little swimming thrown in, that all we value is our supremacy in these two divisions, etc., etc.

All this is pretty feeble. It would be interesting to know, for example, why the thrilling and beautiful riding contests, in which Germans triumphed five times out of a possible six, should be regarded as any more "freakish," or "non-athletic" or "non Olympian" than the dull, interminable, and unlovely competitions in putting the shot, throwing the hammer, hurling the javelin, throwing the discus, etc.

It would also be interesting to us "non-experts" to know why the exacting, skillful, and individualized contests in scull rowing, two men with and without a coxswain—four with and without, etc.—are to be regarded as "freakish" and of no importance in the games, while the mechanized perfection of the Eights is all that matters. If—as we sometimes say—sport is a matter of individual competition, individual excellence—it would seem that in the division of rowing, the Germans have beaten us at our own game.[2]

There used to be a sport-writer in New York named Joe Vila. I think he died a few years ago: I have never forgotten him. I have a deep and true affection for his writings; of all the sports writers that I ever read Joe was the worst—and that is going some! But really the thing that made Joe Vila so good was that he was so bad. He believed everything he said with an earnestness, an enthusiasm, an energy that would have been remarkable in a man half his age—for, if I mistake not, Joe Vila was no chicken; he believed everything he had to say, and he had nothing to say.

I am constantly being accused by feeble people who never go out and look at the life around them of exaggerating things and exaggerating people. Thus, they say the people I write about are from

1. Ambassador Dodd, who was fond of horses, often remarked that only the horses seemed happy in Germany.
2. Germany scored the largest number of points in the Olympic games, 628. The U.S. was second with a total of 451 points, and Italy was third with 164.

seven to twenty feet tall—that everyone is a giant or a monster in my writing—that I exaggerate everything. But they exaggerate. My people are not seven feet or twenty feet tall: it is those people who say so who exaggerate. This brings me back to Joe Vila. I am going to tell you how he wrote—give you an example of his daily style: the prophecies, assurances, suppositions, prognostications, etc.—and when I am through, some people will again say I have exaggerated. But I have not: —No, what is more, I have even understated and tranquilized Joe Vila's way of writing. I can not prove this here since I do not happen to have the files of the N.Y. Sun for the last 20 years ready to hand, as I write this in Innsbruck, but if any reader will take the trouble to go back and examine Joe Vila's columns over that period, he will find that the following illustration—of my own composition—is very far from an exaggeration:

"If Kid Getti's fast left hook is working properly and he manages to connect with it often enough he is likely to be returned the winner in his ten round contest with Petey Glickman, which will be held tonight in the 97th Armory. On the other hand, if Glickman manages to connect often enough with the deadly sleep-producer he carries in his right hand, he may be declared the winner by a knockout. Our own guess is that Getti should win if the fight goes the distance and he manages to land often enough with his lightening-like left to pile up a victory on points. On the other hand, if Glickman lands often enough with that murderous right-hand wollop that put such battlers as Kid Feinberg, Marty Petersen, and Young Jack Ketchell on the canvas within the prescribed limit, Getti may well be on Queer Street before the match is over—etc., etc., etc." [3]

NOTES

Innsbruck, Aug. 20, 1936:

The Idea of Property in American Life

1. The Belief in Property so firmly rooted because Property in America is such an insubstantial thing—A man is likely to lose everything at any moment in America—Floods (a farm destroyed in 3 days —Mark Twain's story of farmer who found himself in Ark. after river

---

3. This sketch was later expanded and included in *A Note on Experts: Dexter Vespasian Joyner.*

changed its course)—drought—The violence of change in America—
after the Civil War, for example, the stricken South—a period of
prosperity in 80's—the collapse in the 90's—revival—collapse again in
1907—etc.

At the September sitting of the Court that year—A negro, for
selling corn whiskey, 18 months in the penitentiary—A negro for
stealing household articles worth 6.00—3 years in the penitentiary—A
mountaineer for cutting his wife's father—nothing.

Thea—arrives tonight—2:53 (2:52 Bhf.-zeit) [*Bahnhof time*].

Alpenbach: Dec. 25, 1936.[4]

The Voyage Over: Mr. Bell, the old liquor salesman—"Water
seeks its own level"—Von Koch, the Prussian who had lived for eight
years in the trapping country of Alberta—There was a kind of silence
in his face—Joe Pearman, the ex-champion walker—Dick, the enormous undertaker from New Jersey—Casey, from the publishers—The
two women at my table, Phyllis Fergus—(?) from Chicago—and Mrs.
Nylander, the lady orchestra conductor and doctor's wife—The trips
to first class: Mrs. [*Katherine*] Cushing, her daughter, the Petty girl,
and the other dark young girl—Captain Scharf of the *Europa*—his red
Germanic face red with weather, [tenderly?] veined.

The lovely looking woman named Mrs. Leonard—University of
Iowa graduate with the slightly nasal cracked note in voice—Husband
a lawyer.

First Class Passengers: Mary Lawton—[*breaks off*]

NOTE
The Hound of Darkness (June 18, 1912)
In Darkness a whitewashed room, a smell of plain boards, old
pine boxes, calamine, a slight smell of piss. From without a smell of
grass, mown grass, of apple leaves, of chestnut trees, of flowers, the lily
beds, the earth. In the room an old iron bed, white—painted many
times, down-sagging in the middle, rustling with corn shucks, there
frail-armed, beneath a shock of raven hair, in cotton night-gown,
summer cool, a boy.

4. The reason for this date is not clear. Wolfe was in Alpbach on August 25,
and the snow may have made him think it more like Christmas weather than
August.

—Boy (upstarting from his bed in darkness, with lean fragile body—[swings?] him supporting on the bed).

—Is it a lion in the mouth sulfurous, a fox in the paw felonius, a hound in dark mysterious, that prowls the walls of night's great earth forever and that will not let us speak? [5]

—Ah, it is too bad, too bad, and not to be endured—to know that I am tongued to famous men, yet have no tongue to speak.

—Oh you, who wait there at the wall of night—you who prowl forever at the porches of our speech—oh tongueless, viewless, speechless—oh aware-full sprite—beast, angel, demon and as now—who wait there watching on the latch of the dark—oh, speak!

BLOCKS (for Spangler's Paul)

Block I   The Town—a Town in the South 25 years ago—what they thought, felt, believed, etc.

Block II   The World Unvisited (The Hound of Darkness—etc.)

Block III   The School ([Refrain?], etc.)

Block IV   The University

Block V

GERMANY

1st Trip: Dec. 1926—Stuttgart—Munich—Zurich—Paris—etc.—2 weeks

2nd Trip: July–Aug. 1927—Munich—Augsburg—Berchtesgarten—Salzburg—Vienna—Prague—Nuremberg—Paris—etc.—2 weeks

3rd Trip: July–Oct. 1928—Köln—Bonn—Mainz—Wiesbaden—Frankfurt—Munich (Oct.-Fair)—Oberammergau—Salzburg—Wien—etc.—3 months

4th Trip: Aug.-Sept. 1930—Basel—Freiburg—Strasbourg—etc.—1 month

5th Trip: May–July 1935—Hanover—Berlin—Leipzig—Weimar—Eisenach—Magdeburg—Hamburg—Bremen—etc.—2 months

6th Trip: Aug.-Sept. 1936—Bremerhaven—Bremen—Berlin—Munich—Garmisch—Innsbruck—Kufstein—etc.—1 mo.

5. This passage exists in many versions and drafts in Wolfe's manuscripts. A revision is included in "A Prologue to America," *Vogue*, Feb. 1, 1938, p. 64.

A NOTE ON TRAVEL
(As She Is Gemacht)

I should like to tell you that Germany is one of the most beautiful and enchanting countries in the world—because it is. I should also like to tell you that the Austrian Tirol is magnificently lovely, and that the people there are among the friendliest, gentlest, kindest, and most neighborly people in the world—because these facts are true. I should like to tell you of all the cities, places, towns, and things I saw in less than six weeks here in Europe—the men and women that I met, the things I found out, the universe of life I apprehended—because all is fresh and clear now—even to the words they spoke, the clothes they wore, the rooms they sat in, the movements and the intonations of their every moment—I have it all, could tell you about it all—and will—but later on.

For that is not the purpose of this little piece. This is a note on travel—just a simple bare anatomy, written with that spare economy for which my style is justly noted. I am just going to tell you what can happen to you—the physical facts, the difficulties, obstructions, delays, etc., that may occur when you want to make a little journey over here from one small country to another.

Here are the facts: In mid-July I decided suddenly to get on a ship and go abroad for a month. Two of my books have been translated in Germany, royalties were due me from my German publisher, it was arranged by cable that if I came, he would have one thousand German marks waiting for me when the boat was docked at Bremerhaven.

Well and good! I got tourist passage, both ways, and made a deal with the Nord-deutsche Lloyd to get half my passage free if I wrote 3 short articles for their travel magazine. I took some spare cash in my pocket for expenses on the ship, and fifty dollars in Am. Ex. Co. travellers checks, thinking I would need no more, sure my German money would be waiting for me.

When I landed at Bremerhaven, the cash was gone, but I had my checks. Before I could land, however, I had to declare my $50 in travellers checks, and received a paper with the gov't. stamp that certified that I was entering the country with this amount of money.

True to his promise, my publisher had money waiting for me at Bremerhaven. For the next two weeks I spent this money lavishly—gave parties—dinners—took my friends around—saw the Olympic games—had a good time.

Then the money was gone, and I cabled to America for more money. This money came; I paid my hotel bill, etc., and decided to take a trip to the Austrian Tirol.

Well and good again. First I went to the Austrian Embassy and got a visa. Then I went to the American Express Co. to buy some Austrian money. They informed me this was impossible unless I had a government permit. Whereupon I showed them the certificate I had received on entering the country, certifying I had only $50 when I entered the country. They informed me that this was not the paper that they meant—that this paper was only a permit which would allow me to take out of the country as much money as I brought in—namely $50.

Whereupon I informed them that I now had more than $50— that I had cabled home for funds, and now had considerably more than $50—$130 in fact, and that I would take this amount with me to Austria.

Politely, they informed me that this could not be done—since my certificate said I had only $50, $50 was all I could take with me on my Austrian journey. What could I do with the rest? I could leave it behind me in Berlin, they said, and retrieve it when I returned. Or, if I wanted to take the whole amount I could make application to the Devisen [*currency*] authorities for a new permit which would certify I had $130 instead of $50. This might be difficult: if I knew people at the American Embassy, it might be better if I went there. I did know people there, and there I went: with the greatest kindness and helpfulness they took charge of the matter. They told me they could get the permit for me, but not before noon of the next day. This meant I would lose the morning train, but it was the best that could be done.

Now, since this is a truthful story, and I a truthful person, I must tell something else. I took a girl with me to Austria, and I am not a married man. However—believe it or not, I care not—I did not take the girl to Austria for what my home-town paper used to refer to, with a gloating coyness, as "immoral purposes." If this girl and I were ever "immoral" we did not have any purposes. The real reason I took her was that I liked her, and she liked me, and we enjoyed being together. Well, then, you may ask, what was the trouble? It seems a simple enough matter to take a trip with a girl if she likes you. How did that increase your travelling difficulties?

Well, the difficulty was that the girl was a German girl [*breaks off*]

[*Wolfe spent a week in Alpbach, and after a stormy quarrel with Frau Voelcker he left on August 27. He returned to Berlin by way of Munich, where he stopped off briefly.*]

[*Munich*] Sat.–Sun., Aug. 29–30:

What I Did Today:
 Got up at 11:00—(or thereabouts)—took bath—left hotel a very few minutes after 12—went to Fleischmann's Bank on st. next to here and cashed 100 M for which rec'd 98.5 (or a little less)—Went then to Fürstengruft (over Karls Platz—seeing all things & people)—then to Frauenkirche—then to Rathaus (end of little neue place) —then by taxi (not needed) to Tal—to Bogen (?) Schack (?) at (?)— Then to Spaten (?) Luisen (?) [6] and Residenz—Then to Pinakothek— Then to Glyptothek, 6th (int.)—then Königsplatz (one of 16—2nd on left hand side) is Wolf—Then Regina Palast—coffee—cake—Then by foot to hotel—Then nap 2 or 3 hrs.—Then by foot to Löwenbräu Keller—In garden there with people at table—Then by taxi to Walter- spiel [*restaurant*] at Vier Jahreszeiten—Then by foot to Annast [*coffee house*]—Then to Central Palast—Then to Atlanta Club (nice) —Then by taxi home.

Berlin, Wed., Sept. 2, 1936:
 Up before noon, bathed, dressed, shaved, etc.; out in Kurfürs- tendamm and into Joachimsthaler Str. to newspaper shop for Paris *Herald;* so to Haus Deutschland for lunch, which was great, with Mosel wine, brandy, coffee, cost 12 M; so by Stadtbahn Am Zoo to Lehrter Bahnhof; so on foot by Reichstag thru Brandenburg Tor on to Unter den Linden and Amexco; no mail there; so to Norddeutscher Lloyd where found could have 1st class ticket *Europa* Sept. 5 for $300, and said I did not think I could afford it but would let them know by 11 o'clock tomorrow morning; so along U.D.L. toward French Line and met Herr Rexroth [7] (Frl. Klem's friend) so he with me to Fr. Line where they promised to cable to Paris for tourist passage on *Norman- die;* so with Herr Rexroth to Lustgarten and museums for exposition of etchings, etc.—but closed—so with Herr R. to Royal Palace Hof for inspection; so with Herr R. to Habels for bottle of wine; so with Herr

6. Bogen, a suburb outside Berlin where people go to drink coffee; Schack, a small gallery emphasizing German Romantic and nineteenth-century painting; Spaten, a brewery; Luisen Garten, a public park.
 7. H. G. Rexroth, a Berlin journalist who worked for the *Frankfurter Zeitung, Berliner Tageblatt,* and *Deutsche Allgemeiner Zeitung.*

R. to Friedrichstrasse subway and then to Zoo; so to hotel for nap (7:00–8:30) so to Scala, where saw second half; so to Schlichters for great dinner; so by foot back to Zoo; to Delphi on Kat. Str. (which was closing) and so home to hotel.

Funds (Thurs., Sept 3, 1936)
R.M 200

Debts and Expenses

Hotel	90	R.M.
French Line	30	R.M.
Voelcker	83	R.M.
Expenses	200	R.M.
	403	

Cash on Hand

Express Check	$ 20
American Currency	8
	$ 28

Cash Required

$100 [*marked out*]

On Freedom of Speech and Thought

We say in America that we are free to speak and write and think as we please, but this is not true. We also say that in Germany people can not speak and write and think as they please. This also is not true. People are free to speak, and write and think some things in Germany that they are not free to speak and write in America. For example, in Germany you are free to speak and write that you do not like Jews and that you think Jews are bad, corrupt, and unpleasant people. In America you are not free to say this.

The Slot Machine

1. We can make any criticism we like, however violent, about the inhabitants of the state of Kansas. But it is very dangerous to make any criticism, even a mild one, about Jews.

2. Nothing good can be said about the Italian or German Dictatorships. If one suggests that benefits from these dictatorships have been considerable, the slot-machine answer, with a slight sneer, is, "Oh, yes, we know—the streets are clean and the trains run on time, but do you think these blessings compensate for the loss of human liberties, freedom of speech, etc., etc."

It is useless to tell the Slot-Machines that the benefits of the Fascist Dictatorships have resulted in far more considerable benefits than "clean streets and trains on time," and that if we are really going to combat the evil of Fascism, we must first begin by understanding its good.

Sunday night, Sept. 6, 1936 (written at Klinger's Weinstube after spending afternoon with Ledig, his girl, and another man, at Potsdam):

A dictatorship at full strength has an impressive aura of glittering success. The reasons for this are not hard to find: A dictatorship starts from ruin and proceeds from chaos. It is the product of a general and conclusive bankruptcy. In modern times the dictatorships that were established in Russia, Italy and Germany have given proof of this.

Sept. 7:

Unter Den Linden is 43 steps or 130 (?) ft.—in addition sidewalks 7 (or 21 T)—with grass entrances.

A LITTLE LIST [8]

Men:

Canby	Mrs. [*Léonie*] Sterner
De Voto	Mrs. [*Katherine Briggs*] Day
Angoff	Mrs. [*Dorothy Williams*] Gardner
Calverton	Mrs. [*Belinda Dobson*] Jelliffe
Burgum	Miss Eda Lou Walton
Chamberlain	

8. A reference to Ko-Ko's song in the first act of *The Mikado:*
"As some day it may happen that a victim must be found,
  I've got a little list—I've got a little list
Of social offenders who might well be underground,
  And who never would be missed—who never would be missed!"

These people were destined for satirical treatment at some time in the future.

Restaurants:
- 4 (or more) Schlichters (Luther Strasse)
- 6 Habel (Unter Den Linden)
- 1 Eden Dach
- 2 Lauers
- 3 or 4 Weisz Czardas
- 1 Strumpf
- 4 or 5 Klinger's (Raabe Strasse)
- 2 Corso
- Burgkeller
- Münchener Hofbrau (Potsdamer Platz)

Anne Menz	1
Rathauskeller	1
Alte Klause	1
Haus Germania (Traube)	1
Bruening's Linde	1

Habel—Once at lunch (Von Treubashoven)—twice with Thea —Two or three times alone.

[*Other places:*]

Rowohlt	1
Embassy	1
Fr. Klem	1
Westrick	1

FASCISM

For	*Against*
Physical Clean-ness	Repression of Free Speech
Healthy People	A Cult of Insular Superiority
Effective Relief	With This A Need For Insular Domination
A Concentration of National Energy	

The Horses Are Happy In A Land I Know
Often I had heard of that beautiful land, and in my dreams I had remembered it—There was a youth—(you knew him well, you hills,

and murmuring waters of the Swannanoa):—That summer I was twelve years old, it was the summer of the veterans' Fifty Year Reunion at Gettysburg.

Great "I" Books of The World:
    Moby Dick
    Huck Finn
    Sorrows of Werther
    David Copperfield
    Gulliver
    Rousseau's Confessions
    Remembrance of Things Past
    Leaves of Grass
    The Confessions of a Fool
    Robinson Crusoe

My name is Wolfe: I am an American.

[*Several of the following passages are Wolfe's notes for a projected political and literary satire in the manner of Swift's "A Modest Proposal."*]

Benefits:
    Let us consider some of the probable benefits of such a system. I should be suppressed, which would be a national loss and a loss to art, but the Malcolm Cowleys, the Mike Golds, the V. F. Calvertons, the Bunny [*Edmund*] Wilsons, etc., etc., would also be suppressed which would be a gain to everyone and everything. Freedom of speech and freedom of the press would be suppressed, but so would freedom of Press-Filth, Press-Lies, etc., be suppressed.

Divisions, Classes, Grades, Degrees, Hierarchies, etc.:
    First: Political Criminals of the First, Second, Third, *et seq.* Degrees:
        National: The Executive Officials: Tugwell, Morgenthau, Roper.
                The Parliamentary Officials: Robert R. Reynolds of N.C., Smith of S.C.
        State: The Governors: Talmadge.
        Municipal: The late James J. Walker of N.Y.C.; Mayor Hague of Jersey City; the Hon. Edw [*breaks off*]

It may be argued that such a [dispensation?] of criminals may be a trifle astonishing and fortuitous.

I confess, of course, that my program may be open to some such objections as these, and my own well-known love of order and regularity being what it is, I can only regret, of course, the inevitability of these slight imperfections. It is a nice question, of course, whether such distinguished candidates as the aforesaid Woollcott belongs more to the list of the criminal [vipers?] of printed type or among the list of Whores (Male and Female), Pimps, Fairies, the Criminally Perverse, etc.

In partial defense and extenuation of these imperfections in my program, I can only offer as a defense (and I hope an entirely good and sufficient one), the necessity for quick and final action in behalf of the general weal.

I realize very well that such a program as I have suggested—however tentative—will arouse spirited argument and even serious dissent among hundreds of other loyal citizens who, like myself, have the interests of our country at heart. The first objection, I am well aware, will be that my program is somewhat too limited and confined, and that an undue sense of caution and moderation has caused me to [*exercise*] an unreasonable and unsalutary restraint.

I think I can hear already the chorus of protest that we may expect from the more radical—or "leftist," as the jargon has it—quarters of our party.

"Come," they will cry—"this program of yours is milk-soppery! You have not even scratched the surface yet:—Certainly, there can be no objection to the seven or eight thousand names you have mentioned, for they are only the names that every school boy knows as standing first in the annals of criminal iniquity—"

Now, to these various objections which I anticipate, I can offer, I think, certain reasonable answers: First of all, to the objection about what seems to be the extreme and unwarranted moderation of my own program, I can offer this argument in answer:

That the experiences of history and of our own lives should teach us that if we err, it is usually better to err on the side of moderation than on the side of excess. For, it is apparent, an error in moderation, when demonstrated, may usually be remedied by an increase in means; an error in excess, however, is by no means so easy to control. In other words, it is easier to increase the velocity of a machine *gradually* (if power for increase be not wanting) than to decrease it suddenly once it has been attained.

Let us consider the possibilities of the scene, for it is a not unpleasing one.

At two o'clock in the morning, the great armored trucks begin to cruise through the bleak, gaunt, almost deserted streets of lower New York. The first haul has been thor[*ough*] and exact: it cont[*ained*] 3,642 of the city's leading murderers, gangsters, vice promotors, and crime-monopolists [*breaks off*]

Ledig

"Zis littel man with his pipe—I s'ink," said Ledig earnestly, "it is ver-ry str-a-a-n-ge" (Or: Zis Littel Man with hiss pipe—do you not s'ink it str-a-a-nge).[9]

Note:

The following volume is an excerpt of chapters of a work that is yet to be published which will bear the title "The Vision of Spangler's Paul." Because of the immense length of that book, as yet uncompleted, and because of a unity of theme and purpose which coheres to the present one, the author desires to publish this one because he believes it has a unity of theme and purpose which makes publication justifiable in this form.

1) The Names of Spangler's Paul
2) The German Lesson
3) Mr. Berniker
4) Old Man Helm
5) The Trip to Pennsylvania
6) The War
7) Dark in The Forest
8) The Oktoberfest
9) Im Dunkeln Wald
10) Bright Star
11) Father Farewell
12) Epilog (Again, Again)

On the Contract:

I submitted Herr Ledig to a very close, exact, and persistent questioning concerning the terms of these contracts, and elicited from him the following amazing information: [10] [*breaks off*]

9. Wolfe is attempting to catch the accent of H. M. Ledig-Rowohlt, who was his model for Franz Heilig in "I Have a Thing to Tell You."

10. Wolfe's dissatisfaction with the terms of Rowohlt's agreement to publish *From Death to Morning* and *The Story of a Novel* and with the method of de-

I do not see how we can go on further. There has been so much disappointment, so much failure, so much unfulfillment—Yes, even so much bitter argument and passionate denial—and it seems to me now there is nothing more to say, for me, nothing more to do. I am filled with the profoundest melancholy, the most hopeless sense of finality when I think of the whole thing.

[*Wolfe left Berlin by train on September 8. At Aachen one of his fellow passengers in the compartment was arrested. Just before the arrest the man had given Wolfe a handful of two-mark pieces to carry across the border for him, and Wolfe still had the money in his pocket when he reached Paris. He immediately began the story of this dramatic event and considered two possible titles. The story was published as "I Have a Thing to Tell You" in the* New Republic *during March, 1937, and later was included in* You Can't Go Home Again.]

I HAVE A THING TO TELL YOU [11]
or
I HAVE THEM YET

I am going to tell you a little story and it is a little story that may hurt me too. I'm taking a chance when I tell it.

. . . . . whereon the pillars of this earth are founded . . . . . oh brothers, we shall rest forever rounded with undated comfort and [choice?] repose (From The Vision of Spangler's Paul).

—My name is ———— and I was born into this world thirty-five years ago.

. . . . I don't like Jews, and if most of the people that I know would tell the truth about their feelings, I wonder how many of them would be able to say that they liked Jews.

—But something has spoken to me in the night, and told me I shall die, I know not where.

. . . . . I have a thing to tell you . . . . . brothers, we must brothers be—or die.

---

termining royalties on *Von Zeit und Strom* (*Of Time and the River*) led him to hire a Berlin law firm. He especially disliked the German system of basing royalites on the paperback edition regardless of the kind of cover the books actually had (paper, boards, or tape), and whether a paperback edition was actually issued or not. In the case of *Von Zeit und Strom*, no paperback edition had been issued, and the tape edition sold for 14 RM and the edition in boards for 12 RM.

11. This was the phrase with which Heinz Ledig-Rowohlt prefaced the atrocity stories he told Wolfe.

. . . . The gate swings back upon its creaking hinges, the screen-door slamming clicks to the lifted latch.

Sunday, Paris, Café Du Rond Pont Des Champs Elysées—(Sept. 13, 1936):

On the question of Freedom:—The Count Orlovski spoke to me the other day on the question of freedom: He spoke of my travel difficulties in Germany, and said that with politics, etc., France would become the same sort of country—and that it was a crime, because "France was the only place where there was any freedom left."

Let us examine this statement:—It is a familiar one, and has been uttered to me by various people at many various times during the past fifteen years.—In the 1920's the Malcolm Cowleys, the Allen Tates, the Bunny Wilsons, the Harry Crosbys, etc., of the Left Bank were uttering it very often. They lived in France they said, because it was the only place where there was any freedom left—and they loved freedom.

Now, I think their love for freedom has somewhat abated. The Malcolm Cowleys and the Bunny Wilsons want the Revolution, the World Union of the Soviets, etc. They do not want freedom. I believe that is now sometimes called "a bourgeois ideal"—and the Allen Tates, etc. want a form of high-toned fascism which bears the high-toned name of Southern Agrarianism.

The Count Orlovski still wants freedom—which means freedom for the Count Orlovski, who is the son of a Chemical National Bank Heiress from N.J. who purchased a Polish Count with her holdings, and so came to France, and very slowly and stupidly drank herself to death over a period of thirty years or so—well, the Count Orlovski wants freedom for Count Orlovskis everywhere, and for Chemical Bank Heiresses to marry Count Orlovskis everywhere and to come to France and very slowly and stupidly drink themselves to death.

Paris—that sad and enervating town—and a feeling of horrible nakedness there—of being watched by *cats*.

The eternal monotony of French life—The banal life of cafés —the people gesticulating and talking—and to what purpose?

[*Apparently Wolfe wrote the following five diary entries from memory, misdating the first.*]

Wed.–Thurs. (Sept. 11–12) [*9 and 10*]:

Arrived at 9:30—to hotel—out to Boulevards—Café de la Paix —Café further down on Capucines—walked down Rue Royale—then to Vendôme to Ritz for money—then to Pharmacie on Rue Faubourg Montmarte—then to Blondel, etc.—then to House near St. Lazare—then home.

Thursday–Friday:

In morning Pole (called me up to invite me to dinner) so later to French Line (where saw Poles)—then in Amexco met the Hayes-es —then to Haussmann to look at clothes—then to Duval's with Hayes-es —then to meet Poles with their beautiful whore—much brandy and wine at dinner—then left Poles—and then everything—Café De La Régence—Montparnasse—Dôme—Jockey Club—Rotonde—trouble —trouble—Harry's New York Bar—across street from Harry's to little "Ciro's"—then to Faubourg Montmartre (with whore house notions) —then passed out and got home at 8 o'clock in morning, with hotel filled with departures.

Friday–Saturday:

Up and felt a wreck—then to Amexco—then to Boulevard café —then to Prunier's for oysters—then to Fouquet's—later to Harry's Bar—said goodbye to people of night before—then to Montmarte and found Graff closed—then to another place and home.

Sat.–Sunday:

Up and to Amexco—then to tailor's—ordered another suit— then to little bar next Café de la Paix—then back to tailor's—then to Boulevard café—then to Adega—then to Cigogne—then to Royale— then to La Rue's (remember W.C. mirrors)—then to Montmartre for choucroute—then home.

Sunday–Monday:

Slept till two—then up and bathed and walked to Boulevards— walked to Régence—had sandwich and whisky—then to Adega—then to send telegram—then by taxi to Champs Elysées—glass champagne at Alsacienne restaurant—then food at Huysmans restaurant—then coffee at two cafés—then by foot to Italiens—by taxi to hotel—charged $1.00—and ate choucroute at bistro opposite Casino de Paris.

"COLLEGE EDUCATION"

Among some of the simpler forms of the national hypocrisy which are likely to puzzle investigators a century from now is that one which tends to idealize the benefits of a "college education" in theory but to sneer at it in practice. Almost any older American—self-made business man, self-made (or machine-made) politicians, heavy-handed son of toil, or person of whatever state in life, is ready to assure the youth of college years that he should be prepared to make every effort, "every sacrifice," to secure "a college education"—that the benefits to be derived are of inestimable value, that the lack of such an education is irremediable.

Yet, in practice, the arguments of these same men are ludicrously opposite. Surely it would be logical to assume that these impassioned pleaders for college education (all the more impassioned —do they not say—because they "never got the chance") would be content with nothing less than the cream of the universities in the highest and most important offices of the nation's life—No, would even insist that the positions of the greatest authority be occupied only by men of great learning—who had spent their lives in the arduous accumulations of knowledge.

But how does this work out in practice? Not at all as we might expect. One of the most bitter charges—the ultimate sneer—that can be made of a man in high office is that he is "nothing but a professor" and "let us, for God's sake, get this moon-eyed theorist out of office and put in someone who has both feet on the ground—someone who knows what it is all about—a business man—a practical man."

Thus Wilson was finally bitterly reviled as the professor, the schoolteacher with his Fourteen Points—the impractical theorist—and the virtues of such men as Coolidge and Hoover extolled as men "who knew what it was all about."

The advantages of French life are largely exaggerated—and first of all, of course, by the French themselves. In the first place, there is the French climate, which is a very unwholesome and unsound one. French propaganda has of course established the myth of the wholesomeness of the French climate—it is, they say, mild, temperate, agreeable, and so on—they fail to add that it is also depressing, enervating, and unconducive to the highest and most accentuated effort.

Berlin, on the other hand, has been pictured by these propagandists of glory and the French weather as a harsh Northern city, with a climate which is harsh, northern, rheumatic, savage, and impossible.

This again is untrue: the climate of Berlin is magnificent: it is so lean, so sweet, so cool, so bracing, so un-harsh.

For years and years the young expatriates of America flocked to Paris to get some work done—and the work that they did?—Alas, it is only necessary to survey the works of the prize possessions of this school—the Cowleys, the Tates, the Jolases, etc. to see how pitiful even the efforts of the prize performers were—

[*Wolfe sailed for home on the French Liner* Paris *on September 17.*]

Aboard the *Paris*—Sunday—Sept. 20, 1936:

Met Aboard Ship: Miller the Writer; his son; the Old Man from Boston—Mr. [*John E.*] Hannigan—the Professor; the man from Milwaukee—Mr. [*C. A.*] Duff; Mlle.—the French teacher and lecturer at our table; Miss Simon—the New York Communist Jewess; [*breaks off*]

Rec'd: 4 Scotches from Duff—2 Beers from Miller.

Given: 8 Scotches—Duff; 5 Champagnes and 2 Scotches—Hannigan; 1 Beer—Miss Simon.

Cost of Trip

$140	ticket
$125	cash
$200	from Chase Bank (Berlin)
$200	from Chase Bank (Austria)
$130	from Chase Bank (Berlin)
$200	from Scribner's (Berlin, Paris)
$995	
— $150	(cash on hand)
$845	

Personae (from First to Last):

On Board *Europa:* Joe Pearman, Mr. Bell, Mary Lawton, Mrs. Skeffington Norton, Mrs. Hoar, The Mexican Girl—7 [*days*].

In Berlin: Ledig, Rowohlt, Martha, Thea Voelcker—18.

In The Tirol and Munich: Thea, Fraulein Lenni, Herr [*Alfons*] Moser [12]—12.

In Berlin Again: Westrick, His wife, Herr Albert [13]—10.

---

12. Proprietor of the Hotel Böglerhof in Alpbach, where Wolfe and Frau Voelcker stayed.

13. G. A. **Westrick** and H. F. **Albert** were lawyers, members of the firm of Albert, Westrick, and Hauss, whom **Wolfe** employed to represent him in dealing

On the Train to Paris: Tommy Majewski,[14] The German Woman, The Young Sculptor, The Little Man—1.

In Paris: Count Orlovski, The Two Beautiful Whores, The Chorus Girls and College Boys of New York Bar—8.

On Board The *Paris:* The Old French Mademoiselle, Miller and Son, The New York Communist Jewess, Mr. Duff, Mr. Hannigan—7.

[*Wolfe landed in New York on September 24, and he made no further entries in this notebook except the address and telephone number of his friends Grace and Beverly Smith and several other New York City addresses, mostly warehouses.*

Not long after his return to America he wrote the following fragment, which is indicative of his thinking at the time.]

For the first time since the inauguration of the modern Olympiad in 1896, we were up against a new kind of competition. Heretofore, the nations of the world had sent teams to represent them in the games—the effort was casual, sporadic, and detached: at this Olympiad one nation at least did not send a team—it *was* the team, and the team the nation. The whole united power of Germany's enormous organizing and disciplining genius went into their effort. No one really knows how strong America is: we are a loose-jointed, shambling, and disengaged people. But from the effort of these games some idea may be gained of Germany's strength. It was an enormous strength, and it was collected in a single stroke as compact as the blow of a fist.

There have been too many false stories—too many distortions of fact, twisting of evidence, and just plain lies. Surely, if the conscience of the men of good will throughout the world is so deeply and earnestly convinced that what has happened in Germany is against the true current of that nation's spirit, and the true current of the spirit of the world—and I, for one, am so convinced—is it not a matter of the deepest urgency that we keep, so far as possible, scrupulously exact our account of what has happened there? Are we to fight fire with fire— subdue contagion by the spreading of a plague?—or meet a lie with another lie of our own formulation? It will not do.

---

with Rowohlt Verlag. Westrick handled most of the negotiations after Wolfe had left Germany and succeeded in getting Rowohlt to base the royalty on the board edition.

14. Tomasz J. Majewski, a New York stockbroker.

Notes from
Fall, 1936

Wolfe made only one or two entries in a notebook during the fall, which was the third great creative period of his career. He began to work in an entirely new way both for recording major notes and outlines and developing his material; he dictated to a secretary who typed his words directly without any intervening shorthand notes. Between early October and December 4, he accumulated, according to his secretary's notation, 721 pages or 180,250 words. This included such blocks of material as "I Have a Thing to Tell You" (both a long and a short version) and "The Child by Tiger"; the bulk of the State College material, the account of the Southerners in New York, and the Oktoberfest material, all of which eventually went into The Web and the Rock; *and all of his hero's European travels, which finally became Part V of* You Can't Go Home Again. *He continued to work on yet a third version of "I Have a Thing to Tell You," for serial publication in the* New Republic, *up until Christmas, when he left for a trip through the South.*

We represent this period of literary outpouring by including samples of his dictation as the typist recorded it. Most of the material is single-spaced with wide margins on both sides, so that the pages look like galley proof. Wolfe then worked in the margins making his revisions. It is not entirely clear, but it is likely, that he set to work first on "I Have a Thing to Tell You" and then followed a simple chronological order for the other sections. We arrange them here in that order.[1] The first sample is the opening four paragraphs of "I Have a Thing to Tell You" in its earliest version.

THE WORLD: THE BRIGHT ANGEL (March 1935–October 1936)
I HAVE A THING TO TELL YOU (Sept. 9, 1936)
(Nun Will Ich Ihnen 'Was Sagen)

Exactly at seven o'clock the phone beside my bed rang quietly. I stirred quickly and uneasily and roused myself sharply, from that fitful

1. When adding up the number of pages, the secretary listed them in this order: "I Have a Thing to Tell You, Octoberfest, Child by Tiger, Characters, Town [*she meant "State"*], City, Earth."

and uneasy half sleep which a man experiences when he has gone to bed late, knowing he must rise early. It was the porter. His low quiet tone had in it the immediate decision of authority. "It is seven o'clock" he said. I answered quickly "Thank you. It's all right. I am awake." I got up, still fighting dismally with the misery of stale fatigue which begged for sleep and with a sharp gnawing tension of necessity which demanded action. But one look about the room reassured me. My old leather trunk lay open on the baggage rest. It had been packed the night before with beautiful, clean efficiency by the maid. Now there was very little more to do except to dress and shave, stow toilet things away, pack my brief case with a few books and the manuscript and letters that had accumulated and drive to the station. Twenty minutes' steady work would find me ready. The train was not due until half past eight, and my station with a taxicab was not three minutes distant. I stood up and stuck my toes into my slippers, walked over to the windows, tugged the cord and pulled up the heavy blinds.

It was a gray morning. Below me, save for an occasional taxicab or motor car, the quiet thrum of a bicycle, or some one walking briskly, with a lean, spare clack of early morning to his work, the Kurfürstendamm was bare and silent. In the center of the street, above the tram tracks, the fine trees had already lost their summer freshness —that deep and dark intensity of German green which is the greenest green on earth and which gives to all their foliage a kind of forest darkness, a sense of coolness and of magic. The leaves looked faded now and dusty. They were already touched here and there by the yellowing tinge of autumn. A tram, cream-yellow, spotless, shining as a perfect toy, slid past, with a kind of hissing sound upon the rails. Aside from this the tram car made no noise. Like everything they did, like everything they made, the tram and tramway were sound and perfect in their function. The rattling and metallic clatter of an American street car was totally absent. Even the little cobblestones that paved the tramway were as clean and spotless as if each of them had just been gone over thoroughly with a whiskbroom, and the strips of grass on either side were as green and velvety as the sward of an Oxford college. On both sides of the street the great restaurants, cafés and terraces of the Kurfürstendamm were also bare and empty. They had the silent loneliness that cafés always have early in the morning. Chairs were racked upon the tables. Everything was clean and bare. Three blocks away, at the head of the street, the clock in the tower of the Gedächtnis Kirche struck seven times. I could see the great bleak masses of the church, and in the trees a few birds sang.

Some one knocked upon my door. I turned and crossed the room again and opened the door. It was the waiter, bringing in the breakfast. He was a boy of fifteen years, perhaps—a blond-haired solemn child with a fresh red face—dressed in a boiled shirt and a waiter's uniform that was always spotlessly clean but that I suspected had been sawed off and shortened down a little from the costume of some more mature inhabitant to fit its present owner. He marched in solemnly, bearing his tray before him straight towards the table in the center of the room, uttering, as he did so, in a stolid and completely toneless voice, his three phrases of English, which were: "Good morning, sir,"—as I opened the door "if you bleeze, sir," as he set the tray down upon the table and "sank you very much, sir" as he marched out, turned and closed the door behind him.

The formula had always been the same for six weeks, and had not varied by an atom, and suddenly as he marched out again I felt a feeling of regret, of affection and of pity. I told him to wait a minute and got my trousers and took some money and gave it to him. His pink face reddened suddenly with happiness. He took the money. I shook hands with him, and then the boy bowed and said gutterally "Sank you very much, sir." And then, very quietly and earnestly, "Gute reise, der Herr." He clicked his heels together and bowed formally and then closed the door. And I stood there for a moment, with that strange and nameless feeling of affection and regret, knowing that I should never see him again.

[*The narrative continues for 50 single-spaced pages. The second version, double-spaced, runs 93 pages and was later used for* You Can't Go Home Again. *The version prepared for the* New Republic *had to be cut back to 67 pages, and it took Miss Nowell's patience and prudence to help Wolfe produce the shortened version.*]

[*Wolfe had unconsciously made some decisions about "The Vision of Spangler's Paul" during his holiday. On his return, he wrote to Thea Voelcker, he found "the whole plan from first to last clear to me." What he seemed to mean is that he was ready now to use his entire experience for the new book. The dictated sections show that Wolfe's autobiographical narrative could become more mythic. His central character could re-enact the classic search for identity, beginning as an orphan boy puzzled about his divided heritage and growing up to continue the search for his place in the world—as his world expanded from town, to state, to nation, to globe. Wolfe started his revisions by going back to what he had written about Spangler's childhood and considering what characters would people his little world. Some of this material eventually became part of* The Web and the Rock, *Chapters 1 and 6.*]

PART I

THE CHILD CALIBAN

THE CHARACTERS

The narrator—"I." (The narrator I of the book is a child known as Spangler's Paul: at the beginning of the book he is twelve years old. When the action starts he is lying in the grass before his uncle's house in North Carolina. This is the chapter which has already been written in a first draft with the title "The Names of the Caliban Paul.") The revisions that must now be made are as follows: The boy, instead of being before his father's house, is before his uncle's. His status, as the story opens, is really that of a charity boy, a kind of sunny orphan. His mother, his uncle's sister and a member of a family of mountain people who have come in to town, has died several years before.

His father, the man Spangler, a man from the Pennsylvania German stock, who came into the hills and settled years before, is now estranged from the hard-bitten and puritanic mountain family into which he married. The situation of the boy is this: Spangler, several years previous to his wife's death, had practically left his wife and child, although he continued to support them, and had begun to live in open defiance of convention and public disapproval with an attractive but notorious woman in the community whose name was Mrs. Winston. After his wife's death this liaison continues, to the scandal of the public and to the horror and outrage of his wife's people, the Creasmans. The Creasmans take the boy from him. In spite of this, the boy's childhood with his mountain kinsmen is a hard and thorny one.

His uncle, Mark Creasman, is a man who, after a childhood and youth of bitter poverty, has accumulated a fortune in the hardware business. As the story opens the boy is lying before his uncle's brand new house. It is one of the showplaces of the town—bright red brick, hard new cement, columns before the house,—everything hard, new, ugly, bold and raw as new-got wealth. Here in this new, raw, splendid house, Mark Creasman lives now with Tett, his wife, and his two sons, Hugh and Gilly. The boy does not live in this fine house. He lives instead in the little one-story frame house which his grandfather John Creasman built with his own hands fifty years before when he came to town. This little frame house of the grandfather is on the same premises as Mark Creasman's fine new house. It is a little to the right and to the rear, obscured and dwarfed, by its more splendid kinsman [*more*] than by the other larger houses of the street. Here Spangler's little boy is growing up, under the guardianship of a rusty old crone of fate, his great aunt Maw, a spinstress, one of his grandfather's sisters.

Aunt Maw is now in her late seventies but like some weird sister who preaches doom forever but who never dies, it seems, that she is ageless and eternal. From this dark old aunt of doom, and from the drawling voices of his Creasman kin, a dark picture of his mother's world, his mother's time, of all the universe of the Creasman lives and blood, is built up darkly, is wrought out, slowly, darkly, with an undefined but overwhelming horror, in the memory, mind and spirit of the boy. He hears lost voices in the mountains long ago. The wind-torn rawness, the desolate bleakness of lost days in March along clay-rutted roads in the bleak hills a hundred years ago. Some one is dead in a hill cabin long ago. It is night. He hears the bleak howling of the wind about the eves of March. He is within the cabin. The rude bare boards creak to the tread of feet. There is no light except the flickering light of pine. The soft swift flare of resinous wood, the crumbling ash, against the wall upon a bed a sheeted figure of some one who has died.

[*The material continues, describing the Creasmans and Spangler's admiration for his father and his father's masculine world. It appears in* The Web and the Rock, *pp. 8–10.*]

The other immediate characters of the boy's life and kin at this moment, as he lies before his uncle's house, are

In his uncle's house:
>   *Mark Creasman*, the boy's uncle
>   *Tett:* Mark Creasman's wife, the boy's aunt
>   *Hugh*, Mark Creasman's oldest son, the boy's cousin
>   *Gilly*, Mark Creasman's younger son, the boy's cousin.

In his grandfather's little House:
>   *Aunt Maw*, the boy's great-aunt, a spinstress, his grandfather's sister
>   *Jim Rickett*, a boy of fourteen, a nephew of Aunt Tett, and one of her dependents
>   *Sam Blalock*, age sixteen, also one of Aunt Tett's nephews and a dependent
>   *Dorcus*, a boy of fourteen, a little better than half-wit, an orphan boy whom Tett has taken from the Baptist orphanage and drudge of all trades about the house

Judy, the girl named Judy Ransom, also taken from the Baptist orphanage by Tett and also drudge of all trades about the house.

The five boys of the street
    the Spangler boy
Nebraska Crane, the son of a policeman, a boy with coarse black hair, a square freckled face, and tar black eyes, is the best and bravest boy in town. He is afraid of nothing. He can do everything better than any one else and can hit a baseball farther. He has a touch of Cherokee blood in him

Jim Shepperton, the son of the lawyer Shepperton. He is the quickest, sharpest, finest. He is also afraid of nothing. He is Mercutio

Vern McCaskill, a poor boy, he is a student, the debater, the reasoner and finally the politician. Has a square, broad forehead, cowlick hair, a blunt nose, thick ugly lips that roll outwards with almost negroid _____,[2] the whole face expressive of a somewhat coarse but tremendous intellectual power—an immense solidity, earnestness and depth of thought and a humor as round, as unctuous, as coarse and devastating as an American river or a mountain—all legible somehow in his calm but powerful and extraordinary features and his coarse and ugly but powerfully expressive mouth.

Augustus Potterham, whom the other boys also call variously the duke, or potted ham. He is a son of a funny shabby little Englishman, Mr. Potterham, with a funny chirping little voice, ruddy apple cheeks and a funny calm little brown mustache. Chance, destiny, the ill health of his wife, has brought this shabby little man to town many years before. He ekes out a modest living for himself and his numerous family by dealing as owner, agent and speculator in negro real estate. In spite of this humble and rather prosaic employment he is big with the importance of his family and the noble traditions of his aristocratic lineage. He is quite testy on the subject of his name and annoyed when any one mispronounces it, and almost every one in town, of course, does mispronounce it. They draw it out, broadly and emphatically, as Pot-ter-ham. Mr. Potterham insists the correct pronounciation is Po-tram, that he has the direct testimony of his noble kinsmen, the Dukes of Potterham, to this effect, etc. Augustus has inherited all this nonsense from his father. For the other boys he is their freak child, their lame duck, the butt of their jokes and ridicule, but something to be

2. The typist left a blank at this point, apparently because she did not understand Wolfe's word. Omissions like this occur in a few other places in the typescript. For example, at one place the word she did not understand is, obviously one of Wolfe's favorite words, "adyt."

taken in hand, to be protected and cared for. They have an unspoken love and sincere affection for him.

The People on the Street
The Cranes

Nebraska At the opening of the story, age 14, and previously described.

John Crane, Nebraska's father, a policeman, an ex-professional wrestler and occasionally still a participant in local exhibitions

Little Buzz, Nebraska's younger brother, at this time aged five, drinks beer and smokes cigars to the huge delight and pride of the rest of the family

Nell, Nebraska's sister, aged thirteen, already as large and as mature as a woman

Mrs. Crane, the daughter of a butcher, a giant of a woman, as brutal, as savage as unhalted nature, also as warm, as true, a natural force of a woman. This completes the Crane family.

The Potterhams

Augustus, already referred to and described, also age 14, very red in the face, with high cheek-bones, unruly, fluffy, carrot-colored hair, stammers when he's excited, voice has something of its father's cockney chirp

Mr. Potterham, also previously described, talks in his chirping little voice of his fine family, his coat of arms, the dukes of Potterham, etc. But relapses into cockney and drops his aitches when angry or excited.

Mrs. Potterham, a little, gentle, ruddy-faced Englishwoman, who in England would belong to the lower middle class. Devoted, motherly, so domestic that she hardly leaves the house twice a year. Meekly adores her husband, her children. Has none of her husband's pretensions to great family and noble birth, keeps tea brewing all day long and when the little man flies off the handle, is angry or exhausted, out of sorts, says " 'ere now, Charlie, do sit down and 'ave a nice 'ot cup of tea."

The Potterham Girls,

Beryl, the eldest, very earnest, very literary, a solemn thinker

Eunice, very musical, emulous of Beryl, also intellectual

Abby, the youngest, a jolly warm-hearted girl with a big laugh and no pretensions of any sort. They are a fine family. It is a good home. There is one day in every week when they bake bread, and the Spangler boy can smell delicious odors of the baking day. They have another day for beating carpets. They have a good life. They go on wonderful camping trips to the mountains. Take lots of food. Stay two or three days.

The Sheppertons

Jim, already referred to and described, age 13 as the story opens, a small lean head, well shaped, set closely with blond hair. Quick as a flash, light, wiry, active. A wonderful natural grace in everything he does. The best for running, swimming, diving, as fine as a blade. Mercutio

James Shepperton, Sr., an attorney, a pleasant, distinguished, mild-mannered man. Outwardly amiable and even-tempered, but inwardly defeated, already broken and disgraced by a marriage to a woman who is very lovely and utterly faithless

The Shepperton Girls,

Margaret, 17, like her mother

Eleanor, 15, also like her mother

The Suggs Family

Captain Suggs, a cripple, both legs amputated far above the knee. The rest of him a gigantic, brutal hulk, enormous shoulders, powerful thick hands, the look of brutal power and determination about the great thick neck, the mighty shoulders and the broad, red, clean-shaven, cruel-lipped mouth. Gets about on crutches when he has his wooden stumps on him. Otherwise crawls about on the stump ends of his amputated legs, which are protected by worn leather pads. Had one leg shot off at Cold Harbor, the other mangled and was amputated 20 years later. In spite of his mutilation and his huge bulk, he can move with amazing speed when he wants to; when he is angered he can use his crutch as a club and can floor any one within a radius of six feet.

His wife, a little frail woman, thoroughly submissive, thoroughly the old man's slave. He has two

Sons, the elder

"Fielder" Suggs, now a little past 30 years of age, and on his way to fortune. Called "Fielder" because at one time in his career he has been a professional baseball player. Has had an unsavory past and will never be accepted in genteel society among the people of the town and does not care. The childhood of the "Fielder" was lived under vicious circumstances. He grew up in a rickety shack, on the edge of the district and early learned agility, astonishing quickness, the ability to think and move fast and to defend himself as a result of his early encounters with the old man's crutch. Was knocked down so often before he was ten years old, he has never been afraid of being knocked down since. Utterly fearless, a little bullet of a man, as solid as a goat,

no more than 5'3 or 4" tall, but afraid of no one. Been told, during his baseball days, and while he was manager of a semi-professional team, that a notorious thug and bully of the neighboring town had threatened to kill him if he ever returned. He immediately sent the man a telegram that he was returning on the first train, and did return and almost killed his enemy.

At the age of 12 when he was nothing but a tough and wiry scrap of a boy, two negroes used him as their accomplice in a robbery. At night the negroes knocked a hole through the wall of Uncle Harry's Pawn Shop, a hole big enough for the little Fielder to worm through. He got inside the shop and cleaned the cases of all the available watches, rings and jewelry of any sort he could lay his hands on. The negroes were captured and sent to the state penitentiary. The Fielder, on account of his youth and his father's position as a crippled Confederate veteran, was treated more leniently and served a term of two years in the county reform school. His youth was spent under vicious and unsavory circumstances. His male companions were the so-called tough element of the little town, the tough team drivers, pool room loafers, brawlers, pimps and touts, the fellows who worked around theatres,—the scene-shifters, curtain raisers, etc. And his female companions, as might be expected, were fit consorts to this life, the small town prostitutes, both congenital and professional, the chorus girls with the little shabby travelling shows that occasionally come through.

Three or four years before, however, the Fielder, with money enough for one month's rent, has rented a vacant store in the town's public square and installed there the first moving picture projection camera the town has known. Its success has been astounding and instantaneous. Within six months he has leased another deserted store on another corner of the square, secured another camera and left his younger brother Stephen to take up the tickets at the first. At the present time the Fielder owns or controls more than thirty of these little places all over the South. He has moved his headquarters to Atlanta and he is on his way to his first million. It is a story as astounding in its miracle of sudden wealth as any that occurred during the days of the gold rush, but the down doesn't know this yet. They cannot believe it. But they pay their nickels and their dimes eagerly through the windows of the Princess and the Gaiety upon the square, and they think of Fielder still as the boy who wormed through the wall of Uncle Harry Finkelstein's one night and cleaned the cases for the negroes.

The Bernikers

Old Man Berniker, an old German of the working class, who learned his trade as a cabinet maker in his boyhood and likes it and who is now employed in the casket factory (this really means coffin factory) three miles out of town upon the river. Is up at five o'clock every morning and works for two hours in his garden before he sets off for his day's work at the factory. It is naturally the finest garden on the street, by all odds the finest garden in town. The onions quilled and stiffened green, stand in their places like a regiment of Prussian soldiers. It is the same with the lettuces, the radishes, the beans, the peas, even the grapevines, trained along the arbor he has built for them. The modest frame house, although flanked by much grander neighbors, is the best kept house upon the street. The lawn is mowed and cropped and watered till every blade of grass seems to have been manicured. The flowers, the geranium beds, the rose bushes, the nasturtiums are arranged with the symmetry of a geometric design. The house itself, a common frame house of two stories, is always spotless, with clean paint. There are three daughters:

Freda, the eldest, a spinstress, plump, vital, jolly, indefatigable worker. She is the best dressmaker in town. All the fine ladies come to her for their dresses. The hum of the sewing machine can be heard all day long

Else, the second, tall, thin, dark, silent, also a spinstress. Is the housekeeper, prepares the meals, keeps the place in order.

Bertha, the youngest, age 21, the most attractive of the three. Dark, slender and graceful, rather pretty, attractive but still, one feels somehow, doomed like her sisters to be an old maid. She teaches music —gives music lessons; every day little girls go in and out to have their music lessons, and every day at three o'clock the Spangler boy can hear the rather melancholy sounds of little girls as they thump up and down the scale, in the Bernikers' shuttered parlor.

The Rutledges

Dr. Rutledge, a man of sixty, or thereabouts, a grizzled mustache, a dry spotted, slightly concave face, a reputation for having been a philanderer in the past—of chasing after women; with a secure position as a member of one of the most prominent families in the community. Besides his wife he has two daughters

Margaret, the elder, who has been married and who has separated from her husband. She is a woman around 30, obviously unbalanced, and has a reputation of being a drug addict

Elizabeth, the youngest, never called Elizabeth, but known everywhere, to every one in town, as Tot. She has done as she pleased all her life. She is a public scandal, but she is also a girl of the greatest charm, and grace and sweetness. She cares not a rap what any one says or thinks of her; in spite of the talk every one likes her.

[*The sequence continues for 131 pages of double-spaced type-script and includes brief characterizations of people in Mrs. Hopper's boarding house, of people who live on the east side of town and of those who live on the west side, of the "People of the Night," and of the "People of the City." It ends with two figures, Spurgeon and John J. O'Mahoney, at the "School for Utility Cultures."*]

[*The following excerpt is the first page of the next block of material, which consists of 23 pages of single-spaced typescript. The running title is "Nigger Dick"; thus this first page may be a revision with a new title. During the winter, Wolfe worked this draft over into two other versions before Miss Nowell sold it to the* Saturday Evening Post *in May, 1937.*]

THE TOWN
THE CHILD BY TIGER
(The Winter's Tale, 1913–14)

One day after school, twenty-five years ago, late in October of that year, several of us were playing with a football in the yard at Randy Shepperton's. Randy was calling signals and handling the ball. Nebraska Crane was kicking it. Augustus Potterham was too clumsy to run or kick or pass. He got in his own way, and in the way of every one else, in everything he did. So we put him at center, where all he'd have to do would be to pass the ball back to Randy when he got the signal. We had several other boys who were not ordinarily members of our own group, but with whom we played. We had Howard Jarvis, Jim Redmond and a boy named Hensley. It wasn't enough to make a team, of course. We didn't have room enough to play a game, even if we had had team enough. What we played was really a kind of skeletonized practice game, with Randy and Nebraska back, Gus at center, two other fellows at the ends and three or four of us on the other "side," whose duty was to get in and "break it up," if we could. Thus, if Randy passed we tried to get in and block or intercept the pass. If Nebraska ran we tried to get in through his "interference" and stop him. According to the rules of this skeletonized and half-imaginary game, we didn't have to tackle. If we could get through and get our hand upon the runner he was considered to be tackled and the ball was put down in that place. When we intercepted a pass, or when Nebraska kicked to us, the ball went over to our "side," of course, and then we were the attacking group—the ones who passed and ran and punted.

It was about four o'clock in the afternoon. There was a smell of smoke, of leaves, of burning in the air. Nebraska had just kicked to us. It was a good kick too—a high, soaring punt that spiraled out above my head, behind me. I ran back and tried to get it, but it was far and away "over the goal line"—that is to say, out in the street. It hit the street and bounded back and forth with that peculiarly erratic bounce a football has. The ball rolled away from me down towards the corner. I was running out to get it when Dick Prosser, Sheppertons' new negro man, came along, gathered it up neatly in his great black paw and tossed it to me. He turned in then, and came on down the alley way, around the house, greeting us as he did. He called all of us "mister" except Randy, and Randy was always "cap'n,"—"Cap'n Shepperton." This formal address,—"Mr." Crane, "Mr." Potterham, "Mr." Spangler, "Cap'n" Shepperton—pleased us immensely, gave us a feeling of mature importance and authority.

[*The following excerpt opens a 47-page sequence of single-spaced typescript*]

THE STATE
(1917–21)

Tank Eubanks, looks like an old walrus; slouch old cap pulled down over one ear, unshaved stubble of beard, walrus mustaches; conveys students to and from the town of Ralston, fourteen miles away. A dissolute old reprobate, bears the name of Tank because of his bibulous capacity. Drives Hudson Supersix over rough and perilous roads like a madman. Has wrecked car time and time again but, with the luck that is supposed to belong to children and to drunk men, lives to tell the tale.

Old Man Pickens, the village cop, known among the students as Two-Gun Pickens, the terror of Hog Wart Hill. Never known to arrest any one yet but is always threatening to do so. When his authority is questioned or ridiculed, will produce an enormous horse pistol, wave it menacingly and will announce no one is going to ridicule the law and get away with it.

Old Man Pendergraf, a slouchy, paunchy, unshaven Southern white; runs a little ramshackle confectionery, tobacco, newspaper, soda pop place and lives upon the student trade. Also has two public service cars, which he runs on the Ralston road. Is a bitter enemy of Tank Eubanks. They have had brawls by the dozen. Is dying of cancer but refuses to believe that anything can hurt him. When drunk will explain to every one how the doctor told him how he has a whole row of cancers down his middle, but will then go on to say he has seen trees with the same disease which would grow right around the affected and eaten out parts until they were as good and sound as they ever were. And will then demand triumphantly, if a tree can do it, why can't a man?

Jimmy McEaver, the university registrar, nervous and dyspeptic man, gray-haired, slender, wears spectacles, yellowed fingers, smokes cigarettes constantly, has secret, or semi-secret vice, of which he is ashamed and which he fears will be discovered by the students, as of course it has been, long ago. This vice is the consumption, day after day, of an incredible quantity of the beverage known as Coca-Cola. Every day at noon he will leave his office in the administration build-ing, cross the campus, come down past fraternity row, duck down an alley way, into the side door of Abernathy's pharmacy, drink three coca-colas in rapid succession, duck out again, cross the street to Spruills' drug store, duck in and drink two more, come out and glance quickly and furtively about to see if he's been observed, then duck into Doc Mason's drug store, get two more and then get out and on his way towards home and lunch before the main crowd and jam of students has arrived.

Uncle Andy, an aged negro, janitor and caretaker and general man-of-all-work over at the medical building. Devoutly religious, a great favorite among the students, is often called upon to make a talk in chapel in the morning or to deliver a sermon, which he does amazingly well, his favorite subject being "De Dry Bones in De Valley." A part of his duties at the medical building is the gruesome task of taking charge of the "stiffs" in the pickling vats and fishing them out with a long hook-like pole when they are needed, laying them out on a wheel table, shoving them into the elevator and taking them to the dissecting room on the top floor. In spite of the disquieting nature of this task, it has not shaken by one atom the old man's piety or the devotion of his religious faith. He lives all alone in a tiny and tidy little shack at the western edge of town. His wife has been dead for years; his daughters have gone off and married. He had a son who ran away from home twenty years before, but some day, says old Andy, with a sweetness of unshaken faith, he come back too. And old Andy is right. The boy comes back. Old Andy hooks him from the pickling vat one day and lays him out upon the table and sees the great white burns of the electrodes on the powerful black arms and legs, and looks into the face, that not sin and violence and death in the electric chair have wholly altered, and knows the boy is home at last and pulls a cloth across the face and, singing an old hymn, wheels him in and takes him up to where the students in the big dissecting room are waiting for him.

Big Ben Jolley, who believes, like his predecessor, Dr. Pangloss, that everything happens for the best, in this best of all possible worlds (so long as it does not happen to Big Ben himself, and he gets a full and generous portion of life's more amiable and agreeable benefits). Big Ben, who is at this time of Spangler's first meeting with him a kind of Mother Machree of the campus, a Mother Confessor of erring freshmen, the brood hen of a whole flock of yearling innocents, the guide and mentor of a whole flock of fledgeling lives, is really, in spite of his name, not a very big Ben at all. At first sight he looked enormous. He was enormous, if avoirdupois alone is to be considered. A youth of 22 or 23 at this time, he weighed close to 300 lbs. But when one really observed him closely, one saw that this enormous weight was carried on a very small frame. In many respects, in fact, he was almost tiny. In height he could not have been more than 5'6 or 7", his feet, for a person of his bulk, were amazingly small, his hands, had it not been for their soft fat padding, were almost the tiny hands of a child. His belly, of course, was enormous; his great fat throat went right back in fold after fold of double chins. When he laughed his laugh came from him in a high, choking explosive scream that set the throat and the enormous belly into jellied tremors. He did have a very rich, a very instant sense of humor, and this humor, with the high choking laugh and the great shaking belly, had given him among many students a reputation for hearty good nature that many fat men have. But more observant people would find out that this impression of hearty and whole-souled good nature was not wholly true. If Big Ben's antagonism and prejudice were aroused, he could be about as venomous and malicious an enemy as one could find. He could still scream with his great fat whah-whah of echoing laughter, but this time the laugh had venom in it, for the great fat belly that shook with such convulsive mirth was also soured with bile.

[*The characterization continues about Big Ben Jolley and his literary tastes, including his clash with Spangler over* Crime and Punishment, *which became Chapters 11 and 12 of* The Web and the Rock.]

[*The next block of material is entitled "The City. Sept. 1923. The Southerners in New York." It begins with the material published in* The Web and the Rock, *pp. 239–48, "I have often observed that there is no one on earth who is more patriotically devoted—verbally, at least—to the region from which he came and which gave him birth than the American from the Southern portion of the United States." The account goes on to cover Jim Ravenal (Randolph, as he appeared in* The Web and the Rock*), Dexter Joyner, Horace Vespasian Alsop, Joe Vila (the sports writer)* [3] *and Beryl Endicott, Lloyd McHarg's first wife, on whom he based the leading character in his novel "The Old Home Town." It ends with a satiric discourse on Greenwich Village dilettantes.*]

[*The following excerpt begins a block of material which is 28 single-spaced pages long.*]

THE WORLD
THE OKTOBERFEST (August to December 1928)

The city of Munich in Bavaria is perhaps unique among the cities of the world. Other cities have their special tone and quality. None has a tone and quality that is more sharply set, more deeply marked, more unmistakable and yet so indefinable, so hard to articulate, as that of Munich. And this difficulty comes from the very depth and strength of Munich's character; the very sharpness of its definition makes it all the harder to define, the very warmth and brilliance of its color harder to describe.

For with places, as with people, I have found it is the place with the strongest character, the most positive and individual temper that it is hardest to describe. And I think the reasons for this are, upon reflection, evident. A place or a person, by the very strength and force of its own character, tends arbitrarily to stamp a pattern and enforce a mode upon the mind and imagination of mankind. Thus it happens that it is precisely the strongest and most unmistakable characters of history about which there is the greatest confusion. The personality of a great man almost inevitably creates a legend. That legend begets other ones, until, as time goes on, the legends have so mixed and multiplied that the original character and personality of their hero is partially obscured. This happened to Napoleon. It happened to George Washington. It

3. Much of this portion was printed in a small posthumous volume, *A Note on Experts: Dexter Vespasian Joyner* (New York, 1939).

happened to Abraham Lincoln. Even after one short century, the true characters of these men have become so obscured by the vast accumulation of legendry that one is forced to pierce through many subtle veils in order to get back to the real man as he was. And in a way this is inevitable because a great man *is* a legend.

For a legend, considered in one light, is only a condensed and heightened form of reality. With every great legendary book, for instance, with the *Odyssey*, with *Don Quixote*, in our own times, in particular, with the *Ulysses* of James Joyce, the legend is not a fanciful interpretation of human life but really an *intense illumination* of that life. Consider Joyce's book as an illustration of this: In *Ulysses* one gets constantly the sense of *looking at a brick wall so intensely that he looks right through the wall*. It is the same with everything in the book: The whole work attains a fabulous and legendary quality from the very intensity of its vision. That now familiar story of a day in Dublin, the story of Stephen Dedalus, Buck Mulligan, Leopold Bloom and Molly Bloom, the whole tremendous gallery of figures has now attained a legendary quality in the minds of those who read it fifteen years ago, and in its essence is not unlike the great legendary epic of the Greeks before Troy and in the end it is apparent that the legend is right. It is apparent that the legend is true.

It is apparent that the legend attains a superior reality through the clarity and intensity of its vision. For every honest man is bound to own that he hardly ever sees a brick wall clearly, that he hardly ever remembers a brick wall correctly, but none the less he knows the brick wall is there and when some one shows it to him, and shows it as it is, he knows it is the truth. But if some one lies about the wall and shows it as it is not he knows instantly that it is a lie. In my own experience I can liken this to this image. I have passed by a certain door a thousand times and always seen that door, yet never saw it as it was. And then one day, when I was far away, years after I'd passed the door, I would suddenly remember it. And instantly I would see that door the way it was. Now, what has happened? Did I see that door as it had looked just once in all those thousand times that I had passed it? No, I think that finally I saw the door as it had looked a thousand times and under a thousand lights and weathers of man's life and spirit. And finally, long afterwards, I saw it, the essential door, the way it was. The final door, therefore, was the legendary door, and yet it was at last the right one. It was, at last, reality.

Again, there is a story of the Chinese painter who painted horses. For twenty years he stayed in the stables of the emperor and looked at horses and never painted them. And then he went away and never looked at horses any more, but painted them. And the horses that he painted were legendary horses, unlike any single horse that ever was but more like horses than any single horse could ever be. Or again, there is the mighty legend of Don Quixote. Cervantes lived and looked at life for sixty years, and then he went away and wrote his legend about it. And the minute that we open his great book we know that both the legend and the man are true. This is reality. Finally, there is Plato, with his concept of the idea which is, it seems to me, just another philosophic way of saying concept of the legend. According to this concept the idea of a wheelbarrow is closer to reality than the wheelbarrow itself, because the idea of the wheelbarrow is the essence from which all wheelbarrows past and present have been derived, and which, therefore, unlike the wheelbarrow itself, is of the essence of reality since it is everlasting and indestructible.[4]

[*The discourse continues on to a description of Munich, of a pension and its sojourners, and of Spangler's fight with other beer-drinkers at the Fair, most of which finally found its way into Chapters 46, 47, and 48 of* The Web and the Rock.]

[*The following excerpt is the beginning of the largest batch of dictated material, 90 pages of single-spaced typescript.*]

CHARACTERS: THE EARTH
ENGLAND (October–April, 1930–1931)

Daisy Purvis

All through the fall and winter of that year I lived in London. It was a memorable year, a year in which, as I later was to discover, I had found out an entire new world, of which the events, the experiences and the people were later to be engraved upon my life with an indelible and unalterable memory; and one of the most memorable experiences of this year was my relationship with Daisy Purvis. Mrs. Purvis was a charwoman who lived at Hammersmith but who for years had worked for "unmarried gentlemen" in the fashionable districts known as Pimlico and Mayfair. I inherited her, so to speak, from a young gentleman of fashion but, from what I could gather, little wealth, who occupied the flat in which I lived in Ebury Street before I took it over.

4. Wolfe is returning here to precepts of Horace Williams, his old philosophy professor at Chapel Hill. The wheelbarrow was one of Williams' classroom examples.

His name, as I remember it, was one of those resounding dou-ble-jointed names that one comes across so often among the members of the upper or near-upper or would-be upper branches of English society. It was something like Maj. Somebody Somebody Somebody Reeves-Proctor. He was a good-looking fellow, a tall young English-man, ruddy, brown-haired, small-mustached, with the clipped speech, the lean and well-conditioned figure of a cavalryman. I liked him too. He was an engaging kind of fellow, so engaging, in fact, that when I sublet his flat—he had the place in lease from an estate and renting agency, with offices at the upper end of the street, and with the unforgettable name of Tooth, Shreve and Willets—he managed also to insinuate into his bill for rent a thumping good bill that covered all the gas and electricity he had used in the preceding quarter. And gas and electricity, as I was shortly to discover, came high in London. You read and worked by one, sometimes not only through the night but also through the pea-soup opacity of a so-called day. And you bathed and shaved and cooked and, what is most important, feebly warmed your-self by the other. I never could figure out exactly just what happened to me, or just how the engaging Maj. Somebody Somebody Somebody Reeves-Proctor did it. He managed it so adroitly that I believe I was on my way back to America before I realized that I had occupied his modest dwelling something less than two quarters, but had paid the gas and electric company four whacking assessments on the entire year.

I thought I was getting a bargain at the time, however, and perhaps I was. I paid Maj. Reeves-Proctor, as I recall it, in quarterly installments, in advance of course, and at the rate of 2 pounds and ten shillings a week. For this sum I had the advantage of being the sole occupant, at night at least, of the greater part of a very small but distinctly authentic London house. It was really a rather tiny house. Certainly, a very inconspicuous one, on a street and in a section noted for the fashionable spaciousness, the chaste magnificence, of its dwell-ings. The building was four stories tall—three, that is, as the English count it. The ground floor was occupied by a small tailor shop, really a place that existed more for the repair, the pressing and cleaning of clothes than for making them. I had a good deal of respect for that little shop. The venerable and celebrated Mr. George Moore had his pants pressed there, and I had myself the honor of being present in the shop one night when the great man called and demanded his trousers.

It was, if I may be candid, a considerable moment in my life. I felt that I was assisting at an impressive and distinguished ceremony. If I had had a personal invitation from his majesty the King of England to his coronation, I don't believe I could have been more overcome with a sense of reverential awe. In the first place, it was the first time I had ever been in such intimate contact with literary greatness, and I think most fair-minded and sensible people will agree that there are few things in the world more intimate than a pair of pants. In the second place, even at the moment that Mr. Moore entered the shop and demanded his own trousers, I was requesting the return of a pair of mine. This homely coincidence gave me a feeling of perfectly delightful intimacy with a gentleman whose talents had for so many years been an object of my veneration. It gave me a feeling of easy and casual familiarity, as who should say to me, "Oh by the way, have you seen anything of George Moore lately?" To which I could of course nonchalantly reply, "Oh yes, I ran into him the other day in the place where we both go to have our pants pressed."

Again, and candor again compels this confession, I must admit that night after night, as I sat alone in my sitting room in the third floor of that little house, at that hour of the night its sole occupant, its only tenant, its solitary lord and master, toiling on the composition of a work which I dared not admit, but which I hoped, would rival in talent and in celebrity some of George Moore's own, I would get at times the most curious and moving sense of companionship, a feeling that I was not utterly alone in that little London house, the feeling that there was a beneficent and approving spirit there with me also, which, through the watches of the night, would speak to me with the eloquence of silence, saying: "Toil on, and do not lose your heart or hope. Let nothing you dismay. Be not afraid. You are not utterly forsaken. I am here as well. Here in the darkness, here waiting, here attentive, here approving of your labor and your dream. Ever sincerely yours, George Moore's Pants."

[*The musings continue in their leisurely way to a full character-ization of Daisy Purvis and accounts of meeting Mr. Lloyd McHarg, of his Dutch publishers Bienden and Stoat, and of his wild journey to an English country house with Spangler, most of which appeared at length in Chapters 32 to 37 of* You Can't Go Home Again.]

Pocket Notebook 31A
October, 1936, to Summer, 1937

This notebook, which was found among the Wolfe papers that were in the possession of John Terry after Terry's death, spans an important but troubled period of Wolfe's life. During this time, the following situations were dominant:

1) His quarrel with Maxwell Perkins, which reached the point at which he broke completely with Scribner's over an expensive settlement of a libel suit.

2) His publication of "I Have a Thing to Tell You."

3) His work on a number of short stories and two short novels: "The Lost Boy" and "The Party at Jack's."

4) His three trips to the South, each one a more determined effort to find a new place for himself there.

5) His development of a plan for a new book, which would focus on the theme of fame, including the price an artist has to pay for it, and which would emphasize satire and social criticism. For this book he intended to draw mostly on his experiences since 1929. His central character was to be a kind of antihero, whose ordinariness is reflected in his name, Joe Doaks.

Unfortunately, very little detail about these activities shows up in the notebook. In fact, a number of the pages are blank, and many of the notations are just names and addresses, most of which we have omitted. As a consequence, we have drawn upon some loose notes and pages among the manuscripts which do reflect Wolfe's chief concerns of the year, and we have rearranged the few significant notebook entries in chronological order.

My Summer as Newsbutch on the R'way.
My Evenings Working at the Drug Store.
I ran away: the summer in South Carolina.
Father and Mrs. Winbourne.
Going to Sunday School: The Undertaker's Doll.

Milly—Wednesday—Oct. 14—at 6:30.[1]

You see the trouble with me is I trust everybody, so I think everybody is like I am—uh-huh—I know, that's what it is.

[*Wolfe began quarreling with Perkins at their first meeting after his return from Europe. In November, Marjorie Dorman and her family filed a libel suit against Wolfe and Scribner's asking $125,000.00 damages. Wolfe, wild with rage, irrationally blamed Perkins for this new catastrophe and spent more and more time brooding about his difficulties. Finally, he wrote two long letters to Perkins declaring a severance with Scribner's, but he delayed mailing them.*[2]

He ate Christmas dinner with the Perkins family and left the following day on a month-long, rambling trip that took him to New Orleans, Chapel Hill, and various other places, but he carefully avoided Asheville. His first stop after leaving New York was Richmond, Virginia, where he ran into the annual meeting of the Modern Language Association and spent a pleasant evening with John Crowe Ransom, Allen Tate, Robert Penn Warren, Cleanth Brooks, and others of the Nashville Agrarians. At one point in the conversation he declared to his surprised listeners that he actually enjoyed the physical act of writing.[3]

After a brief stop in Atlanta, he arrived in New Orleans on New Year's Day, 1937, and remained ten days. During this time he met and was entertained by William B. Wisdom, who even then had begun collecting Thomas Wolfe items. Wolfe was so lavishly wined and dined in New Orleans that he spent much time in an alcoholic haze, and finally mailed one of the letters to Perkins. The list of people he met is badly scrawled and barely legible.]

Hotel Roosevelt Bar.

New Orleans: Antoine's—St. Regis.

Bultman, 1525 Louisiana Ave., Jackson 2725.[4]

1. A dinner party at the Lexington Avenue apartment of Miss Emelia Rebecca Hess was planned for October 14, 1936.
2. The first was a "personal" letter; the second, which was never mailed, was a "business" letter. Both have been published; see *Letters*, pp. 575–603.
3. Edd Winfield Parks was present in the hotel room when Wolfe made this statement. He later informed Paschal Reeves that Wolfe spoke with deep earnestness and obvious sincerity.
4. Wolfe was delighted with the Bultmans' spacious Dutch Colonial home and planned to use it in his writing.

People:

    Lyle Saxon [5]—an old lady—not a phony—[*illegible*]

    The Antonys [6]—phonies.

    Pat O'Donnell and wife [7]—young, phony, fast

    Muriel Bultman [8]—a phony

    Mr. and Mrs. Bultman—not phonies—this is the [hearty?] couple to [defend?] book man. An undertaker and his wife—interesting dark people—not phonies

    Sidney Field [9] and wife—swell

    [*Bernard*] Szold [10] and wife—the man a phony—not wife

    Mrs. Barrie—a phony

    [*Roland*] Ladreyt [11]—an advertising man—not a phony but an advertising man

    John T. McClure [12]—swell

    [*Billy*] Fitzpatrick [13]—swell

    [*Tommy*] Sancton [14]—swell

    Eldred and wife—an advertising man and his N.C. wife—not phonies

    Rice—a phony

    The Godchaux—a phony [cosmopolitanism?]

    Watson Somebody-or-other—a phony

    Joyce Stagg [15]—pretty good—not a phony

    Willie B. Wisdom [16]—an autograph collector, but he likes me

---

5. Author of *Father Mississippi, Fabulous New Orleans, La Fitte: The Pirate, Children of Strangers,* and other works, Saxon was only nine years older than Wolfe.

6. Marc and Lucille Godchaux Antony, interior decorators.

7. He wrote *Great Big Doorstep* and *Green Margins;* Mary King O'Donnell is the author of *Those Other People,* a novel about the French Quarter.

8. The former wife of Owen Francis, a writer whom Wolfe had befriended several years earlier.

9. An architect in Philadelphia, son of Flo Field, a New Orleans writer.

10. Director of the Little Theatre.

11. Advertising manager of the *Times-Picayune.*

12. Sunday editor of the *Times-Picayune,* poet, and former staff member of the *Double Dealer.*

13. A *Times-Picayune* reporter; later, as a writer for the *Wall Street Journal,* he won a Pulitzer Prize.

14. A reporter for the New Orleans *Item.*

15. She worked at Hansell's bookstore and later married John McClure.

16. A New Orleans businessman, Wisdom early recognized Wolfe's greatness and began his collection of Wolfe material. After Wolfe's death, Wisdom bought his library, unpublished manuscripts, and other personal effects and presented them to Harvard University. The William B. Wisdom Collection of Thomas Wolfe is one of the finest and most complete collections of any major author and is now located in the Houghton Library.

Peggy Poor—a nice young blonde
Tony the Barkeep—swell
The Whore—good
The Nigger at Boston Club—the club's black bar[tender—good?]
The Half wit at Tony's—pretty good
Leo Zinser—pretty good
The two girls with Ladreyt—a couple of good pieces but good [girls?] to [whoop?] it up
The piano player at La Lune—good
The German woman at Shell Beach—grand
The opera singer and his pal—a couple of bastards
O'Donnell's friend—a man named Brown—a poisonous Kike

Mr. and Mrs. [*Allen B.*] Eldred, Cedar 2266-W.[17]

Garland [*B. Porter*], 605 Rhodes Bldg., Atlanta, Georgia.[18]

[*Wolfe's next stop on his trek North after leaving Atlanta was the 2500-acre estate of James Boyd at Southern Pines, N.C. Then followed a nostalgic visit to Chapel Hill.*]

The Shotwell Papers, N.C. Historical Commission, Raleigh—Dr. C. C. Crittenden.[19]

Vann Woodward—Chapel Hill—Department of History.[20]

[*After one more stop, with his friend William T. Polk in Warrenton, N.C., Wolfe reached New York about January 25.*]

17. Mrs. Eldred was Margaret Folsom of Asheville. They invited Wolfe to visit them at Ocean Springs, Miss., but after one day there he moved to the Buena Vista Hotel in Biloxi, where he slept a great deal and revised "I Have a Thing to Tell You."

18. After leaving Biloxi, Wolfe stopped for a visit with Porter, advertising manager of the *Atlanta Georgian*, and E. H. Abernethy, magazine publisher. Wolfe was quoted in an interview as saying he had "completed the rough draft of his new book, 'The Hound of Darkness,'" Atlanta *Constitution*, Jan. 17, 1937.

19. The third volume of the memoirs and diaries of Randolph Abbot Shotwell (1844–1885), Confederate soldier and journalist, was soon to be published by the North Carolina Historical Commission, of which C. C. Crittenden was secretary. Shotwell, who had established the *Asheville Citizen*, gives a vivid account of Reconstruction life in North Carolina.

20. Later Sterling Professor of History at Yale University, C. Vann Woodward was then completing his doctorate at the University of North Carolina.

Dear Max Perkins
Does Scribner's Want My Next Book Please Answer Immediately

THOMAS WOLFE [21]

George Stevens, 138 East 94, 7:30 Sat. night.

Ernest Bates, Ki 6–5400.[22]

Ham Basso, Atwater 9–6511.[23]

Douglas Gorsline, 65 W. 56th, Apt. 408, Co 5–4405.[24]

Written or to Be Written:
N.C.—The Middle West—St. Louis—*1904* The Lost Boy (In Progress)
N.C.—The Child By Tiger 1912 (Written)
N.Y.—The Rocky Mtn West—The Girl From Wyoming 1931–1933 (To Be Written)
Pennsylvania—Chicago—The Wind From the West 1934 (In Progress)
Brooklyn—Steve's Place 1934 (In Progress)
Germany—I Have A Thing To Tell You 1936 (Written)

[*The following notes represent the earliest indications of Wolfe's turning to his book about Joe Doaks, an ever-expanding narrative which absorbed his attention more and more during the next year. With this new alter ego, he was indulging in satiric purgation of some of his recent disappointments and frustrations.*]

THE LIFE AND TIMES OF JOSEPH DOAKS

Arrival in the City
Monty Bellamy: The Hotel

21. Elizabeth Nowell dates this draft of a telegram as February but says it was not sent to Perkins.
22. Former literary editor of the *Dictionary of American Biography* and associate editor of the *Modern Monthly*, Bates had just written an article on Wolfe which appeared in the *English Journal*, Sept., 1937.
23. While Basso was in New York in March, Wolfe talked at length to him on two subjects: his differences with Perkins and the adventures of Joe Doaks.
24. Wolfe was sitting for a portrait by Gorsline, who was married to one of Maxwell Perkins' daughters. The portrait now hangs in the Reading Room of the Houghton Library, Harvard University.

The Rock: The Southerners
Alsop
Joyner
Brooklyn
?
?
?
The Voyage
Mrs. Feitlebaum [25]

Return: Utility Cultures, Inc.
Mrs. Feitlebaum
The October Fair
Return: Meeting Fame
The Pursuit
Capture
The Medusa
The Faithful Friend [26]

[*On some separate sheets, Wolfe even provided a comic ances-try for Joe Doaks, a series of dupes and bumblers of whom Sir Guy Le Doakes is representative:*]

THE GENEALOGY OF DOAKS

It is unfortunate that no one has yet attempted a definitive genealogy of that remarkable and numerous family, who, during the past ten centuries, have spread over the entire face of the civilized earth, and who bear the proud old name of Doaks. And yet the reason for this deficiency is not far to seek. It was Carlyle who remarked that history is only the biography of its famous men, and because historians, even today, are still troubled by this superstition, the Doaks family has not received—historically, at any rate—the attention that it deserves. For, as we have already shown, history is a great deal more than the biography of famous men. History is the sum of all the moments of our lives—of all our lives—and from this it will be evident at once that the

25. In the Doaks manuscript the character Rebecca Feitlebaum is drawn from Aline Bernstein.
26. Wolfe sometimes handled the materials on fame allegorically. Fame is a woman, an unfaithful mistress. The Faithful Friend is Dame Care, who always remains with the artist.

most important part of history is the unrecorded part—the history of forgotten days, of sunlight on a wall, of wood notes in the wilderness, of all the million nameless Doakses who have come and lived and died and gone down, unrecorded, to the earth.

But in the end, it may be that it is the unrecorded Doakses who have mattered most. In the end it may be that it has been the word unspoken or the voice forgotten or the language that men knew, but never uttered, that has shaped the tides and currents of this earth. History shows Napoleon on a white horse, his fingers thrust into his breast, brooding about the destiny of mighty battle. But Tolstoi shows him as a kind of fool, sitting upon his horse and giving orders that no one listens to—a hapless, helpless cork tossed back and forth upon the tides of battle. Meanwhile, the Doakses of the earth swarm back and forth. The course of battle veers and changes. Men win or lose, survive or perish. But in the end, it does not matter. The result is just the same. It is the Doakses of the earth who have their way.

Not that all Doakses have been nameless and obscure. There have been notable exceptions. Every one, for example, is familiar with the famous story of Guy Doakes and King Richard of the Lion Heart. Every schoolboy knows that story as it has been recorded in the works of Hume, Macauley, Greene and other writers. Every one remembers how King Richard, in his siege upon Jerusalem, was one day set upon and pressed in battle by a host of Saracens, cut off from his own men, surrounded, beaten down upon one knee, in deadly peril. And then, what schoolboy heart has not been thrilled by that brave story of his rescue. The very words come back, and we remember how the tall young squire appeared to save his king, hewing a path through walls of living steel, cutting his way right through the pagan horde, trampling across their fallen bodies, until he reached the kneeling and sore-stricken figure of his prostrate lord and hewed out a very circle of dead Saracens around him, until the wall broke through, the English came. And then—what boy who has ever read the thrilling story can forget how lion-hearted Richard stood erect and wiped the blood from his beclouded brow and said, "Sir Squire, what is thy name?" And how the squire knelt humbly, saying, "An' it please ye, good my lord, my name is Guy Le Doakes." And then how Richard slowly lifted that great sword, which had cut its way through Europe, to the very walls of old Jerusalem, and laying its broad blade upon the bowed head of his kneeling subject said, "Arise, sir squire, squire no longer. Rise, Sir Guy Le Doakes. For thou hast done a thing this day that men in England shall tell children of, when thou and I are dead. And as a token of this deed, and of this day, I give to thee this pledge, that I shall not forget." So, with these words, the king reached up and plucked a lemon from a bough and gave it to Sir Guy Le Doakes, saying, "Be this fruit from this day on the symbol of thy house, and of thy line, Sir Guy. And when thou back returnest to good English soil, take but the seeds of this fair fruit and plant them where thou wilt—and where these seeds take root and flourish upon English earth, then shalt thou have that domain for thy own. As far around as thou canst measure in a whole day's riding. Yes, though thou choosest for thine own the fairest earth in my whole kingdom, between Cornwall and the Hebrides." And we all know, then, the story, how Sir Guy Le Doakes did humbly take this pledge and token of his master's gratitude, and when the wars were over and he came to English earth again, picked out the fairest spot that he could find and planted all his seeds. And we know also how Sir Guy discovered, then, that no lemon seed could grow on English soil, and how he came before King Richard of the Lion Heart again and told him how no seed had sprouted, how no tree would grow. "Nay, then," said Richard, with a grave yet gentle smile, "Thy domain, Guy, is even larger than thou thoughtest it would be. Thy domain is the very earth itself, the length and breadth of this whole isle, to come and go in as thou choosest, the very winds of English air shall be thy own, the fair firmament above us, stars and moon, and English skies, the very beating of the vexed, tempestuous seas, the very airs that breathe on thee, Sir Guy, shall call thee master, saying, all nature, sire, bows down to pay thee homage. The very birds that sing are choristers for Guy." Now when Sir Guy Le Doakes had heard these words, he rose and was exceedingly happy, because he saw the Deeper Meaning which his own vexed and worldly sense had not revealed to him. He saw that he was truly richer now than he had ever dreamed that he could be, that his domain was far greater than any he had ever thought of owning, that all earth, indeed, moon, sun and skies and starry firmament, belonged to his estate. And so he rode away with a glad heart. And from that day on, the story says, he roamed the roads of England like a conqueror.

How true this story is, in all its elements, no one can say, but the legend, if legend it be, lives on and still remains, until this day,—is given permanence, in fact, by the great Doakes coat-of-arms, which, as every one familiar with such matters knows, is a lemon, pendant, from a spear, above two lions rampant, and below, the famous legend of the Doakses everywhere: "Pour mon Dieu, mon roi et mon citron."

Again, what boy of spirit who has ever read Le Morte d'Arthur can ever forget the touching chronicle of Sir Doakes Le Greal as told by good old Thomas Malory in that famous book:

". . . . And thus it past on from Candylmas until St. Swythin's Eve and after Ester that the moneth of May was come whan every lusty herte begynneth to blossome and to brynge forth fruyte. For lyke as herbes and trees bryngen forth fruyte and florysshen in May, in lyke wyse every lusty herte that is in ony maner a lover spryngeth and floryssheth in lusty dedes. For it gyveth unto al lovers courage, that lusty moneth of May, in some thyng to constrayne hym to some maner of thyng more in that moneth than in ony other moneth, for dyverse causes. For thenne alle herbes and trees renewen a man and woman. And lyke wyse lovers callen ageyne to their mynde old gentilnes and old servyse, and many kynde dedes were forgeten by neclygence. For lyke as wynter rasure doth always arase and deface grene somer, soo fareth it by unstable love in man and woman. For in many persons there is no stabylyté. For we may see al day, for a lytel blast of wynters rasure anone we shalle deface and lay aparte true love, for lytel or noughte, that cost moch thynge. This is no wysedome nor stabylyté, but it is feblenes of nature and grete disworshyp who somever used this. Therfore lyke as May moneth floreth and floryssheth in many gardyns, soo in lyke wyse lete every man of worship florysshe his herte in this world, fyrst unto God, and next unto the ioye of them that he promysed his feythe unto. For there was never worshypful man or worshipfull woman but they loved one better than another. And worshyp in armes may never be foyled, but fyrst reserve the honour to God, and secondly the quarel must come of thy lady, and suche love I calle vertuous love. But now adayes men can not love seven nyghte but they must have alle their desyres. That love may not endure by reason. For where they ben soone accorded, and hasty hete, soone it keleth. Ryghte soo fareth love now adayes: soone hote, soone cold. This is noo stabylyté. But the old love was not so. Men and wymmen coude love togyders seven yeres, and no lycours lustes were bitwene them, and thenne was love trouthe and feythfulnes.

Now speke we I take God to record of the fayrest knyghte that ever in the quest of the Sank Greal forsoke the vanytyes of the world, the clenest mayden hee of al the knyghtes that were in the Sanke Greal, excepte Syr Galahad.

Now speke we of Syr Doakes Le Greal that made such sorowe daye and nyght that he never slepte, ete, nor dranke in servys of the Greal.

So when he had thus endured a ten days, that he febled he must nedes passe out of thys world, then he shryved him clene, and so it was no bote to stryve, but he departed and rode westerly, and there he sought a vij or viij days, and atte last he cam to a kepe where hee went inne and sawe a ladye.

Ladye, sayde syr Doakes Le Greal in a faynt voys, sithen he was lyke to die of febleness, is not thy marster, the good Lord of the Western Kepe within.

Nay, sayd the ladye in the same faynt tone, he is awaye. Com inne.

Then madam, I byseche you, gyve me shelter for the nyghte, sythen I am faynt wyth weariness and lyke to dye.

Syr, sayd the ladye, enter here, for God's love, and bee welcome: we will reste ye here. But fyrst (sayd shee) com wyth mee to my chaymber, for that I would have ye see my knyttinge ere ye slepe.

Madame, quod syr Doakes Le Greal, of knyttinge I have no grete skyl, sythen in the Sufferaunce of God and the Sank Greal it has been all my lyf to fyghte fals knygthes and succour maydens in dystres.

Syr, sayd the ladye, of fals knyghtes I wete not wel, but of maydens inne dystres I know ful sore.

Nay, then, sayd Doakes Le Greal, but lede me to thys mayden. I will succour her.

Sir, sayd the ladye, I am shee.

Ladye, sayd syr Doakes Le Greal, what is the cause of thy dystres. Is hit a dragon, sayd syr Doakes Le Greal.

Hit coude bee, sayd the ladye, yet I wete not wel.

Is hit a fals knyghte, sayd syr Doakes Le Greal.

It coude be, sayd the ladye, wee shall see.

Ladye, but lede me to the spot of thy dystres, an I will succour thee, he sayd.

I will shew it to thee, sayd the ladye, but sythen thou art weary lye thee down (sayd shee) upon this couche that ye maye better see the knyttinge worke I have to shew thee.

Madame, sayd Syr Doakes Le Greal, I never herde that ye must lye down onne a couche to looke at knyttinge worke.

Ye must to see it wel, sayd shee.

Nay, madam, quod syr Doakes Le Greal, I see no knytting worke.

Nay, sayd the ladye, for thatte ye muste fynde hit ferst and ye have never syrched for hit.

Where shal I syrch for hit, sayd Doakes Le Greal.

Heare, in the baskette, Sympel, Sayde the Ladye of the Westerne Kepe.

Now, fayre knygthe (quod she) and yet ye be the fayrest knyghte thatte ever strake wyth suerde Ile shew thee yet the fayrest resting playce of knyttinge worke that ever swerde was couched in. So saying she undid hyr gyrdle and she bad him loke.

Syr Knyghte, sayde she, now dyd ye ever see the lyke of thatte.

Aye, pardy, sayd Syr Doakes Le Greal, but hit was onne my fader's mayre.

Nay then, the ladye sayde this is noe mayre's neste. Ye canne wete it wel wherefore he marvaylled what hit mente. Nay, madam, (quod he), I have no weet in maters such as these, for in the quest of the Sank Greal I never yette saw aught of baskets or of knyttinge worke.

Then gette ye home and syrch for Mayres Nests in your fader's house, the Ladye sayd, for at knyttinge worke ye have no skyl . . . . ."

Such is the story of Sir Doakes Le Greal as Malory recounts it, in his famous chronicle.

NOTE [27]

(The Doaksology is incomplete: it is the author's intention to bring the family's history up to the present and back to the connecting link—the man in the train who is returning home again.)

THE ORDEAL OF THE BONDSMAN DOAKS
With Notes and Introduction
by a Friend

Then Agrippa said unto Paul, almost thou persuadest me to be a Christian.

And Paul said, I would to God, that not only thou, but also all that hear me this day, were both almost, and altogether such as I am, except these bonds.

. . . "Prince Andrey turned away. His heart was heavy and full of melancholy. It was all so strange—so different from what he had anticipated" . . . (*War and Peace*)

27. The manuscript is in typescript, but Wolfe added this handwritten note, probably for Edward Aswell's information when he was preparing to show him some new materials.

"It was all very well to dissemble your love,
But *why* did you kick me downstairs?" [28]

Dedication

To the honored memory of Lemuel Gulliver, Esq., an English
Gentlemen and Explorer of the Eighteenth Century.

THE INTRODUCTION
By
A Friend

. . . "I knew the bird intimately" . . . (*The Mikado*)

It was the first literary party in the life of Joseph Doaks. As he
entered the room, he was smote suddenly by the impression of having
stepped right into a Covarrubias drawing and having all the figures
come to life. He saw them all at once. They rose up and hit him smack
between the eyes, just like the figures in the drawing, looking even
more like their own cartoons than life itself. There was Van Vleeck
with his buck teeth over in a corner talking to a negro man; there was
Stephen Hook looking just the way he knew that Stephen Hook would
look, leaning against the mantle with that air of bored nonchalance that
was really just the screen of his excruciating shyness; there was Mr.
Lloyd McHarg, or "Knuckles" as he was more familiarly known to his
friends, who had done great violence to himself and nature and yet
remained quite splendidly himself—a man—a kind of unruinable ruin,
with pale blue eyes that looked as if they had been slightly poached in
alcohol, the corrugated redness of his puckered face, the essential and
terrific redness of hair, eyebrows, ears and everything about him, the
high staccatto cachination of his speech that was itself like the nervous
clatter of a typewriter or of a page of one of his own books. There was
the famous columnist, V. P. Y., small, swarthy, dry with the grotesquely worn yet attractive face of a very homely horse; Cottswold,
the critic, a little puff-ball of a man, a lover of dear whimsy Barriesque,
a polished adept of envenomed treacle, and many other famous ones
of that lost day and time.

They all looked so much like themselves and as Joe knew that
they *must* look, that like the man who once saw Shelley plain, or like

28. From Isaac **Bickerstaff's** poem " 'Tis Well 'Tis No Worse."

the kid who gets off the train for the first time in Paris, he squared his shoulders, drew a breath and muttered to himself: "Well, here we are."

And then these forms and faces, fixed and burnt there in his memory, in that blinding instant of first recognition, moved and shifted, the whole glittering sheen and interflux of life, of beauty and of talent, came to play again, the rosy smiling face of Mrs. Jack bore on him, wreathed in friendly greeting. She welcomed him and took him with her—then he heard a Voice.

[*The material continues on to introduce Seamus Malone (whose voice Joe has heard) and to present a sketch quite similar to that which appears in* The Web and the Rock, *pp. 527–36.*]

[*Tired after a busy spring, and thinking about the cordial reception he had received in the South in January, Wolfe decided it was time for his long-delayed return to Asheville. He began his trip southward in April by visiting Miss Catherine Brett at Dingman's Ferry, Pennsylvania. She drove him in her car to his father's old home, near York Springs. While there Wolfe went out to Gardner's Church, an Evangelical United Brethren church in the community of Latimore, a few miles north of York Springs, where members of his fathers' family are buried. He copied some of the inscriptions from the tombstones into his notebook.*]

Huldah Emeline
[*Daughter of Jacob and Eleanor J. Wolf*]
Born June 6, 1844
Died Feb. 26, 1858

Susan R.
[*Daughter of Jacob and Eleanor J. Wolf*]
[*Born Dec. 30*] 1846
[*Died July 20*] 1867

Sarah Ellen
Wife of Eli Lentz
Born Dec. 31, 1841
Died July 25, 1864

George [*A. Wolf*]
Died May [*11*] 1901
Aged 61 years, 7 mos. and 16 days

Altamont—1916
—That the richest man in town was the best
—That it was a disgrace bordering on crime to be poor
—That there was a personal God regulating the affairs of the universe and that if we saw things amiss in the life around us, they seemed amiss because we didn't know as much about them as God knew
—That it was the duty of every "real man" to get and hold a job and that if he didn't, it was his fault
—That the American way of life was incomparably the best on earth.

[*Wolfe was welcomed back to Asheville by a friendly citizenry curious to see the hometown boy who had made good. He even renewed acquaintance with some people whom he feared he had offended. Soon after his arrival, he was asked by the local paper to write an article "describing his feelings at being at home again after so long an absence."*]

I have come home for the first time in seven years and, if I may, I should like to make this statement to the people of my native town: I was twenty-nine years old when I was here last; I am thirty-six years old now. I am seven years older; I hope also I am a little wiser. Certainly, I can say sincerely that I am glad to be home again, if only for a day or two.

A good many people here, I believe, are fairly familiar with the general facts of my life. They know that I have tried to follow the profession of the writer and to make the writer's life my own.

May I say that if anything I have written has displeased anyone in my home town, I am genuinely and sincerely sorry for it. May I also say that if people in my home town do not like the books I have written, it is my sincere and earnest hope that the day will come when I write a book that the people in my home town will like.

And may I say finally that I have come home now for the first time in seven years not as a writer, but as a man who was born in this town, who grew up here, whose people have lived here, and who is now sincerely glad to be back again.[29]

[*When Wolfe returned to New York in mid-May, his work immediately began to show that his renewal of contact with his home*

---

29. An early draft found among his papers.

region was stimulating. He turned out the Civil War story "Chicka-mauga," the authentic details for which he had heard from the lips of his great-uncle John Westall over in the mountain area near Burnsville. He also began sketching out a genealogy of the Joyner family, Joe Doaks's maternal forebears. However, it lacks the high spirits and the folk quality of Wolfe's later version. The following passage is a sample:]

THE JOYNER GENEALOGY

Since we have already devoted considerable time and space to giving the historical account of the celebrated tribe of Doaks back to its earliest origins in English history, it is only fair here to give a somewhat briefer summary of another distinguished family whose history will be more than once intimately concerned with the adventures of this book. We refer, of course, to the great Joyner family with whose most distinguished representative, the famous Zachariah, we have already made acquaintance. To come briefly to their Catawba origins, for space does not permit a more extensive investigation of their English–Scotch or continental ancestry, the history of the Catawba Joyners is this: The American ancestor was one Richard Joyner, by birth an Englishman, who emigrated to this country in the first quarter of the eighteenth century, settled in Pennsylvania for a few years and eventually gravitated southward, as did many other of the English and German colonists of that period, to eastern Catawba, where he married and begot children and eventually died. It is with the history of one of these children that we are chiefly concerned, because he it was who was the true parent of the *great* Joyner tribe—the only one that matters—the only one with which our history is concerned. It is true enough that there were other children who in course of time grew up and married and had children of their own, but all of them remained in the eastern part of the state and accordingly never came to much. William Joyner was a pioneer. It was William Joyner who, after an honorable and valued enlistment in the American Revolution, pushed on westward to close the war to the very bases of the Blue Ridge, to take up there a revolutionary land grant that had been bestowed on him as a reward for his services in the American War of Independence.

[The material continues for thirty-eight pages about William Joyner, his sons Zachariah and Lucius (later named Theodore), and the Military Academy which Lucius established.]

[*The hospitable air of home and the dissatisfaction with his relationships in New York persuaded Wolfe to return South and spend the summer writing in a mountain cabin at Oteen, a few miles from Asheville. No notes remain from this two-month period, during which he revised and expanded "The Party at Jack's," a short novel highly critical of New York social and intellectual life. Wolfe left the work in a state of rough completion, and it was published (edited by Edward Aswell) as "The House That Jack Built" in* You Can't Go Home Again, *pp. 147–322. Scattered among the manuscript pages of this piece, which Wolfe wrestled with intermittently during the spring, are three groups of notes that show his concern with structure, point of view, and other technical matters. The last group comes from Wolfe's preparation for his third version (with suggestions perhaps made by Miss Nowell?):*]

1. Young Man—Hook—The Woman.
2. Young Man—Mrs. Jack.
3. Young Man—Mrs. Jack—Farley.
4. Lily Mandell—Mrs. Jack—Young Man.
5. Lily Mandell—Mrs. Jack—Young Man—Hirsch.
6. "Beddoes!"
7. Young Man—Mrs. Jack—Sculptor.
8. Hirsch—Mrs. Jack—Sacco and Vanzetti.
9. Amy Leer—Hook—Portrait.

From the Point of View of the Lover
   (Mrs. Jack the Centre)
He Sees:
   1) Entrance of Miss Mandell and Hirsch
   2) Farley

1. Make Mrs. Jack something else—a dress designer.
2. Turn Ernie [*the son*] into Mr. Jack.
3. Work Train Into Mrs. Jack's room.
4. Make youthful lover think the things about the people at the party.
5. Make Old John tap against the elevator walls.[30]

30. The first three items and the last one are crossed out, indicating that Wolfe made the changes. Item 2 explains why the characterization of Mr. Jack is occasionally troubled. For example, YCGHA, pp. 225–27, presents a worldly, supercilious Mr. Jack because the character had originally been his son (Ernie or Fritz).

[*On August 18, while he was roaring drunk in Asheville, Wolfe was arrested and detained overnight in the city jail. The following morning, after he had sobered up, he was released and no charges were preferred. The arrest was a kind of climax to his growing tension and dissatisfaction with the return to North Carolina and to his growing realization that you can't go home again. The envelope from the Asheville jail which had contained Wolfe's pocket articles ($14.50 in cash) has the following information on it:*]

Date	8–18–37
Name of Defendant	Thos. Wolfe
Arresting Officers	Tweed, J. G. Anderson
Charge	Dis Con
Articles	$14.50
	R
	sergeant.]

[*On the back of an envelope from the Convention Hall-Auditorium Committee addressed to "Mr. Thomas Wolfe, Battery Park Hotel, City," and postmarked August 27, 1937, Asheville, N.C., Wolfe wrote the following notes. This is the beginning of his attempt to make Asheville, its political corruption, and its economic crash a part of his criticism of the American social scene. He brought it to partial fruition in his treatment of Libya Hill in* You Can't Go Home Again:]

THE RUIN OF THE CITY

Characters—George Graves
      —Blochem (the politician)
      —The Civic Clubs
      —Biltmore Forest
      —The S. A. Men
      —McRae
      —Doc Strong
      —Craddux
      —The Mayor's Daughter
      —The Senator's Daughter
      —The Killing at Clingman

Pocket Notebook 32
September 14, 1937, to February, 1938

Wolfe spent the remainder of the year looking for a publisher, a search that became a tragicomedy. Rival publishers at first could not believe that Wolfe had left Scribner's, and his initial attempts to contact them were rebuffed or ignored. He concluded that no one wanted to publish him and then went into seclusion, during which he lived at various hotels. Finally, when the severance with Scribner's was verified, most of the leading publishers made strong overtures to Wolfe. At one point he was on the verge of accepting Houghton-Mifflin's offer, but he finally selected Harper's in mid-December.[1] His choice of a publisher did not settle all his problems, for the lawsuit to recover his manuscripts was still going on. When Wolfe won this case in February, 1938, it was the first time in three years that he was free from litigation.

At the suggestion of Robert N. Linscott of Houghton-Mifflin, Wolfe hauled out "The October Fair" in October and began rewriting it, but he had lost interest in this material. His interest now was in writing about the Asheville scandal in the failure of its main bank in 1930, and in order to set the stage for that event he supplied a background in "The Rise of the Bank." He also began devising ways by which "The October Fair" could be included in his Doaks book.

[Wolfe left Asheville on September 5 and went to Bristol, Virginia, where he was the guest of Mrs. Anne W. Armstrong for a few days.[2] She drove him the forty miles to Marion, where he visited Sherwood Anderson before heading toward New York. During a stopover in Baltimore, he began this notebook.]

1. For Edward C. Aswell's account of Wolfe's change of publishers, see "Thomas Wolfe Did Not Kill Maxwell Perkins," *Saturday Review of Literature*, Oct. 6, 1951, pp. 16–17, 44–46. The anonymous publishers Aswell mentions in the article were: Warder Norton, Alfred Harcourt, Alfred McIntyre of Little Brown, Bernard Smith and Mrs. Blanche Knopf of Knopf's, and Lee Barker, Robert Linscott, and Paul Brooks of Houghton-Mifflin.

2. For Mrs. Armstrong's account of this visit, see "As I Saw Thomas Wolfe," *Arizona Quarterly*, II (Spring, 1946), 5–15.

Baltimore, Sept. 14, 1937:

Arrived at 7:43 this morning—to Hotel Emerson by cab—Big Bag Had Not Arrived—a cool autumnal morning—very bright—Room unmade—B'kfast at lunchroom on Baltimore St.—Bought Boric solution and gargle—then to room—sent suit out to be pressed—slept uneasily (worrying about case until 12)—up—shower—sent in income tax check—got hotel porter to trace bag—he found it—to Bar for 2 Scotch & sodas—drinking now in downstairs night club room.

Events of past 2½ months—left N.Y. July 1 [*breaks off*]

Carolina Banquet, Ambassador [*Hotel*], Oct. 9.

Bets:

That Yankees Will Win Series
That Yankees Make More Homeruns Than the Giants
That Yankees Hit For More Total Bases Than the Giants

Gloucester, Mass., Friday, Oct. (7?) 1937, 4:10 P.M.:

3rd game (today)	Yanks 5
	N.Y. 1
1st game	Yanks 8
	N.Y. 1
2nd game	Yanks 8
	N.Y. 1

Publishers:

Scribners [*crossed out*]
MacMillan (an English House)
Harper's
Viking (a Jewish House)
Knopf (the same—with exhibitionist note added)
Little-Brown (a Boston House)
Houghton-Mifflin (a Boston House)
Harcourt-Brace [3] (It has Cappy Pierce)
Doubleday-Doran (Said To Be Big-Production Factory)

[*A list of the powerful football teams of the season:*]
The East:

3. When Wolfe called Harcourt, Brace, Alfred Harcourt immediately informed Charles Scribner of the fact, and only then did Scribner's realize that the break was irrevocable.

New England: Yale, Dartmouth
N.Y., N.J.: Fordham
Penn., Md., D.C., etc.: Pittsburgh, Villanova [*crossed out*], Lafayette [*crossed out*]
    The South: Alabama, Vanderbilt, Auburn
    Middle West: Nebraska, Minnesota
    S.W.:?

England:	House of the Far and Lost
	'E
France:	The Sun and the Rain
	Paris etc.
Germany:	I Have a Thing to Tell You
	Oktoberfest [4]
	Dark in the Forest
N.C.:	L.H.A.
	The Lost Boy
	The Web of Earth
	Old Catawba
	The Child By Tiger
N.Y.:	Of Time A. T. River
	Death the Proud Brother
	No Door
	Mr. Malone
	Only the Dead
	The Train and The City
	April Late April
New England:	Of T A T R
	Bascom Hawke
St. Louis:	The Lost Boy

Les Célèbres

The Town: Col. "Joyner," The Willets family, "Our Dick," Lon Radiker, Charley Riggs, Dan Emmanuel, Aunt Fern.

The State: Frank Ramsay, Willis Nutter Ramsay, Jeremiah Ransome.

The City: Mrs. Jack, Mr. Jack, Lily Mandell, Saul Levenson, Stephen Hook, Roy Malone, Amy Van Leer, Alsop, Joyner, Van Paget and Page, Rubenstein (The Lawyers), James Rodney, Jr.

4. "Oktoberfest" had been published in *Scribner's Magazine*, June, 1937, and was the last of Wolfe's works to appear there until after his death.

The World: The Ambassador, The Ambassador's Daughter, Willy, The Frau Baronin.

The Best Restaurants I Have Found in New York
(For Consistent Goodness)
Luchow's
The LaFayette
The Blue Ribbon (more middle class but good)
Janssen

A FAREWELL TO THE FOX [5]

[*A number of notes on apartments indicate that Wolfe was looking for a new place to live. Eventually he settled down in the Chelsea Hotel, 222 W. 23rd St.*]

Becker came limping in at half past nine, followed by the intern —The brute was jacketed in coarse clean white: his shoulders made a heavy bulge around the arm pits, his hairy hands were clean: he looked ready to cut anything. "Was ist?" he growled.

5. After the break with Scribner's became final, Wolfe began considering his Maxwell Perkins material for the conclusion of his "big book." This phrase became the title of the final section of the outline he left with Aswell.

"Johann!" He jerked a coarse thumb at the word. "Rasieren," Becker said. He went limping out.

"Was sagt er?" I said as soon as I could get my breath.

"Rasieren," Johann grinned. He knew that I had heard. He was enjoying it.

"Rasieren Sie meinen ganzen kopf?"

"Ja," said Johann grinning from ear to ear. "Ganz."

"Why, that *son* of a bitch—"

"Nein," said Johann gently. "Nein."

He halted looking at the orderly with [angry curses?].

"Sie mussen," Johann said gently. "Wirklich." [6]

Doaks in 1930

Mr. Doaks, in the early months of 1930, was no more than conscious of The Great Collapse. True, the Crash had already occurred—but when he left his country at the beginning of May, its consequence, the repercussions of its tragedy, were unforeseen—by such as he.

And had they been foreseen by anyone? The prophets of woe were few indeed, he was to find in the years that followed that most of those who gained renown as such prophets, had gained it by a kind of afterthought—the fortunate reward that seems to attend the predictions of the "expert" everywhere in America. For an expert is a man who sometimes hits it right. And though an expert is 999 times wrong he is yet an expert and reverenced, if on the thousandth time he hits it right.

The Men of Good Will:

    Else Becker (1935–1937)

    Mrs. Purvis (1930–1931)

    The Scandinavians in Brooklyn

      Steve (1933–

      Carl   1934)

    Johann (1928)

    Thea Schmidtbauer (1928)

    The Girl in Vienna (1928)

    The Boy in "I Have a Thing" (1936–1937)

    Mr. Sykes (London) 1935

6. A draft of the hospital scene, which was summarized into a single sentence in the published version, W&R, p. 675: "The Herr Geheimrat ordered his assistant to shave the hair around the wounds, and this was done."

ELSE BECKER

He called for Mrs. Becker. She came in with an inquiring look on her face.

"I do not know vat you say," she said.

Mrs. Platz rang the bell.

"It's Ian," she said, smiling simply, and came in [*page missing*]

DR. WILBY [7]

The aesthetic development of the great Dr. Wilby—the thing that made him, in the opinion of many Cultured People, "the most rare and balanced of all our critics"—extended probably over a period of some twenty years. There had been a time, for example, when Dr. Wilby had brought joy to the souls of the correct by dismissing the works of some of the leading writers of the time as being the delayed productions of "a dirty little boy." A little later, Dr. Wilby's dirty little boy had been qualified somewhat by the adjectival words "who scrawls bad words upon the walls of privies that he hopes may shock his elders."

A pleasing image was thus subtly conveyed to the readers of the Atlantic Monthly, the Boston Evening Transcript, and Dr. Wilby's own Distinguished Thursday Review of Letters. It conveyed to these cultivated readers a comfortable feeling of urbanity—for what could be more comfortable or urbane for a devoted reader of the Thursday Review—than the sense that just as he was squatting comfortably to attend to the most inevitable of the natural functions he might look up and read with an amused and tolerating eye certain words that various dirty little boys like Anatole France, G. B. Shaw, Dreiser, Wells, Sherwood Anderson, and D. H. Lawrence had scrawled up there with the intention of shocking him.

Obviously the natural reaction of the well-trained Thursday Afternooner would be to—smile and wipe.

The personnel of Dr. Wilby's editorial staff was in all respects worthy the guiding authorities of such a master. There was, first of all, the celebrated stylist and bon vivant of fine letters, Nicholas Crowthorpe, of whom a coarser but impressed contemporary had reverently exclaimed, "He's a whimsical old son of a bitch, ain't he?"

7. An early draft of a satire on Henry Seidel Canby, editor of the *Saturday Review of Literature*. Wolfe later changed the name to Dr. Turner, and the material was put into HB as "Portrait of a Literary Critic," pp. 150–61.

Upon the Germans:

What were some of the notable characteristics of this great people?

High among them, from order, tradition, and from tradition, integrity and high honesty.

A phrase heard frequently in New York at this period was:

"Well, they can afford to do that, they got the name."

One heard this often among Americans, but not among Germans. The familiar Yankee phrase "he can travel now upon his reputation" did not apply here.

First of all, this was evident from their restaurants and their food.

Utility Cultures, Inc.

Dean Harmswell
Barnabas B. Spurgeon
Ella Mae Maird
Alsop

SPURGEON [8]

The career—or, as men were later wont to say, the revolutionary background—of Mr. Barnabas B. Spurgeon, was, externally at least, not propitious.

He was a New Englander by birth, and a graduate of Amherst College. After his graduation, he taught for two or three years at the University of Michigan, and enjoyed while there a fruitful and stimulating intercourse with the late Professor Stuart B. Sherman, who was then in his academic hey-day. Under the sound but stimulating inspirations of Professor Sherman's tutelage, Mr. Spurgeon completed there his "work upon his doctorate," as the process is called in learned circles. His thesis, when published and presented, aroused in the scholarly world a considerable disturbance: there were those progressive spirits of Professor Sherman's own persuasion who were quite enthusiastic and referred to it as "decidedly interesting," "stimulating," "a genuine advance in the field of a more enlightened scholarship."

8. A sketch of a character based on Wolfe's N.Y.U. colleague Edwin Berry Burgum. In other drafts the name is Chester Alonzo Spurgeon. One paragraph on Spurgeon went into Chapter 27, YCGHA, p. 410.

Others, however, of an older generation, and of a more dogmatic cast of mind, shook their heads with an air of weary foreboding: Mr. Spurgeon's thesis was, they grudgingly admitted, "interesting." It was —they unwillingly confessed, "stimulating." But, they demanded, was it "sound"?

The subject was: "The Concept of Primogeniture as Exemplified In The Novels of Edward Bulwer, Lord Lytton."

A FAREWELL TO THE FOX

Oct. 1928—Munich
Nov.–Dec. 1928—Vienna—Budapest
Jan. 1929—The Fox
March–April 1929—Utility Cultures
Early Oct. 1929—Last Return
Oct. 1929—The Book
Oct. 1929–May 1930—Mixed Returns
June 1930—Paris—away
July–Aug.—Switzerland
Sept.—Schwarzwald
Oct. 1930–March 1931—England—Mrs. Purvis
March–Nov. 1931—The Alley
Nov. 1931–Aug. 1932—The House
Aug. 1932–Nov. 1933—The Flat
Nov. 1933–March 1935—The Terrace
March 1935–July 1935—The Bright Medusa
July 1935—Fame and the Poet
July–Sept. 1935—The Great West
Sept. 1935–July 1936—The Dread Medusa
July 1936–Oct. 1936—I Have a Thing to Tell You
Oct. 1936–May 1937—The End of Medusa
May 1937–Sept. 1937—The Big Return

[*Determined to make literary capital of the return to Asheville, Wolfe planned to include it in his Doaks book. In the version which follows, a first draft written in the fall or winter of 1937, Joe Doaks speaks in the first person. Wolfe later changed it to third person and to George Webber. When Aswell published the material, he called the character Eugene Gant.*]

May: 1937.

I had been seven years from home and one day I was back again. And what was there to say? Time passes, and puts halters to debate. There was so much to say that never could be spoken, there had been times, so many times in those long years of absence when I had debated with the tongues of silence and return, saying: "I will go home again. I shall lay bare my purposes, say my piece, speak so that no man living in the world can doubt me—oh, I shall tell them till the thing is crystal clear when I go home again."

I did not know then that you can't go home again.

Down through the Valley of Virginia I had kept the watered course. Each man of us, he has his own America, his own stretch, from which here outward he shall shape his scheme, until the lengths, the patterns, and the prospect is all his, but he must start first with his own; and my own was this: down first from twelve miles North and East of Gettysburg, to Hagarstown, then down the Valley of Virginia: first the great barns, the wide sweep and noble roll of Pennsylvania fields, the neat-kept houses; lower down in the great Valley, still good fields and kept places, but the looser, sparser agriculture of the land; and now, for the first time, the hodden drab of nigger gray, gray barns, gray sheds, gray lean-tos slanting to the weather that had given them the unpaint of their hodden gray: the rains were heavy through Virginia, and every day there were wet pools of light, the sodden land. It was almost the time of apple blossoms, faintly there was smell of rain and apple blossoms on the air.

I went down very slowly: slowly the rains lifted, one day sun and light, the blue veil, the shouldering ramparts of the great Blue Ridge appeared. And suddenly I was back in space and color and in time, the weather of my youth was round me, I was home again. And I had been seven years from home and what was there to say?

The hills draw in out of wide valleydom, and signs of old kept spaciousness into the blue immediate, another life, another language of its own—creek, hill, and hollow, gulch and notch, knob, bald, ridge, and cabins nestling in a patch of bottom land appear: the road from Tennessee is long and roundabout, winds in and out, and goes by rocky waters boiling at the bottom of steep knolls—then climbs, climbs, winds and climbs; and May is late and cold among the upper timber, fume-flaws and torn filaments of mist wash slowly around the shoulders of the hills: here higher up the chestnut blight is evident: ruined, in the blasted sweeps, the great sentries of the heights appear.

[*The narrative continues on through the shooting in the mountain town and the arrival of Joe in his home town, and ends with the long monologue of "Mama." It is an early version of the material which appears in* The Hills Beyond, *pp. 120–41.*]

[*The following entry attempts to estimate the number of novels each writer has published.*]

Anderson—5
Dreiser—4 or five
Lewis—3 or four
Hemingway—2 or three
Does Passos—2 or three (or more)
Caldwell—2 or three
Masters [9]—! ! ! ! ? ? ? ?
Faulkner—3 or four (or more)

WOLFE, WILLIAM OLIVER: STONECUTTER

Born at Gardner's Church, near York Springs, in Adams County, Pennsylvania, April 1851: the fifth child of a family of nine. His parents were Jacob and Eleanor Jane Wolf of that community. He was bound out to Jacob Schaffer, a farmer of that community, in 1863, worked with his brother Wesley at the mule camps of the Union Army in York, Pa., in the winter of 1864–1865. Went to Baltimore in 1865–1866 and was apprenticed to _____ _____, a stonecutter, from whom he learned his trade. He returned to Penn. and worked in York for a year in 1870–71, then went to Raleigh, N.C., where he was employed as a mason and stonecutter in construction of the state penitentiary. Was later engaged in similar employment in Columbia, S.C., returned to Raleigh and set up in business for himself, was married twice in Raleigh, first to Hattie Watson, which marriage was terminated by divorce, then to Cynthia Allen. In 1883, moved to Asheville, N.C., in the western part of the state because of his wife's health: she died one year later and he was married in 1885 for the third time to Julia Elizabeth Westall, a woman from a family of that community. To them were born the following children: Leslie, 1886 (deceased at the age of nine months); Effie 1887; Frank 1888; Mabel 1890; Grover 1892 (deceased 1904); Ben 1892 (deceased 1918); Frederick 1895; and Thomas Clayton Oct. 3, 1900. William Oliver Wolfe, the father of this family, was engaged in business in Asheville, N.C., for

9. Edgar Lee Masters also lived at the Chelsea Hotel, and he and Wolfe had become firm friends.

the remainder of his life and died there in June, 1922, seventy-one years old.

I have of late, dear Fox, been thinking of you very much, and of your simple, yet your strange and fascinating name.[10]

Potential Fascist Literary Groups and Individuals:
  The Saturday Review of Literature
  The Southern Agrarians
  The Virginia Quarterly
  New York Times Sunday Book Review
  Brickell's Column [11]
  Hansen's Column [12]
  The N.Y. Sun
  The Nat'l Academy of Arts and Letters [13]
  The American Academy [*of Arts and Letters*]
  Individuals:
    [*J.*] Donald Adams
    B. De Voto

Jim and Ann Poling, Pl 8-3158, 400 East 49th.[14]

I

THE OCTOBER FAIR

Towards the close of a day near the end of the summer of 1925 a great liner was approaching the coast of the North American continent at her full speed of 22 knots an hour.[15]

10. Draft of the opening sentence of Chapter 45, YCGHA.
11. Herschel Brickell's column appeared in the New York *Post*.
12. Harry Hansen's column was a feature of the New York *World-Telegram*.
13. Wolfe was elected a member of the National Institute of Arts and Letters in January, 1937, but did not attend his first meeting until January, 1938. For his comments, see *Letters*, pp. 702-703. The nominating committee for Literature at the time of Wolfe's election consisted of Van Wyck Brooks, Archibald MacLeish, Dorothy Canfield Fisher, John Livingston Lowes, Stephen Vincent Benét, and Arthur Train. Other members elected in 1937 included Sherwood Anderson, James Branch Cabell, John Dos Passos, Robinson Jeffers, and Robert Sherwood.
14. James W. Poling, Managing Editor of Doubleday, also tried to sign Wolfe. Doubleday offered to match any proposal Wolfe received from any other publisher.
15. Draft of the opening sentence of Chapter 17, W&R.

The Vision of Spangler's Paul
The Lives of the Bondsman Doaks
The Ordeal of the Bondsman Doaks
The Lives of the Bondsman Paul
You Can't Go Home Again

Published:
18 No Door
18 Death the Proud Brother
18 Boomtown
5000 April Late April
───────
59,000

Unpublished:
Party at Jack's (35000)

WORKERS BOOKSHOP, 50 EAST 13TH ST.

Ten Days That Shook the World
Franz Mehring's Life of Marx
Communist Manifesto
Strachey's *Coming Struggle For Power*
Das Kapital
The Letters of Marx and Engles
Carl Marx's Letters On The Civil War

Mr. Saxton, 34 Gr. Park East, 7:45.[16]

Dear Sherwood: [17]

I'm sorry you felt you had to write that second note. I was pretty rough the other day and I am going to write today and tell you

16. Harper's was now wooing Wolfe vigorously. Eugene Saxton, editor-in-chief of Harper's, gave a dinner for Wolfe, at which Cass Canfield, president of the firm, and Aswell were also present. For an account of this dinner, see Andrew Turnbull, *Thomas Wolfe*, pp. 285–86.

17. Draft of a letter to Sherwood Anderson, December 20, 1937. Anderson and Wolfe had quarreled at a party on December 1. Shortly afterward, on December 17, Anderson had written Wolfe a note asking him to a cocktail party for the benefit of the Spanish Loyalists, and he also invited Wolfe to have dinner with him later. Meanwhile, Wolfe bumped into Anderson in a hotel

so. But I think that we got somewhere with our talk and my recollection, however hazy, was pretty clearly that we shook hands at the end and said we weren't going to let anything come between us.

[*On December 18, Wolfe brought his long indecision about publishers to an end by making up his mind to accept the Harper's offer. He spent Christmas with the Edward C. Aswells at Chappaqua, New York, and signed the contract with Harper's on December 31. Aswell then asked for a statement that could be used in a press release, and Wolfe responded by writing the following statement, including the first paragraph.*]

A STATEMENT

Thomas Wolfe has signed a contract with Harper & Brothers for the publication of his next novel. The author, in a letter written to his publishers just before Christmas, says:

"This is a time of year that has some sadness in it for us all. But we can feel happy, too, in the knowledge that nothing gets lost, and that the people we have known will still be our friends, no matter where we are, and that although we can't go home again, the home of every one of us is in the future. And that is why I am looking forward to next year.

"It has been my fortunate lot always to have as publishers in this country people of the finest ability and the highest integrity. For that reason, I am glad to know that with the New Year I shall be associated with a house like yours.

"As you know, like many other young men, I began life as a lyrical writer. I am no longer a very young man—I am thirty-seven years old—and I must tell you that my vision of life has changed since I began to write about ten years ago, and that I shall never again write the kind of book that I wrote then. Like other men, I began to write with an intense and passionate concern with the designs and purposes of my own youth, and, like many other men that preoccupation has

---

lobby and renewed the quarrel. Anderson sent a note the next day, December 18, saying: "When I wrote you yesterday suggesting that you have dinner with me Tuesday evening, I had no notion how you felt. As you have expressed such a hearty desire to chuck our acquaintance—why not?" For a full discussion of the whole matter, see *Letters*, pp. 687–88.

now changed to an intense and passionate concern with the designs and purposes of life.

"For two years now, since I began to work on my new book, I have felt as if I was standing on the shore of a new land. About the book that I am doing, I can only tell you that it is a kind of fable, constructed out of the materials of experience and reality, and permitting me, I hope, a more whole and thorough use of them than I have had before. The book belongs in kind with those books which have described the adventures of the average man—by this I mean the naturally innocent man, every mother's son of us—through life.

"Anyway, for better or for worse, my life, my talent, and my spirit is now committed to it utterly. Like Martin Luther, I can't do otherwise—Ich kann nicht andern—I have no other choice.

"Now I can only hope the end for both of us will be well.

Sincerely yours,
THOMAS WOLFE"

[*The Dooher case came to trial on February 8, 1938, in Jersey City, and Wolfe won a complete victory. After the trial he, Maxwell Perkins, and Mrs. Jelliffe made a festive round of New York in celebration. This was the last time that Wolfe and Perkins met.*]

A PREFACE [18]

The chronology of this book is long and vexed. The plan first occurred to the author, so far as he can remember, as early as the spring of 1929. It clarified itself in some coherent detail during a year abroad in 1930–1931. Parts of it (_____) were written during that year, and a great deal of it (Death the Proud Brother, No Door, The Train and the City, April Late April) during the two years that followed (1931–1933). After 1935, little was done on the book until summer and late autumn 1937 when work was resumed on it. It was completed and designed into its present form in 1938.

[*While Wolfe was in London in 1930, he learned of the failure of the Central Bank of Asheville and of the town's economic collapse. In time he came to think of the condition of his home town, so he was to*

18. This entry, which describes Wolfe's work on "The October Fair," indicates that he was still considering a return to that book for his next published work.

inform his Purdue audience, as "an appalling microcosmos of the whole breakdown—in feverish miniature, a picture of the whole boom that had swept the nation." To provide the background for a fictional account of Asheville's ordeal he wrote "The Rise of the Bank (1916–1924)." A forty-page typed manuscript, it shows the mounting social concern that characterizes Wolfe's late writing.]

THE RISE OF THE BANK (1916–1924)

Some forty years ago, the people of the town of Libya Hill were very familiar with the figure of a weazened, dark complexioned little man, named Willis Riggs. He was such a pathetic, obscure, emaciated, little man that he really stuck in people's memory, with a kind of singular vividness, just because he was so obscure and insignificant. Nobody knew very much about him, or where he was from, except that he had been around the town for a long time, and most of the time was miserable. For a long time he was employed at a great variety of shabby and insecure employments: that wretched little man was so miserably hard up that the poverty of the Riggs' family was a by-word in the town. There was nothing that he would not do to earn a little money just to keep life in his large family. He would run errands, deliver packages, mow lawns, work in stores during "the Christmas rush"—if a mild flurry in trade that occurred in a town of ten thousand inhabitants forty years ago around Christmas-time could be called a rush.

But often, the plain blunt truth of the matter is, the condition of this man and his family was desperate. He was married, and his wife was another pitiful undersized little creature like himself. And they had several children, and these children were also undersized and pitiful, and seemed never to have had enough to eat. The whole family had a kind of terrible fascination for the town because they seemed to have been derived from a different race of people, a different grade and order of the human species. They were really like a race of dwarfs: one does not so often see people of this sort in America, or at least not in the south. God knows, in this abundant land, which, if we are to believe the politicians, offers so much to everyone, there are enough underfed, under-developed, under-cared for people. The south has millions of them: The ranks of its poor whites, its tenant farmers, its hill people, and its textile workers alone can produce enough to afflict the conscience and the soul of man. But usually with these people, one sees what they might have been, if they had had a decent chance. In the gangling mountaineer, the malarial lowlander, the shambling tenant with his tattered overalls, the scrawny neck, his toothless jaws, and his slattern of a wife with her hank of hair, the snuff-stick dripping from the corner of her mouth, and a dozen of her filthy little children clinging to her skirts as she clutches another wretched little waif to her lank bosom, and for the fourteenth time proposes her pregnant belly to the open door of the lean-to-shack—in all the tragic rudiments, one sees the elements of decent, alert, vigorous and full bodied humanity, if only that had had a chance.

[*Then follows a two-page description of the Big People and the Little People, which Aswell used in* "The Universe of Daisy Purvis," You Can't Go Home Again, *pp. 530-31.*]

This was the way it was with Willis Riggs, and his unhappy family. They belonged to the Little People of the earth, and perhaps they literally belonged to that kind of little people one sees in England, for, although people did not know very much about their antecedents, it was said that Mr. Riggs' father had been an Englishman, and had come to this country some time before.

Doaks remembered vividly one tragic story about this family from his own childhood. He remembered it so vividly that the exact date was printed in his memory. It was long before his birth, on Christmas Day, 1893. This, of course, was the year in which there had been another ruinous economic catastrophe, which had already come to be known by the general name of "depression." On the morning of Christmas Day, 1893, his father had gone out and walked over to the cottage in which Willis Riggs' family then lived. There had been a fall of snow the night before, and the weather now had turned clear and cold. The elder Doaks had found a scene of unmitigated wretchedness as he stepped into the little house. The place was freezing cold, or, as Joe's father had put it in his own pungent phrase "Y'God, there wasn't enough fire in the house for Patty the pig to light his corncob pipe with"—for there wasn't a lump of coal or a stick of wood left to light a fire. They had taken most of the wretched furniture, such as it was and split it up into kindling wood, now they had burned all this up. The children—there were three of them—Barrett, who was eight years old, his young brother James, a child of four, and their little sister, who was hardly more than a babe in arms, she was only three years old—were hung together in a big wooden bed, hugging one another for warmth with every manner of bed clothing, or clothing of any sort, that wretched house could offer. The children didn't have any shoes or stockings, and their wretched little clothes were so shabby and ragged that the only way their mother had been able to get warmth for them was to pile them together in this old bed. There wasn't even a curtain at the windows, and this poor family, with the pitiful shame that we have here in America about being poor, had pulled the old ragged shades down to keep out the intrusive glance of neighbors and of passersby. The elder Doaks had walked into this cheerless and tragic scene, and his first response had been immediate and characteristic. Without preliminary, he had cleared his throat and wet his thumb, and then roared out "Merciful God, Mr. Riggs! What is the meaning of all this!" The poor little man had just looked at him with a trembling chin and watering eyes, without waiting for an answer, the other man strode across the floor of the wretched room to the big bed, pulled back the huddle of those wretched covers and seeing those poor half-naked children there, had cried out again: "Merciful God!" As for the poor woman, she had turned away her little wretched huddled figure bowed in shame and bitter misery, and clutched her apron with her worn hands, and with that bitter gesture that women have had in moments of grief since the beginning of time, had covered her face with her apron and wept bitterly.

The next response of the elder Doaks had also been characteristic because that man was a good man when he got started. He walked across the room, and with a single smashing kick tore the wretched door off its hinges and then he smashed it into kindling wood. He had a fire laid and lighted in that room within five minutes, and for the first time in many days, that shabby little cottage had a decent coil of smoke out of the chimney. Then he left the house and warned them not to stir until he got back. He went home, gathered together, from the supply of his own brood, enough shoes and stockings, little shabby garments, jackets, coats, whatever he could lay his hands on, to clothe the children, and he went striding back with these. Then he came back and filled a tow-sack with coal which he carried on his shoulder. He ordered Mrs. Riggs to get a fire going in the range, returned home again, got four fat chickens from the chicken coup, killed them, had his wife pluck them, filled up a flour sack and a basket with every kind of provision he could lay his hands on—potatoes, canned peaches, cherries, preserves, all of his wife's making, butter, bread, flour, coffee, sugar, bunches of celery, raisins, nuts and fruits, big winter apples, the whole provisioning of Christmas. And he took these back with him.

It was a late Christmas dinner in the Doaks household that day, and it was a later one perhaps in the Riggs household. But it was worth it for both of them.

We will pass briefly by almost twenty years in time now in the history of the Riggs family. In the elections of 1894,[19] Benjamin Harrison, a Republican, was elected President of the United States, and, of course, a Republican Postmaster was appointed for the town of Libya Hill. Mr. Riggs was a Republican, and had always quite obediently voted the ticket and through the intercession of some Republicans in town, he got a civil service appointment and was made a mail carrier. After this, his lot was somewhat easier and more secure. The man's meager little figure, carrying his heavy leather mailbag and stumping briskly along his route, became a familiar one. His children were growing up, his two boys were in school: Barrett, the elder of the two, got as far as the eighth grade, but James went the whole way through high school. At the age of fifteen, however, Barrett was taken out of school and went to work. He held a succession of small jobs around the town for two or three years, then in his eighteenth year got a job in one of the banks. When he was twenty, he had an opportunity to go to Florida, and there to go to work in a bank. He went, and he was employed there for several years.[20]

What happened there was never exactly known, but it was known that there had been trouble of some sort: whatever the matter was, it was not a matter that reflected on the honesty of Barrett Riggs, but rather on his competence. At any rate, he lost his job, apparently. Then he returned to Libya Hill, was idle for some months, "looking around," like Mr. Micawber, "for something to turn up" and finally landed a job as teller in a small but apparently substantial institution known as The Merchants National.

In these days he was remembered and spoken of by everybody as a bright young fellow. The elder Doaks, who kept a deposit in this Bank, used to come home and talk about him. Barrett's "background" was still pretty close to him, people were perhaps unconsciously unkind in referring to it, but the reason they did was that they were really delighted by the young man's modest success, everyone was favorably impressed by his pleasant, smiling, and friendly manner, which also seemed to be so businesslike and knowing. It was the day of the "hustler"—the ideal of "the hustler" was held up to American youth as a mark at which they could shoot. And Barrett Riggs, apparently, was trying his best to live up to the idea, and to hit the mark.

In these days, he had none of the pompous manners, the swollen

19. Harrison's election occurred in 1888, and McKinley was elected in 1896.
20. Part of this paragraph about Barrett, whose name was later changed to Jarvis, and portions of the following material went into "The Catastrophe," YCGHA, pp. 360–62.

assurance that were to characterize him in his greater days. He always had a bright and smiling morning face, it was always briskly and cheerfully "good morning, Mr. Doaks"—"good morning, Mr. Brown" —when a customer came in. And really the small dwarf figure of the little fellow was almost an asset to him in these days. It seemed to fit in perfectly with his brisk, cheerful businesslike manner, that was also so friendly, so helpful, so courteous, and so eager to please. He also dressed neatly, and it was known that "he helped support his mother" —his father had died a year or two before. And all these things seemed to touch a warm spot in the hearts of the people in the town who remembered his childhood and from what meager and wretched beginnings he had come. People actually wanted him to succeed: It was a kind of heartening vindication of an American legend—the story of the poor boy, who had not only "made good" but had profited from the poverty and hardship of his early life.

In these ways, when the word began to go around a year or two later that a group of men in town were talking of starting another bank, and that Barrett Riggs was being mentioned as a cashier of the new institution, the feeling was most favorable. The men who were sponsoring the new bank were business and professional men of respectable reputations, but it would not be too much to say that the greatest personal asset they had from the beginning was the fact that they had appointed Barrett Riggs their cashier.

Thus far, out of such unpromising beginnings, he had played his life cards well, he had offended no one, he had made no enemy, he had remained modestly friendly, and yet impersonal, as if not wishing to intrude himself too much upon the attention of his elders, and men of greater substance and authority in the town's life. And the whole feeling about him was favorable. It was thought that here was a young man, who, in slightly later phrase, "had both feet on the ground." Barrett Riggs knew what he was about—that was the general opinion: he had learned about life in the highly thought of "university of hard knocks," and he had learned business and banking in the "hard school of experience." The general feeling was that if Barrett Riggs was going to be cashier of the new bank, the new bank was pretty sure to be all right.

In this way, that sensational and ill-starred institution that was sixteen years later to destroy a town, and to ruin the lives of thousands of its inhabitants, came into being. And its beginning, like the beginnings of so many similar institutions, was deceptively modest. The talk about the new bank presently became a fact—a modest fact. It was presently announced that a group of "conservative business men"—a dentist, an attorney, a merchant—were backing it. They were not going to run in competition with their older and more important brethren. This was not their purpose: it was their feeling that a growing town like Libya Hill was a steady increase in its population, its business and financial interest, could well use a new bank—such a bank as they proposed to found. It was, one gathered, to be an institution conducted on the most eminently approved principles vindicated by years of banking experience, but it was to be a "progressive" bank, too,—a forward looking bank, mindful of the future, of the great golden magnificent future that Libya Hill was sure to have—that it was even heresy to doubt. In this way, also, it was to be a kind of young man's bank. And this was where Barrett Riggs came in.

He could not have come in more fortuitously—the whole idea, the modest way in which it was proposed, found its instant approval. Everything was to be done so simply, so sanely, so conservatively, and without grandiose pretensions, and that was the way, people felt, anything that Barrett Riggs was connected with would be done.

When the project was at length sealed and confirmed, Barrett Riggs himself went around to people in the town and sold stock in the bank. He had no difficulty at all in selling it. People felt that here, if ever, there was a modest and sound investment. Nobody expected to make a fortune. Barrett Riggs made it quite plain that he did not think anyone was going to make a fortune. But, he said, here was a safe and honest investment: The stock sold for $100 a share, the bank was to be modestly capitalized in the sum of $25,000, there was therefore going to be two hundred fifty shares of stock, and, since in Barrett's telling phrase, the bank was really "a community project whose first and only purpose is to serve the community," no one was going to be allowed to buy too much of the stock. The four sponsors, including himself, were taking twenty-five shares apiece. It was their purpose to divide the remaining one hundred fifty shares among "a selected group"—this was another one of Barrett's phrases—of the leading business men in town. The elder Doaks apparently was included in this group and, thus encouraged, he was persuaded to buy ten shares without much difficulty.

This was the way the amazing bank got founded.

[*The narrative continues for thirty more pages describing the way the bank grew in power during the war years and the way it took its place in the social and political structure of the town.*]

Political and Social Notes

1937–1938

Wolfe's recent trips to Europe, his observation of the horrors of the Great Depression and the struggles of the Roosevelt administration to overcome it, and his living in a world threatened by Hitler, Mussolini, Franco, and Stalin had made him more politically sensitive than he had been in his youth. More than this, his growing identification of himself with his nation had turned his customary self-scrutiny to national scrutiny, and he was questioning some of the directions of the national life. These national and international concerns became mixed with his own anxieties about his independence and his accomplishment as an artist. Further stresses related to his recent entanglements in lawsuits confused him even more. As a result of all these areas of thought, a great many notes and fragments about his political views and about the social milieu of the artist are scattered among Wolfe's papers from the last two years of his life.

Although most of these notes cannot be dated exactly, we have gathered a selection of them and placed them here at the beginning of 1938, because early 1938 provided a number of occasions for Wolfe to think and write about his political views. On February 1, he received a letter from Donald Ogden Stewart of the League of American Writers who was conducting a poll of American authors on the question, "Are you for or are you against Franco and Fascism?" Then Freda Kirchway, editor of the Nation, *asked him to contribute an article to the series "How to Keep Out of War," and Clifton Fadiman asked him to set down his credo for the* Nation's *series* Living Philosophies.

The selections begin with some notations which reflect Wolfe's distress about his relationship with Scribner's and with the lawsuits he faced.

A MODEST PAMPHLET

Tending To Prove That Writers (and all others of their Ilk) Shall Be Allowed To Live and if the God-

damned Sons of Bitches Go Not Too Hardly At
The Task To Earn A Living and If It Be Not Too
Much To Suppose Be Allowed To Draw Their
Breath Occasionally Without Agony, Labor, Hor-
ror, Death, Damnation, And Attendant Abomina-
tions In This Home of Free People and Free Speech,
The United States of America

by

Thomas Wolfe

A MODEST COMMERCIAL PROPOSAL

Tending To Prove That Authors Are Members of
the Human Race And That If They Are Properly
Dealt With They Are As Tractable As Most Other
People And That the Publishing Profession Al-
though It Is As Well Known A Beneficent And
Philanthropic Enterprise Established As An Avoca-
tion By Gentlemen of Cultural and Sporting Tastes
Whose Fathers and Kinsmen Made Their Money
Out of Something Else May Still Derive Some Profit
Occasionally, If The Matter Be Shrewdly Dealt
With, Out of An Author, The Body, Bones, Brains,
Sweat Etc. of A Living Man

Code for Noble Lawyers

—He must always spring like a bulldog to the defense of the
imperiled artist who has been menaced in his right to say "shit" and
"fuck" whenever he wants to; but he has nothing to do, of course, in
behalf of the poor devil who is merely trying to use what talent nature
gave him, and who is being fleeced, swindled, harried, blackmailed, and
coerced by every racketeering lawsuit that the benevolent laws of this
great republic offer to every scoundrel who chooses to victimize an
honest man. It would, of course, be utterly ridiculous [*end of page*]

THE MYTHOLOGY OF PUBLISHING

The mythology of Publishing was this: that publishing was
different from other forms of capitalistic enterprise in that it was not
influenced by the profit motive. True, an author's works occasionally

sold in sufficient quantities to reward the publisher with a profit—a very modest one, one was told, in no ways commensurate with the outlay of time, expense, labor, care and risk that had been involved. But even when this happened, and there was a small profit, it was used mainly for the purpose of making up the deficits incurred by the publication of scores and scores of books which had not sold at all. Indeed, one was told that "the average book" did not even pay for itself: if a publisher could just break even on the cost of publication, he was lucky. If one enquired why the publisher published so many books with no hope of selling them, the publisher replied he published them because of his interest in literature, because he took pride in the publication of good books, regardless of whether they sold or not: publishing thus became a kind of handmaiden to the fine arts.

Among the elements of this mythology was an atmosphere of benevolent paternalism. One was forever hearing, in one form or another, of the great benevolence of the house to some outworn veteran of its service—old man Rivers was one of these. As James Rodney said: "I—I—I—why—I could make twice as much if I were ruthless and let them out but—but—but—but—why—I mean to say—money isn't everything."

One heard a great deal about old man Rivers, but very little of the young men and women in the packing department in the basement.

It seemed to him that they had translated the meaningless activity of their former lives into a new series of meaningless activities. The words were different but the music was the same. Formerly they had gone to "cocktail parties": now they went to "cocktail parties" for the Southern share-croppers, for the Spanish loyalists, for the Polish, German, or Roumanian Jews.

Causes (1935–1938)
    The Share Cropper
    The Striking Seamen
    Spain
    The Jews in Germany
(1931–1935)
    Communism
    The Technocrats
    The "Ideologies."

Sunday Evening (10:15) after just returning from open air Communist meeting in Union Square: Two groups—one, the larger one, soliciting funds for Loyalist Spain: at first, a comedian, a little man with a battered face and thinning hair talking the comic Italian dialect to make them laugh—"Duh Trotzky-kikes, an' Mussilina and-a duh castor oil"—not much salvation here: just to make them laugh—then young fellow of twenty or so haranguing them in a high rather hoarse voice—"help these American boys—3200 of them ready to face cold Facist steel—every penny counts"—after 20 or 30 minutes effort got $7.00 from 200 people.

In smaller group, a little man, small moustache, quiet spoken, Jewish, talking against Fascism—a broad-faced Italian worker takes him up—not argumentatively, but to explain why Mussolini got power in [*Italy*] [1] how there were schools now—how he had gone back to his own village and the improvements he had found—stated very simply he was not a fascist but asked the communist simply to recognize these facts—communist then went on with his "definition" of fascism—and what he said was sensible but now, confronted with certain physical facts that did not fit in with his plans, he reverted to the familiar formulas of the communist harangue—"Fascism was governmentalized capitalism"—why it [*had*] [2] to invade Ethiopia, and so on, in order to save itself—and why it meant disaster in the end—all of which I believe is true: but the communist weakness—a critical weakness in their program here in America—is their effort to ignore or evade facts that do not agree with their program—

1) The admission, first of all, that immediate benefits are likely to result from fascist dictatorship—it is useless to deny that this happened both in Italy and Germany, etc. etc.

What are some of the salient characteristics of fascism:
 1. Dictatorship
 2. Suppression of Free Speech, Free Thought, Free Press, In the Interest of Authoritative Purpose
 3. Oppression and Punishment of Minorities
It is obvious that these characteristics are also common to the present Russian regime.

—But, say the supporters of the present Russian regime, these characteristics are necessary for the consummation of an ultimately beneficent plan.

—But? Do not the Fascists say the same thing?

—But, say the opponents of Fascism and the proponents of the present Russian regime—the Russian Plan is a beneficent one and the Fascist Plan is a destructive one.

1. Wolfe had written "Spain" by mistake.
2. Wolfe had repeated "it" by mistake.

—Do not the proponents of the Fascist system say the same—that their Plan is a beneficent one and the Russian Plan a destructive one?

About Dictatorship:—the essential fact about dictatorship—i.e. its reason for *being*—is this: it is produced inevitably by a time of catastrophe or extreme peril—Extreme power is consigned by a people into the hands of an individual by a people in extreme distress, by a disorganized or bankrupt people, or by the people who feel the need of individual leadership in a time of crisis. Thus in this country, the political leaders with the greatest power have been Washington, Lincoln, Wilson, and in our own time, Roosevelt.

In an absolute sense, it is granted that none of these men were dictators—as someone has pungently observed, "When you have a dictator, you will know it, and you will not be permitted to discuss it" —and certainly the authorities of Washington, Lincoln, Wilson, and Roosevelt, have been not only freely discussed but freely and bitterly opposed; but in certain correct and special senses each of these men were given dictatorial powers. The hypothesis of repeal was always included—the idea that the power of the leader to dictate had been given to him by the consent of the people and could, by the dissent of the people, be revoked. Thus, Washington was always in trouble with his Assemblies, Lincoln with the bitterly dissident factions not only in his own government but in his own cabinet, Wilson with his Congress, Roosevelt with his critics, etc.

—But it is impossible to deny that each of these men, in his own way, engaged in a restricted dictatorship. This fact is clearly recognized today by the opponents of Roosevelt, the most sensible of whom agree he enjoys a restricted dictatorship granted freely to him through the free mandate of the people, but who fear that he will manipulate that trust and that mandate to his own purposes in such a way as to secure for himself, or for more dangerous successors, an arbitrary and dictatorial command of power. I, for one, do not share this fear, but everyone is well aware of it.

[*The following letter was never finished and never sent. Wolfe apparently felt that he had something publishable here, and he revised it to become a letter replying to someone who had written to him from Spain. He called it "A Spanish Letter" and later included it in his manuscript stack to be used in his novel about George Webber. Aswell used parts of it, somewhat rearranged, in* You Can't Go Home Again, *Chapter 38.*]

Mr. Donald Ogden Stewart
League of American Writers
38 14th Avenue
New York, New York

Dear Sir:

    I have received your letter of February 1st in which you ask the following questions: "Are you for, or are you against Franco and Fascism? Are you for, or are you against the legal government of the people of Republican Spain?" You say you desire to print my answer. Well, my answer is going to be long. But the reason it is going to be long is that I want to go upon the record here and now in such a clear, exact and unmistakable way that there will never be any doubt in the mind of anyone how I feel, or what it is that I am talking about. Incidentally, this is the first letter I have ever written in my life to any person, organization, or agency of public information either to express my own views on any subject intended for publication or to answer an invitaton to express them.

    What I am going to say is going to be pretty personal, and it is going to be personal because any opinion I may utter here has come not through what I have read, not from anything that has been suggested to me by someone else, nor from the intellectual influence of my associates and friends. It has come, as has every deep conviction of my life, from what I have seen, felt, thought, lived, experienced and found out for myself. It seems to me this is the way every man alive has got to find out things, and therefore, if what one man has found out in this way has any use or value for you, or seems important to you in any way, here it is:

    I came from the state of North Carolina, in the Middle South, and from, I think, the most conservative element of American life. All of my people, although for the most part people of modest and even humble circumstances, were people who had lived in this country and known its life for two hundred years or more, and so far as I know, until the last generation, there was not one of them who has ever lived in a city. My father was a stone-cutter, his father was a farm laborer, my mother's family were mountain people: all of them were politically, socially, religiously, and in every other way, a part of the most traditional element of this country's life; and my own childhood, boyhood, and early training was passed under these influences and under these circumstances.

    When I began to write, I began, as so many young men do, as a lyrical writer. My first book was a book about the life of a small town, and of the people there. I suppose the book followed a pretty familiar pattern, and that the central conflict was between a young fellow with sensitive feelings, and perhaps some talent, and the social forces around him—that is, the life of the small town, and the collisions of his own personality with it.

The solution, or resolution, of this conflict was also a familiar one: the hero solved it by escaping, by leaving the community and the environment with which he had been in conflict. Like many other young men of my age at the time I wrote that book, which appeared in 1929, my mind, while seething with feelings, thoughts, images, and swift and penetrating perceptions, was nevertheless a confused and troubled one. I was in conflict with the whole baffling complex of life, of society, and of the world around me. I was trying to shape a purpose, to find a way, and to know my own position. But, like many other people of that time, although I was not defeated, I was lost.

I suppose if anyone had questioned me to find out what I thought or what I believed, and above all, why I wanted to write books, I should have said that I wrote books because someday I hoped I would write a great one, that I would rather do this than anything in the world, that it seemed to me art was the highest thing in life, and that the life of the artist was the best and highest life a man could have. I might even have said in those days that art is enough, that beauty is enough, in William Morris' words that "Love is enough though the whole world be waning." And I think I should certainly have disagreed positively with anyone who suggested that the artist's life and work were in any way connected with the political and economic movements of his time.

Now that I no longer feel this way, I would not apologize for having felt so, nor sneer at the work I did, or at the work of other young men at that time who felt and thought as I did. It seems to me natural and almost inevitable that a young man should begin life as a lyrical writer, that his first picture of life, as reflected in his first work, should be a very personal one, and that he should see life and the world largely in terms of its impingements on his own personality, in terms of his personal conflicts or agreements with the structure of things as they are. As for the way we felt, or thought we felt, about art and love and beauty in those days, and how they were not only sufficient to all things, but that all things else were alien and remote to them, that too, perhaps, is a natural and inevitable way for young men to feel. And it certainly was a product of the training, the culture, and the aesthetic ideas of that time.

But I have found out something else, for myself at least, in the past few years. And it is this: you can't go home again—back to your childhood, back to the father you have lost, back to the solacements of time and memory—yes, even back to art and beauty and to love. For me, at any rate, it is now manifest that they are not enough. And I do not think that this be treason, but if it be, then—.

I began to find out about it six or seven years ago, when I was living and working on a book in Brooklyn, and I have been finding out about it ever since. I do not know when it first began, perhaps such things as these have no actual moment of beginning, but I do know that one day I got a letter from a person who was speaking about love and art and beauty. It was a good letter, but after I had read it I looked out the window and across the street I saw a man. He was digging with his hand into a garbage can for food: I have a good memory for places and for time and this was half-way through December 1932. And I know that since then I have never felt the same way about love or art or beauty or thought they were enough.

This thing has all come slowly, because although thinking, feeling, perceiving, even working and writing, have always come to me with a rush, upon a kind of furious and tremendous tide, the resolution of things is very slow, because, as I have said, nothing is any good to me, nor I think to any man, until we find it for ourselves. And I know now that you can't go home again.

For four years, then, I lived and worked in Brooklyn. I worked like a locomotive. I certainly did not get around very much in literary circles. But I do not think I missed much of what was going on around me, in Brooklyn—which really *is* the world, or has the whole world in it—among my people down in North Carolina, in my native town, or in the country as a whole. And I think the reason I did not miss much was because I was so hard at work. People have told me that such work shuts one off from life. But that is not true. Such work is life, and enhances the whole sense and understanding of life immeasurably. So was it with me, at any rate.

Early in 1935, I finished a big job of work and went abroad for the first time in four years. I went to Germany, because of all the countries I have ever seen, outside of my own, that, I think, is the country I have liked the best, in which I have felt most at home, with whose people I have felt the most natural, instant, and instinctive sympathy and understanding. It is also the country whose magic and mystery have haunted me the most. I had thought about it many times: after the labor, the fury, and the exhaustion of those four Brooklyn years, it meant peace for me, and release, and happiness, and the old magic again.

I had not been there since the fall of 1930. Then I had stayed in a little town in the Black Forest, and there was great excitement among the people, for a great national election was being held. The state of politics was chaotic, there was a bewildering number of political parties —more than forty million votes, as I recall, were cast in the great Wahl [*election*]. That year the Communists alone got four million votes, or more.

This time, the thing was different. Germany had changed. Some people told me that there was no such confusion or chaos in politics or government now, because everyone was so happy. And I should have been. For I think no man ever went to a foreign land under more propitious conditions than did I early in May, 1935.

It is said that Byron awoke one morning at the age of twenty-four to find himself famous. I had to wait ten years longer. I was thirty-four when I reached Berlin, but it was magic just the same. I suppose I was not really very famous. But it was just as good, because for the first and last time in my life I felt as if I were. A letter had reached me from America telling me that my second book had been successful there, and my first book had been translated and published in Germany a year or two before. The German critics had said tremendous things about it, my name was known. When I got to Berlin people were waiting for me.

It was the month of May: along the streets, in the Tiergarten, in the great gardens, and along the Spree Canal, the horse chestnut trees were in full bloom. The great crowds sauntered underneath the trees on the Kurfürstendamm, the terraces of the cafés were crowded with people, and always, through the golden sparkle of the days, there was a sound of music in the air, the liquid smack of leather boots upon the streets as men in uniform came by with goose precision. There are so many chains of endless lovely lakes around Berlin, and for the first time I knew the wonderful golden bronze upon the tall poles of the Kiefern trees: I had only known the South, the Rhinelands and Bavaria before. And now Brooklyn, and four years of work, the man who prowled into the garbage can, and the memory of grim weather, were far away.

It was a glorious period for a week. I suppose in some way I connected the image of my own success, this happy release after years of toil and desparation, with May, the Kiefern trees, the great crowds thronging the Kurfürstendamm, all of the golden singing of the air— somehow with a feeling that for everyone grim weather was behind and that happy days were here again.

I had heard some ugly things, but I did not see them now. I did not see anyone beaten, I did not see anyone imprisoned, or put to death, I did not see any of the men in concentration camps, I did not see openly anywhere the physical manifestations of a brutal and compulsive force. True, there were men in brown shirts everywhere, there were men in leather boots and black uniforms, in uniforms of olive green around one everywhere, there was about one everywhere in the great streets the solid liquid smack of booted feet, the blare of brass, the tootling fifes, the memory of young faces shaded under iron helmets, with folded arms and ramrod backs, precisely seated in great army lorries.

But all of this was so mixed in with May, and the horse chestnut trees, the great cafés in the Kurfürstendamm, and the genial temper of the people making holiday, as I had seen and known it on so many pleasant times before that even if it did not now seem good, it did not seem sinister or bad.

Then something happened. It didn't happen suddenly. It just happened as a cloud gathers, as fog settles, as rain begins to fall.

Someone I had met was giving me a party and asked me if I should like to ask any of the people I had met to come to it. I mentioned one. My party host was silent for a moment; he looked embarrassed: then he told me the person I had mentioned had formerly been the editorial head of a publication that had been suppressed, and that one of the people who had been instrumental in its suppression had been invited to the party, so would I mind—?

I named another, and again the anxious pause, the embarrassment, the painful silence. This person was—was—well, he knew this person and he knew he did not go to parties, he would not come were he invited, so would I mind—? (A year later I found out why he did not go to parties, and why he would not come: by that time the reason could be talked of openly: he was a Jew.) I named another, a woman I had met, whom I had liked. Again, the anxious pause, the painful silence. How long had I known this woman? Where, under what circumstances, had I met her?

I tried to reassure my host on all these scores. I told him he need have no fear of any sort about this woman. He was instant, swift, in his apologies—oh, by no means: he was sure the lady was eminently all right—only, nowadays—with a mixed gathering—he had tried to pick a group of people I had met and liked, who all knew one another—he had thought that it would be much more pleasant that way—strangers at a party were often shy at first, constrained, and formal with each other—so would I mind—?

A friend came to see me: "In a few days," he said, "you will receive a phone call from a certain person. He will try to meet you, to

talk to you. Have nothing to do with this man. His name is _____."
When I asked him why this man should try to meet me, and why, if he
did, I should be afraid of him, he would not answer, he just muttered:
"This is a bad man. We have a name for him: it is 'the Prince of
Darkness.' " [3] In a few days the man that he had named did call up, and
did want to meet me. I wish that I could say that all of this was as
laughable and as melodramatic as it may sound. But the tragedy is, it
was not.

Not that it was political. I am not trying to suggest that it was.
The roots of it were much more sinister and deep and evil, and in their
whole and tragic implication more far-reaching than politics or even
racial prejudice could ever be. For the first time in my life, I came
upon something, I began to feel and experience the full horror of
something that I had never known before—something that made all the
swift violence and passion of America, the gangster compacts, the swift
killing, all the confusion, harshness, and corruption that infect portions
of our own life seem innocent by comparison. And this was the picture
of a great people who were spiritually sick, psychically wounded: who
had been poisoned by the contagion of an ever-present fear, the
pressure of a constant and infamous compulsion, who had been silenced
into a sweltering and malignant secrecy, until spiritually they were
literally drowning in their own secretions, dying from the distillations
of their own self poison, for which now there was no medicine or
release.

Can anyone be so base as to exult at this great tragedy—a
tragedy in which the whole world shares today—or to feel hatred for
the great and mighty people who have been the victims of it? Cultur-
ally, it seems to me, from the eighteenth century on, the German was
the first citizen of Europe. In Goethe there was made sublimely
articulate the expression of a world spirit which knew no boundary
line of race, or color, or religion, which rejoiced in the inheritance of
all mankind, and which wanted no domination and no conquest of that
inheritance, save the knowledge of his own contribution and participation in it.

From the eighteenth century, in an unbroken line, down to the
present one, that spirit in art, in literature, in music and in philosophy,
has continued, until there is not a man or woman in the world today
who is not, in one way or another, the richer for it. When I first went

---

3. Perhaps Rudolf Diels (1900–1957), the former head of the Secret Police
(Gestapo), who had fallen into disfavor with Hitler but had been spared in the
June purge of 1934. Diels had become a friend of Martha Dodd's. Diels later
wrote a book entitled *Lucifer Ante Portas* (Zurich, 1949?).

to Germany, in 1926, the evidence of that spirit was manifest everywhere, even in the most simple and unmistakable ways. One could not, for example, pass the crowded window of a book shop in any town in Germany without observing instantly the overwhelming evidence of the intellectual and cultural enthusiasm of the German people. Now that the 'indignation' of the world is aroused it is too easy to sneer at these things as evidences of Teutonic ponderosity, Prussian pedagogics, another evidence of the unimaginative heaviness of their temperament. But the plain blunt truth of the matter is that it was a magnificent and noble thing, and, without drawing an invidious comparison, a careful examination of the contents of a German bookshop or of a bookseller's window, in 1926, would have revealed a breadth of vision, an interest in the cultural production of the whole world that would have made the contents of a French bookshop, with its lingual and geographic constriction, seem paltry by comparison.

The best writers of every country in Europe were as well known in Germany as in their own land. The names of such American writers as Theodore Dreiser, Sinclair Lewis, Upton Sinclair, Jack London, were not only well known, but their books were sold and read everywhere throughout the country; and the work of our younger writers was eagerly published, welcomed, read, and judged as was the work of writers everywhere throughout the world.

Even in 1935 when, after an absence of almost five years, I saw the country again, and for the first time under the regime of Adolph Hitler, the evidences of this noble enthusiasm, now submerged and mutilated, were apparent in the most touching way. It has been said by some people that there are no more good books published in Germany, because good books can no longer be published or read. This is not true as so many things one reads about Germany today are not true. And about Germany today we must be very true. And the reason that we must be very true is that the thing we are against is false: we can not turn the other cheek to wrong, but also we cannot be wrong about wrong. We can not meet wrong with wrong: we must be right about it. And we can not meet lies and falsehood with lies and falsehood, although there are people who argue otherwise.

So it is not true to say that good books can no longer be published or read in Germany. And because it is not true, the tragedy of Germany, and the survival of the great German spirit, even in the devious and distorted ways in which it does now manifest itself, is more movingly evident than it would be if it were true. Good books are still published where the substance and material of good books does not in any way controvert or either openly or by implication criticize the present regime. It would simply be foolish and stupid to assert that any good book must so controvert or criticize the present regime, just because it is a good book.

For all these reasons, the eagerness, the curiosity, and the enthusiasm of Germans for the books which they are still allowed to read has been, if anything, movingly intensified. Their eagerness to find out what is going on in the world, what is being written and published outside Germany, their generous enthusiasm for such American writing as they are now allowed to read is as overwhelming as it is pathetic. One might liken the survival of the German spirit, under these conditions, to that of a man dying of thirst in a dry land, gulping greedily at a flask of water; or to a man who is drowning, clutching desperately at the floating spar of his own wrecked ship.

Everywhere about me, as time went on during that spring and summer of 1935, I saw the evidences of this dissolution, this shipwreck of a great spirit, this miasmic poison that sank like a pestilential fog through the very air, tainting, sickening, blighting with its corrosive touch, through fear, pressure, suppression, insane distrust and spiritual disease, the lives of everyone I met. It was, and was everywhere, as invisible as a plague, and as unmistakable as death; it sank in on me through all the golden singing of that May, until at last I felt it, breathed it, lived it, and knew it for the thing it was.

I returned to Germany again for the last time perhaps that I shall ever be allowed to visit or to see that magic land again, in 1936. This time, the welcome that I got was even greater than it had been the year before. My second book had just been published, and it had received a great reception: now everywhere I went there were people who knew my work. But something had gone out of life for me.

The pestilence of the year before had spread and deepened so that there was not a person I had known before who had not perceptibly grown, within the space of one short year, sick and stricken as he had not been before. The evidence of pressure and of fear was everywhere sharply more apparent as soon as one reestablished contact with the lives that he had known. The personal evidences were appalling and too innumerable to relate, but here are a few:

I was told that a little man whom I had known before, and who had been previously employed in a publishing house, wanted to see me. And this time again, I had been invited to a party to meet some old friends and some other people who had read my books. This time also I suggested to my host that he invite this little man. And this time he told me very simply that it was impossible: he said that in the course of the past year, this little man and all others like him in the Reich had been discharged from his employment, for this little man was a Jew; and that therefore it would be impossible for me now to invite him to a party, or unwise to meet him in a public place, but that if I wanted to see him a meeting in a private place could be arranged.

And so I met him in secrecy in a room one afternoon. And this little man came in, and I had known him before, not very well. And now, what was there to say? He was a little scrap of a man, not more than five feet tall, and he had always been a shabby looking little man, and now I saw him and remembered he was wearing the same shabby little suit that he had always worn, except that now his shabby little suit was frayed and patched, and his collar was clean, but he had turned it, and it had the mottled look that collars have when people launder them themselves. He wore a shoe-string of a tie, and his neck and Adam's apple were as thin and stringy as a piece of gristle, and his eyes were like sunk comets in his face. His little claw-like hands were cold as fish and trembled when he talked; and all that I can remember that he said to me, shaking his head upon that gristle of a neck was, "Sir—sir—the world is very sad, sir; the world is very sad."

And this is all I remember that man saying, and then he got up and went out, and I never saw him any more; and, so help me God, this is the truth of it, as exactly and literally as I remember the whole thing.

Well I can't go home again.

A man I knew had asked me to his home for lunch: he was a German of an ancient family, and in scholarship his forbears had had a famous name for a hundred years or more. The year before I had seen him frequently; and there had been one evening at a café when, after much beer, at three o'clock, he talked to me as he had never talked before. He laid bare the secret of his own devotion, and the secret of his hate; and what he said to me that night was such that he would have gone before a firing squad had it been known.

And now, after one year's absence I saw this man again. We sat down to lunch in his apartment, high up, between the thick and ponderous walls of a great house in Berlin; there were geraniums on the window sills, the windows were thrown open, but the sounds of life and of Berlin seemed securely far away. He began to talk again, and then he saw those open windows, and like a man who shuts himself away from the foul contagions of a pestilence, he sprang to his feet, ran to the windows, closed and locked them, and then turned upon his wife and in a trembling voice reviled her for her carelessness.

She tried to quiet him and told him that there was no danger, that the walls were thick, and that they were so high above the street that no one passing by could hear. And like someone trembling on the verge of a hysteria, he told her that in these times no one could be sure of anything, and that there were people listening everywhere.

Before I left that day I asked him and his wife if they would come and dine with me before I left Berlin. I told them I had met a girl,[4] and suggested that I ask her too, in order that our dinner would even up at four. Quick as a flash, with mistrust baleful in his eyes, he pounced on me, and put me through a rapid fire of questioning: Who was this woman? How long had I known her? Under what circumstances had I met her? Who had introduced her to me? What had I heard or known or been able to find out about her?—and when I answered all these things he turned to his wife, and speaking bitterly to her in German, said: "You see the way it is? The minute that a man like this comes here they put a woman on his trail"—which was grotesque, unbelievable, absurd—if it had not been so horrible and so tragic, too.

He turned to me more quietly and said: "I'm sorry, but what you ask is quite impossible. We cannot meet people whom we do not know." I left him then. We shook hands, and said good-bye, and we knew we should not see each other any more.

But when I told the girl, her eyes too grew black and dark with suspicion and mistrust. She said in her somewhat broken English: "Who is this man? Where did you meet him?"—and then, turning away she muttered something I had heard her say before: "You do not understand . . . these things—they cannot be! It is impossible! . . . there is not private life any more." I understood her then.

It was the season of the great Olympic Games, and every day I went to the Stadium in Berlin. And, just as that year of absence had marked the evidence of a cruel and progressive dissolution in the lives of all the people I had known, so had it also marked the overwhelming evidence of an increased concentration, a stupendous organization, a tremendous drawing together and ordering, in the vast collective power of the whole land. And as if these Games had been chosen as a symbol of this new collected might, the means of showing to the world in concrete terms what this new power had come to be. It seemed that every energy and strength in the whole country had been collected and disciplined to this end. It is probable that no more tremendous demonstration has been known in modern times: the Games were no longer Games, no longer a series of competitive exercises to which the nations of the world had sent their chosen teams. The Games were an orderly and overwhelming demonstration in

4. Thea Voelcker.

which the whole nation had been schooled, and in which the whole nation took a part.

No one who witnessed that tremendous demonstration will ever forget it. In the sheer pageantry of the occasion, the games themselves were overshadowed. But the great organizing strength and genius of the German people, which has been used so often to such noble purpose, had never been more thrillingly displayed than it was now. There had never been in the whole history of the Games, such complete and perfect preparation, and such calm and ordered discipline.

With no past experience in such affairs, the German people had constructed a mighty Stadium which was not only the most beautiful, but the most perfect in its design and purpose that any nation has designed in modern times.

And all the attendant and accessory elements of this great plant —the swimming pools, the great halls, and the lesser stadia, had all been laid out and designed with this same cohesion of beauty and of use.

The organization was superb. Day after day enormous crowds, such as no other city in modern times has had to cope with, and such as would certainly have congested and maddened the traffics of New York, and all its transportational facilities, were handled with a quietness, and order, and a speed that was astounding.

The daily spectacle was overwhelming in its beauty and magnificence. From one end of Berlin to another, from the Lustgarten to the Brandenburger Tor, along the whole broad sweep of Unter den Linden, through the vast alleys and avenues of the faery green Tiergarten, out through the great West of Berlin to the very portals of the Stadium, the town was a thrilling pageantry of royal banners—not merely endless yards and miles of looped-up bunting, but banners fifty feet in height, such as might have graced the battle tent of some great emperor. It was a thrilling tournament of color that caught the throat, and that in its massed splendor and grand dignity made all the gaudy decorations of our own Worlds' Fairs, inaugurations, great parades, look like a scheme of shoddy carnivals in the comparison.

And all through the day, from morning on, Berlin became a mighty Ear, attuned, attentive, focused, on the Stadium. From one end of the city to the other, the air became a single voice. The green trees along the Kurfürstendamm began to talk: out of the viewless air, concealed and buried in ten thousand trees, a voice to four million people from the Stadium—and for the first time in his life, a Yankee ear had the strange adventure of hearing the familiar terms of track and field translated in the tongue that Goethe used. He would be informed now that the Vorlauf would be run—and now the Zwischenlauf—at length the Endlauf—and the winner: Owens—Oo–Ess–Ah.[5]

Meanwhile, through those tremendous banner-laden ways, the crowds thronged ceaseless all day long. From end to end the great wide promenade of Unter den Linden was solid with a countless horde of patient, tramping German feet. Fathers, mothers, children, young folks, old, the whole material of the nation was there from every corner of the land, trudged wide-eyed, full of wonder, past the marvel of those ceaseless banner-laden ways from morn to night.

And in between one saw the glint of foreign faces: the dark features of the Frenchman or Italian, the ivory grimace of the Jap, the straw hair and the blue eyes of the Swede, bright stabs of color of Olympic jackets, the big Americans, natty in straw hats, blue coats, crested with Olympic seal, and white flannels; and other teams from other nations, with gay and jaunty colors of their own.

And there were great displays of marching men, sometimes ungunned but rhythmic, great regiments of brown shirts swinging through the streets; again, at ease, young men and laughing, talking with each other, long lines of Hitler's bodyguards, black-uniformed and leather-booted, the Schutz-Staffel men, stretching in unbroken lines from Leader's residence in the Wilhelmstrasse up to the arches of the Brandenburger Tor; then suddenly the sharp command, and instantly, unforgettably, the liquid smack of ten thousand leather boots as they came together, with the sound of war.

By noon, all of the huge approaches to the Games, that enchanted laneway that the Leader would himself take from the Wilhelmstrasse to the Great Stadium, miles away, were walled in by the troops, behind which patient, dense, incredible, the masses of the nation waited day by day.

And if the inside of the Stadium was a miracle of color, structure, planned design, the outside, that enormous mass of people waiting, waiting, was a memory one could not forget. All had been planned and shaped to this triumphant purpose, maybe; but the people—they had not been planned. They just stood there and waited, day by day—the poor ones of the earth, the humble ones of life, the workers and the wives, the mothers and the children of the land. They were there because they had not money enough to buy the magic little

5. Martha Dodd tells the story of Wolfe's whooping so loudly over one of the triumphs of Jesse Owens, the great Negro athlete, that Hitler threw one of his scornful frowns at the diplomatic box, where Wolfe was seated. *Through Embassy Eyes*, p. 212.

cardboard square that would have given them a place within that magic ring. They were there for just one purpose—to wait from morn to night for just two brief and golden moments of the day: the moment when the Leader came, the moment when he went.

And at last he came: and something like a wind across a field of grass was shaken through that crowd, and from afar the tide rolled up with him, in which was born the hope, the voice, the prayer of the land. And Hitler came by slowly in a shining car, erect and standing, moveless and unsmiling, with his hand upraised, palm outward, not in Nazi-wise salute, but straight up, with such blessing and such gesture that the Buddha or Messiahs use [*breaks off*]

[*The following note was probably made in connection with Wolfe's letter to the* Nation, *April 2, 1938, in which he opposed American isolationism and warned that the democracies must get ready to act effectively "to oppose the aggressions of Germany, Italy, and Japan." For the text, see* Letters, *pp. 735–36.*]

A WORD IN TIME OF DOUBT

My own position is not, and has never been, a pacifist position. I do not believe that, in the present structure of society, wars are inevitably useless and inevitably to be avoided.

For example, I think that the Revolutionary War in the United States had to be fought; the Civil War in the United States had to be fought; the participation of the United States [*in the World War*] [6] had to be made. I think such wars as the War of 1812, the Mexican War, the Spanish American War, the Border Wars on Mexico, might have been avoided.

[*The following batch of notes preceded Wolfe's writing a satirical letter directed against Franco in the* Nation, *May 21, 1938. For the final version, see* Letters, *pp. 752–54. Worried about the success of his ironies, Wolfe assured the editor that it was "wrote sarcastical."*]

—I have read with great interest the recent remarks of Mr. Ellery Sedgwick and his account of what General Franco is doing in the interests of his people.

—Spain: the creation of ruins—Germany, of new roads.

—their enterprising governments.

6. Wolfe had started to write "the World War had to be fought," but scratched it out.

—I have never shared the general American disrespect for ruins: Mark Twain's act.

—The encouragement of peaceful trade.

A Letter to the Editor (on Spain)

Sir: I wonder if you could turn this inquiry over to someone in your Travel Department who could inform me if there are going to be any Conducted Tours to Spain this summer.

—I understand that General Franco has not only taken the greatest precautions in preserving the old ruins, but has even shown remarkable ingenuity and enterprise (gone to considerable trouble and expense) in the creation of new ones.

[*The following notes on fascism, communism, and democracy, written on various kinds of paper, reflect perhaps Wolfe's attempt to formulate a credo for Fadiman's series.*]

I believe in neither Fascism nor Communism, and I do not believe that one is forced to choose between the two. But if the decision ever rested on that choice, I should choose Communism. I cannot agree with people who say that both are equally bad and identical.

I believe in the preservation of the idea of democracy at any cost, as the most valuable idea of government and life that has been produced. I do not believe in the preservation of the capitalist system as it now exists; and I believe that it must either change voluntarily by directive force within; or that it will be changed forcibly by pressure from without. I do not hold that the idea of democracy, and the idea of free capitalist enterprise are synonymous.

If it is necessary for me here to define my own political position, I should say it was definitely socialistic veering to the left.

If I had to state my politics I'd call myself a social democrat. And by social democrat I would understand a man who believes in socialism but not in communized socialism, and in democracy but not individualized democracy.[7]

7. When this passage was quoted in Kennedy, *The Window of Memory*, p. 370, the "but not in" before "communized socialism" was omitted by mistake.

I do not believe in the abolition of private property, in the class warfare, or in the so-called dictatorship of the proletariat. I do not believe also in the abolition of free inquiry, or that the ideas represented by "freedom of thought," "freedom of speech," "freedom of press" and "free assembly" are just rhetorical myths. I believe rather that they are among the most valuable realities that men have gained, and that if they are destroyed men will fight to have them.

I do not think there is any grave "Communist danger" in America at the present time.

But I do think there is a grave Fascist danger, and it is with Fascism that I am concerned.

A FEW MILD WORDS,

Modestly Interposed, in time of doubt, with a view toward showing that the ideas of human liberty, freedom of speech, thought, and expression, are not the Victorian clap-trap they are now commonly allowed to be, in the best circles, but may even have a certain value in eternity, and return again; that a man has some right to be heard with some show of respectful attentiveness and some effort at reasonable consideration on the part of the listeners instead of greeted with a convulsed lip, a glittering eye, and a raucous handful of categorical catch-words and hand-me-down cat-calls as a poor benighted son-of-a bitch who doesn't know his ass from the House of Morgan because he doesn't happen to agree with the enlightened ones.

I do not think political democracy has failed, but I think its processes have been so corrupted and weakened everywhere that its failure is possible, and its survival dubious. As a method of individual life and general government the democratic ideal still seems to me to be the best one that men have conceived.

If democracy means social equality, they did not, as we have seen, have it. If it means economic equality, they did not, as we have seen, have it. If it means freedom of speech, they did not have it. If it means freedom of the press, they did not have it. If it means political equality, they had it only insofar as they were allowed to go to the polls and drop in their ballot. In practice, this equality was denied the negro population, which was 30% of the town. As to their actual right to choose and select their leaders, it was almost negative. Their leaders were selected for them in advance by the political groups that controlled the state, the county and the town. If the citizen had any choice at all, it was at best between two or three candidates of contending parties who had been picked in advance by the leaders who controlled the politics of these parties.

We know that, having established the country with a high and consecrated sense of man's spiritual enlargement, we came to care for little save the enlargement of the paunch and of the pocket-book.

—We know these things—we know them with our lives, our hearts, our spirits—yes, our spirits *still* are living in America, even with betrayal.

—Is it not true that on great trains that pound and lengthen to their stride across the continent we have whipped past scrofulic tank towns of the Middle West and seen the station, the stacked oil tanks by the tracks, the big grain elevators, painted red—a moment of light here —and the dreary blistered little rickets of a town, littered around and bogged down in fat thickets of unwholesome weeds—unpainted, joyless, lean-to, stinking as their backyard's privy—the baked sun-made horror of the one main street, flanked by its rows of wretched raw-brick concrete stores and shops, the back yards jumbled up with filth—old crates and boxes, tin-cans, rusty water-cans and slimy mud cobwebbed with hens-feet, stinking with their dung.

—and as we saw all this, did our hearts cry out with joy and did we murmur piously: "O God has smiled upon this favored land—thank God the standard of our living is so high compared to that of Holland, Denmark, Sweden and those other backward nations."

Is it not true that we had Fathers of a Revolution in this country, and devotion to a faith—and that now we have—*Daughters of a Revolution*—and a devotion to—God help us if that vicious scum of filth and lying and betrayal is all we have to be devoted to! Is it not true that having known faith and freedom in this land, and an image of free institutions, the very words that once gave life and hope to us have been so befouled and slobbered over by the politician getting votes, the politician painting his swollen face with spurious rage, that they have now gone dead and stale and foul for us—and that Croesus with his filthy money-bags at stake invokes the Constitution and the Ten Com-

mandments in a single breath, howls out that liberty—his *own* liberty
to get—is in dire peril, and that the ancient rights of Americans—yes!
the dunghill rights of Croesus to his money-bags—is being menaced by
the foes of liberty—foes of Croesus! foes of hell!

It may be well opposed by the readers of these lines that having
spoken of this dark wound of America, I yet have failed to tell them
what it is—and I admit that this is true. But is it easy instantly to name
a nameless thing, at once to probe the sources of a nameless hurt, to
find at once a name, a reason, and a cure for some twisted, dark and
obscure hurt that has been riven in the fundamentals of life? But so
agreeing, that however bad or mixed or hidden our great hurt may be
—so agreeing we must find a name, a cause, a light, a remedy for it—let
me ask you this: is it not true that we are all ashamed? Is it not true
that there is in our hearts the knowledge of betrayal—vicious, cow-
ardly betrayal—self-betrayal of ourselves, America's betrayal of her
self? Is it not true that all of us are conscious in our hearts that there
was hope of high and glorious fulfillment in America—and that that
high and glorious fulfillment has not only never been achieved but that
even the *promise* of that high and glorious fulfillment has been so
aborted, corrupted, made dropsical with disease, that its ancient and
primeval lineaments are no more to be seen? Is it not true that we were
given here for the enrichment and improvement of man's life a golden
wilderness, and that we have made of it a wilderness of horror, ugliness
and confusion? Is it not true that we began here with an ideal of a free
man's life, enlarging and fulfilling its whole purpose in an atmosphere
of free and spacious enlightenment—and is it not true that what we
have is for the most part just a mongrel and disordered mob—a jargon
of a thousand tongues, the mouthpiece of a million vicious and sensational rumours—but with no *faith*, no *freedom*, no *belief*—a slave-like
swarm without the dignities of slavery—a duped, doped horde who
seek or want no remedy for the diseases that prey upon them—and
themselves so vicious, infamous, and base, that one does not know
which is more hateful or more odious—the fools who take it, or the
knaves who dupe?

Or is this all untrue? Is it rather true—as we are now piously
informed every day—that "with all its imperfections the American
system is the best on earth, and offers the highest promise of development to the common man?" Is it really true, and do we believe it?
When we walk out on the streets and make our way along Sixth
Avenue, do our hearts sing out with joy at the glory and excellence of
the life we have achieved? When we see the little rabble—groups of

men all huddled round the signs of the employment agencies along Sixth Avenue, when we see their vicious and defeated faces, the dismal improvender of their lives—not, by the way, "no food," "no clothes," "no joy," and "no security"—but what is worse, bad food, bad clothes, bad joy, and insecurity—when we see the dreary street, tormented by its thousand dreary architectures, tormented by the jungle of its rusty signs, tormented by the rusty rackets of its elevated, tormented by the wasteland horror of its little shops, hot dog stands, grease-and-food emporiums, shooting galleries, etc.—tormented most of all by its racing violence of the million dreary, ill-fed, thrusting, seeking and courting tenants of its ugly little lives—when we see all this, do not our hearts cry out with joy at the richness, glory, and abundance of the life we have produced?

Or, do not our souls sing out for joy when we see Jersey City? When we explore that spreading blot of brick and stone, that rusty, dismal jungle known as Brooklyn that goes on forever wholly without plan or end, middle or beginning—do our spirits sink into the drowning sea-depths of unplumbed, unutterable despair—or do we give thanks for what God and man has wrought—for this triumph of rugged individuals which has sown three million human lice across this waste whenever a vacant lot could be found to build upon?

"To hate America or love her?"—Great God, if by so doing either one, I could find out the hurt in me, if by so doing I could find America's [*breaks off*]

—We've got to *loathe* America, as we loathe ourselves; with loathing, horror, shame, and anguish of the soul unspeakable—as well as with love—we've got to face the total horror of our self-betrayal, the way America has betrayed herself.

Let us do what Whitman dreamed—let us stick to each other as long as we live [8]—and let us find out who and what and why we are!

HOW LITTLE OF AMERICA GETS IN PRINT

(The Reason America Did Not Get In Print Was Not Because of Lack of Consciousness: We Knew About It But We Could Not Say It)

8. A paraphrase of the concluding line of "The Song of the Open Road."

McHarg (His Works As An Illustration In All Ways)
My Self (My Lack to Him and My Superiority)
The Newspapers
Henry Adams (Returning to N.Y.—the view of the explosive architectures—the fault with this now)
Henry James (a letter: the "thin" American landscape, etc.—the truth and fault of this)
Sacco and Vanzetti (the truth and fault of this—? the slot machine used?)

A Note on the Quality of Night and Darkness in American Writing:

It seems to me that all American writing of the first mark has had in it a quality of darkness and night—I mention Poe, Hawthorne, Melville, Whitman (most decidedly), Mark Twain, and Sherwood Anderson.

—The Yankee temper has too often been assumed to be shrewd, pungent, homely, everyday, and matter-of-fact—Caleb Smithers not to be taken in on a horse-trade, Lincoln telling the man who asked him how long his legs were that they were "long enough to reach to the ground"—but, say—think of that face, that gaunt and homely figure for a moment—is Lincoln of the *day* or is he of the *night*—and is the reason that this man belongs indubitably to darkness only that the time and the event that produced him is a dark time and a dark event? I do not think this is the reason.

And if Caleb, Abner, Silas, Artemus, and Will are Yankee types —then are no less Melville, Whitman, Hawthorne, Anderson and Poe the Yankee individuals.

—in Mark Twain—how that huge river moves itself—not like a shining golden serpent of the day—but how it drinks from out the continent, moves forever like a mighty, dark and secret river of the night. Of specific instances, indeed, there is no lack—the nighttime scenes in Huckleberry Finn—etc.

—the great gold ring of Chaucer's coin is not for us—nor Shakespeare—Hamlet [*is*] dark and Macbeth full of midnight hell and Lear storm-Stygian—yet the whole of it is all slashed through with gold and light. It is not so—not in this way—with Whitman, Melville or with Poe—the corn blades standing hot and odorous at noon, the thick hot air and coarse fertility, the humid bottoms of the Mississippi—but what strikes deeper to our hearts are the corn-blades rustling in the night, "Ah, coarse and sweet, ah, coarse and sweet, America."

—and I know—and so do *you*—a million other things about this land as well: the pitchers warming up before the game in May—Grove swinging lightly with his lean left whip, tobacco wadded gauntly in his jaw, eight thousand men in shirtsleeves sprawled out comfortably in the stadium and the look upon their faces. Ruth next at bat and coming up and kneeling swiftly on his bat in a white circle—who that saw *that* will ever more forget it!

—as we go seeking through this huge sprawling and chaotic land—the truth we seek may just be found—and unmistakable, and without a reason—just in little things—a man upon the road eight miles from Gettysburg in apple-orchard time in Pennsylvania and early morning and slanting rain, the wet clean fragrance of the apple-blossoms—"There," said he "are Stokes' Delicious—it's a good apple—but as for me, give me a good Grimes."

Pocket Notebook 33
Early 1938 to April 25, 1938

The first five months of 1938 were devoted to preparing a publishable manuscript to give to Harper's editor Edward Aswell. At first Wolfe worked and reworked his plan for a book about Joe Doaks, which focused on his experiences since the publication of Look Homeward, Angel. *But an inner urge kept compelling him to pull more and more of his material into an ever-lengthening autobiographical narrative. Finally he decided to compile into one mammoth work all his available manuscript: the early history of the Joyners and the brick-mason Wes Spangler, the chapters about childhood and youth associated with George Spangler, the love story about Esther Jack, the satirical materials about the adventures of Joe Doaks—plus whatever else he could salvage from the left-over scraps of "K 19" and* Of Time and the River. *Since he had accepted an invitation to speak at Purdue University on May 19, he set this date as a deadline for himself and was able to put his manuscript into tentative order for delivery to Aswell on the day of his departure.*

YOU CAN'T GO HOME AGAIN

"Once upon a time" etc.
"The time that is lovely" etc.
But you can't go home again.
Heard lost voices in the mountains long ago . . . the men on the roads—the ghost returning.
But—well, you can't go home again.

Jim Agee [1]
121 Le Roy St.

1. James Agee (1909–1957), who had attracted critical attention with his first volume of poems *Permit Me Voyage* in 1934, was eager to meet Wolfe. Miss Nowell brought him over to Wolfe's hotel one afternoon, during the course of which the two voluble Southerners exchanged views at great length about America, about social problems, and about the life of the American artist.

Mike Gold and wife [2]
Friday night, 7:15—Drug Store in Times Building.

Since 1923:
    N.Y.U.
    Europe
    Mrs. B.
    L.H.A. (Asheville)
    Oktoberfest
    Brooklyn
    Max and Scribners
    Of Time and the River
    The Medusa
    You Can't Go Home Again
    Farewell—and Hail!

Tenative:
    Prolog
    Old Catawba
    Libya Hill: The Older Doaks
    The Doaksology
    The Child Caliban
    The Hound of Darkness
    1929   A Preface To Exile
           The Station
           K 19
           The Boom Town
    1930   The Book and the Ring

YOU CAN'T GO HOME AGAIN

Done:
    The Introduction
    . . . The Time that is lovely

---

2. Michael Gold, novelist and Marxist critic, was the editor of *New Masses*. Wolfe liked him very much and gave him without fee his story "The Company" about Joe's brother Jim Doaks and his mistreatment by the Federal Weight and Scales Company. It was published in *New Masses* on January 11, 1938, and later appeared in YCGHA, pp. 129–40 (where Edward Aswell had changed the name to Randy Shepperton.)

Proposed:

. . . Heard lost voices of his kinsmen in the mountains long ago—the imaginations and the stories.

Nebraska Crane was the best boy in town but [*blank*] was poor white trash and a common louse . . . .

Paul, Paul, Paul.

[*From separate typewritten sheets.*]

POSSIBLE MATERIAL FOR MISS NOWELL IN 1938

1. Revision of NO MORE RIVERS.

2. An article on sports (Really a piece about America: The baseball park of a small town when one is a child, the bleachers, the players, the fans and local characters, the time Ty Cobb came to town as the hero of The College Widow by George Ade; after the show Ty Cobb and my cousin Henry Westall and Gil Stikeleather, the two town sports, on terms of familiar intimacy with the great man, going into the Candy Kitchen, etc; the night Frank Gotch, the famous wrestler, wrestled Hansen, the Terrible Swede, at the Auditorium; I thought I might work in here the part about Nebraska Crane and his father, the policeman, who used to wrestle the Masked Marvel at the Auditorium, and how one night the mask came off and the terrible Masked Marvel turned out to be a young Greek who worked in the lunch room down at the depot; the Associated Press tickers clattering in the offices of The Asheville Citizen—"Walter Johnson was invincible today and held the Athletics to four scattered hits"—1912, and all that it brings back, another world before the war, etc.; 1916—"On to Richmond"—riding the day coach of the Seaboard Air Line all night long to see the team play Virginia on Thanksgiving day—and how we beat them for the first time in eleven years—and how a scrub on the Varsity had talked me out of my new overcoat, and how I was wearing his old sweater which had a big N.C. on it, and how proud I was; late summer 1923, the flat up at the edge of Harlem, five of us all from the south, and how we speculated on tickets for the Dempsey-Firpo fight, and were going to get rich, and wound up, after arguing furiously with one another, by going to the fight ourselves: after the fight, Times Square at 1 o'clock and the men collected there arguing passionately with one another about the fight; the whole piece might start out with some reference to the arguments that are always going on in the

sporting columns of the newspapers between the Ancients and the Moderns—"the old timers" and the younger generation—and what Jim Jeffries would have done to Joe Louis, or vice versa, then perhaps leading into boyhood memories of things your father told you, and of how he was in New Orleans the night Corbett knocked out John L. Sullivan; then the baseball bleachers, Ty Cobb, the AP tickers, and the rest of it on up to the present—really a piece about America, the smell of the bleachers, the old Auditorium, the town sports in 1912, etc.)

3. THE STILL-VEX'D BERMOOTHES (A story about a man looking for peace and rest and quiet, and an escape from the violence and conflict of life and of the city, and how he goes to Bermuda, and how he finds upon this little shaving of coral out in the ocean the same conflicts, violence, and confusion he has left behind him. Probably will be used also as a part of the Doaks book).

4. YOU CAN'T GO HOME AGAIN (I believe this may work out into something very interesting, although Nowell may have trouble finding a place where it can go: In design it would be somewhat like THE HOUND OF DARKNESS piece in Vogue, but a great deal more complex, and probably a good deal longer. However, the element of personal narrative will also be very much greater: The texture, of course, is poetic and it moves with a beat, punctuated by the recurrence of the phrase "You can't go home again"—which I believe would pull the whole thing together without further explanation and make the whole narrative element clear. The way I have thought it out, it would begin something like this:

"Once upon a time there was a tiny little boy, and he was a fine boy, smart boy too, and that is the good time because it is the time when the sunlight came and went, and it was warm upon the porch, and Britt's cow was wrenching grass out in the alley way, along the edges of the back yard fence and it made a coarse, cool sound, and there was the sound of sawn ice out in the streets at noon—but—

You can't go home again.

The time that is good is the time of the fatness and the bright colors; it is the elfin time of the calendars, and the sad, mysterious time of the early photographs. It is the time of the early lithographs, it is the time when the world was green and red and yellow. It is the time of the red barn and the windmill, and the house of the seven thousand gables, it is the time of the green lawn, the blue sky, and the white excursion steamer on the river—"

And here would follow the whole Currier and Ives passage of time and memory that Nowell liked. Concluded with the culminating phrase "You can't go home again." The way I have thought it out, the whole piece would develop to this pattern and would really be a kind of spiritual autobiography or narrative: That is, without telling the reader so definitely, I think it would be clear that it is the whole inside story of a man's life, and I think it would be possible to use all the chants and passages of time and memory that I have written—which are, of course, just a form of trying to "go home again"—building right up to the conclusion which would be a final realization and discovery that one can't go home again—home to his childhood, home to his father, home to time and memory and all the things to which he has gone back in his mind and heart so many thousand times—and ending maybe in some such way as this:

"You can't go home again, you can't go home again—oh brothers, friends, comrades—*our* home is in the future: There is no other way.")

5. THE WOMAN OF WEST WYOMING (I have never been able to think of a good title for this story, so in my mind I have always called it this. I suppose you would call it a kind of love story, but it is really about the West, the way I have always wanted to tell about the West. The way it shapes up in my mind, a man returns to the city after having lived abroad, loses himself in a remote and obscure part of the city, and buries himself in work. He is in a very lonely and confused state of mind, and full of doubt and apprehension, and the only answer he has to the problem of his life is work. Then he meets a woman who also lives in the city but is from the West. They fall in love with each other; and for a time the man is at peace, and the doubts and fears and apprehensions he has had about his life are at rest. But then the old fury and torment of work comes back again, he hurls himself back into his work and wrestles with it, work again becomes his whole life, and eventually he drives the woman from him and loses her. Years pass, and then the man one day goes West. And when he sees the West for the first time he knows all about it. It is like a country which he has never visited but which he has known all about because he has had it in him all the time. All the space, the light, the distance, the grand dimension, and the solar energy of the West, its tremendous strength and quietness go home to his heart at once. And then he remembers the woman and understands all about her. This is the way I have thought about the story: I suppose it is a kind of love story, but it is really about the West.)

The State
The Rock
The Voyage

The Woman
The Book
The Exile
The Jungle
The Medusa
The Return
A Farewell to the Fox

Now is duh mont' of March, duh mont' of March. Now it is Brooklyn in duh mont' of March.

In sunlight now the legend shaping to a sharper frame.
 . . . For I have heard that there was one, the great-grandfather, who was strong of thew.
 . . . Have these things altered then: the look of day, or wheel-tracks in a rutted road . . . have these things altered?
 . . . Well, you can't go home again.
 . . . The lean-to porch—plates and the gourd . . . . And he, I've heard, would never put his shoes on when he came in from the fields.
 . . . within closed walls by cast iron heat, within a heat-stale room, heard street boughs creaking and the corner light, the howl of wind in winter, and the sad lost voices of his kinsmen long ago.

Since 1929:
    1929 The Book
    1930 Break with Aline
    1930–31 The Guggenheim
    1931–1935 Brooklyn—The Dormans
              Brooklyn—Columbia Hts.
              Brooklyn—Montague Terrace
              The Fox and Rodneys
    1930–35 Libya Hill and Exile
    1935 Release and Fame
          Germany
          The West
    1935–36 The Darkening Medusa
    1937 Return and End of Exile
          Beginning of Freedom
          You Can't Go Home Again
    1938 Farewell to the Fox

Martha Dodd [3]
1 West 30th Apt. 4E

She had one of the greatest opportunities of any young woman of her generation, and she had made nothing of it. With an unparalleled opportunity for observation, for detachment, for comprehension of the thing about which she professed to know much, she had found out not so much as could be found out by a fifteen-minute conversation with a German sailor on the Hoboken waterfront.

Is a writer political or not?
Is Shakespeare political? Yes.
Is John Keats? No.
Is P. B. Shelley? Yes.
Is Byron? Decidedly.
Is Dickens? Yes.
Is Thackeray? No.
Is Henry James? No.
Is Flaubert? Partly.
Is Zola? Decidedly.
Is Victor Hugo? Decidedly.
Is Gautier? No.
Is Tolstoi? Yes.

The question of whether a great writer can be political or not is not debatable. Obviously, he can be and usually is. What is debatable is whether the function of the great writer is to deal solely with "art and beauty and with love."

The book is full of action, violence, and swift movement but I did not find it convincing because the people did not convince me. I found Cobb hard to visualize as a living person; the Old Man was a movie comic, and the girl, Sugar, just a movie girl who said "You clunk."

Between 1814–1914 one hundred years of so-called peace—a few exceptions:

The American Civil War (1861–1865), The Franco-Prussian War, The War in the Crimea, The Insurrections of 1848, The War of

---

3. The Dodds had returned from Germany in the winter of 1937, and Wolfe renewed his acquaintance with Martha briefly. She was one of the people who tried to interest him in supporting the Spanish Loyalists.

Garibaldi, The Russo-Japanese War, The Spanish-American, The Boxer Rebellion, The War in India, The Boer War.

[*When Wolfe signed the contract with Harper's for a book to be called "The Life and Adventures of the Bondsman Doaks," he promised Aswell a synopsis of its contents. The following notes, outlines, and summaries, which were found among Wolfe's papers, represent his plans for the book during January and February. The "Time Sweeps" show his attempt to work with material (already written) from the earlier part of his experience.*]

A SYNOPSIS

FOR

THE LIVES OF THE BONDSMAN DOAKES

(Title Tentative)
By
Thomas Wolfe

Note: The action of the Book covers the period between September, 1929 and September, 1937.

BOOK I

The Hound of Darkness
(September 18, 1929)

Prologue: A night in September, 1929. Dazzling moonlight over America. At first, from a great height, the body and bones of the American continent. Then the sound of the sea. Then the sound of a great train, Pacific Nine. Then the Corn Blades, rustling stiffly: "Ah, coarse and cool, ah coarse and cool, America."

The Invocation: A Listner speaks: "Is it a lion in the mouth sulfurous"—etc.

The Song: "Where shall we go now? And what shall we do?"—The tongues and voices of America: a panoramic chorus of the whole continent ending with "soon the morning, soon the morning— oh, America."

II

The Station

A description of the mighty station, the ten thousand people arriving and departing, and the sounds of time. Then, the introduction of the man named Doakes.

III

The Doaksology

The genealogy of the Great Doakes (or Doaks) family from the earliest times: the place they have played in history: Doakses the First, who built one of the Great Pyramids; Caesar's reference to them in the Gallic Wars—"doctissimi eorum Doxiensi sunt [*the cleverest of them were the Doxians*]"; the part the Doakes tribe played in the early invasions of England by the Angles, Saxons, and the Jutes; the Doakes among the Norman Conquerors, and the English Doakes who resisted them; the story of Sir Doakes Le Greal in Malory's Morte Darthur; the famous story of Sir Guy Le Doakes at the Siege of Jerusalem and how Richard the Lion Hearted knighted him, and how and why the family coat of arms has ever since been the lemon; the story of Hugh (or Hew) Doakes and how he was part of the first colony to attempt a settlement in Old Catawba: character of Doakes Family here defined as dependable people, people who are good colonizers, able workmen, etc.; early settlements of the Doakes family in America, chiefly in Pennsylvania and in Old Catawba, account of their early history, their history in the Civil War, down to the present times, and the chief members of the present family. A description of the hero, and some account of his past history.

SYNOPSIS FOR "THE ORDEAL OF THE BONDSMAN DOAKS"

Prolog: The Hound of Darkness
                Old Catawba
                The Doaksology
Part I: THE RETURN OF THE NATIVES
                1. The Station
                2. The Train: K 19

3. The Boom Town
4. The Bank
5. Jim Doaks and The Company
6. The Ride
7. Conclusion and Return Scenes: Departure

Part II: THE CITY
1. Utility Cultures
2. Alsop
3. Mrs. Jack
4. Joyner Again: The New Romantic
5. Fame, Half-time, and Exile Whole
6. Morning
7. Noon
8. Party at Jack's

Part III: THE LOCUSTS HAVE NO KING
1. This is Adelaide
2. Mr. Wakefield
3. The Party: "Do you know something?—I think you're pretty swell" etc.
4. The Street of the Night: Where shall we go now? And what shall we do?
5. Death the Proud Brother
6. Morning: The Station again

Part IV: THE WINTER'S TALE
1. Joyner Redivivus
2. Alsop Estranged
3. The Crash: The Crisis at Libya
4. The Conflict with Esther
5. The Fox Awake
6. April, late April
7. No Door
8. The Parting with Esther
9. Morning, a Child, the Bridge: The Hospital

Part V: THE OKTOBERFEST
1. "Summer was kind to us," etc.—A Lyrical Monologue Showing the Events of the Summer—Paris, the Rhineland, the Black Forest in Rapid Interweft, ending up with Dream Passage "Last Night I think I saw the old Demented Moon." (This passage to be punctuated by flashes of actuality weaving through the Time

Dream—Letters to and from the Fox and Mrs. Jack, etc.)

2. Cockaigne: A description of Munich, the Pension in the Theresien Strasse, the American Church, Mrs. Park, etc.

3. "October was approaching and the season of the great Oktoberfest was now at hand"—follow this by THE FIRST VISIT TO THE FAIR (OKTOBERFEST).

4. Time Interlude: "A Letter from Esther—the Americans—the Germans—Conflict

5. The Fight at the Fair

6. The Hospital: Geheimrat Becker, Johann, the Nun, the American, the Doctor, Theresa Bahr

7. Time Interlude Again: "Long, Long into the Night I Lay" etc., the Park, In the Park, the Good Child's River: Esther's revelry [*reverie?*]

8. Unteralpbach: The Passion Players, Mrs. Park; Jesus dead and Jesus living

9. Dark in the Forest

10. The Magic Mountains

Part VI: THE RUIN OF THE CITY

1. London in November: Mrs. Purvis, Hugh Proctor and McHarg

2. America: The Fall of the Bank

3. England Again: Hampstead, the Bloomies, the Commisar's Wife

4. The Swarming Web: the great cloud loaded, crested, just before the storm

5. April: Parting with Proctor, Mrs. Purvis and the Doctor; Home again

Part VII: THE JUNGLE WEB (BROOKLYN)

1. The Alley

2. The Trials of the Bank

3. The Exile of True Jim: Washington

4. Work in the Jungle: Hunger and Love

5. The Quest for the Blessed Isle: The Still Vex'd Bermoothes

6. Joyner as Prophet of the Day to Come: the Technicians

7. The Lowest Depths: Hunger and Work

8. Inauguration

9. The Death of Jim Doaks

Part VIII: THE LION AND THE FOX

1. The Day of the Fox: the Fox awake
2. The Lion awake
3. The Goat awake
4. No more Rivers
5. The great Baboon
6. Others Awake: These tangled threads—Mr. Prince, incoming from New Jersey; young James also; Ed Cole, the little bookkeeper; Worth, the advertising man; Lewelloin Reade; Del Gaynor, with sleepy dissipated looking eyes; Schroeders, big and little; up from the coast Ed Bauer from the Jersey shore—all threading in in the morning from New Jersey. Connecticut Terborgh and poor little Sloan; Brooklyn-wise Miss Dickens, fitly named; Jamaica Young Soulters in the Shipping Department; out-of-the-Bronx, Milt Thorpe and Jimmie, the office boy; out-of-the-village, Susan Flanders, Education, from Eleventh Street, is there. Rip Brent, from his apartment house on Eighty-Seventh Street; Phil Richards, Thorpe's assistant from his home in Chelsea; Mike Mc-Greavey from Fifth Avenue and Brooklyn; Pete Montez, the other elevator boy, a Spaniard from East One Hundred Eleventh Street; Miss Packer, Goat's assistant from somewhere out of New Jersey; Miss Melroy, aggressive as a sparrow, from her single ladies-quite-alone-most-club-like-hotel, lodge and tenement, in pale salmon brick, in the middle East Side; Steve Bissette, out of his second-story walkup on East Sixtieth
7. The Congress of the Threads: morning at Rodney's. Old James, up-coming in the elevator, meets Flipcroft, the religious editor "great work my boy, I didn't think you had it in you" etc.
8. Mid-morning: Fox and Goat—"Is it really a *good* book?"—"Later on, 'Louder. Louder'—have you noticed how deaf he is becoming." Schroeder, Singer, walking up the aisles, rubbing his hands beneath his chin and cackling

fiendish to himself—yes,—Ha ha ha, I believe he expired in considerable agony" etc. Dick gazing mournful from his window—"These little mouths—these feeding little mouths"—so on. The Fox and Miss Terborgh—"Ah, come, honestly. *You* know what to do with it" etc. "Ha ha ha" the sudden dry little cachinations from the Schroeder—Ricky Schroeder and Miss Jensen secretary. The Goat had 'phoned—"Miss Packer will you take a letter?—Just a minute, Bob"—talks on the 'phone to Miss Packer, to Bob and chewed a cigar all at once. The Fox going into Hauser's office and laying manuscript upon the desk—whispers, "You know what to do about this"—goes back to office, hangs on coat lapels, looks out the window with his sea-pale eyes—goes out and talks to McNair—then down to the floor below to talk to Leighton about the Congress

9. Noon time: The Fox and Goats: Chappio's
10. The Afternoon at Rodney's eleven, the annual party at old James: "I'd like to drink to Jimmie Betterton—always thought he was a fine fellow" etc.
11. Night: The Lion and the Fox again—the old Lion in his bed, flat on his back, and very straight and quiet, and dead; the Fox in bed in darkness on his back, in darkness staring with his sea-pale eyes

Part IX: THE END OF THE STORM

1. He struck the board and beat against the wall, etc.
2. Wintringham DeKaye
3. Alsop Redivivus
4. Steve's place
5. The house at Malbourne
6. The Wind from the West: the smell of the apples, the death of Charles Doaks, the burial ground—"again again I plucked the berries harsh and rude."
7. The Wind from the West continued; the smell of the train smoke, the stockyards and the

slaughter pens: "Who's master of the hounds this year?"

8. Mrs. Whelke and the Doctor
9. Emptied of Brooklyn: Departure

Part X: THE CONQUEST OF FAIR MEDUSA

1. The voyage over: Paris as Ghost: "Where are the snows of yester-year?"
2. The channel voyage: Hugh Proctor and the folk of quay, the streets of Hythe, the far and the near, the most familiar fields—the woman in the road, with a painted face, the walk in the woods, the night trip up to London—"Epstein. Yus. Some folks might [*say*] he was as bald as an egg, I'd say he had a fine ['*ed of 'air*]—that's relativity."
3. Spring in England: Mr. Sykes
4. The country garden: Cambridge, Norfolk, Yarmouth, Blakely, the two men in the train—"The grahses and the sedges"
5. The tidy land: "What shall we say of these [*who*] stamp proud feet" etc.
6. "My name is Wachter"
7. The God is captured: the old man's daughter: Hartmann, Lewald, the old man, Mrs. Starnbeck, the party at Newalls, down beneath the kiefern trees, the trip to the center, a rock of [*magic*], return
8. The voyage home: fame of the poet
9. The discovery of the West
10. The maelstrom: dark and gruesome
11. Van Paget and Page
12. The Sirens "What song the sirens sang" etc.
13. Friendship's garland: Alsop and little boy
14. The loss of the Fair Medusa

Part XI: I HAVE A THING TO TELL YOU

1. The great games
2. Theresa Bahr
3. Hartmann and Lewald again
4. Munich revisited
5. The Tirol: Happiness in the valley
6. The old man's family again
7. Departure: I have a thing to tell you

Part XII: YOU CAN'T GO HOME AGAIN
           1. Deep South
           2. One man's Valley
           3. The killing at Clingman
           4. Return
           5. Return and farewell
           6. He can't go home again
Part XIII: A FAREWELL TO THE FOX
Part XIV: CONCLUSION

Nebraska Crane: the man of nature.
Alsop: the man of sentiment—"all things for the best."
Joyner: the man of fashion—the eternal trifler is with us yet.[4]
Jim: the conservative—"a man with both feet on the ground—that's . . . that's the American way of doing things."

Time Sweeps Backward:
    The Train—Nebraska (3 o'clock)
              —Alsop (Just the Hometown parts)
              —Joyner (ibid.)
              —Suggs (The Hometown parts)

The Time Sweeps:
    Tallyho Joyner:
       In his Mother's electric landaulet (1914)
       At Pine Rock (1916)
       Stories from the War: (Joyner in France, 1918)
       Harvard 1919–1921 (Use inflation stuff on Beacon Hill—Joyner's revolutionary background)
       France 1922–1929.
    Alsop:
       Coming along the street (1914)
       In the YMCA at Pine Rock (1916)
       The Room (1917)
       The Rock (1923)
       The Train (1929)
    Jarvis Riggs:
       The Story (1893)

---

4. "The eternal trifler" is a phrase from Matthew Arnold's "Stanzas from the Grande Chartreuse." Wolfe used the phrase occasionally to characterize an aesthete without humanist concerns.

The Young Teller (1911–1912)
The Bank (1912 on)
The Bank (1920–)

THE BANK

By 1916, the structure of the political ring that was to govern Libya for the next twenty years had been formed, and had begun to centre its activities around the Bank. Public borrowing—the floating of bond issues—was recklessly increased, the resulting funds increasing the funds of the "fastest growing bank in Old Catawba." The funds, in turn, were loaned back to the politicians, or to other important individuals of what was later to be known to everyone as "The Ring," for personal and private purposes of their own, upon securities and assurances that were often so tenuous that the meditations of the philosophers in The Clouds of Aristophanes were substantial by comparison.

. . . Far from the castle clinging to the rock, the old chimes in the darkness over Gothic towns, the blond flesh of the lavish women, and the cathedral magic of the kiefern trees—far, far, it seems, immensely far, is winter, winter howling in the oak, the gulched clay, and the desolations of the great unfinished land; far, far from Thuringen to Tennessee; and from the Wartburg to the Appalachian fastnesses of Banner Elk; it is so far as dreams are far, as exile and as memory are far, as all lost voices of lost kinsmen in the hills long, long ago is far and yet . . .

The years slide by like water: one day he is home again.[5]

[*The first version of the following "Statement" was a letter to Aswell dated February 14, 1938. It began:* "I am doing the synopsis of the book which I told you I would make out for you, and I hope to give it to you in a day or two." *Wolfe revised the letter and extended it into its present form. Aswell stated that he never saw the document until after Wolfe's death. Although the "Statement" describes a book and intentions much like* You Can't Go Home Again, *Aswell very inappropriately took some of Wolfe's words about fictional aims from this "Statement," called them an "Author's Note," and placed them at the beginning of* The Web and the Rock. *The result was a good deal*

---

5. This passage, with its theme of wandering and return, appears in similar form in a number of Wolfe manuscripts in which his character makes a homeward journey—such as "K 19" and "Boom Town."

of critical confusion, and reviewers pointed out that Wolfe's stated intentions were not successfully carried out in his book.]

A STATEMENT OF PURPOSE

First of all, so far as the author can now make out—and the reason for any dubiety that may be apparent here is not due to any doubt on the author's part, or any lack of conviction, as to purpose or direction, but rather to the enormous masses of material with which he is working, and the tides and planes and forces which shift and vary constantly, while still holding the same general direction—here is the latest stage of definition as clearly as it can be put, and what the author thinks the book is about:

The book is about one man's discovery of life and of the world, and in this sense it is a book of apprenticeship. The author first thought of the book as a kind of American Gulliver's Travels. He used this comparison deliberately, but he also likened the book to those books that had to do with the adventures of "the innocent man" through life —he mentioned, in addition to Gulliver, such books as Don Quixote, Pickwick, Candide, The Idiot, and Wilhelm Meister. He used these names not as examples of literary models which he intended to follow, but merely as indications of the direction he was taking. Now he thinks the illustration that comes closer to the kind of book he wants to do is Wilhelm Meister's Apprenticeship rather than Gulliver. And the reason for this is that he now believes as the definition of the book grows clearer, the illustration he made about Gulliver might mislead in that as the very name Gulliver implies, it might indicate to one that he was contemplating a book about a man who was "gulled," who was expecting one thing from life and found another, etc.

This element is certainly in the book, but it does not define as directly as it should the author's position and direction at this time about the book. The book will have satire in it, swingeing and scalding satire, it is hoped, but it is not essentially a satiric book. It is a book about discovery—about discovery not in a sudden and explosive sense as when "some new planet breaks upon his ken"—but of discovery as through a process of finding out, and of finding out as a man has to find out, through error and through trial, through fantasy and illusion, through falsehood and his own damn foolishness, through being mistaken and wrong and an idiot and egotistical and aspiring and hopeful and believing and confused, and pretty much what every one of us is and goes through and finds out about and becomes.

And, in order that there may be no doubt as to what this process of discovery involves, the whole book might almost be called "You Can't Go Home Again"—which means back home to one's family, back home to one's childhood, back home to the father one has lost, back home to romantic love, to a young man's dreams of glory and of fame, back home to exile, to escape to "Europe" and some foreign land, back home to lyricism, singing just for singing's sake, back home to aestheticism, to one's youthful idea of the "artist," and the all-sufficiency of "art and beauty and love," back home to the ivory tower, back home to places in the country, the cottage in Bermuda, away from all the strife and conflict of the world, back home to the father one is looking for—to someone who can help one, save one, ease the burden for one, back home to the old forms and systems of things that once seemed everlasting, but that are changing all the time—back home to the escapes of Time and Memory. Each of these discoveries, sad and hard as they are to make and accept, are described in the book almost in the order in which they are named here. But the conclusion is not sad: this is a hopeful book—the conclusion is that although you can't go home again, the home of every one of us is in the future, there is no other way.

This description of the purpose of the book ought to be kept in mind and read pretty carefully, and thought about a lot, because the author is depending on his editor now for so much: he wants him to be thoroughly convinced at the outset that the author knows what he is doing and where he is going, and that although there are many, many doubts in his mind, there is no doubt; and although there are many, many confusions, there is no confusion. To get right down to cases now, even, as it has to be here, in the most broad and general way, here is what the author has in mind:

He intends to use his own experience absolutely—to pour it in, to squeeze it, to get everything out of it that it is worth. He intends for this to be the most objective book that he has ever written, and he also intends by the same token, for it to be the most autobiographical. He has constructed a fable, invented a story and a legend; out of his experience he has derived some new characters who are now compacted not so much from specific recollection as from the whole amalgam and consonance of seeing, feeling, thinking, living, and knowing many people. There are two important ones, for example, named Alsop and Joyner—who, each in his own way are pretty much what the name of each signifies—but each, the author hopes, are as convincing and living people as he has ever created. He now thinks he may be wrong in calling the central figure, the protagonist, Joe Doaks, but

Alsop and Joyner can probably stand as they are—that is, both are real names, both are fairly familiar and common names: the objection to Joe Doaks, of course, is that it may carry with it too much a connotation of newspaper cartooning, slap-stick, the fellow in the bleachers, and so on. The way the author feels now, it should be more of a Wilhelm Meister kind of name—an *American* Wilhelm Meister kind of name.

To get still further to cases: as the editor will remember, when he first talked with the author about what he had to do, the author spoke of the book which he had called "The October Fair" and told something of the conflict in his mind between this book, and the other book which he has been describing here. He told, for example, of the time several years ago when all his heart and life and energy were absorbed by the October Fair and how, at that time, he thought this was the book he had to do and had framed it in a sequence to follow "Look Homeward Angel" and "Of Time and the River." The author explained how he had written and striven on this book for two or three years, how "Of Time and the River" finally grew out of it and preceded it, and of how finally he had gone cold on the October Fair: that is, it was no longer the burning, all-absorbing thing he had to do.

But he described also the feeling of incompletion and discontent in his mind because of this book which had been projected and never published—the feeling that it had in it some of the best and truest work that he had ever done, and the feeling that this work ought to receive the consummation and release of print. He still feels that way, except —and that is what he is trying to explain about his whole position here as concerns his book—his vision has changed: he no longer wishes to write a whole book about a woman and a man in love, and about youth and the city, because it now seems to him that these things, while important, are subordinate to the whole plan of the book he has in mind. In other words, being young and in love and in the city now seem to the author to be only a part of the whole experience of apprenticeship and discovery of which he is talking. They are also a part of the knowledge that you can't go home again.

That plan, as he now sees it in his mind, as he is shaping it in the enormous masses of manuscript which he has already written, and as he is trying to clarify it in the synopsis, is as follows:

The protagonist—the central character, the Wilhelm Meister kind of figure—really the most autobiographical character the author has ever written about because he wants to put everything he has or knows into him—is important now because the author hopes he will be, or illustrate, in his own experience every one of us—not merely the sensitive young fellow in conflict with his town, his family, the little world around him—not merely the sensitive young fellow in love, and so concerned with his little universe of love that he thinks it is the whole universe—but all of these things and much more insofar as they illustrate essential elements of any man's progress and discovery of life and as they illustrate the world itself, not in terms of personal and self-centered conflict with the world, but in terms of ever-increasing discovery of life and the world, with a consequent diminution of the more personal and self-centered vision of the world which a young man has.

In other words, the author has thought of the book as a series of concentric circles—that is, one drops the pebble in the pool—the Wilhelm Meister pebble, or whatever we shall ultimately call him—but instead of pebble and pool simply in personal terms of pebble and pool, one gets a widening ever-enlarging picture of the whole thing—the pebble becomes important, if important at all, only in terms of this general and constant pattern of which it is the temporary and accidental stimulus: in other words, any other pebble would produce the same effect—the important thing is to tell about the thing itself, the thing that happens—the pebble, if you like, is only a means to this end.

THE PROTAGONIST

The author feels that the figure of the protagonist may be, technically and in other ways, the most important and decisive element in this book. As he has told the editor, this book marks not only a turning away from the books he has written in the past, but a genuine spiritual and artistic change. In other words, he feels that he is done with lyrical and identifiable personal autobiography; he is also seeking, and hopes now to obtain, through free creation, a release of his inventive power which the more shackling limitations of identifiable autobiography do not permit.

In other words, the value of the Eugene Gant type of character is his personal and romantic uniqueness, causing conflict with the world around him: in this sense, the Eugene Gant type of character becomes a kind of romantic self-justification, and the greatest weakness of the Eugene Gant type of character lies in this fact.

Therefore, it is first of all vitally important to the success of this book that there be no trace of Eugene Gant-i-ness in the character of the protagonist; and since there is no longer a trace of Eugene Gant-i-ness in the mind and spirit of the creator, the problem should be a technical one rather than a spiritual or emotional one. In other words, this is a book about discovery, and not about self-justification: it hopes to describe the pattern that the life of Everyman must, in general, take, in its process of discovery: and although the protagonist should be, in his own right, an interesting person, his significance lies not in his personal uniqueness and differences, but in his personal identity to the life of every man. The book is a book of discovery, hence union, with life; not a book of personal revolt, hence separation, from life: the protagonist becomes significant not as the tragic victim of circumstances, the romantic hero in conflict and revolt against his environment, but as a kind of polar instrument round which the events of life are grouped, by means of which they are touched, explained, and apprehended, by means of which they are seen and ordered.

Autobiographically, therefore, he should bear perhaps about the same relation to the life of the author, as Wilhelm Meister bears to the life of Goethe, or as Copperfield bears to the life of Dickens: as to the story itself—the legend—it should bear about the same relation to the life of the author as the story of Wilhelm Meister bears to Goethe's life; even perhaps as Don Quixote bears to the life of Cervantes—although this book is perhaps more in the vein of satiric legendry than the book the author has in mind.

But the book certainly should have in it, from first to last, a strong element of the satiric exaggeration of Don Quixote, not only because it belongs to the nature of the legend—"the innocent man" discovering life—but because satiric exaggeration also belongs to the nature of life—and particularly American life. No man, for example, who wants to write a book about America on a grand scale can hardly escape feeling again and again the emotion of the man when he first saw a giraffe: "I don't believe it!"

So, the book certainly must have this element, and it seems to the author the figure of the protagonist must have it too. He must have it because the very process of discovery, of finding out, will be intensified and helped by it.

. . . .

He is somewhat above the middle height, say five feet nine or ten, but he gives the impression of being somewhat shorter than that, because of the way he has been shaped and molded, and the way in which he carries himself. He walks with a slight stoop, and his head, which is carried somewhat forward, with a thrusting movement, is set down solidly upon a short neck between shoulders which, in comparison with the lower part of his figure, and his thighs and legs, are extremely large and heavy. He is barrel-chested, and perhaps the most extraordinary feature of his make-up, which accounts for the nickname he has had since childhood—the boys, of course, called him "Monk"— are the arms and hands: the arms are unusually long, and the hands, as well as the feet are very big with long spatulate fingers which curve naturally and deeply in like paws.

The effect of this inordinate length of arms and hands, which dangle almost to the knees, together with the stooped and heavy shoulders, and the out-thrust head, is to give the whole figure a somewhat prowling and half-crouching posture.

Finally, the features, the face, are small, compact, and somewhat pug-nosed, the eyes set very deep in beneath heavy brows, the forehead is rather low, and the hair begins not far above the brows. The total effect of this, particularly when he is listening or talking to someone, the body prowling downward, the head thrust forward and turned upward with a kind of packed attentiveness, made the Simian analogy inevitable in his childhood; therefore the name of "Monk" has stuck.

In addition to this, it has never occurred to him, apparently, to get his figure clothed in garments suited to his real proportions: he apparently has walked into a store somewhere and picked up and worn out the first thing he could get on—in this way, a way of which he is not wholly conscious, the element of the grotesque is exaggerated.

The truth of the matter is, he is not really grotesque at all: that is to say, his dimensions, while unusual and a little startling at first sight, are in no sense of the word abnormal. He is not in any way a freak of nature, although some people might think so: he is simply a creature with big hands and feet, extremely long arms, a trunk somewhat too large and heavy, the legs, and features perhaps somewhat too small and compact for the big shoulders that support them.

Since he has added to this rather awkward but not distorted figure, certain unconscious tricks and mannerisms of his own, such as his habit of carrying his head thrust forward, and peering upward when he is listening or talking, it is not surprising if the impression he first makes should sometimes arouse laughter and surprise. Certainly he knows of this, and he has sometimes furiously and bitterly resented it; but he has never inquired sufficiently or objectively enough into the reasons for it.

The truth of the matter is that although he has a very intense and apprehensive eye for the appearance of things, he does not have an intense and apprehensive eye for his own appearance: in fact, the absorption of his interest and attention in the world around him is so passionate and eager that it rarely occurs to him what kind of figure and appearance he is himself making.

In other words, he does not realize the kind of effect he has on people, and when as sometimes happens, it is rudely and brutally forced upon his attention, it throws him into a state of furious anger. He is young: and he has not learned the wisdom and tolerant understanding of experience and maturity: in short, he does not see that these things are accidental and of no great consequence—that personal beauty is probably no very great virtue in a man anyway; and that this envelope of flesh and blood in which a spirit happens to be sheathed, has been a very loyal and enduring, even though an ugly, friend.

THE STORY

The Story Begins With a Prologue
Prologue

The prologue as the author now sees it is to be called The Hound of Darkness—and states the setting. The setting is America. This is followed with Old Catawba, a description of the place from which the protagonist comes.

This was followed originally by The Doaksology: a satiric genealogy of the great Doaks family since the earliest times. If the name Doaks is changed, perhaps the genealogy could still be used. Then follows an account of the town of Libya Hill: how it got its name from the first Joyner who settled there, the connection of the Joyners with the family of the protagonist: a description of Libya Hill and the people there. All of this save the part about Libya Hill has been completely written. The Libya parts are incomplete.

THE DIRECT NARRATIVE

To Be Called
The Station or
The One and The Many or
The Pebble and The Pool

The direct narrative begins with the pebble (the protagonist) rolling home. The chapter bears the title of The Station. Perhaps a better name for it would be The Pebble and The Pool. Another, and perhaps the best of all, would be The One and The Many. For the purpose of this beginning—this setting—is to show the tremendous and nameless Allness of The Station—ten thousand men and women constantly arriving and departing, each unknown to the other, but sparked with the special fire of his own destination, the unknown town, the small hand's breadth of earth somewhere out upon the vast body of the continent—all caught together for a moment, interfused and weaving, not lives but life, caught up, subsumed beneath the great roofs of the mighty Station, the vast murmur of these voices drowsily caught up there like the murmurous and incessant sound of time and of eternity, which is and is forever, no matter what men come and go through the portals of the great Station, no matter what men live or die.

And our protagonist is introduced: he is here among them—the one and the many, the pebble and the pool.

K 19

K 19 is the pullman car going home. The moment that the protagonist enters it he is transported instantly from the vast and nameless Allness of general humanity in The Station into the familiar geography of his home town. As he goes down the green aisle of the pullman car, he sees faces, people, characters that are to play an important part throughout the narrative. He hears a dozen voices, words and phrases; he sees a dozen faces, lives, identities—all like himself, drawn out of the tremendous and nameless floodtide of The Station into the narrow frame of a projectile—all like himself, shot forward through time and space toward one small spot eight hundred miles away which is familiar to them all: voices, greetings, behind the green-glazed curtains of the washroom, voices, laughter, greetings.

He sees the squat and swarthy little figure of the banker, Jarvis Riggs; the long dish face of Parson Flack, who manipulates the politics of the town; the round-featured weak amiability of the Mayor; the toothy sandy-visaged angularity of the lawyer; the beak-nosed homeliness of Sol Swartzburg, returning from a buying expedition; Mrs. Morton, gray-haired, attractive, talked about; and Stanley Samuel, the newspaper publisher, potent, sly, contriving in the Parson's ring, and never too near Mrs. Morton, but never very far away from her; these and others, all part of the familiar chronicle of one small town, instantly recaptured—even in the train, in K 19, they are all home again.

With these also, several others: Dexter Joyner is returning home. It is his first visit back in six or seven years: he wears a coat of rough brown tweed, gray English flannels, a beret, he carries a book by André Gide, in French, with a paper cover, tucked underneath his arm —he is easy but cold in his manner, detached: he responds to greetings with a certain cold formality, he keeps his distance: his manner says plainly that he may know them, but he is never of them or with them —his speech and manner have a certain cold impatience—an almost scowling boredom—in a sharp, sharp tone, marked by impatience, he says "What?"—it is plain to see that he has lived in Paris for many years, he has belonged to many movements there, he has lived upon the Left Bank, has written poems and criticisms that are so subtle and obscure that the average person cannot even understand them—he shook the soil of Yankeedom from his feet years before when it became plain to him that there was no hope for it, that there was no art in it, that there was nothing but Philistinism and Babbitry in it, and now he knows about so many things, he has been a part of so many rare and precious movements, of such a foreign and superior life that none of these people could possibly know about, that he contains himself and speaks quietly when they greet him, that he shows his boredom and impatience—he says "What?" to them.

One gathers that he is going home from duty, and that this will be his last visit: his grandfather is very old, and will not live long— when someone asks him if he is going to carry on the military school, he looks bored and puzzled and impatient, then says "What?"—this settles it. Upon what meat has this our Caesar fed, that he has grown so great? What?

Alsop too returning home: unlike Joyner, a lover of his fellow-men, he stands in the aisle talking to people, his face pontifically grave and respectful when he listens to his elders, his great fat belly and the fat white dewlap of his throat shaking with laughter at a joke, building on it, improvising on it, mounting in his great fat throat to a phlegmy scream—people look at him and smile, they hear the great fat scream of laughter and smile, they say "There's Jerry Alsop"—smiling as people smile at jolly fat men, liking him because he is so fat: but behind the winking glimmer of his polished glasses, his eyes contract with laughter that has too much of slyness and mockery in it—sometimes his face composes to a look of grave respectfulness, but there is slyness, mockery at the corners of his mouth.

He greets the protagonist cordially but behind his greeting there is slyness too: they have not seen much of each other since their college days—he has been lost to Alsop's fold, he has escaped from the priestly benevolence of the fat man's wing—he is not approved of any longer, the fat man now greets him with a show of cordiality—a moment later, gravely, shyly, with a show of innocence, the fat man catches up a word that he has spoken, deftly twists and misinterprets it [*into*] lewd meanings, before he can reply builds it up into a high fat scream of throaty laughter—gets everyone to laughing too by the sheer infection of his shaking belly and the trembling throat—behind the glasspoints of the narrowed eyes, the glint of malice and of mockery peer forth. The other's face reddens and he has no answer, he turns away with flags of anger reddening his neck—as he goes down the aisle, he hears sly silence, then the fat man's scream of laughter, and his face burns dark: for a moment he almost wishes he could be as Joyner, armored behind that bored detachment, the cold "What?"

But to one side now, a voice breaks through his anger, speaks to him. A strong and friendly voice, drenched in strong sunlight and the warmth of earth, good-natured, easy, bantering, unafraid, unchanged, exactly as it was when it was fourteen years of age, breaks like a flood of warm and living light upon his consciousness. He turns and stops: it is Nebraska Crane—the square, freckled, sunburned visage looks at him with the same humorous friendliness it has always had: and the brown face, the tar-black Cherokee eyes look out with the same straight deadly fearlessness they have always had—the big brown paw comes out and grips him tolerantly, saying "Whoa, there!—where you goin', Monkus?"—using the same jesting nickname he has used for twenty years. And instantly, it is like coming home to a strong and friendly place: the tremendous strength, and calm, and good-humored fearlessness of the other's life floods in upon him, as it has always done, giving him a sense of restorative power and confidence. In another moment, they are seated talking together with the familiarity of people whom no bridge of years and distance can alter.

Nebraska Crane's right ankle is taped and bandaged: between his knees there is a heavy stick. The other asks him what has happened: the Cherokee boy grins tolerantly and says: "The old man's cracking up, Monkus. I can't stand the gaff any more." The other remembers now that Nebraska is only two years older than himself—just past thirty—he is incredulous. Nebraska smiles good-naturedly again and says: "That's an old man in baseball, Monk, and I went up when I was twenty. I've been around a long time."

The quiet resignation of the player touches the other with a feeling of sadness. Somehow it is hard and painful for him to face the fact that this strong and fearless creature, who has stood in his life always for courage, for triumph, and for victory should now be speaking with such quiet resignation and acceptance of defeat.

And yet he sees instantly that this too is of the essence of

Nebraska's nature—that he was the same as a boy—that the element of his great strength is his cheerful fatalism—that he could face anything, even death, the same way. The fatalism of the player is here explained: seeing the look of regret and disappointment on his friend's face, Nebraska smiles and goes on cheerfully:

[*The narrative continues to develop the reunion between Monk and Nebraska for about five pages. Edward Aswell used most of it in* You Can't Go Home Again, *pp. 64–69.*]

"Yes, Bras," for a moment the other looks out at the flashing landscape of New Jersey, with a feeling of sadness and wonder in his heart, "It all comes back."

Here, as the great train rushes forward across the land, the scene sweeps backward into time: we are back to three o'clock on an afternoon in May in 1914: below the young leaves of the maple tree, a boy lies on his belly in the young and tender grass—Jerry Alsop, aged eighteen, already fat and priestly, his belly buttoned in blue serge, going down along the other side of the street, Dexter Joyner sliding smoothly past at eleven miles an hour, in his mother's electric Landaulet, already something precious and remote, enclosed smoothly behind shining glass, a single red carnation in a small vase just above his head, Nebraska, fifteen years of age, the same square freckled face, the same coal-black grave and steady eyes, advancing steadily up the street upon the other side, the smooth ash of a baseball bat carried sprucely on his shoulder like a soldier marching, the thick leather fingers of a well-oiled fielder's glove protruding from the right hip pocket of his pants, the two young voices raised in quiet and steady greeting, then the boys with the accursed names—Sid, Roy, Victor, Harry, Clarence—from the hated other side of town, the sun-wide regions of the west where desolation is—intruding in a loutish scrabble into this sweet harmony of home, the maple tree, the good green region of the east where boys with good names like Nebraska Crane come from—and then around one the sudden ring of jeering faces and of hated names, and suddenly, in midst of peril, Nebraska back among them with his avenging bat and the black death-giving eyes of the Cherokee—the rout of the enemy, the square brown face, the wide grin, and the quiet word again—then silence in the street again, the drone of afternoon, the booming stroke of three o'clock and the Court House bell across the town—and then the Negro market boys upon their flashing wheels in flashing echelon, in spirals, squadrons, platoons, fours and eights, fantastic sinuosities—then away, away up towards the markets—and as they go, back from their black and happy lips floats back the name that somehow, God knows how, they have bestowed on him by which he is known to them —"Paul! Paul!"

"My name is not Paul! My name is—"

Again the train, the crowded landscape of New Jersey, the black eyes of the Cherokee—Time!

(The time movement to be included here is the section known as "The Boy Caliban, 1914.")

[*The "Statement" continues for another thirty pages describing other characters such as Judge Bland, Parson Flack, and Jerry Alsop and includes flashbacks in time that record such material as the usurious loan business, the public exposure of Judge Bland's visits to Miss Queenie's bawdy house, and Alsop's literary opinions at Pine Rock College.*]

Mrs. [*Anne Morrow*] Lindbergh, Sat. March 5, 17 East 9th St.

Sunday, Feb. 27—Authors' Fund Party at Rainbow Room— 5:30–7:00 (c)—A Dense Mass of People, Tony Sarg, Van Loon, "The Man with the Thousand Voices." Got out then and had Scotch on terrace overlooking city.

The Publishers (1929–1937)
The Lawyers (1935–1938)
The Parasites (1935–1938)
The Women (1925——)
The People (always).

The Publishers—He might have been a good property.

The Lawyers—"In the Murphy matter—"

The Parasites—Remembering our conversation in [Ricardi?] ". . . we'd like you to donate 2 copies of your book to our little library."

"when questioned on the street" etc.

The Women—"Why are you so suspicious . . . don't you know that everybody loves you?"

The People—". . . greatest city in the world . . . always something new . . . marvelous."

THE VISION OF SPANGLER'S PAUL

Introduction by a Friend
Old Catawba
The Doaksology (?)
How Libya Got Its Name
"Son, son" . . . so did he always know
"The time that is good"
"Three o'clock"
The Bridge
The Hound of Darkness
Pine Rock (The State)
The Rock (The City)
Mrs. Jack
The Station
K 19
Boom Town
The Ring and the Book
The Street of the Night
The Party at Jack's
The Oktoberfest

Part II

The Ruin of the City
Winter in England
The Alley

Needed to fill in—The Lawyers:
Van Paget and Page.
Rice, Cohen, Morris, Louis, Schalzberger, and Rappaport.
Fogg, Fulton, Goforth, Roberhorst, and Woon.
Mortimer Davenport Fulton
Fogg, Fulton, Fulton, Fulton, Goforth, Roberhorst, and Woon
Mortimer Davenport

Rongg and Wright
Sylvia Rongg

There lived at this time in the land of Germany (as yet unan-nealed) a writer of books whose name was Ernest Hahn—a great windy fart of a book called Die Hochgebirge [*The High Mountains*].

Yes, the People.

[*The following notes about the Joyners and "the people" are representative of a great many scattered notes and pages reflecting Wolfe's work during the spring with material which was finally published in* The Hills Beyond, *Chapters 2 through 6.*]

THE JOYNER GENEALOGY

Of where they came from there is some doubt: people who came into the hills and hollows of Zebulon County in 1793 were not much interested in family trees, save in their more recent and immediate branches—Zacchariah Joyner was himself impatient of all attempts to dignify him genealogically—in answer to questions where he *came* from, he is known to have answered bluntly: "I don't know where we came from; the point is we're here now."

There is even some doubt as to old William Joyner's origins—it is certainly known that he was a soldier of the Revolutionary Armies, and took part in the none too glorious operations with the Redcoats at Cowpens; and he certainly did come to Zebulon as the result of a Revolutionary land grant. Beyond that, not much has been established as historic fact. The truth is, the whole tribe of Joyner is so much a part of the history of Western Catawba that it is very hard to think of them as belonging now, or in the past to any other place. [*The material goes on about his exploits with the bear. Other pages deal with Zack and Uncle Theodore.*]

And the people! Yes, the people!—to be gloated on by Ph.D.'s —who thought their songs and ballads "almost" those of Elizabeth; to be doted on by Northern ladies who found their ways and customs picturesque; and to be yearned over by invading social service workers, who doted on the squalor, ignorance, and poverty, who did (God bless their souls) their *little* bit—their precious little bit—to help the people, teach the people, prop the [*page missing*] lean-to shacks, rickets, incest, syphilis, fourteen children, hunger—all the rest of it—adored the people, because the people were "so fine."

Dear God, dear Jesus God, it is a lie, protect us and the people from such stuff as this: the people are not "fine"—the people are—the people.

And after a hundred years of it—denudings, minings, lootings, intermarryings, world-lostness—all the rest of it—the people are still there, spite Snake, the lumber thief, who stole their hills and [*breaks off*]

Pounders, Red Roberts, Victor Roncey, Young Tansy, Johnny Dundee, "Captain" Raper, Harry Greb, Frank Gotch, and Hansen and Gilroy, Gilroy of Georgetown, Yank Tandy, Graham Pansy and the Tayloe Brothers, Big Kelly, little Kelly, and Jack Corbett, Lowe and Robert Spaugh.

Bert, Bob, and Jack, the names of horses. Archie Butt.

Ed and Mary Lou [6]
4:08 Chappaqua, Saturday, Upper Level.

After 1929:
 Exile: The Affair in Asheville
 The Break Up of Love
 The Years in Brooklyn
 Friendship with one Perkins
 1935 The Coming of Fame
 1936 Disenchantment
 1937 Return Home
 1938 Announcement of a New Faith

M'ch 1, 1937–M'ch 1, 1938:
 The Child By Tiger
 The Lost Boy
 'E
 Mr. Malone
 Katamoto
 The Party at Jack's
 Return
 A Prologue to America
 April Late April
 Oktoberfest
 The Company

 The Bank
 Alsop

6. Aswell describes this particular visit of Wolfe's to his home in Chappaqua in "Thomas Wolfe Did Not Kill Maxwell Perkins."

Ravenel
Preacher Reed
Dinwood Bland
The Bridge
The Scar

1) The way Webber comes to Town—The Circus
2) Build it with Brick
3) Webber's influence on new city: the Joyner genealogy.
4) The Father and uncle: Theodore
5) The Bell—Looky Thar
6) The Wooden Leg
7) The New World: the Railway—the new hotel, etc.: Webber.
8) The 1900's
9) The Affair at the Bridge

Cupper's on top—He didn't hit him once when he—
Willie took a beer glass—smashed it over Cupper's head . . .
and all Cupper did was just turn his head—and then Willie took a
gallon jug . . . and it went flying all over the girl's dress . . . and then
Cupper really went to work.
(a voice respectful) and Cupper's a good guy.

The Years of the Weaver's Weft
The Years of the Weaver
The Web of the Weaver's Weft
The Years Which the Weaver Hath Spun
Webber
George Webber, Weber, Weaver.

[*Sometime in March, Wolfe changed his mind about the proposed book. He decided to make it a complete autobiographical chronicle, pulling together all he had written for "Spangler's Paul," "The
October Fair," the story of Joe Doaks, and any other assembly of
episodes. He chose a new title and a new name for his hero and worked
determinedly for two months before he placed the manuscript in
Edward Aswell's hands.*

*The notes above show him groping for a name and a title. The
following notes have been selected from loose sheets among Wolfe's
papers to illustrate the shaping process as he moved toward his final
composition.*]

The Weft That the Weaver Hath Woven
The Weft That the Weaver Hath Wrought
The Web That the Weaver Has (Hath) Woven
The Web That the Weaver Has (Hath) Wrought
The Years That the Locust Has Eaten

The City: The Rock

The Web and the Rock
The Web in the Rock

Let his name be Webber.

THE WEB AND THE ROCK

A Story of the Voyage of Everyman: His
Going To and Fro Upon the Earth; His
Walking Up and Down In It; And His Desire
For Home; His Vision of the Lost, the Found,
the Ever-Real, the Never-Here America
by
Thomas Wolfe

The Gaps:
    Webber's family—woman he married.
    After Pine Rock: What did George do? (1918 or 1920 to 1923)
    (Newspaper work? perhaps reporter on the Libya Journal)
    From 1929—No Gaps.

Possibilities (Put in men you know on Libya Courier)—1918–1923. B. Smith, Fowler Hill, George McCoy, Arthur Mann.

I must now speak of things about which, insofar as they affect George Webber's own life, and the lives of people still living, who are known to me, but connected by ties of blood relationship, I should prefer to keep silent. I do not presume to probe into them—the work of explanation I will leave to him—but, since the value of anything I can say is solely and simply a value of necessary illumination, I must mention them here.

As briefly as possible then, here is the record: about 1885, John Webber met a young woman of our community named Amelia Joyner. She was the daughter of one Lafayette, or "Fate" Joyner, with whose figure I became familiar in the 80's, who had some distant relationship to my own family, from their origins in Zebulon County, which I have described before.

It cannot be denied, it was a bad marriage.

Webber's Marriage: that he asked her for a divorce is certain, as it is no less certain that she refused to give him one.

What I've Got Now:
    The Roots: Old Catawba, etc.
    The Joyners: 1593–1896, etc.
    The Stranger's Country—Webber, etc., The Train: 1881–1900.
    Caliban—"Son, son," etc.
    The Boy Caliban—Three O'Clock
                The Winter's Tale, etc. } 1908–1916
                The Child By Tiger, etc.

Pine Rock

Alsop, Joyner, Preacher Reed—1916–1920

The City

The Rock
Monty Bellamy, Alsop, etc.—1923

Mrs. Jack (1925–1929)

The Ship, The Room, Utility Cultures—1925
The Boom Town—1929
April Late April, The October Fair, etc.

The Ring and the Book (1930–1931)

The Book, The Party at Jack's, Mr. Malone, The Party
A Summer in Paris
Switzerland } 1930
The Black Forest
'E—McHarg
The Fall of the Bank } 1931
Return

The Jungle Years

Brooklyn—The Alleyway
Only the Dead Know Brooklyn—Exile
The Lion and the Fox
No More Rivers, etc. ⎬ 1931–1935
The Fox at Morning

You Can't Go Home Again

" 'Tis Passing Great to Be a King," etc.
"I Have a Thing to Tell You"
Return ⎬ 1935–1938
You Can't Go Home Again.

March 2, 1935 to March 2, 1938
The boat: A waiter (stare—eyes ahead)
              others
Paris: No one
England (London):   Pat
                    Mr. Sykes
England (Norfolk):   Mr. Blakely
                     Little boy & his mother at swimming pool
                     The Grahsses and the Sedges
                     The Man who liked women
Holland: Bendien
           What shall they do who stamp proud feet
Hannover: Wachter
Berlin: Martha
          The Old Man
          Ledig
          Rowohlt
          Mrs. Harnack
Copenhagen: Else
              Lammersen.

[*Several pages in the notebook, filled with hastily scrawled
notes on the Max Baer–Tommy Farr fight on March 11, are omitted*

here. Wolfe was apparently interested in the idiom the sports announcer used in radio broadcasting.]

Gwen Jassinoff [7] 162 W. 13th.

Democracy: a kind of living constant, [unsubmissive?] to the changes of its forms.

1934–1938

Alsop, The Fox, Miss Brewster, Mrs. Whelke, Dr. Whelke, Hartmann, Lewald, Van Paget and Page, Grogan, Thea.

A POLITICAL QUESTIONAIRE

Q: Are you a Republican?
A: No.
Q: Democrat?
A: No.
Q: Socialist?
A: No.
Q: Communist?
A: No.
Q: What are your political affiliations?
A: None; save to vote at present for that party in America which at the present time best embodies ideas of social revision in which I believe. At the present moment that party is the Democratic Party.

To Be Done:
Order Shoes, send out laundry, send out suits, make Pullman reservation, see or telephone bank.

To Take With:
Evening clothes, Blue Suit, Gabardine.

7. Miss Jassinoff was Wolfe's typist, who worked for him during the months while he was completing his final manuscript.

Letters:
> Bank
> Arthur Mann [8]
> Pearl Shope [9]
> Mrs. Jelliffe?
> Stoney? [10]
> Someone who wants me to intro. book
> Lum Tamblyn and Fairline [11]
> Miss Nowell

The West

> July–Sept. 1935
> *Col.* Davison and his wife, the Ferrils, Olga.
> *N. Mexico* Sally.[12]
> *California* (Hollywood) The Sayres, an old woman at dawn.
> *San Fran* The whore, Palo Alto, Lee and his wife.
> *Utah* a bartender, the whores at the [Isabelle?]
> *St. Louis* Lesser, the woman at the house.

Winter's Tale

> New York 1935–1936
> The Women: Louise Jackson, Mrs. Gardner, Mrs. Sterner.

> April 24–25
> You Can't Go Home Again
> A Farewell to the Fox

8. Arthur Mann, a sports writer, had taken Wolfe to the annual dinner of the New York Chapter of the Baseball Writers of America on January 30. His introduction of Wolfe to some of the baseball players had helped in the characterization of Nebraska Crane.

9. A friend of the Wolfe family in Asheville, who was the model for Helen Gant's friend Pearl Hines in LHA.

10. George Stoney, a student at the University of North Carolina, was writing an account of Wolfe's visit to Chapel Hill in 1936. It appeared in October, 1938, in *The Carolina Magazine* under the title "Eugene Returns to Pulpit Hill."

11. The law firm in New Jersey which had successfully handled Wolfe's case against Murdach Dooher in the recovery of his manuscripts.

12. Mrs. Sally Saunders, editor of the *Junior League Magazine* and a friend of Wolfe's during the last two years of his life. She and a friend were traveling in New Mexico and were with Wolfe the night of his celebrated encounter with Mabel Dodge Luhan. See Nowell, *Thomas Wolfe: A Biography,* p. 287.

The Cleavages with Fox
—Women
—Economics
—Politics
—The Structure of the World.

[*The remaining entries are names and addresses, including real estate listings. Wolfe was still considering a cottage in the country.*

On May 17, Wolfe delivered to Aswell an enormous package of typescript which represented the assembled episodes and possible episodes for his novel. Earlier he had been uncertain about letting Aswell see it. "I don't know whether it would be a good idea to let him read it now or not," *he had written to Miss Nowell on May 12.* "I know where I stand, but it is like presenting someone with the bones of some great prehistoric animal he has never seen before—he might get bewildered." *But Miss Nowell's encouragement reassured him that, although unrevised and in need of extensive cutting and reweaving, the manuscript was coherent and would give Aswell authentic testimony of the scope and quality of the book. For a fully annotated outline of the manuscript, see the Appendix to Richard S. Kennedy's* The Window of Memory, *where it is entitled* "Thomas Wolfe's Rough Outline of his Last Book."]

PART TEN ~

THE RETURN TO THE WEST

A Western Journal
June 20, 1938, to July 2, 1938

Wolfe's speech at Purdue was a triumph. He gave the students a well-prepared, good-humored account of his career and then soberly turned to reveal the development of his social conscience during the recent years.[1]

Next he traveled on to the Pacific Northwest, with his own special mission to search out the Westall relatives, descendants of his great-uncle Bacchus, who had moved to Seattle. While he was in Portland, he was invited to join a happy experiment in tourism. Edward Miller, Sunday editor of the Portland Oregonian, *and Ray Conway, executive in the Oregon State Motor Association, had decided to try to answer these questions:* "Is it feasible and sensible to tour the Western national parks within the time limits of the average man's vacation? If so, what does it cost?" *They were going to attempt to visit eleven national parks and one of the great federal dams in a two-week period, and they asked Wolfe to be their literary passenger. Because Wolfe felt that he was a medium for the American spirit, he accepted eagerly. He would get one more chance to try to absorb the West, which he felt held a special meaning for Americans. He told Miller:* "Almost every American, no matter where born, is a Westerner at heart. . . . The West is inevitable. Somehow or other the great development in this country is taking the western direction—not north or south—but moving across. The West will be truly great when it has enough people. The West is the American horizon." [2]

He carried along a good-sized notebook, for he thought that a record of his impressions might be developed later into a publishable

1. Wolfe's manuscript for the speech was lost for a number of years, but a large portion of it turned up after the death of John Terry. It was among the manuscript materials Terry had appropriated for himself from the Wolfe papers during the years of his unproductive research. The remaining pages were discovered by William Braswell among the pages of manuscript for YCGHA. The piece has now been published by the Purdue University Press: *Thomas Wolfe's Purdue Speech "Writing and Living,"* ed. William Braswell and Leslie A. Field (Lafayette, Ind., 1964).

2. Edward Miller, "Gulping the Great West," [*Portland*] Oregonian, July 31 and August 7, 1938.

volume, to be called "A Western Journey" or "A Western Journal." [3]
He began the trip with pencil in hand and soon had thousands of
words. At some point he turned back to the beginning and jotted down
a trial epigraph or proem; thus the notebook has a formal or literary
touch on the first page.

Storm-herds of thundering Sioux cloud past in viewless vacancy. Long, long ago, within the anodes of the timeless West—a man felt, saw, heard, thought—or did he vision them?—these things—Oh, time.

A DAILY LOG

OF

THE GREAT PARKS TRIP

Monday, June 20 (Crater Lake):

Left Portland, University Club, 8:15 sharp—Fine day, bright sunlight, no cloud in sky—Went South by East through farmlands of upper Willamette and around base of Mount Hood which was glorious in brilliant sun—Then climbed and crossed Cascades (86 miles), and came down with suddenness of knife into the dry lands of the Eastern slope—Then over high plateau and through bare hills and canyons and irrigated farmlands, here and there, Cow Valley, etc., and into Bend at 12:45—200 miles in 4½ hours.

Then back at hotel and view of the 3 Sisters and Cascade range —then up to the Pilot Butte above the town—the great plain stretching infinite away—and unapproachable the great line of the Cascades with their snowcapped sentinels Hood, Adams, Jefferson, 3 Sisters, etc., and out of Bend at 3 and then through the vast and level pinelands—somewhat reminiscent of the South for 100 miles, then down through the noble pines to the vast plainlike valley of the Klamath—the virgin land of Canaan all again—the far-off ranges infinite—Oregon and the Promised Land—then through the valley floor—past Indian reservation—

---

3. This notebook has been edited previously in two different forms. Miss Nowell produced an abridged version entitled "A Western Journey," which appeared in the *Virginia Quarterly Review* (Summer, 1939). Agnes Lynch Starrett and Percival Hunt edited an almost complete version, *A Western Journal* (Pittsburgh: University of Pittsburgh Press, 1951). We are very much indebted to these previous editors in our labors to decipher Wolfe's handwriting for the present edition.

Capt. Jack [*Mountain*]—The Medocs—the great trees open approaching vicinity of the [*Crater Lake National*] Park—the entrance and the reservation—the forester—the houses—the great snow patches underneath the trees—then the great climb upwards—the forestry administration—up and up again—through the passes, the great plain behind and at length the incredible crater of the lake—the hotel and a certain cheerlessness in spite of cordialness—dry tongues vain-talking for a feast—the rooms, the cottages, the college boys and girls who serve and wait—the cafeteria and the souvenirs—the great crater fading coldly in incredible cold light—at length departure—and the forest rangers down below—long, long talks—too long with them about "our wonders" etc.—then by darkness the sixty or seventy miles down the great dark expanse of Klamath Lake, the decision to stay here for the night—three beers, a shave, and this—revelly [*reveille*] at 5:30 in the morning—and so to bed!

First day: 404 miles.

Tues. June 21, 1938 (Yosemite):

Dies Irae: Wakened at 5:30—dragged weary bones out, dressed, closed baggage, was ready shortly before six, and we were off again "on the dot"—at six o'clock. So out of Klamath, the lake's end, and a thread of silver river in the desert—and immediately the desert, sage brush, and bare, naked hills, great-molded, craterous, cuprous, glaciated, blasted—a demonic heath with reaches of great pine, and volcanic glaciation, cuprous, fiendish, desert, blasted—the ruins of old settlers' homesteads, ghost towns and the bleak little facades of long forgotten post-offices lit luridly by blazing morning sun, and the unending monotone, the deserted station of the incessant railway—all dominated now by the glittering snow-pale masses of Mount Shasta—the pine lands, canyons, sweeps and rises, the naked crateric hills and the volcanic lava masses and then Mount Shasta omnipresent—Mount Shasta all the time—always Mt. Shasta—and at last the town named Weed (with a divine felicity)—and breakfast at Weed at 7:45—and the morning bus from Portland and the tired people tumbling out and *in* for breakfast.

And away from Weed and towering Shasta at 8:15—and up and climbing and at length into the passes of the lovely timbered Siskiyous and now down into canyon of the Sacramento in among the lovely timbered Siskiyous all through the morning down and down and down the canyon, and the road snaking, snaking always with a thousand little punctual gashes, and the freight trains and the engines turned backward with the cabs in *front*—down below along the lovely Sacramento snaking, snaking, snaking—and at last into the town of Redding and the timber fading, hills fading, cuprous lavic masses fading—and almost at once the mighty valley of the Sacramento—as broad as a continent —and all through the morning through the great floor of that great plainlike valley—the vast fields thick with straw grass lighter than Swedes' hair—and infinitely far and unapproachable like time's dream the mountain on both sides—and great herds of fat, brown steers in straw-bright fields—a dry land, with a strange, hot, heady fragrance and fertility—and at last no mountains at all but the great sun-bright, heat-hazed, straw-bright plain and the straight marvel of the road on which the car makes on like magic and no sense of speed at 60 miles an hour.

At 11:30 a brief halt—to look at the hotel—and giant palms now, and Spanish tiles and arches and plasters and a patio in the hotel and swimming pool—and on again and on again across the great, hot, straw-bright plain, and great fields mown new and scattered with infinite bundles of baled hay and occasional clumps of greenery and freshness and house and barns where water is and as Sacramento nears a somewhat greener land, more unguent, and better houses now, and great fat herds of steers innumerable and lighter and more sun—modest towns and at length through the heat-haze the slopes of Sacramento and over an enormous viaduct across a flat and marshy land and herons flying and then the far-flung filling stations, hot dog stores, 3 little pigs, and Bar-B-Q's of a California town and then across the Sacramento into town—the town immediate and houses now and mighty palms and trees and people walking and the state house with its gold-leaf dome and spaghetti at the first Greek's that we found and out again immediate and pressing on—past state house—and past street by street of leafy trees and palms and pleasant houses and out from town now—but traffic flashing past now—and loaded trucks and whizzing cars—no more the lonely fifty mile stretches and sixty miles an hour—but down across the backbone of the state—and the whole backbone of the state —cars and towns and farms and people flashing by—and still that same vast boundless plain—no longer *brown* now—the San Joaquin Valley now—and bursting with God's plenty—orchards—peaches—apricots —and vineyards—orange groves—God's plenty of the best—and glaring little towns now thick with fruit packing houses—[ovenhot?] glittering in the hot and shining air—town after town—each in the middle of God's plenty.

And at length the turn at [*Merced*] toward Yosemite [*National Park*]—90 miles away—and a few miles from town the hills again—the barren, crateric, lavic, volcanic, blasted hills—but signs now telling us we can't get in now across the washed out road save behind the conducter [4]—and now too late—already 5 of six and the last conducter leaves at six and we still fifty miles away—and telephone calls now to rangers, superintendents and so forth, a filling station and hot cabins, and the end of a day of blazing heat and the wind stirring in the sycamores about the cabins, and on again now, and almost immediately the broken ground, the straw-bright mouldings, the rises to the crateric hills and soon among them—climbing, climbing into timber—and down, down, down into pleasant timbered mountain folds—get no sensation yet and winding in and out—and the little hill towns here and there and climbing, climbing, climbing, mountain lodges, cabins, houses, and so on, and now in terrific mountain folds, close packed, precipitous, lapped together and down and over, down again along breath-taking curves and steepnesses and sheer drops down below into a canyon cut a mile below by great knife's blade—and at the bottom the closed gate—the little store.

Calls upon the phone again, and darkness and the sounding waters, and at last success—upon our own heads be the risk but we may enter—and we do—and so slowly up and up along the washed out road—finding it not near so dangerous as we feared—and at length past the bad end and the closed gate and release—and up now cleanly and the sound of mighty waters in the gorge and the sheer blacknesses of beetling masses and stars—and presently the entrance and the ranger's house—a free pass now—and up and up—and boles of trees terrific, and cloven rock above the road and over us and dizzy masses night black as a cloud, a sense of the imminent terrific and at length the valley of the Yosemite, roads forking darkly, but the perfect size—and now a smell of smoke and of gigantic tentings and enormous trees and gigantic cliff walls, night black all around and above the sky-bowl of starred night—and Curry's Lodge and smoky gaiety and wonder—hundreds of young faces and voices—the offices, buildings, stores, the dance floor crowded with its weary hundreds, and the hundreds of tents and cabins and the discovery of the life and the immensity of all —and 1200 little shopgirls and stenogs and maids and school-teachers and boys—all, God bless their little lives, necking, dancing, kissing, feeling, and embracing in the giant darkness of the giant redwood trees —all laying and getting laid tonight—and the sound of the dark gigantic fall of water—so to bed!

And 535 miles today!

4. Edward Miller, supplying some annotations for Miss Nowell's abridged version, "A Western Journey," said: "He was referring to a 'pilot car'—an auto hat leads caravans over roads under construction."

The gigantic *unconscious* humor of the situation [5]—C. "making every national park" without seeing any of them—the main thing is to "make them"—and so on and on tomorrow.

Wednesday, June 22:

Woke at 7:00 after sound sleep—water falling—girls' voices, etc.—Breakfast—and good one at cafeteria—after that visited water-falls, took photographs, talked to people, visited swell hotel, sent postcards, etc., and then on way out—by the South Wawona entrance —then beautiful rockrim drive down through wooded Sierras to foot-hills—the brilliant leafage of scrub pine—then the hay-bright gold of wooded hogbacks—then the hay-gold plain and hay-gold heat—a crowded country road—and Clovis—lunch there—then the ride up to the mountains again—the same approach as the day before—by hay-gold hogbacks—then cuprous masses—then forested peaks—then mar-velous and precipitous ride upward and the great view back across the vast tangle of the Sierras.

Then General Grant [*National Park*] [6] and the great trees—the pretty little girls—then the 30 mile drive along the ridge to the Sequoia [*National Park*]—and General Sherman [*Tree*]—and the giant trees —then straight through to other entrance, then down terrifically the terrific winding road—the tortured view of the eleven ranges—the vertebrae of the Sierras—then the lowlands and sheer hogback—no bends—and Visalia—then by dark straight down the valley—to Bakers-field—then East and desertwards across the Tehachapi range—the vertical brightness of enormous cement plants—and now at 1:30 in Mohave at desert edge—and tomorrow across the desert at 8:00 o'clock —and so to bed—and about 365 miles today.

At Bakersfield:

Enormous electric sign—Frosted Milkshakes—a Drive Inn— And Girls in white sailor pantys serving drinks—I drank Frosted Lime, Miller a Coca Cola float, etc.

Thursday, June 23:

Up at 7 o'clock in hotel at Mohave—and already the room hot and stuffy and the wind that had promised a desert storm the night before was still and the sun already hot and mucoid on the incredibly dirty and besplattered window panes—and a moment's look of hot,

5. Wolfe wrote this paragraph on a page opposite the beginning of the diary entry for June 21.
6. When Wolfe made the trip through the General Grant Grove, it was still a separate National Park.

tarred roof and a dirty ventilator in the restaurant below and [*no*] moving life but the freight cars of the S.P. r.r.—and a slow freight clicking past and weariness—so up and shaved and dressed and snapped the zipper and downstairs and the white-cream Ford awaiting and the two others—in the back—and to the cafe for breakfast—eggs and pancakes, sausages, most hearty—and a company of r.r. men—So out of town at 8:10 and headed straight into the desert—and so straight across the Mohave at high speed for four hours—to Barstow—so in full flight now—the desert yet more desert—blazing heat—102 inside the filling station—the dejected old man and his wife—and so the desert mountains, crateric, lavic and volcanic, and so more fiendish the fiend desert of the lavaed earth like an immense plain of broken tar—and very occasionally a tiny blistered little house—and once or twice the presence of water and the magic greenery of desert trees—and yet hotter and more fiendish through fiend hills—cuprous, ferrous and denuded as slag heaps—and so the filling station and the furnace air fumed by a hot, dry, strangely invigorating breeze and the filling station man who couldn't sign: "I'm only up an hour and my hands shake so with the heat"—and Needles at last in blazing heat and the pleasant station and hotel and Fred Harvey all aircooled, and a good luncheon, and an hour here.

And so out again in blazing heat—106 within the shutters of the station awning—116 or 120 out of it—and so out of Needles—and through heat blasted air along the Colorado 15 miles or so and then across the river into Arizona—pause for inspection, all friendly and immediate—then into the desert world of Arizona—the heat blasted air —the desert mountain shapes draw in now and more devilish—the crateric and volcanic shapes draw in and up and up among them, now and then a blistered little town—a few blazing houses and the fronts of stores—up and up now and fiend desert shapes prodigiously—and into Oatman and the gold mining pits, the [craterholes?] the mine shafts and the signs of new gold digging—Mexicans half-naked before a pit—and up and up and winding up and up to Goldcrest (?)

Across the Mohave the S.P. fringed with black against the blazing crater of the desert sky rushes on, rushes on its monotone of forever and of now—moveless Immediate.

And at last the rim and down and down through blasted shapes, volcanic "pipes" and ancient sea erosions, mesa table heads, columnar swathes, stratifications, and the fiendish wind and below the vast pale lemon-mystic plain—and far away immensely far the almost moveless plume of black, of engine smoke and the double header freight advancing—advanceless moveless—moving through timeless time and on and on across the immense plain backed by more immensities of fiendish mountain shapes to meet it and so almost meeting moveless-moving never meeting, up and up and round and through a pass and down to Kingman and a halt for water and on and on and up and down into another mighty plain, desert, going going—green greener—and some cattle now and always up and up and through fiend blasted shapes and the enormous lemon-magic of the desert plains, fiend mountain shapes from lemon heat mist as from magic seas arising—and a halt for gas at a filling station with a water fountain "Please be careful with the water, we have to haul it 60 miles"—5280 feet above.

And 4800 feet we've climbed since Needles and on and on and up and the country greening now and steers in fields wrenching grey-green grass among the sage brush clumps and trees beginning now—the National Forest beginning—and now greenery—and trees and pines and grass again—a world of desert greenness, still not Oregon —but a different world entirely from the desert world and hell shapes —no longer fiend tormented but now friendly, forested, familiar and around and down and in a pleasant valley, Williams—and for a beer here where I *thought* I was 3 years ago—bartender a Mexican or an Indian or both—and out and on our way again along the great road leading across the continent and 6 or 7 miles out an off-turn to the left for the Grand Canyon.

And not much climbing now, but up and down again the great plateau 7000 feet on top—and green fields now and grass and steers and hills forested and oaks and trees and on and on toward (levelling) the distant twin rims—blue-vague defined—of the terrific canyon—the great sun sinking now below us 7000 feet—we racing on to catch him at the canyon ere he sinks entirely—but too late, too late—at last the ranger's little house [*at the South Rim of Grand Canyon National Park*], the permit and the sticker—the inevitable conversations, the polite goodbyes—and (almost dark now) at 8:35 to the edge of the canyon—to Bright Angel Lodge—and before we enter between the cabins the Big Gagoochy [7]—and the Big Gagoochy there immensely, darkly, almost weirdly there—a fathomless darkness peered at from the very edge of hell with abysmal stoneworks—almost unseen—just fathomlessly there—so to our cabin—and delightful rooms—and so to dinner in the Lodge—and our middlemen in jodhpurs, pajamas, shirts, and cowboy pants, and Fred Harvey's ornate wigwam—and to dinner here—and then to walk along the rear of Big Gagoochy and inspect the big hotel—and at the stars innumerable and immense above the Big

7. In another of Miller's notes, he explained: "This was [*Wolfe's*] nickname for the Grand Canyon. It sounded like 'Big Gaboochy.'"

Gagoochy just a look—a big look—so goodnight—and 500 miles today.

Friday, June 24, 1938:
    At daybreak, a deer outside the window cropping grass—Rose Grand Canyon 8:15—others had been up already for an hour—wakened at four or thereabouts by deer grazing, and by its hard small feet outside of window—Then Miller in at 8:30—but let me sleep—so bathed, dressed, to coffee shop by 9 and good breakfast—then packed and with Miller, Conway and the Ranger to Administration offices, met the Ass't. Superintendent—so to Observation point—the Ranger driving and looked through observation glasses at Old Gagoochy and immortal time—and Alberdene the young geologist with crisp-curly hair and deep sensitivities who talked and remembered me from 3 years ago—an Arizona Ph.D. and at Harvard, too—but now wants no more teaching and applies for Philippines—so down to Lookout Tower where the caravan streams in and listens to lecture by young Ranger Columba and into tower and all the people—the Eastern cowboy with Fred Harvey hat and shirt and cowgirl with broad hat, and wet red mouth, blonde locks and riding breeches filled with buttock—and up into tower and the Painted Desert and the Small Gagoochy gorge—and the vermilion cliffs—and down and goodbye to the rangers.
    And so away—and stop-over for a look at Small Gagoochy gorge—and on to the desert and to Cameron and blazing heat and the demented reds again, and lunch here in an Indian Lodg-ee—and an old dog moving in the shadow of a wall—and so away across the bridge and into the Painted Desert and blazing heat and baked road and Painted Desert through the afternoon by the vermilion cliffs—and four small Indian girls in rags and petticoats beside the road awaiting pennies (dimes they got) two upon a burro—beer, and photographs and heat incredible and the demented reds of Painted Desert and away, away again—good road—bad road—good and bad again by the demented and fiend tortured redness of vermilion cliffs—red, mauve, and violet, passing into red again—and now the gorge, much smaller down, of Big Gagoochy, and the Navajo Bridge—and the Gagoochy, brown-red-yellow—a mere 1000 feet or so below.
    And on and on across the Big Gagoochy now through desert land—now gray-greening sagely into sage and stray Indians merging into road here and there and Indian houses—then the far lift of the rise, the road rising, winding into hills, and up and up into the timber and the forest now, and all the lovely quaking aspens and the vast and rising rim of range and meadow land—a golf course big and narrow on both

sides rising clearly and mysteriously to woods—and then the big woods again, and deep, dense woods, the ranger's house and entrance [*to the North Rim of Grand Canyon National Park*], and at last the Lodge, the mysterious color—a haircut, a clean shirt, and supper with the Browns, and a sweet waitress, and before this part—the sunset moment —the tremendous twilight of the Big Gagoochy—more concise and more collected, more tremendous here and dinner then and darkness and the lights of the South Rim—and later on the moving picture, the two Canadian College youths in crimson blazers—the incredible theatrical performance with the waitresses and bellhops performing—Hiawatha [*charting?*] the U.P.—and naught but the clog dancers passable— and then Brown and his colored picture slides—Bryce, Zion, the Canyon and the Mormon temple, then the dance, the bar, Scotch highballs, and good talk with Miller and the wind in pine trees, and home with Miller to the Cabin, and C. still wakeful, rising, reading costs and mileages excitedly from his records—he all the night with them—and arguments, agreements, and avowals again on costs and mileages and possibilities—the moon in 30 hours is possible—and C. taking pride in all our present luxury because "It makes a better person of you" and the first time he gave a man a tip—and so to bed!—and 210 miles today.

Saturday, June 25, 1938:

Rose 7:30 cabin North Rim Lodge Grand Canyon—shave, bath, dressed—cabin very luxurious—appointed like modern hotel—best we'd seen—sound of waitresses and maids singing farewell songs—"Till we meet again" etc.—to passengers departing on buses—Tendering U.P. sentiment and C. declared there were tears in eyes of the passengers and some of the girls—Into Lodge for view from terrace of the Big Gagoochy in first light—and glorious!—and glorious!—wrote half dozen post cards in brilliant sunlight on ledge—then into breakfast with C. and M. and the Browns—and the inevitable Ranger—and the waitress with the strange and charming smile—and she from Texas and admitted that sentiment, songs, and kicking her legs for Pony Boy in night time entertainment all at 8000 feet for dear old U.P. got her wind and at first "made her awfully tired"—so out and by myself again to terrace—then to cabin to pack—then to hotel—and with Ranger and C. and M. to cafeteria for the inevitable inspection of cabins, cafeterias, etc.—and at long last, at 11 o'clock on our way out—and down through the Forest, and the long sweeping upland meadows and the deer and cattle grazing, quivering the aspen leaves in the bright air, and down and down and then the badlands spread below as ever again, the fierce red earth, the tortured buttes and the vermilion cliffs, the Painted desert.

And on and on across the desert and into Utah, and at 1:30, 3 miles past the line, the Mormon town of Kanab at Perry's Lodge—a white house, pleasant, and almost New England, and the fierce bright heat, the little town, and greenness here, and trees and grass, and a gigantic lovely cool-bright poplar at the corner—and so out and on along the road and presently the turn off to the left for Zion's Canyon —and before, the mountains rising range and range, no longer fierce red and vermilion now, but sandy, whitest limestone, striped with strange stripes of salmon pink—scrub-dotted, paler—Now in the canyon road and climbing, and now pink rock again, strange shapes and scorings in the rock, and even vertices upon huge swathes of stone, and plunging down now in stiff canyon folds the sheer solid beetling soaplike block of salmon red again—deeper yet not so fierce and strange (I thought) as the Grand Canyon earth, and towering soapstone blocks of red incredible, and through a tunnel, out and down and down, and through the great one spaced with even windows in the rock that give on magic casements opening on sheer blocks of soapstone red, and out again in the fierce light and down round dizzy windings of the road into the canyon's depth.

And at the bottom halt inevitable at Administration offices [*of Zion National Park*], visit inevitable to cafeteria and cabins, and away again along the canyon and the Virgin River (how sweet to see sweet water sweetly flowing here between these dizzy soapstone blocks of red) and round the bendings of the river by the soapstone walls of block fierce red, and into the valley floor and trees (a little like Yosemite, this valley, yet not so lush, so cool, nor so enchanted, nor cooled by the *dunkelheit* of towering pines), but an oasis here, a glimpse of Lodge inevitable and—O miracle!—in hot oasis, a swimming pool, a bathing house, and young, wet half-naked forms—a pool surrounded by the cottonwoods and walled round, beetled over by sheer soapstone blocks of red, capped by pinnacles of blazing white—O pool in cottonwoods surrounded by fierce blocks of red and temples and kings' thrones and the sheer smoothness of the blinding vertices of soapstone red—did never pool look cooler nor water wetter, water more inviting.

So by the road down to the canyon's end and all around the beetling block of soapstone red, and river flowing, and trees and shade, a tourist party, and a lecturer—and two old friends—and one from Saginaw and one from somewhere else, and one a coal salesman, and one something else, and one with an enormous belly and a half-sleeved shirt, the other with green-visored helmet and two fingers only on his hand, and both amiable and voluble and willing to pose, and talk and act, and awed by nature dutifully—and so amiably goodbye to them, back to the swimming pool, and snapshots here, and so away, and a shot at a white lime-cap on the way, and up and up again, and through the tunnel, and by the strange carved shapes and vertical and punctual lines, and to the top and down and down again—a vista of the plain and desert, and the white sand-lime peaks with the salmon markings—and one strange, isolate and Painted Desertward (I think) of salmon red and down and down and to the main road finally and to the left and up along it toward Bryce Canyon on the main road north to Salt Lake City—and soon, almost immediate, a greener land, and grass in semi-desert fields, and stock and cattle grazing, and now timbered hills in contour not unlike the fields of home, and now farms and green incredible of fields and hay and mowing and things growing and green trees and Canaan pleasantness and a river flowing (the Sevier) and (by desert comparison) a fruitful valley—and occasional little towns—small Mormon towns—sometimes with little houses of old brick—but mostly little houses of frame, and for the most part mean and plain and stunted looking and hills rising to the left—a vista of salmon pink, vermilion cliffs again—the barricades of Bryce.

And then the turn in—and so halted here by road repair until the convoy from the Canyon passes out—and meanwhile talking to the man with the red flag—"we have no deserts here in Utah"—is Zion then a flowering prairie, and are Salt Lake and the Bonneville Flats the grassy precincts of the King's Paradise? And cars gathered here on bleeding oil from Ohio, New Mexico, Illinois, California, Michigan—and presently the other cavalcade appears upon the crest and flash downwards one by one till all are through—and then we start—the road good but still oil-bloody to the right for seven or ten miles—and up through sage land into timber, past canals, dude ranches, etc., into timber on the high plateau, another Ranger's entrance house in view, the stark curly whippings of the flag—another sticker—seven now—and into the [*Bryce Canyon National*] Park and up and through the timber past the Lodge and to the rim, where stood in setting sun looking out and down upon the least overwhelming, dizzy, and least massive of the lot—but perhaps the most astounding—a million wind-blown pinnacles of salmon pink and faery white all fused together like stick candy—all suggestive of a child's fantasy of heaven, and beyond the open semi-green and semi-desert plain—and lime-white and scrub-dotted mountains. And so back and to the Lodge with sour-pussed oldsters on the veranda, trinkets, souvenirs, and, methought, some superciliousness within, so got our keys, and to our cabin, and so shaved, and to the cafeteria which was clean and much be-Indian-souvenired, betrinketed, somehow depressing and expensive—ice tea 15 cents and 20 for a bad and measly sandwich—and so to the Lodge and peeked in at the inevitable Ranger and the attentive dutiful sourpusses listening to the inevitable lecture—Flora and Fauna of Bryce Canyon —so bought postcards and wrote them—and so to my cabin to write this.

And after this to Lodge where dance going on, and into curio shop where, with some difficulty, bought beer in cans, and had two, feeling more and more dissolute in this most moral state of Utah, and struck up talk with quaint old blondined bag named Florence who imitates bird calls and dark rather attractive woman, Canadian probably French, who sold curios and who had life in her—and was thoroughly willing to share it—so talking with them in lobby until dance broke up at 10:30 and young people coming out looking rather lost and vaguely eager, I thought, as if they wanted something that wasn't there and didn't know how to find it—and had some depressing reflections on Americans in search of gaiety, and National Park Lodges, and Utah and frustration, etc.; so home, where found C. busy with his calculations—"if we do so and so tomorrow, we'll have only so and so much to do on Monday"—and wrote this, my companions sleeping—and so to bed—and 265 miles today.

Sunday, June 26, 1938:
Arose Bryce Canyon 7:30—dressed, walked with M. to Rim and to observation house on point and looked at Canyon. Sky somewhat overcast and no sunlight in Canyon, but it was no less amazing—looked fragile compared to other great canyons "like filigree work" of fantastic loveliness—Great shouldering bulwarks of eroded sand going down to it—made it look very brittle and soft—erodes at rate of one inch a year—something the effect of sugar candy at a carnival—powdery, whitey, melting away—old man, roughly dressed, and with one tooth, and wife, and daughter, surprisingly smart looking young female in pajama slacks and smoked goggles talking geology—the words came trippingly off her tongue—"erosion"—"wind erosion"—"125 million years and so on"—There had been argument with someone whether canyon had been cut with water—"all canyons cut with water—" etc. —M. took pictures "Look out as if you're looking out."

Then quickly back through woods toward Lodge, and after last night's rain everything amazingly pungent, sweet and fragrant—smell

of sage, pine needles, etc.—So breakfast in Lodge and C. as usual
engrossed with hotel manager Hodgin about prices, rates, cabin accom-
modations etc.—wrote post cards and ate hearty breakfast and talked
with waitress who was from Purdue—studying "home economics" and
dress designing and hopes to be a "buyer" for Chicago store—observed
the tourists—two grim-featured females—schoolteachers—at table next
—who glowered darkly at everyone and everything with stiff inflexible
faces and H. says most of the tourists are women and many school-
teachers—so the tourists rise to depart, and presently the sound of
departing and the waitresses, maids, bellhops etc. gathered in front of
Lodge and by bus singing "Till we meet again"—"Goodbye, ladies"
etc.—and one of the dour-looking schoolteachers dabbing furtively at
eyes, and the bus departing, and emotional farewells, and the young
folks departing back to their work, and Hodgin exultantly "We got
tears out of four of 'em this morning. Oh, I love to see 'em cry, it
means business"—Then discussing hotel business again and the art of
pleasing guests and squeezing tears from them—and for me the memory of the dour-faced teacher dabbing at her eyes and stabbing pity in
the heart and something that can not be said.

So into hotel for a final look, and boys and girls practicing the
dances of a show, so to the cabin, packed, back to the Lodge and
farewell conversation with the curio-saleslady of last night, and with
the manager's wife—and so fare-well—and checked out the gates at
9:45 and down from the canyon through the woods, past the lodge-
motor-cabin just outside, on to the road-in-construction—slowly,
down towards the valley, and finally (15 miles away) into the main
road for Salt Lake and turned North—and Salt Lake from this point
250 miles away.

So all through the morning at good speed upon fine roads up
through a great enlarging and constantly growing richer valley—at
first mixed with some desert land—bald, scrub-dotted ridges on each
side ascending into lovely timber then to granite tops—and desert land
now, semi-desert, semi-green—clumped now with sage and dry, but
bursting marvellously into greenery where water is let in—and the
river (the Sevier) refreshing it—still seeing desert with occasional
plunges into sage green—the cool dense green of trees clustered
densely round a little house, and fields ripe with thick green, and the
warm green of hay, and fat steers and cows and horses grazing,
apparent men on Mormon Sunday reaping, mowing hay with reaping
machines and fields strewn with cut mounds of green anise hay, and
water—the wondrousness of water in the West, the muddy viscousness
of irrigation ditches filled with water so incredibly wet—the miracle of

water always in the West—the blazing whiteness of the sunlight now, the bright hot blueness of the skies, the piled cumulousness of snowy clouds.

And then the dirty little Mormon villages—blazing and blistered in that hot dry heat—and the forlorn little houses—sometimes just little cramped and warped wooden boxes, all unpainted, hidden under the merciful screenings of the dense and sudden trees—the blistered little storefronts, the wooden falsefronts of the little towns—sometimes the older Mormon houses of red brick—sometimes still more ancient uses of chinked log—sometimes strangely an old Mormon house of stone—but all in that hot dry immensity of heat and light so curiously warped and small and dirty and forlorn—just a touch of strangeness maybe in the set of eaves, the placing of the tiny porch, the look of the shop gables (temple-wise perhaps)—but of architecture graceless, all denuded, with the curious sterility and coldness and frustration the religion has.

But the earth meanwhile burgeoning into green and fat fertility—the windbreaks of the virgin poplars, the dense cool green of poplars in the hot bright light and the staunch cool shade of cottonwoods—and the valley winding into Canaan and the Promised land—the fields lush now with their green, their planted trees, the great reap of their mowings—strangely Canaan now—hemmed by the desert peaks—the hackled ridges on both sides—denuded and half barren, curiously thrilling in their nakedness—and Canaan magical, the vale irriguous below—the marvellous freshness and fecundity of the great Sevier valley now and in the midst of the great plain of Canaan the town of Richfield (so named because of the fat district)—a stop here.

So on steadily into growing fertilities—a blessed land of Canaan irriguous—by L.D.S.[8] made fertile, promised, and "This is the place"—Jacob, Levan, Nephi, Goshen—the names Biblical in Canaan—or Spanish Fork and American Fork—names like the pioneers—but even the towns arising from the desert now—the brightness of new brick—the stamped hard patterns of new bungalows—and in the bright hot light clean wide streets, neat houses, an air of growing and of prosperousness—but still a graceless lack of architectural taste—but now a kind of cooler sterner magic in the scenery (impassionate, granite, clearly barren in the hackled ridges of the limestone peaks, the austere blackness of the timber)—and the great valley floor burgeoning with Canaan in between—the cool flat silver of the lake at Provo and the full

8. Latter Day Saints, the formal name of the Mormons. The assertion "This is the place" was Brigham Young's pronouncement for the Mormon settlement to take place at Salt Lake.

fat land of plenty now—cherry orchards groaning with their fruit, fields thick with grain and hay, and fertile tillages betwixt the granite semi-arid cleanness of the desert peaks—Provo—its thriving look—the immense smelter plants—in hot bright air the hot bright mileage of the business street, the ugly sparseness, stamped out smartness of the stamped brick bungalows—the marvellousness of poplars and of cottonwoods, the dazzling brightness, richness, fragrance of the rambler roses and full fat land of Canaan all away—great canning plants now, and four-laned roads, and flashing and increasing traffic—and Brigham's great vale irriguous of Canaan and of plenty is marching, marching Northward between hackled peaks, is sweeping Northward through the backbone of the Promised Land, is sweeping onward, onward toward the Temple and The Lake—and by a rise approaching the barriers of the hackled peak, up, up, around the naked shoulder of a gravel mountain and down, down into the great plain of Salt Lake— half desert still, half burgeoning to richness and the irriguous vigor of the sudden green, and walled immensely on three sides by the hackled grandeur of the massive hills—but to the West, the massive peaks also but desert openness and the saline flatness, the thin mist lemon of the Great Salt Lake.

So now the houses thicken on both sides—another town with hot bright central street, and stores, and city hall and, like the others, a decided absence of humanity—then down five miles away to Salt Lake City—the bungalows close-set now on both sides—suddenly—heat-heat-misting in its splendid rise and facing the approach backed by the naked molding of the hills—the capitol—with its dome—looking like a capitol and dome always do—so into Salt Lake—skyscrapers, hotels, office buildings, an appearance of a city greater than its growth, and in 4 directions the broad streets sweeping out and ending cleanly under massed dense green at the rises of the barren magic hills—so into town, past a fantastic dance hall, "the world's largest"—stores, streets, blocks 600 feet in length and Sunday hotness, brightness, emptiness—the old feeling of Mormon coldness, desolation—the cruel, the devoted, the fanatic, and the warped and dead.

So for a hearty dinner at Rotisserie, then to the gleaming whiteness of Utah Hotel, the ornate hotel lobby, and mail for C. and M. Then out into the grounds round the Temple—the harsh ugly temple, the temple sacrosanct, by us unvisited, unvisitable, so ugly, green, grotesque, and black—so curiously warped, grotesque, somehow so cruelly formidable—then the great domed roof of the Tabernacle like a political convention hall—the statues of the town saints, Brothers Smith [*Joseph and Hyrum*], with pious recordings of their fanaticisms —the museum, the first cabin, etc.—the pomposities of bronze rhetoric

—the solemn avowals of "the finding of the plates" for the Book of Mormon, etc.[9]—a visit to The Lion House, The Bee Hive,[10] and so forth—and enough, enough, of all this folly, this cruelty and this superstition—into the white car now and out of town—almost immediate the clear and naked hill beside and to the left the vast meadows sloping to pale flatness, and the saline, citric flatness, paleness of the lake—and Land Of Plenty now indeed.

To the right the hackled, semi-barren ridges, and a strip of arid land, then marvellously the orchards, on both sides the orchards bursting with their fruit, their boughs groaning with their cherries, and greenness, lushness, watery fertility, the like of which was never seen before, flanked in the distant by the pale and misty flatness of the lake, the land merging into saline flatness at the marge, and beyond the misty magic of the hackled peaks—aye, with the cruelty of Mormon in it, but with a quality its own that grips and holds you now—and thriving towns, Ogden—"the fastest growing city in Utah"—and flashing brightness and an air of prosperousness and the clean elevation of the bald and hackled peaks—and ever greater orchards groaning with their fruit, and canning plants, and lush fertility—and Brigham, another thriving and exciting lively town—the strange tabernacled form of the Mormon Temple with its 8 gables on each side—but before we enter the busy main street just before us—a turn-off to the left—and almost immediate a climb up to the hills and over them and down the canyon toward Logan.

And now the greatest beauty of the day—the swift mounting up the canyon among bald and greening knobs, a sense of grandeur, sweetness and familiarity, and suddenly, cupped in the rim of bald hills, a magic valley plain, flat as a floor and green as heaven and more fertile and more magic than the Promised Land, then down and winding down the lovely canyon and cattle, horses, and houses sheltered by the trees, and then below the most lovely and enchanted valley of them all —the great valley around Logan—a valley that makes all that has gone before fade to nothing—the very corn and fruit of Canaan—a vast sweet plain of unimaginable richness—loaded with fruit, bursting with cherry orchards, green with its thick and lush fertility and dotted everywhere with the beauty of incredible trees—clumped cottonwoods and lines and windbreaks of incredible poplars—a land of promise and promise of plenty—and then Logan, a thriving, bright

9. Joseph Smith had declared that he found the Bible of the western continent written on thin gold plates. They were buried on the hill Cumorah, near Palmyra, New York.

10. The Lion House is the house in which Brigham Young's wives lived. The Bee Hive is Brigham Young's mansion.

town, blazing with electric light and an air of cheerfulness—the fresh bungalows and cottages and the more expensive homes—the tabernacle, and, with a curious tightening of the throat a thought of little Alladine [*Bell*] [11] who lived here, loved it and its canyon, and went out, like a million other kids like her, from all this Canaan loveliness to some fortune, fame and glory in the city.

And so out and on, light darkening now, and along that valley incredible, and at length across the line to Idaho, and into Preston, blazing with Idaho's electric light—and here perhaps lost the true road, for we entered now a very rough one "under construction for twenty miles"—and mounted in the darkness with a sense of strangeness and it had rained here and to the North the sky was inky rent with gigantic flashes of Western lightning—and the road perilous and slippery, too, the car sliding sideways as on balls of mercury—but we slogged through it to the good road and so on, between hogback ridges that had closed on us, through what was now, I suspect, desert country, towards Pocatello—on a splendid road—where we arrived just before eleven—registered at the Bannock hotel—out in brightly lighted streets and wakeful noctambuloes for food—a sandwich and some beer—so home—most tired—the others sleeping soundly now—perhaps somewhat too fatigued by the crowded beauty, splendor and magnificence of this day to write it down—and so to bed!

And today 467 miles! (and in our first seven days, about 2760 of our journey.)

SQUARE MILEAGES

Oregon	96,690
California	155,652
Arizona	113,956
Utah	83,990
Idaho	84,000
Wyoming	?
Montana	146,997
Washington	69,127

750,412
+100,000 (?)
(about 30% of entire national area)

11. Miss Bell had been one of Wolfe's typists in 1934. See her reminiscences in "T. Wolfe of 10 Montague Terrace," *Antioch Review,* XX (Fall, 1960), 315–30.

Monday, June 27, 1938:

Up at 8:10—Pocatello—overcast day—dressed, shaved, etc.—down for breakfast in Coffee Shop (Bannock Hotel)—C. and M. already there—so out of Pocatello and two miles out found we had left maps, books, etc.—so back—so finally out about 9:45—and the scoriac peaks about the town—the bald naked slopings.

But all through the morning through the great fertile valley of the Snake [*River*]—most fertile we had seen perhaps—the foliage dense—the field grass thick and natural—beside the road the thick and fecund grasses, herbs, flowers—by the irrigation ditches the thick and fecund growth almost middle western.

Following the train—the Yellowstone Express up through the Snake Valley—[today's ghosts?]—the towns—the whistling at the crossing—the final stop at [*Idaho Falls*].

The potato storage sheds sod roofed on top—the barns with the open loft door and the [overhead?]

The piles of dark straw hay—the stockades, the cattle and the horses, the feel and smell of clay and hay and stockades—the low sheds unpainted tenuous.

The little blistered house.

The farm buildings curiously forgotten in the vast curious landscape.

The towns—blistered—little blistered houses—farm implement stores—the big [*sketch*] of grain elevators etc.—and water, water everywhere—beside the road in fields, in irrigation ditches, under the bridges—wetness of water flowing to the [edges?], full to the floor of bridges, magical full water brown-mud-yellow—wanders everywhere.

At Sugar City the turn off for Jackson Hole—the rises now and then another valley less vast but irriguous upon the western borders of the Tetons.

"Almost a hole itself" says C.—and truly almost "holed" but open to one side—and found the pass through—then up up up at first through pined and hemlocked [Appalachian?]—the pleasant foldings of the hills—and pouring waters and then the steep turnings and the winds—the vision of the timber line and snow and then the Pass and down below the miracle of Jackson Hole—the milky winding of Cottonwood Creek—and Wild West enchantments and the bad-men legendaries—the hole terrific—and so down to it—and into Jackson—the Square of old West now beduded—the western hands by the filling station—smell of horsesweat, hay, a thought of curses, and giggling kids upon two broncs—luncheon in a "coffee shop"—the waitress and a blonde berouged [halfnude?] woman—and so out and round the town again, and up the edges of the valley by the Tetons and Leigh

Lake and [*Jenny*] Lake and Jackson Lake—the [*Grand Teton National*] Park entrance—the Museum, the glacial lake, the coolness and the sweetness and the Tetons.

Then through the Teton Forest, and Moran, and up and through the Forest hemlock, pine and spruce by winding single road, and end of Forest and immediate beginning Yellowstone [*National Park*] and the Park entrance, and the ride up through pine-hemlock etc. trees and then the Snake River foaming in its canyon, then a lake with the thick forest round it, then the "Thumb" of Yellowstone, the paint pots and the boiling waters, sinister, grotesque, carved, like a rhinoceros imbedded moving through hot oatmeal—then by narrow road to Old Faithful, and a bear by privy and the woods, and smoke boiling from the ground, and then the vast bouquet of Old Faithful, the enormous Inn, the tremendous Lodge, the cabins—our own by the small fast flowing river and the crater lid, volcanic, the earth smoking from a hundred holes, and Old Geyser and the people waiting, the hot boiling, overslopping of the pot, and then the vast hot plume of steam and water—and the people watching—middle-American watching—kids, old men, women, young men, women—all—and the hot plume, the tons of water falling and the hot plume dying—so to supper at the Lodge—and drinks first—and all the supper one could eat $1.00—and from the window the hot plume again—and then the explanation—entertainment in the visiting hall—and roaring fire in lobby—and old people reading—and so goodnight to Ray—and then to dance and people dancing—so to the Great Inn to the bar—like liner shipboard bar—more merriment here and people more prosperous, less concerned and singing "We don't give a damn for the whole state of Iowa"—and so talking and drinking with M.—and presently the bar closing—midnight—and the rain ceased—the night cleared to heaven and a billion stars and to our Lodge and to our cabin—Ray awake and talking all together—so to bed.

Tuesday, June 28:

Up at 8:40—chill and cold—and maids knocking at cabin door —and M. in to wake me—so dressed and to cafeteria—and C. waiting outside cabin making notes in book (his closeness, unearthly watchfulness, irked me)—to cafeteria with him then—he having eaten—then all to Old Faithful where people coming in as from 1892 and talking to a man from Kansas, then Old Faithful spurted—So on our way along the crater basins—the hot fierce bubblings of the tormented bowels of earth—the Sapphire Pool—etc.—people people people ("Don't lean over that, I'll have a parboiled boy" said man)—to Geyser swimming pool before—father teaching child to float, etc.—and on our way to Middle Basin, on to Norris basin & museum—(not staying long)—so cars by canyon road, enchanted country, and green meadows, and pine-hemlock-spruce-aspen forests—bears upon the road and lovely streams and water water in the West—Virginia cascades cascading— and the meadows and the Elk haunts and the bears now prowling on the road—all cars stopping—drivers cautious stepping out to photograph a bear—so picked up parking couple for a photo—she worked at Canyon hotel—so to Canyon cafeteria—where lunch—and so across the Bridge to see the mighty falls of Yellowstone and water falling boiling and the rushing current of Canyon's loveliest stream—so clear and bright and fierce compared to Colorado—so photographs and Ranger posing (for himself mayhap) with opera glasses—the steep encircled depths, the somewhat yellow walls (hence Yellowstone).

So back across the Bridge (no stopping for Bear Feeding now —no time) and then to Inspiration Point and the walk out over scenery upon the dizzying wooden Bridge—so on toward Mammoth Hot Springs—and the great climb and enchanted mountain country now and great peaks to the West, and the climb, the patched dirty snow beneath the trees and then the rising eminence of Mount Washburn (?)—and the timber line, the snow, the dizzy steepness to the left, and the desert, the Buffalos like dots grazing to the right—the elk—the enchanted valleys far below—now hackled crag peaks to the north and west, and down and down—and then the halt at [*Tower*] Falls,[12] and the clear snaking picture of the fall into the river—and then on, and buffalo away—and the Elk creeks—and finally below the whited, mined-out bleakness of the Mammoth Springs—and naked cabins huddled into rows, and the blistered erosions of the springs, the Lodge, the old Buildings of the Army Post, the vast slag-barreness of Everts Mtn. and a sense of bleakness—and the ranger and the talk, the questions and the answers and with the ranger up to see the Mammoth Springs, the colored rocks, the terraces—and all bleak and disappointing and so down and goodbye the Ranger and the Army Post and elk bones piled in decorative heaps and postcards written hastily and out and out and farewell Yellowstone and Gardiner.

A photo of the car at the stone arch—erected in 1872 ('twas said) and Gardiner small and somewhat bleak and like the entrance of a Nat'l. Park with a string of pullman cars that came up in the morning and two pullman porters coming down the street, a few stores advertis-

---

12. Wolfe mistakenly wrote Fenton or Teton Falls when he was referring to Tower Falls.

ing army and park equipment and away from Gardiner now along the Valley of the Yellowstone and at first the bleak denuded hills, the rushing river, the clear fast fish—abundant river—and then widening and the naked hills enlarging into rocky crags and forested (the timber deeper now than Utah—and the material granite now, no longer limestone) and the valley greening now with the widening and clean-watered rush of Yellowstone—and an enchanted valley now with upslope to the East and right and timbered Rockies going into snow and granite and the crags, nude spaciousness, and the valley not so green as Mormon land mayhap—but thick with grasses yellowed somewhat from the teeth of steers and the nude ranges going toward the timbered crags and to the west the miracle of evening light and the celebrated river called the Yellowstone and trees most green and marvellous—a scene familiar and unknown and elements like these before in Mormon land but by some miracle transformed into this Itselfness—and barns now painted red upon the upland rise of ranges to the East and fading light.

And so to Livingstone, like places known and come to before, and supper at the N.P. station and the waitress with the tired face, and yet with charm, reticence and intelligence, and the strange wood of old trees and the station and in the living room the free pamphlets of the L.D.S. and Christian Science and Adventists and outside the walls of rain (the moaning of full rivers lapping at the rear) and blaze of neons, bars, and the bald hills about—so out and to the west, the Yellowstone and ripe greenery behind now and the bald ridges closing in, the rise across the Bozeman Pass, a pause to read of Bozeman, Lewis, Clark, and then the steep descent, the N.P. descending steeply with us, and *ascending* too, the double header climbing to the right *above* the cut and then the lights of Bozeman—the broad main street ablaze with power of brightness and abundant light, the hotel, and then out with M. to Bar and talk with Barkeep of Montana (and no depression, said he) and so home with M. and said good night, so out again, and to another bar, then power flashing off, most sinister, the town in darkness and faces in the bar around me, then out to first bar again—and then to cafe for hamburger, milk, etc., and then home—and *this*, and *this*—and so to bed.

Wednesday, June 29, (Glacier Park):

Up at seven—and downstairs—and breakfast with others—then off at 7:20 through valley with Bridger Mtns. right, Rockies on left—and so sweeps of range—"a long country"—and presently the great range with great sweeps—the mtns. fading to the right behind, the giant Rockies to the right—and forestry and the signs and stops to read them—and Helena and the enormous gold dredge in Last Chance going up the hill—then through the pass and over and the valleys and the Gates of The Rockies etc.—and the bank-full Missouri,[13] and so on and at Wolf Creek away again and climbing and now the vast Range—the mtns. to the left—the Continental [*Divide*]—and past the desert moldings of the earth to the right—before, the immense and lovely grey green of the range and great herds grazing—the straight backs of the steers in the bright light and stock grazing on the [runup?]—and the Great American Plain opening with infinite lift and rise and vastness to the fore—so towards the Rockies and the lift and rise and heaving of the Earth Wave.

So the Blackfoot reservation town and Browning—all confused, disorderly and Indian—and so on and on directly toward the shining and bright austerity of the mountains now and through the hogbacks and into the canyons—timber, right away, and in the mountains—and presently the town of Glacier Lake [*East Glacier Park*]—and a sandwich there at the hotel—away and up the [*St. Mary's*] lake again to Babb for [mail?]—and back again and from St. Mary's crossing and the cabins along the Going to the Sun Pass and the stupendous hackled peaks now—the sheer basaltic walls of glaciation, the steep scoopings down below, the dense vertices of glacial valley slopes and forest—and climbing, climbing to the Logan Pass so down again terrifically, and the glacial wall beside, the enormous hackled granite peaks before, the green steep glaciation of the forest, the pouring cascades, and the streams below—and down and down the marvelous road into the forest, and by rushing waters, and down and down to McDonald Lake and Hotel—and a cabin here beside the lake—and Ed away upon the waiting lake steamer and Ray and I to cabin—then to dinner—there meeting Mr. Jack Keyes—Ray's friend—then all together for a space —a drink with Keyes—and beer for Keyes and Miller in the cafeteria —and then all departing, all going, very tired and very sleepy—so to bed!

The vast grey green of the plains—in the land mouldings a silken sheen.

The blue blazing day, the clouds cumulous, constant, crowded against infinity, packed with immeasurable light.

And the Rockies half skewed into both light and cloud—the magic of the sky marvellous.

The faery green of the glacial lakes.

13. The headwaters of the Missouri River are in Montana.

Thursday, June 30 (Day of the lakes):

Slept late and soundly—woke at eight—dressed and to hotel for breakfast—women feeding deer and laughing before hotel—The lake mist-blue in morning light—so back to cabin, packed, put things in car —talked to waitress sitting in grass with deer nestling to her—pretty picture—goodbye to Keyes, and away about 10 o'clock.

The lake marvellous in morning shadow and the Alpine sheerness of the granite peaks—so dipping down to Belton where looked at chalet and rooms and talk with dejected manager, and boys hunting for elk horns—So away and down to Flathead Lake along a pleasant lovely stream (McDonald Creek) and around the loveliness of Flathead Lake for next hour or so—a beautiful lake with the granite masses of the Continental divide rising on the other side and cedar hills on the right —and lumber mills and houses of logs and much timber like Olympia again—so leave the lake at Polson and so down into the Missoula Valley—the Rocky range away eastward and lower ridges to the west —the valley widening, the district of Flathead Indians, opened as late as 1910 for white settlement—the river somewhere away to the right— told by a line of trees but out of sight—so down to the junction at ? [*Ravalli*]—and decide on the road to the right by the bison range instead of Missoula, so along this road and by the bison camp at Flathead reservation, and pick up the stream again, this time a marvelous glorious viscous emerald green now known as Clark's Fork (of the Columbia River) and for 200 miles, to Newport (?) on the Washington state line, along this stream which constantly enlarges and grows deeper.

A lovely ride along a valley, the scenery often almost Appalachian (save for the darkness of the trees), the valley, in this journey and this land of mighty sweeps, surprisingly intimate and narrow now, very sparsely settled, but breaking out now and then into wealths and sweeps of green fertility, the green glacial stream constantly being fed by others, drawing all the water from the hills into itself, being widened and thickened but muddied by the confluence of the Bitter Root River—a strange sight now—the left side of the river glacial green, the right side muddy brown, the country now most thickly forested with dark and lovely trees—and back at Thompson's Falls— the blistered little town (the Montana towns have more of a false-front, shacklike, Old West appearance than any others I have seen) and three little girls dancing in front of the place where we eat and the railway grade above and [opposite?], the N.P. station and the blistered houses.

So away along the river again, and pick up a train and follow down it and at last came upon the Pend Oreille Lake—(in Idaho in the panhandle)—a rather big lake and a lovely one, swollen with rains and increased by flood—and along the lake and at last to Kootenai and big farms, well painted buildings, mown alfalfa and green fields, and so pick up the river (the Clark Fork again) now known as the Pend Oreille, and further speculation on the route of Lewis and of Clark, whose ghosts have haunted us and this country since Three Forks and the upper reaches of the Missouri.

And so along the river until we cross it finally at Newport, and the river sweeping North toward Canada and the great loop and its final return with the mighty Columbia, and we away for the last 40 or 50 miles into Spokane—the country already has a Pacific weathered look (I thought)—the dark trees, pines predominant, and some lakes, and all greener than I thought (the whole journey today has been green and thick with forest, full of water) and so into Spokane in good time (at 6:45 Pacific time) and to the Davenport hotel and a bottle of Scotch and conversation, and C., M. and a friend downstairs to dinner, and presently I go down alone, and eat, and then upstairs and straighten accounts with Conway (the whole trip costing me less than $50) and then down to send telegram to Chase bank, and to Roundup place for beer, and so home a little after one to bed.

Spokane, Friday, June 31: [14]
And the notes, the impressions.
The little slaughtered wild things in the road—in Oregon, in California, across the desert, going up through Utah, in Idaho, Wyoming, and Montana—the little crushed carcasses of the gophers, chipmunks, jackrabbits, birds—in the hot bright Western light the black crows picking at some furry mangled little carcass on the hot road—rises and flaps slowly *waitingly* away as the car approaches.

In that lovely valley of the Clark Fork through Montana, in full afternoon-tide and the brightness of the sun the transcontinental freight of the N.P. blasting toward us up the grade, the interminable heavy cars climbing past, and suddenly—the tops of the great train lined with clusters of hoboes—a hundred of them—some sprawled out, sitting, others erect, some stretched out on their backs lazily inviting the luminous American weather, and the mountain ridges all around, the glacial green of Clark's Fork just beyond—and the 'bos roll past across America silently regarding us—the pity, terror, strangeness, and magnificence of it all.

14. Wolfe apparently made these entries the next morning in Spokane, for June 31 would be July 1. They are placed in the early pages of the notebook.

Friday, July 1:

Up at 7:45—and dressed, packed—downstairs to breakfast with C. and M. in coffee shop of Davenport—and two of their friends—and so talking and at last away at 9:50 and west from Spokane through country becoming more barren all the time and sweeps of wheat fields and desert and sage brush country—so to the turn off for Grand Coulee and mounting up and then down through a dry land and the great walls, the basaltic walls, of the Grand Coulee down down down and the tremendous surge and glacial greenness of the Columbia river sweeping round the bend and the basal ramparts of the terrific dam, and the crews with red helmets working, so to the observation point and fidgeted and listened to a talk on the dimensions and purpose of the dam, so inside to hear another talk with a model—the power bases and the giant pumps, the great figures.

So down and across the bridge to Mason City where the workers live—and as much like the rude West as one can find now—and so back and up again and by crews working, gathered in red helmets, and to the top of the plateau, and now following out the route of the Dry Coulee, the cavernous basaltic walls and the ancient and enormous bed —then to the great basin of the Dry falls and then down down down to the Coulee's end and into the dry sage brush desert, and across this desert that the dam will reclaim, and under burning skies, and curded cloud—by it at great speed—and a pause for lunch and on again and towards the hot blue haze of hills and up and up the canyon for a constantly rising plateau, and the air cool now and the wind howling so the car rocks and swerves like a toy and down and down the gorge of the Yakimas into the upper end of the Yakima valley at Ellensburg, then into the Yakima Gorge and the dry hills again and up and around and along the narrow gorge above the rushing river and at last into Yakima where turning follow back along the valley of the Naches and this too burgeoning with fruit and the dry hills closing in and into the canyon gorge again and the boiling river flowing past and trees now, and climbing climbing, and the forest darkness now of the Cascades—pine, hemlock, spruce, some fir.

And up the American river canyon into blue black cascades and forests, night dark now, and mist gathering and clouds overhead all mists deepening and thickening and blowing ice sheets of spume through the Chinook pass, and through the pass and down and fog and mist more thick than leaden fog, and down the road into the valley past the ranger's gate [*of Mount Rainier National Park*] and up again and the milk white of the Glacier Creek and around and up climbing hard now and all lost vaguely in mist and around again and the great white bowl masses of Rainier descried, and mist blowing in in floods of spume and up and up to timber line and to the Sunrise Lodge and light playing marvellously, and blue cerulean struggling to break through and the glaciers level to the eye and visible but the great mountain massif and the peak obscured.

So over the snow still 4 to 6 feet deep to our cabins—then to dinner at the Lodge—a state of unfurnishment yet, and the cold menace and terror of the mountain, the gigantic fume flaws of bright mist sweeping by below us, above us, and around the mighty mass— then with the Ranger to the administration office to see his collection of rocks, flowers and models, then to the cabin where Ranger built a fire, and talking with M. about the trip—and very tired, and presently to bed.

Saturday, July 2:

Lay late, until 8:20—and C. came in to build the fire, and in both of us quiet greetings, a feeling that our trip was almost done, and in me a sense of the tremendous kindness and decency and humanity of the man. He said: "Tom, look at the mountain." I got up and looked, it was immense and terrific and near and clouds still clung to the great Cloudmaker at the side like a great filament of ectoplasm. C. told me to sleep as long as I wanted, and went out but presently I got up and the room warm now and a brisk fire going in the stove and a basin of water and dressed and shaved, and walked over the packed and dirty snow to the Lodge, where joined C. and Caderon at breakfast—and Caderon a nice boy, doing his level best for us in everything, solicitous and good —the long face and teeth and bony aquilinity of the Y.M.C.A. and Sunday school boy—he spoke frequently of his Sunday school class.

So M. joined us, refreshed from sleep, and the Ranger and another Ranger and so out to take pictures and to look at the Mountain —and the sun out now, the mist ocean still below us—but the great mass of Rainier clearly defined now, save for the white sky—backward —and the great mass faced up squarely with all its perilous overwhelming majesty, and with its tremendous shoulders, the long terrific sweeps of its hackling ridges, and stood trying to get its scale, and this impossible because there was nothing but Mountain—a universe of mountain, a continent of mountain—and nothing else but mountain itself to compare mountain to.

On this trip C.'s great love and knowledge of mountains has revealed itself—upon the summit of the pass at the Continental divide in Glacier the way he pointed out the little trees, the affection and reverence with which he spoke of them—the signs by which the trees of timber-line could be observed and noted, the broadness at the base, etc.—the little mountain flowers—now the astounding revelation that he had climbed Hood 225 times and Rainier 40—the quiet way he told of accidents and rescues—of the ice so hard that the axe bounds off and "ruins a man for life"—of the crevasse—of the man who fell and drove his Alpine stock through him and of how he got him out but didn't dare touch the Alpine stock, and of how they got the man down off the mountain and of how "he lived several hours. He was conscious" —and of another young man that he had rescued two or three years before and of how he could see him lying on a ledge in the crevasse— and how his heart sank for he saw the broken axe and Alpine stock and was "afraid it had gone through him too"—but how he was "all right except that he was all cut up"—and "and I got the rope about him and we got him out and sewed him up with a darning needle and ordinary thread, and he's as good today as he ever was"—and C. laughed.

Made farewells and away by 11:30 or so and down the mountain into the sea of cold fog and mist again—the great forests now— dropping below the mists the enormous forest darkness of the Douglas firs, the towering trunks of the terrific trees, the dense fervid darkness of the undergrowth—then blasted woods, denuded hills and acres of stumps and snags, and then the lowlands—a casual margin land at first of farms and woods and natural growth and nondescript houses, barns, etc.—curiously ragged, casual and unkept looking after the irrigated lands, then out and down into the valley, and the level, farms, the fruit trees, and the towns, and so Tacoma and so out along the broad four-wayed Pacific highway towards Olympia, and the four lanes already busy with their traffic of the Fourth [*of July*] and the strings of market stores, hot dog stands, filling stations, taverns, etc.

So down into the crowded streets of Olympia choked with great tides of traffic for the Fourth, the sidewalks crowded with throngs of people—farmers, seamen, lumberjacks in town for the Fourth—so parked the car and to Crane's famous seafood Restaurant for lunch, and ate a shrimp cocktail of the tiny Puget shrimps, and then a delicious pan roast of the small but succulent Puget Sound oysters, the whole cooked in with crab meat in a delicious pungent sauce, and spread on toast, so eaten, most delicious—and so our farewells now, addresses, final instructions—the casualish wordiness of men with some sadness in their heart avoiding farewells—and C. still avoiding it (how like my brother!) is going to rush me up to see the Capitol and we see it, and still avoiding it, back to see the old State Capitol, and we see it—and they give me the maps and the old Tour Book we have worn black, and write their names in it—and at last, farewell—and they are gone, and a curiously hollow feeling in me as I stand there on the streets of Olympia and watch the white Ford [15] flash away—

So stay an hour or so and watch the town, and miss one bus and catch another at 4:35, and to Seattle, the great bus keeping to the inner side at good speed, the magnificent four-ply highway filled with the flashing traffic of the holiday, the country undulant in long sweeps between the dark and ragged lanes of Douglas fir—the temporary congestion at Tacoma—and the bus halt there—then on our way again on the great highway and presently the outskirts of Seattle, scattered houses, open country, the arms of Puget Sound—blue-black, misty, and exciting under the grey skies—and then the great train yards, flying field, viaducts—the settlements upon the hills, then the Railway stations and the full town, the downtown section, "Big House," the crowded streets, the long pull up the slope of Second Avenue, the bus station, a taxi, the hotel, telegrams there from Nowell and Ed [*Aswell*] [16] that make me very happy, money from the bank, a bottle of Scotch liquor, a midnight meal at Rippe's and the trip over now, to bed!

[*Without waiting to rest after his Western tour, Wolfe took a trip on July 3 to Vancouver, where he promptly came down with influenza. After his return to Seattle, his illness developed into pneumonia and he was hospitalized throughout July and August. He seemed unable to make a complete recovery, and his doctors were worried about his recurring fever and headaches and about a cloudy, uncertain area in the X-ray of his right lung.*

What had happened is that the pneumonia had activated an old tuberculosis lesion in his lung, but the doctors disagreed about this diagnosis. Meanwhile, the temperature and headaches continued, and periods of slight irrationality occurred. After a series of doctors had entered the case and after a brain tumor or abscess was suspected, Wolfe was sent, on September 6, across the country to the Johns Hopkins Hospital in Baltimore. There Dr. Walter Dandy, the brain surgeon, performed an exploratory operation and found Wolfe's brain covered with tubercles. He concluded that the tuberculosis lesion had reopened, that the tuberculosis germs had got into the blood stream

15. They had traveled conspicuously in a white Ford which displayed "Oregon State Motor Association" on its sides.

16. Aswell's telegram said: "Your new book is magnificent in scope and design, with some of the best writing you have ever done . . . ."

and been carried to the brain. Wolfe's case was hopeless. He died of tuberculosis of the brain on September 15, 1938.

The manuscript he had left with Edward Aswell, though unfinished, provided the material for three posthumous volumes: The Web and the Rock, *1939,* You Can't Go Home Again, *1940, and* The Hills Beyond, *1941.]*

Index

Index

Note :

On Travel of The Modern
Man :

re one trip

aged   4 - St Louis - here   1500 miles
aged   6 - Santa Fe " -   500   "
                                                        "
                                                        "
                                                        "

DATE DUE			
1-22 76			
FEB 5	1976		
GAYLORD			PRINTED IN U.S.A.

20 - 23 / Harvard
                Asheville
                Baltimore
                Medford
                N.H.

7 or 8000 miles